Elevating Game Exp Unreal Engine 5

Second Edition

Bring your game ideas to life using the new Unreal Engine 5 and C++

Gonçalo Marques

Devin Sherry

David Pereira

Hammad Fozi

BIRMINGHAM—MUMBAI

Elevating Game Experiences with Unreal Engine 5
Second Edition

Copyright © 2022 Packt Publishing

Group Product Manager: Rohit Rajkumar
Publishing Product Manager: Nitin Nainani
Senior Editor: Aamir Ahmed
Senior Content Development Editor: Feza Shaikh
Technical Editor: Shubham Sharma
Copy Editor: Safis Editing
Project Coordinator: Manthan Patel
Proofreader: Safis Editing
Indexer: Rekha Nair
Production Designer: Prashant Ghare
Marketing Coordinator: Teny Thomas

First published: November 2020
Second edition: September 2022
Production reference: 1300822

Published by Packt Publishing Ltd.
Livery Place
35 Livery Street
Birmingham
B3 2PB, UK.

ISBN 978-1-80323-986-6

www.packt.com

I would like to dedicate this book to my parents and my girlfriend, who always supported my weird and uncertain game development journey.

– Gonçalo Marques

I would like to dedicate this book, and my involvement in its development, to all of my friends and family around the world. I love you all and would not be where I am today without your love, support, kindness, and inspiration. Thank you all.

– Devin Sherry

I would like to thank my girlfriend, my family, and all of my friends for inspiring and supporting me on this journey.

This book is dedicated to my grandmother Teresa ("E vai daí ós'pois…!").

– David Pereira

I would like to dedicate this book to my mom, whose constant support and jolliness meant the world to me. I'm sure wherever she is right now, she'll probably be proud looking at my accomplishments.

– Hammad Fozi

Contributors

About the authors

Gonçalo Marques has been an active gamer since the age of 6. He has been using Unreal Engine since 2016 and has done freelance and consulting work using the engine. Gonçalo also released a free and open source plugin called *UI Navigation*, which has garnered an extremely positive reception with over 100,000 downloads and is still receiving frequent updates and fixes. Thanks to the development of this plugin, he became an Epic MegaGrant recipient. He is now working at Funcom ZPX, a game studio in Lisbon that has contributed to games such as *Conan Exiles*, *Mutant Year Zero*, and *Moons of Madness*. Gonçalo is currently working on a new Funcom game in the *Dune* universe.

Devin Sherry is the principal technical designer at People Can Fly in Poland, having worked on *Outriders* and *Outriders: Worldslayer* using Unreal Engine 4. Before that, he worked on *Aquanox: Deep Descent* as a technical designer at the Digital Arrow studio in Serbia. With a decade of experience ranging from the Unreal Developers' Kit to the newly released Unreal Engine 5, Devin is passionate about creating memorable experiences for players and bringing game mechanics to life.

David Pereira started making games in 1998 when he learned how to use Clickteam's *The Games Factory*. He graduated in computer science from FCT-UNL, where he learned about C++, OpenGL, and DirectX, which allowed him to create more complex games. After working in IT consulting for a few years, he joined Miniclip in Portugal where he worked on popular mobile games such as *8 Ball Pool*, *Gravity Guy 1* and *Gravity Guy 2*, *Extreme Skater*, *iStunt2*, *Hambo*, and many others. Since then, he has been the lead developer for MPC in the John Lewis Christmas VR Experience, worked on an earlier version of *Mortal Shell*, and did volunteer work teaching people with Asperger's how to make games with Unreal Engine 4. Today, he's working on his own game, a soon-to-be-announced first-person action RPG.

Hammad Fozi comes from a gaming background and has been extensively working on Unreal Engine since 2017. He has been part of some very successful AAA projects such as *Virtua FanCave* (and Metaverse), Unnamed AAA Sci-Fi DJ Experience, *Heroes and Generals*, and *Creed: Rise to Glory* VR. Hammad has worked with teams who have had experience working at Ubisoft, Warner Bros. Games, 2K Games, and more! He has successfully helped teams consisting of 10–30 people to scale to 150+ in size over his very short yet impressive career. Hammad currently works as a senior C++ game developer and has extensive experience in working with VR and augmented reality, PC/PS5/Xbox/Android/iOS/macOS game development, and Web3/Metaverse/NFT systems (within Unreal Engine).

About the reviewers

Lennard Fonteijn started BASIC programming in his early teens on an old DOS PC. He developed his skills over the years and programming was always a hobby. Being doubtful that turning his hobby into work would make him lose interest in programming, he decided to study computer science. At his first internship, he realized that programming websites and apps wasn't what he wanted to do for long, so he decided to focus on his other passion besides programming: gaming. He was always fascinated by how games worked internally. Having spent quite some time fiddling around with libraries such as OpenGL and DirectX, he knew this had to become his specialty someday. As a result, he directed his computer science studies toward gaming by following a serious games-related ActionScript 3 class and also minoring in game technology. His final internship was at a local game company and he received his bachelor's degree in 2013. After graduation, Lennard became the CTO of the company where he first interned and was a computer science lecturer at a university. In his spare time, he works on his own game-related projects.

Pranav Paharia is an experienced game programmer who has built gaming solutions with Unreal Engine and Unity3D. He has worked on single-player and multiplayer games, for various platforms such as mobile, PC, and VR. He has been working in the game industry since 2013. He has reviewed another book on Unreal Engine, *Beginning Unreal Engine 4 Blueprints Visual Scripting*. He has worked in various industry domains such as video games, animation, AEC, military, education, and social media. Pranav was keen on playing computer games in childhood. His love for computer games inspired him to make games, and he converted his passion into a profession. You can connect with him at pranavpaharia@gmail.com.

Kacper Prędkiewicz, even though his main role is game design, is doing quite a lot of his work in Unreal Engine 5, giving him a unique view of how non-technical people work in Unreal Engine. He has been making games in engines such as Unity, Goodot, GameMaker, and Unreal Engine, and has worked on games of all kinds – from mobile games and small indie projects to big AAA games. He is a graduate in game design, a game designer at People Can Fly studios, and an avid beekeeper.

Thank you, Devin, for including me as your technical reviewer, and for everything you have taught me.

Table of Contents

3

Character Class Components and Blueprint Setup   89

4

Getting Started with Player Input   107

5

Query with Line Traces   133

6

Setting Up Collision Objects   165

10

Creating the SuperSideScroller Game   295

11

Working with Blend Space 1D, Key Bindings, and State Machines   333

12

Animation Blending and Montages   385

13

Creating and Adding the Enemy Artificial Intelligence   417

14

Spawning the Player Projectile 467

17

Using Remote Procedure Calls

18

Using Gameplay Framework Classes in Multiplayer   665

Preface

Immerse yourself in Unreal game projects with this book, written by four highly experienced industry professionals with many years of combined experience with Unreal Engine. *Elevating Game Experiences with Unreal Engine 5* will walk you through the latest version of Unreal Engine by helping you get hands-on with the game creation projects. The book starts with an introduction to the Unreal Editor and key concepts such as actors, blueprints, animations, inheritance, and player input. You'll then move on to the first of three projects – building a dodgeball game, where you'll learn the concepts of line traces, collisions, projectiles, user interface, and sound effects. You'll also discover how to combine these concepts to showcase your new skills. The second project, a side-scroller game, will help you implement concepts such as animation blending, enemy AI, spawning objects, and collectibles. And finally, you'll cover the key concepts in creating a multiplayer environment as you work on the third project – an FPS game. By the end of the Unreal Engine book, you'll have a broad understanding of how to use the tools that the game engine provides to start building your own games.

Who this book is for

This book is for game developers looking to get started with using Unreal Engine 5 for their game development projects. Anyone who has used Unreal Engine before and wants to consolidate, improve, and apply their skills will find this book useful. To better grasp the concepts explained in this book, prior knowledge of C++ basics (such as variables, functions, classes, polymorphism, and pointers) is required. For full compatibility with the IDE used in this book, a Windows system is recommended.

What this book covers

Chapter 1, Introduction to Unreal Engine, explores the Unreal Engine editor. You will be introduced to the editor's interface, see how to manipulate actors in a level, understand the basics of the blueprint visual scripting language, and discover how to create material assets that can then be used by meshes.

Chapter 2, Working with Unreal Engine, introduces Unreal Engine game fundamentals, along with how to create a C++ project and set up the Content Folder of projects. You'll also be introduced to the topic of animations.

Chapter 3, Character Class Components and Blueprint Setup, introduces you to the Unreal Character class, along with the concept of object inheritance and how to work with input mappings.

Chapter 4, Getting Started with Player Input, introduces the topic of player input. You will learn how to associate a key press or a touch input with an in-game action, such as jumping or moving, through the use of action mappings and axis mappings.

Chapter 5, Query with Line Traces, starts a new project called Dodgeball. In this chapter, you will learn about the concept of line traces and the various ways in which they can be used in games.

Chapter 6, Setting Up Collision Objects, explores the topic of object collision. You will learn about collision components, collision events, and physics simulation. You will also study the topic of timers, the projectile movement component, and physical materials.

Chapter 7, Working with UE5 Utilities, teaches you how to implement some useful utilities available in Unreal Engine, including actor components, interfaces, and blueprint function libraries, which will help keep your projects well structured and approachable for other people that join your team.

Chapter 8, Creating User Interfaces with UMG, explores the topic of game UI. You will learn how to make menus and HUDs using Unreal Engine's UI system, UMG, as well as how to display the player character's health using a progress bar.

Chapter 9, Adding Audio-Visual Elements, introduces the topic of sounds and particle effects in Unreal Engine. You will learn how to import sound files to the project and use them as both 2D and 3D sounds, as well as how to add existing particle systems to the game. Lastly, a new level will be made that uses all the game mechanics built in the last few chapters to conclude the Dodgeball project.

Chapter 10, Creating the SuperSideScroller Game, discusses in detail the goals of the SuperSideScroller project and covers an overview of how animation works in Unreal Engine 5 through examples of manipulating the default Mannequin Skeleton.

Chapter 11, Working with Blend Space 1D, Key Bindings, and State Machines, teaches you how to use Blend Space 1D, Animation State Machines, and the Enhanced Input System in Unreal Engine 5 to create working movement-based animation logic for the player character.

Chapter 12, Animation Blending and Montages, discusses further animation concepts in Unreal Engine 5 such as Animation Blending and Animation Montages to allow for concurrent animation to occur when the player character moves and throws the projectile.

Chapter 13, Creating and Adding the Enemy Artificial Intelligence, teaches you how to use AI Controller, Blackboards, and Behavior Trees in Unreal Engine 5 to create simple AI logic for an enemy that the player can face.

Chapter 14, Spawning the Player Projectile, teaches you how to spawn and destroy game objects, and uses additional animation-based concepts such as Anim Notifies and Anim Notify states to spawn the player projectile during the throwing animation.

Chapter 15, Exploring Collectibles, Power-Ups, and Pickups, introduces you to UI concepts of UMG in Unreal Engine 5 and puts your knowledge to the test in creating additional collectibles and power-ups for the player.

Chapter 16, Getting Started with Multiplayer Basics, introduces you to multiplayer and how the server/client architecture works, as well as covering concepts such as connections, ownership, roles, and variable replication. It also covers 2D Blend Spaces to create an animation grid for 2D movement and the Transform Modify Bone control to change the transform of a bone at runtime.

Chapter 17, Using Remote Procedure Calls, teaches you how remote procedure calls work, the different types, and important considerations when using them. It also shows how to expose enumerations to the editor and how to use array index wrapping to cycle between an array in both directions.

Chapter 18, Using Gameplay Framework Classes in Multiplayer, explains how to use the most important classes in the Gameplay Framework in multiplayer. It also explains more about Game Mode, Player State, Game State, and some useful engine built-in functionality.

To get the most out of this book

Software/hardware covered in the book	Operating system requirements
Unreal Engine 5	Windows, macOS, or Linux

To access the files of the Unreal Engine GitHub repository linked throughout this book, make sure to follow these instructions:

`https://www.unrealengine.com/en-US/ue-on-github`

If you get an error 404 on a link from this book to the Unreal Engine documentation, it means that it hasn't been updated yet to 5.0. You should pick the previous engine version from the dropdown on the top left corner of the page.

Installing Visual Studio

Because we'll be using C++ while working with Unreal Engine 5, we'll need an **Integrated Development Environment** (**IDE**) that easily works alongside the engine. Visual Studio Community is the best IDE you have available for this purpose on Windows. If you're using macOS or Linux, you'll have to use another IDE, such as Visual Studio Code, Qt Creator, or Xcode (available exclusively on macOS).

The instructions given in this book are specific to Visual Studio Community on Windows, so if you are using a different OS and/or IDE, then you will need to do your research on how to set these up for use in your working environment. In this section, you'll be taken through the installation of Visual Studio, so that you can easily edit UE5's C++ files:

1. Go to the Visual Studio download web page at `https://visualstudio.microsoft.com/downloads`. The recommended Visual Studio Community version for the Unreal Engine 5 version we'll be using in this book (5.0.3) is Visual Studio Community 2022. Be sure to download that version.

2. When you do, open the executable file that you just downloaded. It should eventually take you to a window where you'll be able to pick the modules of your Visual Studio installation. There, you'll have to tick the **Game Development with C++** module and then click the **Install** button in the bottom-right corner of the window. After you click that button, Visual Studio will start downloading and installing. When the installation is complete, it may ask you to reboot your PC. After rebooting your PC, Visual Studio should be installed and ready for use.

3. When you run Visual Studio for the first time, you may see a few windows, the first one of which is the login window. If you have a Microsoft Outlook/Hotmail account, you should use that account to log in, otherwise, you can skip login by clicking **Not now, maybe later**.

> **Note**
>
> If you don't input an email address, you will only have 30 days to use Visual Studio before it locks out and you have to input an email address to continue using it.

4. After that, you will be asked to choose a color scheme. The **Dark** theme is the most popular and the one we will be using in this section.

Finally, you can select the **Start Visual Studio** option. When you do so, however, you can close it again. We will be taking a deeper look at how to use Visual Studio in *Chapter 2, Working with Unreal Engine* of this book.

Epic Games Launcher

To access Unreal Engine 5, you'll need to download the Epic Games Launcher, available at this link: `https://store.epicgames.com/en-US/download`.

Before you do so, be sure to check its hardware requirements at this link: `https://docs.unrealengine.com/5.0/en-US/hardware-and-software-specifications-for-unreal-engine/`.

This link will allow you to download the Epic Games Launcher for Windows and macOS. If you use Linux, you'll have to download the Unreal Engine source code and compile it from the source – `https://docs.unrealengine.com/5.0/en-US/downloading-unreal-engine-source-code/`:

1. Click the **Download Launcher** option. A `.msi` file will be downloaded to your computer. Open this `.msi` file when it finishes downloading, which will prompt you to install the Epic Games Launcher. Follow the installation instructions and then launch the Epic Games Launcher. When you do so, you should be greeted with a login screen.

2. If you already have an account, you can simply log in with your existing credentials. If you don't, you'll have to sign up for an Epic Games account by clicking the **Sign Up** text at the bottom.

Once you log in with your account, you should be greeted by the **Home** tab. From there, you'll want to go to the **Unreal Engine** tab by clicking the text that says **Unreal Engine**.

3. When you've done that, you'll be greeted with the **Store** tab. The Epic Games Launcher is not only the place from which you install and launch Unreal Engine 5, but it's also a game store. Press the **Unreal Engine** tab on the left side of the launcher.

4. You will now find several sub-tabs at the top of the Epic Games Launcher, the first of which is the **News** sub-tab. This acts as a hub for Unreal Engine resources. From this page, you'll be able to access the following:

    - The **News** page, on which you'll be able to take a look at all the latest Unreal Engine news

    - The **YouTube** channel, on which you'll be able to watch dozens of tutorials and live streams that go into detail about several different Unreal Engine topics

    - The **Q&A** page, on which you'll be able to see, ask, and answer questions posed and answered by the Unreal Engine community

    - The **Forums** page, on which you'll be able to access the Unreal Engine forums

    - The **Roadmap** page, on which you'll be able to access the Unreal Engine roadmap, including features delivered in past versions of the engine, as well as features that are currently in development for future versions

5. The **Samples** tab will allow you to access several project samples that you can use to learn how to use Unreal Engine 5.

6. To the right of the **Samples** tab is the **Marketplace** tab. This tab shows you several assets and code plugins made by members of the Unreal Engine community. Here, you'll be able to find 3D assets, music, levels, and code plugins that will help you advance and accelerate the development of your game.

7. To the right of the **Marketplace** tab, we have the **Library** tab. Here, you'll be able to browse and manage all your Unreal Engine version installations, your Unreal Engine projects, and your **Marketplace** asset vault. Because we have none of these things yet, these sections are all empty. Let's change that.

8. Click the yellow plus sign to the right of the **ENGINE VERSIONS** text. This should make a new icon show up, where you'll be able to choose your desired Unreal Engine version.

9. Throughout this book, we'll be using version *5.0* of Unreal Engine. After you've selected that version, click the **Install** button:

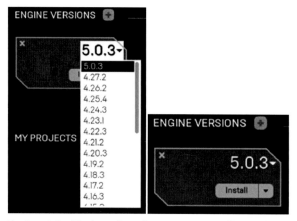

Figure Preface 1.1 – The icon that allows you to install Unreal Engine 5.0

10. After you've done this, you'll be able to choose the installation directory for this Unreal Engine version, which will be of your choosing, and you should then click the **Install** button again.

> **Note**
>
> If you are having issues installing the 5.0 version, make sure to install it on your D drive, with the shortest path possible (that is, don't try to install it too many folders deep, and make sure those folders have short names).

11. This will result in the installation of Unreal Engine 5.0 starting. When the installation is done, you can launch the editor by clicking the **Launch** button of the version icon:

Figure Preface 1.2 – The version icon once installation has finished

If you are using the digital version of this book, we advise you to type the code yourself or access the code from the book's GitHub repository (a link is available in the next section). Doing so will help you avoid any potential errors related to the copying and pasting of code.

Download the example code files

You can download the example code files for this book from GitHub at `https://github.com/PacktPublishing/Elevating-Game-Experiences-with-Unreal-Engine-5-Second-Edition`. If there's an update to the code, it will be updated in the GitHub repository.

We also have other code bundles from our rich catalog of books and videos available at `https://github.com/PacktPublishing/`. Check them out!

You can download videos for Chapters 1, 3, 4-9, and 16-18 which will help to understand the chapters better. Here is the link for it: `https://packt.link/1GnAS`

Download the color images

We also provide a PDF file that has color images of the screenshots and diagrams used in this book. You can download it here: `https://packt.link/iAmVj`.

Conventions used

There are a number of text conventions used throughout this book.

Code in text: Indicates code words in text, database table names, folder names, filenames, file extensions, pathnames, dummy URLs, user input, and Twitter handles. Here is an example: "These lines of code represent the declarations of the `Tick()` and `BeginPlay()` functions that are included in every Actor-based class by default."

A block of code is set as follows:

```
// Called when the game starts or when spawned
void APlayerProjectile::BeginPlay()
{
  Super::BeginPlay();
}
// Called every frame
void APlayerProjectile::Tick(float DeltaTime)
{
  Super::Tick(DeltaTime);
}
```

Bold: Indicates a new term, an important word, or words that you see onscreen. For instance, words in menus or dialog boxes appear in bold. Here is an example: "From the **Open Level** dialog box, navigate to **/ThirdPersonCPP/Maps** to find **SideScrollerExampleMap**."

> **Tips or Important Notes**
> Appear like this.

Get in touch

Feedback from our readers is always welcome.

General feedback: If you have questions about any aspect of this book, email us at customercare@ packtpub.com and mention the book title in the subject of your message.

Errata: Although we have taken every care to ensure the accuracy of our content, mistakes do happen. If you have found a mistake in this book, we would be grateful if you would report this to us. Please visit www.packtpub.com/support/errata and fill in the form.

Piracy: If you come across any illegal copies of our works in any form on the internet, we would be grateful if you would provide us with the location address or website name. Please contact us at copyright@packt.com with a link to the material.

If you are interested in becoming an author: If there is a topic that you have expertise in and you are interested in either writing or contributing to a book, please visit authors.packtpub.com

Share Your Thoughts

Once you've read, we'd love to hear your thoughts! Scan the QR code below to go straight to the Amazon review page for this book and share your feedback.

https://packt.link/r/1803239867

Your review is important to us and the tech community and will help us make sure we're delivering excellent quality content..

1

Introduction to
Unreal Engine

Welcome to *Game Development Projects with Unreal Engine Second Edition*. If this is the first time you're using **Unreal Engine 5** (**UE5**), this book will support you in getting started with one of the most in-demand game engines on the market. You will discover how to build up your game development skills and how to express yourself by creating video games. If you've already tried using UE5, this book will help you develop your knowledge and skills further so that you can build games more easily and effectively.

A game engine is a software application that allows you to produce video games from the ground up. Their feature sets vary significantly but usually allow you to import multimedia files, such as 3D models, images, audio, and video, and manipulate those files through the use of programming, where you can use programming languages such as C++, Python, and Lua, among others.

UE5 uses two main programming languages, C++ and Blueprint, with the latter being a visual scripting language that allows you to do most of what C++ also allows. Although we will be teaching a bit of Blueprint in this book, we will mostly focus on C++, and hence expect you to have a basic understanding of the language, including topics such as **variables**, **functions**, **classes**, **inheritance**, and **polymorphism**. We will remind you about these topics throughout this book where appropriate.

Examples of popular video games made with Unreal Engine 4, the previous Unreal Engine version that UE5 is heavily based on, include *Fortnite*, *Final Fantasy VII Remake*, *Borderlands 3*, *Star Wars: Jedi Fallen Order*, *Gears 5*, and *Sea of Thieves*, among many others. All of these have a very high level of visual fidelity, are well-known, and have (or had) millions of players.

The following link specifies some of the great games that have been made with Unreal Engine 5: `https://youtu.be/kT4iWCxu5hA`. This showcase will show you the variety of games that UE5 allows you to make, both in terms of visuals and gameplay style.

If you'd like to make games such as the ones shown in the video one day or contribute to them in any way, then you've taken your first step in that direction.

This chapter will be an introduction to the Unreal Engine editor. You will learn about the editor's interface; how to add, remove, and manipulate objects in a level; how to use Unreal Engine's Blueprint visual scripting language; and how to use materials in combination with meshes.

By the end of this chapter, you will be able to navigate the Unreal Engine editor, create Actors, manipulate them inside the level, and create materials. Let's start this chapter by learning how to create a new UE5 project in this first exercise.

> **Note**
>
> Before you continue this chapter, make sure you have installed all the necessary software mentioned in the *Preface*.

Technical requirements

The code files for this chapter can be found here: `https://github.com/PacktPublishing/Elevating-Game-Experiences-with-Unreal-Engine-5-Second-Edition`

Exercise 1.01 – creating an Unreal Engine 5 project

In this first exercise, we will learn how to create a new UE5 project. UE5 has predefined project templates that allow you to implement a basic setup for your project. We'll be using the **Third Person** template project in this exercise.

Follow these steps to complete this exercise:

1. After installing Unreal Engine version 5.0, launch the editor by clicking the **Launch** button next to the version icon.

2. After you've done that, you'll be greeted with the engine's **Projects** window, which will show you the existing projects that you can open and work on. It will also give you the option to create a new project. Because we have no projects yet, the **Recent Projects** section will be empty. To create a new project, choose a **Project Category** option, which in our case will be **Games**. Then, click **Next**.

3. After that, you'll see the **Project Templates** window. This window will show all the available project templates in Unreal Engine. When creating a new project, instead of having that project start empty, you have the option to add some assets and code out of the box, which you can then modify to your liking. There are several project templates available for different types of games, but we'll want to go with the **Third Person** project template in this case.

4. Select that template and click the **Next** button, which should take you to the **Project Settings** window.

   In this window, you can choose a few options related to your project:

   - **Blueprint or C++**: Here, you can choose whether you want to be able to add C++ classes. The default option is **Blueprint**, but in our case, we'll want to select the **C++** option.

   - **Quality**: Here, you can choose whether you want your project to have high-quality graphics or high performance. Set this option to **Maximum Quality**.

   - **Raytracing**: Here, you can choose whether you want raytracing enabled or disabled. Raytracing is a novel graphics rendering technique that allows you to render objects by simulating the path of light (using light rays) over a digital environment. Although this technique is rather costly in terms of performance, it also provides much more realistic graphics, especially when it comes to lighting. Set it to **disabled**.

   - **Target Platforms**: Here, you can choose the main platforms you'll want this project to run on. Set this option to **Desktop/Console**.

   - **Starter Content**: Here, you can choose whether you want this project to come with an additional set of basic assets. Set this option to **With Starter Content**.

   - **Location and Name**: At the bottom of the window, you'll be able to choose the location where your project will be stored on your computer and its name.

5. Once you've made sure that all the options have been set to their intended values, click the **Create Project** button. This will cause your project to be created according to the parameters you set. It may take a few minutes for it to be ready. With that, you have created your first UE5 project!

Now, let's learn about some of the basics of UE5.

Getting to know Unreal Engine

In this section, you will be introduced to the Unreal Engine editor, which is a fundamental topic for becoming familiar with UE5.

Once your project has been generated, you should see the Unreal Engine editor open automatically. This screen is likely the one that you will see the most when working with Unreal Engine, so you must get accustomed to it.

Let's break down what we can see in the editor window:

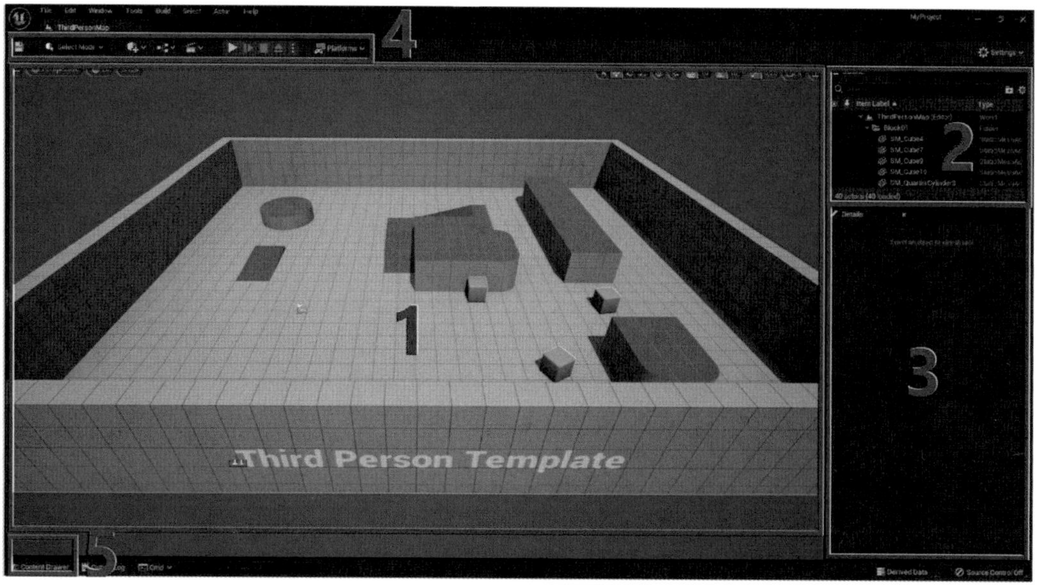

Figure 1.1 – The Unreal Engine editor divided into its main windows

Let's look at these windows in more detail:

1. **Viewport**: At the very center of the screen, you can see the **Viewport** window. This will show you the content of the current level and will allow you to navigate through your level as well as add, move, remove, and edit objects inside it. It also contains several different parameters regarding visual filters, object filters (which objects you can see), and the lighting on your level.

2. **Outliner**: At the top-right corner of the screen, you'll see the **Outliner** window. This allows you to quickly list and manipulate the objects that are on your level. The **Viewport** and **Outliner** windows work hand in hand in allowing you to manage your level, where the former will show you what it looks like and the latter will help you manage and organize it. The **Outliner** window allows you to organize the objects in your level in directories by showing you the *objects* in your level.

3. **Details**: At the far right of the screen, below **Outliner**, you'll be able to see the **Details** panel, which allows you to edit the properties of an object that you have selected in your level. Since no objects have been selected in the preceding screenshot, it is empty. However, if you select any object in your level by *left-clicking* on it, its properties should appear in this window, as shown in the following screenshot:

Figure 1.2 – The Details tab

4. **Toolbar**: At the top of the screen, you'll see the **Toolbar** area, where you'll be able to save your current level, add objects to your level, and play your level, among other things.

> **Note**
> We will only be using some of the buttons from these toolbars, namely, the **Save Current**, **Settings**, **Add**, and **Play** buttons.

5. **Content Drawer**: One of the windows that you'll be using very frequently is the **Content Drawer** window. This window lets you quickly access the **Context Browser** window. You can also open it by using *Ctrl + Space*. The **Content Browser** window will let you browse and manipulate all the files and assets located inside your project's folder. As mentioned at the start of this chapter, Unreal Engine allows you to import several types of multimedia files, and **Content Browser** is the window that will allow you to browse and edit them in their respective sub-editors. Whenever you create an Unreal Engine project, it will always generate a **Content** folder. This folder will be the **root directory** of the **Content Browser** window, meaning you can only browse files inside that folder. You can see the directory you're currently browsing inside the **Content Browser** window by looking at the top of it, which, in our case, is **Content | ThirdPersonCPP**.

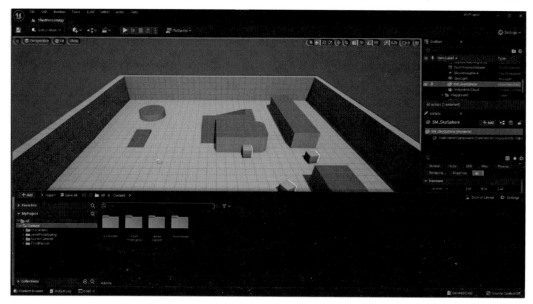

Figure 1.3 – The Content Browser window shown in Unreal Editor interface

If you click the icon to the left of the **Filters** button, at the very left of the **Content Browser** window, you will be able to see the directory hierarchy of the **Content** folder. This directory view allows you to select, expand, and collapse individual directories in the **Content** folder of your project:

Figure 1.4 – The Content Browser window's directory view

> **Note**
>
> The terms **Content Drawer** and **Content Browser** are interchangeable.

Now that we have learned about the main windows of the Unreal Engine editor, let's look at how to manage those windows (hiding and showing their tabs).

Exploring editor windows

As we've seen, the Unreal Engine editor is comprised of many windows, all of which are resizable, movable, and have a corresponding tab on top of them. You can *click and hold* a window's tab and drag it to move it somewhere else. You can hide tab labels by *right-clicking* them and selecting the **Hide Tabs** option:

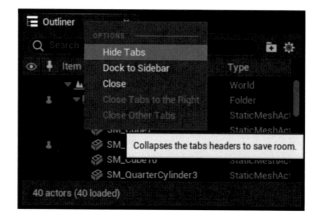

Figure 1.5 – How to hide a tab

If the tab labels have been hidden, you can get them to reappear by clicking the *blue triangle* in the top-left corner of that window, as shown in the following screenshot:

Figure 1.6 – The blue triangle that allows you to show a window's tab

You can also dock the windows to the sidebar to hide them while also having them easily available:

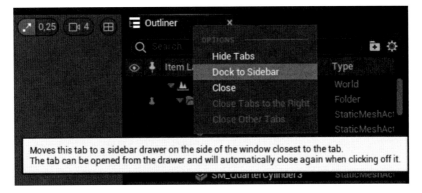

Figure 1.7 – Docking a window to the sidebar

After that, to show or hide them, you simply have to click them:

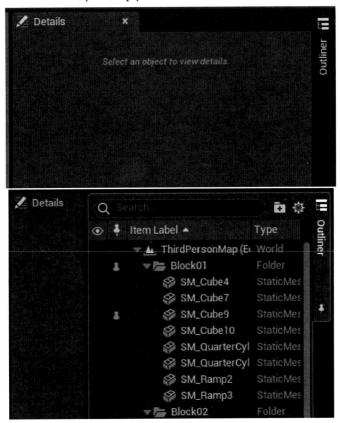

Figure 1.8 – Showing a window docked to the sidebar

When it comes to the windows that are docked to the lower bar, such as the **Content Drawer** window, you can undock them from the lower bar into the editor by clicking **Dock in Layout** in the top-right corner:

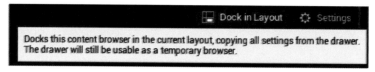

Figure 1.9 – Undocking a window from the lower bar in the editor

Keep in mind that you can browse and open all the windows available in the editor, including the ones that were just mentioned, by clicking the **Window** button in the top-left corner of the editor.

Another very important thing you should know is how to play your level from inside the editor (also known as **PIE**). At the right edge of the **Toolbar** window, you'll see the green **Play** button. If you click it, you'll start playing the currently open level inside the editor:

Figure 1.10 – The green play button, alongside other game playback buttons

Once you hit **Play**, you'll be able to control the player character in the level by using the *W*, *A*, *S*, and *D* keys to move the player character, the *Spacebar* to jump, and moving your mouse to rotate the camera:

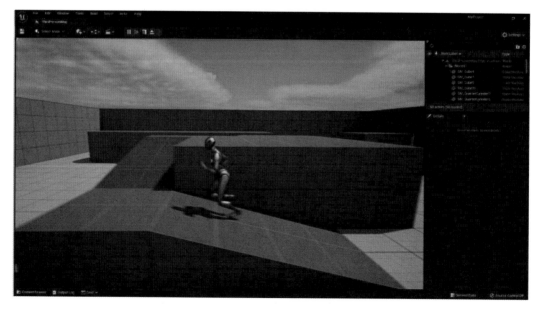

Figure 1.11 – The level being played inside the editor

Then, you can press the *Shift + Esc* keys to stop playing the level.

Now that we've gotten accustomed to some of the editor's windows, let's take a deeper look at the **Viewport** window's navigation.

Viewport navigation

In the previous section, we mentioned that the **Viewport** window allows you to visualize your level, as well as manipulate the objects inside it. Because this is a very important window for you to use and has a lot of functionality, we're going to learn more about it in this section.

Before we start learning about the **Viewport** window, let's quickly get to know **levels**. In UE5, levels represent a **collection of objects**, as well as their locations and properties. The **Viewport** window will always show you the contents of the currently selected level, which in this case was already made and generated alongside the **Third Person** template project. In this level, you can see four wall objects, one ground object, a set of stairs, and some other elevated objects, as well as the player character, which is represented by the UE5 mannequin. You can create multiple levels and switch between them by opening them via the **Content Browser** window.

To manipulate and navigate the currently selected level, you must use the **Viewport** window. If you press and hold the *left mouse button* inside the window, you'll be able to rotate the camera horizontally by moving the mouse *left* and *right*, and move the camera forward and backward by moving the mouse *forward* and *backward*. You can achieve similar results by holding the *right mouse button*, except the camera will rotate vertically when you move the mouse *forward* and *backward*, which allows you to rotate the camera both horizontally and vertically.

Additionally, you can move around the level by clicking and holding the **Viewport** window with the *right mouse button* (the *left mouse button* works too, but using it for movement is not as useful due to there not being as much freedom when rotating the camera) and using the *W* and *S* keys to move forward and backward, the *A* and *D* keys to move sideways, and the *E* and *Q* keys to move up and down.

If you look at the top-right corner of the **Viewport** window, you will see a small camera icon with a number next to it, which will allow you to change the speed at which the camera moves in the **Viewport** window.

Another thing you can do in the **Viewport** window is change its visualization settings. You can change the type of visualization in the **Viewport** window by clicking the button that currently says **Lit**, which will show you all the options available for different lighting and other types of visualization filters.

If you click on the **Perspective** button, you'll have the option to switch between seeing your level from a perspective view, as well as from an orthographic view, the latter of which may help you build your levels faster.

Now that we've learned how to navigate the viewport, let's learn how to manipulate objects, also known as Actors, in your level.

Manipulating Actors

In Unreal Engine, all the objects that can be placed in a level are referred to as Actors. In a movie, an actor would be a human playing a character, but in UE5, every single object you see in your level, including walls, floors, weapons, and characters, is an Actor.

Every Actor must have what's called a **Transform** property, which is a collection of three things:

- **Location**: A `Vector` property signifying the position of that Actor in the level in the X, Y, and Z-axis. A vector is simply a tuple with three floating-point numbers – one for the location of the point on each axis.

- **Rotation**: A `Rotator` property signifying the rotation of that Actor along the X, Y, and Z-axis. A rotator is also a tuple with three floating-point numbers – one for the angle of rotation on each axis.

- **Scale**: A `Vector` property signifying the scale (that is, the size) of that Actor in the level in the X, Y, and Z-axis. This is also a collection of three floating-point numbers – one for the scale value on each axis.

Actors can be moved, rotated, and scaled in a level, which will modify their **Transform** property accordingly. To do this, select any object in your level by *left-clicking* on it. You should see the **Move** tool appear:

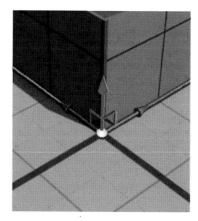

Figure 1.12 – The Move tool, which allows you to move an Actor in the level

The **Move** tool is a three-axis gizmo that allows you to move an object in any of the axes simultaneously. The red arrow of the **Move** tool (pointing to the left in the preceding screenshot) represents the X-axis, the green arrow (pointing to the right in the preceding screenshot) represents the Y-axis, and the blue arrow (pointing up in the preceding screenshot) represents the Z-axis. If you *click and hold* any of these arrows and then drag them around the level, you will move your Actor along that axis in the level. If you click the handles that connect two arrows, you will move the Actor along both those axes simultaneously, and if you click the white sphere at the intersection of all the arrows, you will move the Actor freely along all three axes:

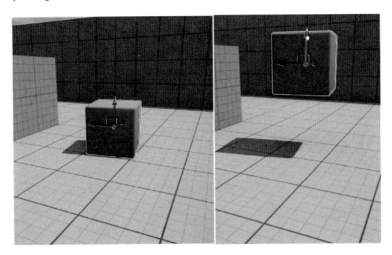

Figure 1.13 – An Actor being moved on the Z-axis using the Move tool

The **Move** tool allows you to move an Actor around the level, but if you want to rotate or scale an Actor, you'll need to use the **Rotate** and **Scale** tools, respectively. You can switch between the **Move**, **Rotate**, and **Scale** tools by pressing the *W*, *E*, and *R* keys, respectively. Press *E* to switch to the **Rotate** tool:

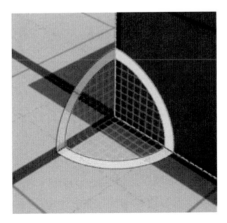

Figure 1.14 – The Rotate tool, which allows you to rotate an Actor

The **Rotate** tool, as expected, allows you to rotate an Actor in your level. You can *click and hold* any of the arcs to rotate the Actor around its associated axis. The red arc (top left in the preceding screenshot) will rotate the Actor around the *X*-axis, the green arc (top right in the preceding screenshot) will rotate the Actor around the *Y*-axis, and the blue arc (lower center in the preceding screenshot) will rotate the Actor around the *Z*-axis:

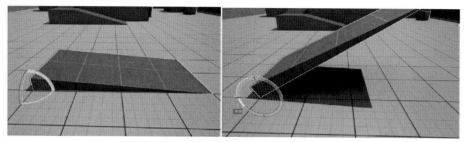

Figure 1.15 – A cube before and after being rotated 30 degrees around the Y-axis

Keep in mind that an object's rotation around the *X*-axis is usually designated as **Roll**, its rotation around the *Y*-axis is usually designated as **Pitch**, and its rotation around the *Z*-axis is usually designated as **Yaw**.

Lastly, we have the **Scale** tool. Press *R* to switch to it:

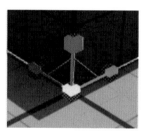

Figure 1.16 – The Scale tool

The **Scale** tool allows you to increase and decrease the scale (size) of an Actor in the *X*, *Y*, and *Z* axes, where the red handle (left in the preceding screenshot) will scale the Actor on the *X*-axis, the green handle (right in the preceding screenshot) will scale the Actor on the *Y*-axis, and the blue handle (top in the preceding screenshot) will scale the Actor on the *Z*-axis:

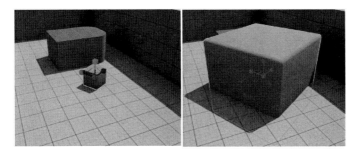

Figure 1.17 – A Cube Actor before and after being scaled on all three axes

You can also toggle between the **Move**, **Rotate**, and **Scale** tools by clicking the following icons at the top of the **Viewport** window:

Figure 1.18 – The Move, Rotate, and Scale tool icons

Additionally, you can change the increments with which you move, rotate, and scale your objects through the grid snapping options to the right of the **Move**, **Rotate**, and **Scale** tool icons. By clicking the buttons highlighted in blue, you'll be able to disable snapping altogether, and by pressing the buttons showing the current snapping increments, you'll be able to change those increments:

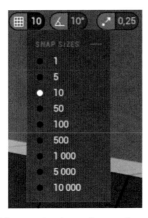

Figure 1.19 – The grid-snapping icons for moving, rotating, and scaling

Now that you know how to manipulate Actors already present in your level, let's learn how to add and remove Actors to and from our level.

Exercise 1.02 – adding and removing Actors

In this exercise, we will be adding and removing Actors from our level.

When it comes to adding Actors to your level, there are two main ways in which you can do so: by dragging assets from the **Content Browser** window or by dragging the default assets from the **Modes** window's **Place Mode**.

Follow these steps to complete this exercise:

1. Go to the **ThirdPersonCPP | Blueprints** directory inside the **Content Browser** window. Here, you will see the ThirdPersonCharacter Actor. If you drag that asset to your level using the *left mouse button*, you will be able to add an instance of that Actor to it. It will be placed wherever you let go of the *left mouse button*:

Figure 1.20 – Dragging an instance of the ThirdPersonCharacter Actor to our level

2. Similarly, drag an Actor to your level by using the **Add** button in the **Toolbar** window (the cube with the green +):

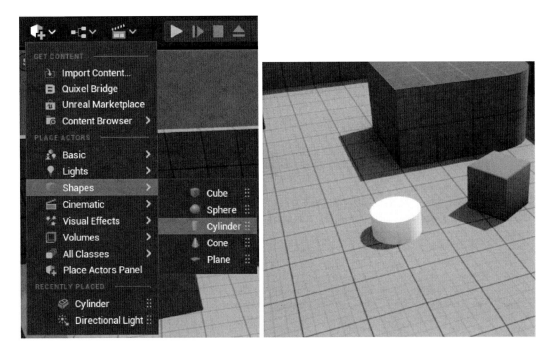

Figure 1.21 – Dragging a Cylinder Actor to our level

3. To delete an Actor, simply select the Actor and press the *Delete* key. You can also *right-click* on an Actor to look at the many other options available to you regarding that Actor.

> **Note**
>
> Although we won't be covering this topic in this book, one of the ways developers can populate their levels with simple boxes and geometry, for prototyping purposes, is BSP Brushes. These can be quickly molded into the desired shape as you build your levels. To find out more about BSP Brushes, go to `https://docs.unrealengine.com/en-US/Engine/Actors/Brushes`.

And with this, we have concluded this exercise and learned how to add and remove Actors to and from our level.

Now that we know how to navigate the **Viewport** window, let's learn about Blueprint Actors.

Understanding Blueprint Actors

In UE5, the word Blueprint can be used to refer to two different things: UE5's visual scripting language or a specific type of asset, also referred to as a Blueprint class or Blueprint asset.

As we've mentioned previously, an Actor is an object that can be placed in a level. This object can either be an instance of a C++ class or an instance of a Blueprint class, both of which must inherit from the Actor class (either directly or indirectly). So, what is the difference between a C++ class and a Blueprint class, you may ask? There are a few:

- If you add programming logic to your C++ class, you'll have access to more advanced engine functionality than you would if you were to create a Blueprint class.

- In a Blueprint class, you can easily view and edit visual components of that class, such as a 3D mesh or a Trigger Box Collision, as well as modify properties defined in the C++ class that are exposed to the editor, which makes managing those properties much easier.

- In a Blueprint class, you can easily reference other assets in your project, whereas in C++, you can also do so but less simply and less flexibly.

- Programming logic that runs on Blueprint visual scripting is slower in terms of performance than that of a C++ class.

- It's simple to have more than one person work on a C++ class simultaneously without conflicts in a source version platform, whereas with a Blueprint class, which is interpreted as a binary file instead of a text file, conflicts will occur in your source version platform if two different people edit the same Blueprint class.

> **Note**
>
> If you don't know what a source version platform is, this is how several developers can work on the same project and have it updated with the work done by other developers. In these platforms, different people can usually edit the same file simultaneously, so long as they edit different parts of that file, and still receive updates that other programmers made without them affecting your work on that same file. One of the most popular source version platforms is GitHub.

Keep in mind that Blueprint classes can inherit either from a C++ class or from another Blueprint class.

Lastly, before we create our first Blueprint class, another important thing you should know is that you can write programming logic in a C++ class and then create a Blueprint class that inherits from that class, but can also access its properties and methods if you specify that in the C++ class. You can have a Blueprint class edit properties defined in the C++ class, as well as call and override functions using the Blueprint scripting language. We will be doing some of these things in this book.

Now that you know a bit more about Blueprint classes, let's create our own.

Exercise 1.03 – creating Blueprint Actors

In this short exercise, we will learn how to create a new Blueprint Actor.

Follow these steps to complete this exercise:

1.   Go to the **ThirdPersonCPP | Blueprints** directory inside the **Content Browser** window and *right-click* inside it. The following window should pop up:

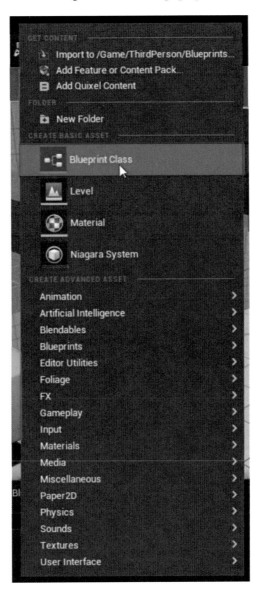

Figure 1.22 – The options window inside the Content Browser window

This options menu contains the types of assets that you can create in UE5 (Blueprints are simply a type of asset, along with other types of assets, such as **Level**, **Material**, and **Sound**).

2.   Click on the **Blueprint Class** icon to create a new Blueprint class. When you do, you will be given the option to choose the C++ or Blueprint class that you want to inherit from:

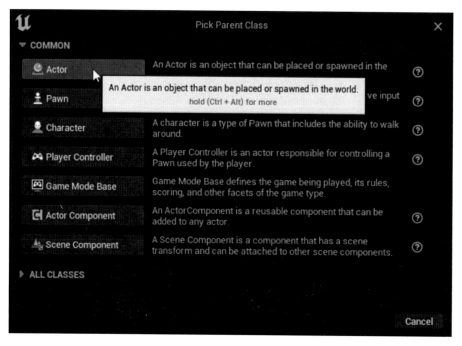

Figure 1.23 – The Pick Parent Class window that pops up when you create a new Blueprint class

3.   Select the first class from this window – that is, the `Actor` class. After this, the text of the new Blueprint class will be automatically selected so that you can easily name it what you want. Name this Blueprint class `TestActor` and press the *Enter* key to accept this name.

After following these steps, you will have created your Blueprint class and completed this exercise. Once you've created this asset, double-click on it with the *left mouse button* to open the Blueprint editor. We will learn more about this in the next section.

Exploring the Blueprint editor

The Blueprint editor is a sub-editor within the Unreal Engine editor specifically for Blueprint classes. Here, you can edit the properties and logic for your Blueprint classes, or those of their parent classes, as well as their visual appearance.

When you open an Actor Blueprint class, you should see the Blueprint editor. This window will allow you to edit your Blueprint classes in UE5. Let's learn about the windows that you're currently seeing:

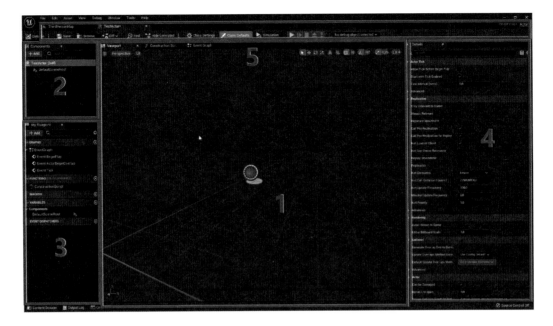

Figure 1.24 – The Blueprint editor window is broken down into five parts

Let's look at these windows in more detail:

1. **Viewport**: Front and center in the editor, you have the **Viewport** window. This window, similar to the **Level Viewport** window that we already learned about, will allow you to visualize your Actor and edit its components. Every Actor can have several Actor Components, some of which have a visual representation, such as Mesh Components and Collision Components. We'll talk about Actor Components in more depth later in this book.

    Technically, this center window contains three tabs, only one of which is the **Viewport** window, but we'll be talking about the other important tab, **Event Graph**, after we tackle this editor's interface. The third tab is the **Construction Script** window, which will not be covered in this book.

2. **Components**: At the top left of the editor, you have the **Components** window. As mentioned previously, Actors can have several Actor Components, and this window is the one that will allow you to add and remove those Actor Components in your Blueprint class, as well as access the Actor Components defined in the C++ classes it inherits from.

3. **My Blueprint**: At the bottom left of the editor, you have the **My Blueprint** window. This will allow you to browse, add, and remove variables and functions defined in both this Blueprint class and the C++ class it inherits from. Keep in mind that Blueprints have a special kind of function, called an **event**, which is used to represent an event that happened in the game. You should see three of them in this window: **BeginPlay**, **ActorBeginOverlap**, and **Tick**. We'll be talking about these shortly.

4. **Details**: At the right of the editor, you have the **Details** window. Similar to the editor's **Details** window, this window will show you the properties of the currently selected Actor Component, function, variable, event, or any other individual element of this Blueprint class. If you currently have no elements selected, this window will be empty.

5. **Toolbar**: At the top center of the editor, you have the **Toolbar** window. This window will allow you to compile the code you wrote in this Blueprint class, save it, locate it in the **Content Browser** window, and access this class's settings, among other things.

You can see the parent class of a Blueprint class by looking at the top-right corner of the Blueprint editor. If you click the name of the parent class, you'll be taken to either the corresponding Blueprint class, through the Unreal Engine editor, or the C++ class, through Visual Studio.

Additionally, you can change a Blueprint class's parent class by clicking on the **File** tab at the top left of the Blueprint editor and selecting the **Reparent Blueprint** option, which will allow you to specify the new parent class of this Blueprint class.

Now that we've learned about the basics of the Blueprint editor, let's look at its **Event Graph**.

Exploring the Event Graph window

The **Event Graph** window is where you'll be writing all of your Blueprint visual scripting code, creating your variables and functions, and accessing other variables and functions declared in this class's parent class.

If you select the **Event Graph** tab, which you should be able to see to the right of the **Viewport** tab, you will be shown the **Event Graph** window instead of the **Viewport** window. On clicking the **Event Graph** tab, you will see the following window:

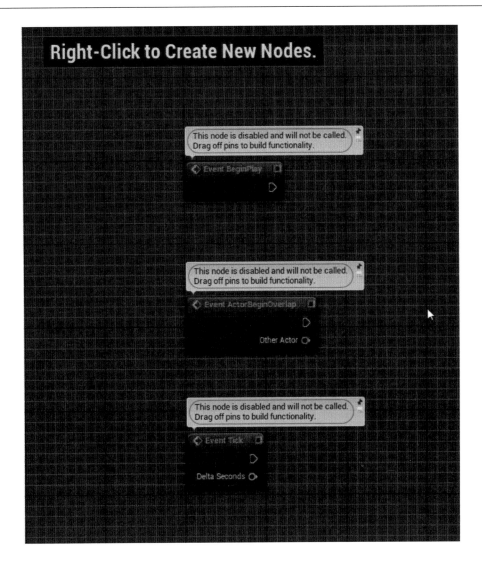

Figure 1.25 – The Event Graph window, showing three disabled events

You can navigate the **Event Graph** window by holding the *right mouse button* and dragging inside the graph, you can zoom in and out by scrolling the *mouse wheel*, and you can select nodes from the graph by either clicking the *left mouse button* or by clicking and holding to select an area of nodes.

You can also *right-click* inside the **Event Graph** window to access the Blueprint's **Actions** menu, which allows you to access the actions you can perform in the **Event Graph** window, including getting and setting variables, calling functions or events, and many others.

The way scripting works in Blueprint is by connecting nodes using pins. There are several types of nodes, such as variables, functions, and events. You can connect these nodes through pins, of which there are two types:

- **Execution pins**: These will dictate the order in which the nodes will be executed. If you want node 1 to be executed first and then node 2, you can link the output execution pin of node 1 to the input execution pin of node 2, as shown in the following screenshot:

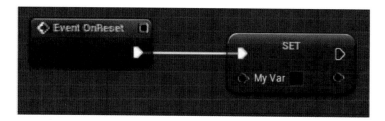

Figure 1.26 – Blueprint execution pins

- **Variable pins**: These work as parameters (also known as input pins), at the left of the node, and return values (also known as output pins), at the right of the node, representing a value of a certain type (integer, float, Boolean, and others):

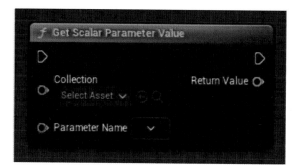

Figure 1.27 – The Get Scalar Parameter Value node

Let's understand this better by completing an exercise.

Exercise 1.04 – creating Blueprint variables

In this exercise, we will learn how to create Blueprint variables by creating a new variable of the **Boolean** type.

In Blueprint, variables work similarly to the ones you would use in C++. You can create them, get their value, and set them.

Follow these steps to complete this exercise:

1. To create a new Blueprint variable, head to the **My Blueprint** window and click the + button in the **Variables** category:

Figure 1.28 – The + button in the Variables category

2. After that, you'll automatically be allowed to name your new variable. Name this new variable `MyVar`:

Figure 1.29 – Naming the new variable MyVar

3. Compile your Blueprint by clicking the **Compile** button on the left-hand side of the **Toolbar** window:

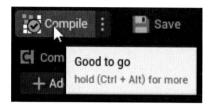

Figure 1.30 – The Compile button

4. Now, if you look at the **Details** window, you should see the following:

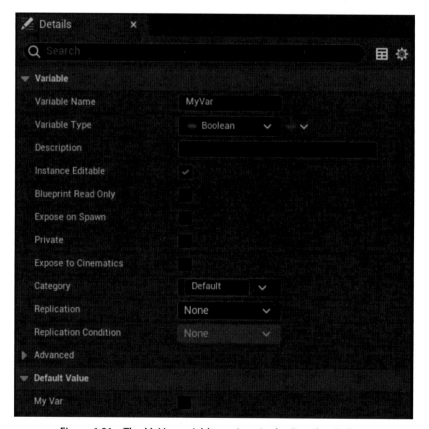

Figure 1.31 – The MyVar variable settings in the Details window

5. Here, you'll be able to edit all the settings related to this variable, with the most important ones being **Variable Name**, **Variable Type**, and **Default Value** at the end of the settings. You can change the values of Boolean variables by clicking the gray box to their right:

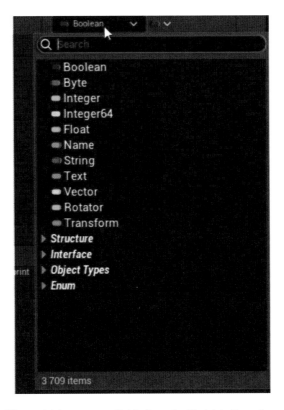

Figure 1.32 – The variable types available from the Variable Type drop-down menu

6. You can also drag a getter or setter for a variable inside the **My Blueprint** tab into the **Event Graph** window:

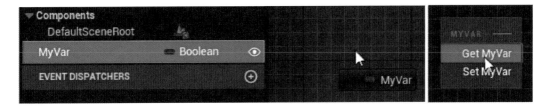

Figure 1.33 – Dragging the MyVar variable into the Event Graph window

Getters are nodes that contain the current value of a variable, while setters are nodes that allow you to change the value of a variable.

7. To allow a variable to be editable in each of the instances of this Blueprint class, you can click the eye icon to the right of that variable inside the **My Blueprint** window:

Figure 1.34 – Clicking the eye icon to expose a variable and allow it to be instance-editable

8. Then, you can drag an instance of this class to your level, select that instance, and see the option to change that variable's value in the **Details** window of the editor:

Figure 1.35 – The exposed MyVar variable that can be edited through the Details panel of that object

And with that, you know how to create Blueprint variables. Now, let's learn how to create Blueprint functions.

Exercise 1.05 – creating Blueprint functions

In this exercise, we will create our first Blueprint function. In Blueprint, functions and events are relatively similar, with the only difference being that an event will only have an output pin, usually because it gets called from outside of the Blueprint class:

Figure 1.36 – An event (left), a pure function call that doesn't need
execution pins (middle), and a normal function call (right)

Follow these steps to complete this exercise:

1. Click the + button inside the **Functions** category of the **My Blueprint** window:

Figure 1.37 – The + Function button being hovered over, which will create a new function

2. Name the new function MyFunc.

   Compile your Blueprint by clicking the **Compile** button in the **Toolbar** window.

3. Now, if you look at the **Details** window, you should see the following:

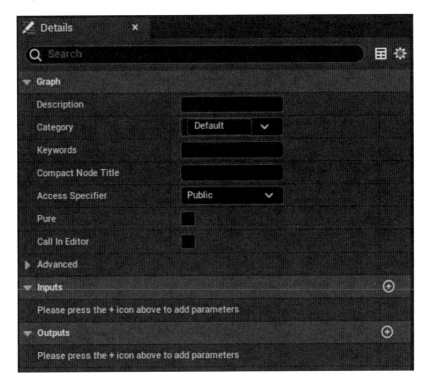

Figure 1.38 – The Details panel for the MyFunc function

Here, you can edit all the settings related to this function, with the most important ones being **Inputs** and **Outputs**. These will allow you to specify the variables that this function must receive and will return.

Lastly, you can edit what this function does by *clicking* it inside the **My Blueprint** window. This will open a new tab in the center window that will allow you to specify what this function will do. In this case, this function will simply return `false` every time it is called:

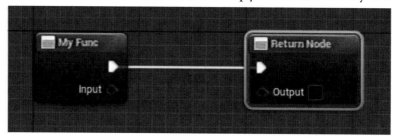

Figure 1.39 – The MyFunc function

4. To save the modifications we made to this Blueprint class, click the **Save** button next to the **Compile** button on the toolbar. Alternatively, you can have it so that the Blueprint automatically saves every time you compile it successfully by selecting that option.

Now, you know how to create Blueprint functions. Next, we will look at the **Multiply** Blueprint node we'll be making use of in this chapter's remaining exercises and activities.

Understanding the Multiply node

Blueprints contain many more nodes that are not related to variables or functions. One such example is arithmetic nodes (that is, adding, subtracting, multiplying, and so on). If you search for `Multiply` in the Blueprint **Actions** menu, you'll find the **Multiply** node:

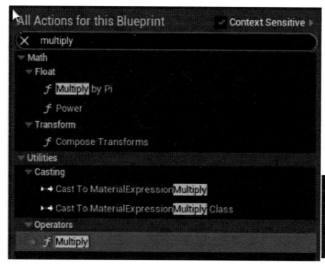

Figure 1.40 – The multiply node

This node allows you to input two or more parameters, which can be of many types (for example, integer, float, vector, and so on; you can add more by clicking the + icon to the right of the **Add pin** text) and output the result of multiplying all of them. We will be using this node later, in this chapter's activity.

Exploring the BeginPlay and Tick events

Now, let's look at two of the most important events in UE5: **BeginPlay** and **Tick**.

As mentioned previously, events will usually be called from outside the Blueprint class. In the case of the **BeginPlay** event, this event gets called either when an instance of this Blueprint class is placed in the level and the level starts being played, or when an instance of this Blueprint class is spawned dynamically while the game is being played. You can think of the **BeginPlay** event as the first event that will be called on an instance of this Blueprint, which you can use for initialization.

The other important event to know about in UE5 is the **Tick** event. As you may know, games run at a certain frame rate, with the most frequent being either 30 **frames per second** (**FPS**) or 60 FPS. This means that the game will render an updated image of the game 30 or 60 times every second. The **Tick** event will get called every time the game does this, which means that if the game is running at 30 FPS, the **Tick** event will get called 30 times every second.

Go to your Blueprint class's **Event Graph** window and delete the three grayed-out events by selecting all of them and clicking the *Delete* key, which should cause the **Event Graph** window to become empty. After that, *right-click* inside the **Event Graph** window, type in **BeginPlay**, and select the **Event BeginPlay** node by either clicking the *Enter* key or by clicking on that option in the Blueprint **Actions** menu. This should cause that event to be added to the **Event Graph** window:

Figure 1.41 – The BeginPlay event being added to the Event Graph
window through the Blueprint Actions menu

Right-click inside the **Event Graph** window, type **Tick**, and select the **Event Tick** node. This should cause that event to be added to the **Event Graph** window:

Figure 1.42 – The Tick event

Unlike the **BeginPlay** event, the **Tick** event will be called with a parameter, **DeltaTime**. This parameter is a float that indicates the amount of time that has passed since the last frame was rendered. If your game is running at 30 FPS, this means that the interval between each of the frames being rendered (the delta time) is going to be, on average, 1/30 seconds, which is around 0.033 seconds (33.33 milliseconds). If frame 1 is rendered and then frame 2 is rendered 0.2 seconds after that, then frame 2's delta time will be 0.2 seconds. If frame 3 gets rendered 0.1 seconds after frame 2, frame 3's delta time will be 0.1 seconds, and so forth.

But why is the **DeltaTime** parameter so important? Let's take a look at the following scenario: you have a Blueprint class that increases its position on the Z-axis by 1 unit every time a frame is rendered using the **Tick** event. However, you are faced with a problem: there's the possibility that players will run your game at different frame rates, such as 30 FPS and 60 FPS. The players that are running the game at 60 FPS will cause the **Tick** event to be called twice as much as the players that are running the game at 30 FPS, and the Blueprint class will end up moving twice as fast because of that. This is where the delta time comes into play: because the game that's running at 60 FPS will have the **Tick** event called with a lower delta time value (the interval between the frames being rendered is much smaller), you can use that value to change the position on the Z-axis. Although the **Tick** event is being called twice as much on the game running at 60 FPS, its delta time is half the value, so it all balances out. This will cause two players playing the game with different frame rates to have the same result.

> **Note**
> In this book, the **Tick** event is used a few times for demonstration purposes. However, because of its performance hit, you should be mindful when using it. If you use the **Tick** event for something that doesn't need to be done every single frame, there's probably a better or more efficient way of doing it.

> **Note**
>
> If you want a Blueprint that is using the delta time to move, you can make it move faster or slower by multiplying the delta time by the number of units you want it to move per second (for example, if you want a Blueprint to move 3 units per second on the Z-axis, you can tell it to move `3 * DeltaTime` units every frame).

Now, let's complete an exercise where we will work with Blueprint nodes and pins.

Exercise 1.06 – offsetting the TestActor class on the Z-axis

In this exercise, you'll be using the `BeginPlay` event to offset (move) the `TestActor` class on the Z-axis when the game starts being played.

Follow these steps to complete this exercise:

1. Open the `TestActor` Blueprint class.

2. Using the **Blueprint Actions** menu, add the `Event BeginPlay` node to the graph, if it's not already there.

3. Add the `AddActorWorldOffset` function and connect the `BeginPlay` event's output execution pin to this function's input execution pin. This function is responsible for moving an Actor in the intended axes (*X*, *Y*, and *Z*) and it receives the following parameters:

    -   `Target`: The Actor that this function should be called on, which will be the Actor calling this function. The default behavior is to call this function on the Actor calling this function, which is exactly what we want and is shown using the `self` property.

    -   `DeltaLocation`: The amount that we want to offset this Actor by in each of the three axes: *X*, *Y*, and *Z*.

    -   We won't be getting into the other two parameters, `Sweep` and `Teleport`, so you can leave them as-is. They are both Boolean types and should be left set to `false`:

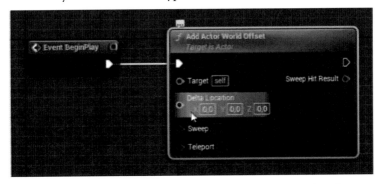

Figure 1.43 – The BeginPlay event calling the AddActorWorldOffset function

4. Split the `Delta Location` input pin, which will cause this `Vector` property to be split into three float properties. You can do this to any variable type that is comprised of one or more subtypes (you wouldn't be able to do this to the float type because it's not comprised of any variable subtypes) by *right-clicking* on them and selecting **Split Struct Pin**:

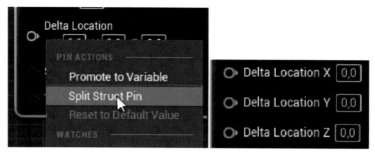

Figure 1.44 – The Delta Location parameter being split from a vector into three floats

5. Set the *Z* property of **Delta Location** to `100` units by using the *left mouse button*, typing that number, and then pressing the *Enter* key. This will cause our **TestActor** to move up on the Z-axis by `100` units when the game starts.

6. Add a cube shape to your **TestActor** using the **Components** window so that we can see our Actor. You can do this by clicking the **+ Add** button, typing **Cube**, and then selecting the first option under the **Basic Shapes** section:

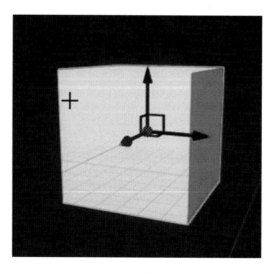

Figure 1.45 – Adding a cube shape

7. Compile and save your Blueprint class by clicking the **Compile** button.

8. Go back to the level's **Viewport** window and place an instance of your **TestActor** Blueprint class inside the level, if you haven't done so already:

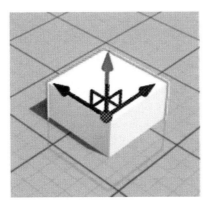

Figure 1.46 – Adding an instance of TestActor to the level

9. When you play the level, you should notice that the **TestActor** class we added to the level is in a more elevated position:

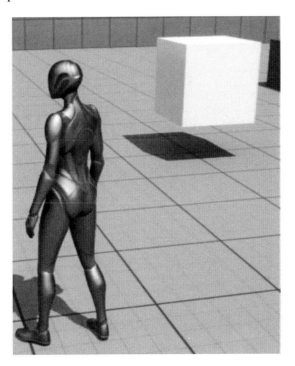

Figure 1.47 – TestActor increasing its position on the Z-axis when the game starts

10. After making these modifications, save the changes that you've made to our level by either pressing *Ctrl + S* or clicking the **Save Current** button in the **Toolbar** window.

In this exercise, you learned how to create your first Actor Blueprint class with Blueprint scripting logic.

> **Note**
>
> Both the `TestActor` Blueprint asset and the `Map` asset, along with the final result of this exercise, can be found here: `https://github.com/PacktPublishing/Elevating-Game-Experiences-with-Unreal-Engine-5-Second-Edition`.

Now, let's learn a bit more about the `ThirdPersonCharacter` Blueprint class.

The ThirdPersonCharacter Blueprint class

Let's take a look at the `ThirdPersonCharacter` Blueprint class, which is the Blueprint that represents the character that the player controls, and look at the Actor Components that it contains.

Go to the **ThirdPersonCPP | Blueprints** directory inside the **Content Browser** window and open the **ThirdPersonCharacter** asset:

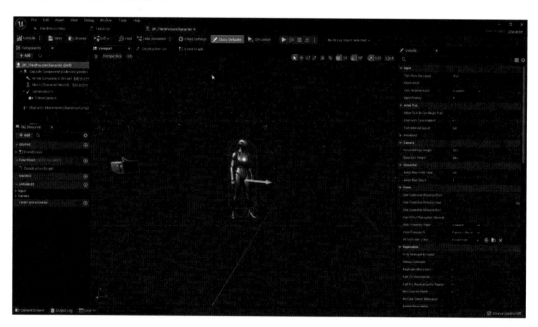

Figure 1.48 – The ThirdPersonCharacter Blueprint class

Previously, when we introduced the **Components** window inside the Blueprint editor, we mentioned **Actor Components**.

Actor Components are entities that must live inside an Actor and allow you to spread the logic of your Actor into several different Actor Components. In this Blueprint, we can see that there are four visually represented Actor Components:

- A Skeletal Mesh Component, which shows the UE5 mannequin

- A Camera Component, which shows where the player will be able to see the game from

- An Arrow Component, which allows us to see where the character is facing (this is mainly used for development purposes, not while the game is being played)

- A Capsule Component, which specifies the collision range of this character

If you look at the **Components** window, you'll see a few more Actor Components than the ones we can see in the **Viewport** window. This is because some Actor Components don't have a visual representation and are purely made up of C++ or Blueprint code. We'll look at Actor Components in more depth in the next chapter and *Chapter 7, Working with UE5 Utilities*.

If you take a look at this Blueprint class's **Event Graph** window, you'll see that it's essentially empty, similar to the one we saw with our **TestActor** Blueprint class, despite it having a bit of logic associated with it. This is because that logic is defined in the C++ class, not in this Blueprint class. We'll look at how to do this in the next chapter.

To explain this Blueprint class's Skeletal Mesh Component, we should first talk about meshes and materials.

Exploring the usage of meshes and materials

For a computer to visually represent a 3D object, it needs two things: a 3D mesh and a material. 3D meshes allow us to specify the shape of an object and its size, while a material allows us to specify its color and visual tones, among other things. We'll dive deeper into both of these in the following sections and see how UE5 allows us to work with them.

Meshes

3D meshes allow you to specify the size and shape of an object, like this mesh representing a monkey's head:

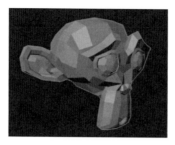

Figure 1.49 – A 3D mesh of a monkey's head

Meshes are comprised of several vertices, edges, and faces. Vertices are simply 3D coordinates with *X*, *Y,* and *Z* positions; an edge is a connection (that is, a line) between two vertices; and a face is a connection of three or more edges. The preceding screenshot shows the individual vertices, edges, and faces of the mesh, where each face is colored between white and black, depending on how much light is reflecting off the face. Nowadays, video games can render meshes with thousands of vertices in such a way that you can't tell the individual vertices apart because there are so many of them so close together.

Materials

Materials, on the other hand, allow you to specify how a mesh is going to be represented. They allow you to specify a mesh's color, draw a texture on its surface, or even manipulate its vertices.

Creating meshes is something that, at the time of writing this book, is not properly supported in UE5 and should be done in another piece of software, such as Blender or Autodesk Maya, so we won't be going into this in great detail here. We will, however, learn how to create materials for existing meshes.

In UE5, you can add meshes through Mesh Components, which inherit from the Actor Component class. There are several types of Mesh Components, but the two most important ones are Static Mesh Components, for meshes that don't have animations (for example, cubes, static level geometry), and Skeletal Mesh Components, for meshes that have animations (for example, character meshes that play movement animations). As we saw earlier, the **ThirdPersonCharacter** Blueprint class contains a Skeletal Mesh Component because it's used to represent a character mesh that plays movement animations. In the next chapter, we'll learn how to import assets such as meshes into our UE5 project.

Now, let's learn how to manipulate materials in UE5.

Manipulating materials in UE5

In this section, we'll learn how materials work in UE5. As mentioned previously, materials are what specify the visual aspects of a certain object, including its color and how it reacts to light. To learn more about them, follow these steps:

1. Go back to your **Level Viewport** window and select the **Cube** object shown in the following screenshot:

Figure 1.50 – The Cube object, next to the text that says Third Person on the floor

2. Take a look at the **Details** window, where you'll be able to see both the mesh and material associated with this object's **Static Mesh** Component:

Figure 1.51 – The Static Mesh and Materials (Element 0) properties
of the Cube object's Static Mesh Component

> **Note**
> Keep in mind that meshes can have more than one material, but must have at least one.

3. Click the *looking glass* icon next to the **Materials** property to be taken to that material's location in the **Content Browser** window. This icon works with any reference to any asset inside the editor, so you can do the same thing with the asset referenced as the cube object's **Static Mesh**:

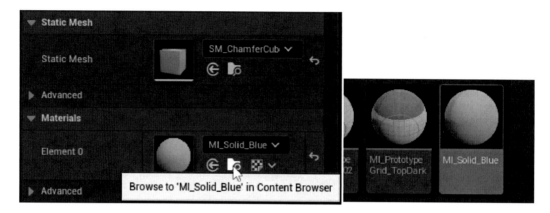

Figure 1.52 – The looking glass icon (left), which takes you to that
asset's location in the Content Browser (right)

4. *Double-click* the asset with the *left mouse button* to open its properties. Because this material is a child of another material, we must select its parent material. In this material's **Details panel**, you'll find the **Parent** property. Click the *looking glass* icon to select it in the **Context Browser** window:

Figure 1.53 – The Parent property

5. After selecting that asset, double-click it with the *left mouse button* to open it in the **Material** Editor. Let's break down the windows present in the **Material** Editor:

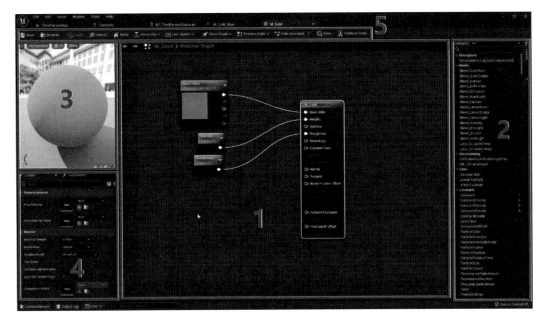

Figure 1.54 – The Material Editor window broken down into five parts

Let's look at these windows in more detail:

1. **Graph**: Front and center in the editor, you have the **Graph** window. Similar to the Blueprint editor's **Event Graph** window, the **Material** Editor's graph is also node-based, where you'll also find nodes connected by pins, although here, you won't find execution pins, only input and output pins.

2. **Palette**: At the right edge of the screen, you'll see the **Palette** window, where you can search for all the nodes that you can add to the **Graph** window. You can also do this the same way as in the Blueprint editor's **Event Graph** window by *right-clicking* inside the **Graph** window and typing in the node you wish to add.

3. **Viewport**: At the top-left corner of the screen, you'll see the **Viewport** window. Here, you can preview the result of your material and how it will appear on some basic shapes such as spheres, cubes, and planes.

4. **Details**: At the bottom-left corner of the screen, you'll see the **Details** window where, similar to the Blueprint editor, you'll see the details of either this **Material** asset or those of the currently selected node in the **Graph** window.

5. **Toolbar**: At the top edge of the screen, you'll see the **Toolbar** window, where you'll be able to apply and save the changes you've made to your material, as well as perform several actions related to the **Graph** window.

In every single Material Editor inside UE5, you'll find a node with the name of that **Material** asset, where you'll be able to specify several parameters related to it by plugging that node's pins into other nodes.

In this case, you can see that there's a node called 0.7 being plugged into the **Roughness** pin. This node is a **Constant** node, which allows you to specify a number associated with it – in this case, 0.7. You can create constant nodes of a single number, a 2 vector (for example, (1, 0.5)), a 3 vector (for example, (1, 0.5, 4)), and a 4 vector (for example, (1, 0.5, 4, 0)). To create these nodes, you can click the **Graph** window with the *left mouse button* while holding the *1, 2, 3,* or *4* number keys, respectively.

Materials have several input parameters, so let's go through some of the most important ones:

- BaseColor: This parameter is simply the color of the material. Generally, constants or texture samples are used to connect to this pin, to either have an object be a certain color or to map to a certain texture.

- Metallic: This parameter will dictate how much your object will look like a metal surface. You can do this by connecting a constant single number node that ranges from 0 (not metallic) to 1 (very metallic).

- Specular: This parameter will dictate how much your object will reflect light. You can do this by connecting a constant single number node that ranges from 0 (doesn't reflect any light) to 1 (reflects all the light). If your object is already very metallic, you will see little to no difference.

- Roughness: This parameter will dictate how much the light that your object reflects will be scattered (the more the light scatters, the less clear this object will reflect what's around it). You can do this by connecting a constant single number node that ranges from 0 (the object essentially becomes a mirror) to 1 (the reflection on this object is blurry and unclear).

> **Note**
> To learn more about material inputs like the ones shown previously, go to https://docs.unrealengine.com/en-US/Engine/Rendering/Materials/MaterialInputs.

UE5 also allows you to import images (.jpeg, .png) as Texture assets, which can then be referenced in a material using Texture Sample nodes:

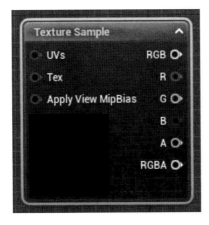

Figure 1.55 – The Texture Sample node, which allows you to specify
a texture and use it or its color channels as pins

> **Note**
> We will learn how to import files into UE5 in the next chapter.

To create a new **Material** asset, *right-click* on the directory inside the **Content Browser** window where you want to create the new asset, which will allow you to choose which asset to create, and then select **Material**.

With that, you know how to create and manipulate materials in UE5.

Now, let's jump into this chapter's activity, which is the first activity in this book.

Activity 1.01 – propelling TestActor on the Z-axis indefinitely

In this activity, you will use the **Tick** event of `TestActor` to move it on the Z-axis indefinitely, instead of doing this only once when the game starts.

Follow these steps to complete this activity:

1. Open the `TestActor` Blueprint class.

2. Add the **Event Tick** node to the Blueprint's **Event Graph** window.

3. Add the **AddActorWorldOffset** function, split its **DeltaLocation** pin, and connect the **Tick** event's output execution pin to this function's input execution pin, similar to what we did in *Exercise 1.01 – creating an Unreal Engine 5 project*.

4. Add a `Float Multiplication` node to the **Event Graph** window.

5. Connect the **Tick** event's **Delta Seconds** output pin to the first input pin of the **Float Multiplication** node.

6. Create a new variable of the `float` type, call it `VerticalSpeed`, and set its default value to `25`.

7. Add a getter to the `VerticalSpeed` variable in the **Event Graph** window and connect its pin to the second input pin of the `Float Multiplication` node. After that, connect the `Float Multiplication` node's output pin to the **Delta Location Z** pin of the **AddActorWorldOffset** function.

8. Delete the **BeginPlay** event and the **AddActorWorldOffset** function connected to it, both of which we created in *Exercise 1.01 – creating an Unreal Engine 5 project*.

9. Delete the existing instance of our actor in the level and drag in a new one.

10. Play the level. You will notice our `TestActor` rising from the ground and up into the air over time:

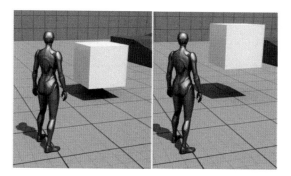

Figure 1.56 – TestActor propelling itself vertically

And with those steps completed, we have concluded this activity – the first of many in this book. We've consolidated adding and removing nodes to and from the Blueprint editor's **Event Graph** window, as well as using the **Tick** event and its **DeltaSeconds** property to create game logic that maintains consistency across different frame rates.

> **Note**
>
> The solution to this activity can be found on GitHub here: `https://github.com/PacktPublishing/Elevating-Game-Experiences-with-Unreal-Engine-5-Second-Edition/tree/main/Activity%20solutions`.
>
> The `TestActor` Blueprint asset can be found here: `https://github.com/PacktPublishing/Elevating-Game-Experiences-with-Unreal-Engine-5-Second-Edition`.

Summary

By completing this chapter, you have taken the first step in your game development journey by learning about UE5. You now know how to navigate the Unreal Engine editor, manipulate the Actors inside a level, create Actors, use the Blueprint scripting language, and how 3D objects are represented in UE5.

Hopefully, you realize that there's a whole world of possibilities ahead of you and that the sky is the limit in terms of the things you can create using this game development tool.

In the next chapter, you will recreate the project template that was automatically generated in this chapter from scratch. You will learn how to create C++ classes and then create Blueprint classes that can manipulate properties declared in their parent class. You will also learn how to import character meshes and animations into Unreal Engine 5, as well as become familiar with other animation-related assets such as *Animation Blueprints*.

2

Working with Unreal Engine

In the previous chapter, we went through the basics of the Epic Games Launcher, along with Unreal Editor fundamentals. We learned how to work with objects and what Blueprints are at a basic level, in addition to exploring the First Person template. In this chapter, we'll be building upon those fundamentals by exploring the Third Person template and working with input and animations.

Game development can be done in a wide variety of languages, such as C, C++, Java, C#, and even Python. While each language has pros and cons, we will be using C++ throughout this book as it is the primary programming language that's used within Unreal Engine.

In this chapter, we will get you up to speed on how to create a C++ project and perform basic-level debugging in UE5. It is very important to be able to debug code as it helps the developer while dealing with bugs. The tools provided come in very handy and are essential for any Unreal Engine developer.

Following this, we will get up close and personal with the core classes involved in creating games and experiences in Unreal Engine. You will explore Game Mode and the relevant class concepts, followed by an exercise to gain a hands-on understanding of this.

The final section in this chapter is all about animations. Almost every single game features animations, some to a very basic extent, but some to a very high level, which includes captivating details that are key to the gameplay experience. Unreal Engine offers several tools you can use to create and deal with animations, including the Animation Blueprint, which provides complex graphs, and a State Machine.

This chapter will focus on many of the basic concepts and features within Unreal Engine. You will be shown how to create a C++ project, how to perform some basic debugging, and how to work with character-specific animations.

In this chapter, we'll cover the following topics:

- Creating and setting up a blank C++ project
- The Content folder's structure in Unreal Engine
- Working with the Visual Studio solution
- Importing the required assets

- The Unreal Game Mode class
- Understanding levels and the Level Blueprint
- Animations

By the end of this chapter, you'll be able to create C++ template projects and debug code within Visual Studio, understand the folder structure and the best practices involved, and be able to set up character animations based on their states.

Technical requirements

This chapter has the following technical requirements:

- UE5 installed
- Visual Studio 2019 installed
- The complete code for this chapter can be downloaded from this book's GitHub repository at `https://github.com/PacktPublishing/Elevating-Game-Experiences-with-Unreal-Engine-5-Second-Edition`.

Creating and setting up a blank C++ project

At the start of every project, you may want to start with any of the templates provided by Epic (which contain ready-to-execute basic code) and build on top of that. Most/some of the time, you may need to set up a blank or empty project that you can mold and sculpt to your requirements. We'll learn how to do that in the following exercise.

Exercise 2.01 – creating an empty C++ project

In this exercise, you will learn how to create an empty C++ project from the template provided by Epic. This will serve as the foundation for many of your future C++ projects.

Follow these steps to complete this exercise:

1. Launch UE5 from the Epic Games Launcher.
2. Click on the **BLANK PROJECT** section and click **Blank**.
3. Under the **Project Defaults** section on the right pane, select **C++**.

> **Note**
> Make sure that the project folder and project name are specified with an appropriate directory and name, respectively.

4. When everything is set up, click on the **Create** button. In this case, our project directory is inside a folder called `UnrealProjects`, which is inside the E drive. The project name is set to `MyBlankProj` (it is recommended that you use these names and project directories, but you can use your own if you wish to do so).

> **Note**
>
> The project name cannot have any spaces in it. It is preferable to have an Unreal directory as close to the root of a drive as possible (to avoid running into issues such as the 256-character path limit when creating or importing assets into your project's working directory; for small projects, it may be fine, but for more large-scale projects, where the folder hierarchy may become too complex, this step is important).

5. After it's done generating the code and creating the project files, the project will open, along with its Visual Studio solution (`.sln`) file.

    Make sure that the Visual Studio solution configuration is set to **Development Editor** and that the solution platform is set to **Win64** for desktop development:

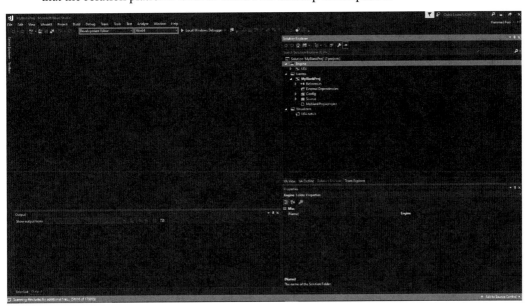

Figure 2.1 – Visual Studio deployment settings

By completing this exercise, you know how to create an empty C++ project on UE5, along with its considerations.

In the next section, we'll talk about the folder structure, along with the most basic and most used folder structure format that's used by Unreal developers.

The Content folder's structure in Unreal Engine

In your project directory (in our case, E:/UnrealProjects/MyBlankProj), you will see a Content folder. This is the primary folder that your project uses for different types of assets and project-relevant data (including Blueprints). The C++ code goes into the Source folder in your project. Please note that the best practice is to create new C++ code files directly through the Unreal Editor as this simplifies the process and results in fewer errors.

There are many different strategies you can use to organize the data inside your Content folder. The most basic and easy-to-understand is using folder names to depict the type of content inside. Therefore, a Content folder directory structure may resemble the example at https://github. com/PacktPublishing/Game-Development-Projects-with-Unreal-Engine/ blob/master/Chapter02/Images/06New.png. In this example, you can see that each file is categorically placed under the name of the folder representing its type at the first level, with the following levels further grouping it into meaningful folders.

> **Note**
> All Blueprints should prefix BP to their name (to differentiate them from the default blueprints used by Unreal Engine). The rest of the prefixes are optional (however, it is best practice to format them with the prefixes shown earlier).

In the next section, we will look at the Visual Studio solution.

Working with the Visual Studio solution

Every C++ project in Unreal Engine has a Visual Studio solution. This, in turn, drives all the code and allows developers to set up execution logic and debug code in its running state.

Solution Analysis

The Visual Studio solution (.sln) file that's produced inside the project directory contains the entire project and any associated code that's been added to it.

Let's have a look at the files present in Visual Studio. Double-click the .sln file to open it within Visual Studio.

In **Solution Explorer**, you will see two projects called Engine and Games.

The Engine Project

At the base level, Unreal Engine itself is a Visual Studio project and has a solution file. This contains all the code and third-party integrations that work together in Unreal Engine. All the code within this project is called the **source** code.

The Engine project consists of the external dependencies, configurations, plugins, shaders, and source code of Unreal Engine that are currently being used for this project. You can, at any time, browse the UE5 | Source folder to view any of the engine code.

> **Note**
>
> As Unreal Engine is open source, Epic allows developers to both view and edit source code to suit their needs and requirements. However, you cannot edit the source code in the version of Unreal Engine that's installed via the Epic Games Launcher. To be able to make and build changes in source code, you need to download the source version of Unreal Engine, which can be found via GitHub. You can use the following guide to download the source version of Unreal Engine: https://docs.unrealengine.com/en-US/GettingStarted/ DownloadingUnrealEngine/index.html.
>
> After downloading, you can also refer to the following guide to compile/build the newly downloaded engine: https://docs.unrealengine.com/en-US/Programming/ Development/BuildingUnrealEngine/index.html.

Game Project

Under the Games directory is the solution folder that's named after your project. Upon expansion, you'll find a set of folders. You will need to understand the following ones:

- **Config folder**: This folder carries all the configurations that have been set up for the project and the build (these can optionally have platform-specific (such as Windows, Android, iOS, Xbox, or PlayStation) settings as well).

- **Plugins folder**: This is an optional folder that's created when you add any third-party plugin (downloaded from the Epic Marketplace or obtained through the internet). This folder will contain all of the source code of the plugins associated with this project.

- **Source folder**: This is the primary folder we're going to be working with. It will contain the Build Target files, as well as all the source code for the project. The following is a description of the default files in the source folder:

  - **Target and Build Files**: These (as shown in *Figure 2.2*) contain code that specifies the Unreal Build Tool (*the program that builds your game*) that you will use to build your game. It contains any extra modules that need to be added to the game, as well as other build-related settings. By default, there are two target files (one for Unreal Editor and another for the build, as depicted by their names), which end with the .Target.cs extension, and one build file that ends with Build.cs.

  - **ProjectName code files (.cpp and .h)**: By default, these files are created for each project and contain the code that's used to run the default game module code.

- **ProjectNameGameModeBase code files (.cpp and .h)**: By default, an empty **Project Game Mode Base** is created. It's not used in most cases.

- **ProjectName.uproject file**: This file contains the descriptors used to provide basic information about the project and the list of plugins associated with it.

Debugging code in Visual Studio

Visual Studio provides powerful debugging features with the help of breakpoints in code. This allows users to pause the game at a particular line of code so that the developer can see the current values of variables and step through the code and game in a controlled fashion (they can proceed line by line, function by function, and so on).

This is useful when you have a lot of variables and code files in your game project, and you want to see the values of the variables being updated and used in a step-by-step fashion to debug the code, find out what issues there are, and solve them. Debugging is a fundamental process of any developer's work, and only after many continuous debugging, profiling, and optimization cycles does a project get polished enough for deployment.

Now that you've got the basic idea of the Visual Studio solution, we'll move on and cover a practical exercise on it.

Exercise 2.02 – debugging the Third Person template code

In this exercise, you'll be creating a project using the **Third Person** template of Unreal Engine and debugging the code from within Visual Studio. We'll be investigating the value of a variable called `BaseTurnRate` in the `Character` class of this template project. We'll learn how the value updates as we move through the code, line by line.

Follow these steps to complete this exercise:

1. Launch Unreal Engine from the Epic Games Launcher.

2. Click on the **Games** section and click **Next**.

3. Select **Third Person** and click **Next**.

4. Select **C++**, set the project's name to `ThirdPersonDebug`, and click the **Create Project** button.

5. Now, close Unreal Editor, go to the Visual Studio solution, and open the `ThirdPersonDebugCharacter.cpp` file:

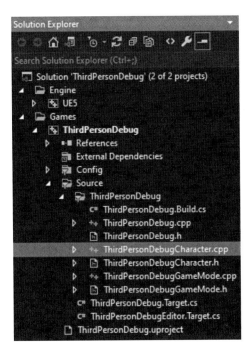

Figure 2.2 – The ThirdPersonDebugCharacter.cpp file's location

6. Left-click on the bar on the left-hand side of line 18. A red dot icon should appear on it (*you can toggle it off by clicking on it again*):

```
16    {
17        // Set size for collision capsule
18        GetCapsuleComponent()->InitCapsuleSize(42.f, 96.0f);
19
```

Figure 2.3 – Collision capsule init code

7. Here, we are getting the capsule component (explained further in *Chapter 3, Character Class Components and Blueprint Setup*) of the character, which, by default, is the root component. Then, we are calling its InitCapsuleSize method, which takes in two parameters: the InRadius float and the InHalfHeight float, respectively.

8. Make sure that the solution configuration setting in VS is set to **Development Editor** and click on the **Local Windows Debugger** button:

Figure 2.4 – Visual Studio build settings

9. Wait until you're able to see the following window in the bottom-left corner:

> **Note**
> If the window doesn't pop up, you can open the window manually by opening **Autos** under **Debug | Windows | Autos**. Additionally, you may also use `locals`.

Figure 2.5 – Visual Studio variable watch window

`this` shows the object itself. The object contains variables and methods that it stores, and by expanding it, we're able to see the state of the entire object and its variables at the current line of code execution.

10. Expand `this`, then `ACharacter`, and then `CapsuleComponent`. Here, you can see the values for the `CapsuleHalfHeight` = `88.0` and `CapsuleRadius` = `34.0` variables. Next to line `18`, where the red dot initially was, you will see an arrow. This means that the code is at the end of line `17` and has not executed line `18` yet.

11. Click the **Step Into** button to go to the next line of code (shortcut: *F11*). **Step Into** will move into code inside the function (if present) on the line. On the other hand, **Step Over** will just execute the current code and move to the next line. Since there is no function on the current line, **Step Into** will mimic the **Step Over** functionality:

Figure 2.6 – Debug step into

12. Notice that the arrow has moved to line `21` and that the variables have been updated. `CapsuleHalfHeight` = `96.0` and `CapsuleRadius` = `42.0` are highlighted in red. Also, notice that the `BaseTurnRate` variable has been initialized to `0.0`:

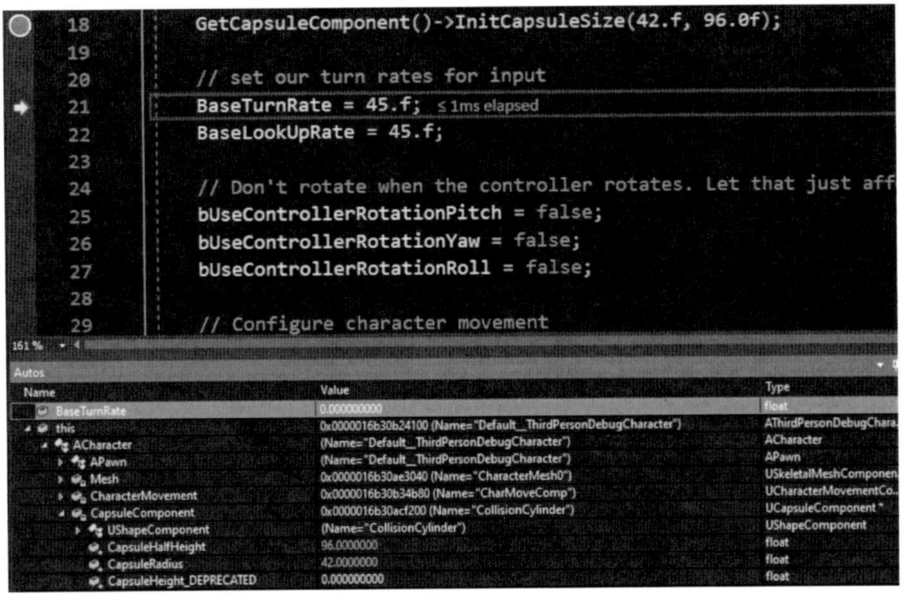

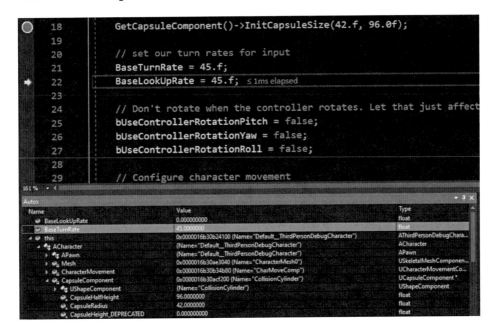

Figure 2.7 – BaseTurnRate initial value

13. Step in (*F11*) once again to go to line 22. Now, the BaseTurnRate variable has a value of 45.0, and BaseLookUpRate has been initialized to 0.0, as shown in the following screenshot:

Figure 2.8 – BaseTurnRate updated value

14. Step in (*F11*) once again to go to line 27. Now, the `BaseLookUpRate` variable has a value of 45.0.

Similarly, you are encouraged to step in and debug other sections of the code to not only familiarize yourself with the debugger but also to understand how the code works behind the scenes.

By completing this exercise, you've learned how to set up debug points in Visual Studio, as well as stop debugging at a point, and then continue line by line while watching an object and its variable's values. This is an important aspect for any developer, and many often use this tool to get rid of pesky bugs within code, especially when there are a lot of code flows and the number of variables is quite large.

At any point, you can stop debugging, restart debugging, or continue with the rest of the code by using the buttons on the top menu bar, as shown here:

Figure 2.9 – Debugging tools in Visual Studio

Now, we'll look at importing assets into an Unreal project.

Importing the required assets

Unreal Engine allows users to import a wide range of file types for users to customize their projects. There are several import options that developers can tweak and play around with to match their required settings.

Some common file types that game developers often import are FBX for scenes, meshes, animations (exported from Maya and other similar software), movie files, images (mostly for the user interface), textures, sounds, data in CSV files, and fonts. These files may be obtained from the Epic Marketplace or any other means (such as the internet) and used within the project.

Assets can be imported by dragging and dropping them into the `Content` folder, or by clicking the **Import** button in the **Content Browser** area.

Now let's tackle an exercise where we'll learn how to import FBX files and see how this is done.

Exercise 2.03 – importing a character FBX file

This exercise will focus on importing a 3D model from an FBX file. FBX files are widely used to export and import 3D models, along with their materials, animations, and textures.

Follow these steps to complete this exercise:

1. Download the `SK_Mannequin.FBX`, `ThirdPersonIdle.FBX`, `ThirdPersonRun.FBX`, and `ThirdPersonWalk.FBX` files from the `Chapter02 | Exercise2.03 | ExerciseFiles` directory, which can be found on GitHub.

> **Note**
>
> The `ExerciseFiles` directory can be found on GitHub at `https://github.com/PacktPublishing/Game-Development-Projects-with-Unreal-Engine/tree/master/Chapter02/Exercise2.03/ExerciseFiles`.

2. Open the blank project we created in *Exercise 2.01 – creating an empty C++ project.*

3. In the **Content Browser** area of the project, click **Import**:

Figure 2.10 – The Content Browser area's Import button

4. Browse to the directory of the files we downloaded in *Step 1*, select `SK_Mannequin.FBX`, and click on the **Open** button.

5. Make sure that the **Import Animations** button is **unchecked** and click the **Import All** button. You may get a warning here stating that **There are no smoothing groups**. You can ignore this for now. With that, you have successfully imported a skeletal mesh from an FBX file. Now, we need to import its animations.

6. Click the **Import** button again, browse to the folder we created in *Step 1*, and select `ThirdPersonIdle.fbx`, `ThirdPersonRun.fbx`, and `ThirdPersonWalk.fbx`. Then, click on the **Open** button.

7.   Make sure that the skeleton is set to the one you imported in *Step 5* and click **Import All**:

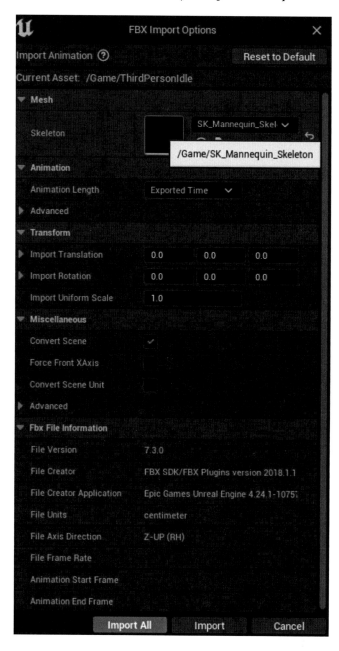

Figure 2.11 – FBX Import Options

8. Now, you will see the three animations (`ThirdPersonIdle`, `ThirdPersonRun`, and `ThirdPersonWalk`) inside the **Content Browser** area.

9. If you double-click on `ThirdPersonIdle`, you'll notice that the left arm is hanging down. This means that there's a retargeting issue. When the animations are imported separately from the skeleton, the Unreal Engine internally maps all the bones from the animation to the skeleton. However, sometimes, that results in a glitch. Let's resolve this:

Figure 2.12 – ThirdPersonIdle UE4 mannequin animation glitch

10. Open the `SK_Mannequin` Skeletal Mesh and open the **Skeleton Tree** tab if it wasn't opened previously:

Figure 2.13 – SK_Mannequin Skeleton Tree tab

11. Under **Options**, enable the **Show Retargeting Options** setting:

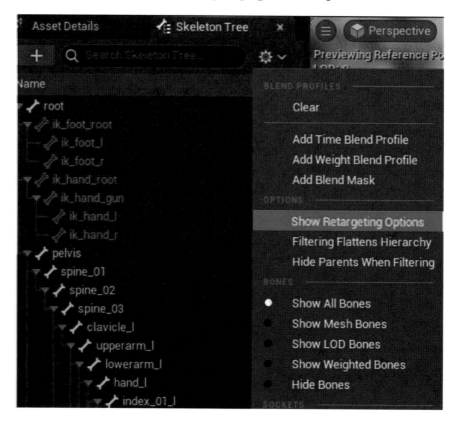

Figure 2.14 – Show Retargeting Options

12. Now, inside the skeleton tree, reduce the `spine_01`, `thigh_l`, and `thigh_r` bones to enable better visibility.

13. Now, select the `spine_01`, `thigh_l`, and `thigh_r` bones. Right-click on them and, in the menu, click the **Recursively Set Translation Retargeting Skeleton** button. This will fix the bone translation issues we encountered previously.

14. Re-open the `ThirdPersonIdle` animation to verify the hanging arm has been fixed:

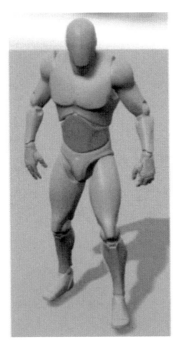

Figure 2.15 – Fixed ThirdPersonIdle animation

> **Note**
>
> You can find the complete exercise code files on GitHub in the `Chapter02 | Exercise2.03 | Ex2.03-Completed.rar` directory by going to the following link: `https://packt.live/2U8AScR`.
>
> After extracting the `.rar` file, double-click the `.uproject` file. You will see a prompt asking **Would you like to rebuild now?**. Click **Yes** on that prompt so that it can build the necessary intermediate files, after which it should open the project in Unreal Editor automatically.

By completing this exercise, you've understood how to import assets and, more specifically, imported an FBX skeletal mesh and animation data into your project. This is crucial for the workflows of many game developers as assets are the building blocks of the entire game.

In the next section, we'll look at the Unreal core classes for creating a game, how important they are for creating a game or experience, and how to use them inside a project.

The Unreal Game Mode class

Consider a situation where you want to be able to pause your game. All the logic and implementation that's required to be able to pause the game will be placed inside a single class. This class will be responsible for handling the game flow when a player enters the game. The game flow can be any action or a set of actions that occur in the game. For example, game pause, play, and restart are considered simple game flow actions. Similarly, in the case of a multiplayer game, we require all the network-related gameplay logic to be placed together. This is exactly what the Game Mode class is there for.

Game Mode is a class that drives the game logic and imposes game-related rules on players. It essentially contains information about the current game being played, including gameplay variables and events, which will be mentioned later in this chapter. Game Mode can hold all the managers of the gameplay objects, it's a singleton class, and it can be accessed by any object or abstract class present in the game.

As with all the other classes, the Game Mode class can be extended in Blueprints or C++. This can be done to include extra functionality and logic that may be required to keep players updated about what's happening inside the game.

Let's go over some example game logic that goes inside the Game Mode class:

- Limiting the number of players that are allowed to enter the game
- Controlling the Spawn location and Player Controller logic of newly connected players
- Keeping track of the Game Score
- Keeping track of the Game Win/Lose condition
- Implementing the Game Over/Restart Game scenario

In the next section, we will look at the default classes provided by Game Mode.

Game Mode default classes

In addition to itself, Game Mode uses several classes to implement game logic. It allows you to specify classes for its following defaults:

- **Game Session Class**: Handles admin-level game flow such as login approval.
- **Game State Class**: Handles the state of the game so that clients can see what's going on inside the game.
- **Player Controller Class**: The main class that's used to possess and control a pawn. It can be thought of as a brain that decides what to do.
- **Player State Class**: Holds the current state of a player inside the game.
- **HUD Class**: Handles the user interface shown to the player.

- **Default Pawn Class**: The main actor that the player controls. This is essentially the player character.

- **Spectator Class**: Being a subclass of the `DefaultPawn` class, the `SpectatorPawn` class specifies the pawn responsible for spectating the game.

- **Replay Spectator Player Controller**: The Player Controller that's responsible for manipulating the replay during playback, within the game.

- **Server Stat Replicator Class**: Responsible for replicating server stat net data.

You can either use the default classes as-is or you can specify your own for custom implementation and behavior. These classes will work in conjunction with Game Mode and will automatically run without being placed inside the world.

Gameplay events

In terms of a multiplayer game, when many players enter the game, it becomes essential to handle logic to allow them to enter the game and maintain their state, as well as viewing other players' states and handling their interactions.

Game Mode provides you with several events that can be overridden to handle such multiplayer gameplay logic. The following events are especially useful for networking features and abilities (which they are mostly used for):

- `On Post Log In`: This event is called after the player is logged into the game successfully. From this point onward, it is safe to call replicated logic (used for networking in multiplayer games) on the `Player Controller` class.

- `Handle Starting New Player`: This event is called after the `On Post Log In` event and can be used to define what happens to the newly entered player. By default, it creates a pawn for the newly connected player.

- `SpawnDefaultPawnAtTransform`: This event triggers the actual pawn spawning within the game. Newly connected players can be spawned at particular transforms or at preset player start positions placed within the level (which can be added by dragging and dropping the `Player Start` from the **Models** window into the world).

- `On Logout`: This event is called when a player leaves the game or is destroyed.

- `On Restart Player`: This event is called to respawn the player. Similar to `SpawnDefaultPawnAtTransform`, the player can be respawned at specific transforms or pre-specified locations (using the player start position).

Networking

The Game Mode class is not replicated to any clients or joined players. Its scope is only limited to the server where it is spawned. Essentially, the client-server model dictates that the clients only act as inputs within the game that is being played on the server. Therefore, the gameplay logic should not exist for the clients; it should only exist for the server.

GameModeBase versus Game Mode

From version 4.14 onward, Epic introduced the `AGameModeBase` class, which acts as the parent class for all Game Mode classes. It is essentially a simplified version of the `AGameMode` class.

However, the Game Mode class contains some additional functionality that is better suited for multiplayer shooter-type games as it implements the `Match State` concept. By default, the Game Mode Base is included in new template-based projects.

Game Mode also contains a State Machine that handles and keeps track of the player's state.

Now that you have some understanding of Game Mode and its relevant classes, in the next section, you will learn about levels and the Level Blueprint, and how they tie to the Game Mode class.

Understanding levels and the Level Blueprint

Levels, in gaming, are sections or parts of a game. Since many games are quite large, they are broken down into different levels. A level of interest is loaded into the game for the player to play. When they are done with that level, another level may be loaded in (while the current one will be loaded out) so that the player can proceed. To complete a game, a player usually needs to complete a set of specific tasks to move on to the next level, eventually completing the game.

A Game Mode can be directly applied to the level. The level, upon loading, will use the assigned Game Mode class to handle all the logic and gameplay for that particular level and override the game mode of the project for this level. This can be applied using the **World Settings** tab after opening a level.

A Level Blueprint is a Blueprint that runs within the level, but cannot be accessed outside the scope of the level. Game Mode can be accessed in any blueprint (including the Level Blueprint) by the `Get Game Mode` node. This can later be cast to your Game Mode class, to obtain a reference to it.

> **Note**
>
> A level can only have one Game Mode class assigned to it. However, a single Game Mode class can be assigned to multiple levels to imitate similar functionality and logic.

The Unreal Pawn class

The Pawn class, in Unreal, is the most basic class of actors that can be possessed (either by a player or AI). It also graphically represents the player/bot in the game. Code inside this class should have everything to do with the game entities, including interaction, movement, and ability logic. The player can still only possess a single pawn at any time in the game. Also, the player can *unpossess* one pawn and *possess* another pawn during gameplay.

The DefaultPawn class

Unreal Engine gives developers a DefaultPawn class (which inherits from the base Pawn class). On top of the Pawn class, this class contains additional code that allows it to move within the world, as you would in the editor version of the game.

The Spectator Pawn class

Some games offer features to spectate games. Let's say you're waiting for a friend to finish their game before joining you, so you go ahead and spectate their game. This allows you to observe the game the player is playing, through a camera that you can move around to get a view of the players or the game. Some games also offer spectate modes that can travel back in time, to show a particular action of the game that happened in the past or at any point in the game.

As the name suggests, this is a special type of pawn that provides sample functionality to spectate a game. It contains all the basic tools (such as the Spectator Pawn Movement component) required to do so.

The Unreal Player Controller class

The Player Controller class can be thought of as the player. It is essentially the *soul* of a pawn. A Player Controller takes input from the user and feeds it to the pawn and other classes for the player to interact with the game. However, you must take note of the following points while dealing with this class:

- Unlike the pawn, there can only be one Player Controller that the player represents in a level. (This is just like when you travel in an elevator. While inside one, you can only control that elevator, but you can then exit it and enter another elevator to control that one.)

- The Player Controller persists throughout the game, but the pawn may not (for example, in a battle game, the player character may die and respawn, but the Player Controller would remain the same).

- Due to the temporary nature of the pawn and the permanent nature of the Player Controller, developers need to keep in mind which code should be added to which class.

Let's understand this better through the next exercise.

Exercise 2.04 – setting up the Game Mode, Player Controller, and Pawn classes

This exercise will use the blank project we created in *Exercise 2.01 – creating an empty C++ project*. We'll be adding our Game Mode, Player Controller, and Pawn classes to the game and testing if our code works in Blueprints.

Follow these steps to complete this exercise:

1. Open the project we created in *Exercise 2.01 – creating an empty C++ project*.

2. Right-click inside the **Content Browser** area and select **Blueprint Class**.

3. Under the **ALL CLASSES** section, find and select **Game Mode**:

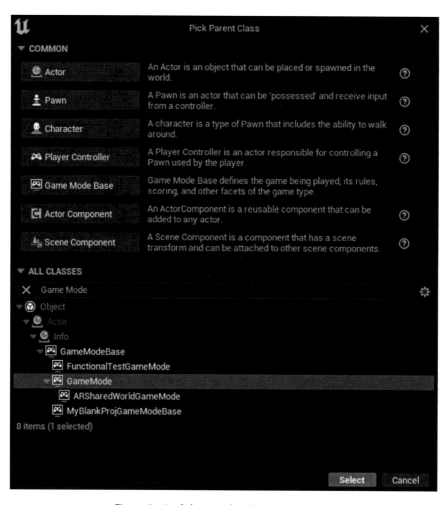

Figure 2.16 – Selecting the Game Mode class

4. Set its name to BP_MyGameMode.

5. Repeat *steps 2* to *4* and select the Pawn class from under the **Common Classes** section, as shown in the preceding screenshot. Set the name of this class to BP_MyPawn.

6. Repeat *steps 2* to *4* and select the Player Controller class under the **Common Classes** section, as shown in the preceding screenshot. Set the name of this class to BP_MyPC:

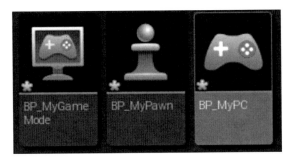

Figure 2.17 – Game Mode, Pawn, and Player Controller names

7. Open BP_MyGameMode and open the **Event Graph** tab:

Figure 2.18 – The Event Graph tab in Blueprint

8.   Left-click and drag from the white pin in the `Event BeginPlay` node and then release the *left mouse button* to open the **Options** menu. Type `print` and select the `print` node highlighted in the list:

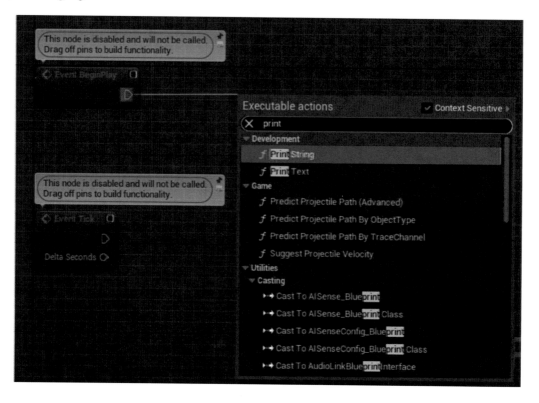

Figure 2.19 – The Print String node (Blueprint)

9.   In the resultant `Print String` node that gets placed under the `In String` parameter, type `My Game Mode has started!`.

10. Now, press the **Compile** and **Save** buttons on the top menu bar.

11. Repeat *steps 7* to *10* for both the `BP_MyPawn` and `BP_MyPC` classes, setting the `In String` parameter to `My Pawn has started!` and `My PC has started!`, respectively.

12. Finally, open the **World Settings** tab by clicking Settings on the right of the editor and clicking on **World Settings**:

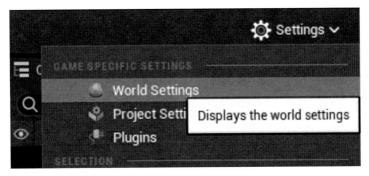

Figure 2.20 – World Settings

13. Under the **Game Mode** section, use the dropdown to set the **GameMode Override**, **Default Pawn Class**, and **Player Controller Class** options to our respective classes:

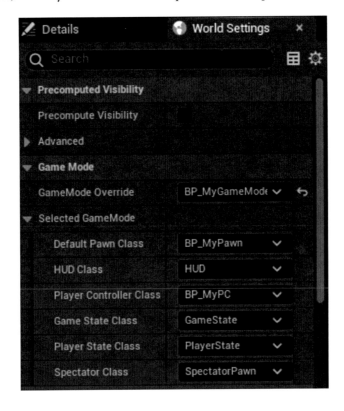

Figure 2.21 – World Settings and Game Mode setup

14. Click **Play** to play your game and see the three print statements on the top. This means that the current **GameMode Override**, **Default Pawn Class**, and **Player Controller Class** options have been set to your specified classes and are running their code:

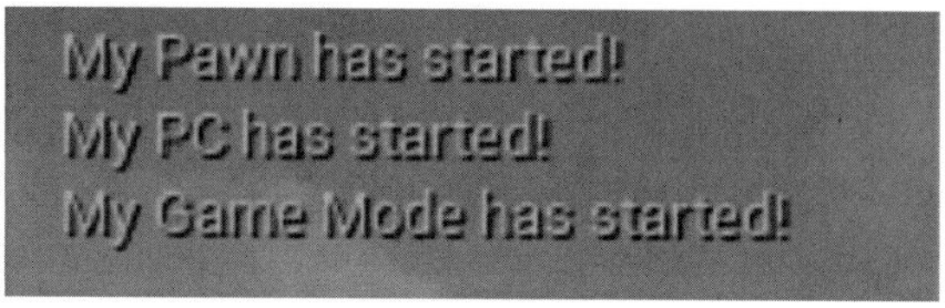

Figure 2.22 – Output prints

> **Note**
>
> You can find the completed exercise code files on GitHub, in the `Chapter02 | Exercise2.04 | Ex2.04-Completed.rar` directory, at `https://packt.live/3k7nS1K`.
>
> After extracting the `.rar` file, double-click the `.uproject` file. You will see a prompt asking **Would you like to rebuild now?**. Click **Yes** on that prompt so that it can build the necessary intermediate files, after which it should open the project in Unreal Editor automatically.

Now that you know the basic classes and how they work in Unreal, in the next section, we will look at animations, what processes are involved, and how they complete them. We'll follow this with an exercise.

Working with animations

Animation is essential for adding life and richness to a game. Superb animations are one of the major factors that differentiate average games from the good and the great from the best. Visual fidelity is what keeps gamers excited and immersed in games, and hence animations are a core part of all games and experiences created in Unreal Engine.

> **Note**
>
> This chapter seeks to cover animation basics. A more in-depth approach to animation will be taken in *Chapter 11, Working with Blend Space 1D, Key Bindings, and State Machines*

Animation Blueprints

An Animation Blueprint is a specific kind of blueprint that allows you to control the animation of a Skeletal Mesh. It provides users with a graph specifically for animation-related tasks. Here, you can define the logic for computing the poses of a skeleton.

> **Note**
> A Skeletal Mesh is a skeleton-based mesh that contains bones, all of which come together to give form to the mesh, whereas a Static Mesh (as the name suggests) is an un-animatable mesh. Skeletal Meshes are normally used for characters and life-like objects (for example, a player hero), whereas Static Meshes are used for basic or lifeless objects (for example, a wall).

Animation Blueprints provide two kinds of graphs: `EventGraph` and `AnimGraph`.

Event Graph

The Event Graph within an Animation Blueprint provides setup events related to animations, as we learned in *Chapter 1, Introduction to Unreal Engine*, that can be used for variable manipulation and logic. Event graphs are mostly used within Animation Blueprints to update Blend Space values, which, in turn, drive the animations within `AnimGraph`. The most common events that are used here are as follows:

- `Event Blueprint Initialize Animation`: Used to initialize the animation.
- `Event Blueprint Update Animation`: This event is executed every frame, allowing developers to perform calculations and update its values as required:

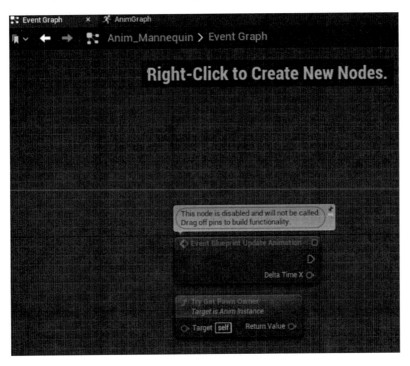

Figure 2.23 – Animation Event Graph

In the preceding screenshot, you can see the default Event Graph. The `Event Blueprint Update Animation` and `Try Get Pawn Owner` nodes are here. You created new nodes and appended them to a graph to complete some meaningful tasks in *Exercise 2.04 – setting up the Game Mode, Player Controller, and Pawn classes.*

The Anim Graph

The Anim Graph is dedicated to and responsible for playing animations and outputting the final pose of the skeleton on a per-frame basis. It provides developers with special nodes to execute different logic. For example, the `Blend` node takes in multiple inputs and is used to decide which input is currently being used in the execution. This decision is usually dependent on some external input (such as an alpha value).

The Anim Graph works by evaluating nodes by following the flow of execution between the exec pins on the nodes being used.

In the following screenshot, you can see a single `Output Pose` node on the graph. This is the final pose output of the animation that will be visible on the relevant Skeletal Mesh within the game. We will be using this in *Exercise 2.05 – creating a mannequin animation*:

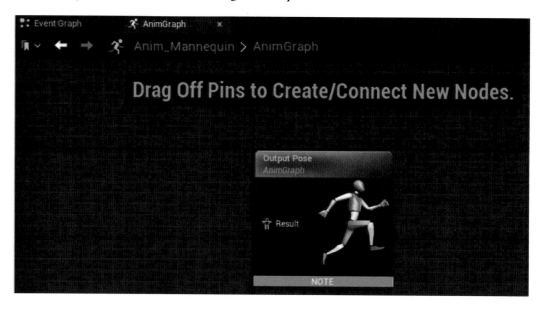

Figure 2.24 – Animation AnimGraph

State Machines

You have already learned how animation nodes and logic can be set up, but one essential component is missing. Who decides when a particular animation or piece of logic should play or execute? This is where State Machines come into the picture. For example, a player may need to shift from crouching to a standing pose, so the animation needs to be updated. The code will call the Animation Blueprint, access the State Machine, and let it know that the state of the animation needs to be changed, resulting in a smooth animation transition.

A State Machine consists of states and rules that can be thought of as depicting the state of an animation. A State Machine can always be in one state at a particular time. A transition from one state to another is carried out when certain conditions (which are defined by rules) are met.

Transition Rules

Each Transition Rule contains a Boolean node called `Result`. If the Boolean is true, the transition can occur and vice versa:

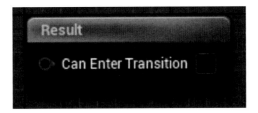

Figure 2.25 – Transition Rules

Blend Spaces

When you're provided with a bunch of animations, you can create a State Machine and run those animations. However, a problem is presented when you need to transition from one animation to another. If you simply switch the animation, it will glitch since the new animation's starting pose might be different from the old animation's ending pose.

Blend Spaces are special assets that are used to interpolate between different animations based on their alpha values. This, in turn, removes the glitch issue and interpolates between the two animations, causing a swift and smooth change in animation.

Blend Spaces are created either in one dimension, known as a Blend Space 1D, or two dimensions, known as a Blend Space. These blend any number of animations based on one or two input(s), respectively.

Exercise 2.05 – creating a mannequin animation

Now that you've gone through most of the concepts related to animations, we'll be diving in hands-on by adding some animation logic to the default mannequin. We'll be creating a Blend Space 1D, a State Machine, and Animation logic.

Our goal here is to create a running animation of our characters and thus gain insight into how animations work, as well as the way they are bound to the actual character in a 3D world.

Follow these steps to complete this exercise:

1. Download and extract all the contents of the `Chapter02|Exercise2.05|ExerciseFiles` directory, which can be found on GitHub. You can extract this to any directory you're comfortable with using on your machine.

> **Note**
>
> The `ExerciseFiles` directory can be found on GitHub at the following link: `https://github.com/PacktPublishing/Game-Development-Projects-with-Unreal-Engine/tree/master/Chapter02/Exercise2.05/ExerciseFiles`.

2. Double-click the `CharAnim.uproject` file to start the project.

3. Press **Play**. Use the keyboard's *W*, *A*, *S*, and *D* keys to move and the spacebar to jump. Notice that, currently, there are no animations on the mannequin.

4. In the `Content` folder, browse to `Content|Mannequin|Animations`.

5. Right-click the `Content` folder and, from the `Animation` section, select `Blend Space 1D`.

6. Select `UE4_Mannequin_Skeleton`.

7. Rename the newly created file `BS_IdleRun`.

8. Double-click `BS_IdleRun` to open it.

9. Under the **Asset Details** tab, inside the **Axis Settings** section, expand the **Horizontal Axis** section and set **Name** to `Speed` and **Maximum Axis Value** to `375.0`:

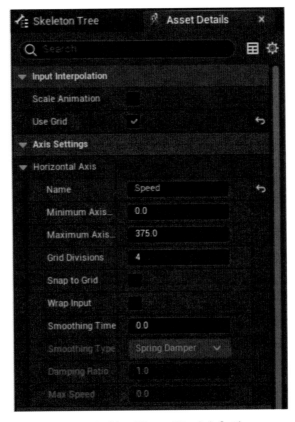

Figure 2.26 – Blend Space 1D – Axis Settings

10. Go to the **Sample Interpolation** section and set **Target Weight Interpolation Speed Per Sec** to 5.0.

11. Drag and drop the ThirdPersonIdle, ThirdPersonWalk, and ThirdPersonRun animations into the graph separately:

Figure 2.27 – Blend Space previewer

12. In the **Asset Details** tab, under **Blend Samples**, set the following variable values:

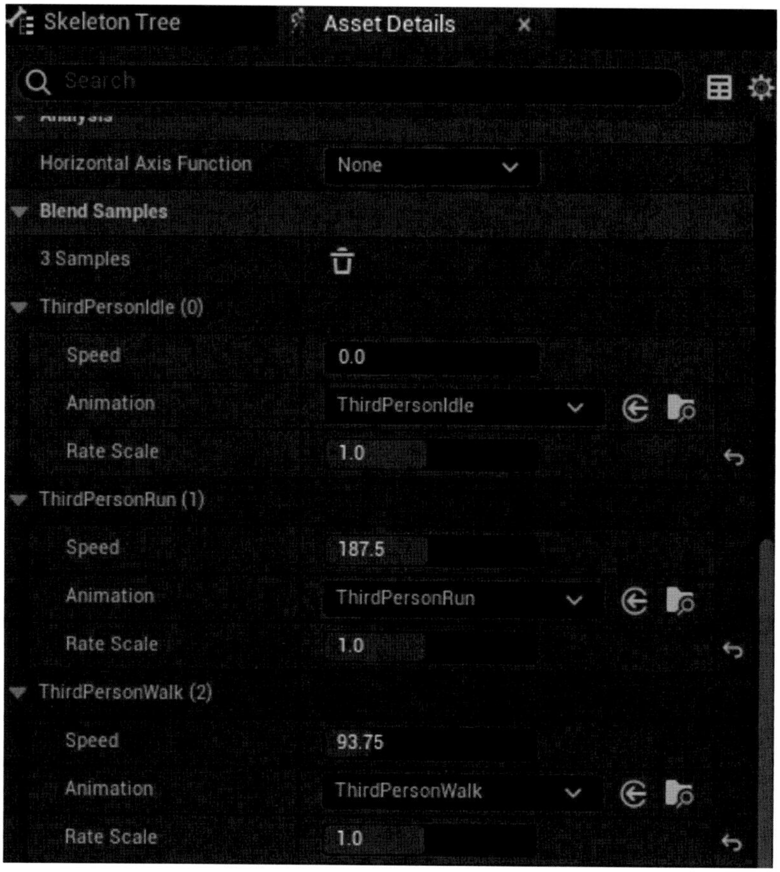

Figure 2.28 – Blend Samples

13. Click **Save** and close this **Asset**.

14. Right-click inside the Content folder and, from the **Animation** section, select Animation Blueprint.

15. In the **Target Skeleton** section, select UE4_Mannequin_Skeleton and then click the **OK** button:

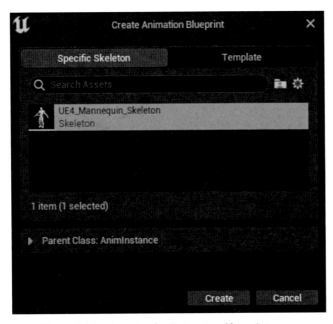

Figure 2.29 – Creating the Animation Blueprint asset

16. Name the file Anim_Mannequin and press *Enter*.

17. Double-click the newly created Anim_Mannequin file.

18. Next, go to the **Event Graph** tab.

19. Create a boolean variable called IsInAir? by clicking the + icon in the variable section on the bottom left-hand side. Be sure to assign the proper type:

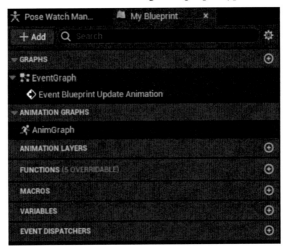

Figure 2.30 – Adding variables

20. Create a float variable called `Speed`.

21. Drag off the `Try Get Pawn Owner` return value node and type `Is Valid`. Select the bottom one:

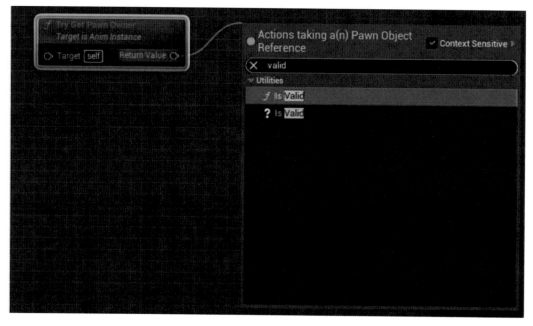

Figure 2.31 – Event Graph Is Valid node

22. Connect the `Exec` pin from the `Event Blueprint Update Animation` node to the `Is Valid` node:

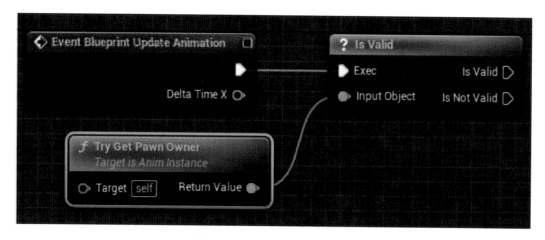

Figure 2.32 – Connecting nodes

23. From the `Try Get Pawn Owner` node, use the `Get Movement Component` node.

24. From the node obtained in *step 22*, get the `Is Falling` node and connect the Boolean return value to a set node for the `Is in Air?` Boolean. Connect the `SET` node exec pin to the `Is Valid` exec pin:

Figure 2.33 – Is in Air Boolean setup

25. From the `Try Get Pawn Owner` node, use the `Get Velocity` node, get its `VectorLength`, and connect the output to the `A Variable Set` node of `Speed`:

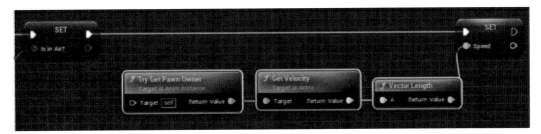

Figure 2.34 – Speed Boolean setup

26. Next, go to the **Anim Graph** tab.

27. Right-click anywhere inside **Anim Graph**, type `state machine`, and click on **Add New State Machine**:

Figure 2.35 – The Add New State Machine option

28. Make sure that the node is selected and press *F2* to rename it `MannequinStateMachine`.

29. Connect the output pin of `MannequinStateMachine` to the input pin of the `Output Pose` node and click the **compile** button on the top bar:

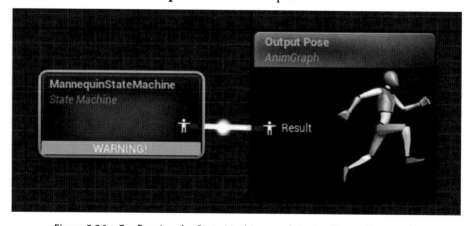

Figure 2.36 – Configuring the State Machine result in the Output Pose node

30. Double-click the `MannequinstateMachine` node to enter the State Machine. You will see an `Entry` node. The state that will be connected to it will become the default state of the mannequin. In this exercise, this will be our `Idle Animation`.

31. Right-click on an empty area inside the State Machine and, from the menu, select **Add State**. Press *F2* to rename it `Idle/Run`.

32. Drag from the icon next to the `Entry` text, point it inside the `Idle/Run` node, and then release it to connect it:

Figure 2.37 – Connecting Added State to Entry

33. Double-click on the `Idle/Run` state to open it.

34. From the **Asset Browser** menu in the bottom-right corner, select and drag the `BS_IdleRun` animation onto the graph. Get the `Speed` variable from the **Variable** section on the left and connect it, as shown here:

Figure 2.38 – Idle/Run state setup

35. Head back to `MannequinStateMachine` by clicking on its breadcrumb in the top banner:

Figure 2.39 – State Machine navigation breadcrumb

36. From the **Asset Browser** menu, drag and drop the `ThirdPersonJump_Start` animation into the graph. Rename it `Jump_Start`.

37. Repeat *step 35* for `ThirdPersonJump_Loop` and `ThirdPerson_Jump` and rename them `Jump_Loop` and `Jump_End`, respectively:

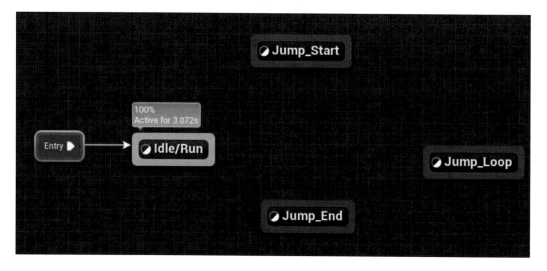

Figure 2.40 – State setup

38. Open the `Jump_Start` state. Click on the `Play ThirdPersonJump_Start` node. *Uncheck* `Loop Animation` in the `Settings` section.

39. Open the `Jump_Loop` state and click on the `Play ThirdPersonJump_Loop` node. Set `Play Rate` to `0.75`.

40. Open the `Jump_End` state and click on the `Play ThirdPerson_Jump` node. *Uncheck* the `Loop Animation` Boolean.

41. Since we can shift from `Idle/Run` to `Jump_Start`, drag from the `Idle/Run` state and drop it to the `Jump_Start` state. Similarly, `Jump_Start` leads to `Jump_Loop`, then to `Jump_End`, and finally back to `Idle/Run`.

Drag and drop the arrows to set up the State Machine, as follows:

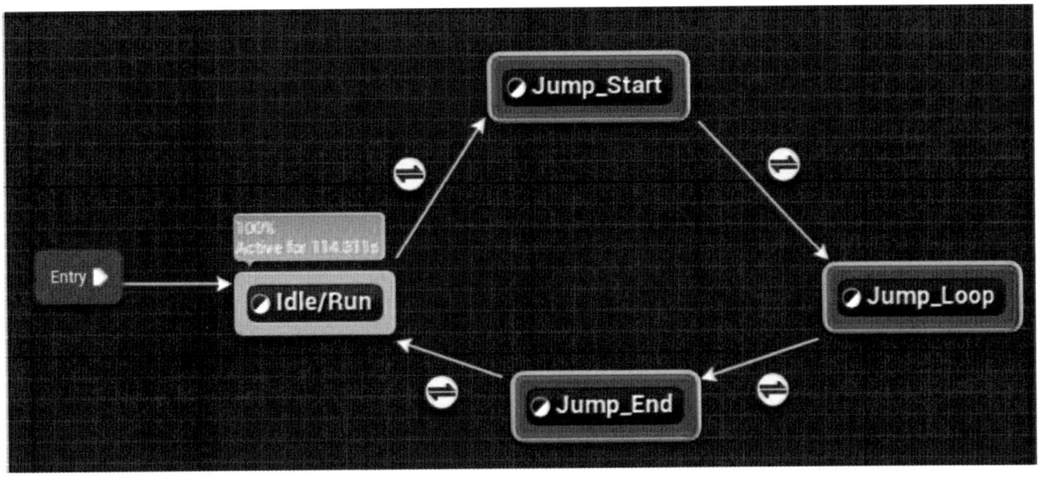

Figure 2.41 – State connections

42. Double-click the `Idle/Run` to `Jump_Start` transition rule icon and connect the output of the `Is in Air?` variable to the result:

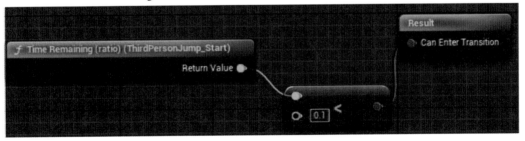

Figure 2.42 – Idle/Run to Jump_Start transition rule setup

43. Open the `Jump_Start` to `Jump_Loop` transition rule. Get the `Time Remaining (ratio)` node for `ThirdPersonJump_Start` and check whether it is less than `0.1`. Connect the resulting bool to the result:

Figure 2.43 – Jump_Start to Jump_End transition rule setup

44. Open the `Jump_Loop` to `Jump_End` transition rule. Connect the output of the inverse of the `Is in Air?` variable to the result:

Figure 2.44 – Jump_Loop to Jump_End transition rule setup

45. Open the `Jump_End` to `Idle/Run` transition rule. Get the `Time Remaining (ratio)` node for `ThirdPerson_Jump` and check whether it is less than `0.1`. Connect the resulting bool to the result:

Figure 2.45 – Jump_End to Idle/Run transition rule setup

46. Close the Animation Blueprint.

47. In the `Content` folder, browse to `Content | ThirdPersonBP | Blueprints` and open the `ThirdPersonCharacter` Blueprint.

48. Select `Mesh` in the **Components** tab:

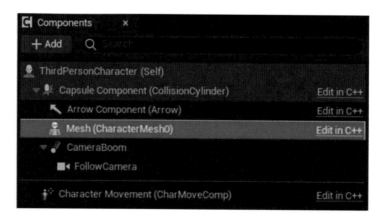

Figure 2.46 – The Mesh component

49. In the **Details** tab, set **Anim Class** to the `Animation Blueprint` class that you created:

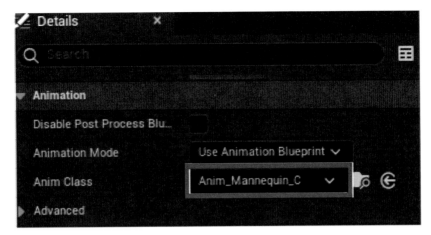

Figure 2.47 – Specifying the Animation Blueprint in the Skeletal Mesh component

50. Close the Blueprint.

51. Play the game again and notice the animations.

You should have achieved the following output. As you can see, our character is running, and the running animation is being shown:

Figure 2.48 – Character running animation

> **Note**
>
> You can find the complete exercise code files on GitHub, in the `Chapter02|Exercise2.05 |Ex2.05-Completed.rar` directory at `https://packt.live/3kdI1SL`.
>
> After extracting the `.rar` file, double-click the `.uproject` file. You will see a prompt asking **Would you like to rebuild now?**. Click **Yes** on that prompt so that it can build the necessary intermediate files, after which it should open the project in Unreal Editor automatically.

By completing this exercise, you've understood how to create State Machines, a Blend Space 1D, an Animation Blueprint, and how to tie it all together with the Skeletal Mesh of a character. You've also worked on play rates, transitional speed, and the transitional states, helping you understand how the world of animation intricately ties in together.

We kicked off this section by understanding how State Machines are used to represent and transition in-between Animation States. Next, we learned how a Blend Space 1D gives us blending in-between those transitions. All this is used by the Animation Blueprint to decide what the current animation of the character is. Now, let's combine all these concepts in an activity.

Activity 2.01 – linking animations to a character

Let's say, as an Unreal games developer, you've been provided with a character Skeletal Mesh and its animations, and you've been tasked with integrating them inside a project. To do that, in this activity, you'll be creating an Animation Blueprint, State Machines, and a Blend Space 1D of a new character. By completing this activity, you should be able to work with animations in Unreal Engine and link them to Skeletal Meshes.

This activity's project folder contains a **Third Person** template project, along with a new character, `Ganfault`.

> **Note**
>
> This character and its animations were downloaded from `mixamo.com`. These have been placed in the `Content |Ganfault` folder of this book's GitHub repository: `https://packt.live/35eCGrk`.
>
> *Mixamo.com* is a website that sells 3D characters with animations and is sort of an asset marketplace for 3D models. It also contains a library of free models, alongside the paid ones.

Follow these steps to complete this activity:

1. Create a Blend Space 1D for the Walking/Running animation and set up the Animation Blueprint.

2. Next, go to `Content | ThirdPersonBP | Blueprints` and open the `ThirdPersonCharacter` Blueprint.

3. Click the Skeletal Mesh component on the left and, inside the **Details** tab on the right, replace the `SkeletalMesh` reference with `Ganfault`.

4. Similarly, update the **Animations Blueprint** section of the Skeletal Mesh component with the Animation Blueprint you created for `Ganfault`.

> **Note**
>
> For the State Machine, only implement Idle/Run and Jump State.

Once you've completed this activity, the Walk/Run and Jump animations should be working properly, as shown in the following output:

Figure 2.49 – Activity 2.01 expected output (left: Run; right: Jump)

> **Note**
>
> The solution to this activity can be found on GitHub here: https://github.com/ PacktPublishing/Elevating-Game-Experiences-with-Unreal-Engine- 5-Second-Edition/tree/main/Activity%20solutions.

By completing this activity, you now know how to navigate Unreal Engine for the project, debug code, and work with animations. You also understand State Machines, which represent transitions between the Animation States and the Blend Spaces 1D that are used in that transition. You can now add animation to 3D models based on gameplay events and inputs.

Summary

In this chapter, we learned how to create an empty project. Then, we learned about the folder structure and how to organize files in the project directory. After that, we looked at template-based projects. We learned how to set breakpoints in code so that we can watch variable values and debug entire objects while the game is running, which would help us find and eradicate bugs in our code.

Thereafter, we saw how Game Mode, Player Pawn, and Player Controller are relevant classes that are used in Unreal Engine for setting up game flows (the execution order of code), as well as how they are set up inside a project.

Finally, we looked at animation basics and worked with State Machines, Blend Spaces 1D, and Animation Blueprints to make our character animate (walk/run and jump) within the game according to the keyboard input.

Throughout this chapter, we became more familiar with the powerful tools in Unreal Engine that are essential for game development. Unreal's Game Mode and its default classes are required to make any kind of game or experience in Unreal Engine. Additionally, animations bring life to your character and help add layers of immersion to your games. All game studios have animations, characters, and game logic since these are the core components that drive any game. These skills will help you numerous times throughout your game development journey.

In the next chapter, we will talk about the `Character` class in Unreal Engine, its components, and how to extend the class for additional setup. You'll be working on various exercises, followed by an activity.

3

Character Class Components and Blueprint Setup

In the previous chapter, we learned how to create empty projects and import files, which folder structure to use, and how to work with animations. In this chapter, we'll explore some other key tools and functionality that you will work with when using Unreal Engine.

Game developers often need to use certain tools that save them time and energy when building game functionality. Unreal Engine's powerful object inheritance capabilities give developers the edge they need to be more efficient. Developers can also work with both C++ and Blueprints interchangeably and use them to their benefit when developing games.

Another value-added benefit developers gain is the ability to extend code for use later in a project. Let's say your client has new requirements that build upon the old ones (as is the case in most game studios). Now, to extend functionality, developers can just inherit a class and add more functionality to it to get results quickly. This is very powerful, and it comes in handy in many situations.

This chapter will focus on the `Character` class in C++. You will be shown how to extend the `Character` class in C++ and then extend this newly created `Character` class further in Blueprints via inheritance. You will also work with player input and some movement logic. We will discuss the Unreal `Character` class, create C++ code, and then extend it in Blueprints, before finally using it to create an in-game character.

In this chapter, we will cover the following topics:

- The Unreal `Character` class
- Extending the C++ class with Blueprints

By the end of this chapter, you will understand how class inheritance works in UE5 and how to utilize it to your advantage. You will also be able to work with Axis Mappings and Action Input Mappings, which are key in driving player-related input logic.

Technical requirements

This chapter has the following technical requirements:

- Unreal Engine 5 installed

- Visual Studio 2019 installed

The complete code for this chapter can be downloaded from GitHub at `https://github.com/PacktPublishing/Elevating-Game-Experiences-with-Unreal-Engine-5-Second-Edition`.

The Unreal Character class

Before we talk about the Unreal `Character` class, let's briefly touch on the concept of inheritance. If you're used to working with C++ or another similar language, you should already be familiar with this concept. Inheritance is the process whereby a class derives characteristics and behavior from another class. A C++ class can be extended to create a new class – a derived class – that retains properties of the base class and allows these properties to be modified or new characteristics to be added. An example of this is the `Character` class.

The `Character` class is a special type of pawn and is a descendant of the Unreal `Pawn` class. Extending upon the `Pawn` class, the `Character` class has some movement capabilities by default, along with some inputs that add movement to the character. As standard, the `Character` class gives users the ability to get a character to walk, run, jump, fly, and swim within the created world.

Since the `Character` class is an extension of the `Pawn` class, it contains all the code/logic of the pawn, and developers can extend this class to add more functionality to it. When extending the `Character` class, its existing components get carried over to the extended class as inherited components (in this case, the Capsule, Arrow, and Mesh components).

> **Note**
> Inherited components cannot be removed. Their settings may be changed, but a component that's added to a base class will always be present in the extended class. In this case, the base class is the `Pawn` class, while the extended (or child) class is the `Character` class.

The `Character` class provides the following inherited components:

- **Capsule component**: This is the root component that serves as the "origin" that other components get attached to within the hierarchy. This component can also be used for collisions and takes the form of a capsule that logically outlines many character forms (especially humanoid ones).

- **Arrow component**: This provides a simple arrow pointing toward the front of the hierarchy. By default, this is set to `hide` when the game starts, but it can be tweaked to be visible. This component can be useful for debugging and adjusting game logic if required.

- **Skeletal Mesh component**: This is the primary component that developers are mostly concerned with within the `Character` class. The Skeletal Mesh, which is the form the character will take, can be set up here, along with all the relevant variables, including animations, collisions, and so on.

Most developers usually prefer to code the game and character logic in C++ and extend that class to Blueprints so that they can perform other simple tasks, such as connecting assets to the class. So, for example, a developer may create a C++ class that inherits from the `Character` class, write all the movement and jumping logic within that class, and then extend this class with a Blueprint, in which the developer updates the components with the required assets (such as the Skeletal Mesh and animation blueprint), and optionally code additional functionality into blueprints.

Extending the Character class

The `Character` class is extended when it is inherited by either C++ or Blueprints. This extended `Character` class will be a child of the `Character` class (*which will be called its parent*). Extending classes is a powerful part of object-oriented programming, and classes can be extended to great depths and hierarchies.

Exercise 3.01 – creating and setting up a third-person Character C++ class

In this exercise, you will create a C++ class based on a `Character` class. You will also initialize the variables that will be set in the default values for the class that will extend this `Character` class.

Follow these steps to complete this exercise:

1. Launch Unreal Engine, select the **Games** category, and click the **Next** button.

2. Select **Blank** and click the **Next** button.

3. Choose **C++** as the project type, set up the project name as `MyThirdPerson`, choose a suitable project directory, and click the **Create Project** button.

4. Right-click in the **Content Browser** area and click the **New C++ Class** button.

5. In the dialog box that opens, select `Character` as the class type and click the **Next** button.

6. Name it `MyThirdPersonChar` and click the **Create Class** button.

7. Upon doing so, Visual Studio will open the `MyThirdPersonChar.cpp` and `MyThirdPersonChar.h` tabs.

> **Note**
>
> On some systems, you might be required to run the Unreal Engine editor with administrator privileges to automatically open the Visual Studio solution with the newly created C++ files.

8. Open the `MyThirdPersonChar.h` tab and add the following code under the `GENERATED_BODY()` text:

    ```
    // Spring arm component which will act as a
    // placeholder for
    // the player camera. This component is recommended to //
    be used as it automatically controls how the
    //camera handles situations
    // where it becomes obstructed by geometry inside the
    // level, etc
    UPROPERTY(VisibleAnywhere, BlueprintReadOnly, Category =
       MyTPS_Cam, meta = (AllowPrivateAccess = "true"))
    class USpringArmComponent* CameraBoom;

    // Follow camera
    UPROPERTY(VisibleAnywhere, BlueprintReadOnly, Category =
       MyTPS_Cam, meta = (AllowPrivateAccess = "true"))
    class UCameraComponent* FollowCamera;
    ```

    In the preceding code, we're declaring two components: the `Camera` component itself and `Camera boom`, which acts as the placeholder for the camera at a certain distance from the player. These components will be initialized in the constructor in *step 11*.

9. Add the following `#include` statements under `#include "CoreMinimal.h"`, in the `MyThirdPersonChar.h` file:

    ```
    #include "GameFramework/SpringArmComponent.h"
    #include "Camera/CameraComponent.h"
    ```

10. Now, go to the `MyThirdPersonChar.cpp` tab and add the following `#include` statements after the `#include MyThirdPersonChar.h` code:

    ```
    #include "Components/CapsuleComponent.h"
    #include "GameFramework/CharacterMovementComponent.h"
    ```

    The preceding code adds the relevant classes to the class, which means we now have access to its methods and definitions.

11. In the AMyThirdPersonChar::AMyThirdPersonChar() function, add the following lines:

```
// Set size for collision capsule
GetCapsuleComponent()->InitCapsuleSize(42.f, 96.0f);

// Don't rotate when the controller rotates. Let that //
just
  affect the camera.
bUseControllerRotationPitch = false;
bUseControllerRotationYaw = false;
bUseControllerRotationRoll = false;

// Configure character movement
GetCharacterMovement()->bOrientRotationToMovement = true;

// Create a camera boom (pulls in towards the
  player if there is a collision)
CameraBoom =
  CreateDefaultSubobject<USpringArmComponent>(
  TEXT("CameraBoom"));
CameraBoom->SetupAttachment(RootComponent);
CameraBoom->TargetArmLength = 300.0f;
CameraBoom->bUsePawnControlRotation = true;

// Create a camera that will follow the character
FollowCamera =
  CreateDefaultSubobject<UcameraComponent>(
  TEXT("FollowCamera"));
FollowCamera->SetupAttachment(CameraBoom,
  USpringArmComponent::SocketName);
FollowCamera->bUsePawnControlRotation = false;
```

The last line of the preceding code snippet will set up the camera to bind its rotation with the pawns'. This means that the camera should, in turn, rotate based on the rotation of the player controller that's associated with this pawn.

12. Head back to the Unreal Engine project and click the **Compile** icon button on the top bar:

Figure 3.1 – The Compile button on the top bar of Unreal Editor

A Live coding succeeded message should appear at the bottom right.

> **Note**
>
> You can find the completed exercise code files on GitHub, in the Chapter03 | Exercise3.01 directory, at https://github.com/PacktPublishing/Game-Development-Projects-with-Unreal-Engine/tree/master/Chapter03/Exercise3.01.

After extracting the .rar file, double-click the .uproject file. You will see a prompt asking Would you like to rebuild now?. Click Yes so that it can build the necessary intermediate files, after which it should open the project in Unreal Editor automatically.

By completing this exercise, you've learned how to extend the Character class. You have also learned how to initialize the default components of the Character class and how to compile the updated code from within Unreal Editor. Next, you will learn how to extend the C++ class you created in Blueprints and why that is feasible in many situations.

Extending the C++ class with Blueprints

As mentioned earlier, most developers extend the C++ code logic to blueprints to link this with the assets they will use. This is done to achieve easy asset assignment compared to finding and setting up the asset in code. Furthermore, it allows developers to use powerful blueprint features such as Timelines, Events, and ready-to-use macros, in combination with their C++ code, to achieve the maximum benefit of developing with both C++ and Blueprints.

So far, we have made a C++ Character class. In it, we have set up components and movement capabilities. Now, we want to specify the assets that are going to be used in our class, as well as add input and movement ability. For this, it is easier to extend with Blueprint and set up the options there. This is what we will be doing in the next exercise.

Exercise 3.02 – extending C++ with Blueprints

In this exercise, you will learn how to extend the C++ class you created with Blueprints to add Blueprint code on top of the pre-existing C++ code. You will also be adding input key bindings, which will be responsible for moving the character.

Follow these steps to complete this exercise:

1. Download and extract the contents of the `Chapter03/Exercise3.02/ExerciseFiles` directory, which can be found on GitHub.

> **Note**
> The `ExerciseFiles` directory can be found on GitHub at `https://github.com/PacktPublishing/Game-Development-Projects-with-Unreal-Engine/tree/master/Chapter03/Exercise3.02/ExerciseFiles`.

2. Browse to the `Content` folder inside the **MyThirdPerson** project we created in *Exercise 3.01 – creating and setting up a third-person Character C++ class*.

3. Copy the `MixamoAnimPack` folder we created in *step 1* and paste it into the `Content` folder directory we opened in *step 2*, as shown in the following screenshot:

Figure 3.2 – MixamoAnimPack placed in the project directory

> **Note**
> The `MixamoAnimPack` assets were obtained from the Epic marketplace via the following link: `https://www.unrealengine.com/marketplace/en-US/product/mixamo-animation-pack`.

4. Open the project. Right-click inside the **Content Browser** area and click `Blueprint Class`.

5.   In the **Search** dialog, type GameMode, right-click the class matching the name, and click the **Select** button. Have a look at the following screenshot:

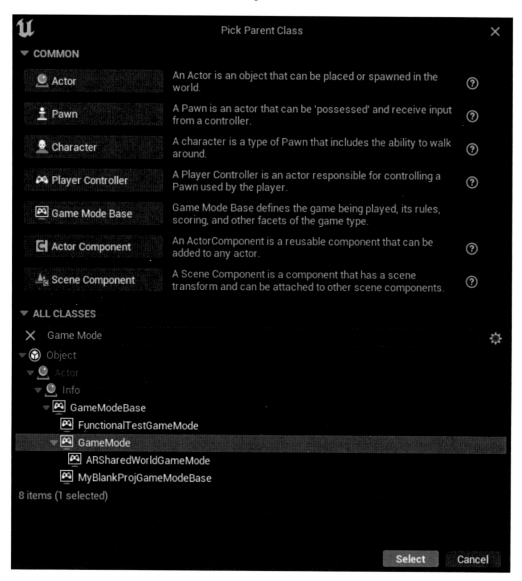

Figure 3.3 – Creating the GameMode class

6.   Name the blueprint we created in *step 6* BP_GameMode.

7.   Now, repeat *step 5*.

8. In the **Search** box, type MyThirdPersonChar, select the class, and then right-click on the **Select** button.

9. Name the blueprint we created in *step 9* BP_MyTPC.

10. In the **World Settings** tab, click the **None** option next to **GameMode Override** and select **BP_GameMode**:

Figure 3.4 – Specifying Game Mode in World Settings

11. Set **Default Pawn Class** to BP_MyTPC:

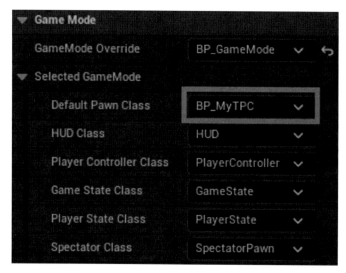

Figure 3.5 – Specifying Default Pawn Class in Game Mode

12. Open **BP_MyTPC** and click on the **Mesh (Inherited)** component in the hierarchy of the **Components** tab on the left-hand side.

13. In the **Details** tab, find the **Mesh** section and set **Skeletal Mesh** to **Maximo_Adam**.

> **Note**
>
> Meshes and Animations will be covered in depth in *Chapter 11, Working with Blend Space 1D, Key Bindings, and State Machines.*

14. In the **Details** tab, find the **Animation** section and set **Anim Class** to **MixamoAnimBP_Adam_C**. You'll note that this class name gets suffixed with _C when selected. This is the instance of the blueprint that was created by UE5. Blueprints, in a working project/build, usually get suffixed this way to differentiate between a Blueprint class and an instance of that class:

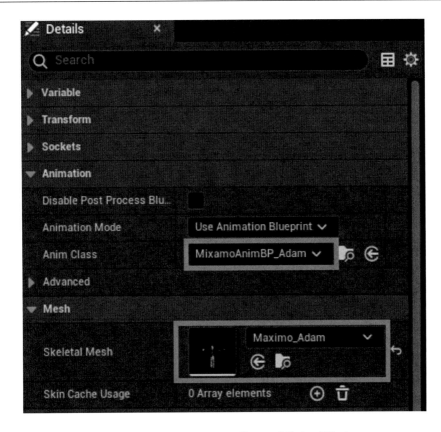

Figure 3.6 – Setting up Anim Class and Skeletal Mesh

15. From the top-most menu, go to the **Edit** drop-down and click **Project Settings**.

16. Click on the **Input** section, which can be found in the **Engine** section:

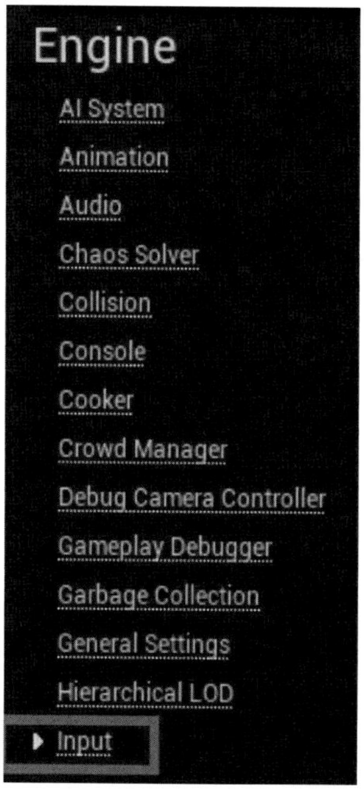

Figure 3.7 – The Input section of Project Settings

17. In the **Bindings** section, click the + icon next to **Axis Mappings** and expand the section.

> **Note**
>
> **Action Mappings** are single keypress actions that are performed, such as jump, dash, or run, while **Axis Mappings** are float values that are assigned that will return a floating-point value based on the keypress of the user. This is more relevant in the case of gamepad controllers or VR controllers, where the analog thumb stick comes into play. In that case, it would return the floating value of the state of the thumb stick, which is very important for managing player movement or related functionalities.

18. Rename **NewAxisMapping_0** so that it's called MoveForward.

19. In the **MoveForward** section, click the drop-down menu and select W.

20. Click the + icon next to the **MoveForward** icon to add another field.

21. Set the new field to S. Set its scale to -1.0 (since we want to move backward with the S key).

22. Create another axis mapping by repeating *step 18*, name it MoveRight, and add two fields – A with -1.0 for the scale and D with 1.0 for the scale:

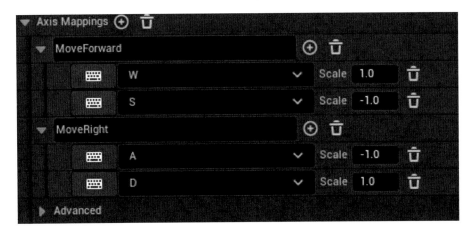

Figure 3.8 – Movement Axis Mappings

23. Open **BP_MyTPC** and click the **Event Graph** tab:

Figure 3.9 – The Event Graph tab

24. Right-click anywhere inside the graph, type Move Forward, and select the first node option:

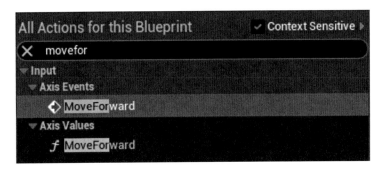

Figure 3.10 – The MoveForward Axis Event

25. Right-click inside the graph, search for **Get Control Rotation**, and select the first node option.

> **Note**
>
> Since the camera associated with a player can choose not to show the pawn's yaw, roll, or pitch, `Get Control Rotation` gives the pawn full aim rotation. This is useful in many calculations.

26. Left-click and drag from **Return Value** of the **Get Control Rotation** node, search for **Break Rotator**, and select it.

27. Right-click inside the graph, search for **Make Rotator**, and select the first node option.

28. Connect the Z (*yaw*) node from **Break Rotator** to the Z (*yaw*) node of **Make Rotator**.

> **Note**
>
> **Make Rotator** creates a rotator with the pitch, roll, and yaw values, while the break rotator splits a rotator into its components (roll, pitch, and yaw).

29. Left-click and drag from **Return Value** of the **Make Rotator** node, search for **Get Forward Vector**, and select it.

30. Left-click and drag from **Return Value** of the **Get Forward Vector** node, search for **Add Movement Input**, and select it.

31. Connect the **Axis Value** node from the **InputAxis MoveForward** node to the **Scale Value** node in the **Add Movement Input** node.

32. Finally, connect the white **Execution** pin from the **InputAxis MoveForward** node to the **Add Movement Input** node.

33. Right-click inside the graph, search for **InputAxis MoveRight**, and select the first node option.

34. Left-click and drag from **Return Value** of the **Make Rotator** node, search for **Get Right Vector**, and select it.

35. Left-click and drag from **Return Value** of the **Get Right Vector** node, search for **Add Movement Input**, and select it.

36. Connect the **Axis Value** pin from the **InputAxis MoveRight** node to the **Scale Value** pin in the **Add Movement Input** node we created in the previous step.

37. Finally, connect the **white Execution** pin from the **InputAxis MoveRight** node to the **Add Movement Input** node we added in *step 36*:

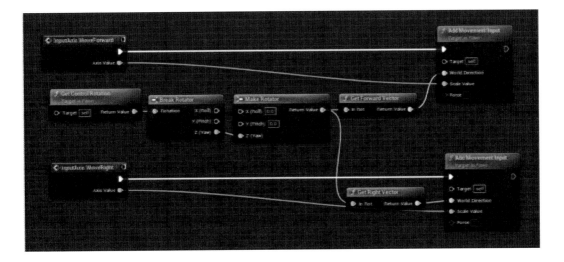

Figure 3.11 – Movement logic

38. Now, head to the **Viewport** tab. Here, you will see that the character's front is not pointing in the direction of the arrow and that the character is displaced above the capsule component. Click on the Mesh component and select the object translation node located at the top of the viewport. Then, drag the arrows on the Mesh to adjust it so that the feet align with the bottom of the capsule component and the Mesh is rotated to point toward the arrow:

Figure 3.12 – The Translation Rotation and Scale Selector section

Once the character is aligned in the capsule, it will look as follows:

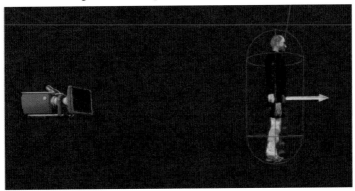

Figure 3.13 – Mesh adjusted within the capsule component

39. In the **Toolbar** menu, press the **Compile** button and then **Save**.

40. Go back to the map tab and press the **Play** button to view your character in-game. Use the *W*, *A*, *S*, and *D* keys to move around.

> **Note**
>
> You can find the completed exercise code files on GitHub, in the `Chapter03 | Exercise3.02` directory, at `https://packt.live/3keGxIU`.

After extracting the `.rar` file, double-click the `.uproject` file. You will see a prompt asking **Would you like to rebuild now?**. Click `Yes` on that prompt so that it can build the necessary intermediate files, after which it should open the project in Unreal Editor automatically.

By completing this exercise, you know how to extend C++ code with Blueprints, and why that is favorable in many situations for developers. You also learned how to add input mappings and how they are used to drive player-related input logic.

In the activity for this chapter, you will be combining the skills you have gained from the previous exercises of this chapter and extending the project you completed in *Activity 2.01 – linking animations to a character* of *Chapter 2, Working with Unreal Engine*. This will allow you to build on your own Blueprint and see how that maps to real-world scenarios.

Activity 3.01 – extending the C++ Character class with Blueprints in the Animation project

Now that you've created a C++ class and extended it with Blueprints, it is time to bring both concepts together in a real-world scenario. In this activity, you will be making our character from *Activity 2.01 – linking animations to a character*, which can be found in *Chapter 2, Working with Unreal Engine*, jump using the spacebar key on your keyboard. However, you need to create the `Character` class from scratch in C++ and then later extend it with Blueprint to reach the final goal.

Follow these steps to complete this activity:

1. Open the project from *Activity 2.01 – linking animations to a character*.

2. Create a `Character` class in C++ that will initialize the character variables, including the camera associated with the player.

3. Map the `Jump` input to the spacebar key in the project settings.

4. Extend the created C++ class with a blueprint to add the associated assets and jump functionality.

Expected Output

The character should be able to jump when you press the spacebar key. The level should use the Blueprint that extends the C++ `Character` class:

Figure 3.14 – Ganfault jump activity expected output

> **Note**
> The solution to this activity can be found on GitHub here: `https://github.com/PacktPublishing/Elevating-Game-Experiences-with-Unreal-Engine-5-Second-Edition/tree/main/Activity%20solutions`.

By completing this activity, you've understood scenarios where C++ code is extended in Blueprints to implement functionalities and logic. This combination of C++ and Blueprints is the most powerful tool game developers possess to create masterful and unique games within Unreal Engine.

Summary

In this chapter, you learned how to create a C++ `Character` class, add initializer code to it, and then use Blueprints to extend it to set up assets and add additional code.

The result obeys the C++ code, as well as the Blueprint code, and can be used in any purposeful scenario.

You also learned how to set up Axis Mappings that have been mapped to the *W*, *A*, *S*, and *D* keys to move players (which is the default movement mapping in many games). You also learned how to make the character jump within the game.

In the next chapter, you will explore Input Mappings in more depth and how to use the Mobile Previewer within Unreal Editor. This will help you create games with solid inputs mapped to game and player logic. It will also allow you to quickly test what your game will look and feel like on a mobile, all within Unreal Editor.

4

Getting Started with Player Input

In the previous chapter, we created our C++ class, which inherits from the `Character` class, and added all the necessary `Actor` components to be able to see the game from the character's perspective, as well as being able to see the character itself. We then created a `Blueprint` class that inherits from that C++ class in order to visually set up all of its necessary components.

In this chapter, we will be looking at these topics in more depth, as well as covering their C++ usage. We will learn about how player input works in UE5, how the engine handles input events (*key presses and releases*), and how we can use them to control logic in our game.

In this chapter, we will cover the following topics:

- Understanding Input Actions and Contexts
- Processing Player Input
- Pivoting the camera around the character

By the end of this chapter, you will know about **Input Actions** and **Input Contexts**, how to create and modify them, how to listen to each of those mappings, and how to execute in-game actions when they're pressed and released.

> **Note**
>
> In this chapter, we will be using an alternative version of the `Character` blueprint we created called BP_MyTPC in the previous chapter. This chapter's version will have the default UE5 Mannequin mesh, not the one from Mixamo.

Let's start this chapter by getting to know how UE5 abstracts the keys pressed by a player to make it easier for you to be notified of those events.

Technical requirements

The project for this chapter can be found in the Chapter04 folder of the code bundle for this book, which can be downloaded here: `https://github.com/PacktPublishing/Elevating-Game-Experiences-with-Unreal-Engine-5-Second-Edition`.

Understanding Input Actions and Contexts

Player input is the thing that distinguishes video games from other forms of entertainment media – the fact that they're interactive. For a video game to be interactive, it must take into account a player's input. Many games do this by allowing the player to control a virtual character that acts upon the virtual world it's in, depending on the keys and buttons that the player presses, which is exactly what we'll be doing in this chapter.

> **Note**
>
> It's important to note that UE5 has two input systems – the Legacy Input System, used since the start of UE4, and the new Enhanced Input System, introduced only in the last version of UE5 as an experimental system and now as a complete plugin in UE5. We will be using the new Enhanced Input System in this book. If you wish to know more about UE5's Legacy Input System, you can do so by accessing this link: `https://docs.unrealengine.com/4.27/en-US/InteractiveExperiences/Input/`

Most game development tools nowadays allow you to abstract keypresses into **actions**, which allow you to associate a name (for example, *Jump*) with several different player inputs (pressing a button, flicking a thumbstick, and so on). In UE5, the way in which you can specify this is through the use of **Input Actions** combined with **Input Contexts** (also referred to as **Input Mapping Contexts**).

Input Contexts contain **Input Actions** that are associated with them, along with which keys will execute them, and **Input Actions** contain specifications as to how they will be executed. The combination of both of these assets allows you to do something when an **Input Action** is triggered but also easily change how that **Input Action** is triggered and by which keys.

In order to better understand how **Input Contexts** and **Input Actions** work together, let's think of a game, such as *GTA*, where you have different gameplay contexts in which you control different people/objects with different keys.

For instance, when you're controlling your player character running around the city, you use the movement keys to move the character around, and you use a different key to make your character jump. However, when you enter a car, the controls will change. The movement keys will now steer the car instead, and the same key that was used for jumping will now be used, for instance, for braking.

In this example, you have two different Input Contexts (controlling the character and controlling the vehicle), each with its own set of Input Actions. Some of those Input Actions are triggered by the same key, but that's fine, because they're done in different Input Contexts (for example, using the same key to cause your character to jump and to stop the vehicle).

Before we start looking into some of the Enhanced Input-related assets, because it's a plugin, we'll have to enable it. To enable it, follow these steps:

1. Go to **Edit** | **Plugins** | **Built-In** | **Input** and tick the **Enabled** box for the **Enhanced Input** plugin. After you have done so, you'll be prompted to restart the editor.

2. Click the **Restart Now** button when this happens. After the editor restarts, and now that the **Enhanced Input** plugin has been enabled, you'll need to tell the engine to use its classes to handle the player's input.

3. To do this, go to **Edit** | **Project Settings** | **Engine** | **Input**, and then, inside the **Default Classes** category (near the end), set the **Default Player Input Class** property to EnhancedPlayerInput and the **Default Input Component Class** property to EnhancedInputComponent. Now that the **Enhanced Input** plugin has been enabled and its classes are being used, we can proceed with this chapter's content.

In order to know more about Input Contexts and Input Actions, let's inspect them. Follow these steps:

1. Right-click on the **Context Browser** and select **Input** | **Input Action**. Name the newly created Input Action IA_Movement, and then open it. You should see the Input Action window, which has the following properties:

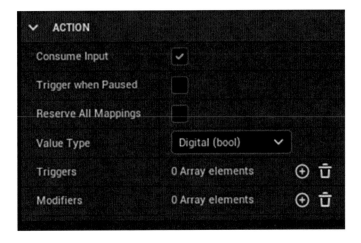

Figure 4.1 – The Action window

Now, let's take a look at its options in detail:

- **Consume Input**: This specifies whether this Input Action will block other actions that are triggered by the same key simultaneously. If it's set to `true`, another Input Action with a lower priority that will be triggered by the same key won't be triggered.

- **Trigger when Paused**: This specifies whether this Input Action can be triggered if the game is paused.

- **Reserve All Mappings**: This specifies whether a higher priority Input Action will be triggered if it's triggered by the same key.

- **Value Type**: This specifies the type of value for this Input Action. Its values can be the following:

  - **Digital (bool)**: Used for Input Actions that have a binary state – for instance, a jumping Input Action, in which the player is either pressing it or not, would use this value.

  - **Axis 1D (float)**: Used for Input Actions that have a scalar state in one dimension – for instance, accelerating in a racing game, where you can use the gamepad's triggers to control the throttle.

  - **Axis 2D (Vector2D)**: Used for Input Actions that have a scalar state in two dimensions – for instance, actions for moving your character, which are done using two axes (the forward axis and the sideways axis), would be good candidates for using this value.

- **Axis 3D (Vector)**: Used for Input Actions that have a scalar state in three dimensions. This value isn't as likely to be used as the others, but you may find a use for it.

- **Triggers**: This specifies the key events that will execute this Input Action. The values for this can be a combination of the following:

  - **Chorded Action**: The Input Action is triggered as long as a different specified Input Action is also triggered.

  - **Down**: The Input Action is triggered for every frame that the key exceeds the actuation threshold.

Note

The actuation threshold is the value at which a key's input will be considered for executing an action. Binary keys (like the ones on a keyboard) have an input value of either 0 (not pressed) or 1 (pressed), while scalar keys, like the triggers on a gamepad, have an input value that goes continuously from 0 to 1 or, like the individual axes of the thumbsticks, that go continuously from −1 to 1.

- **Hold**: The Input Action is triggered when the key has exceeded the actuation threshold for a specified amount of time. You can optionally specify whether it's triggered once or for every frame.

- **Hold and Release**: The Input Action is triggered when the key has exceeded the actuation threshold for a specified amount of time and then stops exceeding that actuation threshold.

- **Pressed**: The Input Action is triggered once the key exceeds the actuation threshold and won't be triggered again until it's released.

- **Pulse**: The Input Action is triggered at a specified interval as long as the key exceeds the actuation threshold. You can specify whether the first pulse triggers the Input Action and whether there's a limit to how many times it can be called.

- **Released**: The Input Action is triggered once the key stops exceeding the actuation threshold.

- **Tap**: The Input Action is triggered when the key starts and then stops exceeding the Actuation Threshold, as long as it's done within the specified amount of time.

- **Modifiers**: This specifies the ways in which this Input Action's input will be modified:

- **Dead Zone**: The key's input will be read as 0 if it's lower than the lower threshold and as 1 if it's higher than the upper threshold.

- **FOV Scaling**: The key's input will be scaled alongside the FOV (if the FOV increases, the key's input will increase, and vice versa).

- **Modifier Collection**: The key's input will be modified according to the specified list of modifiers.

- **Negate**: The key's input will be inverted.

- **Response Curve – Exponential**: An exponential curve will be applied on the key's input.

- **Response Curve – User Defined**: A user-defined curve will be applied on the key's input.

- **Scalar**: The key's input will be scaled at each axis according to the scalar specified.

- **Smooth**: The key's input will be smoothed out across multiple frames.

- **Swizzle Input Axis Values**: The key's axis order will be switched.

- **To World Space**: The key's axes will be converted toworld space.

2. After doing this, right-click on **Context Browser** and select **Input | Input Context**. Name the newly created input context `IC_Character` and open it.

    You should see the Input Action window pop up. Note that it has an empty **MAPPINGS** property.

Figure 4.2 – The MAPPINGS property

3. Let's now add a new mapping. Press the + button next to the **Mappings** property. You'll notice a new property show up where you can specify the Input Action this mapping will be associated with.

This action can be triggered by several different keys, each of which can have its own triggers and modifiers, which work the same as the corresponding properties in the Input Action asset.

> **Note**
>
> When it comes to modifying the **Triggers** and **Modifiers** properties, the usual practice is to change the modifiers in the Input Context asset and the triggers in the Input Action asset.

> **Note**
>
> We will not be using these properties in this book, but for each Input Mapping Context, you can specify whether it can be modified by a player by ticking the **Is Player Mappable** property and specifying **Player Mappable Options**.

When we generated the `Third Person` template project back in *Chapter 1, Introduction to Unreal Engine*

, it came with some inputs already configured, which were the *W, A, S,* and *D* keys, as well as the `left thumbstick` for movement, the *spacebar* key, and the `gamepad bottom face` button for jumping.

For context, let's consider an Xbox One controller, which can be broken down into the following:

*   The **left analog stick**, usually used for controlling movement in games
*   The **D-pad**, which can control movement and also has a variety of other uses
*   The **right analog stick**, usually used for controlling the camera and view perspective

- The **face buttons** (**X**, **Y**, **A**, and **B**), which can have various uses depending on the game but usually allow the player to perform actions in the game world

- The **bumpers and triggers** (**LB**, **RB**, **LT**, and **RT**), which can be used for actions such as aiming and shooting or accelerating and braking

Now that we've learned how to set up `Input Actions`, let's add some of them in the next exercise.

Exercise 4.01 – creating the movement and jump input actions

In this exercise, we'll be adding the mappings for the *Movement* and *Jump* Input Actions.

To achieve this, follow these steps:

1. Open the **IA_Movement** Input Action.

2. Set its value type as **Axis2D**. We'll make this an Input Action of type **Axis2D** because the character's movement is done on two axes – the forward axis (the *Y* axis for this Input Action) and the sideways or right axis (the *X* axis for this Input Action):

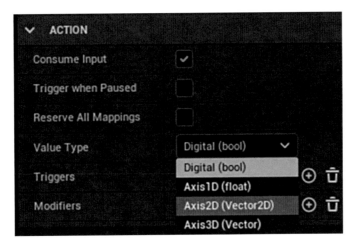

Figure 4.3 – The Value Type options

3. Add a new trigger of type **Down** with an actuation threshold of **0,1**. This will ensure that this Input Action is called when one of its keys has an actuation threshold of at least **0,1**:

Figure 4.4 – The Down trigger

4. Open the **IC_Character** Input Context.

5. Click the + icon to the right of the **Mappings** property to create a new mapping:

Figure 4.5 – Adding a new action mapping

6. When you've done so, you should see a new empty mapping with its properties either empty or set to **None**:

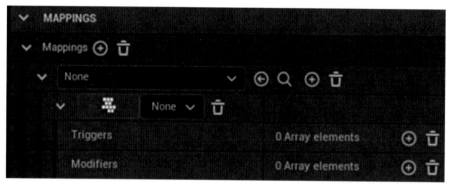

Figure 4.6 – The default settings of a new action mapping

7. Set the Input Action of this mapping (the first property that's set to **None**) to **IA_Movement**:

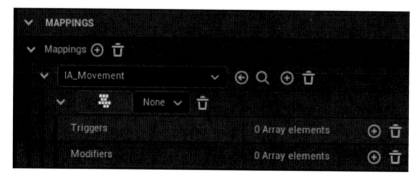

Figure 4.7 – The new IA_Movement mapping

8. Set the first key in this mapping to **Gamepad Left Thumbstick Y-Axis**.

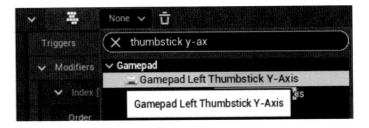

Figure 4.8 – The Gamepad Left Thumbstick Y-Axis key

> **Note**
>
> If the key you want to set is from one of the input devices you have connected (for example, mouse, keyboard, or gamepad), you can click the button to the left of the key dropdown and then press the actual key you want to set, instead of searching for it in the list. For instance, if you want to set a mapping to use the *F* key on the keyboard, you can click that button, then press the *F* key, and then that key will be set for that mapping.

Because we want this key to control the Input Action's *Y* axis instead of its *X* axis, we need to add the **Swizzle Input Axis Values** modifier with the **YXZ** value.

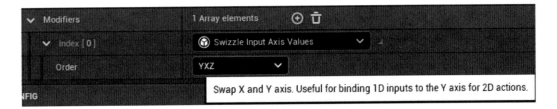

Figure 4.9 – The Swizzle Input Axis modifier

9. Click the + button to the right of the Input Action set for this mapping in order to add a new key and execute that Input Action:

Figure 4.10 – The + button to the right of IA_Movement

10. Set the new key to **Gamepad Left Thumbstick X-Axis**. Because this will already control the movement Input Action's *X* axis, we won't need to add any modifiers.

11. Add another key to the Input Action, this time the *W* key. Because this key will be used for moving forward, and therefore use the *Y* axis, it will need the same modifier that we added before – the **Swizzle Input Axis** modifier with the **YXZ** value.

12. Add another key to the Input Action, this time the *S* key. Because this key will be used for moving backward, and therefore use the *Y* axis, it will need the same modifier we added before – the **Swizzle Input Axis** modifier with the **YXZ** value, as well as a new modifier – **Negate**. The reason for this is that we want the value of the movement Input Action to be –1 on the *Y* axis when this key is pressed (that is, when its input is 1):

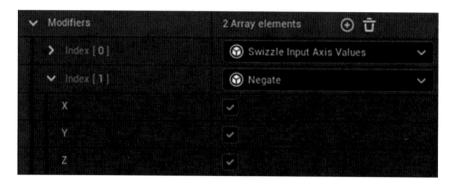

Figure 4.11 – The Swizzle Input Axis Values and Negate modifiers

13. Add another key to the Input Action, this time the *D* key. Because this key will be used for moving right, and therefore use the positive end of the *X* axis, it won't need any modifiers.

14. Add another key to the Input Action, this time the *A* key. Because this key will be used for moving left, and therefore use the negative end of the *X* axis, it will need the Negate modifier, just like the *S* key.

15. Create a new Input Action asset called IA_Jump, and then open it.

16. Add a **Down** trigger and leave its actuation threshold as **0,5**:

Figure 4.12 – The Down trigger

17. Go back to the **IC_Character** Input Context asset and add a new Input Action to the **Mappings** property – this time, the **IA_Jump** Input Action we just created:

Figure 4.13 – The IA_Jump mapping

18. Add two keys to this mapping – **Space Bar** and **Gamepad Face Button Bottom**. If you're using an Xbox controller, this will be the *A* button, and if you're using a PlayStation controller, this will be the *X* button:

Figure 4.14 – The IA_Jump mapping keys

And with those steps completed, we've completed this chapter's first exercise, where you've learned how you can specify Input Action Mappings in UE5, allowing you to abstract which keys are responsible for which in-game actions.

Let's now take a look at how UE5 handles player input and processes it within the game.

Processing Player Input

Let's think about a situation where the player presses the **Jump** Input Action, which is associated with the *spacebar* key, to get the player character to jump. Between the moment the player presses the *Spacebar* key and the moment the game makes the player character jump, quite a few things have to happen to connect those two events.

Let's take a look at all of the necessary steps that lead from one event to the other:

1. `Hardware Input`: The player presses the *spacebar* key. UE5 will be listening to this keypress event.

2. The `PlayerInput` class: After the key is pressed or released, this class will translate that key into an Input Action. If there is a corresponding Input Action, it will notify all classes that are listening to the action that it was just pressed, released, or updated. In this case, it will know that the *Spacebar* key is associated with the *Jump* Input Action.

3. The `Player Controller` class: This is the first class to receive these keypress events, given that it's used to represent a player in the game.

4. The `Pawn` class: This class (and consequently the `Character` class, which inherits from it) can also listen to those keypress events, as long as they are possessed by a Player Controller. If so, it will receive these events after that class. In this chapter, we will be using our `Character` C++ class to listen to action and axis events.

Now that we know how UE5 handles player inputs, let's see how we can listen to Input Actions in C++ in the next exercise.

Exercise 4.02 – listening to movement and jump input actions

In this exercise, we will register the Input Actions we created in the previous section with our character class by binding them to specific functions in our character class using C++.

The main way for a **Player Controller** or **Character** to listen to Input Actions is by registering the Input Action delegates using the `SetupPlayerInputComponent` function. The `MyThirdPersonChar` class should already have a declaration and an implementation for this function. Let's have our character class listen to those events by following these steps:

1. Open the `MyThirdPersonChar` class header file in Visual Studio, and make sure there's a declaration for a `protected` function called `SetupPlayerInputComponent` that returns nothing and receives a `class UInputComponent* PlayerInputComponent` property as a parameter. This function should be marked as both `virtual` and `override`:

    ```
    virtual void SetupPlayerInputComponent(class
    UInputComponent*
    PlayerInputComponent) override;
    ```

2. Add a declaration for a `public class UInputMappingContext*` property called `IC_Character`. This property must be a UPROPERTY and have the `EditAnywhere` and `Category = Input` tags. This will be the Input Context we'll be adding for the character's input:

    ```
    UPROPERTY(EditAnywhere, Category = Input)
    class UInputMappingContext* IC_Character;
    ```

3. After that, we'll need to add the Input Actions to listen for the character's input. Add three `public class UInputAction*` properties, all of which must be UPROPERTY and have the `EditAnywhere` and `Category = Input` tags. Those two properties will be called the following:

    - IA_Move

    ```
    IA_JumpUPROPERTY(EditAnywhere, Category = Input)
    class UInputAction* IA_Move;


    UPROPERTY(EditAnywhere, Category = Input)
    class UInputAction* IA_Jump
    ```

4. Open this class's source file and make sure that this function has an implementation:

    ```
    void AMyThirdPersonChar::SetupPlayerInputComponent(class
    UInputComponent* PlayerInputComponent)
    {
    }
    ```

5. Because in UE5 you can use either the legacy Input Component or the Enhanced Input Component, we need to account for this. Inside the previous function's implementation, start by casting the `PlayerInputComponent` parameter to the `UEnhancedInputComponent` class and saving it inside a new `EnhancedPlayerInputComponent` property of type `UEnhancedInputComponent*`:

    ```
    UEnhancedInputComponent* EnhancedPlayerInputComponent =
    Cast<UEnhancedInputComponent>(PlayerInputComponent);
    ```

    Because we'll be using `UEnhancedInputComponent`, we need to include it:

    ```
    #include "EnhancedInputComponent.h"
    ```

6. If it's not `nullptr`, cast the `Controller` property to `APlayerController` and save it in a local `PlayerController` property:

    ```
    if (EnhancedPlayerInputComponent != nullptr)
    {
      APlayerController* PlayerController =
      Cast<APlayerController>(GetController());
    }
    ```

If the newly created `PlayerController` property isn't `nullptr`, then we'll need to fetch `UEnhancedLocalPlayerSubsystem` so that we can tell it to add the `IC_Character` Input Context and activate its Input Actions.

7. To do this, create a new `UEnhancedLocalPlayerSubsystem*` property called `EnhancedSubsystem` and set it to return the value of the `ULocalPlayer::GetSubsystem` function. This function receives a template parameter representing the subsystem we want to fetch, which is `UEnhancedLocalPlayerSubsystem`, and a normal parameter of type `ULocalPlayer*`. This last parameter's type is a representation of a player who's controlling a pawn in the current instance of the game, and we'll pass it by calling `PlayerController->GetLocalPlayer()`:

```
UEnhancedInputLocalPlayerSubsystem* EnhancedSubsystem =
ULocalPlayer::GetSubsystem<UEnhancedInputLocalPlayerSubsy
stem>(PlayerController->GetLocalPlayer());
```

Because we'll be using the `UEnhancedLocalPlayerSubsystem`, we need to include it:

```
#include "EnhancedInputSubsystems.h"
```

8. If the `EnhancedSubsystem` property isn't `nullptr`, call its `AddMappingContext` function, which receives the following parameters:

- `UInputMappingContext* Mapping Context`: The Input Context we want to activate – in this case, the `IC_Character` property

- `int32 Priority`: The priority we want this Input Context to have, which we'll pass as 1

```
EnhancedSubsystem->AddMappingContext(IC_Character, 1);
```

9. Because we'll be using `UInputMappingContext`, we need to include it:

```
#include "InputMappingContext.h"
```

10. Now that we've added the logic to activate the Input Context, let's add the logic for listening to the Input Actions. Add the code for the following steps after we check whether `PlayerController` is `nullptr`, but still inside the brackets where we check whether `EnhancedPlayerInputComponent` is `nullptr`:

```
if (EnhancedPlayerInputComponent != nullptr)
{
  APlayerController* PlayerController =
  Cast<APlayerController>(GetController());
  if (PlayerController != nullptr)
  {
```

```
    . . .
}

// Continue here
}
```

In order to listen to the `IA_Movement` Input Action, we'll call the `EnhancedPlayer InputComponent BindAction` function, which receives as parameters the following:

- `UInputAction* Action`: The Input Action to listen to, which we'll pass as the `IA_Movement` property.

- `ETriggerEvent TriggerEvent`: The input event that will cause the function to be called. Because this Input Action is triggered for every frame in which it's being used, and it's triggered using the Down trigger, we'll pass this as the `Triggered` event.

- `UserClass* Object`: The object that the `callback` function will be called on – in our case, that's the `this` pointer.

- `HANDLER_SIG::TUObjectMethodDelegate <UserClass> ::FMethodPtr Func`: This property is a bit wordy, but it's essentially a pointer to the function that will be called when this event happens, which we can specify by typing &, followed by the class's name, then `::`, and finally, the function's name. In our case, we want this to be the Move function, which we'll be creating in a following step, so we'll specify it with & `AMyThirdPersonChar::Move`:

```
EnhancedPlayerInputComponent->BindAction(IA_Move,
ETriggerEvent::Triggered, this, &AMyThirdPersonChar
::Move);
```

Because we'll be using `UInputAction`, we need to include it:

```
#include "InputAction.h"
```

11. Let's now bind the function that will make the player character start jumping. In order to do this, duplicate the `BindAction` function call we added for the `IA_Move` Input Action, but make the following changes:

- Instead of passing the `IA_Move` Input Action, pass the `IA_Jump` Input Action.

- Instead of passing the `&AMyThirdPersonChar::Move` function, pass `&ACharacter::Jump`. This is the function that will make the character jump.

- Instead of passing `ETriggerEvent::Trigger`, pass `ETriggerEvent::Started`. This is so that we can be notified when the key starts and stops being pressed:

```
EnhancedPlayerInputComponent->BindAction(IA_Jump,
ETriggerEvent::Started, this, &ACharacter::Jump);
```

12. In order to bind the function that will make the player character stop jumping, let's now duplicate the last `BindAction` function call that we did, but make the following changes to it:

- Instead of passing the `ETriggerEvent::Started`, we'll pass `ETriggerEvent::Completed`, so that the function gets called when this Input Action stops being triggered.

- Instead of passing the `&ACharacter::Jump` function, pass `&ACharacter::StopJumping`. This is the function that will make the character stop jumping:

```
EnhancedPlayerInputComponent->BindAction(IA_Jump,
ETriggerEvent::Completed, this, &ACharacter::StopJumping);
```

> **Note**
>
> All functions used to listen to Input Actions must receive either no parameters or a parameter of type `FInputActionValue&`. You can use this to check its value type and fetch the right one. For instance, if the Input Action that triggers this function has a `Digital` value type, its value will be of type `bool`, but if it has an `Axis2D` value type, its value will be of type `FVector2D`. The latter is the type we'll be using for the `Move` function because that's its corresponding value type.
>
> Another option for listening to Input Actions is to use `Delegates`, which is outside the scope of this book.

13. Let's now create the `Move` function that we referenced in a previous step. Go to the class's header file and add a declaration for a `protected` function called `Move`, which returns nothing and receives a `const FInputActionValue& Value` parameter:

```
void Move(const FInputActionValue& Value);
```

14. Because we're using `FInputActionValue`, we have to include it:

```
#include "InputActionValue.h"
```

15. In the class's source file, add this function's implementation, where we'll start by fetching the Value parameter's input as FVector2D. We'll do this by calling its Get function, passing as a template parameter the FVector2D type. We'll also save its return value in a local variable called InputValue:

```
void AMyThirdPersonChar::Move(const FInputActionValue&
Value)
{
  FVector2D InputValue = Value.Get<FVector2D>();
}
```

16. Next, check whether the Controller property is valid (not nullptr) and whether the InputValue property's X or Y value is different to 0:

```
if (Controller != nullptr && (InputValue.X != 0.0f ||
InputValue.Y != 0.0f))
```

If all of these conditions are true, we'll then get the camera's rotation on the z axis (yaw), so that we can move the character relative to where the camera is facing. To achieve this, we can create a new FRotator property called YawRotation with a value of 0 for pitch (rotation along the y axis) and roll (rotation along the x axis) and the value of the camera's current yaw for the property's yaw. To get the camera's yaw value, we can call the Player Controller's GetControlRotation function and then access its Yaw property:

```
const FRotator YawRotation(0, Controller->
   GetControlRotation().Yaw, 0);
```

> **Note**
> The FRotator property's constructor receives the Pitch value, the Yaw value, and then the Roll value.

- After that, we'll check whether the InputValue's X property is different to 0:

```
if (InputValue.X != 0.0f)
{
}
```

- If it is, get the right vector of YawRotation and store it in an Fvector RightDirection property. You can get a rotator's right vector by calling the KistemMathLibrary object's GetRightVector function. A rotator or vector's right vector is simply its perpendicular vector that points to its right. The result of this will be a vector that points to the right of where the camera is currently facing:

```
const Fvector RightDirection =
    UkismetMathLibrary::GetRightVector(YawRotation);
```

- We can now call the AddMovementInput function, which will make our character move in the direction we specify, passing as parameters the RightDirection and InputValue X properties:

```
AddMovementInput(RightDirection, InputValue.X);
```

- Because we'll be using both the KismetMathLibrary and Controller objects, we'll need to include them at the top of this source file:

```
#include "Kismet/KismetMathLibrary.h"
#include "GameFramework/Controller.h"
```

17. After checking whether the X property of InputValue is different to 0, check whether its Y property is different to 0:

```
if (InputValue.X != 0.0f)
{
    ...
}
if (InputValue.Y != 0.0f)
{
}
```

18. If it is, call the YawRotation property's Vector function and store its return value in an FVector ForwardDirection property. This function will convert FRotator to FVector, which is equivalent to getting a rotator's ForwardVector. The result of this will be a vector that points forward of where the camera is currently facing:

```
const FVector ForwardDirection = YawRotation.Vector();
```

We can now call the AddMovementInput function, passing as parameters the ForwardDirection and InputValue Y properties:

```
AddMovementInput(ForwardDirection, InputValue.Y);
```

19. Before we compile our code, add the `EnhancedInput` plugin to our project's `Build.cs` file in order to notify UE5 that we'll be using this plugin in our project. If we don't do this, parts of our project won't compile.

20. Open the `.Build.cs` file inside your project's `Source/<ProjectName>` folder, which is a C# file and not a C++ file, located inside your project's source folder.

21. Open the file, and you'll find the `AddRange` function from the `PublicDependencyModuleNames` property being called. This is the function that tells the engine which modules this project intends to use. As a parameter, an array of strings is sent with the names of all the intended modules for the project. Given that we intend on using UMG, we'll need to add the `EnhancedInput` module after the `InputCore` module:

```
PublicDependencyModuleNames.AddRange(new string[] {
"Core",
"CoreUObject", "Engine", "InputCore", "EnhancedInput",
"HeadMountedDisplay" });
```

22. Now that you've notified the engine that we'll be using the `EnhancedInput` module, compile your code, open the editor, and open your `BP_MyTPS` blueprint asset. Delete the `InputAction` Jump event, as well as the nodes connected to it. Do the same for the **InputAxis MoveForward** and **InputAxis MoveRight** events. We will be replicating this logic in C++ and need to remove its Blueprint functionality so that there are no conflicts when handling input.

23. Next, set the **IC Character** property to the **IC_Character** Input Context, the **IA Move** property to the **IA_Movement** Input Action, and the **IA Jump** property to the **IA_Jump** Input Action:

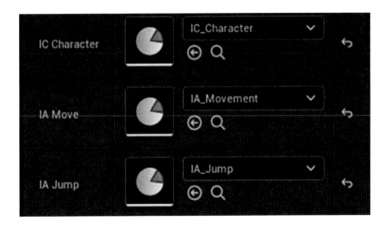

Figure 4.15 – The IC Character, IA Move, and IA Jump properties

24. Now, play the level. You should be able to move the character using the keyboard's *W*, *A*, *S*, and *D* keys or the controller's *left thumbstick*, as well as jumping with the *Spacebar* key or *gamepad face button bottom*:

Figure 4.16 – The player character moving

After following all these steps, you will have concluded this exercise. You now know how to create and listen to your own **Input Action** events using C++ in UE5. Doing this is one of the most important aspects of game development, so you've just completed an important step in your game development journey.

Now that we've set up all of the logic necessary to have our character move and jump, let's add the logic responsible for rotating the camera around our character.

Turning the camera around the character

Cameras are an extremely important part of games, as they dictate what and how the player will see in your game throughout the play session. When it comes to third-person games, which is what this project is about, the camera allows a player not only to see the world around them but also the character they're controlling. Whether the character is taking damage, falling, or something else, it's important for the player to always know the state of the character they are controlling and to be able to have the camera face the direction they choose.

Like every modern third-person game, we will always have the camera rotate around our player character. To have our camera rotate around our character, after setting up the **Camera** and **Spring Arm** components in *Chapter 2, Working with Unreal Engine*, let's continue by adding a new **Look** Input Action. Follow these steps:

1. Do this by duplicating the **IA_Move** Input Action (by either selecting it in **Content Browser** and pressing *Ctrl + D*, or by *right-clicking* it and selecting **Duplicate**) and name the new asset IA_Look. Because this new Input Action's setup is similar to that of the **IA_Move** Input Action, we'll leave this duplicated asset as is.

2. Then, open the **IA_Character** Input Context and add a new mapping for the **IA_Look** Input Action.

3. Add the following keys to this new mapping – **Mouse X**, **Mouse Y**, **Gamepad Right Thumbstick X-Axis**, and **Gamepad Right Thumbstick Y-Axis**. Because the *Y* keys will be controlling the Input Action's *Y* axis, we'll have to add the **Swizzle Input Axis Values** modifier to them (the **Mouse Y** and **Gamepad Right Thumbstick Y-Axis** keys). Additionally, because the **Mouse Y** key will make the camera go down when you mose the mouse up, we'll have to also add a **Negate** modifier to it:

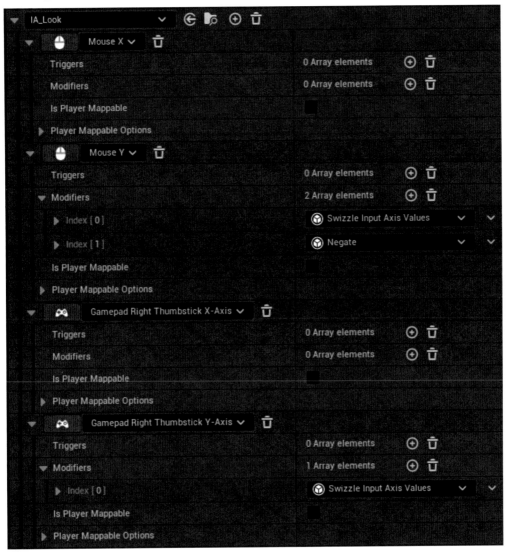

Figure 4.17 – The mappings for the IA_Look Input Action

Let's now add the C++ logic responsible for turning the camera with the player's input:

1. Go to the `MyThirdPersonChar` class's header file and add a `public class UInputAction* IA_Look` property, which must be `UPROPERTY` and have the `EditAnywhere` and `Category = Input` tags:

    ```
    UPROPERTY(EditAnywhere, Category = Input)
    class UInputAction* IA_Look;
    ```

2. Next, add a declaration for a `protected` function called `Look`, which returns nothing and receives a `const FInputActionValue& Value` parameter:

    ```
    void Look(const FInputActionValue& Value);
    ```

3. Next, go to the `SetupPlayerInputComponent` function implementation, in the class's source file, and duplicate the line responsible for listening to the `IA_Move` Input Action. In this duplicated line, change the first parameter to `IA_Look` and the last parameter to `&AMyThirdPersonChar::Look`:

    ```
    EnhancedPlayerInputComponent->BindAction(IA_Look,
    ETriggerEvent::Triggered, this,
    &AMyThirdPersonChar::Look);
    ```

4. Then, add the `Look` function's implementation, where we'll start by fetching the `Value` parameter's input as `FVector2D`. We'll do this by calling its `Get` function, passing as a `template` parameter the `FVector2D` type. We'll also save its `return` value in a local variable called `InputValue`:

    ```
    void AMyThirdPersonChar::Look(const FInputActionValue&
    Value)
    {
        FVector2D InputValue = Value.Get<FVector2D>();
    }
    ```

5. If the `InputValue` X property is different to 0, we'll call the `AddControllerYawInput` function, passing this property as a parameter. After that, check whether the `InputValue` Y property is different to 0, and then we'll call the `AddControllerPitchInput` function, passing this property as a parameter:

    ```
    if (InputValue.X != 0.0f)
    {
        AddControllerYawInput(InputValue.X);
    }
    ```

```
if (InputValue.Y != 0.0f)
{
    AddControllerPitchInput(InputValue.Y);
}
```

> **Note**
>
> The `AddControllerYawInput` and `AddControllerPitchInput` functions are responsible for adding rotation input around the *z* (turning left and right) and *y* (looking up and down) axes respectively.

6. After you've done this, compile your code, open the editor, and open your **BP_MyTPS** Blueprint asset. Set its **IA_Look** property to the **IA_Look** Input Action:

Figure 4.18 – The camera is rotated around the player

When you play the level, you should now be able to move the camera by rotating the mouse or by tilting the controller's *right thumbstick*:

Figure 4.19 – The camera is rotated around the player

And that concludes the logic for rotating the camera around the player character with the player's input. Now that we've learned how to add inputs to our game and associate them with in-game actions, such as jumping and moving the player character, let's consolidate what we've learned in this chapter by going through how to add a new `Walk` action to our game from start to finish in the next activity.

Activity 4.01 – adding walking logic to our character

In the current game, our character runs by default when we use the movement keys, but we need to reduce the character's speed and make it walk.

So, in this activity, we'll be adding logic that will make our character walk when we move it while holding the *Shift* key on the keyboard or the **Gamepad Face Button Right** key (*B* for the Xbox controller and *O* for the PlayStation controller).

To do this, follow these steps:

1. Duplicate the **IA_Jump** Input Action and name the new asset `IA_Walk`. Because this new Input Action's setup is similar to that of the **IA_Jump** Input Action, we'll leave this duplicated asset as is.

2. Then, open the **IA_Character** Input Context and add a new mapping for the **IA_Walk** Input Action. Add the following keys to this new mapping – **Left Shift**, and **Gamepad Face Button Right**.

3. Open the `MyThirdPersonChar` class's header file and add a `class UInputAction*` `IA_Walk` property, which must be `UPROPERTY` and have the `EditAnywhere` and `Category = Input` tags.

4. Then, add declarations for two `protected` functions that return nothing and receive no parameters, called `BeginWalking` and `StopWalking`.

5. Add the implementations for both these functions in the class's source file. In the implementation of the `BeginWalking` function, change the character's speed to 40% of its value by modifying the `CharacterMovementComponent` property's `MaxWalkSpeed` property accordingly. To access the `CharacterMovementComponent` property, use the `GetCharacterMovement` function.

   The implementation of the `StopWalking` function will be the inverse of that of the `BeginWalking` function, which will increase the character's walk speed by 250%.

6. Listen to the `Walk` action by going to the `SetupPlayerInputComponent` function's implementation and adding two calls to the `BindAction` function, the first one of which passes as parameters the `IA_Walk` property, the `ETriggerEvent::Started` event, the `this` pointer, and this class's `BeginWalking` function, while the second passes the `IA_Walk` property, the `ETriggerEvent::Completed` event, the `this` pointer, and this class's `StopWalking` function.

7. Compile your code, open the editor, open your `BP_MyTPS` Blueprint asset, and set the **IA_Walk** property to the **IA_Walk** Input Action.

   After following these steps, you should be able to have your character walk, which decreases its speed and slightly changes its animation, by pressing either the keyboard's *Left Shift* key or the controller's **Face Button Right** key:

Figure 4.20 – The character running (left) and walking (right)

And that concludes our activity. Our character should now be able to walk slowly as long as the player is holding the **Walk** Input Action.

> **Note**
> The solution to this activity can be found on GitHub here:
> `https://github.com/PacktPublishing/Elevating-Game-Experiences-with-Unreal-Engine-5-Second-Edition/tree/main/Activity%20solutions`.

Summary

In this chapter, you've learned how to create and modify **Input Actions**, as well as add their mappings to an **Input Context**, which gives you some flexibility when determining which keys trigger a specific action or axis, how to listen to them, and how to execute in-game logic when they're pressed and released.

Now that you know how to handle the player's input, you can allow the player to interact with your game and offer the agency that video games are so well known for.

In the next chapter, we'll start making our own game from scratch. It'll be called **Dodgeball** and will consist of the player controlling a character trying to run away from enemies that are throwing dodgeballs at it. In that chapter, we will have the opportunity to start learning about many important topics, with a heavy focus on collisions.

5

Query with Line Traces

In previous chapters, we learned about how we can reproduce the Third Person template project offered to us by the Unreal Engine team in order to understand some of the basic concepts of UE5's workflow and framework.

In this chapter, you will start creating another game from scratch. In this game, the player will control a character from a top-down point of view (similar to games such as Metal Gear Solid 1, 2, and 3). A top-down perspective implies that the player controls a character that is seen as if it was being looked down upon, usually with the camera rotation being fixed (the camera doesn't rotate). In our game, the player character must go from point A to point B without being hit by dodgeballs, which are being thrown at the player by the enemies that are spread throughout the level. The levels in this game will be maze-like in nature, and the player will have multiple paths to choose from, all of which will have enemies trying to throw dodgeballs at them.

In this chapter, we'll cover the following topics:

- Introduction to collision
- Understanding and visualizing Line Traces (Single and Multi)
- Sweep Traces
- Trace Channels
- Trace Responses

In the first section, we begin by getting to know what collision is in the world of video games.

Technical requirements

The project for this chapter can be found in the Chapter05 folder of the code bundle for this book, which can be downloaded here: `https://github.com/PacktPublishing/Elevating-Game-Experiences-with-Unreal-Engine-5-Second-Edition`.

Introduction to collision

A collision is basically a point at which two objects come into contact with each other (for example, two objects colliding, an object hitting a character, a character walking into a wall, and so on). Most game development tools have their own set of features that allow for collision and physics to exist inside the game. This set of features is called a physics engine, which is responsible for everything related to collisions. It is responsible for executing Line Traces, checking whether two objects are overlapping each other, blocking each other's movement, or bouncing off of a wall, and much more. When we ask the game to execute or notify us of these collision events, the game is essentially asking the physics engine to execute it and then show us the results of these collision events.

In the **Dodgeball** game you will be building, examples of where collision needs to be taken into account include checking whether enemies are able to see the player (which will be achieved using a Line Trace, which is covered in this chapter), simulating physics on an object that will behave just like a dodgeball, checking whether anything is blocking the player character's movement, and much more.

Collision is one of the most important aspects of most games, so understanding it is crucial in order to get started with game development.

Before we start building our collision-based features, we will first need to set up our new **Dodgeball** project in order to support the game mechanics we will be implementing. This process starts with the steps described in the following section.

Setting up your project

Let's begin by creating our Unreal Engine project:

1. Launch UE5. Select the **Games** project category, then click on **Next**.
2. Select the **Third Person template**, then click on **Next**.
3. Make sure the first option is set to **C++** and not **Blueprint**.
4. Select the location of the project according to your preference and name your project Dodgeball, then click on **Create Project**.

When the project is done being generated, you should see the following on your screen:

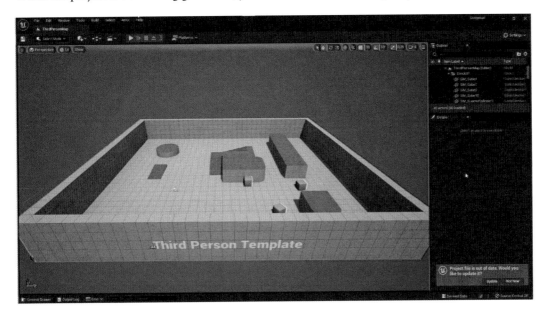

Figure 5.1 – Dodgeball project loaded up

5. After the code has been generated and the project opens up, enable the Enhanced Input plugin, just like we did in steps 1-3 of the *Understanding input actions and contexts* section in *Chapter 4, Getting Started with Player Input*.

6. After that, close the UE5 editor and open the files of the generated third-person `Character` class, `DodgeballCharacter`, in Visual Studio, as shown in the following figure:

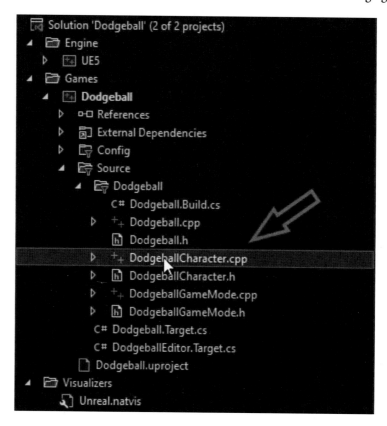

Figure 5.2 – Files generated in Visual Studio

As mentioned earlier, your project is going to have a top-down perspective. Given that we're starting this project from the Third Person template, we'll have to change a few things before we turn this into a top-down game. This will mainly involve changing some lines of code in the existing `Character` class.

Exercise 5.01: Converting DodgeballCharacter to a top-down perspective

In this exercise, you'll be performing the necessary changes to your generated `DodgeballCharacter` class. Remember, it currently features a third-person perspective where the rotation of the character is dictated by the player's input (*namely the mouse or right analog stick*).

In this exercise, you will change this to a top-down perspective, which remains the same regardless of the player's input and the camera always follows the character from above.

The following steps will help you complete this exercise:

1. Head to the `DodgeballCharacter` class's constructor and update the `CameraBoom` properties, as mentioned in the following steps.

2. Change `TargetArmLength`, which is a property of `CameraBoom`, to `900.0f` in order to add some distance between the camera and the player as follows:

    ```
    // The camera follows at this distance behind the
    // character
    CameraBoom->TargetArmLength = 900.0f;
    ```

3. Next, add a line that sets the relative pitch to `-70°` using the `SetRelativeRotation` function so that the camera looks down at the player. The `FRotator` constructor's parameters are `pitch`, `yaw`, and `roll`, respectively, as follows:

    ```
    //The camera looks down at the player
    CameraBoom->SetRelativeRotation(FRotator(-70.f, 0.f,
    0.f));
    ```

4. Change `bUsePawnControlRotation` to `false` so that the camera's rotation isn't changed by the player's movement input as follows:

    ```
    // Don't rotate the arm based on the controller
    CameraBoom->bUsePawnControlRotation = false;
    ```

5. Add a line that sets `bInheritPitch`, `bInheritYaw`, and `bInheritRoll` to `false` so that the camera's rotation isn't changed by the character's orientation as follows:

    ```
    // Ignore pawn's pitch, yaw and roll
    CameraBoom->bInheritPitch = false;
    CameraBoom->bInheritYaw = false;
    CameraBoom->bInheritRoll = false;
    ```

    After we've made these modifications, we're going to remove the character's ability to jump (we don't want the player to escape from the dodgeballs that easily) and to rotate the camera from the player's rotation input.

6. Go to the `SetupPlayerInputComponent` function in the `DodgeballCharacter`'s source file and remove the following lines of code in order to remove the ability to jump:

    ```
    // REMOVE THESE LINES
    PlayerInputComponent->BindAction("Jump", IE_Pressed,
    this,
        &ACharacter::Jump);
    ```

```
PlayerInputComponent->BindAction("Jump", IE_Released,
this,
    Acharacter::StopJumping);
```

7. Next, add the following lines in order to remove the player's rotation input:

```
// REMOVE THESE LINES
PlayerInputComponent->BindAxis("Turn", this,
    &APawn::AddControllerYawInput);
PlayerInputComponent->BindAxis("TurnRate", this,
    &ADodgeballCharacter::TurnAtRate);
PlayerInputComponent->BindAxis("LookUp", this,
    &APawn::AddControllerPitchInput);
PlayerInputComponent->BindAxis("LookUpRate", this,
    &ADodgeballCharacter::LookUpAtRate);
```

This step is optional, but in order to keep your code clean, you should remove the declarations and implementations of the `TurnAtRate` and `LookUpAtRate` functions.

8. After that, we'll have to adapt this project to use the Enhanced Input system instead of the Legacy Input system. Go to this class's header file and add a property for the Character's Input Context as well as the Move Input Action, just like we did in steps 2 and 3 of *Exercise 4.02*. Add a declaration for the `Move` function, just like we did in step 14 of *Exercise 4.02*.

9. Add the logic for adding the Character's Input Context as well as binding the Move Input Action, just like we did in steps 4-10 of *Exercise 4.02*.

10. Add the implementation to the `Move` function, just like we did in steps 14-18 of *Exercise 4.02*.

11. Add the Enhanced Input dependency, just like we did in steps 19 and 20 of *Exercise 4.02*.

12. Finally, after you've made these changes, run your project from Visual Studio.

13. When the editor has loaded, go to **Edit | Project Settings | Engine | Input** and then, inside the **Default Classes** category (near the end), set the **Default Player Input Class** property to `EnhancedPlayerInput` and the **Default Input Component Class** property to `EnhancedInputComponent`.

14. After this, create the `IA_Move` Input Action asset and set it up just like we did in steps 1-3 of *Exercise 4.01*.

15. Then, create the `IC_Character` Input Context asset and add a mapping for the `IA_Move` Input Action, just like we did in steps 4-14 of *Exercise 4.01*.

16. The last thing you need to do to complete the Enhanced Input setup is to open the **ThirdPersonCharacter** blueprint and set the `IC_Character` and `IA_Move` properties, just like we did in step 22 of *Exercise 4.01*.

17. After that, play the level. The camera's perspective should look like the following and should not rotate based on the player's input or the character's rotation:

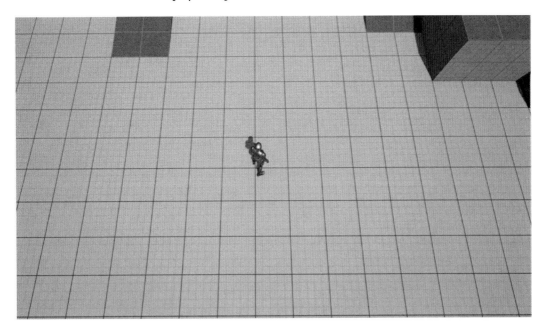

Figure 5.3 – Locked camera rotation to a top-down perspective

That concludes the first exercise of this chapter and the first step of your new project, **Dodgeball**.

Next, you will be creating the `EnemyCharacter` class. This character will be the enemy that throws dodgeballs at the player while the player is in view. But the question that arises here is this: how will the enemy know whether it can see the player character or not?

That will be achieved with the power of **Line Traces** (also known as **Raycasts** or **Raytraces**), which you will be looking at in the following section.

Understanding Line Traces

One of the most important features of any game development tool is its ability to execute Line Traces. These are available through the physics engine that the tool is using.

Line Traces are a way of asking the game to tell you whether anything stands between two points in the game world. The game will *shoot a ray* between those two points, specified by you, and return the objects that were hit (if any), where they were hit, at what angle, and much more.

In *Figure 5.4*, you can see a representation of a Line Trace where we assume object **1** is ignored and object **2** is detected,due to their Trace Channel properties (further explained in the following paragraphs):

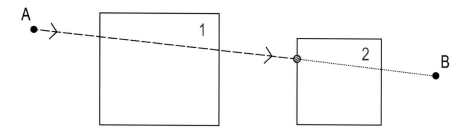

Figure 5.4 – A Line Trace being executed from point A to point B

Figure 5.4 is explained as follows:

- The dashed line represents the Line Trace before it hits an object.
- The arrows represent the direction of the Line Trace.
- The dotted line represents the Line Trace after it hits an object.
- The striped circle represents the Line Trace's impact point.
- The big squares represent two objects that are in the path of the Line Trace (objects **1** and **2**).

We notice that only object **2** was hit by the Line Trace and not object **1**, even though it is also in the path of the Line Trace. This is due to assumptions made about object **1**'s Trace Channel properties, which are discussed later in this chapter.

Line Traces are used for many game features, such as the following:

- Checking whether a weapon hits an object when it fires
- Highlighting an item that the player can interact with when the character looks at it
- Rotating the camera around the player character automatically as it goes around corners

A common and important feature of Line Traces is **Trace Channels**. When you execute a Line Trace, you may want to check only specific types of objects, which is what Trace Channels are for. They allow you to specify filters to be used when executing a Line Trace so that it doesn't get blocked by unwanted objects. Check the following examples:

- You may want to execute a Line Trace only to check for objects that are visible. These objects would block the `Visibility` Trace Channel. For instance, invisible walls, which are invisible pieces of geometry used in games to block the player's movement, would not be visible and therefore would not block the `Visibility` Trace Channel.

- You may want to execute a Line Trace only to check for objects that can be interacted with. These objects would block the `Interaction` Trace Channel.

- You may want to execute a Line Trace only to check for pawns that can move around the game world. These objects would block the `Pawn` Trace Channel.

You can specify how different objects react to different Trace Channels so that only some objects block specific Trace Channels and others ignore them. In our case, we want to know whether anything stands between the enemy and the player character so that we know whether the enemy can see the player. We will be using Line Traces for this purpose by checking for anything that blocks the enemy's line of sight of the player character, using a `Tick` event.

In the next section, we will be creating the `EnemyCharacter` class using C++.

Creating the EnemyCharacter C++ class

In our **Dodgeball** game, the `EnemyCharacter` class will constantly be looking at the player character if they're within view. This is the same class that will later throw dodgeballs at the player; however, we'll leave that for the following chapter. In this chapter, we will be focusing on the logic that allows our enemy character to look at the player.

So, let's get started as follows:

1. Right-click on the **Content Browser** inside the editor and select **New C++ Class**.
2. Choose the `Character` class as the parent class.
3. Name the new class `EnemyCharacter`.

After you've created the class and opened its files in Visual Studio, let's add the `LookAtActor` function declaration in its `header` file. This function should be `public` and not return anything, only receiving the `AActor* TargetActor` parameter, which will be the Actor it should be facing. Have a look at the following code snippet, which shows this function:

```
// Change the rotation of the character to face the given
// actor
void LookAtActor(AActor* TargetActor);
```

> **Note**
>
> Even though we only want the enemy to look at the player character, in order to execute good software development practices, we're going to abstract this function a bit more and allow EnemyCharacter to look at any Actor. This is because the logic that allows an Actor to look at another Actor or the player character will be exactly the same.
>
> Remember, you should not create unnecessary restrictions when writing code. If you can write similar code and simultaneously allow more possibilities, you should do so if that doesn't overcomplicate the logic of your program.

Moving on ahead, if EnemyCharacter can't see the Target Actor, it shouldn't be looking at it. In order to check whether the enemy can see the Actor, it should be looking at the LookAtActor function that will call another function, which is the CanSeeActor function. This is what you'll be doing in the following exercise.

Exercise 5.02: Creating the CanSeeActor function that executes Line Traces

In this exercise, we will create the CanSeeActor function, which will return whether the enemy character can see the given Actor.

The following steps will help you complete this exercise:

1. Create the declaration for a public CanSeeActor function in the header file of the EnemyCharacter class; it will return bool and receive a const Actor* TargetActor parameter, which is the Actor we want to look at. This function will be a const function, because it doesn't change any of the class's attributes, and the parameter will also be const because we won't need to modify any of its properties, we'll only need to access them, as follows:

    ```
    // Can we see the given actor
    bool CanSeeActor(const AActor* TargetActor) const;
    ```

    Now, let's get to the fun part, which is executing the Line Trace.

    In order to call functions related to line tracing, we'll have to fetch the enemy's current world with the GetWorld function. However, we haven't included the World class in this file, so let's do so in the following step.

> **Note**
>
> The GetWorld function is accessible to any Actor and will return the World object that the Actor belongs to. Remember, the world is necessary in order to execute the Line Trace.

2. Open the `EnemyCharacter` source file and find the following code line:

    ```
    #include "EnemyCharacter.h"
    ```

    Add the following line right after the preceding line of code:

    ```
    #include "Engine/World.h"
    ```

3. Next, create the implementation of the `CanSeeActor` function in the `EnemyCharacter` source file where you'll start by checking whether our `TargetActor` is `nullptr`. If it is, then we return `false`, given that we have no valid Actor to check our sight o,f as follows:

    ```cpp
    bool AEnemyCharacter::CanSeeActor(const AActor *
    TargetActor)
      const
    {
      if (TargetActor == nullptr)
      {
        return false;
      }
    }
    ```

    Next, before we add our `Line Trace` function call, we need to set up some necessary parameters; we will be implementing these in the following steps.

4. After the preceding `if` statement, create a variable to store all of the necessary data relative to the results of the Line Trace. Unreal Engine already has a built-in type for this called the `FHitResult` type, as follows:

    ```cpp
    // Store the results of the Line Trace
    FHitResult Hit;
    ```

    This is the variable we will send to our Line Trace function, which will populate it with the relevant info of the executed Line Trace.

5. Create two `FVector` variables for the `Start` and `End` locations of our Line Trace and set them to our enemy's current location and our target's current location, respectively, as follows:

    ```cpp
    // Where the Line Trace starts and ends
    FVector Start = GetActorLocation();
    FVector End = TargetActor->GetActorLocation();
    ```

6. Next, set the Trace Channel we wish to compare against. In our case, we want to have a `Visibility` Trace Channel specifically designated to indicate whether an object blocks another object's view. Luckily for us, such a Trace Channel already exists in UE5, as shown in the following code snippet:

```
// The trace channel we want to compare against
ECollisionChannel Channel = ECollisionChannel::ECC_
Visibility;
```

The `ECollisionChannel` enum represents all of the possible Trace Channels available to compare against. We will be using the `ECC_Visibility` value, which represents the `Visibility` Trace Channel.

7. Now that we've set up all our necessary parameters, we can finally call the `LineTrace` function, `LineTraceSingleByChannel`, as follows:

```
// Execute the Line Trace
GetWorld()->LineTraceSingleByChannel(Hit, Start, End,
    Channel);
```

This function will consider the parameters we send it, execute the Line Trace, and return its results by modifying our `Hit` variable.

Before we continue, there are still a couple more things we need to consider.

If the Line Trace starts from within our enemy character, which is what will happen in our case, that means it's very likely that the Line Trace will simply hit our enemy character immediately and just stop there because our character might block the `Visibility` Trace Channel. In order to fix that, we need to tell the Line Trace to ignore it.

8. Use the built-in `FCollisionQueryParams` type, which allows us to give even more options to our Line Trace, as follows:

```
FCollisionQueryParams QueryParams;
```

9. Now, update the `Line Trace` to ignore our enemy by adding itself to the list of Actors to ignore, as follows:

```
// Ignore the actor that's executing this Line Trace
QueryParams.AddIgnoredActor(this);
```

We should also add our target to our list of Actors to ignore because we don't want to know whether it blocks the `EnemySight` channel; we simply want to know whether something between the enemy and the player character blocks that channel.

10. Add the `Target Actor` to the list of Actors to be ignored, as shown in the following code snippet:

```
// Ignore the target we're checking for
QueryParams.AddIgnoredActor(TargetActor);
```

11. Next, send our `FCollisionQueryParams` to the Line Trace by adding it as the last parameter of the `LineTraceSingleByChannel` function as follows:

```
// Execute the Line Trace
GetWorld()->LineTraceSingleByChannel(Hit, Start, End,
Channel,
  QueryParams);
```

12. Finalize our `CanSeeActor` function by returning whether the Line Trace hits anything or not. We can do that by accessing our `Hit` variable and checking whether there was a blocking hit, using the `bBlockingHit` property. If there was a blocking hit, that means we can't see our `TargetActor`. This can be achieved with the following code snippet:

```
return !Hit.bBlockingHit;
```

> **Note**
>
> Although we won't need any more information from the `Hit` result other than whether there was a blocking hit, the `Hit` variable can give us much more information on the Line Trace, such as the following:
>
> Information on the Actor that was hit by the Line Trace (`nullptr` if no Actor was hit) by accessing the `Hit.GetActor()` function.
>
> Information on the Actor component that was hit by the Line Trace (`nullptr` if no Actor component was hit) by accessing the `Hit.GetComponent()` function.
>
> Information on the location of the hit by accessing the `Hit.Location` variable.
>
> The distance of the hit can be found by accessing the `Hit.Distance` variable.
>
> The angle at which the Line Trace hit the object, which can be found by accessing the `Hit.ImpactNormal` variable.

Finally, our `CanSeeActor` function is complete. We now know how to execute a Line Trace and we can use it for our enemy's logic.

By completing this exercise, we have finished the `CanSeeActor` function; we can now get back to the `LookAtActor` function. However, there is something we should look at first, which is visualizing our Line Trace.

Visualizing the Line Trace

When creating new logic that makes use of Line Traces, it is very useful to actually visualize the Line Trace while it's being executed, which is something that the Line Trace function doesn't allow you to do. In order to do that, we must use a set of helper debug functions that can draw objects dynamically at runtime, such as lines, cubes, spheres, and so on.

Let's then add a visualization of our Line Trace. The first thing we must do in order to use the debug functions is to add the following `include` line of code under our last `include` line:

```
#include "DrawDebugHelpers.h"
```

We will want to call the `DrawDebugLine` function in order to visualize the Line Trace, which needs the following inputs (that are very similar to the ones received by the Line Trace function):

- The current `World`, which we will supply with the `GetWorld` function
- The `Start` and `End` points of the line, which will be the same as the `LineTraceSingleByChannel` function
- The desired color of the line in the game, which can be set to `Red`

Then, we can add the `DrawDebugLine` function call under our Line Trace function call, as shown in the following code snippet:

```
// Execute the Line Trace
GetWorld()->LineTraceSingleByChannel(Hit, Start, End, Channel,
  QueryParams);


// Show the Line Trace inside the game
DrawDebugLine(GetWorld(), Start, End, FColor::Red);
```

This will allow you to visualize the Line Trace as it is being executed, which is very useful.

> **Note**
>
> If you feel the need for it, you can also specify more of the visual Line Trace's properties, such as its lifetime and thickness.
>
> There are many `DrawDebug` functions available that will draw cubes, spheres, cones, donuts, and even custom meshes.

Now that we can both execute and visualize our Line Trace, let's use the `CanSeeActor` function, which we created in the last exercise, inside the `LookAtActor` function.

Exercise 5.03: Creating the LookAtActor function

In this exercise, we will be creating the definition of our `LookAtActor` function, which will change the enemy's rotation so that it faces the given Actor.

The following steps will help you complete the exercise:

1. Create the `LookAtActor` function definition in the `EnemyCharacter` source file.

2. Start by checking whether our `TargetActor` is `nullptr` and returns nothing immediately if it is (because it's not valid), as shown in the following code snippet:

```
void AEnemyCharacter::LookAtActor(AActor * TargetActor)
{
  if (TargetActor == nullptr)
  {
    return;
  }
}
```

3. Next, we want to check whether we can see our `Target Actor`, using our `CanSeeActor` function:

```
if (CanSeeActor(TargetActor))
{

}
```

If this `if` statement is `true`, that means we can see the Actor, and we will set our rotation in such a way that we are facing that Actor. Luckily for us, there's already a function within UE5 that allows us to do that: the `FindLookAtRotation` function. This function will receive as input two points in the level, point A (the `Start` point) and point B (the End point), and return the rotation that the object at the start point must have in order to face the object at the end point. Perform the following steps in order to use this function.

4. Include `KismetMathLibrary` as shown in the following code snippet:

```
#include "Kismet/KismetMathLibrary.h"
```

5. The `FindLookAtRotation` function must receive a `Start` and End points, which will be our enemy's location and our Target Actor's location, respectively, as follows:

```
FVector Start = GetActorLocation();
FVector End = TargetActor->GetActorLocation();
// Calculate the necessary rotation for the Start
```

```
// point to face the End point
FRotator LookAtRotation =
   UKismetMathLibrary::FindLookAtRotation(Start, End);
```

6. Finally, set your enemy character's rotation to the same value as our `LookAtRotation`, as follows:

```
//Set the enemy's rotation to that rotation
SetActorRotation(LookAtRotation);
```

And that's it for the `LookAtActor` function.

Now, the last step is to call the `LookAtActor` function inside the `Tick` event and send the player character as the `TargetActor`, as in the Actor that we want to look at.

7. For us to fetch the character that is currently being controlled by the player, we use the `GameplayStatics` object. As with other UE5 objects, we must first include them as follows:

```
#include "Kismet/GameplayStatics.h"
```

8. Next, head to your `Tick` function's body and call the `GetPlayerCharacter` function from `GameplayStatics`, as follows:

```
// Fetch the character currently being controlled by
// the player
ACharacter* PlayerCharacter =
   UGameplayStatics::GetPlayerCharacter(this, 0);
```

This function receives the following as input:

- A `World` context object, which is, essentially, an object that belongs to our current world and is used to let the function know which `World` object to access. This `World` context object can simply be the `this` pointer.

- A player index, which, given that our game is supposed to be a single-player game, we can safely assume to be 0 (the first player).

9. Next, call the `LookAtActor` function, sending the player character that we just fetched, as follows:

```
// Look at the player character every frame
LookAtActor(PlayerCharacter);
```

10. The last step of this exercise is to compile your changes in Visual Studio.

Now that you've completed this exercise, your `EnemyCharacter` class has all of the necessary logic to face the player character, if it's within view, and we can start creating the `EnemyCharacter` Blueprint Class.

Creating the EnemyCharacter Blueprint Class

Now that we have finished the logic for our `EnemyCharacter` C++ class, we must create our Blueprint Class that derives from it, as follows:

1. Open our project in the editor.

2. Go to the `Blueprints` folder inside the `ThirdPersonCPP` folder in the `Content Browser`.

3. Right-click and select the option to create a new Blueprint Class.

4. Expand the **All Classes** tab near the bottom of the **Pick Parent Class** window, search for our `EnemyCharacter` C++ class, and select it as the Parent Class.

5. Name the Blueprint Class `BP_EnemyCharacter`.

6. Open the Blueprint Class, select the **SkeletalMeshComponent** (called **Mesh**) from the **Components** tab, and set its **Skeletal Mesh** property to `SKM_Quinn_Simple` and its **Anim Class** property to `ABP_Quinn`.

7. Change the **Yaw** of **SkeletalMeshComponent** to `-90°` (on the *z-axis*) and its position on the *z-axis* to `-83` units.

8. After you've set up the Blueprint Class, its mesh setup should look very similar to that of our **DodgeballCharacter** Blueprint Class.

9. Drag an instance of the `BP_EnemyCharacter` class to your level in a location near an object that can block its line of sight, such as following location (the selected character is `EnemyCharacter`):

Figure 5.5 – Dragging the BP_EnemyCharacter class into the level

Now we can finally play the game and verify that our enemy does look at our player character whenever it's within view, as follows:

Figure 5.6 – The enemy character with a clear view of the player using a Line Trace

10. We can also see that the enemy stops seeing the player whenever it's not within view, as shown in *Figure 5.7*:

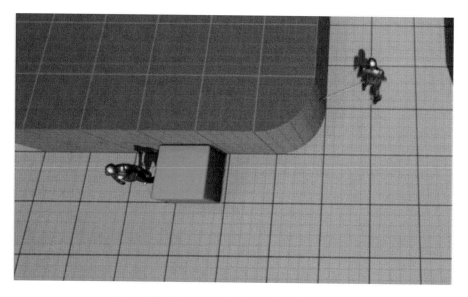

Figure 5.7 – The enemy losing sight of the player

And that concludes our `EnemyCharacter`'s logic. In the following section, we will be looking at Sweep Traces.

Sweep Traces

Before we continue with our project, it is important to know about a variant of the Line Trace, which is the **Sweep Trace**. Although we won't be using these in our project, it is important to know about them and how to use them.

While the Line Trace basically *shoots a ray* between two points, the Sweep Trace will simulate *throwing an object* between two points in a straight line. The object that is being *thrown* is simulated (it doesn't actually exist in the game) and can have various shapes. In the Sweep Trace, the `Hit` location will be the first point at which the virtual object (which we will call **shape**) hits another object if it were thrown from the start point to the end point. The shapes of the Sweep Trace can be either a box, a sphere, or a capsule.

The following is a representation of a Sweep Trace from point A to point B, where we assume that object 1 is ignored due to its Trace Channel properties, using a box shape:

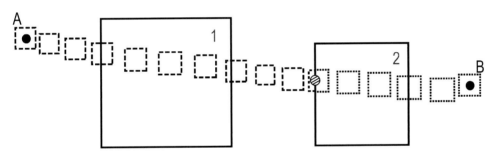

Figure 5.8 – Representation of a Sweep Trace

In *Figure 5.8*, we notice the following:

- A Sweep Trace, using a box shape, being executed from point A to point B.
- The dashed boxes represent the Sweep Trace before it hits an object.
- The dotted boxes represent the Sweep Trace after it hits an object.
- The striped circle represents the Sweep Trace's impact point with object **2**, which is the point at which the Sweep Trace box shape's surface and object **2**'s surface collide with each other.
- The big squares represent two objects that are in the path of the Line Sweep Trace (objects **1** and **2**).
- Object **1** is ignored in the Sweep Trace due to assumptions based on its Trace Channel properties.

Sweep Traces are more useful than regular Line Traces in a few situations. Let's take the example of our enemy character, which can throw dodgeballs. If we wanted to add a way for the player to constantly visualize where the next dodgeball that the enemy throws will land, that could be better achieved with a Sweep Trace. We would do a Sweep Trace with the shape of our dodgeball (a sphere) toward our player, check the impact point, and show a sphere on that impact point, which would be visible to the player. If the Sweep Trace hits a wall or a corner somewhere, the player would know that if the enemy were to throw a dodgeball at that moment, that's where it would hit first. You could use a simple Line Trace for the same purpose, but the setup would have to be rather complex in order to achieve the same quality of results, which is why Sweep Traces are a better solution in this case.

Let's now take a quick look at how we can do a Sweep Trace in code.

Exercise 5.04: Executing a Sweep Trace

In this exercise, we will implement a Sweep Trace in code. Although we won't be using it for our project, by performing this exercise you will become familiar with such an operation.

Go to the end of the `CanSeeActor` function created in the preceding sections and perform the following steps:

1. The function responsible for the Sweep Trace is `SweepSingleByChannel`, which is available within UE5 and requires the following parameters as inputs:

    An `FHitResult` type to store the results of the sweep (we already have one of these, so there's no need to create another variable of this type) as follows:

    ```
    // Store the results of the Line Trace
    FHitResult Hit;
    ```

    `Start` and `End` points of the sweep (we already have both of these, so there's no need to create another variable of this type) as follows:

    ```
    // Where the Sweep Trace starts and ends
    FVector Start = GetActorLocation();
    FVector End = TargetActor->GetActorLocation();
    ```

2. Use the intended rotation of the shape, which is in the form of an `FQuat` type (representing a quaternion). In this case, it's set to a rotation of 0 on all axes, by accessing the `FQuat`'s `Identity` property as follows:

    ```
    // Rotation of the shape used in the Sweep Trace
    FQuat Rotation = FQuat::Identity;
    ```

3. Now, use the intended Trace Channel to compare it against (we already have one of these, so there's no need to create another variable of this type) as follows:

```
// The trace channel we want to compare against
ECollisionChannel Channel = ECollisionChannel::ECC_
Visibility;
```

4. Finally, use the shape of a box for the Sweep Trace by calling the FcollisionShape MakeBox function and supplying it with the radius (on all three axes) of the box shape we want. This is shown in the following code snippet:

```
// Shape of the object used in the Sweep Trace
FCollisionShape Shape =
FCollisionShape::MakeBox(FVector(20.f,
    20.f, 20.f));
```

5. Next, call the SweepSingleByChannel function as follows:

```
GetWorld()->SweepSingleByChannel(Hit,
                                Start,
                                End,
                                Rotation,
                                Channel,
                                Shape);
```

With these steps completed, we finish our exercise on Sweep Traces. Given that we won't be using Sweep Traces in our project, you should comment out the SweepSingleByChannel function so that our Hit variable doesn't get modified and lose the results from our Line Trace.

Now that we've concluded the section on Sweep Traces, let's get back to our **Dodgeball** project and learn how to change an object's response to a Trace Channel.

Changing the Visibility Trace Response

In our current setup, every object that is visible blocks the `Visibility` Trace Channel; however, what if we wanted to change whether an object blocks that channel completely? In order to do this, we must change a component's response to that channel. Have a look at the following example:

1. We select the cube that we've been using to block the enemy's sight in our level as shown in *Figure 5.9*:

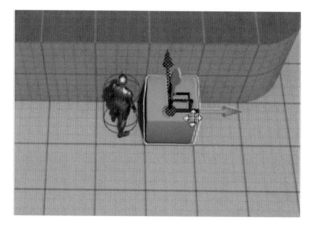

Figure 5.9 – Default spawn of the character

2. Then, you go to the **Collision** section of this object's **Details Panel** (its default place in the **Editor**'s interface) as follows:

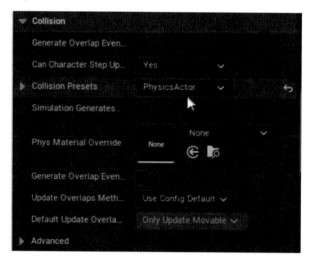

Figure 5.10 – Collision tab in the Details Panel in Unreal Engine

3. Here, you'll find several collision-related options. The one we want to pay attention to right now is the **Collision Presets** option. Its current value is **Default**; however, we want to change it according to our own preferences, so we will click on the drop-down box and change its value to **Custom**.

4. Once you do this, you'll notice a whole group of new options pop up as follows:

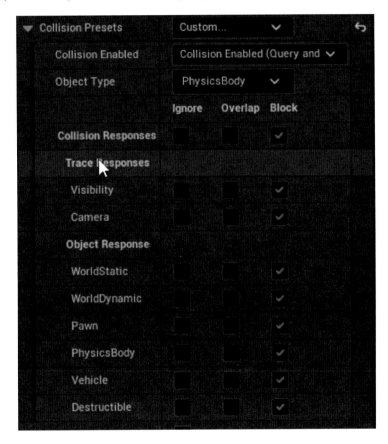

Figure 5.11 – Collision Presets set to Custom

This group of options allows you to specify how this object responds to Line Traces and object collision, and the type of collision object it is.

The option you should be paying attention to is **Visibility**. You'll notice it's set to **Block**, but you can also set it to **Overlap** and **Ignore**.

Right now, the cube is blocking the **Visibility** channel, which is why our enemy can't see the character when it's behind this cube. However, if we change the object's response to the **Visibility** channel to either **Overlap** or **Ignore**, the object will no longer block Line Traces that check for **Visibility** (which is the case for the Line Trace you've just written in C++).

5.   Let's change the cube's response to the **Visibility** channel to **Ignore**, and then play the game. You'll notice that the enemy is still looking toward the player character, even when it's behind the cube:

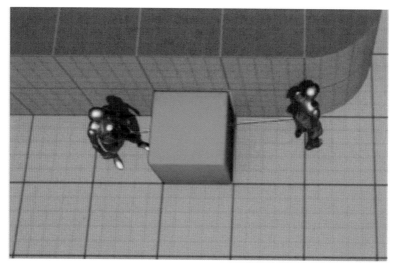

Figure 5.12 – The enemy character looking through an object at the player

This is because the cube no longer blocks the **Visibility** channel, and so the Line Trace the enemy is executing no longer hits anything when trying to reach the player character.

Now that we've seen how we can change an object's response to a specific Trace Channel, let's change the cube's response to the **Visibility** channel back to **Block**.

However, there's one thing that's worth mentioning. If we were to set the cube's response to the **Visibility** channel to **Overlap** instead of **Ignore**, the result would be the same. But why is that, and what is the purpose of having these two responses? In order to explain that, we'll look at Multi Line Traces.

Multi Line Traces

When using the `CanSeeActor` function in *Exercise 5.02, Creating the CanSeeActor function that executes Line Traces*, you might have wondered to yourself about the name of the Line Trace function we used, `LineTraceSingleByChannel`, specifically about why it used the word *Single*. The reason for that is that you can also execute `LineTraceMultiByChannel`.

But how do these two Line Traces differ?

While the Single Line Trace will stop checking for objects that block it after it hits an object and tell us that was the object that it hit, the Multi Line Trace can check for any objects that are hit by the same Line Trace.

The Single Line Trace will do the following:

- Ignore the objects that have their response set to either `Ignore` or `Overlap` on the Trace Channel being used by the Line Trace
- Stop when it finds an object that has its response set to `Block`

However, instead of ignoring objects that have their response set to `Overlap`, the Multi Line Trace will add them as objects that were found during the Line Trace and only stop when it finds an object that blocks the desired Trace Channel (*or when it reaches the end point*). In the next figure, you'll find an illustration of a Multi Line Trace being executed:

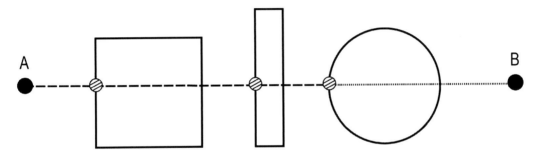

Figure 5.13 – A Multi Line Trace being executed from point A to point B

In *Figure 5.13*, we notice the following:

- The dashed line represents the Line Trace before it hits an object that blocks it.
- The dotted line represents the Line Trace after it hits an object that blocks it.
- The striped circles represent the Line Trace's impact points, and only the last one of which is a blocking hit in this case.

The only difference between the `LineTraceSingleByChannel` and the `LineTraceMultiByChannel` functions, when it comes to their inputs, is that the latter must receive a `TArray<FHitResult>` input instead of a single `FHitResult`. All other inputs are the same.

Multi Line Traces are very useful when simulating the behavior of bullets with strong penetration that can go through several objects before stopping completely. Keep in mind that you can also do Multi Sweep Traces by calling the `SweepMultiByChannel` function.

> **Note**
>
> Another thing about the `LineTraceSingleByChannel` function that you might be wondering about is the `ByChannel` portion. This distinction has to do with using a Trace Channel, as opposed to the alternative, which is an Object Type. You can do a Line Trace that uses Object Types instead of Trace Channels by calling the `LineTraceSingleByObjectType` function, also available from the `World` object. Object Types are related to topics we will be covering in the following chapter, so we won't be going into detail on this function just yet.

The Camera Trace Channel

When changing our cube's response to the `Visibility` Trace Channel, you may have noticed the other out-of-the-box Trace Channel: **Camera**.

This channel is used to specify whether an object blocks the line of sight between the camera's spring arm and the character it's associated with. In order to see this in action, we can drag an object to our level and place it in such a way that it will stay between the camera and our player character.

Have a look at the following example:

1. We duplicate the `floor` object.

> **Note**
>
> You can easily duplicate an object in the level by holding the *Alt* key and dragging one of the *Move Tool*'s arrows in any direction.

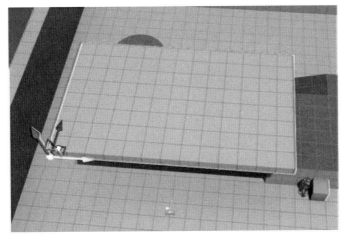

Figure 5.14 – Floor object being selected

2.   Next, we change its **Transform** values as shown in the following figure:

Figure 5.15 – Updating the Transform values

3.   Now when you play your game, you'll notice that when the character goes under our duplicated `floor` object, you won't lose sight of the player character, but; the spring arm will cause the camera to move down until you can see the character, as follows:

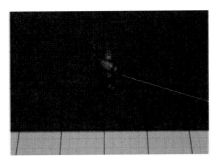

Figure 5.16 – Changes in the camera angle

4. In order to see how the spring arm's behavior differs when an object isn't blocking the `Camera` Trace Channel, change our duplicated floor's response to the `Camera` channel to `Ignore` and play the level again. What will happen is that when our character goes under the duplicated floor, we will lose sight of the character.

After you've done these steps, you can see that the `Camera` channel is used to specify whether an object will cause the spring arm to move the camera closer to the player when it intersects that object.

Now that we know how to use the existing Trace Channels, what if we wanted to create our own Trace Channels?

Exercise 5.05: Creating a custom EnemySight Trace Channel

As we've discussed before, UE5 comes with two out-of-the-box Trace Channels: `Visibility` and `Camera`. The first one is a general-use channel that we can use to specify which objects block the line of sight of an object, whereas the second one allows us to specify whether an object blocks the line of sight between the camera's spring arm and the character it's associated with.

But how can we create our own Trace Channels? That's what we'll be looking into in this exercise. We will create a new `EnemySight` Trace Channel and use it to check whether the enemy can see the player character, instead of the built-in `Visibility` channel, as follows:

1. Open **Project Settings** by pressing the **Edit** button at the top-left corner of the editor and go to the **Collision** section. There you'll find the **Trace Channels** section. It's currently empty because we haven't yet created any of our own Trace Channels.

2. Select the **New Trace Channel** option. A window should pop up, giving you the option to name your new channel and set its default response by the objects in your project. Name your new Trace Channel `EnemySight` and set its default response to `Block`, because we want most objects to do exactly that.

3. After you've created the new Trace Channel, we must go back to our `EnemyCharacter` C++ class and change the trace we're comparing against in our Line Trace, as follows:

    ```
    // The trace channel we want to compare against
    ECollisionChannel Channel = ECollisionChannel::ECC_
    Visibility;
    ```

Given that we are no longer using the `Visibility` channel, we must reference our new channel. But how do we do that?

In your project's directory, you'll find the `Config` folder. This folder contains several `ini` files related to your project, such as `DefaultGame.ini`, `DefaultEditor.ini`, `DefaultEngine.ini`, and so on. Each of these contains several properties that will be initialized when the project is loaded. The properties are set by name-value pairs (`property=value`), and you can change their values as desired.

4. When we created our `EnemySight` channel, the project's `DefaultEngine.ini` file was updated with our new Trace Channel. Somewhere in that file, you'll find the following line:

```
+DefaultChannelResponses=(Channel=ECC_GameTraceChannel1,
    DefaultResponse=ECR_Block,bTraceType=True,
    bStaticObject=False,
    Name="EnemySight")
```

> **Note**
>
> The preceding code line can be found highlighted at the following link: `https://packt.live/3eFpz5r`.

The preceding line says that there is a custom Trace Channel called `EnemySight` that has a default response of `Block` and, most importantly, is available in C++ using the `ECC_GameTraceChannel1` value of the collision enum we mentioned earlier, `ECollisionChannel`. This is the channel we'll be referencing in the following code:

```
// The trace channel we want to compare against
ECollisionChannel Channel =
    ECollisionChannel::ECC_GameTraceChannel1;
```

5. Verify that our enemy's behavior remains the same after all of the changes we've made. This means that the enemy must still face the player character, as long as it's within view of said enemy.

By completing this exercise, we now know how to make our own Trace Channels for any desired purpose.

Going back to our enemy character, there are still ways that we can improve its logic. Right now, when we fetch our enemy's location as the start point of the Line Trace, that point is somewhere around the enemy's hip, because that's where the origin of the Actor is. However, that's not usually where people's eyes are, and it wouldn't make much sense to have a humanoid character looking from its hip instead of its head.

So, let's change that and have our enemy character check whether it sees the player character starting from its eyes, instead of its hip.

Activity 5.01: Creating the SightSource property

In this activity, we will be improving our enemy's logic to determine whether it should look at the player. Currently, the Line Trace that's being done to determine that is being *shot* from around our character's hips, (0, 0, 0) in our `BP_EnemyCharacter` blueprint. We want this to make a bit more sense, so we'll make it so that the Line Trace starts somewhere close to our enemy's eyes.

The following steps will help you complete the activity:

1. Declare a new `SceneComponent` in our `EnemyCharacter` C++ class called `SightSource`. Make sure to declare this as a UPROPERTY with the `VisibleAnywhere`, `BlueprintReadOnly`, `Category = LookAt`, and `meta = (AllowPrivateAccess = "true")` tags.

2. Create this component in the `EnemyCharacter` constructor by using the `CreateDefaultSubobject` function, and attach it to `RootComponent`.

3. Change the start location of the Line Trace in the `CanSeeActor` function to the `SightSource` component's location, instead of the Actor's location.

4. Open the `BP_EnemyCharacter` Blueprint Class and change the `SightSource` component's location to the location of the enemy's head, `10, 0, 80`, as was done in the *Creating the EnemyCharacter Blueprint Class* section to the `SkeletalMeshComponent` property of `BP_EnemyCharacter`.

Hint: This can be achieved from the **Transform** tab in the **Editor panel** as shown in *Figure 5.17*.

▼ Transform				
Location ⌄	10,0	0,0	80,0	↶
Rotation ⌄	0,0 °	0,0 °	0,0 °	
Scale ⌄ 🔓	1,0	1,0	1,0	
Mobility	Static	Stationary	**Movable**	

Figure 5.17 – Updating the SightSource component's values

The following is the expected output:

Figure 5.18 – The expected output showing the updated Line Trace from the hip to the eye

> **Note**
>
> The solution for this activity can be found on GitHub here: `https://github.com/PacktPublishing/Elevating-Game-Experiences-with-Unreal-Engine-5-Second-Edition/tree/main/Activity%20solutions`.

By completing this activity, we have updated our `SightSource` property for our `EnemyCharacter`.

Summary

By completing this chapter, you have added a new tool to your belt: Line Traces. You now know how to execute Line Traces and Sweep Traces, both Single and Multi, how to change an object's response to a specific Trace Channel, and how to create your own Trace Channels.

You will quickly realize in the following chapters that these are essential skills when it comes to game development, and you will make good use of them on your future projects.

Now that we know how to use Line Traces, we're ready for the next step, which is Object Collision. In the following chapter, you will learn how to set up collisions between objects and how to use collision events to create your own game logic. You will create the Dodgeball Actor, which will be affected by real-time physics simulation, the Wall Actors, which will block both the characters' movements and the dodgeball, and the Actor responsible for ending the game when the player comes into contact with it.

6

Setting Up Collision Objects

In the previous chapter, we covered some of the basic concepts of collision, namely Line Traces and Sweep Traces. We learned how to execute different types of Line Traces, how to create custom Trace Channels, and how to change how an object responds to a specific channel. Many of the things you learned in the previous chapter will be used in this chapter, where we'll learn about object collision.

Throughout this chapter, we will continue to build upon our top-down Dodgeball game by adding game mechanics that revolve around object collision. We will create the Dodgeball actor, which will act as a dodgeball that bounces off of the floor and walls; the Wall actor, which will block all objects; the Ghost Wall actor, which will only block the player, not the enemies' lines of sight or the dodgeball; and the Victory Box actor, which will end the game when the player enters the Victory Box, representing the end of the level.

We will cover the following topics in this chapter:

- Understanding object collision in UE5
- Understanding collision components
- Understanding collision events
- Understanding collision channels
- Creating physical materials
- Introducing timers
- Understanding how to spawn actors

Before we start creating our `Dodgeball` class, we will go over the basic concepts of object collision.

Technical requirements

The project for this chapter can be found in the Chapter06 folder of the code bundle for this book, which can be downloaded here: `https://github.com/PacktPublishing/Elevating-Game-Experiences-with-Unreal-Engine-5-Second-Edition`.

Understanding object collision in UE5

Every game development tool must have a physics engine that simulates collision between multiple objects, as explained in the previous chapter. Collision is the backbone of most games released nowadays, whether 2D or 3D. In many games, it's the main way in which the player acts upon the environment, be it running, jumping, or shooting, and the environment acts accordingly by making the player land, get hit, and so on. It is no understatement to say that, without simulated collision, it wouldn't be possible to make many games at all.

So, let's understand how object collision works in UE5 and how we can use it, starting with collision components.

Understanding collision components

In UE5, two types of components can affect and be affected by collision; they are as follows:

- Meshes
- Shape objects

Meshes can be as simple as a cube, or as complex as a high-resolution character with tens of thousands of vertices. A mesh's collision can be specified with a custom file imported alongside the mesh into UE5 (which is outside the scope of this book), or it can be calculated automatically by UE5 and customized by you.

It is generally a good practice to keep the collision mesh as simple (for example, a few triangles) as possible so that the physics engine can efficiently calculate collision at runtime. The types of meshes that can have collision are as follows:

- **Static Meshes**: Meshes that are defined as static and do not change.
- **Skeletal Meshes**: Meshes that can have a skeleton and change their poses, which allows them to be animated. Character meshes, for instance, are skeletal meshes.
- **Procedural Meshes**: Meshes that can be generated automatically according to certain parameters.

Shape objects, which are simple meshes represented in wireframe mode, are used to behave as collision objects by causing and receiving collision events.

> **Note**
> Wireframe mode is a commonly used visualization mode in game development, usually for debugging purposes, which allows you to see meshes without any faces or textures – they can only be seen through their edges, which are connected by their vertices. You will see what wireframe mode is when we add a **Shape** component to an actor.

Please note that Shape objects are essentially invisible meshes and that their three types are as follows:

- Box Collision (Box Component in C++)

- Sphere Collision (Sphere Component in C++)

- Capsule Collider (Capsule Component in C++)

> **Note**
>
> There's a class that all the components that provide geometry and collision inherit from, which is the Primitive component. This component is the basis for all components that contain any sort of geometry, which is the case for mesh components and shape components.

So, how can these components collide, and what happens when they do? We shall have a look at this in the next section.

Understanding collision events

Let's say that two objects are colliding with one another. Two things can happen:

- They overlap each other, as if the other object weren't there, in which case the Overlap event is called.

- They collide and prevent each other from continuing their course, in which case the Block event is called.

In the previous chapter, we learned how to change an object's response to a specific Trace channel. During this process, we learned that an object's response can be either Block, Overlap, or Ignore.

Now, let's see what happens in each of these responses during a collision:

- **Block**: Two objects will only block each other if both of them have their response to the other object set to Block:

  - Both objects will have their OnHit events called. This event is called whenever two objects block each other's path at the moment they collide. If one of the objects is simulating physics, that object must have its SimulationGeneratesHitEvents property set to true.

  - Both objects will physically stop each other from continuing with their course.

The following diagram shows an example of when two objects are thrown and bounce off each other:

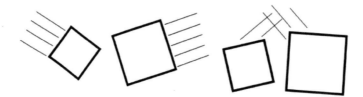

Figure 6.1 – Object A and object B blocking each other

- **Overlap**: Two objects will overlap each other if they don't block each other and neither of them is ignoring the other:

  - If both objects have the `GenerateOverlapEvents` property set to `true`, they will have their `OnBeginOverlap` and `OnEndOverlap` events called. These overlap events are called when an object starts and stops overlapping another object, respectively. If at least one of them doesn't have this property set to `true`, neither of them will call these events.

  - The objects act as if the other object doesn't exist and will overlap each other.

As an example, suppose the player's character walks into a trigger box that marks the end of the level, which only reacts to the player's character.

The following diagram shows an example of two objects overlapping each other:

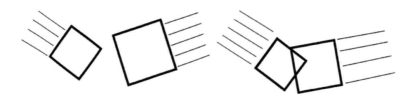

Figure 6.2 – Object A and object B overlapping each other

- **Ignore**: Two objects will ignore each other if at least one of them is ignoring the other:

  - No events will be called on either object.

  - Similar to the `Overlap` response, the objects will act as if the other object doesn't exist and will overlap each other.

An example of two objects ignoring each other would be when an object other than the player's character goes into a trigger box that marks the end of the level, which only reacts to the player's character.

> **Note**
> You can look at the previous diagram, where two objects overlap each other, to understand **Ignore**.

The following table will help you understand the necessary responses that two objects must have to trigger the previously described situations:

Object B Object A	Block	Overlap	Ignore
Block	Block	Overlap	Ignore
Overlap	Overlap	Overlap	Ignore
Ignore	Ignore	Ignore	Ignore

Figure 6.3 – Resulting responses on objects based on Block, Overlap, and Ignore

Following this table, consider that you have two objects – object A and object B:

- If object A has set its response to object B to **Block** and object B has set its response to object A to **Block**, they will **Block** each other.

- If object A has set its response to object B to **Block** and object B has set its response to object A to **Overlap**, they will **Overlap** each other.

- If object A has set its response to object B to **Ignore** and object B has set its response to object A to **Overlap**, they will **Ignore** each other.

> **Note**
> You can find a full reference to UE5's collision interactions at https://docs.unrealengine.com/en-US/Engine/Physics/Collision/Overview.

A collision between objects has two aspects to it:

- **Physics**: All collisions related to physics simulation, such as a ball being affected by gravity and bouncing off the floors and walls.

  The physically simulated response of the collision within the game can be either of the following:

  - Both objects continue their trajectories as if the other object wasn't there (no physical collision).

  - Both objects collide and change their trajectories, usually with at least one of them continuing its movement – that is, they are blocking each other's paths.

- **Query**: A query can be divided into two aspects of collision, as follows:

  - The events related to the collision of the objects that are called by the game and that you can use to create additional logic. These events are the same ones we mentioned previously:

  - The OnHit event

  - The OnBeginOverlap event

  - The OnEndOverlap event

  - The physical response to the collision within the game, which can be either of the following:

    - Both objects continued their movement as if the other object wasn't there (no physical collision)

    - Both objects collide and block each other's path

The physical response from the physics aspect may sound similar to the physical response from the query aspect; however, although they are both physical responses, they will cause objects to behave differently.

The physical response from the physics aspect (physics simulation) only applies when an object is simulating physics (for example, being affected by gravity, bouncing off the walls and ground, and so on). Such an object, when hitting a wall, for instance, will bounce back and continue moving in another direction.

On the other hand, the physical response from the query aspect applies to all objects that don't simulate physics. An object can move without simulating physics when being controlled by code (for example, by using the SetActorLocation function or by using the **Character Movement** component). In this case, depending on which method you use to move the object and its properties, when an object hits a wall, it will simply stop moving instead of bouncing back. This is because you're simply telling the object to move in a certain direction and something is blocking its path, so the physics engine doesn't allow that object to continue moving.

Now that we've learned about collision events, let's move on to the next section, where we will be looking at collision channels.

Understanding collision channels

In the previous chapter, a looked at the existing Trace Channels (*Visibility* and *Camera*) and learned how to make a custom channel. Now that you know about Trace Channels, it's time to talk about Object Channels, also known as Object Types.

While Trace Channels are only used for Line Traces, Object Channels are used for object collision. You can specify a "purpose" for each Object channel, much like with Trace Channels, such as **Pawn**, **Static Object**, **Physics Object**, **Projectile**, and so on. Then, you can specify how you want each Object Type to respond to all the other Object Types by blocking, overlapping, or ignoring objects of that type.

Now that we've taken a look at how collision works, let's go back to the collision settings of the cube we selected in the previous chapter, where we changed its response to the Visibility Channel.

Follow these steps to learn more about collision channels:

1. The cube can be seen in the following screenshot:

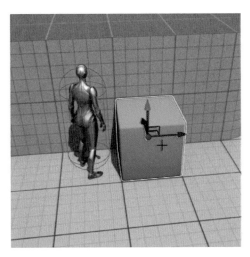

Figure 6.4 – Cube blocking the SightSource of the enemy

2. With the level open in the editor, select the cube and go to the **Collision** section of its **Details** panel:

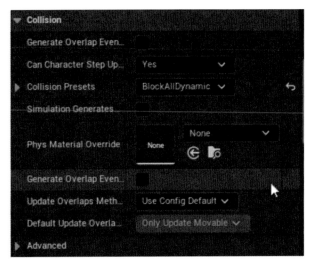

Figure 6.5 – The changes in the level editor

Here, we can see some options that are important to us:

- **Simulation Generates Hit Events**, which allows the OnHit events to be called when an object is simulating physics (we'll talk about this later in this chapter).

- **Generate Overlap Events**, which allows the OnBeginOverlap and OnEndOverlap events to be called.

- **Can Character Step Up On**, which allows a character to easily step onto this object.

- **Collision Presets**, which allows us to specify how this object responds to each Collision Channel.

3. Let's change the **Collision Presets** value from Default to Custom and take a look at the new options that show up:

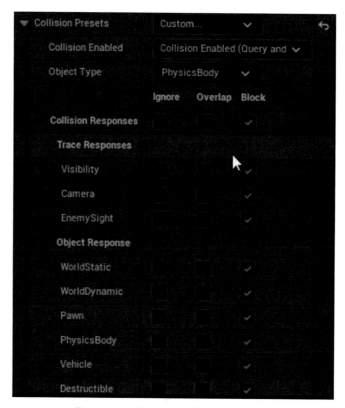

Figure 6.6 – Changes in Collision Presets

The first of these options is the **Collision Enabled** property. It allows you to specify which aspects of collision you want this object to be considered for: **Query**, **Physics**, **Both**, or **None**. Again, physics collision is related to physics simulation (whether this object will be considered by other objects that simulate physics), while query collision is related to collision events and whether objects will block each other's movement:

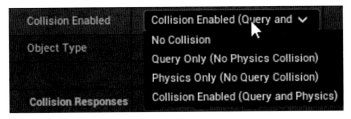

Figure 6.7 – Collision Enabled for Query and Physics

The second option is the **Object Type** property. This is very similar to the Trace Channel concept but is specifically for object collision and, most importantly, dictates what type of collision object this is. The Object Type values that come with UE5 are as follows:

- `WorldStatic`: An object that doesn't move (structures, buildings, and so on)
- `WorldDynamic`: An object that may move (objects whose movement is triggered by code, objects the player can pick up and move, and so on)
- `Pawn`: Used for Pawns that can be controlled and moved around the level
- `PhysicsBody`: Used for objects that simulate physics
- `Vehicle`: Used for Vehicle objects
- `Destructible`: Used for destructible meshes

As mentioned previously, you can create custom object types (which will be mentioned later in this chapter) as well, similar to how you can create Trace Channels (*which was covered in the previous chapter*).

The last option we have is related to **Collision Responses**. Given that this `Cube` object has the default collision options, all the responses are set to `Block`, which means that this object will block all the Line Traces and all objects that block `WorldStatic` objects, given that that is this object's type.

Because there are so many different combinations of collision properties, UE5 allows you to group collision property values in the form of Collision Presets.

Let's go back to the **Collision Presets** property, which is currently set to **Custom**, and *click it* so that we can see all the possible options. Some of the existing **Collision Presets** are as follows:

- **No Collision**: Used for objects that aren't affected by collision whatsoever:

  - **Collision Enabled**: NoCollision
  - **Object Type**: WorldStatic
  - Responses: Irrelevant
  - Example: Objects that are purely visual and distant, such as an object that the player will never reach

- **Block All**: Used for objects that are static and block all other objects:

  - **Collision Enabled**: Query and Physics
  - **Object Type**: WorldStatic
  - Responses: Block all channels
  - Example: Objects that are close to the player character and block their movement, such as the floor and walls, which will always be stationary

- **Overlap All**: Used for objects that are static and overlap all other objects:

  - **Collision Enabled**: Query only
  - **Object Type**: WorldStatic
  - Responses: Overlap all channels
  - Example: Trigger boxes placed in the level, which will always be stationary

- **Block All Dynamic**: Similar to the Block All preset, but for dynamic objects that may change their transform during gameplay (Object Type: WorldDynamic)

- **Overlap All Dynamic**: Similar to the Overlap All preset, but for dynamic objects that may change their transform during gameplay (Object Type: WorldDynamic)

- Pawn: Used for pawns and characters:

  - **Collision Enabled**: Query and Physics
  - **Object Type**: Pawn
  - Responses: Block all channels, Ignore Visibility Channel
  - Example: Player character and non-playable characters

- **Physics Actor**: Used for objects that simulate physics:

  - **Collision Enabled**: `Query` and `Physics`

  - **Object Type**: `PhysicsBody`

  - Responses: `Block` all channels

  - Example: Objects that are affected by physics, such as a ball that bounces off the floor and walls

Just like the other collision properties, you can also create your own collision presets.

> **Note**
> You can find a full reference to UE5's collision responses here: `https://docs.`
> `unrealengine.com/en-US/Engine/Physics/Collision/Reference`.

Now that we know about the basic concepts of collision, let's go ahead and start creating the `Dodgeball` class. The next exercise will guide you toward doing just that.

Exercise 6.01 – creating the Dodgeball class

In this exercise, we'll be creating our `Dodgeball` class, which will be thrown by our enemies and bounce off the floor and walls, just like an actual dodgeball.

Before we start creating the `Dodgeball` C++ class and its logic, we should set up all the necessary collision settings for it.

The following steps will help you complete this exercise:

1. Open **Project Settings** and go to the **Collision** subsection within the **Engine** section. Currently, there are no Object Channels, so you need to create a new one.

2. Press the **New Object Channel** button, name it `Dodgeball`, and set its **Default Response** to **Block**.

3. Once you've done this, expand the **Preset** section. Here, you'll find all the default presets available in UE5. If you select one of them and press the **Edit** option, you can change that **Preset Collision** settings.

4. Create your own **Preset** by pressing the **New** button. We want our **Dodgeball** preset settings to be as follows:

   - **Name**: `Dodgeball`

   - **Collision Enabled**: `Collision Enabled (Query and Physics)` (we want this to be considered for physics simulation as well as collision events)

- **Object Type**: `Dodgeball`

- **Collision Responses**: Select *Block* for most of the options, but *Ignore* the Camera and `EnemySight` (we don't want the dodgeball to block the camera or the enemy's line of sight)

5. Once you've selected the correct options, press **Accept**.

    Now that the `Dodgeball` class's collision settings have been set up, let's create the `Dodgeball` C++ class.

6. Inside the **Content Browser** area, *right-click* and select **New C++ Class**.

7. Choose **Actor** as the parent class.

8. Choose **DodgeballProjectile** as the name of the class (our project is already named `Dodgeball`, so we can't name this new class that too).

9. Open the `DodgeballProjectile` class files in Visual Studio. The first thing we'll want to do is add the collision component of the dodgeball, so we'll add a `SphereComponent` to our class header (*actor component properties are usually private*):

    ```
    UPROPERTY(VisibleAnywhere, BlueprintReadOnly, Category =
        Dodgeball, meta = (AllowPrivateAccess = "true"))
    class USphereComponent* SphereComponent;
    ```

10. Next, include the `SphereComponent` class at the top of our source file:

    ```
    #include "Components/SphereComponent.h"
    ```

> **Note**
> Keep in mind that all header file includes must be before the `.generated.h` include.

Now, head to the `DodgeballProjectile` class's constructor, within its source file, and perform the following steps:

11. Create the `SphereComponent` object:

    ```
    SphereComponent =
    CreateDefaultSubobject<USphereComponent>(TEXT("Sphere
        Collision"));
    ```

12. Set its `radius` to 35 units:

    ```
    SphereComponent->SetSphereRadius(35.f);
    ```

13. Set its **Collision Preset** to the Dodgeball preset we created:

```
SphereComponent->SetCollisionProfileName(FName("Dodgeb
all"));
```

14. We want Dodgeball to simulate physics, so notify the component of this, as shown in the following code snippet:

```
SphereComponent->SetSimulatePhysics(true);
```

15. We want Dodgeball to call the OnHit event while simulating physics, so call the SetNotifyRigidBodyCollision function to set that to true (this is the same as the SimulationGeneratesHitEvents property that we saw in the Collision section of an object's properties):

```
//Simulation generates Hit events
SphereComponent->SetNotifyRigidBodyCollision(true);
```

We will also want to listen to the OnHit event of SphereComponent.

16. Create a declaration for the function that will be called when the OnHit event is triggered, in the DodgeballProjectile class's header file. This function should be called OnHit. It should be public, return nothing (void), have the UFUNCTION macro, and receive some parameters, in this order:

   I.   UPrimitiveComponent* HitComp: The component that was hit and belongs to this actor. A primitive component is an actor component that has a Transform property and some sort of geometry (for example, a Mesh or Shape component).

   II. AActor* OtherActor: The other actor involved in the collision.

   III. UPrimitiveComponent* OtherComp: The component that was hit and belongs to the other actor.

   IV. FVector NormalImpulse: The direction in which the object will be moving after it has been hit, and with how much force (by checking the size of the vector). This parameter will only be non-zero for objects that are simulating physics.

   V.   FHitResult& Hit: The data of the hit resulting from the collision between this object and the other object. As we saw in the previous chapter, it contains properties such whether as the location of the hit is normal, which component and actor it hit, and so on. Most of the relevant information is already available to us through the other parameters, but if you need more detailed information, you can access this parameter:

```
UFUNCTION()
void OnHit(UPrimitiveComponent* HitComp, AActor*
OtherActor,
```

```
UPrimitiveComponent* OtherComp, FVector
NormalImpulse, const
FHitResult& Hit);
```

Add the OnHit function's implementation to the class's source file and within that function, at least for now, destroy the dodgeball when it hits the player.

17. Cast the OtherActor parameter to our DodgeballCharacter class and check if the value is not a nullptr. If it's not, which means that the other actor we hit is a DodgeballCharacter, we'll destroy this DodgeballProjectile actor:

```
void ADodgeballProjectile::OnHit(UPrimitiveComponent *
    HitComp, AActor * OtherActor, UPrimitiveComponent *
    OtherComp, FVector NormalImpulse, const FHitResult &
    Hit)
{
    if (Cast<ADodgeballCharacter>(OtherActor) !=
    nullptr)
    {
        Destroy();
    }
}
```

Given that we're referencing the DodgebalCharacter class, we'll need to include it at the top of this class's source file:

```
#include "DodgeballCharacter.h"
```

> **Note**
>
> In the next chapter, we'll change this function so that we have the dodgeball damage the player before destroying itself. We'll do this when we talk about Actor components.

18. Head back to the DodgeballProjectile class's constructor and add the following line at the end to listen to the OnHit event of SphereComponent:

```
// Listen to the OnComponentHit event by binding it to
// our function
SphereComponent->OnComponentHit.AddDynamic(this,
    &ADodgeballProjectile::OnHit);
```

This will bind the OnHit function we created to this SphereComponent OnHit event (because this is an actor component, this event is called OnComponentHit), which means our function will be called alongside that event.

19. Lastly, make SphereComponent this actor's RootComponent, as shown in the following code snippet:

```
// Set this Sphere Component as the root component,
// otherwise collision won't behave properly
RootComponent = SphereComponent;
```

> **Note**
>
> For a moving actor to behave correctly on collision, whether it's simulating physics or not, it is usually necessary for the main collision component of the actor to be its RootComponent.
>
> For example, the RootComponent component of the Character class is a Capsule Collider component, because that actor will be moving around and that component is the main way the character collides with the environment.

Now that we've added the DodgeballProjectile C++ class's logic, let's go ahead and create our Blueprint class.

20. Compile your changes and open the editor.

21. Go to **Content | ThirdPersonCPP | Blueprints** in the **Content Browser** area, right-click, and create a new Blueprint class.

22. Expand the **All Classes** section and search for the DodgeballProjectile class. Then, set it as the parent class.

23. Name the new Blueprint class BP_DodgeballProjectile.

24. Open this new Blueprint class.

25. Notice the wireframe representation of the **SphereCollision** component in the actor's **Viewport** window (this is hidden by default during the game, but you can change that property in this component's **Rendering** section by changing its HiddenInGame property):

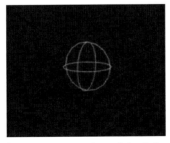

Figure 6.8 – Visual wireframe representation of the SphereCollision component

26. Now, add a new **Sphere** mesh as a child of the existing **Sphere Collision** component:

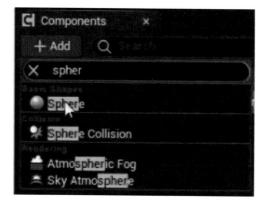

Figure 6.9 – Adding a Sphere mesh

27. Change its scale to 0.65, as shown in the following screenshot:

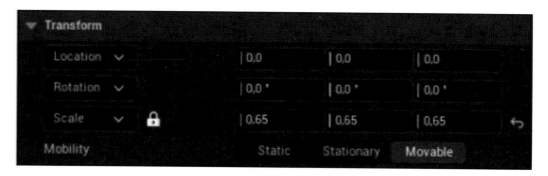

Figure 6.10 – Updating the scale

28. Set its **Collision Presets** to NoCollision:

Figure 6.11 – Updating Collision Presets to NoCollision

29. Finally, open our level and place an instance of the `BP_DodgeballProjectile` class near the player (this one was placed at a height of 600 units):

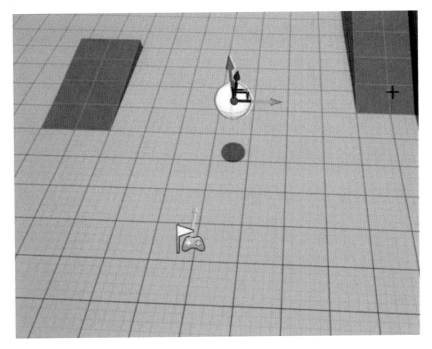

Figure 6.12 – Dodgeball bouncing on the ground

After you've done this, play the level. You'll notice that the dodgeball will be affected by gravity and bounce off the ground a couple of times before coming to a standstill.

By completing this exercise, you've created an object that behaves like a physics object.

You now know how to create collision object types, use the `OnHit` event, and change an object's collision properties.

> **Note**
>
> In the previous chapter, we briefly mentioned `LineTraceSingleByObjectType`. Now that we know how object collision works, we can briefly mention its use: when executing a Line Trace that checks for a Trace Channel, you should use the `LineTraceSingleByChannel` function; when executing a Line Trace that checks for an Object Channel (Object Type), you should use the `LineTraceSingleByObjectType` function. It should be made clear that this function, unlike the `LineTraceSingleByChannel` function, will not check for objects that block a specific Object Type, but those that are of a specific Object Type. Both those functions have the same parameters and both the Trace Channels and Object Channels are available through the `ECollisionChannel` enum.

But what if you wanted the ball to bounce off the floor more times? What if you wanted to make it bouncier? Well, that's where Physical Materials come in.

Creating Physical Materials

In UE5, you can customize how an object behaves while simulating physics using Physical Materials. To get into this new type of asset, let's create our own:

1. Create a new folder inside the `Content` folder called `Physics`.

2. *Right-click* on the **Content Browser** area while inside that folder and, under the **Create Advanced Asset** section, go to the **Physics** subsection and select **Physical Material**.

3. Name this new Physical Material **PM_Dodgeball**.

4. Open the asset and take a look at the available options:

Figure 6.13 – Asset options

The main options we should note are as follows:

- **Friction**: This property goes from 0 to 1 and specifies how much friction will affect this object (0 means this object will slide as if it was on ice, while 1 means this object will stick like a piece of gum).

- **Restitution** (also known as **Bounciness**): This property goes from 0 to 1 and specifies how much velocity will be kept after colliding with another object (0 means this object will never bounce off of the ground, while 1 means this object will bounce for a long time).

- **Density**: This property specifies how dense this object is (that is, how heavy it is relative to its mesh). Two objects can be of the same size, but if one is twice as dense as the other, that means it will be twice as heavy.

To have our `DodgeballProjectile` object behave closer to an actual dodgeball, it'll have to suffer quite a bit of friction (the default value is 0.7, which is high enough) and be quite bouncy. Let's increase the `Restitution` property of this Physical Material to 0.95.

After you've done this, open the **BP_DodgeballProjectile** Blueprint class and change the **Sphere Collision** component's Physical Material, inside its **Collision** section, to the one we just created, **PM_Dodgeball**:

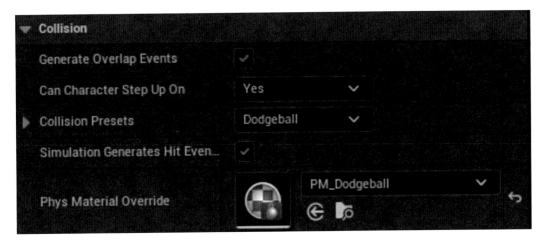

Figure 6.14 – Updating the BP_DodgeballProjectile Blueprint class

> **Note**
> Make sure the instance of the `Dodgeball` actor you added to your level also has this physical material.

If you play the level that we created in *Exercise 6.01 - creating the Dodgeball class*, again, you'll notice that our BP_DodgeballProjectile will now bounce off the ground several times before coming to a standstill, behaving much more like an actual dodgeball.

With all that done, we're just missing one thing to make our Dodgeball actor behave like an actual dodgeball. Right now, there is no way for us to be able to throw it. So, let's address that by creating a Projectile Movement Component, which is what we'll be doing in the next exercise.

In the previous chapters, when we replicated the Third Person template project, we learned that the Character class that comes with UE5 has a CharacterMovementComponent. This actor component is what allows an actor to move around in the level in various ways, and has many properties that allow you to customize that to your preference. However, there is another movement component that is also frequently used: ProjectileMovementComponent.

The ProjectileMovementComponent actor component is used to attribute the behavior of a projectile to an actor. It allows you to set an initial speed, gravity force, and even some physics simulation parameters such as Bounciness and Friction. However, given that our Dodgeball Projectile is already simulating physics, the only property that we'll be using is InitialSpeed.

Exercise 6.02 – adding a ProjectileMovementComponent to DodgeballProjectile

In this exercise, we will be adding a ProjectileMovementComponent to our DodgeballProjectile so that it has an initial horizontal speed. We're doing this so that it can be thrown by our enemies and doesn't just fall vertically.

The following steps will help you complete this exercise:

1. Add a ProjectileMovementComponent property to the DodgeballProjectile class's header file:

    ```
    UPROPERTY(VisibleAnywhere, BlueprintReadOnly, Category =
        Dodgeball, meta = (AllowPrivateAccess = "true"))
    class UProjectileMovementComponent* ProjectileMovement;
    ```

2. Include the ProjectileMovementComponent class at the top of the class's source file:

    ```
    #include "GameFramework/ProjectileMovementComponent.h"
    ```

3. At the end of the class's constructor, create the ProjectileMovementComponent object:

    ```
    ProjectileMovement =
    CreateDefaultSubobject<UProjectileMovementComponent>
    (TEXT("Pro
        jectile Movement"));
    ```

4. Then, set its `InitialSpeed` to `1500` units:

```
ProjectileMovement->InitialSpeed = 1500.f;
```

Once you've done this, compile your project and open the editor. To demonstrate the dodgeball's initial speed, lower its position on the *Z*-axis and place it behind the player (*this one was placed at a height of 200 units*):

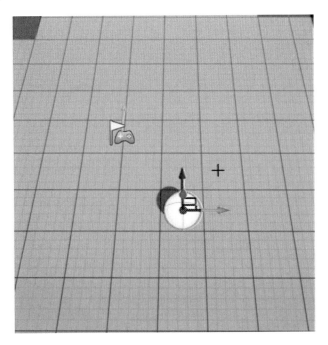

Figure 6.15 – Dodgeball moving along the X-axis

When you play the level, you'll notice that the dodgeball starts moving toward its *X*-axis (*red arrow*)

And with that, we can conclude our exercise. Our `DodgeballProjectile` now behaves like an actual dodgeball. It falls, bounces, and gets thrown.

The next step in our project is going to be adding logic to our `EnemyCharacter` so that it throws these dodgeballs at the player. However, before we address that, we must address the concept of timers.

Introducing timers

Given the nature of video games and the fact that they're strongly event-based, every game development tool must have a way for you to cause a delay, or a wait time, before something happens. For instance, when you're playing an online deathmatch game, where your character can die and then respawn, usually, the respawn event doesn't happen the instant your character dies but a few seconds later. There is a multitude of scenarios where you want something to happen, but only after a certain amount of time. This will be the case for our `EnemyCharacter`, which will be throwing dodgeballs every few seconds. This delay, or wait time, can be achieved through timers.

A **timer** allows you to call a function after a certain amount of time. You can choose to loop that function call with an interval and also set a delay before the loop starts. If you want the timer to stop, you can also do that.

We will be using timers so that our enemy throws a dodgeball every X amount of time, indefinitely, so long as it can see the player character, and then stop that timer when the enemy can no longer see its target.

Before we start adding logic to our `EnemyCharacter` class that will make it throw dodgeballs at the player, we should take a look at another topic, which is how to spawn actors.

Understanding how to spawn actors

In *Chapter 1, Introduction to Unreal Engine*, you learned how to place an actor that you created in the level through the editor, but what if you wanted to place that actor in the level as the game is being played? That's what we're going to be taking a look at now.

UE5, much like most other game development tools, allows you to place an actor in the game while the game itself is running. This process is called **spawning**. To spawn an actor in UE5, we need to call the `SpawnActor` function, available from the `World` object (which we can access using the `GetWorld` function, as mentioned previously). However, the `SpawnActor` function has a few parameters that need to be passed, as follows:

- A `UClass*` property, which lets the function know the class of the object that will be spawned. This property can be a C++ class, available through the `NameOfC++Class::StaticClass()` function, or a Blueprint class, available through the `TSubclassOf` property. It is generally a good practice not to spawn actors from a C++ class directly, but to create a Blueprint class and spawn an instance of that instead.

- The `TSubclassOf` property is a way for you to reference a Blueprint class in C++. It's used for referencing a class in C++ code, which might be a Blueprint class. You must declare a `TSubclassOf` property with a template parameter, which is the C++ class that the class must inherit from. We will be taking a look at how to use this property in practice in the next exercise.

- Either an `FTransform` property or the `FVector` and `FRotator` properties, which will indicate the location, rotation, and scale of the object we want to spawn.

- An optional `FActorSpawnParameters` property, which allows you to specify more properties specific to the spawning process, such as who caused the actor to spawn (that is, `Instigator`), how to handle the object spawning if the location that it spawns at is being occupied by other objects, which may cause an overlap or a block event, and so on.

The `SpawnActor` function will return an instance to the actor that was spawned from this function. Given that it is also a template function, you can call it in such a way that you receive a reference to the type of actor you spawned directly using a template parameter:

```
GetWorld()->SpawnActor<NameOfC++Class>(ClassReference,
    SpawnLocation, SpawnRotation);
```

In this case, the `SpawnActor` function is being called, where we're spawning an instance of the `NameOfC++Class` class. Here, we have provided a reference to the class with the `ClassReference` property and the location and rotation of the actor to be spawned using the `SpawnLocation` and `SpawnRotation` properties, respectively.

You will learn how to apply these properties in *Exercise 6.03 – adding projectile-throwing logic to the EnemyCharacter class*.

Before we continue with the exercise, though, I'd like to briefly mention a variation of the `SpawnActor` function that may also come in handy: the `SpawnActorDeferred` function. While the `SpawnActor` function will create an instance of the object you specify and then place it in the world, this new `SpawnActorDeferred` function will create an instance of the object you want, and only place it in the world when you call the actor's `FinishSpawning` function.

For instance, let's say we want to change the `InitialSpeed` of our dodgeball at the moment we spawn it. If we use the `SpawnActor` function, there's a chance that the dodgeball will start moving before we set its `InitialSpeed` property. However, by using the `SpawnActorDeferred` function, we can create an instance of the dodgeball, then set its `InitialSpeed` to whatever we want, and only then place it in the world by calling the newly created dodgeball's `FinishSpawning` function, whose instance is returned to us by the `SpawnActorDeferred` function.

Now that we know how to spawn an actor in the world, and also about the concept of timers, we can add the logic that's responsible for throwing dodgeballs to our `EnemyCharacter` class, which is what we'll be doing in the next exercise.

Exercise 6.03 – adding projectile-throwing logic to the EnemyCharacter class

In this exercise, we will be adding the logic that's responsible for throwing the **Dodgeball** actor that we just created to our `EnemyCharacter` class.

Open the class's files in Visual Studio to get started. We will begin by modifying our `LookAtActor` function so that we can save the value that tells us whether we can see the player and use it to manage our timer.

Follow these steps to complete this exercise:

1. In the `EnemyCharacter` class's header file, change the `LookAtActor` function's return type from `void` to `bool`:

    ```
    // Change the rotation of the character to face the
    // given actor
    // Returns whether the given actor can be seen
    bool LookAtActor(AActor* TargetActor);
    ```

2. Do the same in the function's implementation, inside the class's source file, while also returning `true` at the end of the `if` statement where we call the `CanSeeActor` function. Also, return `false` in the first `if` statement, where we check if `TargetActor` is a `nullptr`, and also at the end of the function:

    ```
    bool AEnemyCharacter::LookAtActor(AActor * TargetActor)
    {
        if (TargetActor == nullptr) return false;

        if (CanSeeActor(TargetActor))
        {
            FVector Start = GetActorLocation();
            FVector End = TargetActor->GetActorLocation();
            // Calculate the necessary rotation for the Start
            // point to face the End point
            FRotator LookAtRotation =
            UKismetMathLibrary::FindLookAtRotation(
            Start, End);

            //Set the enemy's rotation to that rotation
            SetActorRotation(LookAtRotation);
    ```

```
        return true;
    }

    return false;
}
```

3. Next, add two `bool` properties, `bCanSeePlayer` and `bPreviousCanSeePlayer`, set to `protected` in your class's header file, which will represent whether the player can be seen in this frame from the enemy character's perspective and whether the player could be seen in the last frame, respectively:

```
//Whether the enemy can see the player this frame
bool bCanSeePlayer = false;
//Whether the enemy could see the player last frame
bool bPreviousCanSeePlayer = false;
```

4. Then, go to your class's `Tick` function implementation and set the value of `bCanSeePlayer` to the return value of the `LookAtActor` function. This will replace the previous call to the `LookAtActor` function:

```
// Look at the player character every frame
bCanSeePlayer = LookAtActor(PlayerCharacter);
```

5. After that, set the value of `bPreviousCanSeePlayer` to the value of `bCanSeePlayer`:

```
bPreviousCanSeePlayer = bCanSeePlayer;
```

6. In-between the previous two lines, add an `if` statement that checks whether the values of `bCanSeePlayer` and `bPreviousCanSeePlayer` are different. This will mean that either we couldn't see the player in the last frame and now we can, or that we could see the player in the last frame and now we can't:

```
bCanSeePlayer = LookAtActor(PlayerCharacter);

if (bCanSeePlayer != bPreviousCanSeePlayer)
{

}

bPreviousCanSeePlayer = bCanSeePlayer;
```

7. Inside this `if` statement, we want to start a timer if we can see the player and stop that timer if we can no longer see the player:

```
if (bCanSeePlayer != bPreviousCanSeePlayer)
{
  if (bCanSeePlayer)
  {
    //Start throwing dodgeballs
  }
  else
  {
    //Stop throwing dodgeballs
  }
}
```

8. To start a timer, we'll need to add the following properties to our class's header file, which can all be `protected`:

- An `FTimerHandle` property, which is responsible for identifying which timer we want to start. It works as the identifier of a specific timer:

```
FTimerHandle ThrowTimerHandle;
```

- A `float` property, which represents the amount of time to wait between throwing dodgeballs (the interval) so that we can loop the timer. We give this a default value of 2 seconds:

```
float ThrowingInterval = 2.f;
```

- Another `float` property, which represents the initial delay before the timer starts looping. Let's give it a default value of `0.5` seconds:

```
float ThrowingDelay = 0.5f;
```

- A function to be called every time the timer ends, which we will create and call `ThrowDodgeball`. This function doesn't return anything and doesn't receive any parameters:

```
void ThrowDodgeball();
```

Before we can call the appropriate function to start the timer, we will need to add an `#include` to the object responsible for that, `FTimerManager`, in our source file.

Each `World` has one Timer Manager, which can start and stop timers and access relevant functions related to them, such as whether they're still active, how long they will be running for, and so on:

```
#include "TimerManager.h"
```

9. Now, access the current `World` Timer Manager by using the `GetWorldTimerManager` function:

```
GetWorldTimerManager()
```

10. Next, call the `SetTimer` function of the Timer Manager, if you can see the player character, to start the timer responsible for throwing dodgeballs. The `SetTimer` function receives the following parameters:

   - An `FTimerHandle` that represents the desired timer: `ThrowTimerHandle`.

   - The object that the function to be called belongs to: `this`.

   - The function to be called, which must be specified by prefixing its name with `&ClassName::`, resulting in `&AEnemyCharacter::ThrowDodgeball`.

   - The timer's rate, or interval: `ThrowingInterval`.

   - Whether this timer will loop: `true`.

   - The delay before this timer starts looping: `ThrowingDelay`.

The following code snippet comprises these parameters:

```
if (bCanSeePlayer)
{
  //Start throwing dodgeballs
  GetWorldTimerManager().SetTimer(ThrowTimerHandle,
  this,
  &AEnemyCharacter::ThrowDodgeball, ThrowingInterval,
  true,
  ThrowingDelay);
}
```

11. If we can no longer see the player and we want to stop the timer, we can do so using the `ClearTimer` function. This function only needs to receive an `FTimerHandle` property as a parameter:

```
else
{
  //Stop throwing dodgeballs
```

```
        GetWorldTimerManager().ClearTimer(ThrowTimerHandle);
    }
```

The only thing left is to implement the ThrowDodgeball function. This function will be responsible for spawning a new DodgeballProjectile actor. To do this, we'll need a reference to the class we want to spawn, which must inherit from DodgeballProjectile. So, the next thing we need to do is create the appropriate property using the TSubclassOf object.

12. Create the TSubclassOf property in the EnemyCharacter header file, which can be public:

```
//The class used to spawn a dodgeball object
UPROPERTY(EditDefaultsOnly, BlueprintReadOnly, Category =
    Dodgeball)
TSubclassOf<class ADodgeballProjectile> DodgeballClass;
```

13. Because we'll be using the DodgeballProjectile class, we also need to include it in the EnemyCharacter source file:

```
#include "DodgeballProjectile.h"
```

14. Then, within the ThrowDodgeball function's implementation in the source file, start by checking if this property is a nullptr. If it is, we return immediately:

```
void AEnemyCharacter::ThrowDodgeball()
{
    if (DodgeballClass == nullptr)
    {
        return;
    }
}
```

15. Next, we will be spawning a new actor from that class. Its location will be 40 units in front of the enemy and its rotation will be the same as the enemy. To spawn the dodgeball in front of the enemy character, we'll need to access the enemy's ForwardVector property, which is a unitary FVector (*meaning that its length is 1*) that indicates the direction an actor is facing, and multiply it by the distance at which we want to spawn our dodgeball, which is 40 units:

```
FVector ForwardVector = GetActorForwardVector();
float SpawnDistance = 40.f;
FVector SpawnLocation = GetActorLocation() +
(ForwardVector *
```

```
    SpawnDistance);
//Spawn new dodgeball
GetWorld()->SpawnActor<ADodgeballProjectile>(DodgeballCl
ass,
    SpawnLocation, GetActorRotation());
```

This concludes the modifications we need to make to the `EnemyCharacter` class. Before we finish setting up the Blueprint of this logic, let's make a quick modification to our `DodgeballProjectile` class.

16. Open the `DodgeballProjectile` class's source file in Visual Studio.

17. Within its **BeginPlay** event, set its `LifeSpan` to 5 seconds. This property, which belongs to all actors, dictates how much longer they will remain in the game before being destroyed. By setting our dodgeball's `LifeSpan` to 5 seconds on its `BeginPlay` event, we are telling UE5 to destroy that object 5 seconds after it's spawned (*or if it's already been placed in the level, 5 seconds after the game starts*). We will do this so that the floor isn't filled with dodgeballs after a certain amount of time, which would make the game unintentionally difficult for the player:

```
void ADodgeballProjectile::BeginPlay()
{
    Super::BeginPlay();

    SetLifeSpan(5.f);
}
```

Now that we've finished our C++ logic related to the `EnemyCharacter` class's dodgeball-throwing logic, let's compile our changes, open the editor, and then open our `BP_EnemyCharacter` Blueprint. There, head to the **Class Defaults** panel and change the Dodgeball Class property's value to `BP_DodgeballProjectile`:

Figure 6.16 – Updating Dodgeball Class

After you've done this, you can remove the existing instance of the BP_DodgeballProjectile class we placed in our level if it's still there.

Now, we can play our level. You'll notice that the enemy will almost immediately start throwing dodgeballs at the player and will continue to do so, so long as the player character is in view:

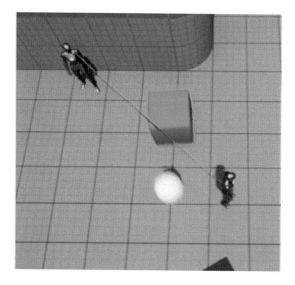

Figure 6.17 – Enemy character throwing dodgeballs if the player is in sight

With that, we have concluded our dodgeball-throwing logic for `EnemyCharacter`. You now know how to use timers, an essential tool for any game programmer.

Now, let's jump into the next section, where we'll be creating walls that handle collision differently.

Creating the Wall classes

The next step in our project is going to be creating the `Wall` classes. We will have two types of walls:

- A normal wall, which will block the enemy's line of sight, the player character, and the dodgeball.

- A ghost wall, which will only block the player character, and ignore the enemy's line of sight and the dodgeball. You may find this type of collision setup in specific types of puzzle games.

We'll create both these Wall classes in the next exercise.

Exercise 6.04 – creating Wall classes

In this exercise, we will be creating the `Wall` classes that represent both a normal `Wall` and a `GhostWall`, which will only block the player character's movement, but not the enemies' lines of sight or the dodgeballs they throw.

Let's start with the normal `Wall` class. This C++ class will be empty because the only thing that it'll need is a mesh to reflect the projectiles and block the enemies' lines of sight, which will be added through its Blueprint class.

The following steps will help you complete this exercise:

1. Open the editor.

2. In the top-left corner of the **Content Browser** area, press the green **Add New** button.

3. Select the first option at the top; that is, **Add Feature or Content Pack**.

4. A new window will appear. Select the **Content Packs** tab, select the **Starter Content** pack, and then press the **Add To Project** button. This will add some basic assets to the project, which we'll use in this chapter and some of the following chapters.

5. Create a new C++ class, called `Wall`, with the `Actor` class as its parent.

6. Next, open the class's files in Visual Studio and add a `SceneComponent` as our Wall's `RootComponent`:

   - The `Header` file will be as follows:

   ```
   private:
   UPROPERTY(VisibleAnywhere, BlueprintReadOnly, Category =
   Wall,
      meta = (AllowPrivateAccess = "true"))
   class USceneComponent* RootScene;
   ```

   - The `Source` file will be as follows:

   ```
   AWall::AWall()
   {
      // Set this actor to call Tick() every frame.  You
      // can turn this off to improve performance if you
      // don't need it.
      PrimaryActorTick.bCanEverTick = true;

      RootScene = CreateDefaultSubobject<USceneComponent>(
      TEXT("Root"));
      RootComponent = RootScene;
   }
   ```

7. Compile your code and open the editor.

Next, go to **Content | ThirdPersonCPP | Blueprints** inside the **Content Browser** area, create a new Blueprint class that inherits from the `Wall` class, name it `BP_Wall`, and open that asse:.

1. Add a **Static Mesh** component and set its **StaticMesh** property to `Wall_400x400`.

2. Set its **Material** property to `M_Metal_Steel`.

3. Set the **Static Mesh** component's location on the *X*-axis to `-200` units (*so that the mesh is centered relative to our actor's origin*):

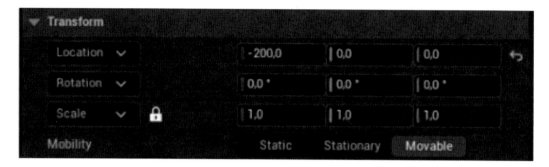

Figure 6.18 – Updating the Static Mesh component's location

This is what your Blueprint class's Viewport should look like:

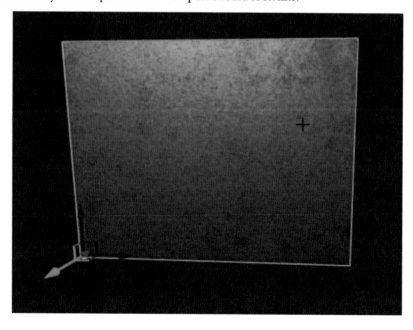

Figure 6.19 – The Blueprint class's Viewport Wall

2

> **Note**
>
> It is generally good practice to add a `SceneComponent` as an object's `RootComponent`, when a collision component isn't necessary, to allow for more flexibility with its child components.
>
> An actor's `RootComponent` cannot have its location or rotation modified, which is why, in our case, if we had created a **Static Mesh** component in the `Wall` C++ class and set that as its root component, instead of using a scene component, we'd have a hard time offsetting it.

Now that we've set up the regular `Wall` class, let's create our `GhostWall` class. Because these classes don't have any logic set up, we're just going to create the `GhostWall` class as a child of the `BP_Wall` Blueprint class and not our C++ class:

1. *Right-click* the **BP_Wall** asset and select **Create Child Blueprint Class**.

2. Name the new Blueprint `BP_GhostWall`.

3. Open it.

4. Change the **Static Mesh** component's collision properties:

   - Set its `CollisionPreset` to `Custom`.

   - Change its response to both the `EnemySight` and `Dodgeball` channels to `Overlap`.

5. Change the **Static Mesh** component's `Material` property to `M_Metal_Copper`.

   The `BP_GhostWall` Viewport should now look like this:

Figure 6.20 – Creating the GhostWall class

Now that you've created both these `Wall` actors, place each in the level to test them. Set their transforms to the following transform values:

- **Wall**: `Location: (710, -1710, 0)`

- **Ghost Wall**: `Location: (720, 1720, 0)`; `Rotation: (0, 0, 90)`:

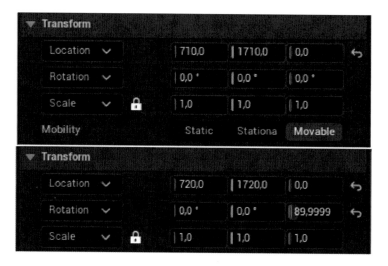

Figure 6.21 – Updating the GhostWall class's locations and rotation

The outcome should look like this:

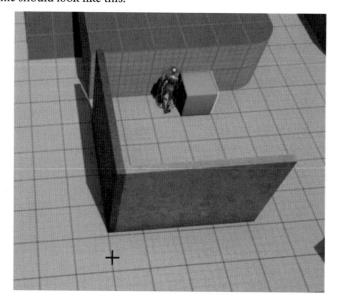

Figure 6.22 – Outcome of the GhostWall and Wall classes

You'll notice that when you hide your character behind the normal `Wall` (the one on the right), the enemy won't throw dodgeballs at the player; however, when you try to hide your character behind `GhostWall` (the one on the left), even though the enemy can't go through it, the enemy will throw dodgeballs at the character and they will pass through the wall as if it wasn't there!

And that concludes our exercise. We have made our `Wall` actors, which will either behave normally or ignore the enemies' lines of sight and dodgeballs!

Creating the VictoryBox actor

The next step in our project is going to be creating the `VictoryBox` actor. This actor will be responsible for ending the game when the player character enters it, given that the player has beaten the level. To do this, we'll be using the `Overlap` event. The following exercise will help us understand `VictoryBox`.

Exercise 6.05 – creating the VictoryBox class

In this exercise, we will be creating the `VictoryBox` class, which, when entered by the player character, will end the game.

The following steps will help you complete this exercise:

1. Create a new C++ class that inherits from the actor and call it `VictoryBox`.

2. Open that class's files in Visual Studio.

3. Create a new `SceneComponent` property, which will be used as a `RootComponent`, just like we did with our `Wall` C++ class:

    *   Header file:

    ```
    private:

    UPROPERTY(VisibleAnywhere, BlueprintReadOnly, Category =
        VictoryBox, meta = (AllowPrivateAccess = "true"))
    class USceneComponent* RootScene;
    ```

    *   Source file:

    ```
    AVictoryBox::AVictoryBox()
    {
        // Set this actor to call Tick() every frame.  You
        // can turn this off to improve performance if you
        // don't need it.
        PrimaryActorTick.bCanEverTick = true;
    ```

```
RootScene =
CreateDefaultSubobject<USceneComponent>(TEXT("Root"));
RootComponent = RootScene;
}
```

4. Declare a BoxComponent in the header file that will check for overlap events with the player character, which should also be private:

```
UPROPERTY(VisibleAnywhere, BlueprintReadOnly, Category =
    VictoryBox, meta = (AllowPrivateAccess = "true"))
class UBoxComponent* CollisionBox;
```

5. Include the BoxComponent file in the class's source file:

```
#include "Components/BoxComponent.h"
```

6. After creating the RootScene component, create BoxComponent, which should also be private:

```
RootScene =
CreateDefaultSubobject<USceneComponent>(TEXT("Root"));
RootComponent = RootScene;

CollisionBox =
    CreateDefaultSubobject<UBoxComponent>(
    TEXT("Collision Box"));
```

7. Attach it to RootComponent using the SetupAttachment function:

```
CollisionBox->SetupAttachment(RootComponent);
```

8. Set its BoxExtent property to 60 units on all axes. This will cause BoxComponent to be double that size – that is, (120 x 120 x 120):

```
CollisionBox->SetBoxExtent(FVector(60.0f, 60.0f, 60.0f));
```

9. Offset its relative position on the Z-axis by 120 units using the SetRelativeLocation function:

```
CollisionBox->SetRelativeLocation(FVector(0.0f, 0.0f,
    120.0f));
```

10. Now, you will require a function that will listen to the BoxComponent's `OnBeginOverlap` event. This event will be called whenever an object enters `BoxComponent`. This function must be preceded by the `UFUNCTION` macro, be `public`, return nothing, and have the following parameters:

```
UFUNCTION()
void OnBeginOverlap(UPrimitiveComponent* OverlappedComp,
  AActor* OtherActor, UPrimitiveComponent* OtherComp,
  int32
  OtherBodyIndex, bool bFromSweep, const FHitResult&
  SweepResult);
```

These parameters are as follows:

- `UPrimitiveComponent* OverlappedComp`: The component that was overlapped and belongs to this actor.

- `AActor* OtherActor`: The other actor involved in the overlap.

- `UPrimitiveComponent* OtherComp`: The component that was overlapped and belongs to the other actor.

- `int32 OtherBodyIndex`: The index of the item in the primitive that was hit (usually useful for Instanced Static Mesh components).

- `bool bFromSweep`: Whether the overlap originated from a Sweep Trace.

- `FHitResult& SweepResult`: The data of the Sweep Trace resulting from the collision between this object and the other object.

> **Note**
>
> Although we won't be using the `OnEndOverlap` event in this project, you will most likely need to use it sooner or later, so here's the required function signature for that event, which looks very similar to the one we just learned about:
>
> ```
> UFUNCTION()
> void OnEndOverlap(UPrimitiveComponent* OverlappedComp, AActor*
> OtherActor, UPrimitiveComponent* OtherComp, int32 OtherBodyIndex);
> ```

11. Next, we need to bind this function to the BoxComponent's `OnComponentBeginOverlap` event:

```
CollisionBox->OnComponentBeginOverlap.AddDynamic(this,
  &AVictoryBox::OnBeginOverlap);
```

12. Within our `OnBeginOverlap` function implementation, we're going to check whether the actor we overlapped is a `DodgeballCharacter`. Because we'll be referencing this class, we also need to include it:

```
#include "DodgeballCharacter.h"

void AVictoryBox::OnBeginOverlap(UPrimitiveComponent *
  OverlappedComp, AActor * OtherActor,
  UPrimitiveComponent *
  OtherComp, int32 OtherBodyIndex, bool bFromSweep,
  const
  FHitResult & SweepResult)
{
  if (Cast<ADodgeballCharacter>(OtherActor))
  {


  }
}
```

If the actor we overlapped is a `DodgeballCharacter`, we want to quit the game.

13. We will use `KismetSystemLibrary` for this purpose. The `KismetSystemLibrary` class contains useful functions for general use in your project:

```
#include "Kismet/KismetSystemLibrary.h"
```

14. To quit the game, we will call the `QuitGame` function of `KismetSystemLibrary`. This function receives the following:

```
UKismetSystemLibrary::QuitGame(GetWorld(),
  nullptr,
  EQuitPreference::Quit,
  true);
```

The important parameters from the preceding code snippet are as follows:

- A `World` object, which we can access with the `GetWorld` function.

- A `PlayerController` object, which we will set to `nullptr`. We're doing this because this function will automatically find one this way.

- An `EQuitPreference` object, which means how we want to end the game, by either quitting or just putting it as a background process. We will want to quit the game, and not just put it as a background process.

- A `bool`, which indicates whether we want to ignore the platform's restrictions when it comes to quitting the game, which we will set to `true`.

Next, we're going to create our Blueprint class.

15. Compile your changes, open the editor, go to **Content** | **ThirdPersonCPP** | **Blueprint** inside the **Content Browser** area, create a new Blueprint class that inherits from `VictoryBox`, and name it `BP_VictoryBox`. Open that asset and make the following modifications:

    - Add a new **Static Mesh** component
    - Set its **StaticMesh** property to `Floor_400x400`
    - Set its **Material** property to `M_Metal_Gold`
    - Set its scale to `0.75` units on all three axes
    - Set its location to `(-150, -150, 20)`, on the *X*, *Y*, and *Z* axes, respectively.

Once you've made those changes, your Blueprint's **Viewport** tab should look something like this:

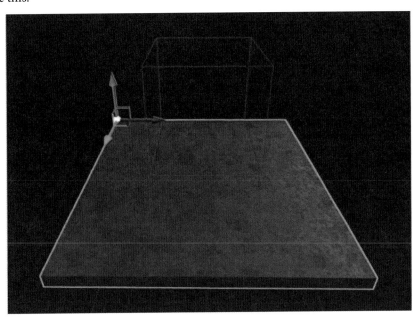

Figure 6.23 – VictoryBox placed in the Blueprint's Viewport tab

Place that Blueprint inside your level to test its functionality:

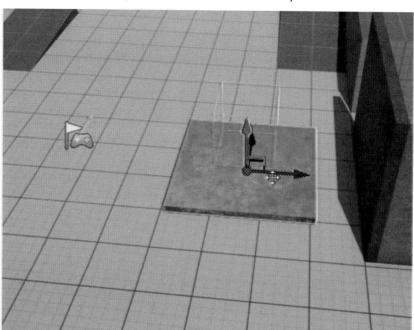

Figure 6.24 – VictoryBox Blueprint in the level for testing

If you play the level and step onto the golden plate (and overlap the collision box), you'll notice that the game abruptly ends, as intended.

And with that, we conclude our `VictoryBox` class! You now know how to use the overlap events in your projects. There's a multitude of game mechanics that you can create using these events, so congratulations on completing this exercise.

We are now very close to reaching the end of this chapter, where we'll be completing a new activity, but first, we'll need to make some modifications to our `DodgeballProjectile` class, namely adding a getter function to its `ProjectileMovementComponent`. We'll do this in the next exercise.

A getter function is a function that only returns a specific property and does nothing else. These functions are usually marked as inline, which means that when the code compiles, a call to that function will simply be replaced with its content. They are also usually marked as `const`, given that they don't modify any of the class's properties.

Exercise 6.06 – adding the ProjectileMovementComponent getter function to DodgeballProjectile

In this exercise, we will be adding a getter function to the `DodgeballProjectile` class's `ProjectileMovement` property so that other classes can access it and modify its properties. We will be doing the same in this chapter's activity.

To do this, you'll need to follow these steps:

1. Open the `DodgeballProjectile` class's header file in Visual Studio.

2. Add a new `public` function called `GetProjectileMovementComponent`. This function will be an inline function, which in UE5's version of C++ is replaced with the `FORCEINLINE` macro. The function should also return a `UProjectileMovementComponent*` and be a `const` function:

```
FORCEINLINE class UProjectileMovementComponent*
   GetProjectileMovementComponent() const
{
   return ProjectileMovement;
}
```

> **Note**
> When using the `FORCEINLINE` macro for a specific function, you can't add the declaration of that function to the header file and its implementation to the source file. Both must be done simultaneously in the header file, as shown previously.

With that, we have concluded this quick exercise. Here, we have added a simple `getter` function to our `DodgeballProjectile` class, which we will be using in this chapter's activity, where we'll replace the `SpawnActor` function within the `EnemyCharacter` class with the `SpawnActorDeferred` function. This will allow us to safely edit our `DodgeballProjectile` class's properties before we spawn an instance of it.

Activity 6.01 – replacing the SpawnActor function with SpawnActorDeferred in EnemyCharacter

In this activity, you will be changing the EnemyCharacter's `ThrowDodgeball` function to use the `SpawnActorDeferred` function instead of the `SpawnActor` function so that we can change the DodgeballProjectile's `InitialSpeed` before spawning it.

The following steps will help you complete this activity:

1. Open the EnemyCharacter class's source file in Visual Studio.

2. Go to the ThrowDodgeball function's implementation.

3. Because the SpawnActorDeferred function can't just receive a spawn location and rotation properties and must receive an FTransform property instead, we'll need to create one of those before we call that function. Let's call it SpawnTransform and send the spawn rotation and location, in that order, as inputs for its constructor, which will be this enemy's rotation and the SpawnLocation property, respectively.

4. Then, update the SpawnActor function call in the SpawnActorDeferred function call. Instead of sending the spawn location and spawn rotation as its second and third parameters, replace those with the SpawnTransform properties we just created, as the second parameter.

5. Make sure you save the return value of this function call inside an ADodgeballProjectile* property called Projectile.

   Once you've done this, you will have successfully created a new DodgeballProjectile object. However, we still need to change its InitialSpeed property and spawn it.

6. Once you've called the SpawnActorDeferred function, call the Projectile property's GetProjectileMovementComponent function, which returns its ProjectileMovementComponent, and change its InitialSpeed property to 2200 units.

7. Because we'll be accessing properties that belong to ProjectileMovementComponent inside the EnemyCharacter class, we'll need to include that component, just like we did in *Exercise 6.02 – adding a ProjectileMovementComponent to DodgeballProjectile*.

8. Once you've changed the value of the InitialSpeed property, the only thing left to do is call the Projectile property's FinishSpawning function, which will receive the SpawnTransform property we created as a parameter.

9. Once you've done this, compile your changes and open the editor.

Expected output:

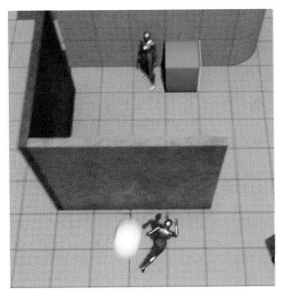

Figure 6.25 – Dodgeball thrown at the player

> **Note**
>
> The solution for this activity can be found on https://github.com/PacktPublishing/
> Elevating-Game-Experiences-with-Unreal-Engine-5-Second-Edition/
> tree/main/Activity%20solutions.

By completing this activity, you've consolidated the use of the `SpawnActorDeferred` function and know how to use it in your future projects.

Summary

In this chapter, you learned how to affect an object with physics simulations, create Object Types and Collision Presets, use the `OnHit`, `OnBeginOverlap`, and `OnEndOverlap` events, update an object's Physical Material, and use timers.

Now that you've learned about these fundamental collision topics, you'll be able to come up with new and creative ways to use them when creating projects.

In the next chapter, we'll be taking a look at actor components, interfaces, and Blueprint Function Libraries, which are very useful for keeping your project's complexity manageable and highly modular, thereby allowing you to easily take parts of one project and add them to another.

Working with UE5 Utilities

In the previous chapter, we learned about the remaining collision-related concepts in UE5, such as collision events, object types, physics simulation, and collision components. We learned how to have objects collide against one another, changing their responses to different collision channels, as well as how to create collision presets, spawn actors, and use timers.

In this chapter, we will look at several UE5 utilities that will allow you to easily move logic from one project to another and keep your project well-structured and organized, which will make life much easier for you in the long run and also make it easier for other people in your team to understand your work and modify it in the future. Game development is a tremendously hard task and is rarely done individually, but rather in teams, so it's important to take these things into account when building your projects.

We'll cover the following topics in this chapter:

- Good practices – loose coupling
- Blueprint Function Libraries
- Actor components
- Exploring interfaces
- Blueprint native events

Technical requirements

The project for this chapter can be found in the Chapter07 folder of the code bundle for this book, which can be downloaded here: `https://github.com/PacktPublishing/Elevating-Game-Experiences-with-Unreal-Engine-5-Second-Edition`.

Good practices – loose coupling

We can use Blueprint Function Libraries to move some generic functions in our project from a specific actor to a Blueprint Function Library so that they can be used in other parts of our project's logic.

We will use Actor components to move part of some actor classes' source code into an Actor component so that we can easily use that logic in other projects. This will keep our project loosely coupled. Loose coupling is a software engineering concept that refers to having your project structured in such a way that you can easily remove and add things as you need. The reason you should strive for loose coupling is if you want to reuse parts of one of your projects for another project. As a game developer, loose coupling will allow you to do that much more easily.

A practical example of how you could apply loose coupling is if you had a player character class that was able to fly and also had an inventory that contained several usable items. Instead of implementing the code responsible for both of those things in that player character class, you would implement the logic for each of them in separate Actor components, which you would then add to the class. This will not only make it easier to add and remove things that this class will do, by simply adding and removing the Actor components responsible for those things, but also allow you to reuse those Actor components in other projects where you have a character that has an inventory or can fly. This is one of the main purposes of Actor components.

Interfaces, much like Actor components, make our project better structured and organized.

Let's start by talking about Blueprint Function Libraries.

Blueprint Function Libraries

In UE5, there's a class called `BlueprintFunctionLibary` that is meant to contain a collection of static functions that don't belong to any specific actor and can be used in multiple parts of your project.

For instance, some of the objects that we used previously, such as the `GameplayStatics` object and `Kismet` libraries such as `KismetMathLibrary` and `KismetSystemLibrary`, are Blueprint Function Libraries. These contain functions that can be used in any part of your project.

There is at least one function in our project that's been created by us that can be moved to a Blueprint Function Library: the `CanSeeActor` function defined in the `EnemyCharacter` class.

In the first exercise of this chapter, we will create a Blueprint Function Library so that we can move the `CanSeeActor` function from the `EnemyCharacter` class to the `BlueprintFunctionLibrary` class.

Exercise 7.01 – moving the CanSeeActor function to the Blueprint Function Library

In this exercise, we will be moving the CanSeeActor function that we created for the EnemyCharacter class to a Blueprint Function Library.

The following steps will help you complete this exercise:

1. Open Unreal Editor.

2. *Right-click* inside the **Content Browser** area and select **New C++ Class**.

3. Choose **BlueprintFunctionLibrary** as the parent class of this C++ class (you'll find it by scrolling to the end of the panel).

4. Name the new C++ class DodgeballFunctionLibrary.

5. After the class's files have been generated in Visual Studio, open them and close the editor.

6. In the header file of DodgeballFunctionLibrary, add a declaration for a public function called CanSeeActor. This function will be similar to the one we created in the EnemyCharacter class; however, there will be some differences.

   The new CanSeeActor function will be static, will return a bool, and will receive the following parameters:

   - A const UWorld* World property, which we will use to access the Line Trace functions.

   - An FVector Location property, which we will use as the location of the actor that is checking whether it can see the target actor.

   - A const AActor* TargetActor property, which will be the actor we're checking visibility for.

   - A TArray<const AActor*> IgnoreActors property, which will specify the actors that should be ignored during the Line Trace functions. This property can have an empty array as a default argument:

```
public:
// Can we see the given actor
static bool CanSeeActor(
const UWorld* World,
FVector Location,
const AActor* TargetActor,
TArray<const AActor*> IgnoreActors = TArray<const
AActor*>());
```

7. Create the implementation of this function in the class's source file and copy the implementation of the EnemyCharacter class's version into this new class. Once you've done that, make the following modifications to the implementation:

  - Change the value of the Start location of the Line Trace to the Location parameter:

    ```
    // Where the Line Trace starts and ends
    FVector Start = Location;
    ```

  - Instead of ignoring this actor (using the this pointer) and TargetActor, ignore the entire IgnoreActors array using the AddIgnoredActors function of FCollisionQueryParams and send that array as a parameter:

    ```
    FCollisionQueryParams QueryParams;
    // Ignore the actors specified
    QueryParams.AddIgnoredActors(IgnoreActors);
    ```

  - Replace both calls to the GetWorld function with the received World parameter:

    ```
    // Execute the Line Trace
    World->LineTraceSingleByChannel(Hit, Start, End, Channel,
        QueryParams);


    // Show the Line Trace inside the game
    DrawDebugLine(World, Start, End, FColor::Red);
    ```

  - Add the necessary includes to the top of the DodgeballFunctionLibrary class, as shown in the following code snippet:

    ```
    #include "Engine/World.h"
    #include "DrawDebugHelpers.h"
    #include "CollisionQueryParams.h"
    ```

8. Once you've created the new version of the CanSeeActor function inside DodgeballFunctionLibrary, head to our EnemyCharacter class and make the following changes:

  - Remove the declaration and implementation of the CanSeeActor function, inside its header and source file, respectively.

- Remove the `DrawDebugHelpers` include, given that we will no longer need that file:

```
// Remove this line
#include "DrawDebugHelpers.h"
```

- Add an include for `DodgeballFunctionLibrary`:

```
#include "DodgeballFunctionLibrary.h"
```

- Inside the class's `LookAtActor` function, just before the `if` statement that calls the `CanSeeActor` function, declare a `const TArray<const AActor*> IgnoreActors` variable and set it to both the `this` pointer and the `TargetActor` parameter:

```
const TArray<const AActor*> IgnoreActors = {this,
    TargetActor};
```

> **Note**
>
> Introducing the preceding code snippet may give you an IntelliSense error in Visual Studio. You can safely ignore it, as your code should compile with no issues regardless.

9. Replace the existing call to the `CanSeeActor` function with the one we just created by sending the following as parameters:

- The current world, through the `GetWorld` function
- The `SightSource` component's location, using its `GetComponentLocation` function
- The `TargetActor` parameter
- The `IgnoreActors` array we just created:

```
if (UDodgeballFunctionLibrary::CanSeeActor(
    GetWorld(),
    SightSource->GetComponentLocation(),
    TargetActor,
    IgnoreActors))
```

Now that you've made all those changes, compile your code, open your project, and verify that the `EnemyCharacter` class still looks at the player as it walks around, so long as it's in the enemy character's sight, as shown in the following screenshot:

Figure 7.1 – The enemy character still looking at the player character

And that concludes our exercise. We've put our `CanSeeActor` function inside a Blueprint Function Library and can now reuse it for other actors that require the same type of functionality.

The next step in our project is going to be learning more about Actor components and how we can use them to our advantage. Let's take a look.

Actor components

As we saw in the first few chapters of this book, Actors are the main way to create logic in UE5. However, we've also seen that Actors can contain several Actor components.

Actor components are objects that can be added to an Actor and can have multiple types of functionality, such as being responsible for a character's inventory or making a character fly. Actor components must always belong to and live inside an Actor, which is referred to as their **Owner**.

There are several different types of existing Actor components. Some of these are as follows:

- Code-only Actor components, which act as their own class inside an actor. They have their own properties and functions and can both interact with the Actor they belong to and be interacted with by it.

- Mesh components, which are used to draw several types of Mesh objects (Static Meshes, Skeletal Meshes, and so on).

- Collision components, which are used to receive and generate collision events.

- Camera components.

This leaves us with two main ways to add logic to our Actors: directly in the `Actor` class or through `Actor` components. To follow good software development practices, namely loose coupling (mentioned previously), you should strive to use Actor components instead of placing logic directly inside an Actor whenever possible. Let's take a look at a practical example to understand the usefulness of Actor components.

Let's say you're making a game where you have the player character and enemy characters, both of which have health, and where the player character must fight enemies, who can also fight back. If you had to implement the health logic, which includes gaining health, losing health, and tracking the character's health, you'd have two options:

- You can implement the health logic in a base character class, from which both the player character class and the enemy character class would inherit.

- You can implement the health logic in an Actor component and add that component to both the player character and enemy character classes separately.

There are a few reasons why the first option is not a good option, but the main one is this: if you wanted to add another piece of logic to both character classes (for example, stamina, which would limit the strength and frequency of the characters' attacks), doing so using the same approach of a base class wouldn't be a viable option. Given that, in UE5, C++ classes can only inherit from one class and there's no such thing as multiple inheritance, that would be very hard to manage. It would also only get more complicated and unmanageable the more logic you decided to add to your project.

With that said, when adding logic to your project that can be encapsulated in a separate component, allowing you to achieve loose coupling, you should always do so.

Now, let's create a new Actor component that will be responsible for keeping track of an actor's health, as well as gaining and losing that health.

Exercise 7.02 – creating the HealthComponent Actor component

In this exercise, we will be creating a new actor component responsible for gaining, losing, and keeping track of an actor's health (its Owner).

For the player to lose, we'll have to make the player character lose health and then end the game when it runs out of health. We'll want to put this logic inside an actor component so that we can easily add all this health-related logic to other actors if we need to.

The following steps will help you complete the exercise:

1. Open the editor and create a new C++ class, whose parent class will be the `ActorComponent` class. Its name will be `HealthComponent`.

2. Once this class has been created and its files have been opened in Visual Studio, go to its header file and add a protected `float` property called `Health`, which will keep track of the Owner's current health points. Its default value can be set to the number of health points its Owner will start the game with. In this case, we'll initialize it with a value of `100` health points:

```
// The Owner's initial and current amount health
// points
UPROPERTY(EditDefaultsOnly, Category = Health)
float Health = 100.f;
```

3. Create a declaration for the function that's responsible for taking health away from its Owner. This function should be `public`; return nothing; receive a `float` `Amount` property as input, which indicates how many health points its Owner should lose; and be called `LoseHealth`:

```
// Take health points from its Owner
void LoseHealth(float Amount);
```

Now, in the class's source file, let's start by notifying it that it should never use the `Tick` event so that its performance can be slightly improved.

4. Change the `bCanEverTick` property's value to `false` inside the class's constructor:

```
PrimaryComponentTick.bCanEverTick = false;
```

5. Create the implementation for our `LoseHealth` function, where we'll start by removing the `Amount` parameter's value from our `Health` property:

```
void UHealthComponent::LoseHealth(float Amount)
{
    Health -= Amount;
}
```

6. Now, in that same function, we'll check whether the current amount of health is less than or equal to 0, which means that it has run out of health points (*has died or been destroyed*):

```
if (Health <= 0.f)
{

}
```

7. If the `if` statement is true, we'll do the following things:

    •   Set the Health property to 0 to make sure that our Owner doesn't have negative health points:

        ```
        Health = 0.f;
        ```

    •   Quit the game, the same way we did in *Chapter 6, Setting Up Collision Objects*, when creating the `VictoryBox` class:

        ```
        UKismetSystemLibrary::QuitGame(this,
                                nullptr,
                                EQuitPreference::Quit,
                                true);
        ```

    •   Don't forget to include the `KismetSystemLibrary` object:

        ```
        #include "Kismet/KismetSystemLibrary.h"
        ```

With this logic done, whenever any actor that has `HealthComponent` runs out of health, the game will end. This isn't exactly the behavior we want in our **Dodgeball** game. However, we'll change it when we talk about interfaces later in this chapter.

In the next exercise, we'll be making the necessary modifications to some classes in our project to accommodate our newly created `HealthComponent`.

Exercise 7.03 – integrating the HealthComponent Actor component

In this exercise, we will be modifying our `DodgeballProjectile` class so that it damages the player's character when it comes into contact with it, as well as the `DodgeballCharacter` class so that it has a `HealthComponent`.

Open the `DodgeballProjectile` class's files in Visual Studio and make the following modifications:

1. In the class's header file, add a protected `float` property called `Damage` and set its default value to `34` so that our player character will lose all of its health points after being hit three times. This property should be a UPROPERTY and have the `EditAnywhere` tag so that you can easily change its value in its Blueprint class:

    ```
    // The damage the dodgeball will deal to the player's
      character
    UPROPERTY(EditAnywhere, Category = Damage)
    float Damage = 34.f;
    ```

In the class's source file, we'll have to make some modifications to the OnHit function.

2. Since we'll be using the HealthComponent class, we'll have to add the include statement for it:

    ```
    #include "HealthComponent.h"
    ```

3. The existing cast that is being done for DodgeballCharacter from the OtherActor property, which we did in *step 17* of *Exercise 6.01 – creating the Dodgeball class*, and is inside the if statement, should be done before that if statement and be saved inside a variable. Then, you should check whether that variable is nullptr. We are doing this to access the player character's HealthComponent inside the if statement:

    ```
    ADodgeballCharacter* Player =
       Cast<ADodgeballCharacter>(OtherActor);
    if (Player != nullptr)
    {

    }
    ```

4. If the if statement is true (that is, if the actor we hit is the player's character), we want to access that character's HealthComponent and reduce the character's health. To access HealthComponent, we must call the character's FindComponentByClass function and send the UHealthComponent class as a template parameter (to indicate the class of the component we want to access):

    ```
    UHealthComponent* HealthComponent = Player->
    FindComponentByClass<UHealthComponent>();
    ```

> **Note**
>
> The FindComponentByClass function, included in the Actor class, will return a reference(s) to the actor component(s) of a specific class that the actor contains. If the function returns nullptr, that means the actor doesn't have an Actor component of that class.
>
> You may also find the GetComponents function inside the Actor class useful, which will return a list of all the Actor components inside that actor.

5. After that, check whether HealthComponent is nullptr. If it isn't, we'll call its LoseHealth function and send the Damage property as a parameter:

    ```
    if (HealthComponent != nullptr)
    {
       HealthComponent->LoseHealth(Damage);
    ```

```
}
Destroy();
```

6. Make sure the existing `Destroy` function is called after doing the null check for `HealthComponent`, as shown in the previous code snippet.

    Before we finish this exercise, we'll need to make some modifications to our `DodgeballCharacter` class. Open the class's files in Visual Studio.

7. In the class's header file, add a `private` property of the `class UhealthComponent*` type called `HealthComponent`:

    ```
    class UHealthComponent* HealthComponent;
    ```

8. In the class's source file, add an `include` statement to the `HealthComponent` class:

    ```
    #include "HealthComponent.h"
    ```

9. At the end of the class's constructor, create `HealthComponent` by using the `CreateDefaultSubobject` function and name it `HealthComponent`:

    ```
    HealthComponent =
        CreateDefaultSubobject<UHealthComponent>(
        TEXT("Health
        Component"));
    ```

    Once you've made all these changes, compile your code and open the editor. When you play the game, if you let your player character get hit by a dodgeball three times, you'll notice that the game abruptly stops, as intended:

Figure 7.2 – The enemy character throwing dodgeballs at the player character

Once the game is stopped, it will look as follows:

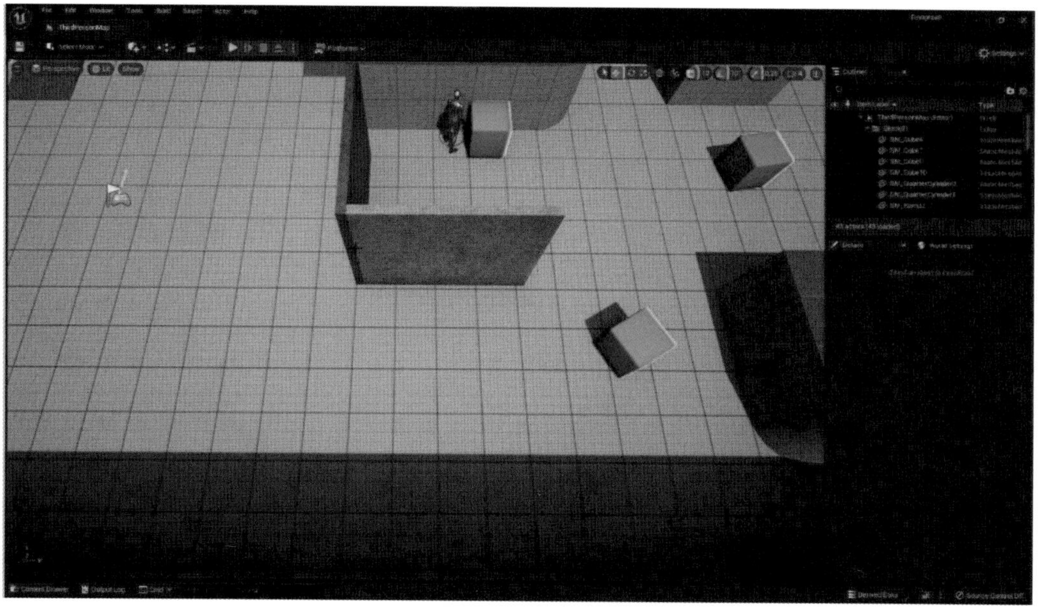

Figure 7.3 – The editor after the player character runs out of health points and the game stops

And that completes this exercise. You now know how to create Actor components and how to access an actor's Actor components. This is a very important step toward making your game projects more understandable and better structured, so good job.

Now that we've learned about Actor components, let's learn about another way to make our projects better structured and organized: by using interfaces.

Exploring interfaces

There's a chance that you may already know about interfaces, given that other programming languages, such as Java, already have them. If you do, they work pretty similarly in UE5, but if you don't, let's see how they work, taking the example of the `HealthComponent` class we created.

As you saw in the previous exercise, when the `Health` property of the `HealthComponent` class reaches `0`, that component will simply end the game. However, we don't want that to happen every time an actor's health points run out: some actors may simply be destroyed, some may notify another actor that they have run out of health points, and so on. We want each actor to be able to determine what happens to them when they run out of health points. But how can we handle this?

Ideally, we would simply call a specific function that belongs to Owner of the `HealthComponent` class, which would then choose how to handle the fact that Owner has run out of health points. But in which class should you implement that function, given that our Owner can be of any class, so long as it inherits from the Actor class? As we discussed at the beginning of this chapter, having a class that's responsible just for this would quickly become unmanageable. Luckily for us, interfaces solve this problem.

Interfaces are classes that contain a collection of functions that an object must have if it implements that interface. It essentially works as a contract that the object signs, saying that it will implement all the functions present on that interface. Then, you can simply check whether an object implements a specific interface and call the object's implementation of the function defined in the interface.

In our specific case, we'll want to have an interface that has a function that will be called when an object runs out of health points so that our `HealthComponent` class can check whether its Owner implements that interface and then call that function from the interface. This will make it easy for us to specify how each actor behaves when running out of health points: some actors may simply be destroyed, others may trigger an in-game event, and others may simply end the game (which is the case with our player character).

However, before we create our first interface, we should talk a bit about Blueprint native events.

Blueprint native events

When using the `UFUNCTION` macro in C++, you can turn a function into a Blueprint native event by simply adding the `BlueprintNativeEvent` tag to that macro.

So, what is a Blueprint native event? It's an event that is declared in C++ that can have a default behavior, which is also defined in C++, but that can be overridden in Blueprint. Let's declare a Blueprint native event called `MyEvent` by declaring a `MyEvent` function using the `UFUNCTION` macro with the `BlueprintNativeEvent` tag, followed by the virtual `MyEvent_Implementation` function:

```
UFUNCTION(BlueprintNativeEvent)
void MyEvent();
virtual void MyEvent_Implementation();
```

The reason why you have to declare these two functions is that the first one is the Blueprint signature, which allows you to override the event in Blueprint, while the second one is the C++ signature, which allows you to override the event in C++.

The C++ signature is simply the name of the event followed by `_Implementation`, and it should always be a `virtual` function. Given that you declared this event in C++, to implement its default behavior, you must implement the `MyEvent_Implementation` function, not the `MyEvent` function (that one should remain untouched). To call a Blueprint native event, you can simply call the normal function without the `_Implementation` suffix; in this case, `MyEvent()`.

In the next exercise, we'll learn how to use Blueprint native events in practice, where we'll create a new interface.

Exercise 7.04 – creating the HealthInterface class

In this exercise, we will be creating an interface that's responsible for handling how an object behaves when it runs out of health points.

To do this, follow these steps:

1. Open the editor and create a new C++ class that inherits from `Interface` (called `Unreal Interface` in the scrollable menu) and call it `HealthInterface`.

2. Once the class's files have been generated and opened in Visual Studio, go to the newly created class's header file. You'll notice that the generated file has two classes – `UHealthInterface` and `IHealthInterface`.

3. These will be used in combination when checking whether an object implements the interface and calls its functions. However, you should only add function declarations in the class prefixed with `I` – in this case, `IHealthInterface`. Add a `public` Blueprint native event called `OnDeath` that returns nothing and receives no parameters. This function will be called when an object runs out of health points:

```
UFUNCTION(BlueprintNativeEvent, Category = Health)
void OnDeath();
virtual void OnDeath_Implementation() = 0;
```

Note that the `OnDeath_Implementation` function declaration needs its own implementation. However, there is no need for the interface to implement that function because it would simply be empty. To notify the compiler that this function has no implementation in this class, we added `= 0` to the end of its declaration.

4. Go to the `DodgeballCharacter` class's header file. We'll want this class to implement our newly created `HealthInterface`, but how do we do that? The first thing we have to do is include the `HealthInterface` class. Make sure you include it before the `.generated.h` include statement:

```
// Add this include
#include "HealthInterface.h"
#include "DodgeballCharacter.generated.h"
```

5. Then, replace the line in the header file that makes the `DodgeballCharacter` class inherit from the `Character` class with the following line, which will make this class implement `HealthInterface`:

```
class ADodgeballCharacter : public ACharacter, public
    IHealthInterface
```

6. The next thing we have to do is implement the `OnDeath` function in the `DodgeballCharacter` class. To do this, add a declaration for the `OnDeath_Implementation` function that overrides the interface's C++ signature. This function should be `public`. To override a `virtual` function, you must add the `override` keyword to the end of its declaration:

```
virtual void OnDeath_Implementation() override;
```

7. In this function's implementation, within the class's source file, simply quit the game, the same way that is being done in the `HealthComponent` class:

```
void ADodgeballCharacter::OnDeath_Implementation()
{
  UKismetSystemLibrary::QuitGame(this,
                                 nullptr,
                                 EQuitPreference::Quit,
                                 true);
}
```

8. Because we're now using `KismetSystemLibrary`, we'll have to include it:

```
#include "Kismet/KismetSystemLibrary.h"
```

9. Now, we must go to our `HealthComponent` class's source file. Because we'll no longer be using `KistemSystemLibrary` and will be using the `HealthInterface` instead, replace the `include` statement for the first class with an `include` statement for the second one:

```
// Replace this line
#include "Kismet/KismetSystemLibrary.h"
// With this line
#include "HealthInterface.h"
```

10. Then, change the logic that is responsible for quitting the game when Owner runs out of health points. Instead of doing this, we'll want to check whether Owner implements `HealthInterface` and, if it does, call its implementation of the `OnDeath` function. Remove the existing call to the `QuitGame` function:

```
// Remove this
UKismetSystemLibrary::QuitGame(this,
                               nullptr,
                               EQuitPreference::Quit,
                               true);
```

11. To check whether an object implements a specific interface, we can call that object's `Implements` function, using the interface's class as a template parameter. The class of the interface that you should use in this function is the one that is prefixed with `U`:

```
if (GetOwner()->Implements<UHealthInterface>())
{

}
```

12. Because we'll be using methods that belong to the `Actor` class, we'll also need to include it:

```
#include "GameFramework/Actor.h"
```

If this `if` statement is true, that means that our Owner implements `HealthInterface`. In this case, we'll want to call its implementation of the `OnDeath` function.

13. To do this, call it through the interface's class (this time, the one that is prefixed with `I`). The function inside the interface that you'll want to call is `Execute_OnDeath` (note that the function you should call inside the interface will always be its normal name prefixed with `Execute_`). This function must receive at least one parameter, which is the object that the function will be called on and that implements that interface; in this case, Owner:

```
if (GetOwner()->Implements<UHealthInterface>())
{
    IHealthInterface::Execute_OnDeath(GetOwner());
}
```

> **Note**
>
> If your interface's function receives parameters, you can send them in the function call after the first parameter mentioned in the preceding step. For instance, if our `OnDeath` function received an `int` property as a parameter, you would call it with `IHealthInterface::Execute_ OnDeath(GetOwner(), 5)`.
>
> The first time you try to compile your code after adding a new function to an interface and then calling `Execute_ version`, you may get an `Intellisense` error. You can safely ignore this error.

Once you've made all these changes, compile your code and open the editor. When you play the game, try letting the character get hit by three dodgeballs:

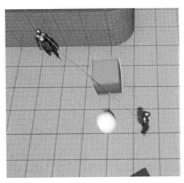

Figure 7.4 – The enemy character throwing dodgeballs at the player character

If the game ends after that, then that means that all our changes worked and the game's logic remains the same:

Figure 7.5 – The editor after the player character runs out of health points and the game stops

And with that, we conclude this exercise. You now know how to use interfaces. The benefit of the change that we just made is that we can now have other actors that lose health, as well as specify what happens when they run out of health points by using the Health interface.

Now, we will complete an activity where we'll move all of the logic related to the LookAtActor function to its own Actor component and use it to replace the SightSource component we created.

Activity 7.01 – moving the LookAtActor logic to an Actor component

In this activity, we'll be moving all of the logic related to the LookAtActor function, inside the EnemyCharacter class, to its own Actor component (similarly to how we moved the CanSeeActor function to a Blueprint Function Library). This way, if we want an actor (that isn't an EnemyCharacter) to look at another actor, we will simply be able to add this component to it.

Follow these steps to complete this activity:

1. Open the editor and create a new C++ class that inherits from SceneComponent, called LookAtActorComponent.

    Head to the class's files, which are open in Visual Studio.

2. Go to its header file and add a declaration for the LookAtActor function, which should be protected, return a bool, and receive no parameters.

> **Note**
>
> While the LookAtActor function of EnemyCharacter received the AActor* TargetActor parameter, this Actor component will have its TargetActor as a class property, which is why we won't need to receive it as a parameter.

3. Add a protected AActor* property called TargetActor. This property will represent the actor we want to look at.

4. Add a protected bool property called bCanSeeTarget, with a default value of false, which will indicate whether TargetActor can be seen.

5. Add a declaration for a public FORCEINLINE function, as covered in *Chapter 6, Setting Up Collision Objects*, called SetTarget, which will return nothing and receive AActor* NewTarget as a parameter. The implementation of this function will simply set the TargetActor property to the value of the NewTarget property.

6. Add a declaration for a public FORCEINLINE function called CanSeeTarget, which will be const, return a bool, and receive no parameters. The implementation of this function will simply return the value of the bCanSeeTarget property.

    Now, go to the class's source file.

7. In the class's `TickComponent` function, set the value of the `bCanSeeTarget` property to the return value of the `LookAtActor` function call.

8. Add an empty implementation of the `LookAtActor` function and copy the `EnemyCharacter` class's implementation of the `LookAtActor` function into the implementation of `LookAtActorComponent`.

9. Make the following modifications to the `LookAtActorComponent` class's implementation of the `LookAtActor` function:

   i. Change the first element of the `IgnoreActors` array to the Actor's component's Owner.

   ii. Change the second parameter of the `CanSeeActor` function call to this component's location.

   iii. Change the value of the `Start` property to the location of Owner.

   Finally, replace the call to the `SetActorRotation` function with a call to the `SetActorRotation` function of Owner.

10. Because of the modifications we've made to the implementation of the `LookAtActor` function, we'll need to add some includes to our `LookAtActorComponent` class and remove some includes from our `EnemyCharacter` class. Remove the includes to `KismetMathLibrary` and `DodgeballFunctionLibrary` from the `EnemyCharacter` class and add them to the `LookAtActorComponent` class.

   We'll also need to add an include to the `Actor` class since we'll be accessing several functions belonging to that class.

Now, let's make some further modifications to our `EnemyCharacter` class:

1. In its header file, remove the declaration of the `LookAtActor` function.

2. Replace the `SightSource` property with a property of the `UlookAtActorComponent *` type called `LookAtActorComponent`.

3. In the class's source file, add an include to the `LookAtActorComponent` class.

4. Inside the class's constructor, replace the references to the `SightSource` property with a reference to the `LookAtActorComponent` property. Additionally, the `CreateDefaultSubobject` function's template parameter should be the `ULookAtActorComponent` class and its parameter should be "Look At Actor Component".

5. Remove the class's implementation of the `LookAtActor` function.

6. In the class's `Tick` function, remove the line of code where you create the `PlayerCharacter` property, and add that exact line of code to the end of the class's `BeginPlay` function.

7. After this line, call the `SetTarget` function of `LookAtActorComponent` and send the `PlayerCharacter` property as a parameter.

8. Inside the class's `Tick` function, set the `bCanSeePlayer` property's value to the return value of the `CanSeeTarget` function call of `LookAtActorComponent`, instead of the return value of the `LookAtActor` function call.

Now, there's only one last step we have to do before this activity is completed.

9. Close the editor (if you have it opened), compile your changes in Visual Studio, open the editor, and open the `BP_EnemyCharacter` Blueprint. Find `LookAtActorComponent` and change its location to `(10, 0, 80)`.

Expected output:

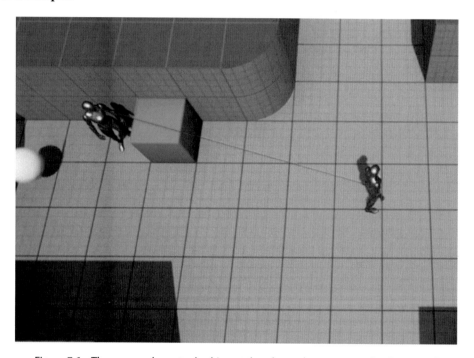

Figure 7.6 – The enemy character looking at the player character remains functional

And with that, we conclude our activity. You have applied your knowledge of refactoring part of an actor's logic into an Actor component so that you can reuse it in other parts of your project, or even in other projects of your own.

> **Note**
> The solution for this activity can be found on `https://github.com/PacktPublishing/Elevating-Game-Experiences-with-Unreal-Engine-5-Second-Edition/tree/main/Activity%20solutions`.

Summary

You now know about several utilities that will help you keep your projects more organized and allow you to reuse the things that you make.

You learned how to create a Blueprint Function Library, create Actor components and use them to refactor the existing logic in your project, and create interfaces and call functions from an object that implements a specific interface. Altogether, these new topics will allow you to refactor and reuse all the code that you write in a project in that same project or another project.

In the next chapter, we'll look at UMG, UE5's system for creating user interfaces, and learn how to create user interfaces.

8

Creating User Interfaces with UMG

In the previous chapter, we learned about general-purpose utilities that allow you to properly structure and organize the code and assets in your project by using blueprint function libraries, actor components, and interfaces.

In this chapter, we will dive into the topic of game **User Interfaces** (**UIs**), which are present in almost every video game. The game UI is one of the main ways in which to show information to the player, such as how many lives they have left, how many bullets are in their weapon, which weapon they are carrying, and more. It also allows the player to interact with the game by choosing whether to continue the game, create a new game, choose which level they want to play in, and more. This is shown to the player mostly in the form of images and text.

In this chapter, we'll cover the following topics:

- Game UI
- UMG basics
- Introducing anchors
- Understanding progress bars

Technical requirements

The project for this chapter can be found in the Chapter08 folder of the code bundle for this book, which can be downloaded here: `https://github.com/PacktPublishing/Elevating-Game-Experiences-with-Unreal-Engine-5-Second-Edition`.

Game UI

Usually, UIs are added on top of the rendering of the game, which means that they are in front of everything else you see in the game and behave as layers (you can add them on top of one another just like in Photoshop). However, there is an exception to this: *diegetic UI*. This type of UI isn't layered onto the game's screen but rather exists inside the game itself. A great example of this can be found in the game *Dead Space*, where you control a character in a third-person view, and can see their health points by looking at the contraption attached to their back, inside the game world.

There are usually two different types of game UI: **menus** and **HUDs**.

Menus are UI panels that allow the player to interact with them, either by pressing a button or a key on their input device.

This can be done in the form of many different menus, including the following:

- Main menus, where the player can choose whether to continue the game, create a new game, exit the game, and more
- Level select menus, where the player can choose which level to play
- Many other options

HUDs are UI panels that are present during gameplay. They give the player information that they should always know, such as how many lives they have left, which special abilities they can use, and more.

In this chapter, we will be covering game UI and how to make both a menu and a HUD for our game.

> **Note**
> We won't be covering diegetic UI here, as it is beyond the scope of this book.

So, how do we go about creating a game UI in UE5? The main way to do it is by using **Unreal Motion Graphics** (**UMG**), which is the tool that allows you to make a game UI (also called widgets in UE5 terms), featuring menus and HUDs, and add them to the screen.

Let's jump into this topic in the following section.

UMG basics

In UE5, the main way to create a game UI is by using the **UMG** tool. This tool will allow you to make a game UI in the form of **Widgets**, which can be created using UMG. This will allow you to easily edit your game UI in a visual manner, through **UMG's Designer** tab, while also allowing you to add functionality to your game UI through UMG's Graph tab.

Widgets are the way UE5 allows you to represent a game UI. Widgets can be basic UI elements such as **Button** elements, **Text** elements, and Image elements, but they can also be combined to create more complex and complete widgets, such as menus and HUDs, which is exactly what we will be doing in this chapter.

In the following exercise, let's create our first widget in UE5 using the UMG tool.

Exercise 8.01 – creating a Widget Blueprint

In this exercise, we will be creating our first Widget Blueprint. Additionally, we will be learning about the basic elements of UMG and how we can use them to create a game UI.

The following steps will help you to complete this exercise:

1. In order to create our first widget, open the editor, go to the **ThirdPersonCPP -> Blueprints** folder inside the **Content Browser** section, and *right-click*.

2. Go to the very last section, **User Interface**, and select **Widget Blueprint**.

3. After that, select **UserWidget** from the list of parent classes available:

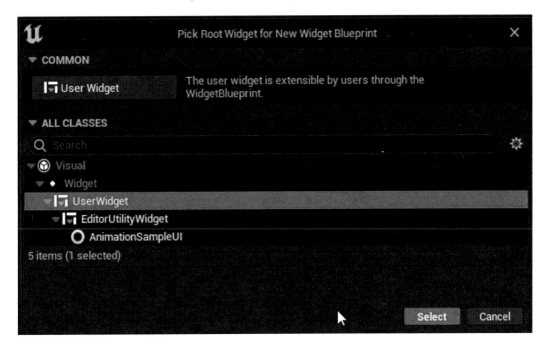

Figure 8.1 – Selecting the UserWidget parent class

Selecting this option will create a new Widget Blueprint asset, which is the name of a widget asset in UE5.

4. Name this widget `TestWidget` and open it. You will see the interface for editing a Widget Blueprint, where you'll be creating your own widgets and UI. Here's a breakdown of all the tabs present in this window:

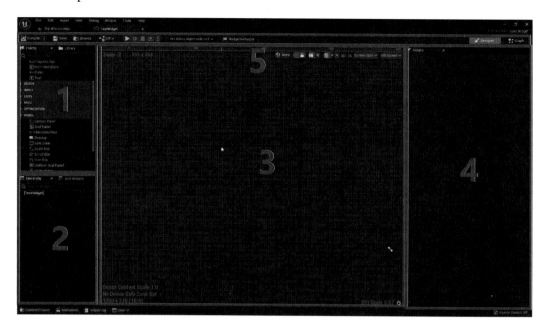

Figure 8.2 – The Widget Blueprint editor broken down into six windows

The details about the tabs in the preceding screenshot are listed as follows:

- **Palette** – This tab shows you all the individual UI elements that you can add to your widget. This includes `Button` elements, `Text Box` elements, `Image` elements, `Slider` elements, `Check Box` elements, and more.

- **Hierarchy** – This tab shows you all the UI elements currently present in your widget. As you can see, currently, we only have a **Canvas Panel** element in our hierarchy.

- **Designer** – This tab shows you how your widget looks visually, according to the elements present in the hierarchy, and how they're laid out. Because the only element we currently have in our widget doesn't have a visual representation, this tab is currently empty.

- **Details** – This tab shows you the properties of the UI element you have currently selected. If you select the existing **Canvas Panel** element, all the options in the preceding screenshot should appear.

- Because this asset is a `Widget Blueprint` asset, these two buttons allow you to switch between the **Designer** view, which is the one presented in the screenshot, and the **Graph** view, which looks exactly like the window of a normal blueprint class.

5. Now, let's look at some of the available UI elements in our **Widget**, starting with the `Canvas Panel` element.

6. Usually, **Canvas Panel** elements are added to the root of Widget Blueprints because they allow you to drag a UI element to any position you want in the **Designer** tab. This way, you can lay out these elements as you wish: at the center of the screen, in the upper-left corner, at the bottom center of the screen, and more. Now, let's drag another very important UI element into our widget: a **Button** element. In order to add a **Canvas Panel** element to your widget, go to the **Panel** category inside the **Palette** window and drag a **Canvas Panel** element into your widget's root inside the **Hierarchy** window (the first piece of text that says [**TestWidget**]) or inside the **Designer** window:

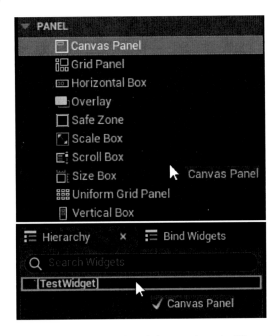

Figure 8.3 – Dragging the Canvas Panel element into the Hierarchy window

7.   In the **Palette** tab, find the **Button** element and drag it into the **Designer** window (hold the left mouse button while you drag):

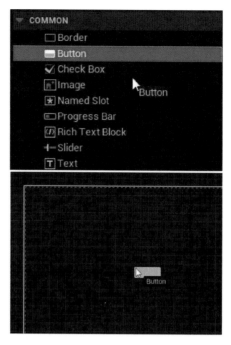

Figure 8.4 – A Button element being dragged from the Palette window into the Designer window

Once you have done this, you'll be able to resize the button to the size you want by dragging the little white dots around it (keep in mind that you'll only be able to do this to an element that is inside a **Canvas Panel** element):

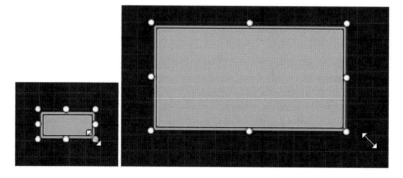

Figure 8.5 – The result of resizing a UI element using the white dots around it

Another way for you to drag elements inside each other in a widget is to drag them inside the **Hierarchy** tab instead of the **Designer** tab.

8. Now drag a `Text` element inside our **Button** element, but this time, use the **Hierarchy** tab:

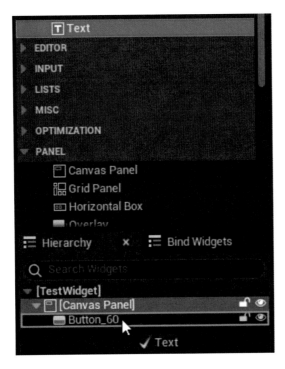

Figure 8.6 – Dragging a Text element from the Palette window into the Hierarchy window

`Text` elements can contain text specified by you with a certain size and font that you can modify in the `Details` panel. After you've dragged the `Text` element inside the `Button` element using the `Hierarchy` tab, this is what the `Designer` tab should look like:

Figure 8.7 – The Button element in the Designer tab, after adding a Text element as its child

Let's change a few properties of the preceding `Text` block.

9. Select it in either the Hierarchy tab or the **Designer** tab, and take a look at the **Details** panel:

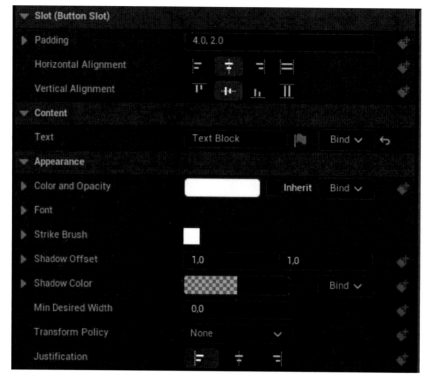

Figure 8.8 – The Details panel, showing the properties of the Text element we added

Here, you'll find several properties that you can edit to your liking. For now, we just want to focus on two of them: the content of the text and its color and opacity.

10. Update the **Content** tab of the **Text element** from **Text Block** to **Button 1**:

Figure 8.9 – Changing the Text property of the Text element to Button 1

Next, let's change the Color and Opacity property setting from White to Black.

11. Click on the **Color and Opacity** property and take a look at the window that pops up: **Color Picker**. This window pops up whenever you edit a Color property in UE5. It allows you to input colors in many different ways, including a color wheel, **Saturation** and **Value** bars, **RGB** and **HSV** value sliders, and more.

12. For now, change the color from white to black by dragging the **Value** bar (the one that goes from white to black from top to bottom) all the way to the bottom and then pressing **OK**:

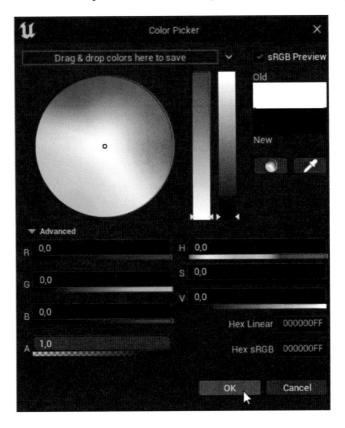

Figure 8.10 – Selecting the color black in the Color Picker window

13. After these changes, this is what the button should look like:

Figure 8.11 – The Button element after we change the Text element's Text property and its color

And with that, we conclude our first exercise of this chapter. You now know some of the essential basics of UMG, such as how to add `Button` and `Text` elements to your widgets.

Before we jump into our next exercise, first, let's learn about anchors.

Introducing anchors

As you might be aware, video games are played on many different screen sizes with many different resolutions. Because of that, it is important to make sure that the menus you create can adapt to all these different resolutions effectively. That is the main purpose of **Anchors**.

Anchors allow you to specify how you want a UI element's size to adapt as the screen resolution changes by specifying the proportion of the screen you want it to occupy. Using anchors, you can always have a UI element in the upper-left corner of the screen, or always occupying half of the screen, no matter the size and resolution of that screen.

As the size of the screen or resolution changes, your widget will scale and move relative to its anchor. Only elements that are direct children of a `Canvas Panel` element can have an anchor, which you can visualize through the **Anchor Medallion** (which is a white flower-like shape in the `Designer` tab) when you select said element:

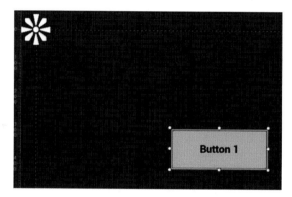

Figure 8.12 – The Anchor Medallion in the upper-left corner of
the outline, as shown in the Designer window

By default, the anchor is collapsed into the upper-left corner, which means that you won't have much control over how the button is scaled as the resolution changes. Let's change that in the next exercise.

Exercise 8.02 – editing UMG anchors

In this exercise, we will be changing the anchors in our widget in order to have our button's size and shape adapt to a wide range of screen resolutions and sizes.

The following steps will help you to complete this exercise:

1. Select the button we created in the previous exercise. Then, head to the **Details** panel and press the very first property you see: the **Anchors** property. Here, you'll be able to see the `Anchor` presets, which will align the UI element according to the pivots shown.

We'll want to have our button centered on the screen.

2. Click on the pivot that's at the center of the screen:

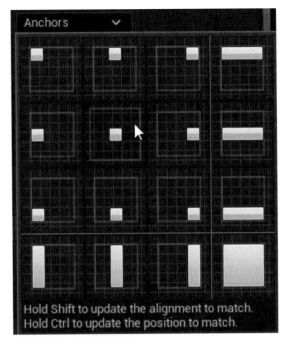

Figure 8.13 – The button's Anchors property, with the center Anchor preset outlined in a box

You'll see that our Anchor Medallion has now changed places:

Figure 8.14 – The Anchor Medallion after we change the button's Anchor property to the center

Now that the Anchor Medallion is at the center of the screen, we still won't have much control over how the button will scale across different resolutions, but at least we know that it'll scale relative to the center of the screen.

In order to have our button centered on the screen, we'll have to change the button's position to be at the center of the screen, too.

3. Repeat the previous step of picking the center anchor, but this time, before you select it, hold the *Ctrl* key in order to snap the button's position to this anchor. After you click on it, release the *Ctrl* key. You should see a result similar to the following screenshot:

Figure 8.15 – The Button element being moved near its selected anchor in the center

As you can see from the preceding screenshot, our button has changed position, but it isn't properly centered on the screen yet. That is because of its alignment.

The `Alignment` property is of the `Vector2D` type (a tuple with two `float` properties: `X` and `Y`) and dictates the center of the UI element relative to its total size. By default, it's set to `(0,0)`, meaning the center of the element is its upper-left corner, which explains the result in the preceding screenshot. It can go all the way to `(1,1)`, which is the lower-right corner. In this case, given that we want the alignment to center the button, we want it to be `(0.5, 0.5)`.

4. In order to update a UI element's alignment when picking an `Anchor` point, you have to hold the *Shift* key and repeat the previous step. Alternately, to update both the position and the alignment of the button, picking the center `Anchor` point while holding both the *Ctrl* and *Shift* keys will do the job. The following screenshot should then be the result:

Figure 8.16 – The Button element being centered relative to its selected Anchor point in the center

At this point, when changing the resolution of the screen, we know that this button will always remain at the center of the screen. However, in order to maintain the button's size relative to the resolution, we'll need to make a few more modifications.

5. Drag the lower-right *petal* of the Anchor Medallion all the way to the lower-right corner of the button:

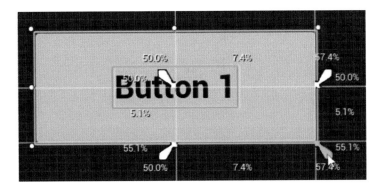

Figure 8.17 – Dragging the lower-right petal of the Anchor Medallion
to update the Button element's Anchor point

6. Drag the upper-left *petal* of the Anchor Medallion all the way to the upper-left corner of the button:

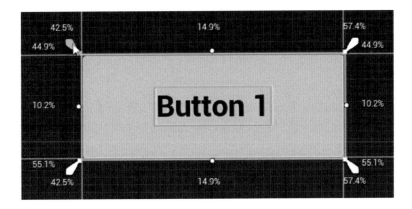

Figure 8.18 – Dragging the upper-left petal of the Anchor
Medallion to update the Button element's Anchor

Note

The percentages you see around the button when changing the Anchor point are the space the element is occupying on the screen, shown as a percentage. For instance, looking at the preceding screenshot, we can see that the button is occupying 11.9% of the widget's space on the X coordinate and 8.4% of the widget's space on the Y coordinate.

You can set the size of a UI element to the size of its anchor by holding the *Ctrl* key while moving the Anchor Medallion *petals*.

Now our button will, finally, adapt to varying screen sizes and resolutions due to these changes to its anchor.

Additionally, you can use the Details panel to manually edit all of the properties we just edited by using the Anchor Medallion and moving the button:

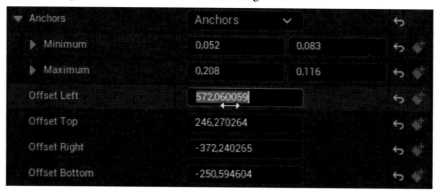

Figure 8.19 – The properties we changed using the Anchor Medallion, as shown in the Details window

Lastly, we need to know how we can visualize our widget with different resolutions in the Designer tab.

7.   Drag the double arrow in the lower-right corner of the outlined box inside the Designer tab:

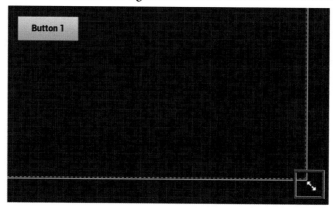

Figure 8.20 – The double arrow in the lower-right corner of the outlined box inside the Designer tab

By dragging the double arrow, you can resize the canvas to any screen resolution you want. In the following screenshot, you'll see the most used resolutions for a variety of devices, and you can preview your widget in each of them:

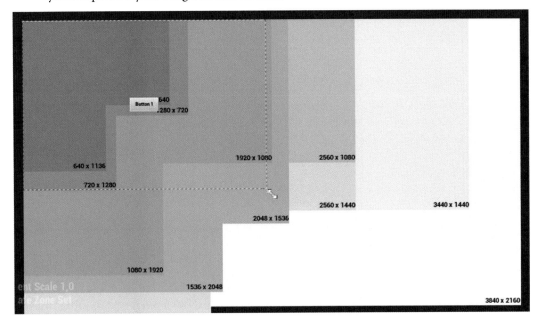

Figure 8.21 – The resolutions we can choose to preview in the Designer window

> **Note**
> You can find a full reference to UMG's anchors at `https://docs.unrealengine.com/en-US/Engine/UMG/UserGuide/Anchors`.

And that concludes our exercise. You've learned about anchors and how to adapt your widgets to varying screen sizes and resolutions.

Now that we've learned about some of the basics of UMG, let's see how we can create a widget C++ class for this Widget Blueprint. That is what we're going to do in the next exercise.

Exercise 8.03 – creating the RestartWidget C++ class

In this exercise, we will learn how to create a widget C++ class, which the Widget Blueprint that we created will inherit from. It will get added to the screen when the player dies in our **Dodgeball** game so that the player can have the option to restart the level. This widget will have a button that will restart the level when the player clicks on it.

The first step of this exercise will be adding the UMG-related modules to our project. Unreal Engine comprises several different modules, and in each project, you have to specify which ones you're going to use. Our project came with a few general modules when the source code files were generated, but we'll need to add a few more.

The following steps will help you complete this exercise:

1. Open the `Dodgeball.build.cs` file, which is a C# file and not a C++ file, located inside your project's `Source` folder.

2. Open the file, and you'll find the `AddRange` function from the `PublicDependency ModuleNames` property being called. This is the function that tells the engine which modules this project intends to use. As a parameter, an array of strings is sent, with the names of all the intended modules for the project. Given that we intend on using UMG, we'll need to add the UMG-related modules: UMG, `Slate`, and `SlateCore`:

```
PublicDependencyModuleNames.AddRange(new string[] {
"Core",
  "CoreUObject", "Engine", "InputCore",
  "EnhancedInput", "HeadMountedDisplay", "UMG",
  "Slate", "SlateCore" });
```

Now that we've notified the engine that we'll be using the UMG modules, let's create our widget C++ class:

3. Open the Unreal Editor interface.

4. Right-click on the **Content Browser** section and select **New C++ Class**.

5. Set the **Show All Classes** checkbox to **true**.

6. Search for the `UserWidget` class and choose that as the new class's parent class.

7. Name the new C++ class `RestartWidget`.

   After the files have been opened in Visual Studio, start making modifications to our widget C++ class, as mentioned in the next steps.

8. The first thing we'll add to this class is a `public class UButton*` property, called `RestartButton`, which represents the button the player will press in order to restart the level. You will want it to be bound to a button in the blueprint class that inherits from this class, by using the `UPROPERTY` macro with the `BindWidget` meta tag. This will force that Widget Blueprint to have a `Button` element, called `RestartButton`, that we can access in C++ through this property and then freely edit its properties, such as its size and position, in the blueprint:

```
UPROPERTY(meta = (BindWidget))
class UButton* RestartButton;
```

> **Note**
>
> Using the `BindWidget` meta tag will cause a compilation error if the Widget Blueprint that inherits from this C++ class doesn't have an element with the same type and name. If you don't want this to happen, you will have to mark UPROPERTY as an optional `BindWidget` like so:
>
> `UPROPERTY(meta = (BindWidget, OptionalWidget = true))`
>
> This will make it so that binding this property is optional and doesn't cause a compilation error when compiling the Widget Blueprint.

Next, we're going to add the function that will be called when the player clicks on the `RestartButton` property, which will restart the level. We will be doing this using the `GameplayStatics` object's `OpenLevel` function and then sending the name of the current level.

9. In the widget class's header file, add a declaration for a `protected` function called `OnRestartClicked` that returns nothing and receives no parameters. This function must be marked as UFUNCTION:

   ```
   protected:
   UFUNCTION()
   void OnRestartClicked();
   ```

10. In the class's source file, add an `include` for the `GameplayStatics` object:

    ```
    #include "Kismet/GameplayStatics.h"
    ```

11. Then, add an implementation for our `OnRestartClicked` function:

    ```
    void URestartWidget::OnRestartClicked()
    {
    }
    ```

12. Inside this implementation, call the `GameplayStatics` object's `OpenLevel` function. This function receives, as parameters, a world context object, which will be the `this` pointer, and the name of the level, which we'll have to fetch using the `GameplayStatics` object's `GetCurrentLevelName` function. Additionally, this last function must receive a world context object, which will also be the `this` pointer:

    ```
    UGameplayStatics::OpenLevel(this,
        FName(*UGameplayStatics::GetCurrentLevelName(
        this)));
    ```

> **Note**
> The call to the `GameplayStatics` object's `GetCurrentLevelName` function must be preceded with `*` because it returns an `FString` type, UE5's string type, and must be dereferenced in order to be passed to the `FName` constructor.

The next step will be to bind this function in such a way that it is called when the player presses the `RestartButton` property:

13. In order to do this, we'll have to override a function that belongs to the `UserWidget` class, called `NativeOnInitialized`. This function is only called once, similarly to the actor's `BeginPlay` function, which makes it appropriate to do our setup. Add a declaration for the `public NativeOnInitialized` function with both the `virtual` and `override` keywords in our widget class's header file:

```
virtual void NativeOnInitialized() override;
```

14. Next, in the class's source file, add the implementation of this function. Inside it, call its `Super` function and add an `if` statement that checks whether our `RestartButton` property is different from `nullptr`:

```
void URestartWidget::NativeOnInitialized()
{
    Super::NativeOnInitialized();
    if (RestartButton != nullptr)
    {
    }
}
```

15. If the `if` statement is true, we'll want to bind our `OnRestartClicked` function to the button's `OnClicked` event. We can do this by accessing the button's `OnClicked` property and calling its `AddDynamic` function. This sends, as parameters, the object we want to call that function on, the `this` pointer, and a pointer to the function to be called, that is, the `OnRestartClicked` function:

```
if (RestartButton != nullptr)
{
    RestartButton->OnClicked.AddDynamic(this,
    &URestartWidget::OnRestartClicked);
}
```

16. Because we're accessing functions related to the `Button` class, we'll also have to include it:

```
#include "Components/Button.h"
```

> **Note**
>
> A button's `OnClicked` event will be called when the player presses and releases that button with the mouse. There are other events related to the button, including the `OnPressed` event (when the player presses the button), the `OnReleased` event (when the player releases the button), and the `OnHover` and `OnUnhover` events (when the player, respectively, starts and stops hovering the mouse over that button).
>
> The `AddDynamic` function must receive, as a parameter, a pointer to a function marked with the `UFUNCTION` macro. If it doesn't, you will get an error when calling that function. This is why we marked the `OnRestartClicked` function with the `UFUNCTION` macro.

After you've done these steps, compile your changes and open the editor.

17. Open the `TestWidget` Widget Blueprint that you created earlier. We'll want to associate this Widget Blueprint with the `RestartWidget` class we just created, so we need to reparent it.

18. From the Widget Blueprint's **File** tab, select the **Reparent Blueprint** option and choose the `RestartWidget` C++ class as its new parent class:

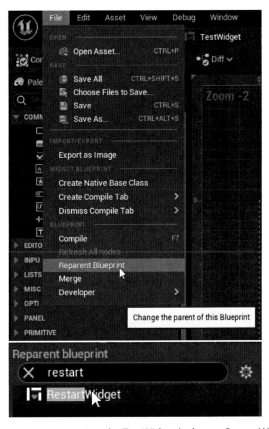

Figure 8.22 – Reparenting the TestWidget's class to RestartWidget

You'll notice that the Widget Blueprint now has a compilation error related to the `BindWidget` meta tag that we created in the C++ class:

Figure 8.23 – Compiler errors after setting the parent class to the RestartWidget class

This is caused by the fact that the C++ class couldn't find a `Button` property called `RestartButton`.

In order to fix this, we'll need to rename our `Button` element inside the Widget Blueprint to `RestartButton`:

Figure 8.24 – Renaming the Button element to RestartButton

After you've done this, close the Widget Blueprint and change its name from `TestWidget` to `BP_RestartWidget`, the same way you just did in the previous step.

That concludes the creation of our widget class. Now, you understand how to connect a widget C++ class to a Widget Blueprint, which is a very important step toward handling game UI in UE5.

The next thing we need to do is create our `Player Controller` C++ class, which will be responsible for instantiating our `RestartWidget` class and adding it to the screen. We will be doing this in the following exercise.

Exercise 8.04 – creating the logic for adding the RestartWidget class to the screen

In this exercise, we will create the logic responsible for adding our newly created `RestartWidget` class to the screen. It will appear on the screen when the player dies so that they have the option to restart the level.

In order to do this, we'll have to create a new `Player Controller` C++ class, which you can do by following these steps:

1. Open the Unreal Editor interface.

2. *Right-click* on the `Content Browser` section and select `New C++ Class`.

3. Search for the `Player Controller` class and choose that as the new class's parent class.

4. Name the new C++ class `DodgeballPlayerController`.

5. Open the class's files in Visual Studio.

    When our player runs out of health points, the `DodgeballCharacter` class will access this `Player Controller` class and call a function that will add the `RestartWidget` class to the screen. Follow these next steps in order to make this happen.

    In order to know the class of the widget to add to the screen (which will be a Widget Blueprint asset and not a Widget C++ class), we'll need to use the `TSubclassOf` type.

6. In the class's header file, add a `public TSubclassOf<class URestartWidget>` property called `BP_RestartWidget`. Be sure to make it a UPROPERTY function with the `EditDefaultsOnly` tag so that we can edit it in the blueprint class:

    ```
    public:
    UPROPERTY(EditDefaultsOnly)
    TSubclassOf<class URestartWidget> BP_RestartWidget;
    ```

    In order to instantiate this widget and add it to the screen, we'll need to save a reference to it.

7. Add a new `private` variable of the `class URestartWidget*` type and call it `RestartWidget`. Be sure to make it a UPROPERTY function with no tags:

    ```
    private:
    UPROPERTY()
    class URestartWidget* RestartWidget;
    ```

> **Note**
> Although this property isn't supposed to be editable in a blueprint class, we have to make this reference a UPROPERTY function; otherwise, the garbage collector will destroy the contents of this variable.

The next thing we need is a function responsible for adding our widget to the screen.

8. Add a declaration for a `public` function that returns nothing and receives no parameters, called `ShowRestartWidget`:

```
void ShowRestartWidget();
```

9. Now, head to our class's source file. First, add an `include` to the `RestartWidget` class:

```
#include "RestartWidget.h"
```

10. Then, add the implementation of our `ShowRestartWidget` function, where we'll start by checking whether our `BP_RestartWidget` variable is not a `nullptr` variable:

```
void ADodgeballPlayerController::ShowRestartWidget()
{
    if (BP_RestartWidget != nullptr)
    {
    }
}
```

11. If that variable is valid (different from `nullptr`), we want to pause the game using the `SetPause` function of **Player Controller**. This will ensure that the game stops until the player decides to do something (which, in our case, will be pressing the button that restarts the level):

```
SetPause(true);
```

The next thing we'll do is change the input mode. In UE5, there are three input modes: `Game Only`, `Game and UI`, and `UI Only`. If your Input mode includes `Game`, that means that the player character and the player controller will receive inputs through the input actions. If your `Input` mode includes `UI`, that means that the widgets that are on the screen will receive inputs from the player. When we show this widget on the screen, we won't want the player character to receive any input.

12. Hence, update to the `UI Only` Input mode. You can do this by calling the `Player Controller` `SetInputMode` function and passing the `FInputModeUIOnly` type as a parameter:

```
SetInputMode(FInputModeUIOnly());
```

Following this, we want to show the mouse cursor so that the player can see which button they are hovering the mouse on.

13. We will do this by setting the `Player Controller` `bShowMouseCursor` property to true:

```
bShowMouseCursor = true;
```

14. Now, we can actually instantiate our widget using the `Player Controller`'s `CreateWidget` function, passing as a template parameter the C++ Widget class, which, in our case, is `RestartWidget`. Then, as normal parameters, we will pass Owning Player, which is the `Player Controller` class that owns this widget and that we'll send using the `this` pointer, and the widget class, which will be our `BP_RestartWidget` property:

```
RestartWidget = CreateWidget<URestartWidget>(this,
    BP_RestartWidget);
```

15. After we instantiate the widget, we'll want to add it to the screen, using the widget's `AddToViewport` function:

```
RestartWidget->AddToViewport();
```

16. That concludes our `ShowRestartWidget` function. However, we also need to create the function that will remove the `RestartWidget` class from the screen. In the class's header file, add a declaration for a function just like the `ShowRestartWidget` function, but this time called `HideRestartWidget`:

```
void HideRestartWidget();
```

17. In the class's source file, add the implementation for the `HideRestartWidget` function:

```
void ADodgeballPlayerController::HideRestartWidget()
{
}
```

18. The first thing we should do in this function is to remove the widget from the screen by calling its `RemoveFromParent` function, and destroy it using the `Destruct` function:

```
RestartWidget->RemoveFromParent();
RestartWidget->Destruct();
```

19. Then, we want to unpause the game using the `SetPause` function we used in the previous function:

```
SetPause(false);
```

20. Finally, let's set the Input mode to Game Only and hide the mouse cursor in the same way we did in the previous function (this time, we pass the FInputModeGameOnly type instead):

```
SetInputMode(FInputModeGameOnly());
bShowMouseCursor = false;
```

And that concludes the logic for our Player Controller C++ class. The next thing we should do is call the function that will add our widget to the screen.

21. Go to the DodgeballCharacter class's source file and add the include keyword to our newly created DodgeballPlayerController class:

```
#include "DodgeballPlayerController.h"
```

22. Within the DodgeballCharacter class's implementation of the OnDeath_ Implementation function, replace the call to the QuitGame function with the following:

- Get the character's player controller using the GetController function. You'll want to save the result in a variable of the DodgeballPlayerController* type, called PlayerController. Because the function will return a variable of the Controller type, you'll also need to cast it to our PlayerController class:

```
ADodgeballPlayerController* PlayerController =
Cast<ADodgeballPlayerController>(GetController());
```

- Check whether the PlayerController variable is valid. If it is, call its ShowRestartWidget function:

```
if (PlayerController != nullptr)
{
    PlayerController->ShowRestartWidget();
}
```

After these modifications, the last thing left for us to do is to call the function that will hide our widget from the screen. Open the RestartWidget class's source file and implement the following modifications.

23. Add an include to the DodgeballPlayerController class, which contains the function that we will be calling:

```
#include "DodgeballPlayerController.h"
```

24. Inside the `OnRestartClicked` function implementation, before the call to the `OpenLevel` function, we must fetch the widget's `OwningPlayer`, which is of the `PlayerController` type, using the `GetOwningPlayer` function, and cast it to the `DodgeballPlayerController` class:

```
ADodgeballPlayerController* PlayerController =
    Cast<ADodgeballPlayerController>(GetOwningPlayer());
```

25. Then, if the `PlayerController` variable is valid, we call its `HideRestartWidget` function:

```
if (PlayerController != nullptr)
{
    PlayerController->HideRestartWidget();
}
```

After you've followed all these steps, close the editor, compile your changes, and open the editor again.

You have now concluded this exercise. We have added all the necessary logic to add our `RestartWidget` class to the screen. The only thing left for us to do is create the blueprint class of our newly created `DodgeballPlayerController` class, which we'll be doing in the next exercise.

Exercise 8.05 – setting up the DodgeballPlayerController blueprint class

In this exercise, we will be creating the blueprint class for `DodgeballPlayerController` in order to specify which widget we want to add to the screen. Then, we will tell UE5 to use this blueprint class when the game starts.

In order to do that, follow these steps:

1. Go to the **ThirdPersonCPP -> Blueprints** directory in the **Content Browser** section, right-click on it, and create a new blueprint class.

2. Search for the **DodgeballPlayerController** class and select it as the parent class.

3. Rename this blueprint class to `BP_DodgeballPlayerController`. After that, open this blueprint asset.

4. Go to its `Class Defaults` tab and set the class's `BP_RestartWidget` property to the `BP_RestartWidget` Widget Blueprint we created.

   Now, the only thing left for us to do is to make sure that this `Player Controller` blueprint class is being used in the game.

   In order to do this, we'll have to follow a few more steps.

5. Go to the `ThirdPersonCPP -> Blueprints` directory in the **Content Browser** section, *right-click* on it, and create a new blueprint class. Search for the `DodgeballGameMode` class and select it as the parent class. Then, rename this `Blueprint` class to `BP_DodgeballGameMode`.

    This class is responsible for telling the game which classes to use for each element of the game, such as which `Player Controller` class to use, among other things.

6. Open the asset, go to its **Class Defaults** tab, and set the class's `PlayerControllerClass` property to the `BP_DodgeballPlayerController` class we just created:

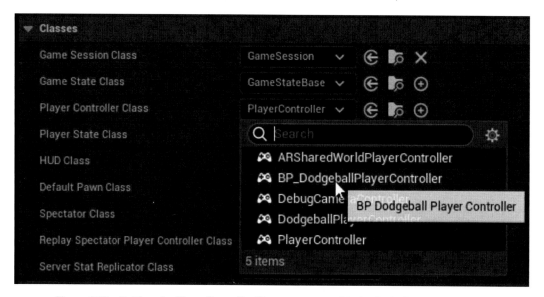

Figure 8.25 – Setting the PlayerControllerClass property to BP_DodgeballPlayerController

7. Close the asset and select the **Blueprints** drop-down option inside the editor toolbar that is at the top of the **Level Viewport** window. From there, select the second **Game Mode** option, inside the **World Override** category (which should, currently, be set to **DodgeballGameMode**), -> **Select GameModeBase Class** -> **BP_DodgeballGameMode**. This will tell the editor to use this new **Game Mode** option in the current level.

> **Note**
> Additionally, you can set the **Game Mode** option inside the **Project Settings** category, which will tell the editor to use that **Game Mode** option on all levels. However, if a level overrides this option by setting the **Game Mode** option in the **World Override** category, that option will be ignored.

Now, play the game and let your character get hit by a dodgeball `three` times. After the third time, you should see the game get paused and show `BP_RestartWidget`:

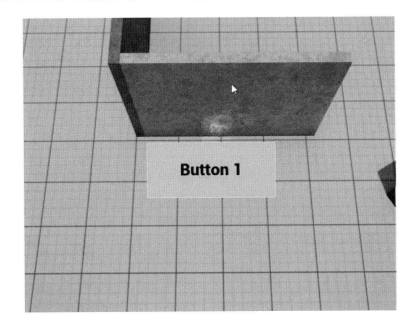

Figure 8.26 – Our BP_RestartWidget property being added to the
screen after the player runs out of health points

And when you click on Button 1 using your mouse, you should see the level reset to its initial state:

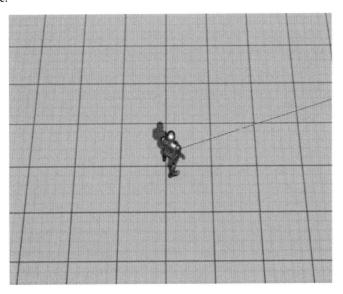

Figure 8.27 – The level restarts after the player presses the button shown in the previous screenshot

And that concludes our exercise. Now you know how to create widgets and show them in your game. This is another crucial step in your journey toward becoming a skilled game developer.

Before we move on to the next exercise, in the next section, let's take a look at progress bars.

Understanding progress bars

One of the ways that video games can represent character stats such as health, stamina, and more is through **Progress Bars**, which are what we'll use to communicate to the player how much health their character has. Essentially, progress bars are a shape, usually rectangular, that can be filled and emptied in order to show the player how a specific stat is progressing. If you want to show the player that their character's health is only half its maximum value, you could do this by showing the progress bar as half full. In this section, that is exactly what we'll be doing. This progress bar will be the only element in our **Dodgeball** game's HUD.

In order to create this **Health Bar** progress bar, first, we'll need to create our HUD widget. Open the editor, go to the `ThirdPersonCPP -> Blueprints` directory inside the **Content Browser** section, and right-click to create a new `Widget Blueprint` class from the `User Interface` category. Then, select **User Widget** from the list of parent classes available. Name this new Widget Blueprint `BP_HUDWidget`. After that, open the new Widget Blueprint.

Add a `Canvas Panel` element to the root of this widget, just like we did in *step 6* of *Exercise 8.01 – improving the RestartWidget class*.

In UE5, progress bars are just another UI element, such as `Button` elements and `Text` elements, which means we can drag them from the **Palette** tab into our **Designer** tab. Take a look at the following example:

Figure 8.28 – Dragging a Progress Bar element into the Designer window

At first, this progress bar might look similar to a button; however, it contains two specific properties that are important for a progress bar:

- **Percent** – This allows you to specify this progress bar's progress, from 0 to 1.

- **Bar Fill Type** – This allows you to specify how you want this progress bar to fill (from left to right, top to bottom, and so on):

Figure 8.29 – The progress bar's Percent and Bar Fill Type properties

If you set the **Percent** property to 0.5, the progress bar will be updated accordingly to fill half of its length:

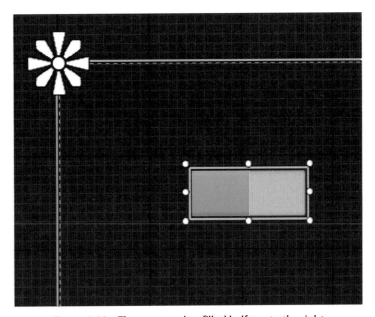

Figure 8.30 – The progress bar filled halfway to the right

Before you continue, set the **Percent** property to 1.

Now, let's change the progress bar's color from blue (its default color) to red. In order to do this, go to the **Details** tab and, inside the **Appearance** category, set the **Fill Color and Opacity** property to red (RGB(1,0,0)):

Figure 8.31 – The progress bar's color being changed to red

After you've done this, your progress bar should now use red as its fill color.

To conclude our progress bar's setup, let's update its position, size, and anchors. Follow these steps to achieve this:

1. In the **Slot** (**Canvas Panel Slot**) category, expand the **Anchors** property and set its properties to these values:

    - **Minimum**: **0.052** on the X axis, and 0.083 on the Y axis

    - **Maximum**: 0.208 on the X axis, and 0.116 on the Y axis

2. Set the **Offset Left**, **Offset Top**, **Offset Right**, and **Offset Bottom** properties to 0.

Your progress bar should now look like this:

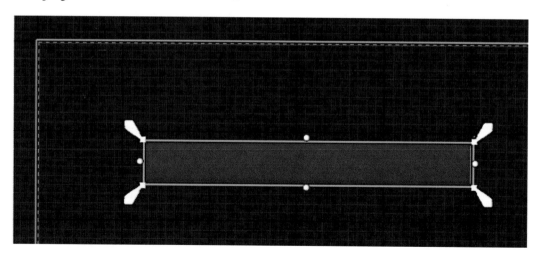

Figure 8.32 – The progress bar after all the modifications in this section have been completed

And with that, we can conclude the topic of progress bars. Our next step is going to be to add all the logic necessary to use this progress bar as a health bar, by updating its **Percent** property alongside the player character's health. In the next exercise, we'll do exactly that.

Exercise 8.06 – creating the health bar C++ logic

In this exercise, we will be adding all the necessary C++ logic to update the progress bar inside our HUD as the player character's health changes.

In order to do this, follow these steps:

1. Open the editor and create a new C++ class that inherits from `UserWidget`, similar to how we did in *Exercise 8.03 – creating the RestartWidget C++ class*. However, this time, call it `HUDWidget`. This will be the C++ class that will be used for our HUD widget.

2. In the `HUDWidget` class's header file, add a new `public` property of the `class UProgressBar*` type called `HealthBar`. This type is used to represent a progress bar, like the one we created in the previous section, in C++. Be sure to declare this property as a `UPROPERTY` function with the `BindWidget` tag:

   ```
   UPROPERTY(meta = (BindWidget))
   class UProgressBar* HealthBar;
   ```

3. Add a declaration for a `public` function, called `UpdateHealthPercent`, which returns nothing and receives a `float HealthPercent` property as a parameter. This function will be called in order to update the **Percent** property of our progress bar:

   ```
   void UpdateHealthPercent(float HealthPercent);
   ```

4. In the `HUDWidget` class's source file, add the implementation for the `UpdateHealthPercent` function, which will call the `HealthBar` property's `SetPercent` function, passing the `HealthPercent` property as a parameter:

   ```
   void UHUDWidget::UpdateHealthPercent(float HealthPercent)
   {
       HealthBar->SetPercent(HealthPercent);
   }
   ```

5. Because we'll be using the `ProgressBar` C++ class, we'll need to add an `include` to it at the top of the class's source file:

   ```
   #include "Components/ProgressBar.h"
   ```

The next step will be to add all the necessary logic to our `Player Controller` class, which is responsible for adding the `HUDWidget` class to the screen. Implement the following steps in order to achieve this:

6. Inside the `DodgeballPlayerController` class's header file, add a `public` property of the `TSubclassOf<class UHUDWidget>` type, called `BP_HUDWidget`. Be sure to mark it as a UPROPERTY function with the `EditDefaultsOnly` tag.

   This property will allow us to specify, in the `DodgeballPlayerController` blueprint class, which widget we want to use as our HUD:

   ```
   UPROPERTY(EditDefaultsOnly)
   TSubclassOf<class UHUDWidget> BP_HUDWidget;
   ```

7. Add another property, this time `private`, of the `class UHUDWidget *` type, called `HUDWidget`. Mark it as a UPROPERTY function, but without any tags:

   ```
   UPROPERTY()
   class UHUDWidget* HUDWidget;
   ```

8. Add a `protected` declaration for the `BeginPlay` function, and mark it as both `virtual` and `override`:

   ```
   virtual void BeginPlay() override;
   ```

9. Add a declaration for a new `public` function, called `UpdateHealthPercent`, which returns nothing and receives `float HealthPercent` as a parameter.

   This function will be called by our player character class in order to update the health bar in our HUD:

   ```
   void UpdateHealthPercent(float HealthPercent);
   ```

10. Now head over to the `DodgeballPlayerController` class's source file. Start by adding an `include` to our `HUDWidget` class:

    ```
    #include "HUDWidget.h"
    ```

11. Then, add the implementation for the `BeginPlay` function, where we'll start by calling the `Super` object's `BeginPlay` function:

    ```
    void ADodgeballPlayerController::BeginPlay()
    {
        Super::BeginPlay();
    }
    ```

12. After that function call, check whether the `BP_HUDWidget` property is valid. If it is, call the `CreateWidget` function with the `UHUDWidget` template parameter and pass `Owning Player`, `this`, and the `BP_HUDWidget` widget class, as parameters. Be sure to set the `HUDWidget` property to the return value of this function call:

```
if (BP_HUDWidget != nullptr)
{
   HUDWidget = CreateWidget<UHUDWidget>(this,
   BP_HUDWidget);
}
```

13. After setting the `HUDWidget` property, call its `AddToViewport` function:

```
HUDWidget->AddToViewport();
```

14. Lastly, add the implementation for the `UpdateHealthPercent` function, where we'll check whether the `HUDWidget` property is valid. If it is, call its `UpdateHealthPercent` function and pass the `HealthPercent` property as a parameter:

```
void ADodgeballPlayerController::UpdateHealthPercent(float
   HealthPercent)
{
   if (HUDWidget != nullptr)
   {
      HUDWidget->UpdateHealthPercent(HealthPercent);
   }
}
```

Now that we've added the logic responsible for adding the HUD to the screen and allowing it to be updated, we'll need to make some modifications to the other classes. Follow the next steps in order to do so.

Currently, our `Health` interface, which we created in the previous chapter, only has the `OnDeath` event, which is called whenever an object runs out of health points. In order to update our health bar every time the player takes damage, we need to allow our `HealthInterface` class to notify an object whenever that happens.

15. Open the `HealthInterface` class's header file and add a declaration similar to the one we did for the `OnDeath` event in *Exercise 7.04 – creating the HealthInterface class*, but this time for the `OnTakeDamage` event. This event will be called whenever an object takes damage:

```
UFUNCTION(BlueprintNativeEvent, Category = Health)
void OnTakeDamage();
virtual void OnTakeDamage_Implementation() = 0;
```

16. Now that we have added this event to our `Interface` class, let's add the logic that calls that event: open the `HealthComponent` class's source file and, inside its implementation of the `LoseHealth` function, after subtracting the `Amount` property from the `Health` property, check whether the `Owner` implements the `Health` interface and, if it does, call its `OnTakeDamage` event. Do this the same way we already did later in that same function for our `OnDeath` event, but this time, simply change the name of the event to `OnTakeDamage`:

```
if (GetOwner()->Implements<UHealthInterface>())
{
    IHealthInterface::Execute_OnTakeDamage(GetOwner());
}
```

Because our health bar will require the player character's health points as a percentage, we need to perform the following steps.

17. Add a `public` function to our `HealthComponent` class that returns just that: in the `HealthComponent` class's header file, add a declaration for a `FORCEINLINE` function that returns a `float` property. This function should be called `GetHealthPercent` and be a `const` function. Its implementation will simply consist of returning the `Health` property divided by `100`, which we will assume is the maximum amount of health points an object can have in our game:

```
FORCEINLINE float GetHealthPercent() const { return
Health /
    100.f; }
```

18. Now go to the `DodgeballCharacter` class's header file and add a declaration for a `public` `virtual` function called `OnTakeDamage_Implementation`, which returns nothing and receives no parameters. Mark it as `virtual` and `override`:

```
virtual void OnTakeDamage_Implementation() override;
```

19. In the `DodgeballCharacter` class's source file, add an implementation for the `OnTakeDamage_Implementation` function we just declared. Copy the content of the `OnDeath_Implementation` function to this new function's implementation, but make this change: instead of calling the `ShowRestartWidget` function of `PlayerController`, call its `UpdateHealthPercent` function, and pass the return value of the `HealthComponent` property's `GetHealthPercent` function as a parameter:

```
void ADodgeballCharacter::OnTakeDamage_Implementation()
{
  ADodgeballPlayerController* PlayerController =
  Cast<ADodgeballPlayerController>(GetController());
  if (PlayerController != nullptr)
  {
    PlayerController->
    UpdateHealthPercent(HealthComponent
    ->GetHealthPercent());
  }
}
```

This concludes this exercise's code setup. After you've done these changes, compile your code, open the editor, and perform the following steps.

20. Open the `BP_HUDWidget` Widget Blueprint and reparent it to the `HUDWidget` class, in the same way you did in *Exercise 8.03 – creating the RestartWidget C++ class*.

21. This should cause a compilation error, which you'll be able to fix by renaming our progress bar element to `HealthBar`.

22. Close this Widget Blueprint, open the `BP_DodgeballPlayerController` blueprint class, and set its `BP_HUDWidget` property to the `BP_HUDWidget` Widget Blueprint:

Figure 8.33 – Setting the BP_HUDWidget property to BP_HUDWidget

After you've done these changes, play the level. You should notice the **Health Bar** progress bar in the upper-left corner of the screen:

Figure 8.34 – The progress bar showing in the upper-left corner of the screen

When the player character gets hit by a dodgeball, you should notice the `Health Bar` progress bar being emptied:

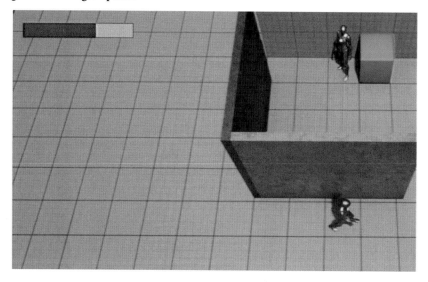

Figure 8.35 – The progress bar being emptied as the player character loses health points

And with that, we conclude this exercise. You've learned all the necessary steps in order to add a HUD to the screen and update it during the game.

Activity 8.01 – improving the RestartWidget class

In this activity, we will be adding a **Text** element to our `RestartWidget` class that reads **Game Over** in order for the player to know that they just lost the game; adding an **Exit** button, which will allow the player to exit the game; and also updating the text of our existing button to **Restart** so that the players know what should happen when they click on that button.

The following steps will help you complete this activity:

1. Open the `BP_RestartWidget` Widget Blueprint.

2. Drag a new `Text` element into the existing `Canvas Panel` element.

3. Modify the `Text` element's properties:

    • Expand the **Anchors** property and set its **Minimum** to `0.291` on the X axis and `0.115` on the Y axis. Then, set its **Maximum** to `0.708` on the X axis and `0.255` on the Y axis.

    • Set the **Offset Left**, **Offset Top**, **Offset Right**, and **Offset Bottom** properties to 0.

    • Set the **Text** property to GAME OVER.

    • Set the **Color and Opacity** property to red: `RGBA(1.0, 0.082, 0.082, 1.0)`.

    • Expand the **Font** property and set its **Size** value to `100`.

    • Set the **Justification** property to **Align Text Center**.

4. Select the other `Text` element inside the `RestartButton` property, and change its **Text** property to `Restart`.

5. Duplicate the `RestartButton` property and change the copy's name to `ExitButton`.

6. Change the **Text** property of the `Text` element inside the `ExitButton` property to `Exit`.

7. Expand the **Anchor** property of the `ExitButton` property, and set its **Minimum** to `0.425` on the *X* axis and `0.615` on the *Y* axis. Then, set its **Maximum** to `0.574` on the *X* axis and `0.725` on the *Y* axis.

8. Set the `ExitButton` properties of **Offset Left**, **Offset Top**, **Offset Right**, and **Offset Bottom** to 0.

    After you've done these changes, we'll need to add the logic responsible for handling the `ExitButton` property click, which will exit the game:

9. Save the changes made to the `BP_RestartWidget` Widget Blueprint and open the `RestartWidget` class's header file in Visual Studio. In this file, add a declaration for a `protected` function called `OnExitClicked` that returns nothing and receives no parameters.

Be sure to mark it as `UFUNCTION`.

10. Duplicate the existing `RestartButton` property, but call it `ExitButton` instead.

11. Inside the `RestartWidget` class's source file, add an implementation for the `OnExitClicked` function. Copy the contents of the `OnBeginOverlap` function from inside the `VictoryBox` class's source file into the `OnExitClicked` function, but remove the cast being done to the `DodgeballCharacter` class.

12. In the `NativeOnInitialized` function implementation, bind the `OnExitClicked` function we created to the `OnClicked` event of the `ExitButton` property, in the same way that we did for the `RestartButton` property in *Exercise 8.03 – creating the RestartWidget C++ class*.

And that concludes our code setup for this activity. Compile your changes, and open the editor. Then, open the `BP_RestartWidget` property and compile it just to make sure there are no compilation errors due to the `BindWidget` tags.

Once you've done this, play the level again, let the player character be hit by three dodgeballs, and notice the `Restart` widget appear with our new modifications:

Figure 8.36 – The updated BP_RestartWidget property being
shown after the player runs out of health points

If you press the `Restart` button, you should be able to replay the level, and if you press the `Exit` button, the game should end.

And that concludes our activity. You've consolidated the basics of using a **Widget blueprint** and changing its element's properties. Now you are ready to start making your own menus.

> **Note**
> The solution for this activity can be found on GitHub here: `https://github.com/PacktPublishing/Elevating-Game-Experiences-with-Unreal-Engine-5-Second-Edition/tree/main/Activity%20solutions`.

Summary

With this chapter concluded, you have now learned how to make a game UI in UE5, understanding things such as menus and HUDs. You've seen how to manipulate a Widget Blueprint's UI elements, including Button elements, Text elements, and Progress Bar elements; work with anchors effectively, which is instrumental in allowing your game UI to adapt elegantly to multiple screens; listen to mouse events in C++, such as the `OnClick` event, and use that to create your own game logic; and how to add the widgets you create to the screen, either at specific events or have them present at all times.

In the next chapter, we'll be taking a look at polishing our **Dodgeball** game by adding audiovisual elements, such as sound and particle effects, as well as making a new level.

9

Adding Audio-Visual Elements

In the previous chapter, we learned about the game UI and how to create and add a user interface (also known as a widget) to the screen.

In this chapter, we will learn how to add audio and particle effects to our game. Both of these aspects will increase the quality of our game and produce a much more immersive experience for the player.

Sound in video games can come in the form of either sound effects (also known as SFX) or music. Sound effects make the world around you more believable and alive, while the music helps set the tone for your game. Both these aspects are very important to your game.

In competitive games such as **Counter-Strike: Global Offensive (CS: GO)**, sound is also extremely important because players need to hear the sounds around them, such as gunshots and footsteps, and which direction they came from, to gather as much information about their surroundings as possible.

In this chapter, we will cover the following topics:

- Audio in UE5
- Sound attenuation
- Understanding Particle Systems
- Exploring level design
- Extra features

Particle effects are important for the same reason that sound effects are important: they make your game world more believable and immersive.

Let's start this chapter by learning how audio works in UE5.

Technical requirements

The project for this chapter can be found in the Chapter09 folder of the code bundle for this book, which can be downloaded here: `https://github.com/PacktPublishing/Elevating-Game-Experiences-with-Unreal-Engine-5-Second-Edition`.

Audio in UE5

One of the essential components of any game is sound. Sounds make your game more believable and immersive, which will provide a much better experience for your player. Video games usually have two types of sounds:

- 2D sounds
- 3D sounds

2D sounds don't have any consideration for the listener's distance and direction, while 3D sounds can be higher or lower in volume and pan to the right or left, depending on the player's location. 2D sounds are usually used for music, while 3D sounds are usually used for sound effects. The main sound file types are `.wav` and `.mp3`.

Here are some of the assets and classes related to audio in UE5:

- `Sound Base`: Represents an asset that contains audio. This class is mainly used in C++ and Blueprint to reference an audio file that can be played.

- `Sound Wave`: Represents an audio file that has been imported into UE5. It inherits from `Sound Base`.

- `Sound Cue`: An audio asset that can contain logic related to things such as attenuation (how the volume changes as the listener's distance varies), looping, sound mixing, and other audio-related functionality. It inherits from `Sound Base`.

- `Sound Class`: An asset that allows you to separate your audio files into groups and manage some of their settings, such as volume and pitch. An example of this would be grouping all your sounds related to sound effects in the `SFX` sound class, all your character dialog in the Dialog sound class, and so on.

- `Sound Attenuation`: An asset that allows you to specify how a 3D sound will behave; for example, at which distance it will start to lower the volume, at which distance it will become inaudible (can't be heard), whether its volume will change linearly or exponentially as the distance increases, and so on.

- `Audio Component`: An actor component that allows you to manage the playback of audio files and their properties. This is useful for setting up continuous playback of sounds, such as background music.

> **Note**
>
> UE5 has a new audio system called **Meta Sounds**, which allows developers to create sounds using **Digital Signal Processing** (**DSP**). Because this topic is outside the scope of this book, we will not be covering this system. If you want to know more about the system and how it works, you can do so by going to
>
> `https://docs.unrealengine.com/5.0/en-US/AudioFeatures/MetaSounds/`.

In UE5, we can import existing sounds the same way we would any other asset: either by dragging a file from Windows File Explorer into the **Content Browser** area or by clicking the **Import** button in the **Content Browser** area. We'll do this in the next exercise.

Exercise 9.01 – Importing an audio file

In this exercise, you will import an existing sound file from your computer into UE5. This audio file will be played when the dodgeball bounces off a surface.

> **Note**
>
> If you don't have an audio file (either a .mp3 or .wav file) available to complete this exercise, you can download the .mp3 or .wav file available at `https://www.freesoundeffects.com/free-track/bounce-1-468901/`.
>
> Save this file as BOUNCE.wav.

Once you have an audio file, follow these steps:

1. Open the editor.
2. Go to the `Content` folder inside the **Content Browser** area and create a new folder called `Audio`:

Figure 9.1 – The Audio folder in the Content Browser area

3. Go to the `Audio` folder you just created.

4. Import your audio file into this folder. You can do this by *dragging* the audio file from **Windows File Explorer** into **Content Browser**.

5. Once you've done this, a new asset should appear with the same name as your audio file, which you can listen to when clicking on it:

Figure 9.2 – The imported audio file

6. Open this asset. You should see many properties available for editing. However, we'll be focusing solely on some of the properties inside the **Sound** category:

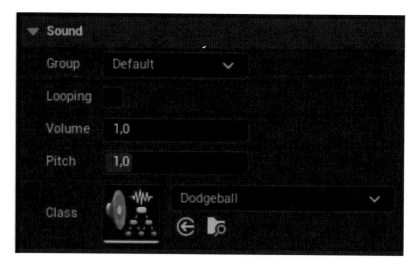

Figure 9.3 – The Sound asset's settings

The following properties are available in the **Sound** category:

- **Looping**: Whether this sound will loop while being played.

- **Volume**: The volume of this sound.

- **Pitch**: The pitch of this sound. The higher the pitch, the higher the frequency, and the higher in tone this sound will be.

- **Class**: The sound class of this sound.

The only property we'll be changing is the `Class` property. We could use one of the existing `Sound` classes that comes with UE5, but let's create our own for the `Dodgeball` game to create a new group of sounds for our game.

7. Go to the `Audio` folder inside the **Content Browser** area.

8. Right-click, go to the **Sounds** category (the penultimate category), then the **Classes** category, and select **Sound Class**. This will create a new `Sound Class` asset. Rename this asset `Dodgeball`.

9. Open your imported sound asset and set its **Class** property to `Dodgeball`:

Figure 9.4 – Changing the Class property to the Dodgeball Sound Class

Now that this imported sound asset belongs to a specific class, you can group other sound effects related to the dodgeball in the same `Sound Class` and edit their properties through that `Sound Class`, which includes `Volume`, `Pitch`, and many others.

And with that, we can conclude our exercise. You have learned how to import sounds into your project and how to change their basic properties. Now, let's move on to the next exercise, where we'll be playing a sound whenever a dodgeball bounces off a surface in our game.

Exercise 9.02 – Playing a sound when the dodgeball bounces off a surface

In this exercise, we will add the necessary functionality to our `DodgeballProjectile` class so that a sound will play when the dodgeball bounces off a surface.

To do this, follow these steps:

1. Close the editor and open Visual Studio.

2. In the header file for the `DodgeballProjectile` class, add a protected `class USoundBase*` property called `BounceSound`. This property should be a `UPROPERTY` and have the `EditDefaultsOnly` tag so that it can be edited in the Blueprint:

    ```
    // The sound the dodgeball will make when it bounces off
    of a
      surface
    UPROPERTY(EditAnywhere, Category = Sound)
    class USoundBase* BounceSound;
    ```

3. Once you've done this, go to the `DodgeballProjectile` class's source file and add an include for the `GameplayStatics` object:

    ```
    #include "Kismet/GameplayStatics.h"
    ```

4. Then, at the beginning of the class's implementation of the `OnHit` function, before the cast to the `DodgeballCharacter` class, check whether our `BounceSound` is a valid property (different than `nullptr`) and whether the magnitude of the `NormalImpulse` property is greater than `600` units (we can access the magnitude by calling its `Size` function).

    As we saw in *Chapter 6, Setting Up Collision Objects*, the `NormalImpulse` property indicates the direction and magnitude of the force that will change the dodgeball's trajectory after it has been hit. The reason why we want to check whether its magnitude is greater than a certain amount is that when the dodgeball starts losing momentum and bounces off the floor several times per second, we don't want to play `BounceSound` several times per second; otherwise, it will generate a lot of noise. So, we will check whether the impulse that the dodgeball is suffering is greater than that amount to make sure this doesn't happen. If both these things are true, we'll call the `GameplayStatics` object's `PlaySoundAtLocation`. This function is responsible for playing 3D sounds. It receives five parameters:

    *   A world context object, which we'll pass as the `this` pointer.

    *   A `SoundBase` property, which will be our `HitSound` property.

    *   The origin of the sound, which we'll pass using the `GetActorLocation` function.

    *   `VolumeMultiplier`, which we'll pass with a value of `1`. This value indicates how much higher or lower the volume of this sound will be when it's played. For instance, a value of 2 means it will have a volume twice as high.

- `PitchMultiplier`, which indicates how much higher or lower the pitch of this sound will be when it's played. We'll be passing this value by using the `FMath` object's `RandRange` function, which receives two numbers as parameters and returns a random number between those two. To randomly generate a number between `0.7` and `1.3`, we'll be calling this function with these values as parameters.

Have a look at the following code snippet:

```
if (BounceSound != nullptr && NormalImpulse.Size() >
600.0f)
{
   UGameplayStatics::PlaySoundAtLocation(this,
BounceSound,
   GetActorLocation(), 1.0f, FMath::RandRange(0.7f,
1.3f));
}
```

> **Note**
>
> The function responsible for playing 2D sounds is also available from the `GameplayStatics` object, and it's called `PlaySound2D`. This function will receive the same parameters as the `PlaySoundAtLocation` function, except for the third parameter, which is the origin of the sound.

5. Compile these changes and open Unreal Editor.

6. Open the `BP_DodgeballProjectile` Blueprint, go to its **Class Defaults** tab, and set the `BounceSound` property to the `Sound` asset you imported:

Figure 9.5 – Setting the BounceSound property to our imported sound

7. Play the level again and enter the enemy character's line of sight. You should notice a sound playing with different pitch values every time the dodgeball that's thrown by the enemy character hits a wall or the floor (not the player character):

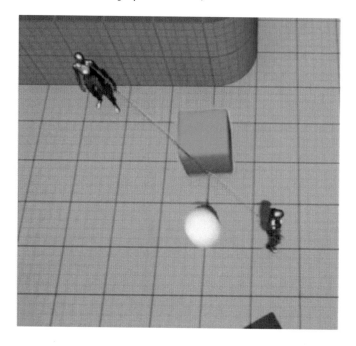

Figure 9.6 – The player character causing the enemy character to throw dodgeballs

If this happens, congratulations – you've successfully played a sound using UE5! If you can't hear the sound playing, make sure that it is audible (it has a level of volume that you can hear).

However, another thing you'll probably notice is that the sound is always played at the same volume, regardless of the distance that the character is from the dodgeball that is bouncing; the sound isn't playing in 3D but rather in 2D. To play a sound in 3D using UE5, we'll have to learn about **Sound Attenuation** assets.

Sound attenuation

For a sound to be played in 3D inside UE5, you'll have to create a **Sound Attenuation** asset, as we mentioned previously. A **Sound Attenuation** asset will let you specify how you want a specific sound to change volume as its distance from the listener increases. Have a look at the following example.

Open Unreal Editor, go to the `Audio` folder inside the **Content Browser** area, right-click, go to the **Sounds** category, and select **Sound Attenuation**. Name this new asset `BounceAttenuation`:

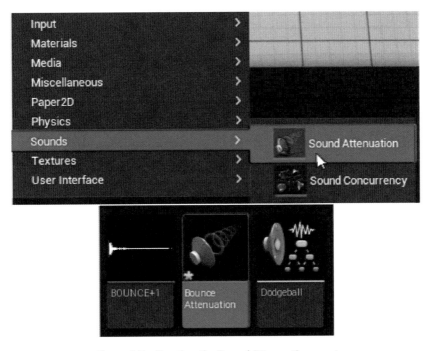

Figure 9.7 – Creating the Sound Attenuation asset

Open this `BounceAttenuation` asset.

Sound Attenuation assets have many settings; however, we'll want to focus mainly on a couple of settings from the **Attenuation Distance** section:

- `Inner Radius`: This `float` property allows us to specify at what distance the sound will start lowering in volume. If the sound is played at a distance less than this value, the volume won't be affected. Set this property to `200` units.

- Falloff Distance: This float property allows us to specify at what distance we want the sound to be inaudible. If the sound is played at a distance greater than this value, we won't hear it. The volume of the sound will vary according to its distance to the listener and whether it's closer to Inner Radius or Falloff Distance. Set this property to 1500 units:

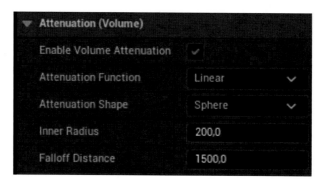

Figure 9.8 – The Sound Attenuation asset settings

Think of this as two circles around the player, with the smaller circle being the inner circle (with a radius value of Inner Radius) and the bigger circle being the falloff circle (with a radius value of Falloff Distance). If a sound originates from inside the inner circle, it is played at full volume, while a sound that originates from outside the falloff circle is not played at all.

> **Note**
> You can find more information on **Sound Attenuation** assets here: https://docs.
> unrealengine.com/en-US/Engine/Audio/DistanceModelAttenuation.

Now that you know about **Sound Attenuation** assets, let's move on to the next exercise, where we'll turn the sound that plays when the dodgeball bounces off the ground into a 3D sound.

Exercise 9.03 – Turning the bounce sound into a 3D sound

In this exercise, we'll be turning the sound that plays when a dodgeball bounces off the ground, which we added in the previous exercise, into a 3D sound. This means that when the dodgeball bounces off a surface, the sound it plays will vary in volume, depending on its distance from the player. We're doing this so that when the dodgeball is far away, the sound volume will be low, and when it's close, its volume will be high.

To use the BounceAttenuation asset we created in the previous section, follow these steps:

1. Go to the header file for DodgeballProjectile and add a protected class USoundAttenuation* property called BounceSoundAttenuation. This property should be a UPROPERTY and have the EditDefaultsOnly tag so that it can be edited in the Blueprint:

    ```
    // The sound attenuation of the previous sound
    UPROPERTY(EditAnywhere, Category = Sound)
    class USoundAttenuation* BounceSoundAttenuation;
    ```

2. Go to the DodgeballProjectile class's implementation of the OnHit function in its source file and add the following parameters to the call to the PlaySoundAtLocation function:

    *   StartTime, which we'll pass with a value of 0. This value indicates the time that the sound will start playing. If the sound lasts 2 seconds, we can have this sound start at its 1-second mark by passing a value of 1. We pass a value of 0 to have the sound play from the start.

    *   SoundAttenuation, to which we'll pass our BounceSoundAttenuation property:

    ```
    UGameplayStatics::PlaySoundAtLocation(this, BounceSound,
        GetActorLocation(), 1.0f, 1.0f, 0.0f,
        BounceSoundAttenuation);
    ```

> **Note**
>
> Although we only want to pass the additional SoundAttenuation parameter, we must pass all the other parameters that come before it as well.

3. Compile these changes and then open the editor.

4. Open the BP_DodgeballProjectile Blueprint, go to its **Class Defaults** tab, and set the BounceSoundAttenuation property to our BounceAttenuation asset:

Figure 9.9 – Setting the BounceSoundAttenuation property to the BounceAttenuation asset

5. Play the level again and enter the enemy character's line of sight. You should notice that the sound that plays every time the dodgeball thrown by the enemy character hits a wall or the floor will be played at different volumes, depending on its distance, and that you won't hear it if the dodgeball is far away:

Figure 9.10 – The player character causing the enemy character to throw dodgeballs

With that, we can conclude this exercise. You now know how to play 3D sounds using UE5. We'll add background music to our game in the next exercise.

Exercise 9.04 – Adding background music to our game

In this exercise, we will add game background music to our game. We will do this by creating a new Actor with an Audio component, which, as we mentioned earlier, is appropriate for playing background music. To achieve this, follow these steps:

1. Download the audio file located at `https://packt.live/3pg21sQ` and import it into the **Audio** folder of the **Content Browser** area, just like we did in *Exercise 9.01 – Importing an audio file*.

2. Right-click inside the **Content Browser** area and create a new C++ class with the `Actor` class as its parent class. Name this new class `MusicManager`.

3. When the files for this class are generated and Visual Studio has opened automatically, close the editor.

4. In the `MusicManager` class's header file, add a new `protected` property of the `class UAudioComponent *` type called `AudioComponent`. Make this a UPROPERTY and add the `VisibleAnywhere` and `BlueprintReadOnly` tags:

```
UPROPERTY(VisibleAnywhere, BlueprintReadOnly)
class UAudioComponent* AudioComponent;
```

5. In the `MusicManager` class's source file, add an `#include` for the `AudioComponent` class:

```
#include "Components/AudioComponent.h"
```

6. In the constructor for this class, change the `bCanEverTick` property to `false`:

```
PrimaryActorTick.bCanEverTick = false;
```

7. After this line, add a new one that creates the `AudioComponent` class by calling the `CreateDefaultSubobject` function and passing the `UAudioComponent` class as a template parameter and "`Music Component`" as a normal parameter:

```
AudioComponent =
    CreateDefaultSubobject<UAudioComponent>(TEXT("Music
    Component"));
```

8. After making these changes, compile your code and open the editor.

9. Go to the `ThirdPersonCPP | Blueprints` folder in the **Content Browser** area and create a new **Blueprint** class that inherits from the `MusicManager` class. Name it `BP_MusicManager`.

10. Open this asset, select its `Audio` component, and set that component's `Sound` property to your imported sound:

Figure 9.11 – The Sound property being updated

11. Drag an instance of the `BP_MusicManager` class into the level.

12. Play the level. You should notice the music start playing when the game starts and it should also loop automatically when it reaches the end (this is done due to the `Audio` component).

> **Note**
>
> **Audio** components will automatically loop whatever sound they're playing, so there's no need to change that `Sound` asset's `Looping` property.

With that, we've completed this exercise. You now know how to add simple background music to your game.

Now, let's jump into the next topic, which is Particle Systems.

Understanding Particle Systems

Let's talk about another very important element of many video games: Particle Systems.

In video game terms, a particle is essentially a position in a 3D space that can be represented with an image. A Particle System is a collection of many particles, potentially with different images, shapes, colors, and sizes. The following figure shows an example of two Particle Systems made in UE5:

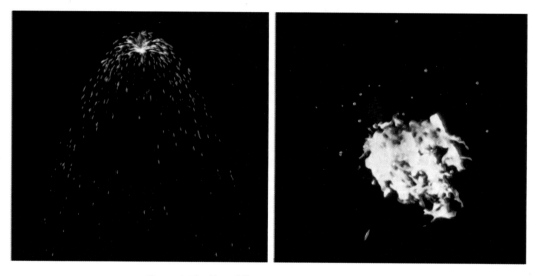

Figure 9.12 – Two different Particle Systems in UE5

The Particle System on the left is supposed to be electrical sparks that could come from a cable that has been sliced and is now in short-circuit, while the one on the right is supposed to be a fire. Although the particle system on the left is relatively simple, you can tell that the one on the right has more than one type of particle inside it, which can be combined in the same system.

> **Note**
>
> UE5 has two different tools for creating Particle Systems: **Cascade and Niagara**. Cascade has been present since the beginning of UE5, while Niagara is a system that is more recent and sophisticated and has only been production-ready since May 2020, as of Unreal Engine version 4.25.
>
> Creating Particle Systems in UE5 is outside the scope of this book, but it is recommended that you use Niagara over Cascade, given that it is a more recent addition to the engine.
>
> In this chapter, we will only be using Particle Systems that are already included in UE5, but if you want to create your own, these links will give you more information about both Cascade and Niagara:
>
> Cascade:
>
> ```
> https://docs.unrealengine.com/en-US/Engine/Rendering/
> ParticleSystems/Cascade
> ```
>
> ```
> https://www.youtube.com/playlist?list=PLZlv_N0_
> O1gYDLyB3LVfjYIcbBe8NqR8t
> ```
>
> Niagara:
>
> ```
> https://docs.unrealengine.com/en-US/Engine/Niagara/
> EmitterEditorReference/index.html
> ```
>
> ```
> https://docs.unrealengine.com/en-US/Engine/Niagara/QuickStart
> ```

We'll learn how to add Particle Systems to our game in the next exercise. In this chapter, we will simply be using existing Particle Systems that were already made by the UE5 team.

Exercise 9.05 – Spawning a Particle System when the dodgeball hits the player

In this exercise, we will learn how to spawn a Particle System in UE5. In this case, we will be spawning an `explosion` Particle System when a dodgeball thrown by the enemy hits the player.

To achieve this, follow these steps:

1. Close the editor and open Visual Studio.
2. In the `DodgeballProjectile` class's header file, add a protected `class UParticleSystem*` property called `HitParticles`.

The UParticleSystem type is the designation for a Particle System in UE5. Be sure to make this a UPROPERTY and give it the EditDefaultsOnly tag so that it can be edited in the Blueprint class:

```
// The particle system the dodgeball will spawn when it
hits
   the player
UPROPERTY(EditAnywhere, Category = Particles)
class UParticleSystem* HitParticles;
```

3. In the DodgeballProjectile class's source file, inside its implementation of the OnHit function, before the call to the Destroy function, check whether our HitParticles property is valid. If it is, call the GameplayStatics object's SpawnEmitterAtLocation function.

This function will spawn an actor that will play the Particle System we pass as a parameter. It receives the following parameters:

- A World object, which we'll pass using the GetWorld function

- A UParticleSystem* property, which will be our HitParticles property

- The FTransform of the actor that will play the Particle System, which we'll pass using the GetActorTransform function:

```
if (HitParticles != nullptr)
{
    UGameplayStatics::SpawnEmitterAtLocation(GetWorld(),
    HitParticles, GetActorTransform());
}
```

> **Note**
> Although we won't be using it in this project, there is another function related to spawning Particle Systems available from the GameplayStatics object, which is the SpawnEmitterAttached function. This function will spawn a Particle System and attach it to an actor, which might be useful if you want to, for instance, make a moving object light on fire so that the Particle System will always remain attached to that object.

4. Compile these changes and open the editor.

5. Open the BP_DodgeballProjectile Blueprint, go to its **Class Defaults** tab, and set the HitParticles property to the P_Explosion Particle System asset:

Figure 9.13 – Setting the HitParticles property to P_Explosion

6. Now, play the level and let your player character get hit by a dodgeball. You should see the explosion Particle System being played:

Figure 9.14 – The explosion particle system being played when the dodgeball hits the player

And that concludes this exercise. You now know how to play Particle Systems in UE5. Particle Systems add visual flair to your game and make it more visually appealing.

In the next activity, we'll be consolidating our knowledge of playing audio in UE5 by playing a sound when the dodgeball hits the player.

Activity 9.01 – Playing a sound when the dodgeball hits the player

In this activity, we will be creating the logic responsible for playing a sound every time the player character gets hit by a dodgeball. In a video game, it's very important to transmit the player's crucial information in many ways, so in addition to changing the player character's health bar, we'll also be playing a sound when the player gets hit so that the player knows that the character is taking damage.

To do this, follow these steps:

1.   Import a sound file that will be played when the player character gets hit into the `Audio` folder inside the **Content Browser** area.

> **Note**
>
> If you don't have a sound file, you can use the one available at `https://www.freesoundeffects.com/free-track/punch-426855/`.

2.   Open the `DodgeballProjectile` class's header file. Add a `SoundBase*` property, just like we did in *Exercise 9.02 – Playing a sound when the dodgeball bounces off a surface*, but this time, call it `DamageSound`.

3.   Open the `DodgeballProjectile` class's source file. In the `OnHit` function's implementation, once you've damaged the player character and before you call the `Destroy` function, check whether the `DamageSound` property is valid. If it is, call the `GameplayStatics` object's `PlaySound2D` function (mentioned in *Exercise 9.02 – Playing a sound when the dodgeball bounces off a surface*), passing `this` and `DamageSound` as the parameters to that function call.

4.   Compile your changes and open the editor.

5.   Open the `BP_DodgeballProjectile` Blueprint and set its `DamageSound` property to the sound file you imported at the start of this activity.

When you play the level, you should notice that every time the player gets hit by a dodgeball, you will hear the sound you imported being played:

Figure 9.15 – A sound should play when the player character gets hit

And with those steps complete, you have finished this activity and consolidated the use of playing both 2D and 3D sounds in UE5.

> **Note**
>
> The solution for this activity can be found on `https://github.com/PacktPublishing/ Elevating-Game-Experiences-with-Unreal-Engine-5-Second-Edition/ tree/main/Activity%20solutions`.

Now, let's wrap up this chapter by learning a bit about the concept of level design.

Exploring level design

Since *Chapter 5, Query with Line Traces*, which was related to our dodgeball game, we added a few game mechanics and gameplay opportunities, as well as some audio-visual elements, all of which were handled in this chapter. Now that we have all these game elements, we must bring them together into a level that can be played from start to finish by the player. To do that, let's learn a bit about level design and level blockouts.

Level design is a specific game design discipline that focuses on building levels in a game. The goal of a level designer is to make a level that is fun to play, introduces new gameplay concepts to the player by using the game mechanics built for that game, contains good pacing (a good balance of action-packed and relaxed gameplay sequences), and much more.

To test the structure of a level, level designers must build what is called a **level blockout**. This is a very simple and boiled-down version of the level that uses most of the elements that the final level will contain, but it is made using only simple shapes and geometry. This is so that it will be easier and less time-consuming to modify the level in case parts of it need to be changed:

Figure 9.16 – An example of a level blockout made in UE5 using BSP Brushes

> **Note**
> It should be noted that level design is its own specific game development skill and is worthy of its own book, of which there are quite a few, but diving into this topic is outside the scope of this book.

In the next exercise, we will be building a simple level blockout using the mechanics we built in the last few chapters.

Exercise 9.06 – Building a level blockout

In this exercise, we will be creating a new level blockout that will contain some structure, where the player will start in a certain place in the level and have to go through a series of obstacles to reach the end of the level. We will be using all the mechanics and objects that we built in the last few chapters to make a level that the player will be able to complete.

Although we will be providing you with a solution in this exercise, you are encouraged to let your creativity loose and come up with a solution yourself, given that there is no right or wrong answer in this case.

To start this exercise, follow these steps:

1. Open the editor.

2. Go to the `ThirdPersonCPP | Maps` folder in the **Content Browser** area, duplicate the `ThirdPersonExampleMap` asset, and name it `Level1`. You can do this by either selecting the asset and pressing *Ctrl + D* or by right-clicking on the asset and selecting **Duplicate** (the third option). This may not be available in some situations, so you'll have to do this by copying and pasting the existing level (*Ctrl + C* and *Ctrl + V*).

3. Open the newly created `Level1` map.

4. Delete all the objects that have a mesh inside the map, except for the following:

   - The `PlayerStart` object
   - The enemy character (note that both characters will look the same)
   - The `floor` object
   - Both `Wall` objects that we created
   - The `VictoryBox` object

   Keep in mind that assets related to lighting and sound should remain untouched.

5. Build the lighting for `Level1` by pressing the **Build** button. This button is to the left of the **Play** button, in the **Toolbar** area at the top of the editor window.

6. At this point, you should have an empty floor with just the objects you'll be needing for this level (the ones mentioned in *Step 4*). Here's the `Level1` map before and after you followed *Steps 4* and *5*, respectively:

Figure 9.17 – Before deleting the required objects

Once you have deleted the objects, your floor should look as follows:

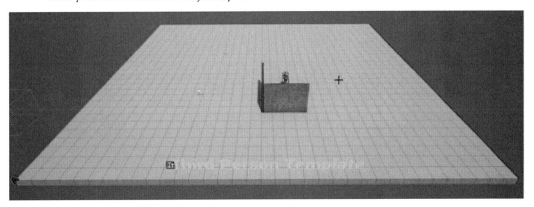

Figure 9.18 – After deleting the required objects

Because building a level, even a simple one, is something that takes a lot of steps and instructions, you will simply be shown a few screenshots of a possible level and, again, be encouraged to come up with your own.

7. In this case, we have simply used the existing `EnemyCharacter`, `Wall`, and `GhostWall` objects and duplicated them several times to create a simple layout that the player can traverse from start to finish. We also moved the `VictoryBox` object so that it matches the new level's end location:

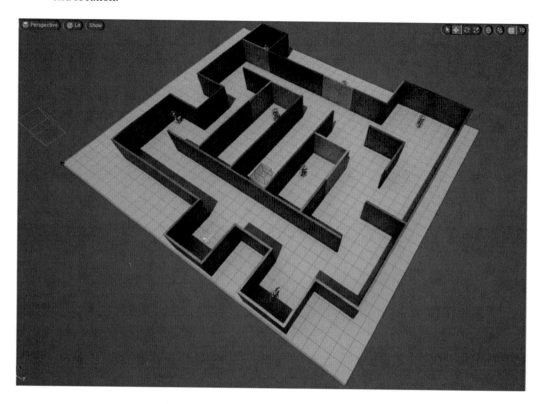

Figure 9.19 – The created level – isometric view

The level can be seen in a top-down view too, as follows:

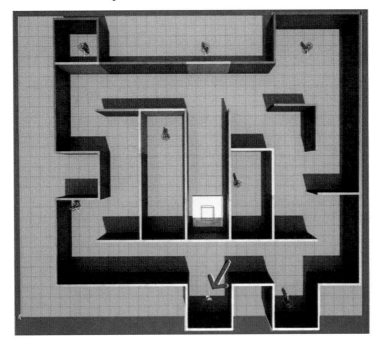

Figure 9.20 – The created level – top-down view with the player character marked with an arrow

Once you're happy with the result, this means you have finished your dodgeball game and can now ask your friends and family to play it and see what they think. Great job – you are one step closer to mastering the art of game development!

Extra features

Before we conclude this chapter, here are some suggestions on what you can do next in this dodgeball project:

- Make it so that the normal `Wall` class we created in *Chapter 6, Setting Up Collision Objects*, doesn't block the enemy's line of sight. This way, the enemy will always throw dodgeballs at the player, which should still be blocked from going through this wall.

- Add a new feature that will allow the player to visualize where the dodgeball thrown by the enemy character will impact first, using the concept of **Sweep Traces**.

- Add a new type of wall that blocks the player character, the enemy character, and the dodgeballs, but that also takes damage from dodgeballs and gets destroyed when it runs out of health points.

There is a whole world of possibilities for expanding the scope of this project. You are encouraged to use the skills you've learned and do further research to build new features and add more complexity to your game.

Summary

You have now completed the dodgeball game project. In this chapter, you learned how to add polish to your game by playing audio and using Particle Systems. You now know how to add 2D and 3D sounds to your game, as well as some of the tools at your disposal regarding that. Now, you can try to add even more sound effects to your game, such as a special sound effect for when an enemy character sees you for the first time (such as in *Metal Gear Solid*), a footstep sound effect, or a victory sound effect.

You also built a level using all the tools that you have made throughout the last few chapters, thus culminating all the logic we have built in this project.

In the next chapter, we'll be starting a new project: the `SuperSideScroller` game. In that project, you'll be introduced to such topics as power-ups, collectibles, enemy **artificial intelligence (AI)**, character animation, and much more. You will be creating a side-scrolling platform game where you control a character that must complete a level, collect gems, and use power-ups to avoid the enemies. The two most important topics you will learn about are UE5's behavior trees and Blackboards, which fuel the AI system, and Animation Blueprints, which allow you to manage your character's animations.

10

Creating the SuperSideScroller Game

So far, we have learned a lot about Unreal Engine, C++ programming, and general game development techniques. In the previous chapters, we covered collisions, tracing, how to use C++ with UE5, and even the Blueprint Visual Scripting system. On top of that, we gained crucial knowledge of skeletons, animations, and Animation Blueprints, all of which we will utilize in the upcoming project.

In this chapter, we will set up the project for a new SuperSideScroller game. You will be introduced to the different aspects of a side-scroller game, including power-ups, collectibles, and enemy AI, all of which we will be using in our project. You will also learn about the character animation pipeline in game development and learn how to manipulate the movement of our game's character.

For our newest project, SuperSideScroller, we will use many of the same concepts and tools that we have used in previous chapters to develop our game features and systems. Concepts such as collision, input, and the HUD will be at the forefront of our project; however, we will also be diving into new concepts involving animation to recreate the mechanics of popular side-scrolling games. The final project will be a culmination of everything we have learned thus far in this book.

In this chapter, we're going to cover the following main topics:

- Project breakdown
- The player character
- Exploring the features of our side-scroller game
- Understanding animations in Unreal Engine 5

By the end of this chapter, we'll have a better idea of what we want to accomplish with our SuperSideScroller game, and we will have the project foundation to begin development.

Technical requirements

For this chapter, you will need to have Unreal Engine 5 installed.

This chapter does not feature any C++ code, and all the exercises are performed within the UE5 editor. Let's begin this chapter with a brief breakdown of the `SuperSideScroller` project.

The project for this chapter can be found in the Chapter10 folder of the code bundle for this book, which can be downloaded here: `https://github.com/PacktPublishing/Elevating-Game-Experiences-with-Unreal-Engine-5-Second-Edition`.

Project breakdown

Let's consider the example of the classic game *Super Mario Bros*, released on the **Nintendo Entertainment System (NES)** console in 1985. For those unfamiliar with the franchise, the general idea is this: the player takes control of Mario, who must traverse the many hazardous obstacles and creatures of the Mushroom Kingdom in the hope of rescuing Princess Peach from the sinister King Koopa, Bowser.

> **Note**
> To have an even better understanding of how the game works, check out this video of its gameplay: `https://www.youtube.com/watch?v=rLl9XBg7wSs`.

The following are the core features and mechanics of games in this genre:

- **Two-Dimensional Movement**: The player can only move in the X and Y directions, using a 2D coordinate system. Refer to *Figure 10.1* to see a comparison of 2D and 3D coordinate systems if you are unfamiliar with them. Although our `SuperSideScroller` game will be in 3D and not pure 2D, the movement of our character will work identically to that of Mario, only supporting vertical and horizontal movement:

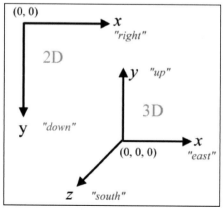

Figure 10.1 – A comparison of 2D and 3D coordinate vectors

- **Jumping**: Jumping is a crucial aspect of any platformer game, and our `SuperSideScroller` game will be no different. There are many different games, such as *Celeste, Hollow Knight*, and *Super Meat Boy*, as mentioned previously, that use the jumping feature – all of which are in 2D.

- **Character Power-Ups**: Without character power-ups, many side-scrolling games lose their sense of chaos and replayability. For instance, in the game *Ori and the Blind Forest*, the developers introduce different character abilities that change how the game is played. Abilities such as the triple-jump or the air dash open a variety of possibilities to navigate the level and allow level designers to create interesting layouts based on the movement abilities of the player.

- **Enemy AI**: Enemies with various abilities and behaviors are introduced to add a layer of challenge for the player, on top of the challenge of navigating the level solely through the use of the available movement mechanics.

> **Note**
>
> What are some ways that AI in games can interact with the player? For example, in *The Elder Scrolls V: Skyrim*, there are AI characters in various towns and villages that can have conversations with the player to exposit world-building elements such as history, sell items to the player, and even give quests to the player.

- **Collectibles**: Many games support collectible items in one form or another; *Sonic the Hedgehog* has rings, while *Ratchet & Clank* has bolts to collect. Our `SuperSideScroller` game will allow players to collect coins.

Now that we have evaluated the game mechanics that we want to support, we can break down the functionality of each mechanic as it relates to our `SuperSideScroller` game and what we need to do to implement these features.

The player character

At the core of any game is the player character; that is, the entity in which our player will interact and play our game. For our `SuperSideScroller` project, we will be creating a simple character with custom meshes, animations, and logic behind it to give it the proper feel for a side-scroller game.

Almost all of the functionality that we want for our character is given to us by default when using the `Side Scroller` game project template in UE5.

> **Note**
>
> At the time of writing, we are using Unreal Engine version 5.0.0; using another version of the engine could result in some differences in the editor, the tools, and how your logic will work later, so please keep this in mind.

In the next exercise, we will create our game project and set up our player character, while also exploring how we can manipulate the parameters of the character to improve upon its movement.

Converting the Third Person template into a side-scroller

Back in Unreal Engine 4, the engine came with a `Side-Scroller` template that could be used as the base template for the `SuperSideScroller` project; however, in UE5, no such template exists. As a result, we will be using the `Third Person` template project provided by UE5 and updating some parameters to make it look and feel like a side-scroller game.

Let's begin by creating our project.

Exercise 10.01 – Creating the side-scroller project and using the Character Movement component

In this exercise, you will be setting up UE5 with the `Third Person` template. This exercise will help you get started with our game.

Follow these steps to complete the exercise:

1. First, open the Epic Games Launcher, navigate to the **Unreal Engine** tab at the bottom of the options on the left-hand side, and select the **Library** option at the top.

2. Next, you will be prompted with a window asking you to either open an existing project or create a new project of a certain category. Among these options is the **Games** category; select this option for our project. With your project category selected, you will be prompted to select the template for your project.

3. Next, click on the **Third Person** option; because the **Side Scroller** template no longer exists, the **Third Person** template is the closest option we have.

    Lastly, we need to set up the default project settings before Unreal Engine will create our project for us.

4. Choose to base the project on `C++`, not `Blueprints`, include `Starter Content`, and use `Desktop/Console` as our platform. The remaining project settings can be left as their defaults. Select the desired location, name the project `SuperSideScroller`, and save the project in an appropriate directory of your choice.

5. After these settings are applied, select **Create Project**. When it's done compiling the engine, both Unreal Editor and Visual Studio will open, and we can move on to the next steps of this exercise:

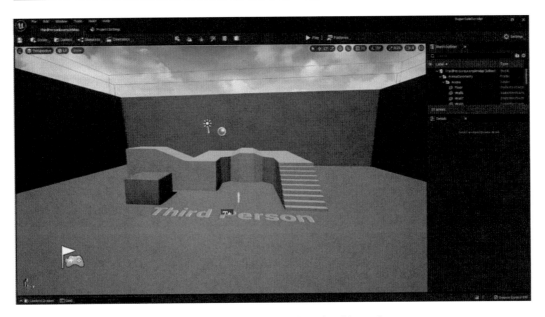

Figure 10.2 – The Unreal Engine editor should now be open

Now that our project has been created, we need to perform a handful of steps to change the Third Person template to a Side Scroller, starting with updating the input **Axis Mappings**. Follow these steps:

1. We can access **Axis Mappings** via **Project Settings** by selecting the **Edit** drop-down menu at the top-left of the editor and selecting the **Project Settings** option.

2. In **Project Settings**, we can find the **Input** option under the **Engine** category. Select the **Input** option to find the **Bindings** section, which contains both **Action** and **Axis Mappings** for the project:

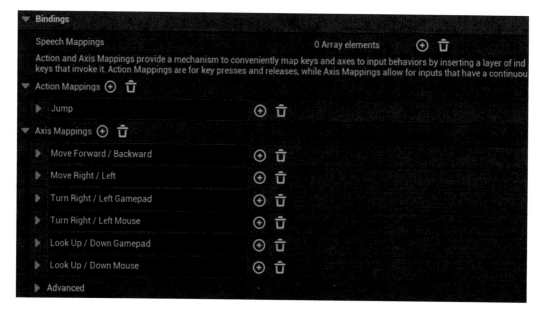

Figure 10.3 – The default Axis and Action Mappings

3. For the needs of the SuperSideScroller project, we simply have to remove **Axis Mappings** for MoveForward, TurnRate, Turn, LookUpRate, and LookUp. You can remove a mapping by left-clicking the garbage can icon next to it.

These mappings are unnecessary for our project due to the behavior of the character controls for a side-scroller game. Now that the mappings have been updated, we can update the parameters within the **ThirdPersonCharacter** Blueprint. Follow these steps:

1. Find the **ThirdPersonCharacter** Blueprint by opening the **Content Drawer** area and navigating to the Content/ThirdPersonCPP/Blueprints directory. Then, open the asset.

2. With the **ThirdPersonCharacter** Blueprint open, navigate to the **Components** tab and select the **Mesh** component. Find the **Rotation** parameter under the **Transform** category and set the **Yaw** value to -90.0f. The final rotation should be (Pitch=0.0,Yaw=-90.0,Roll=0.0). This will ensure that the character mesh will be facing the axis in which our side-scroller will move:

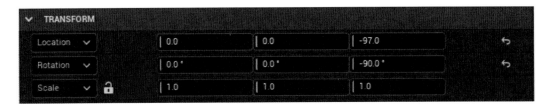

Figure 10.4 – The updated Rotation values of the Mesh component

3. Next, we need to update the parameters within the **Camera Boom** component so that we are facing the same axis as the character mesh. Select the component and find the **Rotation** parameter under the **Transform** category, similar to what we did in the previous step with the **Mesh** component. Set the **Yaw** value to `180.0f`, with the final rotation as `(Pitch=0.0,Yaw=180.0,Roll=0.0)`:

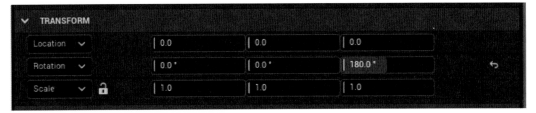

Figure 10.5 0 – The updated Rotation values of the Camera Boom component

4. Now, we need to update the **Target Arm Length** and **Socket Offset** parameters to adjust the positioning of the child **Follow Camera** component. Under the **Camera** category of the **Camera Boom** component, set **Target Arm Length** to `500.0f` and set the Z value of **Socket Offset** to `75.0f`. This will give us a good relative positioning of the **Follow Camera** component to the character mesh:

Figure 10.6 – The updated Target Arm Length and Target Offset parameters

5. The final parameter we need to update in the **Camera Boom** component is the **Do Collision Test** parameter, which determines whether the positioning of **Camera Boom** needs to be adjusted based on collisions it may have with the environment. For our project, we can set that parameter to `False`.

The next set of parameters can be within **Character Movement Component**, which we will talk about more later in this chapter. For now, all you need to know is that this component controls all aspects of the character's movement and allows us to customize it in a way to give us the game feel we desire. Follow these steps:

1. Select **Character Movement Component** at the bottom of the **Components** tab. Under the **General Settings** category of its **Details** panel, find **Gravity Scale** and set it to 2.0f. This will increase the gravity for our character:

Figure 10.7 – The updated Gravity Scale parameter

2. Next, we need to decrease the value of the **Ground Friction** parameter under the **Character Movement: Walking** section so that our character will turn a little slower. Set this parameter to 3.0f. The higher the value of **Ground Friction**, the more difficult it will be for the character to turn and move:

CHARACTER MOVEMENT: WALKING	
Max Step Height	45.0
Walkable Floor Angle	44.765083
Walkable Floor Z	0.71
Ground Friction	3.0

Figure 10.8 – The updated Ground Friction parameter

Let's adjust the parameters that control the jump velocity and the air control the player has while the character is in the air. We can find both parameters under **Character Movement: Jumping / Falling**. Let's increase **Jump Z Velocity** to 1000.0f, and **Air Control** to 0.8f. Updating these values gives our character an interesting jump height and movement while in the air:

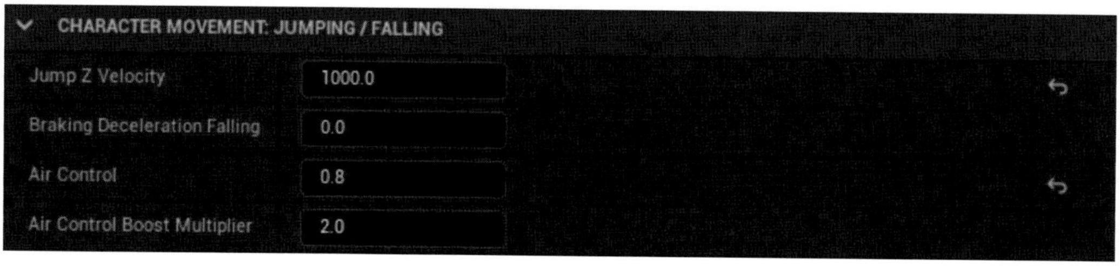

CHARACTER MOVEMENT: JUMPING / FALLING	
Jump Z Velocity	1000.0
Braking Deceleration Falling	0.0
Air Control	0.8
Air Control Boost Multiplier	2.0

Figure 10.9 – The updated Jump Z Velocity and Air Control parameters

The next set of parameters need to be set to help us later on in *Chapter 13, Creating and Adding the Enemy Artificial Intelligence*, when we work with **Nav Meshes**. Under the **Nav Movement** section of **Character Movement Component**, we need to update both **Nav Agent Radius** and **Nav Agent Height** to fit the bounds of **Capsule Component** on our player character. Follow these steps:

1. Set **Nav Agent Radius** to 42.0f and **Nav Agent Height** to 192.0f:

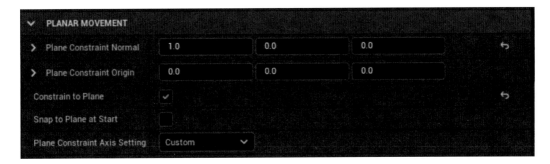

Figure 10.10 – The updated values of the Nav Agent Radius and Nav Agent Height parameters

2. Lastly, we need to adjust the **Planar Movement** section parameters to ensure that the player can only move in the axis that we want. Set **Constrain to Plane** to **True**, and then set the **X** value of **Plane Constraint Normal** to 1.0f; the final value will be (X=1.0f,Y=0.0,Z=0.0):

Figure 10.11 – The updated values of the Constrain to Plane and Plane Constraint Normal parameters

The final step is to add some simple Blueprint logic to the `Event Graph` area of `ThirdPersonCharacter` to allow our character to move from left to right. Follow these steps:

1. In the **Event Graph** area, right-click in an empty space of the graph to open the context-sensitive menu, where we will look for the **InputAxis MoveRight** event. Select the **InputAxis MoveRight** event to add it to the graph:

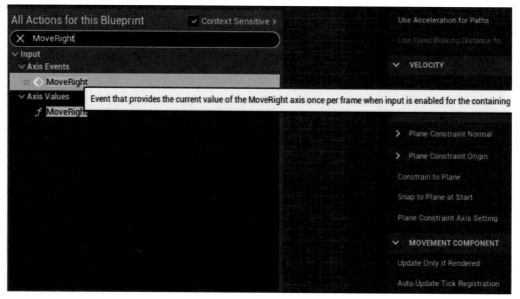

Figure 10.12 – This is the Axis Mapping we kept at the beginning of this exercise

2. The output parameter of the **InputAxis MoveRight** event is a float value called **Axis Value**. This returns a float value between 0 and 1, indicating the strength of the input in that direction. We will need to feed this value into a function called **Add Movement Input**. Right-click in another empty space and find this function to add it to the graph:

Figure 10.13 – The Add Movement Input function

3. Connect the **Axis Value** output parameter of the **InputAxis MoveRight** event to the **Scale Value** input parameter of the **Add Movement Input** function, then connect the white execution pins, as shown in the following screenshot. This allows us to add character movement in a specified direction, as well as strength:

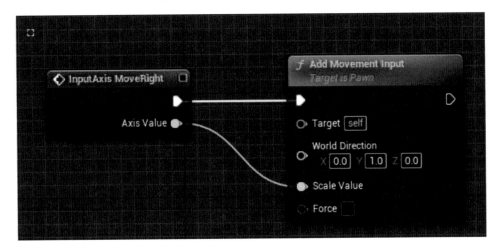

Figure 10.14 – The final Blueprint logic of our character

4. Lastly, we need to ensure that we pass in the right **World Direction** value; in our case, we need to set the *Y*-axis to 1.0f and leave the other axes at their default values of 0.0f.

Now that you have completed the exercise, you have experienced first-hand the control you have over how the character moves and how small tweaks to **Character Movement Component** can drastically change how the character feels! Try changing the values such as **Max Walk Speed** and observe in-game how such changes affect the character.

Activity 10.01 – Making our character jump higher

In this activity, we will be manipulating a new parameter (jump) that exists within the CharacterMovement component of the default Side Scroller Character Blueprint to observe how these properties affect how our character moves.

We will be implementing what we learned in the previous exercise and applying that to how to create our character power-ups and the general movement feel of our character.

Follow these steps to complete this activity:

1. Head to the SideScrollerCharacter Blueprint and find the **Jump Z Velocity** parameter in the CharacterMovement component.

2. Change this parameter from the default value of 1000.0f to 2000.0f.

3. Compile and save the `SideScrollerCharacter` Blueprint and play it in the editor. Observe how high our character can jump using the *space bar* on your keyboard.

4. Stop playing in the editor, return to the `SideScrollerCharacter` Blueprint, and update **Jump Z Velocity** from a value of `2000.0f` to `200.0f`.

5. Compile and save the Blueprint again, play it in the editor, and watch the character jump.

Expected output:

Figure 10.15 – The expected output with the jumping character

---

Note

The solution to this activity can be found on GitHub here: `https://github.com/PacktPublishing/Elevating-Game-Experiences-with-Unreal-Engine-5-Second-Edition/tree/main/Activity%20solutions`.

Now that we have completed this activity, we have a better understanding of how making a few changes to the `CharacterMovement` component parameters can affect our player character. We can use this later on when we need to give our character basic movement behaviors such as **Walking Speed** and **Jump Z Velocity** to achieve the character feel we want. Before moving on, return the **Jump Z Velocity** parameter to its default value `1000.0f`.

We will also keep these parameters in mind when we develop our player character power-ups later in our project.

Now that we have established our game project and player character, let's explore the other features of our `SuperSideScroller` game.

Exploring the features of our side-scroller game

Now, we'll take some time to lay out the specifics of the game we'll be designing. Many of these features will be implemented in later chapters, but now is a good time to lay out the vision for the project. In the following sections, we will be discussing how we want to handle the different aspects of our game, such as the enemies the player will face, the power-ups available to the player, the collectibles for the player to collect, and how the **user interface** (**UI**) will work. Let's begin by discussing the enemy character.

Enemy character

One thing you should have noticed while playing the `SuperSideScroller` project is that there is no enemy AI by default. Let's discuss the type of enemy we will want to support and how they will work.

The enemy will have a basic back-and-forth movement pattern and will not support any attacks; only by colliding with the player character will they be able to inflict any damage. However, we need to set the two locations to move between for the enemy AI, as well as decide whether the AI should change locations. Should they constantly move between locations, or should there be a pause before selecting a new location to move to? In *Chapter 13, Creating and Adding the Enemy Artificial Intelligence*, we will use the tools available in UE5 to develop this AI logic.

Power-ups

The `SuperSideScroller` game project will support one type of power-up, in the form of a potion that the player can pick up from the environment. This potion power-up will increase the movement speed of the player and the maximum height to which the player can jump. These effects will only last a short duration before they are removed.

Keeping in mind what you implemented in *Exercise 10.01 – Creating the side-scroller project and using the Character Movement component*, and *Activity 10.01 – Making our character jump higher*, for the `CharacterMovement` component, you could develop a power-up that changes the effect of gravity on the character, which would provide interesting new ways to navigate the level and combat enemies.

Collectibles

Collectibles in video games serve different purposes. In some cases, collectibles are used as a form of currency to purchase upgrades, items, and other goods. In others, collectibles serve to improve your score or reward you when enough collectibles have been collected. For the SuperSideScroller game project, the coins will serve a single purpose: to give the player the goal of collecting as many coins as they can without being destroyed by the enemy.

Let's break down the main aspects of our collectible:

- The collectible needs to interact with our player; this means that we need to use collision detection for the player to collect it and for us to add information to our UI.

- The collectible needs a visual static mesh representation so that the player can identify it in the level.

The final element of our SuperSideScroller project is the brick block. The brick block will serve the following purposes for the SuperSideScroller game:

- Bricks are used as an element of the level's design. Bricks can be used to access otherwise unreachable areas; enemies can be placed on different elevated sections of bricks to provide variation in gameplay.

- Bricks can contain collectible coins. This gives the player an incentive to try and see which blocks contain collectibles and which do not.

Heads-Up Display (HUD)

The HUD UI can be used to display important and relevant information to the player, based on the type of game and the mechanics that you support. For the SuperSideScroller project, there will be one HUD element, which will show the player how many coins they have collected. This UI will be updated each time the player collects a coin, and it will reset back to 0 when the player is destroyed.

Now that we have laid out some of the specifics that we will be working toward as part of this project, let's learn more about the default skeletal mesh provided by the project template in UE5.

Exercise 10.02 – Exploring the Persona Editor and manipulating the default mannequin skeleton weights

Now that we have a better understanding of the different aspects of the SuperSideScroller project, let's go ahead and take a deeper look into the default mannequin skeletal mesh that is given to us in the **Side Scroller** template project.

Our goal here is to learn more about the default skeletal mesh and the tools that are given to us in the Persona Editor so that we have a better understanding of how bones, bone weighting, and skeletons work inside UE5.

Follow these steps to complete the exercise:

1. Open Unreal Editor and navigate to **Content Drawer**.

2. Navigate to the `/Characters/Mannequins/Meshes/` folder and open the `SK_Mannequin` asset:

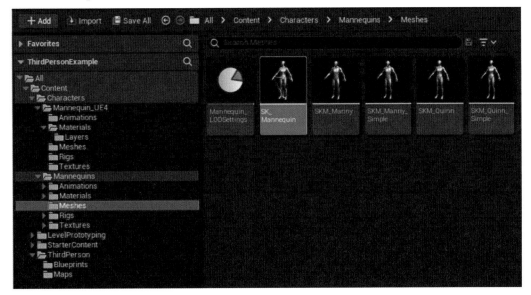

Figure 10.16 – The SK_Mannequin asset is highlighted and visible here

Upon opening the **Skeleton** asset, the **Persona Editor** area will appear:

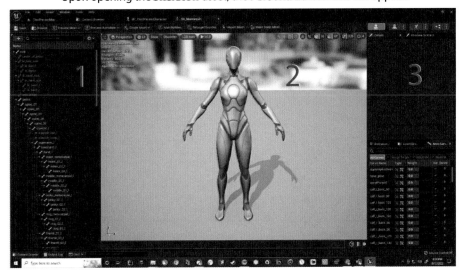

Figure 10.17 – The Persona Editor

Let's briefly break down the Skeleton Editor of the Persona Editor:

- On the left-hand side (*marked with a 1*), we can see the hierarchy of bones that exist in the skeleton. This is the skeleton that was made during the rigging process of this character. The `root` bone, as its name suggests, is the root of the skeletal hierarchy. This means that transformative changes to this bone will affect all of the bones in the hierarchy. From here, we can select a bone or a section of bones and see where they are on the character mesh.

- Next, we see the **Skeletal Mesh** preview window (*marked with a 2*). It shows us our character mesh, and there are several additional options that we can toggle on/off that will give us a preview of our skeleton and weight painting.

- On the right-hand side (*marked with a 3*), we have basic transformation options where we can modify individual bones or groups of bones. If the **Details** panel is not available, navigate to the **Window** tab at the top of the Persona Editor; you will find it in the list of options there. There are additional settings available that we will take advantage of in the next exercise. Now that we know more about what it is and what we are looking at, let's see what the actual skeleton looks like on our mannequin.

3.   Navigate to **Character**, as shown in *Figure 10.10*:

Figure 10.18 – The Character options menu

This menu allows you to display the skeleton of the mannequin over the mesh itself.

4.   From the drop-down menu, select the **Bones** option. Then, make sure the option for **All Hierarchy** is selected. With this option selected, you will see the outlined skeleton rendering above the mannequin mesh:

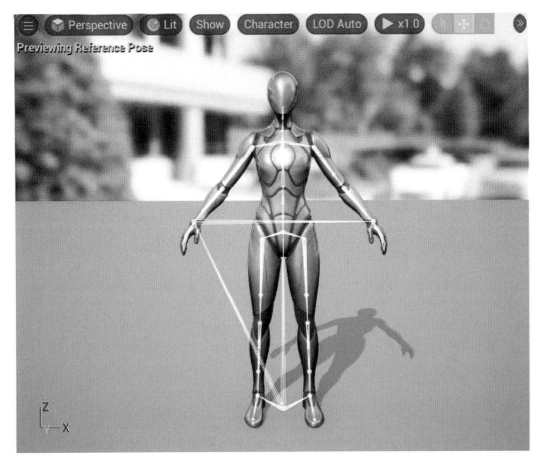

Figure 10.19 – The skeleton overlayed on top of the mannequin Skeletal Mesh

5. Now, hide the mesh and simply preview the skeletal hierarchy, for which we can disable the **Mesh** property:

    • Navigate to **Character** and, from the drop-down menu, select the **Mesh** option.

- Deselect the option for **Mesh**. The result should be as follows:

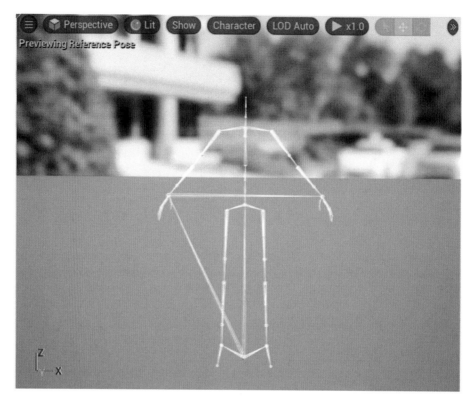

Figure 10.20 – The skeletal hierarchy of the default character

For this exercise, let's toggle the **Mesh** visibility back on so that we can see both the mesh and the skeleton hierarchy.

Finally, we'll look at the weight scaling for our default character.

6. To preview this, navigate to **Character** and, from the drop-down menu, select the **Mesh** option. Then, select the **Selected Bone Weight** option toward the bottom in the **Mesh Overlay Drawing** section:

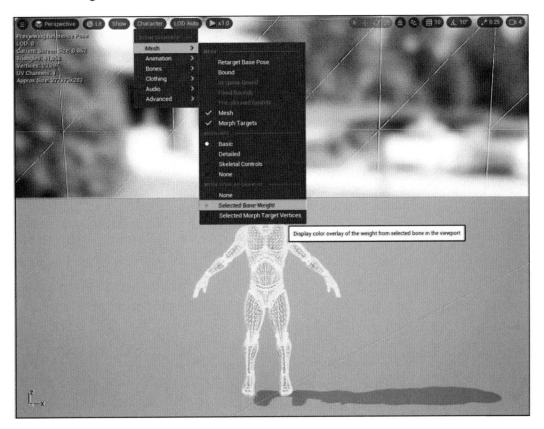

Figure 10.21 – The Selected Bone Weight option

7. Now, if we select a bone or a group of bones from our hierarchy, we can see how each bone affects a certain area of our mesh:

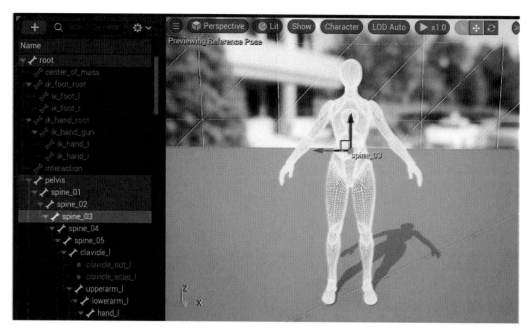

Figure 10.22 – This is the weight scaling for the spine_03 bone

You will notice that when we are previewing the weight scaling for a particular bone, there is a spectrum of colors across different sections of the Skeletal Mesh. This is the weight scaling shown visually instead of numerically. Colors such as `red`, `orange`, and `yellow` indicate larger weighting for a bone, meaning that the highlighted area of the mesh in these colors will be more affected. In areas that are `blue`, `green`, and `cyan`, they will still be affected, but not as significantly. Lastly, areas that have no overlay highlight will not be affected at all by the manipulation of the selected bone. Keep the hierarchy of the skeleton in mind –even though the left arm does not have an overlay color, it will still be affected when you are rotating, scaling, and moving the `spine_03` bone, since the arms are children of the `spine_03` bone. Please refer to the following screenshot to see how the arms are connected to the spine:

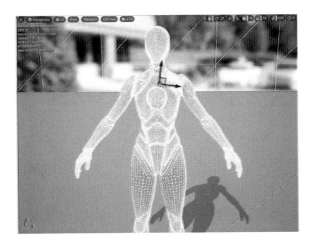

Figure 10.23 – The clavicle_l and clavicle_r bones are children of the spine_03 bone

Let's continue by manipulating one of the bones on the mannequin Skeletal Mesh and see how these changes affect its animation. Follow these steps:

1. In the **Persona Editor** area, left-click the `thigh_l` bone in the skeletal hierarchy:

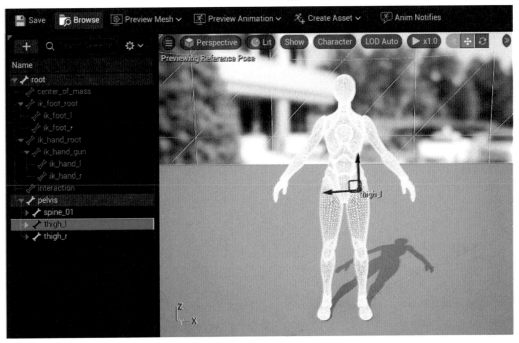

Figure 10.24 – Here, the thigh_l bone is selected

With the `thigh_l` bone selected, we have a clear indication of how the weight scaling will affect other parts of the mesh. Also, because of how the skeleton is structured, any modifications to this bone will not impact the upper body of the mesh:

Figure 10.25 – On the skeletal bone hierarchy, the thigh_l bone is a child of the pelvis bone

2. Using our knowledge from earlier chapters, change the **Local Location**, **Local Rotation**, and **Scale** values to offset the transform of the `thigh_l` bone. The following screenshot shows an example of the values you can use:

Figure 10.26 – The thigh_l values updated

After making these changes to the bone transform, you will see that the mannequin's left leg has completely changed and looks ridiculous:

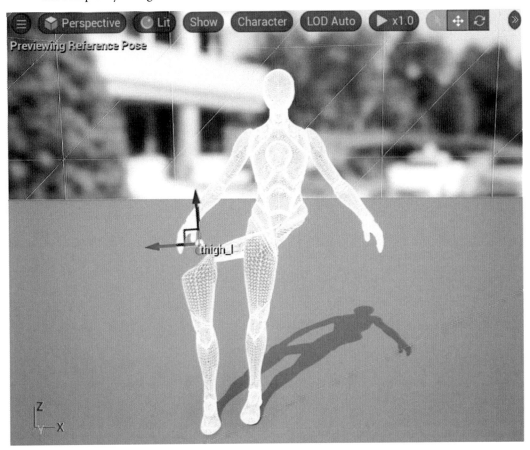

Figure 10.27 – The left leg of the mannequin has completely changed

3. Next, in the **Details** panel, go to the **Preview Scene Settings** tab. Upon left-clicking this tab, you will see new options, displaying some default parameters and an **Animation** section. If **Preview Scene Settings** is not available, navigate to the **Window** tab at the top of the **Persona Editor** area; you will find it in the list of options there.

4. Use the **Animation** section to preview animations and how they are affected by the changes that are made to the skeleton. For the **Preview Controller** parameter, change that to the **Use Specific Animation** option. By doing this, a new option labeled **Animation** will appear. The **Animation** parameter allows us to choose an animation associated with the character skeleton to preview.

5. Next, left-click on the drop-down menu and select the `MF_Walk_Fwd` animation.

6. Finally, you will see the mannequin character playing the walking animation, but their left leg is completely misplaced and mis-scaled:

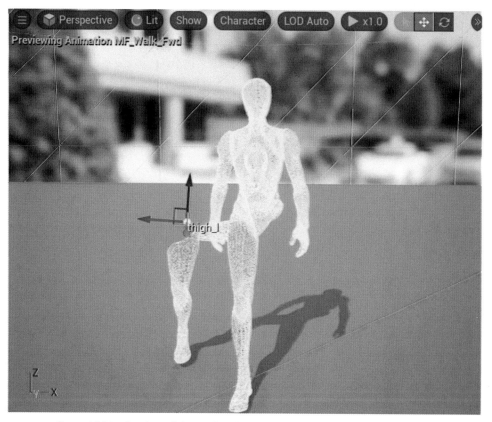

Figure 10.28 – Preview of the updated animation for the mannequin character

Before moving on, make sure to return the `thigh_l` bone to its original **Local Location**, **Local Rotation**, and **Scale**; otherwise, the animations moving forward will not look correct.

Now that you have completed the final part of our second exercise, you have experienced first-hand how skeletal bones affect characters and animations.

Now, let's move on to our second activity. Here, we will manipulate a different bone on the mannequin character and observe the results of applying different animations.

Activity 10.02 – Skeletal bone manipulation and animations

For this activity, we will put the knowledge we have gained about manipulating bones on the default mannequin into practice and affect how the animations are played out on the skeleton.

Follow these steps to complete this activity:

1. Select the bone that will affect the entire skeleton.

2. Change the scale of this bone so that the character is half its original size. Use these values to change **Scale** to (X=0.500000, Y=0.500000, Z=0.500000).

3. Apply the running animation to this Skeletal Mesh from the **Preview Scene Settings** tab and observe the animation for the half-sized character.

   Here is the expected output:

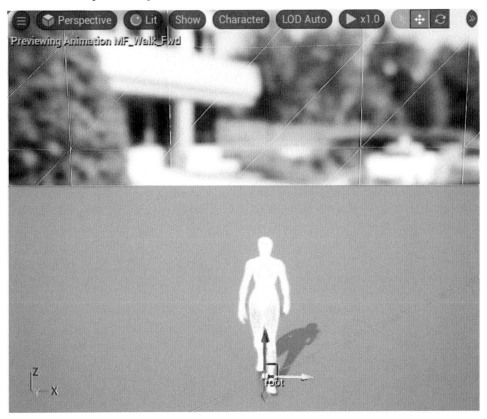

Figure 10.29 – The character has been halved in size and is performing the running animation

> **Note**
>
> The solution to this activity can be found on GitHub here: `https://github.com/PacktPublishing/Elevating-Game-Experiences-with-Unreal-Engine-5-Second-Edition/tree/main/Activity%20solutions`.

With this activity complete, you now have practical knowledge of how bone manipulation of skeletons and Skeletal Meshes affects how animations are applied. You have also seen first-hand the effects weight scaling have on the bones of a skeleton.

Now that we have some experience with Skeletal Meshes, skeletons, and animations within UE5, let's have a deeper discussion about these elements and how they work.

Understanding animations in Unreal Engine 5

Let's break down the main aspects of animations as they function inside Unreal Engine. More in-depth information about the topics in this section can be found in the documentation that is available directly from Epic Games: `https://docs.unrealengine.com/en-US/Engine/Animation`.

Skeletons

Skeletons are Unreal Engine's representation of the character rig that was made in external 3D software; we saw this in *Activity 10.02 – Skeletal bone manipulation and animations*. There isn't much more to skeletons that we haven't discussed already, but the main takeaway is that once the skeleton is in the engine, we can view the skeleton hierarchy, manipulate each bone, and add objects known as sockets. What sockets allow us to do is attach objects to the bones of our character. We can use these sockets to attach objects such as meshes and manipulate the transformation of the sockets without disrupting the bones' transformation. In first-person shooters, typically, a weapon socket is made and attached to the appropriate hand.

Skeletal Meshes

A Skeletal Mesh is a specific kind of mesh that combines the 3D character model and the hierarchy of bones that make up its skeleton. The main difference between a Static Mesh and a Skeletal Mesh is that Skeletal Meshes are required for objects that use animations, while Static Meshes cannot use animations due to their lack of a skeleton. We will look more into our main character Skeletal Mesh in the next chapter, but we will be importing our main character Skeletal Mesh in *Activity 10.03 – Importing more custom animations to preview the character running*, later in this chapter.

Animation sequences

Finally, an animation sequence is an individual animation that can be played on a specific Skeletal Mesh; the mesh it applies to is determined by the skeleton selected while importing the animation into the engine. We will look at importing a character Skeletal Mesh and a single animation asset together in *Activity 10.03 – Importing more custom animations to preview the character running*.

Included in our animation sequence is a timeline that allows us to preview the animation frame by frame, with additional controls to pause, loop, rewind, and so on.

In the next exercise, you will import a custom character and an animation. The custom character will include a Skeletal Mesh and a skeleton, and the animation will be imported as an animation sequence.

Exercise 10.03 – Importing and setting up the character and animation

For our final exercise, we will import our custom character and a single animation that we will use for the `SuperSideScroller` game's main character, as well as create the necessary Character Blueprint and Animation Blueprint.

> **Note**
>
> Included with this chapter is a set of files in a folder labeled `Assets`, and it is these files that we will import into the engine. These assets come from Mixamo: `https://www.mixamo.com/`. Feel free to create an account and view the free 3D character and animation content available there.
>
> The `Assets` content is available in this book's GitHub repository: `https://github.com/PacktPublishing/Elevating-Game-Experiences-with-Unreal-Engine-5-Second-Edition`.

Follow these steps to complete this exercise:

1. Open Unreal Editor.

2. In the **Content Drawer** area, create a new folder named `MainCharacter`. Within this folder, create two new folders called `Animation` and `Mesh`. The **Content Browser** area should now look as follows:

Figure 10.30 – Folders added to the MainCharacter directory in the Content Browser area

3. Next, let's import our character mesh. Inside the `Mesh` folder, right-click and select the **Import** option. This will open the **File Explorer** menu. Navigate to the directory where you saved the `Assets` folder that accompanies this chapter and find the `MainCharacter.fbx` asset inside the `Character Mesh` folder – for example, `\Assets\Character Mesh\ MainCharacter.fbx` – and open that file.

4. When selecting this asset, the **FBX Import Options** window will appear. Make sure that the options for `Skeletal Mesh` and `Import Mesh` are set to `check` in their respective checkboxes and leave every other option set to its default setting.

5. Lastly, we can select the **Import** option so that our FBX asset will be imported into the engine. This will include the necessary materials created within the FBX; a `Physics Asset`, which will automatically be created for us and assigned to `Skeletal Mesh`; and a `Skeleton Asset`.

> **Note**
> Ignore any warnings that may appear when importing the FBX file; they are unimportant and will not affect our project moving forward.

Now that we have our character, let's import an animation. Follow these steps:

1. Inside our `Animation` folder in the `MainCharacter` folder directory, right-click and select **Import**.

2. Navigate to the directory where you saved the `Assets` folder that accompanies this chapter and locate the `Idle.fbx` asset inside the `Animations/Idle` folder – for example, \ `Assets\Animations\Idle\Idle.fbx` – and open that file.

    When selecting this asset, an almost identical window will appear as when we imported our character Skeletal Mesh. Since this asset is only an animation and not a Skeletal Mesh/ skeleton, we don't have the same options as before, but there is one crucial parameter that we need to set correctly: `Skeleton`.

    The `Skeleton` parameter under the **Mesh** category of our **FBX** import options tells the animation to which skeleton the animation applies. Without this parameter set, we cannot import our animation, and applying the animation to the wrong skeleton can have disastrous results or cause the animation to not import altogether. Luckily for us, our project is simple, and we have already imported our character's Skeletal Mesh and skeleton.

3. Select `MainCharacter_Skeleton` and choose **Import All** at the bottom; leave all the other parameters set to their defaults:

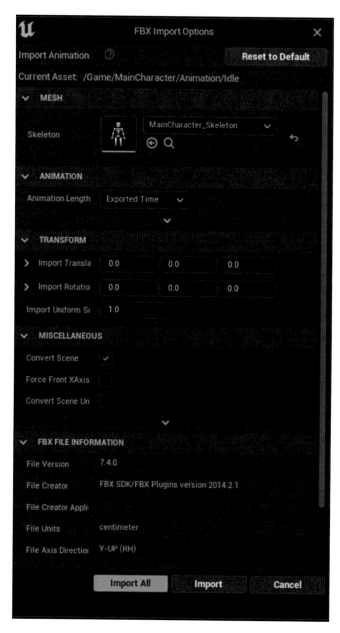

Figure 10.31 – The settings when importing the Idle.fbx animation

Understanding the importing process for both skeletal meshes and animations is crucial, and in the next activity, you will import the remaining animations. Let's continue this exercise by creating both the Character Blueprint and the Animation Blueprint for the SuperSideScroller game's main character.

Now, although the **Side Scroller** template project does include a Blueprint for our character and other assets such as an Animation Blueprint, we will want to create our own versions of these assets for the sake of organization and good practice as game developers.

4. Create a new folder under our MainCharacter directory in the **Content Drawer** area and name this folder Blueprints. In this directory, create a new Blueprint based on the SideScrollerCharacter class under All Classes. Name this new Blueprint BP_SuperSideScroller_MainCharacter:

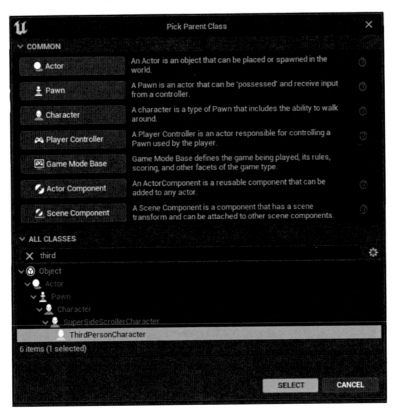

Figure 10.32 – The SideScrollerCharacter class to be used as the parent class for our character Blueprint

5. In our `Blueprints` directory, right-click in an empty area of the **Content Browser** area, hover over the **Animation** option, and select **Animation Blueprint**:

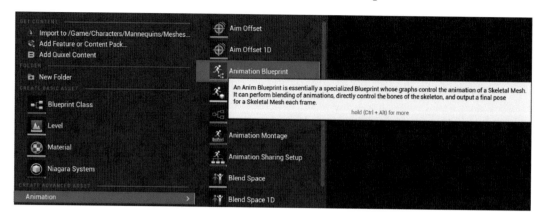

Figure 10.33 – The Animation Blueprint option under the Animation category

6. After we select this option, a new window will appear. This new window requires us to apply a parent class and a skeleton to our Animation Blueprint. In our case, use `MainCharacter_Skeleton`, select **OK**, and name the Animation Blueprint asset `AnimBP_SuperSideScroller_MainCharacter`:

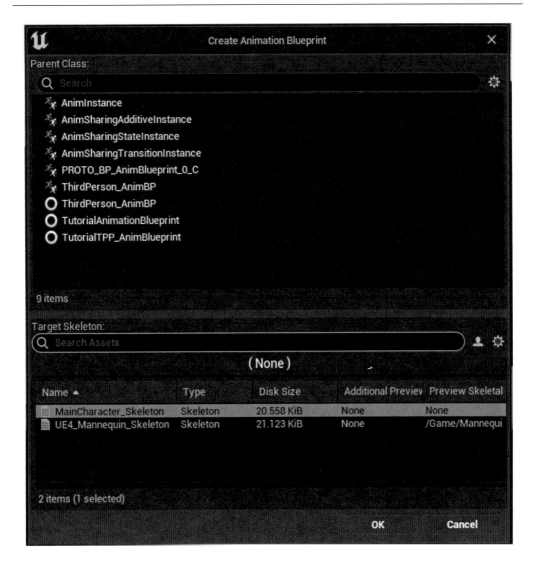

Figure 10.34 – The settings we need when creating our Animation Blueprint

7. When we open our Character Blueprint, BP_SuperSideScroller_MainCharacter, and select the **Mesh** component, we will find a handful of parameters that we can change:

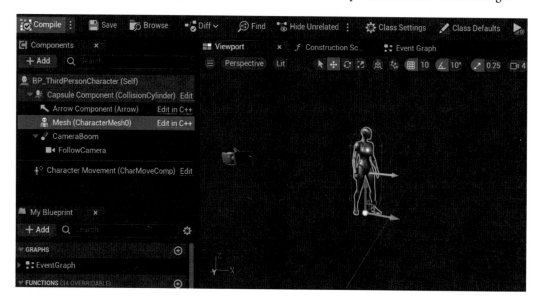

Figure 10.35 – The SuperSideScroller Character Blueprint using the mannequin Skeletal Mesh

8. Under the **Mesh** category, we have the option to update the Skeletal Mesh. Find our MainCharacter Skeletal Mesh and assign it to this parameter:

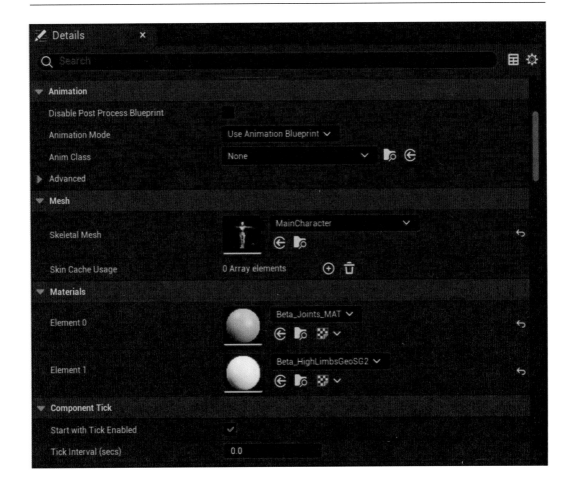

Figure 10.36 – The settings we need for our Mesh component

While still in our Character Blueprint and with the **Mesh** component selected, we can find the **Animation** category just above the **Mesh** category. Luckily, by default, the **Animation Mode** parameter is already set to **Use Animation Blueprint**, which is the setting we need.

9. Now, assign the `Anim` class parameter to our new Animation Blueprint, `AnimBP_ SuperSideScroller_MainCharacter`. Finally, head back to our default `SideScrollerExampleMap` level and replace the default character with our new Character Blueprint.

10. Next, make sure that we have `BP_SuperSideScroller_MainCharacter` selected in the **Content Browser** area, right-click on the default character in our map, and choose to replace it with our new character:

With our new character in the level, we can play in the editor and move around the level. The result should look something like what's shown in the following screenshot; our character is in the default T-pose and moving around the level environment:

Figure 10.37 – You now have the custom character running around the level

With our final exercise complete, you have a full understanding of how to import custom Skeletal Meshes and animations. Additionally, you learned how to create a Character Blueprint and an Animation Blueprint from scratch and how to use those assets to create the base for the SuperSideScroller character.

Let's move on to the final activity of this chapter, where you will be challenged to import the remaining animations for the character and preview the running animation inside Persona Editor.

Activity 10.03 – Importing more custom animations to preview the character running

This activity aims to import the remaining animations, such as running for the player character, and preview the running animation on the character skeleton to ensure that it looks correct.

By the end of the activity, all of the player character animations will be imported into the project and you will be ready to use these animations to bring the player character to life in the next chapter.

Follow these steps to complete this activity:

1. As a reminder, all of the animation assets we need to import exist in the `\Assets\Animations` directory, wherever you may have saved the original .zip folder. Import all of the remaining animations in the `MainCharacter/Animation` folder. Importing the remaining animation assets will work the same way as in *Exercise 10.03 – Importing and setting up the character and animation*, when you imported the `Idle` animation.

2. Navigate to the `MainCharacter` skeleton and apply the `Running` animation you imported in the previous step.

3. Finally, with the `Running` animation applied, preview the character animation in the **Persona Editor** area.

    Here is the expected output:

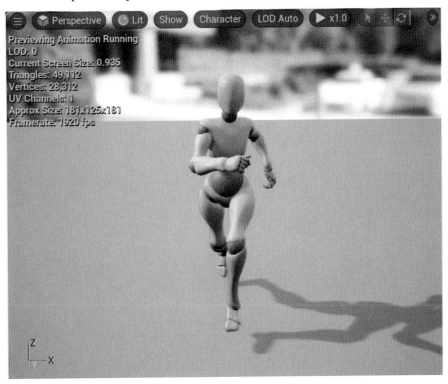

Figure 10.38 – The expected output of the character with additional custom imported assets

> **Note**
>
> The solution to this activity can be found on GitHub here: `https://github.com/PacktPublishing/Elevating-Game-Experiences-with-Unreal-Engine-5-Second-Edition/tree/main/Activity%20solutions`.

With this final activity completed, you have now experienced first-hand the process of importing custom skeletal and animation assets into UE5. This import process, regardless of the type of asset you are importing, is commonplace in the games industry, and you must be comfortable with it.

Summary

With the player character skeleton, Skeletal Mesh, and animations imported into the engine, we can move on to the next chapter, where we will prepare the character movement and Update Animation Blueprint so that the character can animate while moving around the level.

From the exercises and activities of this chapter, you learned about how the skeleton and bones are used to animate and manipulate the character. With first-hand experience in importing and applying animations in UE5, you now have a strong understanding of the animation pipeline, from the character concept to the final assets being imported for your project.

We also took the necessary steps to outline what we want to accomplish with our `SuperSideScroller` game; that is, establishing how we want enemies to work, which power-ups to develop, how collectibles will work, and how the player HUD will look. Lastly, we explored how the character movement component works and how to manipulate its parameters to establish the character movement we desire for our game.

Additionally, you learned about what we will use in the next chapter, such as blend spaces for character movement animation blending. With the `SuperSideScroller` project template created and the player character ready, in the next chapter, we'll animate the character with an Animation Blueprint.

11
Working with Blend Space 1D, Key Bindings, and State Machines

In the previous chapter, we had a high-level look at animation and developing the game design for our `SuperSideScroller` project. You were provided with just the beginning steps in terms of developing the project itself. Then, you prepared the player character's Animation Blueprint and character Blueprint, and also imported all of the required skeletal and animation assets.

In this chapter, we will set up the walking and jumping animations of our player character so that the movement has a sense of locomotion. To accomplish this, you will be introduced to **Blend Spaces**, **Animation Blueprints**, and **Animation State Machines**, the three pillars behind how character animations are controlled.

At this point, the character can move around the level, but is stuck in the T-Pose and does not animate at all. This can be fixed by creating a new Blend Space for the player character, which will be done in the very first exercise of this chapter. Once the Blend Space is complete, you will use it to implement the character Animation Blueprint for the character to animate while moving.

In this chapter, we're going to cover the following main topics:

- Creating Blend Spaces
- Main character Animation Blueprint
- What are velocity vectors?
- Enhanced input system
- Using Animation State Machines

By the end of the chapter, the player character will be able to walk, sprint, and jump, thus providing a better game feel to how the character will move in our game. By creating and learning about Blend Space 1D and Animation Blueprint assets, you will add a layer of sophistication to how the player movement is handled, while also establishing the groundwork for further animations, such as the projectile throw.

Technical requirements

For this chapter, you will need the following:

- Unreal Engine 5 installed
- Visual Studio 2019 installed

The project for this chapter can be found in the `Chapter11` folder of the code bundle for this book, which can be downloaded here: `https://github.com/PacktPublishing/Elevating-Game-Experiences-with-Unreal-Engine-5-Second-Edition`.

We'll start this chapter by learning about Blend Spaces before creating the Blend Space asset that you will need to animate the player character.

Creating Blend Spaces

Blend Spaces allow you to blend between multiple animations based on one or more conditions. Blend Spaces are used in different types of video games, but, more often than not, in games where the player can view the entire character. Blend Spaces are not usually used when the player can only see the character's arms, such as in the **First-Person** project template provided in UE5, as shown here:

Figure 11.1 – The first-person perspective of the default character
in the First-Person project template in UE5

It is more common in third-person games where there is a need to use Blend Spaces to smoothly blend movement-based animations of the character. A good example is the **Third-Person** template project provided in UE5, as shown here:

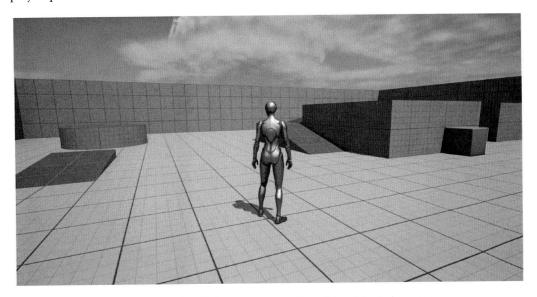

Figure 11.2 – The third-person perspective of the default character
in the First-Person project template in UE5

Let's look at the Blend Space asset provided by Unreal Engine when creating the `Third Person template` project template by opening `/Characters/Mannequins/Animations/Quinn/ BS_MF_Unarmed_WalkRun`. This is a Blend Space 1D asset created for the `Side Scroller` mannequin skeletal mesh so that the player character can smoothly blend between `Idle`, `Walking`, and `Running` animations based on the speed of the character.

If you check **Persona** in the **Asset Details** panel on the left-hand side, you will see the **AXIS SETTINGS** category, which contains the `Horizontal Axis` parameter, where we have settings for this axis, which essentially acts as a variable that we can reference in our Animation Blueprint. Please refer to the following screenshot to see the **AXIS SETTINGS** category within **Persona**:

Figure 11.3 – The axis settings for the Blend Space 1D

Below the preview window, we will also see a small graph with points along the line from left to right; one of these points will be highlighted `green`, while the others will be `white`. We can hold *Shift* and drag this `green` point along the horizontal axis to preview the blended animation based on its value. At speed `0`, our character is in an `Idle` state. As we move our preview along the axis, the animation will begin to blend into `Walking`, followed by `Running`. The following screenshot shows the single-axis graph:

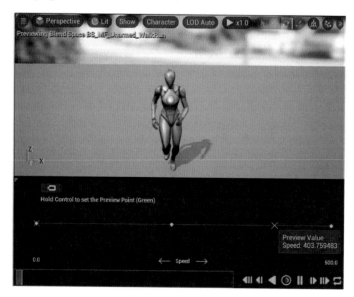

Figure 11.4 – The key frame timeline of the 1D Blend Space 1D

In the next section, we will look at Blend Space 1Ds versus a normal Blend Space, and when to use them based on your animation needs.

Blend Space 1D versus normal Blend Space

Before moving forward with the Blend Space 1D, let's take a moment to look at the main differences between a Blend Space 1D and a normal Blend Space in UE5:

- The Blend Space in Unreal Engine is controlled by two variables, represented by the X and Y axes of the Blend Space graph.
- On the other hand, the Blend Space 1D only supports one axis.

Try to imagine this as a 2D graph. Since you know that each axis has a direction, you can visualize why and when you would need to use this Blend Space rather than a Blend Space 1D, which only supports a single axis.

Say, for example, you wanted to make the player character strafe left and right while also supporting forward and backward movement. If you were to map this movement out on a graph, it would look as follows:

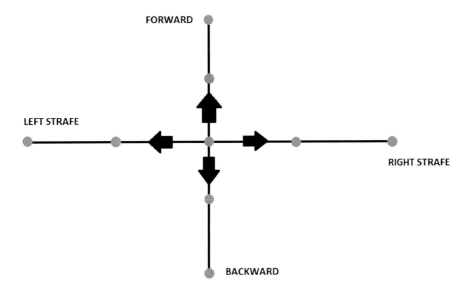

Figure 11.5 – What a Blend Space movement would look like on a simple graph

Now, visualize the movement of the player character, keeping in mind the fact that the game is a Side Scroller. The character won't be supporting left or right strafing or forward and backward movement. The player character will only need to animate in one direction because the Side Scroller character rotates toward the direction of movement by default. Having to only support one direction is why you are using a Blend Space 1D instead of a normal Blend Space.

We will need to set up this type of Blend Space asset for our main character and use the Blend Space for the same purpose, for movement-based animation blending. In the next exercise, we'll create the Blend Space asset using our custom animation assets.

Exercise 11.01 – creating the CharacterMovement Blend Space 1D

To get the player character to animate while they move, you need to create a Blend Space.

In this exercise, you will create the **Blend Space** asset, add the idle animation, and update the CharacterMovement component so that you assign an appropriate walking speed value that corresponds with the Blend Space.

Follow these steps to complete this exercise:

1. Navigate to the /MainCharacter/Animation folder in the **Content Drawer** window, where all the new animations you imported in the previous chapter are located.

2. Now, *right-click* in the main area of the **Content Drawer** window and, from the drop-down menu, hover over the **Animation** option. From its additional drop-down menu, select **Blend Space 1D**.

3. Make sure to select MainCharacter_Skeleton, not UE4_Mannequin_Skeleton, as the skeleton for the Blend Space.

> **Note**
>
> If you apply the incorrect skeleton, the Blend Space will not be functional for the player character, nor will the custom skeletal mesh when you select the skeleton assets, such as Blend Spaces or Animation Blueprints, that are required. Here, you are telling this asset which skeleton it is compatible with. By doing so, in the case of a Blend Space, you can use animations that have been made for this skeleton, thereby ensuring that everything is compatible with everything else.

4. Name this Blend Space asset SideScroller_IdleRun_1D.

5. Next, open the SideScroller_IdleRun_Blend Space 1D asset. You can see the single-axis graph below the preview window:

Figure 11.6 – The editing tool used to create Blend Spaces in UE5

On the left-hand side of the editor, you have the **Asset Details** panel, which contains the **AXIS SETTING** category. Here, you can label the axis and provide both a minimum and maximum float value that will be of use to you in the `Animation Blueprint` property for the player character. The following screenshot shows the default values that have been set for `Horizontal Axis`:

Figure 11.7 – The axis settings that affect the axis of the Blend Space

6. Now, change the name of **Horizontal Axis** to `Speed`:

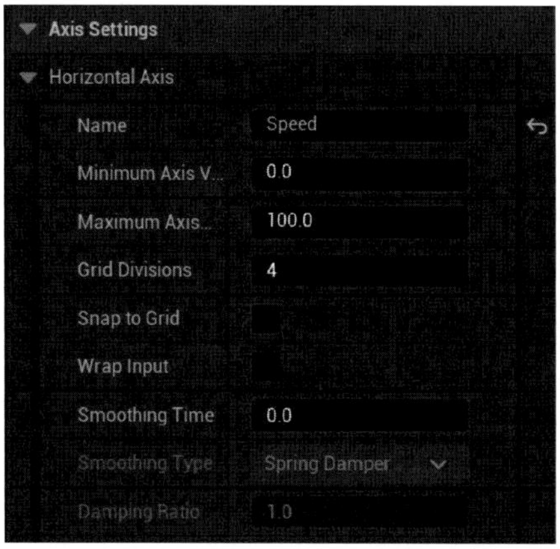

Figure 11.8 – The horizontal axis is now named Speed

7. The next step is to establish **Minimum Axis Value** and **Maximum Axis Value**. You will want the minimum value to be `0.0f`, which is set by default, because the player character will be in an `Idle` state when they are not moving at all.

    But what about **Maximum Axis Value**? This one is a little trickier because you need to bear the following points in mind:

    *   You will be supporting a sprinting behavior for the character that allows the player to move faster when holding down the *Left Shift* keyboard button. When released, the player will return to the default walking speed.

    *   The walking speed must match the characters' `Max Walk Speed` parameter of `CharacterMovementComponent`.

    *   Before you set **Maximum Axis Value**, you need to set the character's **Max Walk Speed** to a value that suits the `SuperSideScroller` game.

8. For this, navigate to `/Game/MainCharacter/Blueprints/` and open the `BP_SuperSideScroller_MainCharacter` Blueprint.

9. Select the `Character Movement` component and, in the **Details** panel, under the **Character Movement: Walking** category, find the `Max Walk Speed` parameter and set its value to `300.0f`.

    With the `Max Walk Speed` parameter set, return to the `SideScroller_IdleRun_` Blend Space 1D and set the `Maximum Axis Value` parameter. If the walking speed was `300.0f`, what should the maximum value be? Keeping in mind that you will support sprinting for the player character, this maximum value needs to be more than the walking speed.

10. Update the `Maximum Axis Value` parameter so that its value is `500.0f`.

11. Lastly, set the `Number of Grid Divisions` parameter to a value of 5. The reason for this is that when working with divisions, a `100` unit spacing between each grid point makes it easier to work with since `Maximum Axis Value` is `500.0f`. This is useful in the case of grid point snapping when you apply the movement animations along the grid.

12. Leave the remaining properties set as their defaults:

Figure 11.9 – The final axis settings for the Blend Space

With these settings, you are telling the Blend Space to use an incoming float value between `0.0f` and `500.0f` to blend between the animations that you will place in the next step and the activity. By dividing the grid into 5 divisions, you can easily add the animations needed at the correct float value along the axis graph.

Let's continue creating the Blend Space by adding our first animation to the axis graph: the `Idle` animation.

13. To the right of the grid, there is the **Asset Browser** tab. Notice that the list of assets includes all of the animations of the player character that you imported in *Chapter 10, Creating the SuperSideScroller Game*. This is because you selected the `MainCharacter_Skeleton` asset when creating the Blend Space.

14. Next, left-click and drag the `Idle` animation to our grid at position `0.0`:

Figure 11.10 – Dragging the Idle animation to our grid at position 0.0

Notice that when dragging this animation to the grid, it will snap to the grid point. Once the animation has been added to the Blend Space, the player character will change from its default T-Pose and start to play the `Idle` animation:

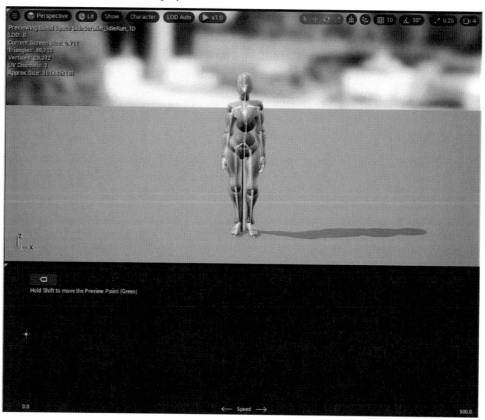

Figure 11.11 – With the Idle animation added to the Blend Space
1D, the player character begins to animate

With this exercise complete, you now have an understanding of how to create a Blend Space 1D and, more importantly, you know the differences between a Blend Space 1D and a normal Blend Space. Additionally, you know the importance of aligning the values between the player character movement component and the Blend Space and why you need to ensure that the walking speed correlates appropriately with the values in the Blend Space.

Now, let's move on to the first activity of this chapter, where you will be applying the remaining `Walking` and `Running` animations to the Blend Space, just as you added the `Idle` animation.

Activity 11.01 – adding the Walking and Running animations to the Blend Space

The 1D movement Blend Space is coming together nicely so far, but you are missing the `Walking` and `Running` animations. In this activity, you will finish the Blend Space by adding these animations to the Blend Space at the appropriate horizontal axis values that make sense for the main character.

Using the knowledge you acquired from *Exercise 11.01 – creating the CharacterMovement Blend Space 1D*, follow these steps to finish up the character movement Blend Space:

1. Continuing from *Exercise 11.01 – creating the CharacterMovement Blend Space 1D*, head back to the **Asset Browser** window.

2. Now, add the `Walking` animation to the horizontal grid position `300.0f`.

3. Finally, add the `Running` animation to the horizontal grid position `500.0f`.

> **Note**
> Remember that you can hold *shift* and drag the green preview grid point along the grid axis to see how the animation blends together based on the axis value, so pay attention to the character animation preview window to make sure that it looks correct.

The expected output is as follows:

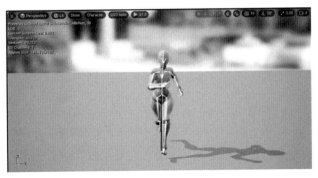

Figure 11.12 – The Running animation in the Blend Space

At this point, you should have a functional Blend Space that blends the character movement animations from `Idle` to `Walking` to `Running` based on the value of the horizontal axis that represents the player character's speed.

> **Note**
>
> The solution to this activity can be found on GitHub here: `https://github.com/PacktPublishing/Elevating-Game-Experiences-with-Unreal-Engine-5-Second-Edition/tree/main/Activity%20solutions`.

The Main Character Animation Blueprint

With the animations added to the Blend Space, you should be able to walk around and see those animations at work, right? Well, no. If you select **Play-In-Editor**, you will notice that the main character is still moving in the T-Pose. The reason is that you aren't telling the Animation Blueprint to use our Blend Space asset yet, which you will do later in this chapter.

Animation Blueprints

Before jumping into using the Animation Blueprint you created in the previous chapter, let's briefly discuss what this type of Blueprint is, and what its main function is. An Animation Blueprint is a type of Blueprint that allows you to control the animation of a skeleton and skeletal mesh – in this instance, the player character skeleton and mesh you imported in the previous chapter.

An Animation Blueprint is broken into two main graphs:

- Event Graph
- Anim Graph

The Event Graph works as in a normal Blueprint where you can use events, functions, and variables to script gameplay logic. The Anim Graph, on the other hand, is unique to an Animation Blueprint, and this is where you use logic to determine the final pose of the skeleton and skeletal mesh at any given frame. It is here where you can use elements such as State Machines, anim slots, Blend Spaces, and other animation-related nodes to then output the final animation for the character.

Let's look at an example.

Open the `AnimBP_SuperSideScroller_MainCharacter` Animation Blueprint in the `MainCharacter/Blueprints` directory.

By default, **AnimGraph** should open, where you will see the character preview, the **Asset Browser** window, and the main graph. It is inside this **AnimGraph** that you will implement the Blend Space you just created to have the player character animate correctly when moving around the level.

Let's get started with the next exercise, where we will do this and learn more about Animation Blueprints.

Exercise 11.02 – adding the Blend Space to the character Animation Blueprint

For this exercise, you will add the Blend Space to the Animation Blueprint and prepare the necessary variable to help control this Blend Space based on the movement speed of the player character. Let's begin by adding the Blend Space to **AnimGraph**.

Follow these steps to complete this exercise:

1. Add the Blend Space to **AnimGraph** by finding the **Asset Browser** window on the right-hand side and left-clicking and dragging the `SideScroller_IdleRun_`Blend Space 1D asset into **AnimGraph**.

    Notice that the variable input for this Blend Space node is labeled `Speed`, just like the horizontal axis inside the Blend Space. Please refer to *Figure 11.14* to see the Blend Space in the **Asset Browser** window:

> **Note**
>
> If you were to name **Horizontal Axis** differently, the new name would be shown as the input parameter of the Blend Space.

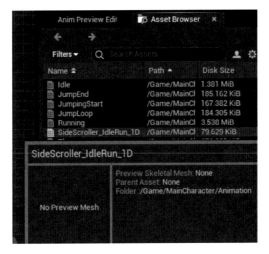

Figure 11.13 – Asset Browser gives you access to all animation assets related to MainCharacter_Skeleton

2. Next, connect the `Output Pose` asset of the Blend Space node to the `Result` pin of the `Output Pose` node. Now, the animation pose in the preview will show the character in the `Idle` animation pose:

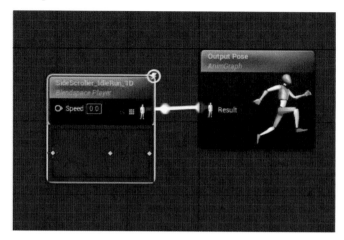

Figure 11.14 – You now have limited control of the Blend Space and can manually enter values into the Speed parameter

3. If you use **Play In Editor** (**PIE**), the player character will be moving around, but will play the `Idle` animation instead of remaining in the T-Pose position:

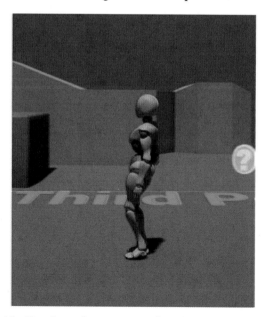

Figure 11.15 – The player character now plays the Idle animation in-game

Now, we can control our Blend Space with our `Speed` input variable. With the ability to use the Blend Space in place, you need a way to store the character's movement speed and pass that value to the `Speed` input parameter of the Blend Space. Let's learn how to do this.

4. Navigate to the `Event Graph` property of our Animation Blueprint. By default, there will be the `Event Blueprint Update Animation` event and a pure `Try Get Pawn Owner` function. The following screenshot shows the default setup of `Event Graph`. The event is updated each frame that the animation is updated, and returns the **Delta Time** property between each frame update and the owning pawn of this Animation Blueprint. You need to make sure that the owning pawn is of the `SuperSideScroller` player character Blueprint class before attempting to get any more information:

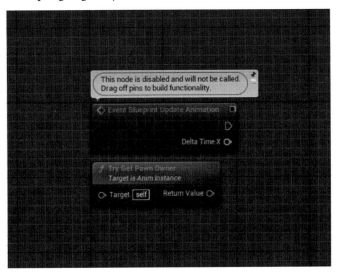

Figure 11.16 – Animation Blueprints include this event and function
pair by default for use in your Event Graph

> **Note**
>
> The main difference between a `Pure` and `Impure` function in UE5 is that a `Pure` function implies that the logic it contains will not modify a variable or member of the class that it is being used in. In the case of `Try Get Pawn Owner`, it is simply returning a reference to the `Pawn` owner of the Animation Blueprint. `Impure` functions do not have this implication and are free to modify any variable or member it wants.

5. Get the `Return Value` property from the `Try Get Pawn Owner` function and, from the `Context Sensitive` menu that appears, search for the cast to `SuperSideScrollerCharacter`:

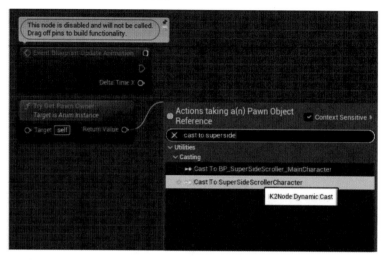

Figure 11.17 – Casting ensures we are working with the correct class

6. Connect the execution output pin from `Event Blueprint Update Animation` to the execution input pin of the cast:

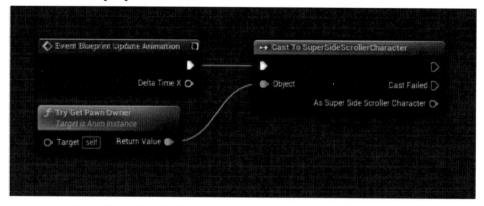

Figure 11.18 – Use the Try Get Pawn Owner function to cast the returned
Pawn object to the SuperSideScrollerCharacter class

The character Blueprint you created inherits from the `SuperSideScrollerCharacter` class. Since the owning pawn of this Animation Blueprint is your `BP_SuperSideScroller_MainCharacter` character Blueprint and this Blueprint inherits from the `SuperSideScrollerCharacter` class, the cast function will execute successfully.

7. Next, store the returned value from the cast to its own variable; that way, we have a reference to it in case we need to use it again in our Animation Blueprint. Refer to *Figure 11.20* and make sure to name this new variable `MainCharacter`:

> **Note**
>
> The `Promote to Variable` option is available in the context-sensitive dropdown, and allows you to store any valid value type in its own variable.

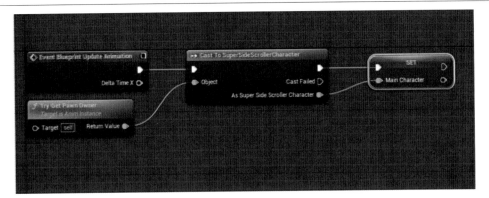

Figure 11.19 – So long as the cast is successful, you will want to keep track of the owning character

8. Now, to track the character's speed, use the `Get Velocity` function from the `MainCharacter` variable. Every object from the `Actor` class has access to this function and returns the magnitude and direction vector that the object is moving in:

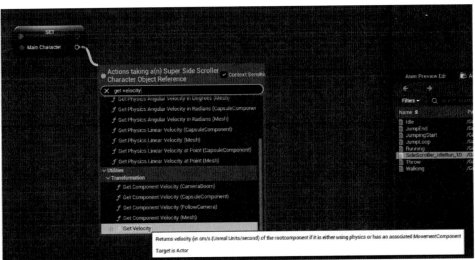

Figure 11.20 – The GetVelocity function can be found under Utilities/Transformation

9.   From `Get Velocity`, you can use the `VectorLength` function to get the actual speed:

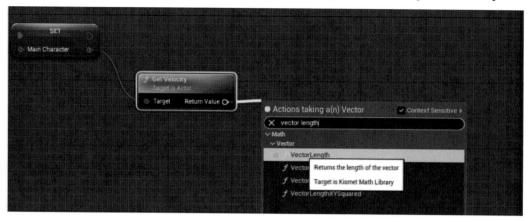

Figure 11.21 – The VectorLength function returns the magnitude of the vector

10.   `Return Value` from the `VectorLength` function can then be promoted to its own variable named `Speed`:

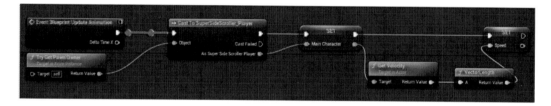

Figure 11.22 – Every actor has the Get Velocity function

In this exercise, you obtained the player character speed by using the `GetVelocity` function. The vector that was returned from the `GetVelocity` function gives the length of the vector to ascertain the actual speed. By storing this value in the `Speed` variable, you can now reference this value in the **AnimGraph** property of the Animation Blueprint to update your Blend Space, which you will do in the next exercise. But first, let's briefly discuss velocity vectors and how we use vector mathematics to determine the speed of our player character.

What are velocity vectors?

Before moving on to the next step, let's explain what you are doing when you get the velocity of the character and promote the vector length of that vector to the `Speed` variable.

What is velocity? Velocity is a vector that has a given **magnitude** and **direction**. To think about it another way, a vector can be drawn like an *arrow*.

The l*ength of the arrow* represents the **magnitude**, or *strength*, while *the direction of the arrowhead* represents the **direction**. So, if you want to know how fast the player character is moving, you will want to get the length of that vector. That is exactly what you are doing when you use the `GetVelocity` function and the `VectorLength` function on the returned velocity vector; you are getting the value of the `Speed` variable of your character. That is why you store that value in a variable and use it to control the Blend Space, as shown in the following diagram. Here, you can see an example of vectors. One has a positive (right) direction with a magnitude of `100`, while the other has a negative (left) direction with a magnitude of `35`:

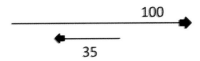

Figure 11.23 – Two different vectors

In the following exercise, you will use the `Speed` variable you created from the `VectorLength` function of the velocity parameter of the player character from the previous exercise to drive how the Blend Space 1D will animate the character.

Exercise 11.03 – passing the character's Speed variable into the Blend Space

Now that you have a better understanding of vectors and how to store the `Speed` variable of the player character from the previous exercise, let's apply the speed to the Blend Space 1D you created earlier in this chapter.

Follow these steps to complete this exercise:

1. Navigate to the **AnimGraph** property within your `AnimBP_SuperSideScroller_MainCharacter` Animation Blueprint.

2. Use the `Speed` variable to update the Blend Space in real time in **AnimGraph** by *left-clicking* and dragging the `Speed` variable onto the graph, and connecting the variable to the input of the `Blendspace Player` function:

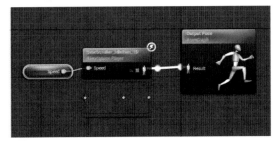

Figure 11.24 – Using the Speed variable to update the Blend Space on every frame

3.   Next, compile the Animation Blueprint.

With that, you can update the Blend Space based on the speed of the player character. When you use PIE, you will see the character in the `Idle` state and the `Walking` state when you move:

Figure 11.25 – The player character is finally able to walk around in the level

Finally, the main character is using the movement animations based on movement speed. In the next activity, you will update the character movement component so that you can preview the character's `Running` animation from the Blend Space.

Activity 11.02 – previewing the Running animation in-game

With the Animation Blueprint updating and getting the speed of the player character, you can preview the `Idle` and `Walking` animations in-game.

In this activity, you will update the `CharacterMovement` component of the player character Blueprint so that you can preview the `Running` animation in-game as well.

Follow these steps to complete this activity:

1.   Navigate to, and open, the `BP_SuperSideScroller_MainCharacter` player character Blueprint.

2. Access the `CharacterMovement` component.

3. Modify the `Max Walk Speed` parameter to a value of `500.0` so that your character can move fast enough to blend its animation from `Idle` to `Walking` and, finally, to `Running`.

By doing this, the player character can reach a speed that allows you to preview the `Running` animation in-game.

The expected output is as follows:

Figure 11.26 – The player character running

> **Note**
>
> The solution to this activity can be found on GitHub here: `https://github.com/PacktPublishing/Elevating-Game-Experiences-with-Unreal-Engine-5-Second-Edition/tree/main/Activity%20solutions`.

Now that you have handled the player character movement blending from `Idle` to `Walking` and finally to `Running`, let's add the functionality that allows the player character to move even quicker by sprinting.

Enhanced input system

Every game requires input from the player, whether it is the keys on a keyboard such as *W*, *A*, *S*, and *D* for moving the player character, or the thumb sticks on a controller; this is what makes video games an interactive experience. We will be using the Enhanced Input System to add an input binding for the sprint action of the player character. For a refresher on how to enable and set up the Enhanced Input System plugin, please review *Chapter 4, Getting Started with Player Input*; moving forward, the exercises in this chapter assume you have enabled the plugin.

UE5 allows us to map keyboard, mouse, gamepad, and other types of controls to labeled actions or axes that you can then reference in Blueprints or C++ to allow character or gameplay functionality to occur. It is important to point out that each unique action or axis mapping can have one or more key bindings, and that the same key binding can be used for multiple mappings. Input bindings are saved into an initialization file called `DefaultInput.ini` and can be found in the `Config` folder of your project directory.

> **Note**
>
> Legacy input bindings can be edited directly via the `DefaultInput.ini` file or through **Project Settings** in the editor itself. The latter is more easily accessible and less error-prone when editing.

In the next exercise, we'll add a new input binding for the player character's `Sprint` functionality.

Exercise 11.04 – adding input for sprinting

With the player character moving around the level, you will now implement a unique character class for the player character that derives from the base `SuperSideScrollerCharacter` C++ class. The reason to do this is so that you can easily differentiate between classes of the player character and the enemy later on, instead of relying solely on unique Blueprint classes.

While creating the unique C++ character class, you will implement the *sprinting* behavior to allow the player character to *walk* and *sprint* as desired.

Let's begin by implementing the `Sprinting` mechanic by adding an `Input Action` for `Sprint`:

1. Navigate to the **Content Drawer** window and, under the `Content` directory, add a new folder called `Input`.

2. In the **Input** directory, create another folder called `Sprint`. It is in this directory that we will create both the `Input Action` and `Input Mapping Context` assets.

3. In the `Sprint` folder, right-click and find the **Input Action** option, under the **Input** category of the menu, as shown here:

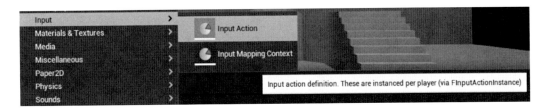

Figure 11.27 – The Input Action class

4. Name this **Input Action** IA_Sprint and open the asset.

5. Under the **Triggers** section, add a new **Trigger** by left-clicking on the + icon. Under the **Index[0]** parameter, select the **Down** type:

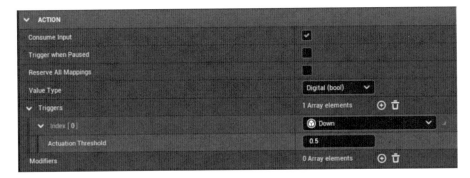

Figure 11.28 – The IA_Sprint Input Action class using the Down Trigger type

Now that we have our **Input Action**, let's create the **Input Mapping Context** asset and add the action to it.

6. In the **Input** directory, right-click and find the **Input Mapping Context** option, under the **Input** category of the menu, as shown here:

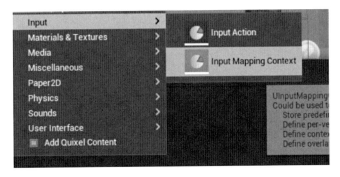

Figure 11.29 – The Input Mapping Context class

7. Name this **Input Mapping Context** `IC_SideScrollerCharacter` and open the asset.

8. In the **Mappings** section, add a new mapping by left-clicking the + icon and then assigning `IA_Sprint`.

9. Next, we want to assign *Left Shift* as the binding to use for sprinting.

10. In the **Triggers** section, add a new **Trigger** by left-clicking on the + icon. Under the **Index[0]** parameter, select **Down**. The final **Input Mapping Context** should look like this:

Figure 11.30 – IC_SideScrollerCharacter using the IA_Sprint Input Action mapping

With the `Sprint` input binding in place, you need to create a new C++ class for the player character based on the `SuperSideScrollerCharacter` class.

11. Make sure that you update the `SuperSideScroller.Build.cs` file so that it includes the Enhanced Input plugin; otherwise, your code will not compile. Add the following line inside the `public SuperSideScroller(ReadOnlyTargetRues Target) : base(Target)` function:

```
PrivateDependencyModuleNames.AddRange(new string[]
{"EnhancedInput"});
```

12. Then, head back inside the editor, navigate to **Tools**, and, from the drop-down list, select the **New C++ Class** option.

13. The new player character class will inherit from the `SuperSideScrollerCharacter` parent class because this base class contains the majority of the functionality needed for the player character. After selecting the parent class, click **Next**. The following screenshot shows where you can find the `SuperSideScrollerCharacter` class:

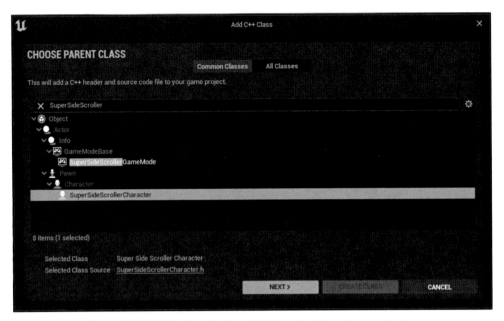

Figure 11.31 – Selecting the SuperSideScrollerCharacter parent class

14. Name this new class `SuperSideScroller_Player`. Leave the path as the default that Unreal Engine provides for you unless you need to adjust the file directory of this new class. After naming the new class and selecting the directory to save the class in, click `Create Class`.

    After selecting `Create Class`, Unreal Engine will generate the source and header files for you, and Visual Studio will automatically open these files. You will notice that both the header file and the source file are almost empty. This is OK because you are inheriting from the `SuperSideScrollerCharacter` class and much of the logic you want is done in that class.

15. In `SuperSideScroller_Player`, you will only add the functionality you need on top of what you inherit. You can view the line where the inheritance is taking place inside `SuperSideScroller_Player.h`:

    ```
    class SUPERSIDESCROLLER_API ASuperSideScroller_Player :
    public ASuperSideScrollerCharacter
    ```

    This class declaration is saying that the new `ASuperSideScroller_Player` class inherits from the `ASuperSideScrollerCharacter` class.

By completing this exercise, you added an **Enhanced Input Binding** for the `Sprint` mechanic that can then be referenced in C++ and used to allow the player to sprint. Now that you have also created the C++ class for the player character, you can update the code with the `Sprint` functionality, but first, you will need to update the `Blueprint` character and the Animation Blueprint to reference this new class. We'll do this in the next exercise.

What happens when you reparent a Blueprint to a new class? Each Blueprint inherits from a parent class. In most cases, this is Actor, but in the case of your character Blueprint, its parent class is SuperSideScrollerCharacter. Inheriting from a parent class allows a Blueprint to inherit the functionality and variables of that class so that the logic can be reused at the Blueprint level.

For example, when inheriting from the SuperSideScrollerCharacter class, the Blueprint inherits components such as the CharacterMovement component and the Mesh skeletal mesh component, which can then be modified in the Blueprint.

Exercise 11.05 – reparenting the character Blueprint

Now that you have created a new character class for the player character, you need to update the BP_SuperSideScroller_MainCharacter Blueprint so that it uses the SuperSideScroller_Player class as its parent class. If you don't, then any logic you add to the new class will not affect the character made in the Blueprint.

Follow these steps to reparent the Blueprint to the new character class:

1. Navigate to /Game/MainCharacter/Blueprints/ and open the BP_SuperSideScroller_MainCharacter Blueprint.

2. Select the **File** option on the toolbar and, from the drop-down menu, select the **Reparent Blueprint** option.

3. When selecting the **Reparent Blueprint** option, Unreal Engine will ask for the new class to reparent the Blueprint to. Search for SuperSideScroller_Player and select that option from the dropdown by left-clicking.

   Once you select the new parent class for the Blueprint, Unreal Engine will reload the Blueprint and recompile it, both of which will happen automatically.

> **Note**
> Be careful when reparenting Blueprints to new parent classes as this can lead to compile errors or settings to be erased or reverted to class defaults. Unreal Engine will display any warnings or errors that may occur after compiling the Blueprint and reparenting it to a new class. These warnings and errors usually occur if there is Blueprint logic that references variables or other class members that no longer exist in the new parent class. Even if there are no compile errors, it is best to confirm that any logic or settings you have added to your Blueprint are still present after the reparenting before moving on with your work.

   Now that your character Blueprint has been correctly reparented to the new SuperSideScroller_Player class, you need to update the AnimBP_SuperSideScroller_MainCharacter Animation Blueprint to ensure that you are casting to the correct class when using the Try Get Pawn Owner function.

4. Next, navigate to the `/MainCharacter/Blueprints/` directory and open the `AnimBP_SuperSideScroller_MainCharacter` Animation Blueprint.

5. Open **Event Graph**. From the `Return Value` property of the `Try Get Pawn Owner` function, search for `Cast to SuperSideScroller_Player`:

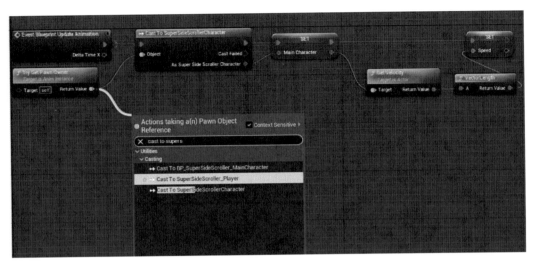

Figure 11.32 – Casting to the new SuperSideScroller_Player class

6. Now, you can connect the output as a `SuperSideScroller_Player` cast to the `MainCharacter` variable. This works because the `MainCharacter` variable is of the `SuperSideScrollerCharacter` type and the new `SuperSideScroller_Player` class inherits from that class:

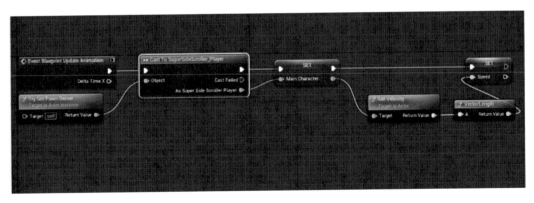

Figure 11.33 – You can still use the MainCharacter variable because SuperSideScroller_Player is based on SuperSideScrollerCharacter due to inheritance

Now that both the `BP_SuperSideScroller_MainCharacter` character Blueprint and the `AnimBP_SuperSideScroller_MainCharacter` Animation Blueprint are referencing your new `SuperSideScroller_Player` class, it is safe to venture into C++ and code the character's sprint functionality.

Exercise 11.06 – coding the character's sprint functionality

With the new `SuperSideScroller_Player` class reference correctly implemented in a Blueprint, it is time to start coding the functionality that will allow the player character to sprint.

Follow these steps to add the `Sprinting` mechanic to the character:

1. The first thing to take care of is the constructor of the `SuperSideScroller_Player` class. Navigate back to Visual Studio and open the `SuperSideScroller_Player.h` header file.

2. You will use the `constructor` function later in this exercise to set initialized values for variables. For now, it will be an empty constructor. Make sure that the declaration is made under the `public` access modifier heading, as shown in the following code:

   ```
   //Constructor
   ASuperSideScroller_Player();
   ```

3. With the constructor declared, create the constructor function definition in the `SuperSideScroller_Player.cpp` source file:

   ```
   ASuperSideScroller_Player::ASuperSideScroller_Player()
   {

   }
   ```

   With the constructor in place, it's time to create the `SetupPlayerInputComponent` function so that you can use the key bindings you created earlier to call functions within the `SuperSideScroller_Player` class.

   The `SetupPlayerInputComponent` function is a function that the character class has built-in by default, so you need to declare it as a `virtual` function with the `override` specifier. This tells Unreal Engine that you are using this function and intend to redefine its functionality in this new class. Make sure that the declaration is made under the `Protected` access modifier heading.

4. The `SetupPlayerInputComponent` function requires an object of the `UInputComponent` class to be passed into the function, like so:

```
protected:
//Override base character class function to setup our
//player
   input component
virtual void SetupPlayerInputComponent(class
UInputComponent*
   PlayerInputComponent) override;
```

The `UInputComponent* PlayerInputComponent` variable is inherited from the `UCharacter` base class that our `ASuperSideScroller_Player()` class derives from, so it must be used as the input parameter of the `SetupPlayerInputComponent()` function. Using any other name will result in a compilation error.

5. Now, in the source file, create the definition of the `SetupPlayerInputComponent` function. In the body of the function, we will use the `Super` keyword to call it:

```
//Not always necessary, but good practice to call the
//function inthe base class with Super.
Super::SetupPlayerInputComponent(PlayerInputComponent);
```

The `Super` keyword enables us to call the `SetupPlayerInputComponent` parent method. With the `SetupPlayerInputComponent` function ready, you need to include the following header files to continue with this exercise without any compile errors:

- `#include "Components/InputComponent.h"`

- `#include "GameFramework/CharacterMovementComponent.h"`

You will need to include the header for the input component to bind the key mappings to the sprint functions you will be creating next. The header for the `Character Movement` component will be necessary for the sprint functions because you will be updating the `Max Walk Speed` parameter based on whether the player is sprinting. The following code contains all of the headers that need to be included for the player character:

```
#include "SuperSideScroller_Player.h"
#include "Components/InputComponent"
#include "GameFramework/CharacterMovementComponent.h"
```

With the necessary headers included in the source file of the `SuperSideScroller_Player` class, you can create the sprint functions to make the player character move faster. Let's begin by declaring the required variable and functions.

6. Under the `Private` access modifier in the header file of the `SuperSideScroller_Player` class, declare a new Boolean variable called `bIsSprinting`. This variable will be used as a failsafe so that you know whether the player character is sprinting before making any changes to the movement speed:

    ```
    private:
    //Bool to control if we are sprinting. Failsafe.
    bool bIsSprinting;
    ```

7. Next, declare two new functions, `Sprint();` and `StopSprinting();`. These two functions will not take any arguments and will not return anything. Declare these functions under the `Protected` access modifier:

    ```
    //Sprinting
    void Sprint();

    //StopSprinting
    void StopSprinting();
    ```

    The `Sprint();` function will be called when the player presses/holds the `Sprint` key mapped to the binding; `StopSprinting()` will be called when the player releases the key mapped to the binding.

8. Start with the definition of the `Sprint();` function. In the source file of the `SuperSideScroller_Player` class, create the definition for this function, as shown here:

    ```
    void ASuperSideScroller_Player::Sprint()
    {
    }
    ```

9. Within the function, you will want to check the value of the `bIsSprinting` variable. If the player is *NOT* sprinting, meaning that `bIsSprinting` is `False`, then you can create the rest of the function.

10. Within the `If` statement, set the `bIsSprinting` variable to `True`. Then, access the `GetCharacterMovement()` function and modify the `MaxWalkSpeed` parameter. Set `MaxWalkSpeed` to `500.0f`. Remember that the `Maximum Axis Value` parameter of the movement Blend Space is `500.0f`. This means that the player character will reach the speed necessary to use the `Running` animation:

    ```
    void ASuperSideScroller_Player::Sprint()
    ```

```
    {
        if (!bIsSprinting)
          {
            bIsSprinting = true;
            GetCharacterMovement()->MaxWalkSpeed = 500.0f;
          }
    }
```

The `StopSprinting()` function will look almost identical to the `Sprint()` function you just wrote, but it works in the opposite manner. First, you want to check whether the player is sprinting, meaning that `bIsSprinting` is `True`. If so, you can create the rest of the function.

11. Inside the `If` statement, set `bIsSprinting` to `False`. Then, access the `GetCharacterMovement()` function to modify `MaxWalkSpeed`. Set `MaxWalkSpeed` back to `300.0f`, which is the default speed for the player character when they're walking. This means that the player character will only reach the speed that's necessary for the `Walking` animation:

```
    void ASuperSideScroller_Player::StopSprinting()
    {
        if (bIsSprinting)
          {
            bIsSprinting = false;
            GetCharacterMovement()->MaxWalkSpeed = 300.0f;
          }
    }
```

Now that you have the functions needed for sprinting, it is time to bind these functions to the action mappings you created earlier. To do this, you need to create variables that hold a reference to the Input Mapping Context and Input Action that were created earlier in this chapter.

12. Inside the `SuperSideScroller_Player` header file, under the **Protected** category, add the following lines of code to create the properties for the Input Mapping Context and Input Action:

```
    UPROPERTY(EditAnywhere, Category = "Input")
    class UInputMappingContext* IC_Character;
    UPROPERTY(EditAnywhere, Category = "Input")
    class UInputAction* IA_Sprint;
```

We must remember to assign these properties within our character Blueprint before we attempt to test the sprinting functionality.

13. Next, inside the `SuperSideScroller_Player` source file, within the `SetupPlayerInputComponent()` function, we need to get a reference to the Enhanced Input Component by writing the following code:

```
UEnhancedInputComponent* EnhancedPlayerInput =
Cast<UEnhancedInputComponent>(PlayerInputComponent);
```

Now that we are referencing `UEnhancedInputComponent`, we need to remember to include this class as well:

```
#include "EnhancedInputComponent.h"
```

Since we want to support both legacy input and the Enhanced Input System, let's add a specific `if` statement to our code to check if the `EnhancedPlayerInput` variable is valid:

```
if(EnhancedPlayerInput)
{}
```

If the `EnhancedPlayerInput` variable is valid, then we want to get a reference to our Player Controller so that we can get access to the `EnhancedInputLocalPlayerSubsystem` class, which will allow us to assign our Input Mapping Context:

```
if(EnhancedPlayerInput)
{
    APlayerController* PlayerController =
    Cast<APlayerController>(GetController());
UEnhancedInputLocalPlayerSubsystem* EnhancedSubsystem =
ULocalPlayer::GetSubsystem<UEnhancedInputLocal
PlayerSubsystem> (PlayerController->GetLocalPlayer());
}
```

14. Now that we are referencing the `UEnhancedInputLocalPlayerSubsystem` class, we need to add the following `include` header file:

```
#include "EnhancedInputSubsystems.h"
```

15. Finally, we will add another `if` statement that checks if the `EnhancedSubsystem` variable is valid and then call the `AddMappingContext` function to add our `IC_Character` Input Mapping Context to our Player Controller:

```
if(EnhancedSubsystem)
{
```

```
EnhancedSubsystem->AddMappingContext(IC_Character,
1);
}
```

Now that we have applied the Input Mapping Context to the player characters' `EnhancedSubsystem`, we can bind the `Sprint()` and `StopSprinting()` functions to the Input Action we created earlier.

16. At the end of the `if (EnhancedPlayerInput)` statement, we will add a `BindAction` to bind `ETriggerEvent::Triggered` to the `Sprint()` function:

```
//Bind pressed action Sprint to your Sprint function
EnhancedPlayerInput->BindAction(IA_Sprint,
ETriggerEvent::Triggered, this, &ASuperSideScroller_
Player::Sprint);
```

17. Finally, we can add our `BindAction` to bind `ETriggerEvent::Completed` to the `StopSprinting()` function:

```
//Bind released action Sprint to your StopSprinting
//function
EnhancedPlayerInput->BindAction(IA_Sprint,
ETriggerEvent::Completed, this, &ASuperSideScroller_
Player::StopSprinting);
```

> **Note**
>
> For more information regarding the `ETriggerEvent` enumerator type, as well as more details about the Enhanced Input System, please revisit *Chapter 4, Getting Started with Player Input*, or refer to the following documentation from Epic Games: `https://docs.unrealengine.com/5.0/en-US/GameplayFeatures/EnhancedInput/`.

With `Action Mappings` bound to the sprint functions, the last thing you need to do is set the default initialized values of the `bIsSprinting` variable and the `MaxWalkSpeed` parameter from the `Character Movement` component.

18. Inside the `constructor` function in the source file of your `SuperSideScroller_Player` class, add the `bIsSprinting = false` line. This variable is constructed as false because the player character should not be sprinting by default.

19. Finally, set the `MaxWalkSpeed` parameter of the character movement component to `300.0f` by adding `GetCharacterMovement()->MaxWalkSpeed = 300.0f`. Please review the following code:

```
ASuperSideScroller_Player::ASuperSideScroller_Player()
{
    //Set sprinting to false by default.
    bIsSprinting = false;

    //Set our max Walk Speed to 300.0f
    GetCharacterMovement()->MaxWalkSpeed = 300.0f;

}
```

With the variables that have been added to the constructor initialized, the `SuperSideScroller_Player` class is done, for now. Return to Unreal Engine and left-click on the **Compile** button on the toolbar. This will recompile the code and perform a hot-reload of the editor.

After recompiling and hot-reloading the editor, we need to remember to assign both the Input Mapping Context and the Input Action inside our player character.

20. Navigate to the `MainCharacter/Blueprints` directory and open the `BP_SuperSideScroller_MainCharacter` Blueprint.

21. In the **Details** panel, under the **Input** category, you will find parameters for `IC_Character` and `IA_Sprint`. Assign the Input Context Mapping and Input Action assets we created earlier to these parameters:

Figure 11.34 – The IC_Character and IA_Sprint parameters

Upon compiling the `BP_SuperSideScroller_MainCharacter` Blueprint, you can use **Play In Editor** to see the fruits of your labor. The base movement behavior is the same as it was previously, but now, if you hold *Left Shift* or *Gamepad Right Shoulder* on a controller, the player character will sprint and begin to play the `Running` animation:

Figure 11.35 – The player character can now sprint

With the player character able to sprint, let's move on to the next activity, where you will implement the base Throw functionality in a very similar way.

Activity 11.03 – implementing the throwing input

One of the features included with this game is the ability for the player to throw projectiles at the enemy. You won't be creating the projectile or implementing the animation in this chapter, but you will set up the key bindings and the C++ implementation for use in the next chapter.

In this activity, you need to set up the Enhanced Input Mapping for the Throw projectile functionality and implement a debug log in C++ for when the player presses the key(s) mapped to Throw.

Follow these steps to complete this activity:

1. Create a new folder inside of the **Input** directory named Throw, and create a new **Input Action** called IA_Throw.

2. Use the Trigger type called Pressed inside IA_Throw.

3. Add the new IA_Throw **Input Action** to IC_SideScrollerCharacter with bindings to both Left Mouse Button and Gamepad Right Trigger.

4. Within Visual Studio, add a new UInputAction variable called IA_Throw and add the appropriate UPROPERTY() macro to the variable.

5. Add a new function to the header file of SuperSideScroller_Player. Name this function ThrowProjectile(). This will be a void function without parameters.

6. Create the definition in the source file of the `SuperSideScroller_Player` class. In the definition of this function, use `UE_LOG` to print a message that lets you know that the function is being called successfully.

7. Add a new `BindAction` function call using the `EnhancedPlayerInput` variable to bind the new Throw **Input Action** to the `ThrowProjectile()` function.

> **Note**
>
> You can learn more about `UE_LOG` here: `https://nerivec.github.io/old-ue4-wiki/pages/logs-printing-messages-to-yourself-during-runtime.html`.

8. Compile the code and return to the editor. Next, add `IA_Throw` to the `BP_SuperSideScroller_MainCharacter` parameter, `IA_Throw`.

The expected result is that when you use the *left mouse button* or the *gamepad right trigger*, a log will appear in `Output Log`, letting you know that the `ThrowProjectile` function is being called successfully. You will use this function later to spawn your projectile.

The expected output is as follows:

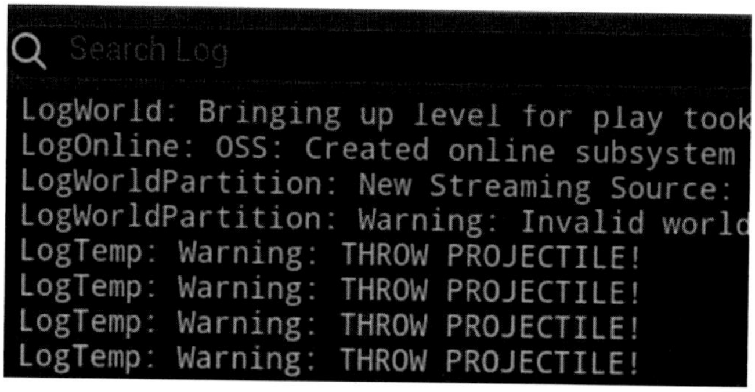

Figure 11.36 – The expected output log

> **Note**
>
> The solution to this activity can be found on GitHub here: `https://github.com/PacktPublishing/Elevating-Game-Experiences-with-Unreal-Engine-5-Second-Edition/tree/main/Activity%20solutions`.

With this activity complete, you now have functionality in place for when you create the player projectile in *Chapter 13, Creating and Adding the Enemy Artificial Intelligence*. You also have the knowledge and experience of adding new key mappings to your game and implementing functionality in C++ that utilizes these mappings to enable gameplay functionality. Now, you will continue updating the player character's movement to allow the jumping animation to play correctly when the player jumps. But first, let's take a moment to learn about Animation State Machines.

Using Animation State Machines

State Machines are a means of categorizing an animation, or sets of animations, into a state. A state can be thought of as a condition that the player character is in at a specific time. Is the player currently walking? Is the player jumping? In many third-person games such as *The Last of Us*, this involves separating the movement, jumping, crouching, and climbing animations into their own states. Each state is then accessible when certain conditions are met while the game is played. Conditions can include whether the player is jumping, the speed of the player character, and whether or not the player is in the crouched state. The job of the state machine is to transition between each state using logical decisions called **Transition Rules**. When you create multiple states with multiple Transition Rules that intertwine with one another, the state machine begins to look like a web. Please refer to the following screenshot to see what the state machine looks like for the `ThirdPerson_AnimBP` Animation Blueprint:

> **Note**
>
> A general overview of State Machines can be found here: `https://docs.unrealengine.com/en-US/Engine/Animation/StateMachines/Overview/index.html`.

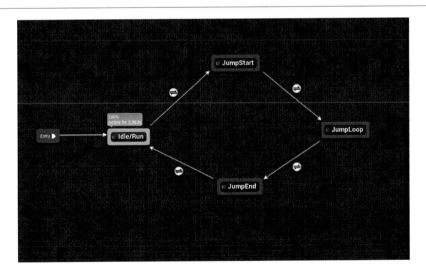

Figure 11.37 – The state machine of ThirdPerson_AnimBP

In the case of the state machine for the player character, this state machine will handle the states of the default player's movement and jumping. Currently, you have the player character animating simply by using a Blend Space that is controlled by the speed of the character. In the next exercise, you will create a new state machine and move the movement Blend Space logic into its own state within that state machine. Let's start creating the new state machine.

Exercise 11.07 – player character movement and jump state machine

In this exercise, you will implement a new animation state machine and integrate the existing movement Blend Space into the state machine. Additionally, you will set up the states for when the player jump starts, and for when the player is in the air during that jump.

Let's start by adding this new state machine:

1. Navigate to the /MainCharacter/Blueprints/ directory and open the AnimBP_SuperSideScroller_MainCharacter Animation Blueprint.

2. In **AnimGraph**, *right-click* in the empty space of the graph and search for state machine inside the context-sensitive search to find the Add New State Machine option. Name this new state machine Movement.

3. Now, instead of plugging the output pose of the SideScroller_IdleRun Blend Space, we can connect the output pose of the new state machine, Movement, to the output pose of the animation:

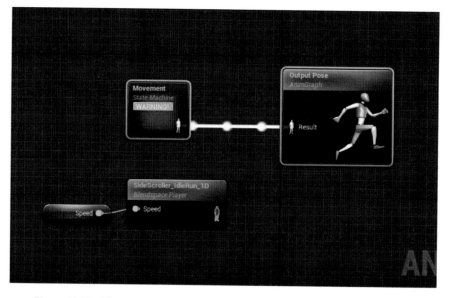

Figure 11.38 – The new Movement state machine replaces the old Blend Space

Connecting an empty state machine to the Output Pose property of the Animation Blueprint will result in the warnings shown in the following screenshot. All this means is that nothing is happening within that state machine and that the result will be invalid to Output Pose. Don't worry; you will fix this next:

Figure 11.39 – The empty state machine results in compile warnings

Double left-click on the Movement state machine to open the state machine itself.

You will start by adding a new state that will handle what the character was doing previously; that is Idle, Walking, or Running.

4. From the Entry point, left-click and drag out to open the context-sensitive search. You will notice that there are only two options – Add Conduit and Add State. For now, you will add a new state and name this state Movement. The following screenshot shows how the Movement state was created:

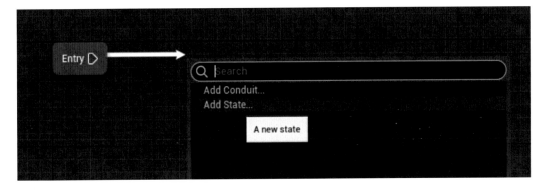

Figure 11.40 – Inside the state machine, you need to add a new state

5. After selecting Add State, you can rename the state to Movement and it should automatically connect to the Entry node of the State Machine.

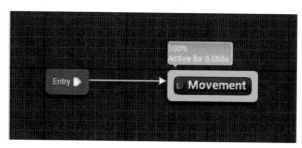

Figure 11.41 – The new Movement state

6. Copy and paste the logic you had where you connected the Speed variable to the SideScroller_IdleRun Blend Space into the new Movement state you created in the previous step. Connect it to the Result pin of the Output Animation Pose node of this state:

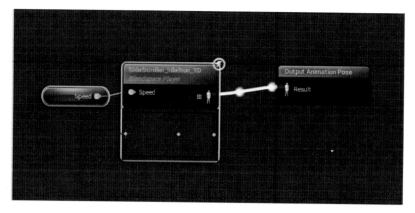

Figure 11.42 – Connecting the output pose of the Blend Space to the output pose of this state

Now, if you recompile the Animation Blueprint, you will notice that the warnings you saw earlier are now gone. This is because you added a new state that outputs an animation to Output Animation Pose instead of having an empty state machine.

By completing this exercise, you have constructed your very first state machine. Although it is a very simple one, you are now telling the character to enter and use the Movement state by default. Now, if you use PIE, you will see that the player character is moving around like they were earlier before you made the state machine. This means that your state machine is functioning and that you can continue to the next step, which will be adding the initial states that are required for jumping. Let's start by creating the JumpStart state.

Transition rules

Conduits are a way of telling each state the conditions under which it can transition from one state to another. In this case, a Transition Rule is created as a connection between the `Movement` and `JumpStart` states. This is indicated by the directional arrow of the connection between the states again. The tooltip mentions the term Transition Rule, which means that you need to define how the transition between these states will happen, using a Boolean value to do so:

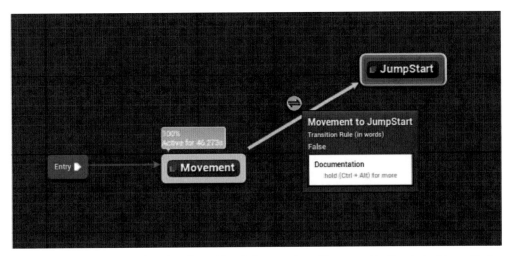

Figure 11.43 – There needs to be a Transition Rule to go from Movement to the start of JumpStart

The main difference between a simple Transition Rule and a conduit is that a Transition Rule can only connect between two states, whereas a conduit can serve as a means to transition between one and many other states. For more information, please refer to the following documentation: `https://docs.unrealengine.com/5.0/en-US/state-machines-in-unreal-engine/#conduits`.

In the next exercise, you will be adding this new `JumpStart` state and adding the proper Transition Rule necessary for the character to go from the `Movement` state to the `JumpStart` state.

Exercise 11.08 – adding states and transition rules to the state machine

In the case of transitioning from the player character's default movement Blend Space to the beginning of the jump animation, you will need to know when the player decides to jump. This can be done using a useful function called `IsFalling` from the `Character Movement` component of the player character. You will want to track whether the player is currently falling to transition in and out of jumping. The best way to do this is to store the result of the `IsFalling` function in its own variable, just like you did when tracking the player's speed.

Follow these steps to complete this exercise:

1. Back in the overview of the state machine itself, left-click and drag from the edge of the Movement state to open the context-sensitive menu.

2. Select the **Add State** option and name this state JumpStart. When you do this, Unreal Engine will automatically connect these states and implement an empty Transition Rule for you:

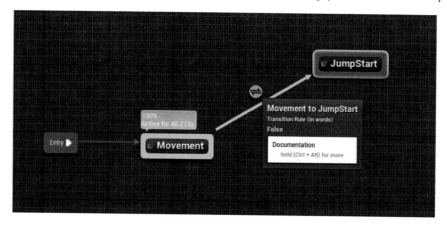

Figure 11.44 – The Transition Rule that Unreal automatically creates for you when connecting two states

3. Navigate back to **Event Graph** inside the Animation Blueprint, where you used the Event Blueprint update animation event to store the Speed value of the player character:

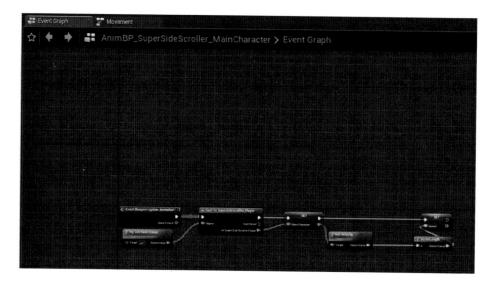

Figure 11.45 – We are now storing the Vector Length of the Main Character as Speed

4. Create a getter variable for `MainCharacter` and access the `Character Movement` component. From the `Character Movement` component, left-click and drag to access the context-sensitive menu. Search for `IsFalling`:

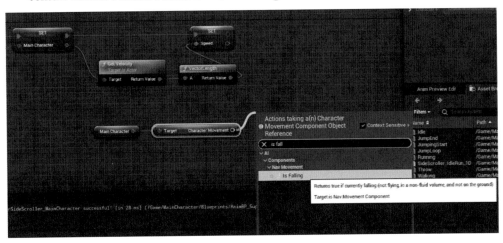

Figure 11.46 – How to find the IsFalling function

5. The character movement component can tell you whether the player character is currently in the air with the help of the `IsFalling` function:

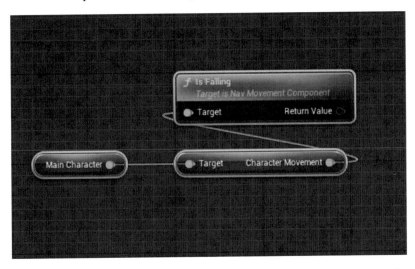

Figure 11.47 – The Character Movement component showing the state of the player character

6. From the `Return Value` Boolean of the `IsFalling` function, left-click and drag to search for the **Promote to Variable** option from the context-sensitive menu. Name this variable `bIsInAir`. When promoting to a variable, the `Return Value` output pin should automatically connect to the input pin of the newly promoted variable. If it doesn't, remember to connect them:

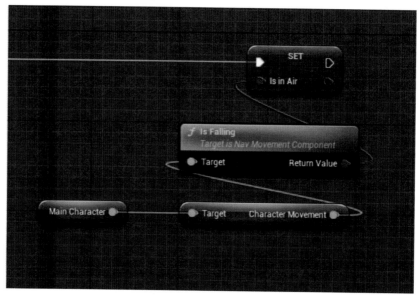

Figure 11.48 – A new variable, bIsInAir, that contains the value of the IsFalling function

Now that you are storing the state of the player and whether or not they are falling, this is the perfect candidate for the Transition Rule between the `Movement` and `JumpStart` states.

7. In the `Movement State` machine, double left-click on `Transition Rule` to enter its graph. You will find only one output node, `Result`, with the `Can Enter Transition` parameter. All you need to do here is use the `bIsInAir` variable and connect it to that output. Now, `Transition Rule` is saying that if the player is in the air, the transition between the `Movement` state and the `JumpStart` states can happen:

Figure 11.49 – When in the air, the player will transition to the start of the jumping animation

With your `Transition Rule` in place between the `Movement` and `JumpStart` states, all you must do is tell the `JumpStart` state which animation to use.

8.   From the state machine graph, double left-click on the `JumpStart` state to enter its graph. From the **Asset Browser** window, left-click and drag the `JumpingStart` animation to the graph:

Figure 11.50 – Ensure you have the JumpingStart animation selected in Asset Browser

9.   Connect the output of the `Play JumpingStart` node to the `Result` pin of the `Output Animation Pose` node:

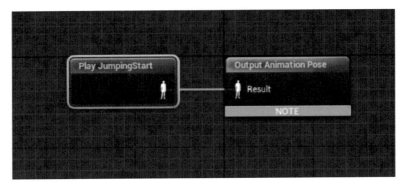

Figure 11.51 – Connecting the JumpingStart animation to Output Animation Pose of the JumpStart state

Before you can move forward with the next state, some settings need to be changed on the `JumpingStart` animation node.

10. Left-click on the `Play JumpingStart` animation node and update the **Details** panel so that it contains the following settings:

- `Loop Animation = False`

- `Play Rate = 2.0`

The following screenshot shows the final settings for the `Play JumpingStart` animation node:

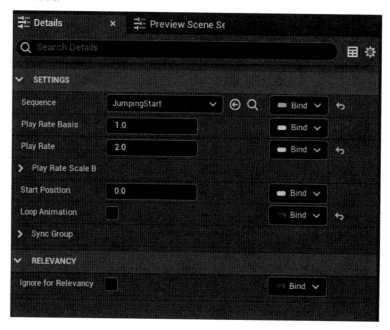

Figure 11.52 – Increasing the play rate will result in a smoother jumping animation overall

Here, you are setting the `Loop Animation` parameter to `False` because there is no reason that this animation should loop; it should only play once in any case. The only way that this animation would loop is if the player character is somehow stuck in this state, but this will never happen because of the next state you will create. The reason for setting `Play Rate` to `2.0` is because the animation itself, `JumpingStart`, is too long for the game you are making. The animation has the character bend their knees drastically, and jump upward for more than a second. For the `JumpStart` state, you want the character to play this animation quicker so that it is more fluid and offers a smoother transition to the next state; that is, `JumpLoop`. To give additional context to the `Play Rate` parameter that's available in an animation, there is both `Play Rate` and `Play Rate Basis`. The `Play Rate Basis` parameter allows you to change where the `Play Rate` parameter is expressed; so, by default, this is set to 1.0. If you wanted to, you could change this value to 10.0, meaning that the `Play Rate` input will be divided by 10. So, depending on `Play Rate Basis`, the value that's used in `Play Rate` can lead to different results; for simplicity, we will keep `Play Rate Basis` at its default value of 1.0.

Once the player character has begun the `JumpStart` animation, there is a point in time during that animation where the player is in the air and should transition to a new state. This new state will loop until the player is no longer in the air and can transition into the final state of ending the jump. Next, we will create a new state that will transition from the `JumpStart` state.

11. From the state machine graph, *left-click* and drag from the `JumpStart` state and select the `Add State` option. Name this new state `JumpLoop`. Again, Unreal Engine will automatically provide you with a `Transition Rule` between these states that you will add to in the next exercise. Finally, recompile the Animation Blueprint and ignore any warnings that may appear under **Compiler Results**:

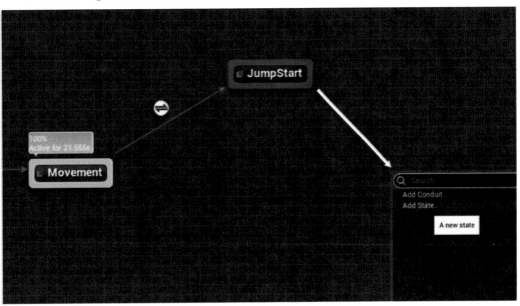

Figure 11.53 – A new state to handle the animation of the character while they're in the air

By completing this exercise, you have added and connected states for `JumpStart` and `JumpLoop`. Each of these states is connected via a `Transition Rule`. You should now have a better understanding of how states within a state machine transition from one to another via the rules established in each Transition Rule.

In the next exercise, you will learn how to transition from the `JumpStart` state to the `JumpLoop` state via the `Time Remaining Ratio` function.

Exercise 11.09 – The Time Remaining Ratio function

For the `JumpStart` state to smoothly transition to the `JumpLoop` state, you need to take a moment to think about exactly how you want this transition to work. Based on how the `JumpStart` and `JumpLoop` animations work, it is best to transition to the `JumpLoop` animation after a specified set of time has elapsed on the `JumpStart` animation. That way, the `JumpLoop` state plays smoothly after X seconds of the `JumpStart` animation playing.

Perform the following steps to achieve this:

1. Double left-click on the `Transition Rule` property between `JumpStart` and `JumpLoop` to open its graph. This `Transition Rule` will check how much time is remaining from the `JumpingStart` animation. This is done because a certain percentage of time remains in the `JumpingStart` animation, and you can safely assume that the player is in the air and is ready to transition to the `JumpingLoop` animation state.

2. To do this, make sure that the `JumpingStart` animation is selected in the **Asset Browser** window. Then, right-click `Event Graph` of `Transition Rule` and find the `Time Remaining Ratio` function.

   Let's take a moment to talk about the `Time Remaining Ratio` function and what it is doing. This function returns a float between `0.0f` and `1.0f` that tells you how much time is remaining in the specified animation. The values `0.0f` and `1.0f` can directly be translated into a percentage value so that they are easier to consider. In the case of the `JumpingStart` animation, you want to know whether less than 60% of the animation is remaining to transition successfully to the `JumpingLoop` state. This is what you will do now.

3. From the `Return Value` float output parameter of the `Time Remaining Ratio` function, search for the `Less Than comparative operative` node from the context-sensitive search menu. Since you are working with a returned value between `0.0f` and `1.0f` to find out whether less than 60% of the animation remains, you need to compare this returned value with a value of `0.6f`. The final result is as follows:

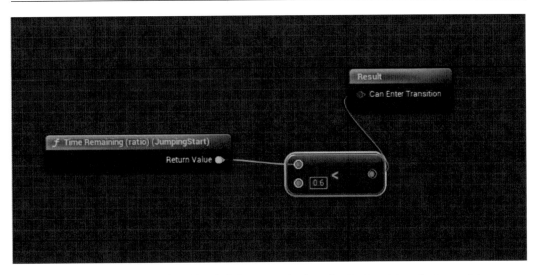

Figure 11.54 – The new Transition Rule between the JumpingStart and JumpingLoop states

With this `Transition Rule` in place, all you need to do is add the `JumpLoop` animation to the `JumpLoop` state.

4.   In the `Movement` state machine, double left-click on the `JumpLoop` state to enter its graph. With the `JumpLoop` animation asset selected in the **Asset Browser** window, left-click and drag it onto the graph. Connect its output to the `Result` input of `Output Animation Pose`, as shown in the following screenshot. The default settings of the `Play JumpLoop` node will remain unchanged:

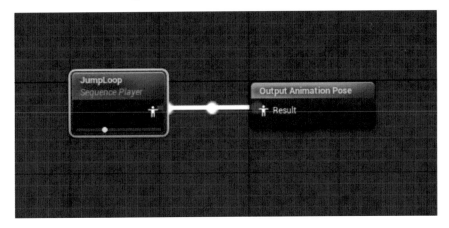

Figure 11.55 – The JumpLoop animation connected to Output Animation Pose of the new state

With the `JumpLoop` animation in place in the `JumpLoop` state, you can compile the Animation Blueprint and PIE. You will notice that the movement and sprinting animations are still present, but what happens when you try to jump? The player character begins the `JumpStart` state and plays the `JumpLoop` animation while in the air. This is great – the state machine is working, but what happens when the player character reaches the ground and is no longer in the air? The player character does not transition back to the `Movement` state, which makes sense because you haven't added the state for `JumpEnd`, nor the transitions between `JumpLoop` and `JumpEnd`, and from `JumpEnd` back to the `Movement` state. You will do this in the next activity. The following screenshot shows an example of a player character stuck in the `JumpLoop` state:

Figure 11.56 – The player character can now play the JumpingStart and JumpLoop animations

By completing this exercise, you successfully transitioned from the `JumpStart` state to the `JumpLoop` state by using the `Time Remaining Ratio` function. This function allows you to know how far along an animation has played, and with this information, you had the state machine transition into the `JumpLoop` state. The player can now successfully transition from the default `Movement` state to the `JumpStart` state and then to the `JumpLoop` state. However, this results in an interesting issue: the player is now stuck in the `JumpLoop` state because the state machine does not contain the transition backs to the `Movement` state. We'll fix this in the next activity.

Activity 11.04 – finishing the Movement and Jumping state machines

With half of the state machine completed, it's time to add the state for when the jump ends, as well as the Transition Rules that allow you to transition from the `JumpLoop` state to this new state, and then transition from this new state back to the `Movement` state.

Follow these steps to complete the Movement state machine:

1. Add a new state for Jump End that transitions from JumpLoop. Name this state JumpEnd.

2. Add the JumpEnd animation to the new JumpEnd state.

3. Based on the JumpEnd animation and how quickly we want to transition between the JumpLoop, JumpEnd, and Movement states, consider modifying the parameters of the animation like you did for the JumpStart animation. The loop animation parameter needs to be False and the Play Rate parameter needs to be set to 3.0.

4. Add a Transition Rule from the JumpLoop state to the JumpEnd state based on the bIsInAir variable.

5. Add a Transition Rule from the JumpEnd state to the Movement state based on the Time Remaining Ratio function of the JumpEnd animation. (Look at the JumpStart to JumpLoop Transition Rule).

By the end of this activity, you will have a fully functioning movement state machine that allows the player character to idle, walk, and sprint, as well as jump and animate correctly at the start of the jump, while in the air, and when landing.

The expected output is as follows:

Figure 11.57 – The player character can now idle, walk, sprint, and jump

> **Note**
> The solution to this activity can be found on GitHub here: https://github.com/PacktPublishing/Elevating-Game-Experiences-with-Unreal-Engine-5-Second-Edition/tree/main/Activity%20solutions.

By completing this activity, you have finished the `Movement` state machine for the player character. By adding the remaining `JumpEnd` state and `Transition Rules` to transition to the `JumpEnd` state from the `JumpLoop` state, and to transition from the `JumpEnd` state back to the `Movement` state, you have successfully created your first animation state machine. Now, you can run around the map and jump onto elevated platforms, all while animating correctly and transitioning between the `Movement` and jump states.

Summary

With the player movement Blend Space created and the player character Animation Blueprint using a State Machine to transition from movement to jumping, you are ready to move on to the next chapter, where you will prepare the required animation slot and animation montage, and then update the Animation Blueprint for the throw animation, which will only use the upper body of the character.

From the exercises and activities in this chapter, you learned how to create a Blend Space 1D that allows you to smoothly blend movement-based animations such as idling, walking, and running using the speed of the player character to control the blending of animations.

Additionally, you learned how to integrate new key bindings into the project settings and bind those keys in C++ to enable character gameplay mechanics such as sprinting and throwing.

Lastly, you learned how to implement your very own animation state machine within the character Animation Blueprint for the player to transition between movement animations, to the various states of jumping, and back to movement again. With all of this logic in place, in the next chapter, we'll create the assets and logic that allow the player character to play the throwing animation, and set up the base class for the enemy.

12
Animation Blending and Montages

In the previous chapter, you were able to bring the player character to life by implementing movement animations in a Blend Space and using that Blend Space in an Animation Blueprint to drive the animations based on the player's speed. You were then able to implement functionality in C++ based on player input to allow the character to sprint. Lastly, you took advantage of the Animation State Machine built-in Animation Blueprints to drive the character's movement state and jumping states to allow fluid transitions between walking and jumping.

With the player character's Animation Blueprint and State Machine working, it's time to introduce Animation Montages and Anim Slots by implementing the character's `Throw` animation. In this chapter, you will learn more about animation blending, see how Unreal Engine handles the blending of multiple animations by creating an Animation Montage, and work with a new Anim Slot for the player's throwing animation. From there, you will use the Anim Slot in the player's Animation Blueprint by implementing new functions such as `Save Cached Pose` and `Layered blend per bone` so that the player can correctly blend the movement animations you handled in the previous chapter with the new throwing animation you will implement in this chapter.

In this chapter, you'll learn about the following topics:

- How to use Anim Slots to create layered animation blending for the player character
- Creating an Animation Montage for the character's `Throw` animation
- Using the `Layered blend per bone` node within the Animation Blueprint to blend together the upper body `Throw` animation and the lower body movement animations of the character

By the end of this chapter, you will be able to use the `Animation Montage` tool to create a unique throwing animation using the `Throw` animation sequence you imported in *Chapter 10, Creating the SuperSideScroller Game*. With this montage, you will create and use Anim Slots that will allow you to blend animations in the Animation Blueprint for the player character. You will also get to know how to use blending nodes to effectively blend the movement and throwing animations of the character.

After finalizing the player character animation, you will create the required class and assets for the enemy AI and learn more about Materials and Material Instances, which will give this enemy a unique visual color so that it can be differentiated in-game. Finally, the enemy will be ready for *Chapter 13, Creating and Adding the Enemy Artificial Intelligence*, where you will begin to create the AI behavior logic.

Technical requirements

For this chapter, you will need Unreal Engine 5 installed

Let's start by learning about what Animation Montages and Anim Slots are and how they can be used for character animation.

The project for this chapter can be found in the Chapter12 folder of the code bundle for this book, which can be downloaded here: `https://github.com/PacktPublishing/Elevating-Game-Experiences-with-Unreal-Engine-5-Second-Edition`.

Animation blending, Anim Slots, and Animation Montages

Animation blending is the process of transitioning between multiple animations on a skeletal mesh as seamlessly as possible. You are already familiar with the techniques of animation blending because you created a `Blend Spaces` asset for the player character in *Chapter 11, Working with Blend Space 1D, Key Bindings, and State Machines*. In this Blend Space, the character smoothly blends between the `Idle`, `Walking`, and `Running` animations. You will now extend this knowledge by exploring and implementing new additive techniques to combine the movement animations of the character with a throwing animation. Through the use of an Anim Slot, you will send the throwing animation to a set of upper body bones, and its children's bones, to allow movement and throwing animations to apply at the same time without negatively impacting the other. But first, let's talk more about Animation Montages.

Animation Montages are very powerful assets that allow you to combine multiple animations and split these combined animations into what are called **Sections**. Sections can then be played back individually, in a specific sequence, or even looped.

Animation Montages are also useful because you can control animations through montages from Blueprints or C++; this means you can call logic, update variables, replicate data, and so on, based on the animation section being played, or if any Notifies are called within the montage. In C++, there is the `UAnimInstance` object, which you can use to call functions such as `UAnimInstance::Montage_Play`, which allows you to access and play montages from C++.

> **Note**
>
> This method will be used in *Chapter 14*, *Spawning the Player Projectile*, when you will begin to add polish to the game. More information about how animations and Notifies are handled by Unreal Engine 5 in C++ can be found at `https://docs.unrealengine.com/en-US/API/Runtime/Engine/Animation/AnimNotifies/UAnimNotifyState/index.html`. You will learn more about Notifies in the first exercise of this chapter, and you will code your own notify state in *Chapter 14*, *Spawning the Player Projectile*.

The following figure shows the Persona editor for Animation Montages. However, this will be broken down even further in *Exercise 12.01*, *Setting up the Animation Montage*:

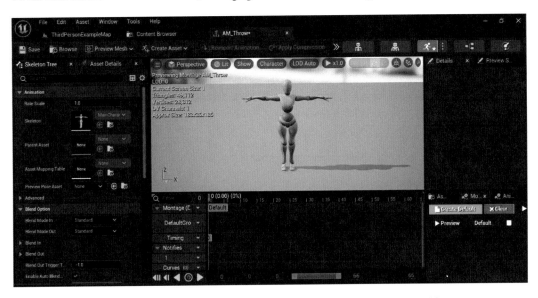

Figure 12.1 – The Persona editor, which opens when editing an Animation Montage

Just like in Animation Sequences, Animation Montages allow Notifies to be triggered along the timeline of a section of an animation, which can then trigger sounds, particle effects, and events. Event Notifies will allow us to call logic from Blueprint or C++. Epic Games provides an example in their documentation of a weapon reload Animation Montage that is split between animations for `reload start`, `reload loop`, and `reload complete`. By splitting these animations and applying Notifies for sounds and events, developers have complete control over how long the `reload loop` animation will play based on internal variables, and control over any additional sounds or effects to play during the course of the animation.

Lastly, Animation Montages support **Anim Slots**. Anim Slots allow you to categorize an animation, or a set of animations, that can later be referenced in Animation Blueprints to allow unique blending behavior based on the slot. This means that you can define an Anim Slot that can later be used in Animation Blueprints to allow animations using this slot to blend on top of the base movement animations in any way you want; in our case, only affecting the upper body of the player character and not the lower body.

Let's begin by creating the Animation Montage for the player character's `Throw` animation in the first exercise.

Exercise 12.01 – Setting up the Animation Montage

One of the first things you need to do for the player character is to set up the Anim Slot that will separately categorize this animation as an upper-body animation. You will use this Anim Slot in conjunction with blending functions in the Animation Blueprint to allow the player character to throw a projectile, while still correctly animating the lower body while moving and jumping.

By the end of this exercise, the player character will be able to play the `Throw` animation only with their upper body, while their lower body will still use the movement animation that you defined in the previous chapter.

Let's begin by creating the Animation Montage for the character, throwing and setting up the Anim Slot there:

1. First, navigate to the `/MainCharacter/Animation` directory, which is where all of the animation assets are located.

2. Now, right-click in the content drawer and hover over the **Animation** option from the available drop-down menu.

3. Then, left-click to select the **Animation Montage** option from the additional drop-down menu that appears.

4. Just as with creating other animation-based assets, such as `Blend Spaces` or `Animation Blueprints`, Unreal Engine will ask you to assign a `Skeleton` object for this Animation Montage. In this case, select `MainCharacter_Skeleton`.

5. Name the new Animation Montage `AM_Throw`. Now, double-left-click to open the montage.

When you open the `Animation Montage` asset, you are presented with a similar editor layout as you would when opening an Animation Sequence. There is a **Preview** window that shows the main character skeleton in the default T pose, but once you add animations to this montage, the skeleton will update to reflect those changes.

With this exercise complete, you have successfully created an **Animation Montage** asset for the **Super SideScroller** project. Now, it is time to learn more about Animation Montages and how you can add the `Throw` animation and Anim Slot you need in order to blend the `Throw` animation with the existing character movement animations.

Animation Montages

Have a look at the following figure:

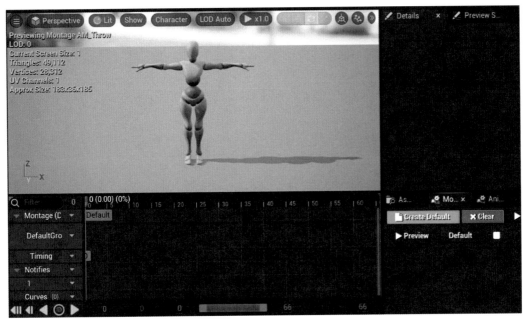

Figure 12.2 – The Preview window alongside the Montage and Sections areas

Underneath the **Preview** window, you have the main montage timeline, in addition to other sections. Let's evaluate these sections from top to bottom:

- **Montage**: The **Montage** section is a collection of animations that can have one or more animations. You can also right-click on any point in the timeline to create a section.

- **Montage Sections**: Sections allow you to compartmentalize the different parts of the montage into their own self-contained section, which allows you to set the order of how the individual animation sequences are played and whether a section should loop.

For the purposes of the Throw montage, you do not need to use this feature since you will only be using one animation in this montage:

- **Timing**: The **Timing** section gives you a preview of the montage and the sequential order of the varied aspects of the montage. The playback order of **Notifies**, the **Montage** section, and other elements will be visually displayed here to give you a quick preview of how the montage will work.

- **Notifies**: This gives you the ability to add points to an animation time frame that can then notify other systems to perform an action or to call logic from both Blueprints and C++. Notify options, such as `Play Sound` or `Play Particle Effect`, allow you to play a sound or particle at a specific time in the animation. You will use these Notifies later on in this project when you implement the throwing projectile:

Figure 12.3 – The Timing and Notifies areas

Now that you are familiar with the interface for Animation Montages, you can add the `Throw` animation to the montage by following the next exercise.

Exercise 12.02 – Adding the Throw animation to the montage

Now that you have a better understanding of what Animation Montages are and how these assets work, it is time to add the `Throw` animation to the montage you created in *Exercise 12.01, Setting up the Animation Montage*. Although you will only be adding one animation to this montage, it is important to emphasize that you can add multiple unique animations to a montage that you can then play back. Now, let's start by adding the `Throw` animation you imported into the project in *Chapter 10, Creating the SuperSideScroller Game*:

1. In **Asset Browser**, find the `Throw` animation asset. Then, left-click and drag it onto the timeline in the **Montage** section:

Figure 12.4 – The Asset Browser window with animation-based assets

Once an animation is added to the Animation Montage, the character skeleton in the **Preview** window will update to reflect this change and begin playing the animation:

Figure 12.5 – The player character begins to animate

Now that the `Throw` animation has been added to the Animation Montage, you can move on to create the Anim Slot.

The **Anim Slot Manager** tab should be docked next to the **Asset Browser** tab on the right-hand side. If you don't see the **Anim Slot Manager** tab, you can access it by navigating to the **Window** tab in the toolbar at the top of the **Animation Montage** editor window. There, left-click to select the option for **Anim Slot Manager**, and the window will appear.

By completing this exercise, you have added the `Throw` animation to your new Animation Montage and you were able to play back the animation to preview how it looks in the editor through **Persona**.

Now, you can move on to learn more about Anim Slots and Anim Slot Manager before adding your own unique Anim Slot to use for animation blending later in this chapter.

Anim Slot Manager

Anim Slot Manager is where you, as the name suggests, manage your Anim Slots. From this tab, you can create new groups, which allows greater organization of your slots. For example, you can create a group by left-clicking on the **Add Group** option and labeling it `Face` to articulate to others that the slots within this group affect the face of the character. By default, Unreal Engine provides you with a group called `DefaultGroup` and an Anim Slot called `DefaultSlot`, which is in that group.

In the following exercise, we will create a new Anim Slot specifically for the upper body of the player character.

Exercise 12.03 – Adding a new Anim Slot

Now that you have a better understanding of Anim Slots and **Anim Slot Manager**, you can follow these steps to create a new Anim Slot, which you will call `Upper Body`. Once you have this new slot created, it can then be used and referenced in your Animation Blueprint to handle animation blending, which you will do in a later exercise.

Let's create the Anim Slot by doing the following:

1. In **Anim Slot Manager**, left-click on the **Add Slot** option.

2. When adding a new slot, Unreal will ask you to give this Anim Slot a name. Name this slot `Upper Body`. Anim Slot naming is important, much like naming any other assets and parameters, as you will be referencing this slot in the Animation Blueprint later.

   With the Anim Slot created, you can now update the slot used for the Throw montage.

3. In the **Montage** section, there is a drop-down menu that displays the applied Anim Slot; by default, it's set to `DefaultGroup.DefaultSlot`. Left-click, and from the drop-down menu, select `DefaultGroup.Upper Body`:

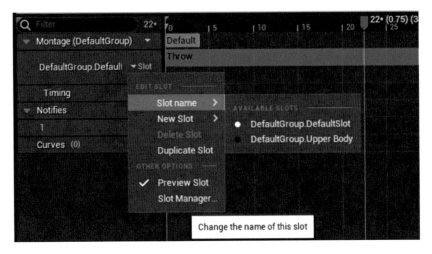

Figure 12.6 – The new Anim Slot will appear in the drop-down list

> **Note**
>
> After changing the Anim Slot, you may notice that the player character stops animating and returns to the T pose. Don't worry – if this happens, just close the Animation Montage and reopen it. Once reopened, the character will play the `Throw` animation again.

With your Anim Slot created and in place in the `Throw` montage, it is now time for you to update the Animation Blueprint so that the player character is aware of this slot and animates correctly based on it.

With this exercise complete, you have created your first Anim Slot using Anim Slot Manager, available in the Animation Montage. With this slot in place, it can now be used and referenced in the player character Animation Blueprint to handle the animation blending required to blend the `Throw` animation and the movement animations you implemented in the previous chapter. Before you do this, you need to learn more about the `Save Cached Pose` node in Animation Blueprints.

Save Cached Pose

There are cases when working with complex animations and characters requires you to reference a pose that is outputted by a State Machine in more than one place. If you hadn't noticed already, the output pose from your `Movement` State Machine cannot be connected to more than one other node. This is where the `Save Cached Pose` node comes in handy; it allows you to cache (or store) a pose that can then be referenced in multiple places at once. You will need to use this to set up the new Anim Slot for the upper body animation.

In the next exercise, you will implement the `Save Cached Pose` node to cache the `Movement` State Machine.

Exercise 12.04 – Save Cached Pose of the Movement State Machine

To effectively blend the `Throw` animation, which uses the `Upper Body` Anim Slot you created in the previous exercise with the movement animations already in place for the player character, you need to be able to reference the `Movement` State Machine in the Animation Blueprint. To do this, do the following to implement the `Save Cached Pose` node in the Animation Blueprint:

1. In the Anim Graph of `AnimBP_SuperSideScroller_MainCharacter`, right-click and search for `New Save Cached Pose`. Name this `Movement Cache`:

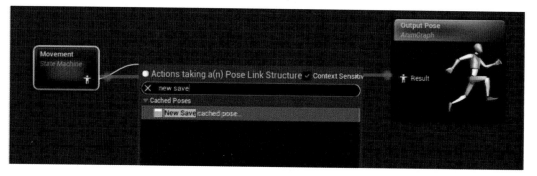

Figure 12.7 – The pose will be evaluated once per frame and then cached

2. Now, instead of connecting your `Movement` state machine directly to the output pose, connect it to the cache node:

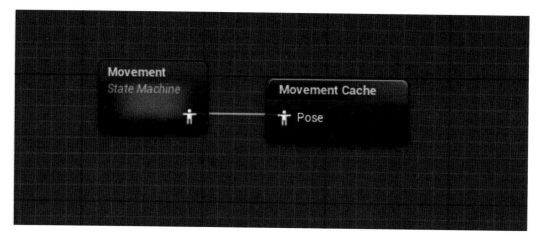

Figure 12.8 – The Movement State Machine is being cached

3. With the Movement State Machine pose being cached, all you have to do now is reference it. This can be done by searching for the Use Cached Pose node.

Note

All cached poses will show in the context-sensitive menu. Just make sure you select the cached pose with the name you gave it in *step 1*.

---

4. With the cached pose node available, connect it to Output Pose of the Anim Graph:

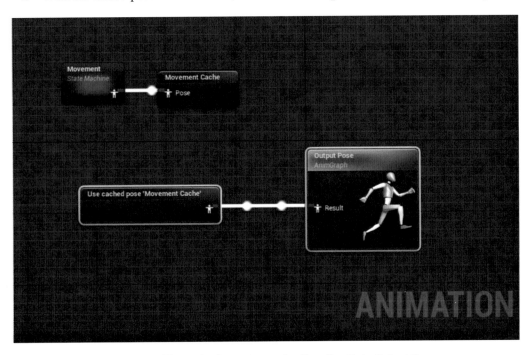

Figure 12.9 – The cached pose is now feeding directly to Output Pose

You will notice now, after *step 4*, that the main character will animate correctly and move as you expect after the last chapter. This proves that the caching of the `Movement` State Machine is working. The following figure shows the player character back in his `Idle` animation in the **Preview** window of the Animation Blueprint:

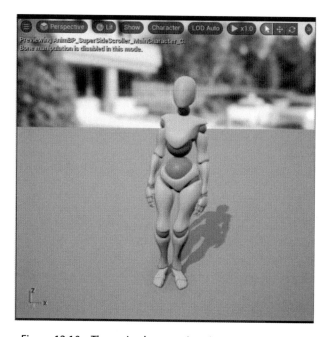

Figure 12.10 – The main character is animating as expected

Now that you have the caching of the `Movement` State Machine working, you will use this cache to blend animations through the skeleton based on the Anim Slot you created:

With this exercise complete, you now have the ability to reference the cached `Movement` State Machine pose anywhere you would like within the Animation Blueprint. With this accessibility in place, you can now use the cached pose to begin the blending between the cached movement pose and the `Upper Body` Anim Slot using a function called `Layered blend per bone`.

Layered blend per bone

The node that you will use to blend animations here is called `Layered blend per bone`. This node masks out a set of bones on the character's skeleton for an animation to ignore those bones.

In the case of our player character and the `Throw` animation, you will mask out the lower body so that only the upper body animates. The goal is to be able to perform the `Throw` and movement animations at the same time and have these animations blend together; otherwise, when you perform the throw, the movement animations would completely break.

In the following exercise, you will use Layered blend per bone to mask out the lower half of the player character so that the Throw animation only affects the upper body of the character.

Exercise 12.05 – Blending animation with the Upper Body Anim Slot

The Layered blend per bone function allows us to blend the Throw animation with the movement animations you implemented in the previous chapter, and give you control over how much influence the Throw animation will have on the player character's skeleton.

In this exercise, you will use the Layered blend per bone function to completely mask out the lower body of the character when playing the Throw animation so that it does not influence the character movement animation of the lower body.

Let's begin by adding the Layered blend per bone node and discussing its input parameters and its settings:

1. Inside the Animation Blueprint, right-click and search for Layered blend per bone in the **Context Sensitive** search. *Figure 12.11* shows the Layered blend per bone node and its parameters:

    *   The first parameter, Base Pose, is for the base pose of the character; in this case, the cached pose of the Movement State Machine will be the base pose.

    *   The second parameter is the Blend Poses 0 node that you want to layer on top of Base Pose; keep in mind that selecting **Add pin** will create additional Blend Poses and Blend Weights parameters. For now, you will only be working with one Blend Poses node.

    *   The last parameter is Blend Weights, which is how much Blend Poses will affect Base Pose on a scale from 0.0 to 1.0 as an alpha:

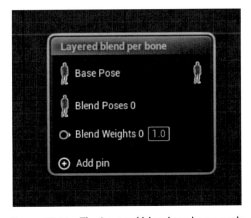

Figure 12.11 – The Layered blend per bone node

Before you connect anything to this node, you will need to add a layer to its properties.

2. Left-click to select the node and navigate to **Details**. You will need to left-click on the arrow next to **Layer Setup** to find the first index, 0, of this setup. Left-click on + next to **Branch Filters** to create a new filter.

There are again two parameters here, namely the following:

*   Bone Name: The bone to specify where the blending will take place and determine the child hierarchy of bones masked out. In the case of the main character skeleton for this project, set Bone Name to Spine. *Figure 12.12* shows how the Spine bone and its children are unassociated with the lower body of the main character. This can be seen in the Skeleton asset, MainCharacter_Skeleton:

Figure 12.12 – The Spine bone and its children are associated with the upper body of the main character

*   Blend Depth: The depth in which bones and their children will be affected by the animation. A value of 0 will not affect the rooted children of the selected bone.

*   Mesh Space Rotation Blend: Determines whether or not to blend bone rotations in mesh space or local space. Mesh space rotation refers to the skeletal mesh's bounding box as its base rotation, while local space rotation refers to the local rotation of the bone name in question. In this case, we want the rotation blend to occur in mesh space, so we will set this parameter to true.

Blending is propagated to all the children of a bone to stop blending on particular bones, add them to the array, and make their blend depth value 0. The final result is as follows:

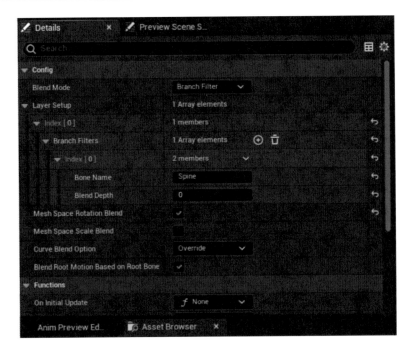

Figure 12.13 – You can set up multiple layers with one blend node

3. With the settings in place on the Layered blend per bone node, you can connect the Movement Cache cached pose into the Base Pose node of the layered blend. Make sure you connect the output of the Layered blend per bone node to Output Pose of the Animation Blueprint:

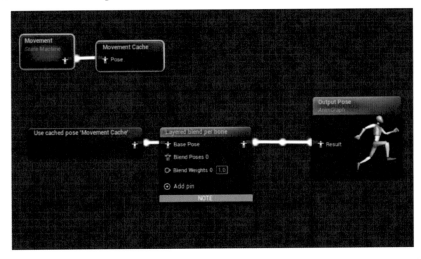

Figure 12.14 – Add the cached pose for the Movement State Machine to the Layered blend per bone node

Now, it's time to use the Anim Slot you created earlier to filter only the animations using this slot through the `Layered blend per bone` node.

4. Right-click in the Anim Graph and search for `DefaultSlot`. Left-click to select the `Slot` node and navigate to **Details**. There, you will find the `Slot Name` property. Left-click on this dropdown to find and select the `DefaultGroup.Upper Body` slot.

When changing the `Slot Name` property, the `Slot` node will update to represent this new name. The `Slot` node requires a source pose, which will again be a reference to the `Movement` State Machine. This means that you need to create another `Use Cached Pose` node for the `Movement Cache` pose.

5. Connect the cached pose to the source of the `Slot` node:

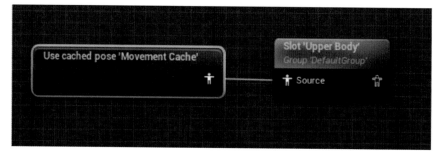

Figure 12.15 – Filtering the cached movement pose through the Anim Slot

6. All that is left to do now is to connect the `Upper Body` slot node to the `Blend Poses 0` input. Then, connect the final pose of the `Layered blend per bone` to the result of the `Output Pose` Animation Blueprint:

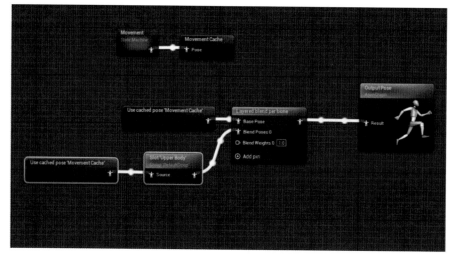

Figure 12.16 – The final setup of the main character's Animation Blueprint

With the Anim Slot and the `Layered blend per bone` node in place within the main character's Animation Blueprint, you are finally done with the animation side of the main character.

With the Animation Blueprint updated, we can now move on to the next exercise, where we can finally preview the `Throw` animation in action.

Exercise 12.06 – Previewing the Throw animation

In the previous exercise, you did a lot of work to allow animation blending between the player character's `Movement` animations and the `Throw` animation by using the `Save Cached Pose` and `Layered blend per bone` nodes. Perform the following steps to preview the `Throw` animation in-game and see the fruits of your labor:

1. Navigate to the `/MainCharacter/Blueprints/` directory and open the character's `BP_SuperSideScroller_MainCharacter` Blueprint.

2. If you recall, in the last chapter, you created `Enhanced Input Action` for throwing with `IA_Throw`.

3. Inside `Event Graph` of the character's Blueprint, right-click and search for `EnhancedInputAction IA_Throw` in the **Context Sensitive** drop-down search. Select it with a left-click to create the event node in the graph.

    With this event in place, you need a function that allows you to play an Animation Montage when the player uses the left mouse button to throw.

4. Right-click in `Event Graph` and search for `Play Montage`. Make sure not to confuse this with a similar function, `Play Anim Montage`.

    The `Play Montage` function requires two important inputs:

    • `Montage to Play`

    • `In Skeletal Mesh Component`

    Let's first handle the `Skeletal Mesh` component.

5. The player character has a `Skeletal Mesh` component that can be found in the **Components** tab labeled `Mesh`. Left-click and drag out a `Get` reference to this variable and connect it to the `In Skeletal Mesh Component` input of this function:

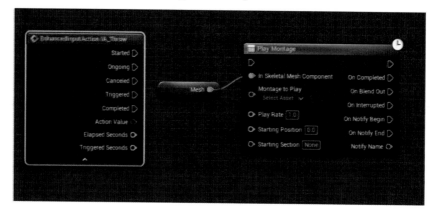

Figure 12.17 – The mesh of the player character connected to the In Skeletal Mesh Component input

The last thing to do now is to tell this function which montage to play. Luckily for you, there is only one montage that exists in this project: `AM_Throw`.

6. Left-click on the drop-down menu under the `Montage to Play` input and left-click to select `AM_Throw`.

7. Finally, connect the `Triggered` execution output of the `EnhancedInputAction IA_Throw` event to the execution input pin of the `Play Montage` function:

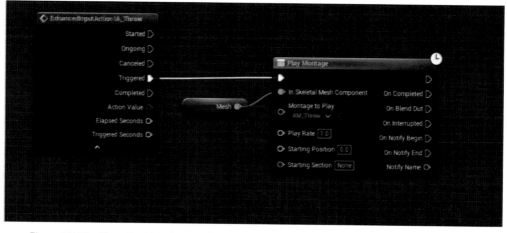

Figure 12.18 – Now the AM_Throw montage plays when the ThrowProjectile input is pressed

8. Now, when you click your left mouse button, the player character will play the throwing Animation Montage.

Notice now how you can walk and run at the same time as throwing, and each animation blends together so as not to interfere with one another:

Figure 12.19 – The player character can now move and throw

Don't worry about any bugs you might see when using the left mouse button action repeatedly to play the `Throw` montage; these issues will be addressed when you implement the projectile that will be thrown in a later chapter for this project. For now, you just want to know that the work done on the Anim Slot and the Animation Blueprint give the desired result for animation blending.

Let's continue with the **SuperSideScroller** project by now creating the C++ class, the Blueprints, and the materials necessary to set up the enemy for use in the next chapter.

The SuperSideScroller game enemy

With the player character animating correctly when moving and performing the `Throw` animation, it is time to talk about the enemy type that the **SuperSideScroller** game will feature.

This enemy will have a basic back-and-forth movement pattern and will not support any attacks; only by colliding with the player character will it be able to inflict damage.

In the next exercise, you will set up the base enemy class in C++ for the first enemy type and configure the enemy's Blueprint and Animation Blueprint in preparation for *Chapter 13, Creating and Adding the Enemy Artificial Intelligence*, where you will implement the AI of this enemy. For the sake of efficiency and time, you will use the assets already provided by Unreal Engine 5 in the **SideScroller** template for the enemy. This means you will be using the skeleton, skeletal mesh, animations, and the Animation Blueprint of the default mannequin asset. Let's begin by creating the first enemy class.

Exercise 12.07 – Creating the enemy base C++ class

The goal of this exercise is to create a new enemy class from scratch and to have the enemy ready to use in *Chapter 13, Creating and Adding the Enemy Artificial Intelligence*, when you will develop the AI. To start, create a new enemy class in C++ by following these steps:

1. In the editor, navigate to **Tools** and select **New C++ Class** to get started with creating your new enemy class. In the editor, create a new C++ class that derives from the `SuperSideScrollreCharacter` parent class.

2. Give this class a name and select a directory. Name this class `EnemyBase` and do not change the directory path. When ready, left-click on the **Create Class** button to have Unreal Engine create the new class for you.

    Let's create the folder structure in the content drawer for the enemy assets next.

3. Head back to the Unreal Engine 5 editor, navigate to the content drawer, and create a new folder called Enemy:

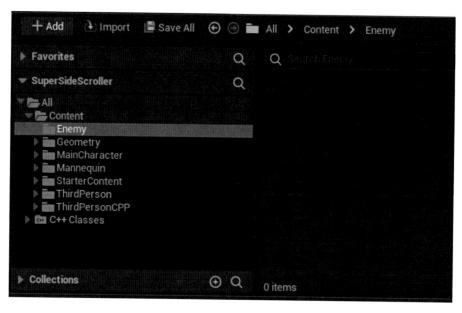

Figure 12.20 – The new Enemy folder

4. In the Enemy folder, create another folder called `Blueprints`, where you will create and save the Blueprint assets for the enemy. Right-click and select **Blueprint Class**. From **Pick Parent Class**, search for the new C++ class you just made, `EnemyBase`, as shown here:

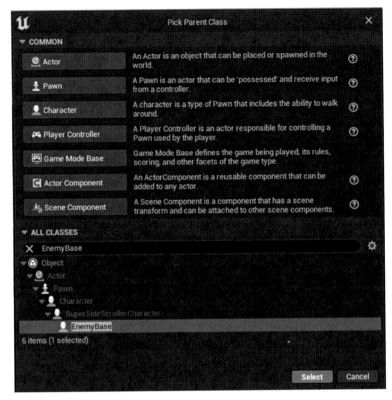

Figure 12.21 – Now, the new EnemyBase class is available for you to create a Blueprint from

5.   Name this `BP_Enemy`.

Now that you have the Blueprint for the first enemy using the `EnemyBase` class as the parent class, it is time to handle the Animation Blueprint. You will use the default Animation Blueprint that is provided to you by Unreal Engine in the **SideScroller** template project. Follow the steps in the next exercise to create a duplicate of the existing Animation Blueprint and move it to the `/Enemy/Blueprints` directory.

Exercise 12.08 – Creating and applying the enemy Animation Blueprint

In the previous exercise, you created a Blueprint for the first enemy using the `EnemyBase` class as the parent class. In this exercise, you will be working with the Animation Blueprint.

The following steps will help you complete this exercise:

1.   Navigate to the `/Mannequin/Animations` directory and find the `ThirdPerson_AnimBP` asset.

2. Now, duplicate the `ThirdPerson_AnimBP` asset. There are two ways to duplicate an asset:

    I.   Select the desired asset in the content drawer and press *Ctrl + W*.

    II.   Right-click on the desired asset in the content drawer and select `Duplicate` from the drop-down menu.

3. Now, left-click and drag this duplicate asset into the `/Enemy/Blueprints` directory and select the option to move when you release the left-click mouse button.

4. Name this duplicate asset `AnimBP_Enemy`. It is best to create a duplicate of an asset that you can later modify if you so desire without risking the functionality of the original.

   With the enemy Blueprint and Animation Blueprint created, it's time to update the enemy Blueprint to use the default `Skeletal Mesh` mannequin and the new Animation Blueprint duplicate.

5. Navigate to `/Enemy/Blueprints` and open `BP_Enemy`.

6. Next, navigate to the `Mesh` component and select it to access its **Details** panel. First, assign **SK_Mannequin** to the **Skeletal Mesh** parameter, as shown here:

Figure 12.22 – You will use the default SK_Mannequin skeletal mesh for the new enemy

7. Now, you need to apply the `AnimBP_Enemy` Animation Blueprint to the `Mesh` component. Navigate to the `Animation` category of the `Mesh` component's **Details** panel, and under **Anim Class**, assign `AnimBP_Enemy`:

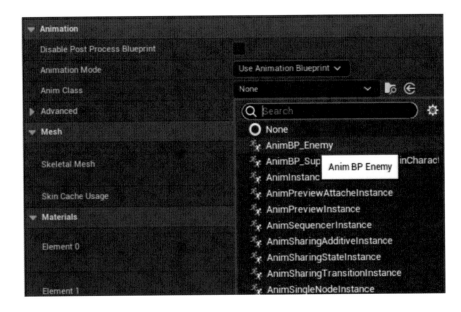

Figure 12.23 – Assign the new AnimBP_Enemy as the Anim class

8. Lastly, you will notice that the character mesh is positioned and rotated incorrectly when previewing the character in the **Preview** window. Fix this by setting the **Transform** property of the **Mesh** component to the following:

- **Location**: ($X = 0.000000$, $Y = 0.000000$, $Z = -90.000000$)
- **Rotation**: (Roll= 0.000000, Pitch= 0, Yaw= -90.000000)
- **Scale**: ($X = 1.000000$, $Y = 1.000000$, $Z = 1.000000$)

The `Transform` settings will appear as follows:

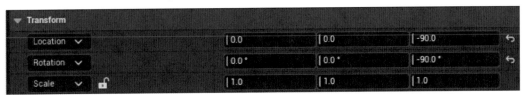

Figure 12.24 – The final Transform settings for the enemy character

The following figure shows the settings of the **Mesh** component so far. Please make sure your settings match what is displayed in *Figure 12.25*:

Figure 12.25 – The settings for the Mesh component of your enemy character

The last thing to do here is to create a Material Instance of the mannequin's primary material so that this enemy can have a unique color that helps differentiate it from the other enemy type.

Let's begin by first learning more about Materials and Material Instances.

Materials and Material Instances

Before moving on to the next exercise, we need to first briefly discuss what Material Instances are before you can work with these assets and apply them to the new enemy character. Although this book is more focused on the technical aspects of game development using Unreal Engine 5, it is still important that you know, on a surface level, what Material Instances are and how they are used in video games. A Material Instance is an extension of a Material, where you do not have access or control over the base Material from which the Material Instance derives, but you do have control over the parameters that the creator of the Material exposes to you. Many parameters can be exposed to you to work with from inside Material Instances.

> **Note**
>
> For more information about Materials and Material Instances, please refer to the following Epic Games documentation pages: `https://docs.unrealengine.com/en-US/Engine/Rendering/Materials/index.html` and `https://docs.unrealengine.com/4.27/en-US/API/Runtime/Engine/Materials/UMaterialInstanceDynamic/`.

Unreal Engine provides us with an example of a Material Instance in the Side Scroller template project called `M_UE4Man_ChestLogo`, found in the `/Mannequin/Character/Materials/` directory. The following figure shows the set of exposed parameters given to the Material Instance based on the parent material, `M_Male_Body`. The most important parameter to focus on is the `Vector` parameter, called `BodyColor`. You will use this parameter in the Material Instance you create in the next exercise to give the enemy a unique color:

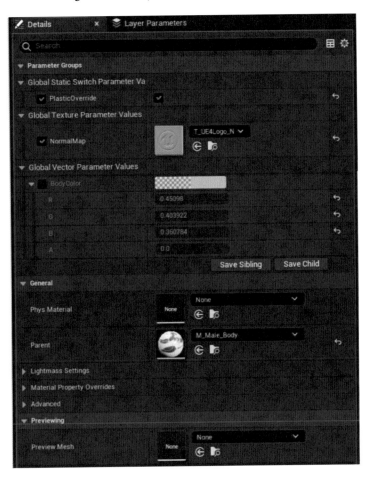

Figure 12.26 – The list of parameters for the M_UE4Man_ChestLogo Material Instance asset

In the following exercise, you will take this knowledge of Material Instances and apply them to create a unique Material Instance to be used for the enemy character you created earlier.

Exercise 12.09 – Creating and applying the enemy Material Instance

Now that you have a basic understanding of what Material Instances are, it is time to create your own Material Instance from the M_MannequinUE4_Body asset. With this Material Instance, you will adjust the BodyColor parameter to give the enemy character a unique visual representation.

The following steps will help you complete this exercise:

1. Navigate to the Characters/Mannequin_UE4/Materials directory to find the Material used by the default mannequin character, M_MannequinUE4_Body.

2. A Material Instance can be created by right-clicking on the Material asset, M_MannequinUE4_Body, and left-clicking on the **Create Material Instance** option. Name this asset as MI_Enemy01.

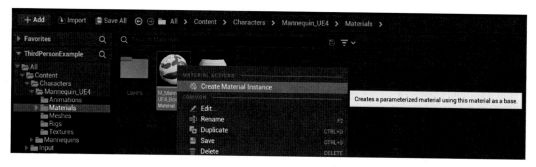

Figure 12.27 – Any material can be used to create a Material Instance

Create a new folder called Materials in the Enemy folder. Left-click and drag the Material Instance into the /Enemy/Materials directory to move the asset to this new folder:

Figure 12.28 – Rename the Material Instance MI_Enemy

3. Double-left-click the Material Instance and find the **Details** panel on the left-hand side. There, you will find a **Vector Parameter** property called **BodyColor**. Make sure the checkbox is checked to enable this parameter, and then change its value to a red color. Now, the Material Instance should be colored red, as shown here:

Figure 12.29 – Now, the enemy material is red

4. Save the **Material Instance** asset and navigate back to the `BP_Enemy01` Blueprint. Select the **Mesh** component and update the **Element 0** material parameter to `MI_Enemy`:

Figure 12.30 – Assign the MI_Enemy material instance to the enemy character Mesh

5. Now, the first enemy type is visually ready and has the appropriate Blueprint and Animation Blueprint assets prepared for the next chapter, where you will develop its AI:

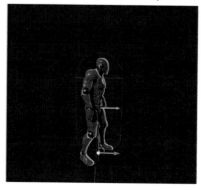

Figure 12.31 – The final enemy character set up

With this exercise complete, you have now created a Material Instance and applied it to the enemy character so that it has a unique visual representation.

Let's conclude this chapter by moving on to a short activity that will help you better understand the blending of animations using the `Layered blend per bone` node that was used in the earlier exercises.

Activity 12.01 – Updating Blend Weights

At the end of *Exercise 12.06, Previewing the Throw animation,* you were able to blend the movement animations and the `Throw` animation so that they could be played in tandem without negatively influencing each other. The result is the player character animating correctly when walking or running, while also performing the `Throw` animation on the upper body.

In this activity, you will experiment with the blend bias values and parameters of the `Layered blend per bone` node to have a better understanding of how animation blending works.

The following steps will help you complete the activity:

1. Update the `Blend Weights` input parameter of the `Layered blend per bone` node so that there is absolutely no blending of the `Throw` animation additive pose with the base movement pose. Try using values here such as `0.0f` and `0.5f` to compare the differences in the animation.

> **Note**
> Make sure to return this value to `1.0f` after you are done so as not to affect the blending you set up in the previous exercise.

2. Update the settings of the `Layered blend per bone` node to change which bone is affected by the blend so that the whole character's body is affected by the blend. It's a good idea to start with the root bone in the skeleton hierarchy of the `MainCharacter_Skeleton` asset.

3. Keeping the settings from the previous step in place, add a new array element to the branch filters and, in this new array element, add the bone name and a blend depth value of `−1.0f`, which allows only the character's left leg to continue to animate the movement correctly when blending the `Throw` animation.

> **Note**
> After this activity, make sure to return the settings of the `Layered blend per bone` node to the values you set at the end of the first exercise to ensure no progress is lost in the character's animation.

The expected output for the first part of the activity is shown here:

Figure 12.32 – Output showing the entire character's body affected

The expected output for the last part of the activity is shown here:

Figure 12.33 – The left leg continues to animate the movement
correctly when blending the Throw animation

> **Note**
>
> The solution to this activity can be found on GitHub here: `https://github.com/PacktPublishing/Elevating-Game-Experiences-with-Unreal-Engine-5-Second-Edition/tree/main/Activity%20solutions`.
>
> Before concluding this activity, please return the `Layered blend per bone` settings to the values you set at the end of *Exercise 12.05, Blending animation with the Upper Body Anim Slot*. If you do not return these values back to their original settings, the animation results in upcoming exercises and activities in the next chapters will not be the same. You can either set the original values manually or refer to the file with these settings at the following link: `https://github.com/PacktPublishing/Elevating-Game-Experiences-with-Unreal-Engine-5-Second-Edition/tree/main/Chapter12/Exercise12.05`.

With this activity complete, you now have a stronger understanding of how animation blending works and how blending weighting can affect the influence of additive poses on base poses using the `Layered blend per bone` node.

> **Note**
>
> There are a lot of techniques for animation blending that you haven't used in this project, and it's strongly recommended that you research these techniques, starting with the documentation at `https://docs.unrealengine.com/en-US/Engine/Animation/AnimationBlending/index.html`.

Summary

With the enemy set up with the C++ class, Blueprint, and Material, you are ready to move on to the next chapter, where you will create the AI for this enemy by taking advantage of systems such as behavior trees in Unreal Engine 5.

From the exercises and activities of this chapter, you learned how to create an Animation Montage that allows the playing of animations. You also learned how to set up an Anim Slot within this montage to categorize it for the player character's upper body.

Next, you learned how to cache the output pose of a State Machine by using the `Use Cached Pose` node so that this pose can be referenced in multiple instances for more complex Animation Blueprints. Then, by learning about the `Layered blend per bone` function, you were able to blend the base movement pose with the additive layer of the `Throw` animation by using the Anim Slot.

Lastly, you put together the base of the enemy by creating the C++ class, Blueprint, and other assets so that they will be ready for the next chapter. With the enemy ready, let's move on to creating the AI of the enemy so that it can interact with the player.

13

Creating and Adding the Enemy Artificial Intelligence

In the previous chapter, you added layered animations for the player character using animation blending with a combination of Anim Slots, Animation Blueprints, and blending functions such as `Layered blend per bone`. With this knowledge, you were able to smoothly blend the throwing animation montage with the base movement state machine to create layered animations for the character.

The primary focus of this chapter is to take the C++ enemy class you created in *Chapter 12, Animation Blending and Montages*, and bring this enemy to life using AI. UE5 uses many different tools to achieve AI, such as AI Controllers, Blackboards, and Behavior Trees, all of which you will learn about and use in this chapter.

In this chapter, we will cover the following topics:

- How to use a Navigation Mesh to create a navigable space inside of the game world that the enemy can move in.

- How to create an enemy AI pawn that can navigate between patrol point locations inside the game world using a combination of the AI tools present inside **Unreal Engine 5** (**UE5**), including `Blackboards` and `Behavior Trees`.

- How to use a Transform Vector to convert local transform into world transform.

- How to create a player projectile class in C++, and how to implement the `OnHit()` collision event function to recognize and log when the projectile hits an object in the game world.

By the end of this chapter, you will be able to create a navigable space where the enemy can move. You will also be able to create an enemy AI pawn and navigate it across locations using `Blackboards` and `Behavior Trees`. Lastly, you will know how to create and implement a player projectile class and add visual elements to it. Before you jump into these systems, let's take a moment to learn about how AI has been used in games in recent history. AI has certainly evolved since the days of *Super Mario Bros.*

Technical requirements

For this chapter, you will need the following technical requirements:

- Unreal Engine 5 installed
- Visual Studio 2019 installed

The project for this chapter can be found in the `Chapter13` folder of the code bundle for this book, which can be downloaded from

`https://github.com/PacktPublishing/Elevating-Game-Experiences-with-Unreal-Engine-5-Second-Edition`.

Enemy AI

What is **artificial intelligence** (**AI**)? This term can mean many things, depending on the field and context where it is used, so let's define it in a way that makes sense regarding the subject of video games.

AI is an entity that is aware of its environment and performs choices that will help it optimally achieve its intended purpose. AI uses what are called **finite state machines** to switch between more than one state based on the input it receives from the user or its environment. For example, a video game AI can switch between an offensive state to a defensive state based on its current health.

In games such as *Hello Neighbor*, which was developed in Unreal Engine 4, and *Alien: Isolation*, the goal of the AI is to find the player as efficiently as possible, but also to follow some predetermined patterns defined by the developers to ensure that the player can outsmart it. *Hello Neighbor* adds a very creative element to its AI by having it learn from the players' past actions and try to outsmart the player based on the knowledge it learns.

You can find an informative breakdown of how the AI works in the following video by the publishers of the game, *TinyBuild Games*: `https://www.youtube.com/watch?v=Hu7Z52RaBGk`.

Interesting and fun AI is crucial to any game, and depending on the game you are making, this can mean a very complex or very simplistic AI. The AI that you will be creating for the `SuperSideScroller` game will not be as sophisticated as those mentioned previously, but it will fill the needs of the game we are seeking to create.

Let's break down how the enemy will behave:

- The enemy will be a very simple enemy that has a basic back and forth movement pattern and will not support any attacks; only by colliding with the player character will they be able to inflict any damage.

- However, we need to set the locations for the enemy AI to move between.

- Next, we must decide whether the AI should change locations, should constantly move between locations, or whether there should be a pause inbetween selecting a new location to move to.

Fortunately for us, UE5 provides us with a wide array of tools that we can use to develop such complex AI. In the case of our project, however, we will use these tools to create a simplistic enemy type. Let's start by discussing what an AI Controller is in UE5.

AI Controller

Let's discuss what the main difference is between a **Player Controller** and an **AI Controller**. Both of these actors derive from the base **Controller** class. A **Controller** is used to take control of a **Pawn** or **Character** to control the actions of said pawn or character.

While a **Player Controller** relies on the input of an actual player, an **AI Controller** applies AI to the characters they possess and responds to the environment based on the rules set forth by the AI. By doing so, the AI can make intelligent decisions in response to the player and other external factors, without the player explicitly telling it to do so. Multiple instances of the same AI pawn can share the same **AI Controller**, and the same **AI Controller** can be used across different AI pawn classes. AI, like all actors inside UE5, is spawned through the UWorld class.

> **Note**
>
> You will learn more about the UWorld class in *Chapter 14*, *Spawning the Player Projectile*, but as a reference, you can read more here: https://docs.unrealengine.com/en-US/API/Runtime/Engine/Engine/UWorld/index.html.

The most important aspect of both the Player Controller and the AI Controller is the pawns they will control. Let's learn more about how AI Controllers handle this.

Auto Possess AI

Like all Controllers, the AI Controller must possess a *pawn*. In C++, you can use the following function to possess a pawn:

```
void AController::Possess(APawn* InPawn)
```

You can also use the following function to unpossess a pawn:

```
void AController::UnPossess()
```

There's also the `void AController::OnPossess(APawn* InPawn)` and `void AController::OnUnPossess()` functions, which are called whenever the `Possess()` and `UnPossess()` functions are called, respectively.

When it comes to AI, especially in the context of UE5, there are two methods in which AI Pawns or Characters can be possessed by an AI Controller. Let's take a look at these options:

- `Placed in World`: This first method is how you will be handling AI in this project; you will manually place these enemy actors into your game world, and the AI will take care of the rest once the game begins.

- `Spawned`: This second method is only a little more complicated because it requires an explicit function call, either in C++ or Blueprint, to Spawn an instance of a specified class. The Spawn Actor method requires a handful of parameters, including the `World` object and `Transform` parameters such as `Location` and `Rotation`, to ensure that the instance that is spawned is spawned correctly.

- `Placed in World or Spawned`: If you are unsure of which method you want to use, a safe option would be `Placed in World or Spawned`; that way, both methods are supported.

- For the `SuperSideScroller` game, you will be using the `Placed in World` option because the AI you will create will be manually placed in the game level.

Let's move to our first exercise where we will implement the AI Controller for the enemy.

Exercise 13.01 – implementing AI Controllers

Before the enemy pawn can do anything, it needs to be possessed by an AI Controller. This also needs to happen before any logic can be performed by the AI. By the end of this exercise, you will have created an AI Controller and applied it to the enemy that you created in the previous chapter. Let's begin by creating the AI Controller.

Follow these steps to complete this exercise:

1. Head to the **Content Drawer** interface and navigate to the `Content/Enemy` directory.

2. *Right-click* on the Enemy folder and select the **New Folder** option. Name this new folder `AI`. In the new `AI` folder directory, *right-click* and select the **Blueprint Class** option.

3. From the **Pick Parent Class** dialog box, expand **All Classes** and manually search for the `AIController` class.

4. *Left-click* this class option and then *left-click* on the blue **Select** option at the bottom to create a new Blueprint from this class. Please refer to the following screenshot to know where to find the AIController class. Also, take note of the tooltip that appears when hovering over the class option; it contains useful information about this class from the developers:

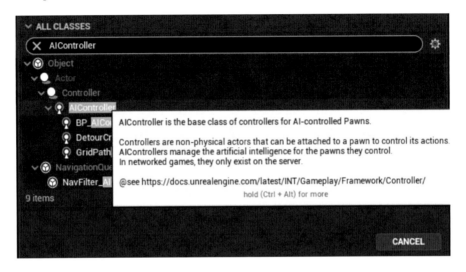

Figure 13.1 – The AIController asset class, as found in the Pick Parent Class dialog box

5. With this new AIController Blueprint created, name this asset BP_AIControllerEnemy.

   With the AI Controller created and named, it's time to assign this asset to the first enemy Blueprint that you made in the previous chapter.

6. Navigate to the /Enemy/Blueprints directory to find BP_Enemy. *Double-click* to open this Blueprint.

7. In the **Details** panel of the first enemy Blueprint, there is a section labeled Pawn. This is where you can set different parameters regarding the AI functionality of Pawn or Character.

8. The AI Controller Class parameter determines, as its name suggests, which AI Controller to use for this enemy. *Left-click* on the dropdown to find and select the AI Controller you made earlier–that is, BP_AIController_Enemy.

With this exercise complete, the enemy AI now knows which AI Controller to use. This is crucial because it is in the AI Controller where the AI will use and execute the Behavior Tree you will create later in this chapter.

The AI Controller is now assigned to the enemy, which means you are almost ready to start developing the actual intelligence for this AI. However, there is still one important topic to discuss before doing so, and that is the **Navigation Mesh**.

Navigation Mesh

One of the most crucial aspects of any AI in video games is the ability to navigate the environment in a sophisticated manner. In UE5, there is a way for the engine to tell the AI which parts of an environment are navigable and which parts are not. This is done through a **Navigation Mesh**, or **Nav Mesh** for short.

The term *mesh* is misleading here because it's implemented through a volume in the editor. We will need a Nav Mesh in our level so that our AI can effectively navigate the playable bounds of the game world. We'll add one together in the following exercise.

UE5 also supports a **Dynamic Navigation Mesh**, which allows the Nav Mesh to update in real time as dynamic objects move around the environment. This results in the AI recognizing these changes in the environment and updating their pathing/navigation appropriately. This book will not cover this, but you can access the configuration options via **Project Settings | Navigation Mesh | Runtime Generation**.

Now that we have learned about the **Navigation Mesh**, let's start our first exercise where we will add the **Navigation Mesh** to our level.

Exercise 13.02 – implementing a Nav Mesh Volume for the AI enemy

In this exercise, you will add a Navigation Mesh to `SideScrollerExampleMap` and explore how Navigation Meshes work in UE5. You'll also learn how to parameterize this volume for the needs of your game. This exercise will be performed within the UE5 editor.

By the end of this exercise, you will have a stronger understanding of the Nav Mesh. You will also be able to implement this volume in your levels in the activity that follows this exercise. Let's begin by adding the Nav Mesh Volume to the level.

Follow these steps to complete this exercise:

1. If you do not already have the map open, please open **ThirdPersonExampleMap** by navigating to **File** and *left-clicking* on the **Open Level** option. From the **Open Level** dialog box, navigate to **/ThirdPersonCPP/Maps** to find **SideScrollerExampleMap**. Select this map by *left-clicking* and then *left-click* **Open** at the bottom to open the map.

2. With the map opened, navigate to the **Window** menu at the top-left of the editor, and make sure you select the **Place Actors** panel option. The **Place Actors** panel contains a set of easily accessible actor types such as **Volumes**, **Lights**, **Geometry**, and others. Under the **Volumes** category, you will find the **Nav Mesh Bounds Volume** option.

3. *Left-click* and drag this volume into the map/scene. By default, you will see the outline of the volume in the editor. Press the *P* key to visualize the **Navigation** area that the volume encompasses, but make sure that the volume is intersecting with the ground geometry to see the green visualization, as shown in the following screenshot:

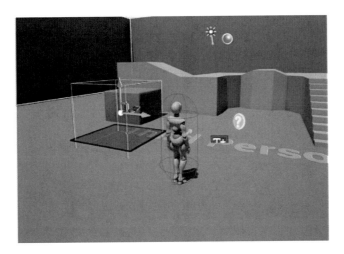

Figure 13.2 – Areas outlined in green are perceived as navigable by the engine and the AI

With the Nav Mesh Volume in place, let's adjust its shape so that the volume extends to the entire area of the level. After this, you'll learn how to adjust the parameters of the Nav Mesh Volume for the game.

4. *Left-click* to select **NavMeshBoundsVolume** and navigate to its **Details** panel. There's a section labeled **Brush Settings** that allows you to adjust the shape and size of the volume. Find the values that fit best for you. Some suggested settings are **Brush Type: Additive**, **Brush Shape: Box**, X: 3000.0, Y: 3000.0, and Z: 3000.0.

Notice that when the shape and dimensions of **NavMeshBoundsVolume** change, **Nav Mesh** will adjust and recalculate the navigable area. This can be seen in the following screenshot. You will also notice that the upper platforms are not navigable; you will fix this later:

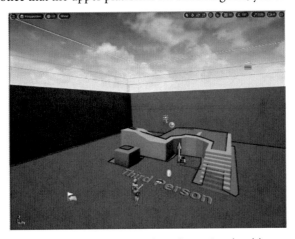

Figure 13.3 – Now, NavMeshBoundsVolume extends to the entire playable area of the example map

By completing this exercise, you have placed your first **NavMeshBoundsVolume** actor into the game world and, using the debug key, *P*, visualized the navigable area in the default map. Next, you will learn more about the `RecastNavMesh` actor, which is also created when placing `NavMeshBoundsVolume` in the level.

Recasting the Nav Mesh

When you added **NavMeshBoundsVolume**, you may have noticed that another actor was created automatically: a **RecastNavMesh** actor called **RecastNavMesh-Default**. This **RecastNavMesh** acts as the "brain" of the Nav Mesh because it contains the parameters needed to adjust the Nav Mesh that directly influences how the AI navigates the given area.

The following screenshot shows this asset, as seen from the **World Outliner** tab:

Figure 13.4 – The RecastNavMesh actor, as seen from the World Outliner tab

> **Note**
>
> There are a lot of parameters that exist in `RecastNavMesh`, and we will only be covering the important parameters in this book. For more information, check out `https://docs.unrealengine.com/en-US/API/Runtime/NavigationSystem/NavMesh/ARecastNavMesh/index.html`.

There are only two primary sections that are important to you right now:

- **Display**: The **Display** section, as its name suggests, only contains parameters that affect the visual debug display of the generated navigable area of **NavMeshBoundsVolume**. It is recommended that you try toggling each of the parameters under this category to see how they affect the display of the generated Nav Mesh.

- **Generation**: The **Generation** category contains a set of values that act as a rule set for how the Nav Mesh will generate and determine which areas of geometry are navigable, and which are not. There are many options here, which can make the concept very daunting, but let's discuss just a handful of the parameters under this category:

  - **Cell Size** refers to the accuracy with which the Nav Mesh can generate navigable space within an area. You will be updating this value in the next step of this exercise, so you'll see how this affects the navigable area in real time.

  - **Agent Radius** refers to the radius of the actor that will be navigating this area. In the case of your game, the radius to set here is the radius of the collision component of the character with the largest radius.

  - **Agent Height** refers to the height of the actor that will be navigating this area. In the case of your game, the height to set here is the **Half Height** value of the collision component of the character with the largest **Half Height**. You can multiply it by 2.0f to get the full height.

  - **Agent Max Slope** refers to the slope angle for inclines that can exist in your game world. By default, the value is 44 degrees, and this is a parameter you will leave alone unless your game requires it to change.

  - **Agent Max Step Height** refers to the height of steps, in terms of staircase steps, that can be navigated by the AI. Much like **Agent Max Slope**, this is a parameter that you will more than likely leave alone unless your game specifically requires this value to change.

Now that you have learned about the Recast Nav Mesh parameters, let's put this knowledge into practice in the next exercise, which will walk you through changing a few of these parameters.

Exercise 13.03 – recasting Nav Mesh Volume parameters

Now that you have the **Nav Mesh** Volume in the level, it is time to change the parameters of the **Recast Nav Mesh** actor so that the Nav Mesh allows the enemy AI to navigate across platforms that are thinner than others. This exercise will be performed within the UE5 editor.

Here, you will simply be updating `Cell Size` and `Agent Height` so that they fit the needs of your character and the accuracy needed for the Nav Mesh:

```
Cell Size: 5.0f
Agent Height: 192.0f
```

The following screenshot shows that the extended platform is now navigable because of the changes we made to `Cell Size`:

Figure 13.5 – Changing Cell Size from 19.0f to 5.0f allows for the narrow extended platform to be navigable

With `SuperSideScrollerExampleMap` set up with its own **Nav Mesh**, you can now move on and create the AI logic for the enemy. Before doing so, complete the following activity to create a level with a unique layout and `NavMeshBoundsVolume` actor that you can use for the remainder of this project.

Activity 13.01 – creating a new level

Now that you have added `NavMeshBoundsVolume` to the example map, it is time to create a map for the rest of the `Super SideScroller` game. By creating a map, you will have a better understanding of how `NavMeshBoundsVolume` and the properties of `RecastNavMesh` affect the environment they are placed in.

> **Note**
>
> Before moving on to the solution for this activity, if you need an example level that will work for the remaining chapters that cover the `SuperSideScroller` game, then don't worry – this chapter comes with the `SuperSideScroller.umap` asset, as well as a map called `SuperSideScroller_NoNavMesh`, which does not contain `NavMeshBoundsVolume`. You can use `SuperSideScroller.umap` as a reference for how to create a level or to get ideas on how to improve your level. You can download the map from https://packt. live/3lo7v2f.

Follow these steps to create a simplistic map:

1. Create a **New Level**.

2. Name this level `SuperSideScroller`.

3. Using the **Static Mesh** assets provided by default in the **Content Drawer** interface of this project, create an interesting space with different elevations to navigate. Add your player character's **Blueprint** to the level, and make sure it is possessed by **Player Controller 0**.

4. Add the **NavMeshBoundsVolume** actor to your level and adjust its dimensions so that it fits the space you created. In the example map provided for this activity, the dimensions set should be `1000.0`, `5000.0`, and `2000.0` in the *X*, *Y*, and *Z* axes, respectively.

5. Make sure that you enable debug visualization for **NavMeshBoundsVolume** by pressing the *P* key.

6. Adjust the parameters of the **RecastNavMesh** actor so that **NavMeshBoundsVolume** works well for your level. In the case of the provided example map, the `Cell Size` parameter is set to `5.0f`, `Agent Radius` is set to `42.0f`, and `Agent Height` is set to `192.0f`. Use these values as a reference.

Expected Output

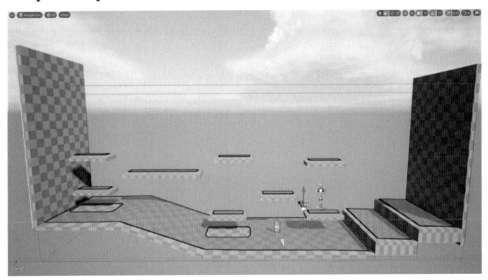

Figure 13.6 – The SuperSideScroller map

By the end of this activity, you will have a level that contains the required `NavMeshBoundsVolume` and settings for the `RecastNavMesh` actor. This will allow the AI we'll develop in the upcoming exercises to function correctly. Again, if you are unsure of how the level should look, please refer to the provided example map, `SuperSideScroller.umap`. Now, it is time to jump into developing the AI for the `SuperSideScroller` game.

Note

The solution for this activity can be found on GitHub here: `https://github.com/ PacktPublishing/Elevating-Game-Experiences-with-Unreal-Engine- 5-Second-Edition/tree/main/Activity%20solutions.`

Behavior trees and Blackboards

Behavior Trees and Blackboards work together to allow our AI to follow different logical paths and make decisions based on a variety of conditions and variables.

A **behavior tree** is a visual scripting tool that allows you to tell a pawn what to do based on certain factors and parameters. For example, a Behavior Tree can tell an AI to move to a certain location based on whether the AI can see the player.

To give an example of how `Behavior Trees` and `Blackboards` are used in games, let's look at the game *Gears of War 5*, which was developed with UE5. The AI in **Gears of War 5**, and throughout the **Gears of War** series, always tries to flank the player or force the player out of cover. To do this, a key component of the AI logic is to know who the player is and where they are. A reference variable to the player, and a location vector to store the location of the player, exist in the `Blackboard`. The logic that determines how these variables are used and how the AI will use this information is performed inside the Behavior Tree.

The `Blackboard` is where you define the set of variables that are required to have the Behavior Tree perform actions and use those values for decision-making.

The `Behavior Tree` is where you create the tasks that you want the AI to perform, such as moving to a location or performing a custom task that you create. Like many of the in-editor tools in UE5, `Behavior Trees` are, for the most part, a very visual scripting experience.

`Blackboards` are where you define the variables, also known as **Keys**, that will then be referenced by the Behavior Tree. The keys you create here can be used in **Tasks**, **Services**, and **Decorators** to serve different purposes based on how you want the AI to function. The following screenshot shows an example set of variable **Keys** that can be referenced by its associated Behavior Tree. Without a `Blackboard`, `Behavior Trees` would have no way of passing and storing information across different Tasks, Services, or Decorators, rendering it useless:

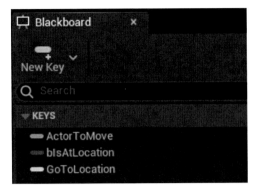

Figure 13.7 – An example set of variables inside a Blackboard that can be accessed in the behavior tree

Behavior Trees are composed of a set of **objects** – that is, **Composites**, **Tasks**, **Decorators**, and **Services** – that work together to define how the AI will behave and respond based on the conditions and logic flow that you set. All Behavior Trees begin with what is called the Root where the logic flow begins; this cannot be modified and has only one execution branch. Let's take a look at these objects in more detail.

> **Note**
>
> For more information regarding the C++ API for `Behavior Tree` Behavior Tree, please refer to the following documentation: `https://docs.unrealengine.com/4.27/en-US/API/Runtime/AIModule/BehaviorTree/Composites`.

Composite nodes tell the `Behavior Tree` how to go about performing tasks and other actions. The following screenshot shows the full list of Composite nodes that Unreal Engine gives you by default: **Selector**, **Sequence**, and **Simple Parallel**.

Composite nodes can also have Decorators and Services attached to them so that optional conditions can be applied before a `Behavior Tree` branch is executed:

Figure 13.8 – Composite nodes – Selector, Sequence, and Simple Parallel

Let's look at these nodes in more detail:

- **Selector**: The **Selector** Composite node executes its children from left to right and will stop executing when one of the child tasks succeeds. Using the example shown in the following screenshot, if the `FinishWithResult` task is successful, the parent **Selector** succeeds, which will cause the `Root` to execute again and `FinishWithResult` to execute once more. This pattern will continue until `FinishWithResult` fails. The **Selector** node will then execute `MakeNoise`. If `MakeNoise` fails, the **Selector** node fails, and the `Root` will execute again. If the `MakeNoise` task succeeds, then the Selector will succeed, and the `Root` will execute again. Depending on the flow of the behavior tree, if the Selector fails or succeeds, the next Composite branch will begin to execute. In the following screenshot, there are no other Composite nodes, so if the Selector fails or succeeds, the `Root` node will be executed again. However, if there were a **Sequence** Composite node with multiple **Selector** nodes underneath, each Selector would attempt to successfully execute its children. Regardless of success or failure, each **Selector** will attempt execution sequentially:

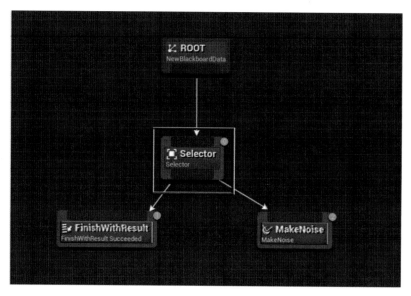

Figure 13.9 – An example of how a Selector Composite node can be used in a behavior tree

Note that when adding tasks and `Composite` nodes, you will notice numeric values on the top-right corners of each node. These numbers indicate the order in which these nodes will be executed. The pattern follows the *top* to *bottom*, *left* to *right* paradigm, and these values help you keep track of the ordering. Any disconnected task or `Composite` node will be given a value of −1 to indicate that it is unused.

- **Sequence**: The **Sequence** Composite node executes its children from left to right and will stop executing when one of the child tasks fails. Using the example shown in the following screenshot, if the Move To task is successful, then the parent **Sequence** node will execute the Wait task. If the Wait task is successful, then the Sequence is successful, and Root will execute again. If the Move To task fails, however, the **Sequence** node will fail and Root will execute again, causing the Wait task to never execute:

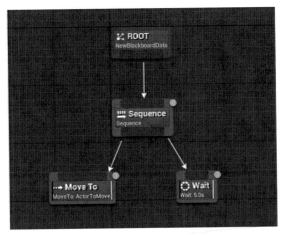

Figure 13.10 – An example of how a Sequence Composite node can be used in a behavior tree

- **Simple Parallel**: The **Simple Parallel** Composite node allows you to execute a task and a new standalone branch of logic simultaneously. The following screenshot shows a very basic example of what this will look like. In this example, a task that's used to **Wait** for 5 seconds is being executed at the same time as a new **Sequence** of tasks is being executed:

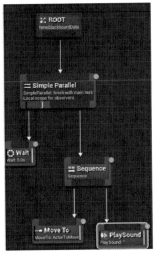

Figure 13.11 – An example of how a Selector Composite node can be used in a behavior tree

The **Simple Parallel** Composite node is also the only **Composite** node that has a parameter in its **Details** panel, which is **Finish Mode**. There are two options:

- **Immediate**: When set to **Immediate**, the **Simple Parallel** Composite node will finish successfully once the main task finishes. In this case, after the `Wait` task finishes, the background tree Sequence will abort and the entire **Simple Parallel** will execute again.

- **Delayed**: When set to **Delayed**, the **Simple Parallel** Composite node will finish successfully once the background tree finishes its execution and the task finishes. In this case, the `Wait` task will finish after 5 seconds, but the entire **Simple Parallel** will wait for the **Move To** and **PlaySound** tasks to execute before restarting.

> **Note**
>
> For more information regarding the C++ API for Composites, please refer to the following documentation: `https://docs.unrealengine.com/4.27/en-US/API/Runtime/AIModule/BehaviorTree/Composites/`.

Now that we have a better understanding of Composite nodes, let's take a look at a few examples of Task nodes.

Tasks

These are tasks that our AI can perform. Unreal Engine provides us with built-in tasks for us to use by default, but we can also create our own in both Blueprints and C++. This includes tasks such as telling our AI to **Move To** a specific location, **Rotate To Face Target**, and even telling the AI to fire its weapon. It's also important to know that you can create custom tasks using Blueprints. Let's briefly discuss two of the tasks you will be using to develop the AI for the enemy character:

- **Move To Task**: This is one of the more commonly used tasks in `Behavior Trees`, and you will be using this task in the upcoming exercises in this chapter. **Move To task** uses the navigation system to tell the AI how and where to move based on the location it is given. You will use this task to tell the AI enemy where to go.

- **Wait Task**: This is another commonly used task in `Behavior Trees` because it allows a delay inbetween task execution if the logic requires it. This can be used to allow the AI to wait a few seconds before moving to a new location.

> **Note**
>
> For more information regarding the C++ API for tasks, please refer to the following documentation: `https://docs.unrealengine.com/4.27/en-US/API/Runtime/AIModule/BehaviorTree/Tasks/`.

Decorators

Decorators are conditions that can be added to tasks or **Composite** nodes, such as a **Sequence** or **Selector**, that allow branching logic to occur. As an example, we can have a **Decorator** that checks whether or not the enemy knows the location of the player. If so, we can tell that enemy to move toward that last known location. If not, we can tell our AI to generate a new location and move there instead. It is also important to know that you can create custom decorators using Blueprints.

Let's also briefly discuss the decorator you will be using to develop the AI for the enemy character – the **Is At Location** Decorator. This determines whether the controlled pawn is at the location specified in the decorator itself. This will be useful to you to ensure that the `Behavior Trees` is not executing until you know the AI has reached its given location.

> **Note**
> For more information regarding the C++ API for decorators, please refer to the following documentation: `https://docs.unrealengine.com/4.27/en-US/API/Runtime/AIModule/BehaviorTree/Decorators/UBTDecorator_BlueprintBase/`.

Now that we have a better understanding of Task nodes, let's briefly discuss Service nodes.

Services

Services work a lot like decorators because they can be linked with tasks and `Composite` nodes. The main difference is that a **Service** allows us to execute a branch of nodes based on the interval defined in the service. It is also important to know that you can create custom services using Blueprints.

> **Note**
> For more information regarding the C++ API for services, please refer to the following documentation: `https://docs.unrealengine.com/4.27/en-US/API/Runtime/AIModule/BehaviorTree/Services/`.

With knowledge of Composite, Task, and Service nodes under our belt, let's move on to the next exercise where we will create the `Behavior Tree` and `Blackboard` for the enemy.

Exercise 13.04 – creating the AI behavior tree and Blackboard

Now that you have had an overview of `Behavior Trees` and `Blackboards`, this exercise will guide you through creating these assets, telling the AI Controller to use the `Behavior Tree` you created, and assigning the `Blackboard` to the `Behavior Tree`. The `Blackboard` and `Behavior Tree` assets you will create here will be used for the `SuperSideScroller` game. This exercise will be performed within the UE5 editor.

Follow these steps to complete this exercise:

1. Within the **Content Drawer** interface, navigate to the /Enemy/AI directory. This is the same directory where you created the AI Controller.

2. In this directory, *right-click* within the blank area of the **Content Drawer** interface, navigate to the **Artificial Intelligence** option, and select **Behavior Tree** to create the Behavior Tree asset. Name this asset BT_EnemyAI.

3. In the same directory as the previous step, *right-click* again within the blank area of the **Content Drawer** interface, navigate to the **Artificial Intelligence** option, and select **Blackboard** to create the Blackboard asset. Name this asset BB_EnemyAI.

   Before we move on to telling the AI Controller to run this new Behavior Tree, let's assign the Blackboard to this Behavior Tree so that they are connected.

4. Open BT_EnemyAI by *double-clicking* the asset in the **Content Drawer** interface. Once opened, navigate to the **Details** panel on the right-hand side and find the Blackboard Asset parameter.

5. *Left-click* the drop-down menu on this parameter and find the BB_EnemyAI Blackboard asset you created earlier. Compile and save the Behavior Treebefore closing it.

6. Next, open the AI Controller's BP_AIController_Enemy asset by *double-clicking* it inside the **Content Drawer** interface. Inside the Controller, *right-click* and search for the Run Behavior Tree function.

   The Run Behavior Tree function is very straightforward: you assign a **Behavior Tree** to the Controller and the function returns whether the Behavior Tree successfully began its execution.

7. Lastly, connect the **Event BeginPlay** event node to the execution pin of the Run Behavior Tree function and assign **Behavior Tree asset** BT_EnemyAI, which you created earlier in this exercise:

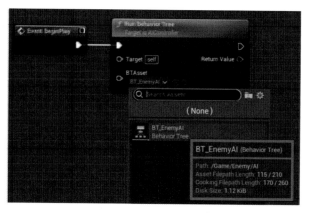

Figure 13.12 – Assigning the BT_EnemyAI behavior tree

8. With this exercise complete, the enemy AI Controller now knows to run the **BT_EnemyAI** Behavior Tree, and this Behavior Tree knows to use the Blackboard asset called **BB_EnemyAI**. With this in place, you can begin to use the Behavior Tree logic to develop the AI so that the enemy character can move around the level.

Exercise 13.05 – creating a new behavior tree task

The goal of this exercise is to develop an AI task for the enemy AI that will allow the character to find a random point to move to within the bounds of the **Nav Mesh** Volume in your level.

Although the `SuperSideScroller` game will only allow two-dimensional movement, let's get the AI to move anywhere within the 3D space of the level that you created in *Activity 13.01 – creating a new level*, and then work to constrain the enemy to two dimensions.

Follow these steps to create this new task for the enemy:

1. First, open the `Blackboard` asset you created in the previous exercise, `BB_EnemyAI`.

2. *Left-click* on the **New Key** option at the top-left of `Blackboard` and select the **Vector** option. Name this vector **MoveToLocation**. You will use this **vector** variable to track the next move for the AI as it decides where to move to.

    For this enemy AI, you will need to create a new **Task** because the currently available tasks inside Unreal do not fit the needs of the enemy behavior.

3. Navigate to and open the `Behavior Tree` asset you created in the previous exercise, `BT_EnemyAI`.

4. *Left-click* on the **New Task** option on the top toolbar. When creating a new `Task`, it will automatically open the task asset for you. However, if you have already created a task, a dropdown list of options will appear when selecting the **New Task** option. Before working on the logic of this **Task**, you must rename the asset.

5. Close the **Task** asset window and navigate to **/Enemy/AI/**, which is where the task was saved to. By default, the name provided is `BTTask_BlueprintBase_New`. Rename this asset `BTTask_FindLocation`.

6. With the new **Task** asset named, *double-click* to open **Task Editor**. New tasks will have empty Blueprint graphs and will not provide you with any default events to use in the graph.

7. *Right-click* within the graph and from the context-sensitive search, find the **Event Receive Execute AI** option.

8. *Left-click* the **Event Receive Execute AI** option to create the event node in the **Task** graph, as shown in the following screenshot:

Figure 13.13 – Event Receive Execute AI returns both Owner Controller and Controlled Pawn

> **Note**
>
> The `Event Receive Execute AI` event will give you access to both **Owner Controller** and **Controlled Pawn**. You will use **Controlled Pawn** for this task in the upcoming steps.

9. Each **Task** requires a call to the `Finish Execute` function so that the `Behavior Tree` asset knows when it can move on to the next **Task** or branches of the tree. *Right-click* in the graph and search for `Finish Execute` via the context-sensitive search.

10. *Left-click* the **Finish Execute** option from the context-sensitive search to create the node inside the Blueprint graph of your **Task**, as shown in the following screenshot:

Figure 13.14 – The Finish Execute function, which has a Boolean parameter that determines whether the task is successful

11. The next function that you need is called **GetRandomLocationInNavigableRadius**. This function, as its name suggests, returns a random vector location within a defined radius of the navigable area. This will allow the enemy character to find random locations and move to those locations.

12. *Right-click* in the graph and search for `GetRandomLocationInNavigableRadius` inside the context-sensitive search. *Left-click* the **GetRandomLocationInNavigableRadius** option to place this function inside the graph.

    With these two functions in place, and with **Event Receive Execute** AI-ready, it is time to obtain the random location for the enemy AI.

13. From the **Controlled Pawn** output of **Event Receive Execute AI**, find the `GetActorLocation` function via the context-sensitive search:

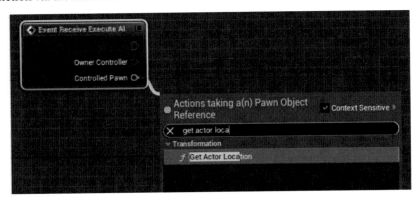

Figure 13.15 – The enemy pawn's location will serve as the origin of the random point selection

14. Connect the vector return value from **GetActorLocation** to the **Origin** vector input parameter of the `GetRandomLocationInNavigableRadius` function, as shown in the following screenshot. Now, this function will use the enemy AI pawn's location as the origin for determining the next random point:

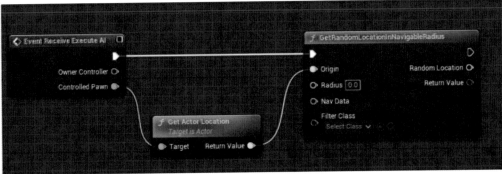

Figure 13.16 – Now, the enemy pawn location will be used as the origin of the random point vector search

15. Next, you need to tell the `GetRandomLocationInNavigableRadius` function the radius in which to check for the random point in the navigable area of the level. Set this value to `1000.0f`.

The remaining parameters, `Nav Data` and `Filter Class`, can remain as is. Now that you are getting a random location from `GetRandomLocationInNavigableRadius`, you will need to be able to store this value in the `Blackboard` vector that you created earlier in this exercise.

16. To get a reference to the `Blackboard` vector variable, you need to create a new variable inside of this `Task` that's of the `Blackboard Key Selector` type. Create this new variable and name it `NewLocation`.

17. Now, you need to make this variable a `Public` variable so that it can be exposed inside the `Behavior Tree`. *Left-click* on the "eye" icon so that the eye is visible.

18. With the `Blackboard Key Selector` variable ready, *left-click* and drag out a `Getter` of this variable. Then, pull from this variable and search for `Set Blackboard Value as Vector`, as shown in the following screenshot:

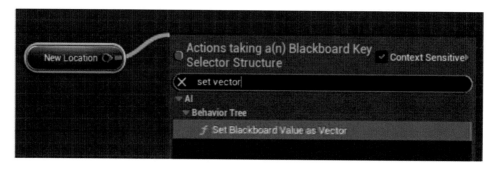

Figure 13.17 – Set Blackboard Value has a variety of different types to support
the different variables that can exist inside the Blackboard

19. Connect the `RandomLocation` output vector from `GetRandomLocationInNavigableRadius` to the `Value` vector input parameter of `Set Blackboard Value as Vector`. Then, connect the execution pins of these two function nodes. The result will look as follows:

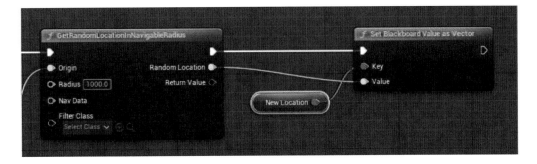

Figure 13.18 – Now, the Blackboard vector value is assigned to this new random location

Lastly, you will use the `Return Value` Boolean output parameter of the `GetRandomLocationInNavigableRadius` function to determine whether the task executes successfully.

20. Connect the Boolean output parameter to the `Success` input parameter of the `Finish Execute` function and connect the execution pins of the **Set Blackboard Value as Vector** and **Finish Execute** function nodes. The following screenshot shows the final result of the **Task** logic:

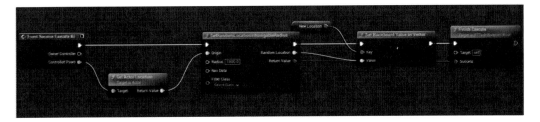

Figure 13.19 – The final setup for the task

> **Note**
> You can find the preceding screenshot in full resolution for better viewing at the following link: `https://packt.live/3lmLyk5`.

By completing this exercise, you have created your first custom **Task** using Blueprints in UE5. You now have a task that finds a random location within the navigable bounds of the **Nav Mesh** volume of your level that uses the enemy pawn as the origin of this search. In the next exercise, you will implement this new **Task** in the `Behavior Tree` and see the enemy AI move around your level.

Exercise 13.06 – creating the behavior tree logic

The goal of this exercise is to implement the new task you created in the previous exercise inside the `Behavior Tree` to have the enemy AI find a random location within the navigable space of your level and then move to this location. You will use a combination of the **Composite, Task**, and **Service** nodes to accomplish this behavior. This exercise will be performed within the UE5 editor.

Follow these steps to complete this exercise:

1. To start, open the `Behavior Trees` you created in *Exercise 13.04 – creating the AI behavior tree and Blackboard*, which is `BT_EnemyAI`.

2. Inside this `Behavior Tree`, *left-click* and drag from the bottom of the `Root` node and select the **Sequence** node from the context-sensitive search. The result will be the `Root` that's connected to the **Sequence** Composite node.

3. Next, from the **Sequence** node, *left-click* and drag to bring up the context-sensitive menu. In this menu, search for the task you created in the previous exercise – that is, **BTTask_FindLocation**.

4. By default, the **BTTask_FindLocation** task should automatically assign the **New Location** Key Selector variable to the **MovetoLocation** vector variable from the `Blackboard`. If this doesn't happen, you can assign this Selector manually in the **Details** panel of the task.

   Now, **BTTask_FindLocation** will assign the **NewLocation** Selector to the **MovetoLocation** vector variable from `Blackboard`. This means that the random location that's returned from the task will be assigned to the `Blackboard` variable and you can reference this variable in other tasks.

   Now that you have found a valid random location and assigned this location to the `Blackboard` variable – that is, **MovetoLocation** – you can use the **Move To** task to tell the AI to move to this location.

5. *Left-click* and pull from the **Sequence** Composite node. Then, from the context-sensitive search, find the **Move To** task. Your `Behavior Tree` will now look as follows:

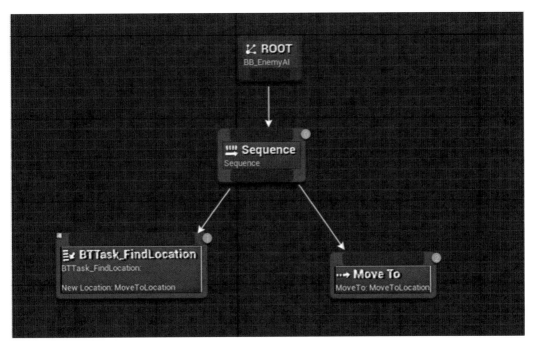

Figure 13.20 – After selecting the random location, the Move
To task will let the AI move to this new location

6. By default, the **Move To** task should assign **MoveToLocation** as its **Blackboard Key** value. If it doesn't, select the task. In its **Details** panel, you will find the **Blackboard Key** parameter, which is where you can assign the variable. While in the **Details** panel, also set **Acceptable Radius** to 50.0f.

    Now, the `Behavior Tree` finds the random location using the **BTTask_FindLocation** custom task and tells the AI to move to that location using the **Move To** task. These two tasks communicate the location to each other by referencing the `Blackboard` vector variable called **MoveToLocation**.

    The last thing to do here is to add a decorator to the **Sequence** Composite node so that the enemy character is not at a random location before the tree is executed again to find and move it to that new location.

7. *Right-click* on the top area of the **Sequence** node and select **Add Decorator**. From the dropdown, *left-click* and select **Is at Location**.

8. Since you already have a vector parameter inside `Blackboard`, the **Is at Location** decorator should automatically assign the **MoveToLocation** vector variable as **Blackboard Key**. Verify this by selecting the decorator and making sure **Blackboard Key** is assigned to **MoveToLocation**.

9.   With the decorator in place, you have completed the `Behavior Tree`. The final result will look as follows:

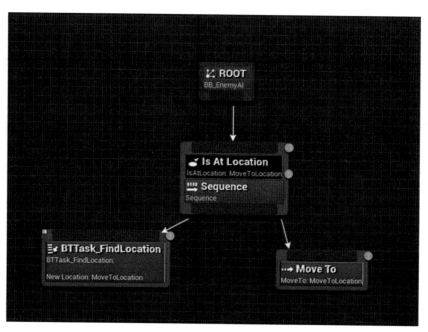

Figure 13.21 – The final setup for the behavior tree for the AI enemy

This `Behavior Tree` is telling the AI to find a random location using **BTTask_FindLocation** and assign this location to the `Blackboard` **MoveToLocation** value. When this task is successful, the `Behavior Tree` will execute the **Move To** task, which will tell the AI to move to this new random location. The **Sequence** node is wrapped in a decorator that ensures that the enemy AI is at **MoveToLocation** before executing again, just as a safety net for the AI.

10. Before you can test the new AI behavior, make sure that you have placed **BP_Enemy AI** into your level if one is not already there from previous exercises and activities.

11. Now, if you use **PIE** or **Simulate**, you will see the enemy AI run around the map and move to random locations within the **Nav Mesh Volume**:

Figure 13.22 – The enemy AI will now move from location to location

> **Note**
>
> There can be some cases where the enemy AI will not move. This can be caused by the GetRandomLocationInNavigableRadius function not returning `True`. This is a known issue, and if it occurs, please restart the editor and try again.

12. By completing this exercise, you have created a fully functional `Behavior Tree` that allows the enemy AI to find and move to a random location within the navigable bounds of your level using the **Nav Mesh Volume**. The task you created in the previous exercise allows you to find this random point, while the **Move To** task allows the AI character to move toward this new location.

Due to how the **Sequence** Composite node works, each task must complete successfully before it can move on to the next task, so first, the enemy successfully finds a random location and then moves toward this location. Only when the **Move To** task completes will the entire `Behavior Tree` start over and choose a new random location.

Now, you can move on to the next activity, where you will add to this `Behavior Tree` to have the AI wait between selecting a new random point so that the enemy isn't constantly moving.

Activity 13.02 – AI moving to the player's location

In the previous exercise, you made the AI enemy character move to random locations within the bounds of **Nav Mesh** Volume by using a custom **Task** and the **Move To** task together.

In this activity, you will continue from the previous exercise and update the `Behavior Tree`. You will take advantage of the **Wait** task by using a decorator, and also create a new custom task to have the AI follow the player character and update its position every few seconds.

Follow these steps to complete this activity:

1. Inside the **BT_EnemyAI Behavior Tree** that you created in the previous exercise, you will continue from where you left off and create a new task. Do this by selecting **New Task** from the toolbar and choosing **BTTask_BlueprintBase**. Name this new task **BTTask_FindPlayer**.

2. In the **BTTask_FindPlayer** task, create a new event called **Event Receive Execute AI**.

3. Find the `Get Player Character` function to get a reference to the player; make sure that you use **Player Index 0**.

4. From the player character, call the `Get Actor Location` function to find the player's current location.

5. Create a new `Blackboard Key Selector` variable inside this task. Name this variable `NewLocation`.

6. *Left-click* and drag the `NewLocation` variable into the graph. From this variable, search for the `Set Blackboard Value` function as a `Vector`.

7. Connect **Set Blackboard Value** as a `Vector` function to the execution pin of the event's **Receive Execute AI** node.

8. Add the `Finish Execute` function, ensuring that the Boolean **Success** parameter is `True`.

9. Lastly, connect **Set Blackboard Value** as a `Vector` function to the `Finish Execute` function.

10. Save and compile the task Blueprint and return to the`BT_EnemyAI Behavior Tree`.

11. Replace the **BTTask_FindLocation** task with the new **BTTask_FindPlayer** task so that this new task is now the first task underneath the **Sequence** Composite node.

12. Add a new `PlaySound` task as the third task underneath the **Sequence** Composite node by following the custom **BTTask_FindLocation** and **Move To** tasks.

13. In the `Sound to Play` parameter, add the **Explosion_Cue SoundCue** asset.

14. Add an **Is At Location** decorator to the **PlaySound** task and ensure that the **MovetoLocation** Key is assigned to this **Decorator**.

15. Add a new **Wait** task as the fourth task underneath the **Sequence** Composite node following the **PlaySound** tasks.

16. Set the **Wait** task to wait `2.0f` seconds before completing successfully.

The expected output is as follows:

Figure 13.23 – Enemy AI following the player and updating to the player's location every 2 seconds

The enemy AI character will move to the player's last known location in the navigable space of the level and pause for `2.0f` seconds between each player position.

Note

The solution for this activity can be found on GitHub here: `https://github.com/PacktPublishing/Elevating-Game-Experiences-with-Unreal-Engine-5-Second-Edition/tree/main/Activity%20solutions`.

With this activity complete, you have learned how to create a new task that allows the AI to find the player's location and move to the player's last known position. Before moving on to the next set of exercises, remove the **PlaySound** task and replace the **BTTask_FindPlayer** task with the **BTTask_FindLocation** task you created in *Exercise 13.05 – creating a new behavior tree task*. Please refer to *Exercise 13.05 – creating a new behavior tree task*, and *Exercise 13.06 – creating the behavior tree logic*, to ensure the `Behavior Tree` is returned correctly. You will be using the **BTTask_FindLocation** task in the upcoming exercises.

In the next exercise, you will address this issue by developing a new Blueprint actor that will allow you to set up specific positions that the AI can move toward.

Exercise 13.07 – creating the enemy patrol locations

The current issue with the AI enemy character is that they can move freely around the 3D navigable space because the Behavior Tree allows them to find a random location within that space. Instead, the AI needs to be given patrol points that you can specify and change in the editor. Then, it will choose one of these patrol points at random to move to. This is what you will do for the SuperSideScroller game: create patrol points that the enemy AI can move to. This exercise will show you how to create these patrol points using a simple **Blueprint** actor. This exercise will be performed within the UE5 editor.

Follow these steps to complete this exercise:

1. First, navigate to the **/Enemy/Blueprints/** directory. This is where you will create the new Blueprint actor that will be used for the AI patrol points.

2. In this directory, *right-click* and choose the **Blueprint Class** option by *left-clicking* this option from the menu.

3. From the **Pick Parent Class** menu prompt, *left-click* the **Actor** option to create a new Blueprint based on the Actor class:

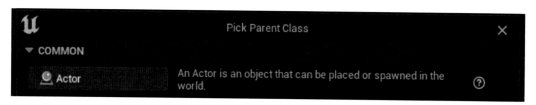

Figure 13.24 – The Actor class is the base class for all objects that
can be placed or spawned in the game world

4. Name this new asset **BP_AIPoints** and open this Blueprint by *double-clicking* the asset in the **Content Drawer** interface.

> **Note**
> The interface for Blueprints shares many of the same features and layouts as other systems, such as Animation Blueprints and tasks, so this should all look familiar to you.

5. Navigate to the **Variables** tab on the left-hand side of the Blueprint UI and *left-click* on the **+Variable** button. Name this variable Points.

6. From the **Variable Type** dropdown, *left-click* and select the **Vector** option.

7. Next, you will need to make this vector variable an **Array** so that you can store multiple patrol locations. *Left-click* the yellow icon next to **Vector** and *left-click* to select the **Array** option.

8. The last step for setting up the **Points** vector variable is to enable **Instance Editable** and **Show 3D Widget**:

    - The **Instance Editable** parameter allows this vector variable to be publicly visible on the actor when placed in a level, allowing each instance of this actor to have this variable available to edit.

    - **Show 3D Widget** allows you to position the vector value by using a visible 3D transform widget in the editor viewport. You will see what this means in the next steps of this exercise. It is also important to note that the Show **3D Widget** option is only available for variables that involve an actor transform, such as vectors and transforms.

    With the simple actor set up, it is time to place the actor in the level and begin setting up the patrol point locations.

9. Add the **BP_AIPoints** actor Blueprint to your level, as shown in the following screenshot:

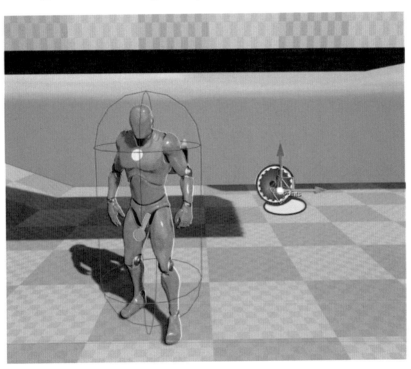

Figure 13.25 – The BP_AIPoints actor is now in the level

10. With the **BP_AIPoints** actor selected, navigate to its **Details** panel and find the **Points** variable.

11. Next, you can add a new element to the vector array by *left-clicking* on the + symbol, as shown here:

Figure 13.26 – You can have many elements inside an array, but
the larger the array, the more memory is allocated

12. When you add a new element to the vector array, you will see a 3D widget appear that you can then *left-click* to select and move around the level, as shown here:

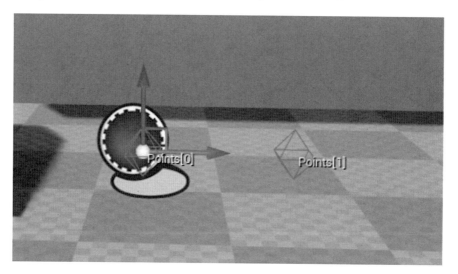

Figure 13.27 – The first patrol point vector location

> **Note**
> As you update the position of the 3D widget that represents the element of the vector array, the 3D coordinates will update in the **Details** panel for the **Points** variable.

13. Finally, add as many elements into the vector array as you would like for the context of your level. Keep in mind that the positions of these patrol points should line up so that they make a straight line along the horizontal axis, parallel to the direction in which the character will move. The following screenshot shows the setup in the example SideScroller.umap level that's included in this exercise:

Figure 13.28 – The example patrol point path, as seen in the SideScroller.umap example level

14. Continue to repeat the previous step to create multiple patrol points and position the 3D widgets as you see fit. You can use the provided **SideScroller.umap** example level as a reference on how to set up these patrol points.

By completing this exercise, you have created a new **Actor** Blueprint that contains a **Vector** array of positions that you can now manually set using a 3D widget in the editor. With the ability to manually set the patrol point positions, you have full control over where the AI can move. However, there is a problem: there is no functionality in place to choose a point from this array and pass it to the `Behavior Tree` so that the AI can move between these patrol points. Before you set up this functionality, let's learn a bit more about vectors and Vector Transformation, as this knowledge will prove useful in the next exercise.

Vector Transformation

Before you jump into the next exercise, it is important that you learn about Vector Transformation and, more importantly, what the `Transform Location` function does. When it comes to an actor's location, there are two ways of thinking of its position: in terms of world space and local space. An actor's position in world space is its location relative to the world itself; in more simple terms, this is the location where you place the actor in the level. An actor's local position is its location relative to either itself or a parent actor.

Let's consider the **BP_AIPoints** actor as an example of what world space and local space are. Each of the locations of the **Points** array is a local-space vector because they are positions relative to the world-space position of the **BP_AIPoints** actor itself. The following screenshot shows the list of vectors in the **Points** array, as shown in the previous exercise. These values are positions relative to the location of the **BP_AIPoints** actor in your level:

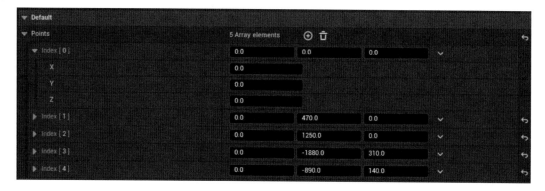

Figure 13.29 – The local-space position vectors of the Points array, relative
to the world-space position of the BP_AIPoints actor

To have the enemy AI move to the correct world space location of these points, you need to use a function called `Transform Location`. This function takes in two parameters:

- `T`: This is the supplied transform that you will use to convert the vector location parameter from a local-space value into a world-space value.

- `Location`: This is the location that is to be converted from local space into world space.

The result of this Vector Transformation is then returned as the return value of the function. You will use this function in the next exercise to return a randomly selected vector point from the `Points` array and convert that value from a local-space vector into a world-space vector. This new world-space vector will then be used to tell the enemy AI where to move relative to the world. Let's implement this now.

Exercise 13.08 – selecting a random point in an array

Now that you know more about vectors and Vector Transformation, in this exercise, you will create a simple `Blueprint` function to select one of the *patrol point* vector locations and transform its vector from a local space value into a world space value using a built-in function called **Transform Location**. By returning the world space value of the vector position, you can then pass this value to the `Behavior Tree` so that the AI will move to the correct position. This exercise will be performed within the UE5 editor.

Follow these steps to complete this exercise. Let's start by creating the new function:

1. Navigate back to the **BP_AIPoints** Blueprint and create a new function by *left-clicking* the + button next to the **Functions** category on the left-hand side of the Blueprint editor. Name this function GetNextPoint.

2. Before you add logic to this function, select this function by *left-clicking* it under the **Functions** category to access its **Details** panel.

3. In the **Details** panel, enable the **Pure** parameter so that this function is labeled as a **Pure Function**. You learned about **Pure Functions** in *Chapter 11, Working with Blend Space 1D, Key Bindings, and State Machines*, when working in the Animation Blueprint for the player character; the same thing is happening here.

4. Next, the GetNextPoint function needs to return a vector that the Behavior Tree can use to tell the enemy AI where to move to. Add this new output by *left-clicking* on the + symbol under the **Outputs** category of the **Details** function. Make the variable of the **Vector** type and name it NextPoint, as shown in the following screenshot:

Figure 13.30 – Functions can return multiple variables of different
types, depending on the needs of your logic

5. When adding an **Output** variable, the function will automatically generate a **Return** node and place it in the function graph, as shown in the following screenshot. You will use this output to return the new vector patrol point for the enemy AI to move to:

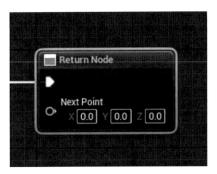

Figure 13.31 – The automatically generated Return Node for the
function, including the Next Point vector output variable

Now that the function's groundwork is completed, let's start adding the logic.

6. To pick a random position, first, you need to find the length of the `Points` array. Create a **Getter** of the `Points` vector and from this vector variable, *left-click* and drag to search for the `Length` function, as shown in the following screenshot:

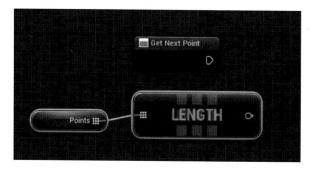

Figure 13.32 – The Length function is a pure function that returns the length of the array

7. With the integer output of the `Length` function, *left-click* and drag out to use the context-sensitive search to find the `Random Integer` function, as shown in the following screenshot. The `Random Integer` function returns a random integer between 0 and `Max value`; in this case, this is the length of the `Points` vector array:

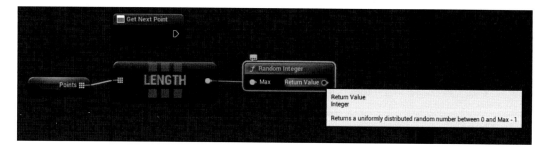

Figure 13.33 – Using Random Integer will allow the function to
return a random vector from the Points vector array

Here, you are generating a random integer between 0 and the length of the `Points` vector array. Next, you need to find the element of the `Points` vector array at the index position of the returned `Random Integer` function.

8. Do this by creating a new `Getter of the Points` vector array. Then, *left-click* and drag to search for the `Get (a copy)` function.

9. Next, connect the return value of the `Random Integer` function to the input of the `Get (a copy)` function. This will tell the function to choose a random integer and use that integer as the index to return from the `Points` vector array.

Now that you are getting a random vector from the `Points` vector array, you need to use the `Transform Location` function to convert the location from a local space vector into a world space vector.

As you have learned already, the vectors in the `Points` vector array are local space positions relative to the position of the `BP_AIPoints` actor in the level. As a result, you need to use the `Transform Location` function to convert the randomly selected local space vector into a world space vector so that the AI enemy moves to the correct position.

10. *Left-click* and drag from the vector output of the `Get (a copy)` function and, via the context-sensitive search, find the `Transform Location` function.

11. Connect the vector output of the `Get (a copy)` function to the `Location` input of the `Transform Location` function.

12. The final step is to use the transform of the Blueprint actor itself as the T parameter of the `Transform Location` function. Do this by *right-clicking* inside the graph and, via the context-sensitive search, finding the `GetActorTransform` function and connecting it to the `Transform Location` parameter, T.

13. Finally, connect the `Return Value` vector from the `Transform Location` function and connect it to the `NewPoint` vector output of the function:

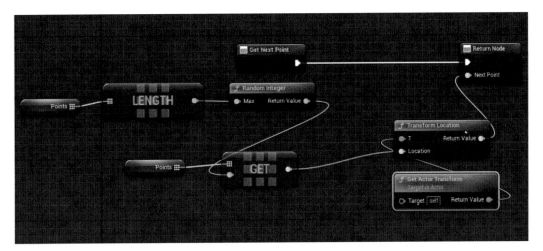

Figure 13.34 – The final logic has been set up for the GetNextPoint function

Note

You can find the preceding screenshot in full resolution for better viewing at the following link: `https://packt.live/35jlilb`.

By completing this exercise, you have created a new Blueprint function inside the **BP_AIPoints** actor that takes a random index from the `Points` array variable, transforms it into a world space vector value using the `Transform Location` function, and returns this new vector value. You will use this function inside the **BTTask_FindLocation** task, inside the AI `Behavior Tree`, so that the enemy will move to one of the points you have set up. Before you can do this, the enemy AI needs a reference to the **BP_AIPoints** actor so that it knows which points it can select from and move to. We'll do this in the following exercise.

Exercise 13.09 – referencing the patrol point actor

Now that the **BP_AIPoints** actor has a function that returns a random transformed location from its array of vector patrol points, you need to have the enemy AI reference this actor in the level so that it knows which patrol points to reference. To do this, you will add a new `Object Reference` variable to the enemy character Blueprint and assign the **BP_AIPoints** actor that you placed in your level earlier. This exercise will be performed within the UE5 editor. Let's get started by adding the `Object Reference` variable.

> **Note**
>
> An `Object Reference` variable stores a reference to a specific class object or actor. With this variable, you can get access to the publicly exposed variables, events, and functions that this class has available.

Follow these steps to complete this exercise:

1. Navigate to the `/Enemy/Blueprints/` directory and open the enemy character Blueprint, **BP_Enemy**, by *double-clicking* the asset from **the Content Drawer** interface.

2. Create a new variable of the `BP_AIPoints` type and make sure the variable is of the `Object Reference` variable type.

3. To reference the existing **BP_AIPoints** actor in your level, you need to make the variable from the previous step a **Public Variable** by enabling the `Instance Editable` parameter. Name this variable `Patrol Points`.

4. Now that you have set the object reference, navigate to your level and select your enemy AI. The following screenshot shows the enemy AI placed in the provided example level – that is, `SuperSideScroller.umap`. If you don't have an enemy in your level, please place one now:

> **Note**
>
> Placing an enemy into a level works the same as it does for any other actor in UE5: *left-click* and drag the enemy AI Blueprint from the **Content Drawer** interface into the level.

Figure 13.35 – The enemy AI placed in the SuperSideScroller.umap level

5. From its **Details** panel, find the `Patrol Points` variable under the **Default** category. The last thing to must do is assign the `BP_AIPoints` actor we already placed in the level in *Exercise 13.07 – creating the enemy patrol locations*. Do this by *left-clicking* the dropdown menu for the `Patrol Points` variable and finding the actor from the list.

With this exercise complete, the enemy AI in your level now has a reference to the **BP_AIPoints** actor in your level. With a valid reference in place, the enemy AI can use this actor to determine which set of points to move between inside the **BTTask_FindLocation** task. All that is left to do now is update the **BTTask_FindLocation** task so that it uses these points instead of finding a random location.

Exercise 13.10 – updating BTTask_FindLocation

The final step in completing the enemy AI patrolling behavior is to replace the logic inside **BTTask_FindLocation** so that it uses the `GetNextPoint` function from the **BP_AIPoints** actor instead of finding a random location within the navigable space of your level. This exercise will be performed within the UE5 editor.

As a reminder, go back to *Exercise 13.05 – creating a new behavior tree task*, and see what the **BTTask_FindLocation** task looked like before you start.

Follow these steps to complete this exercise:

1. First, you must take the returned **Controlled Pawn** reference from **Event Receive Execute AI** and cast it to **BP_Enemy**, as shown in the following screenshot. This way, you can access the `Patrol Points` object reference variable from the previous exercise:

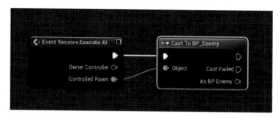

Figure 13.36 – Casting also ensures that the returned Controlled Pawn is of the BP_Enemy class type

2. Next, you can access the `Patrol Points` object reference variable by *left-clicking* and dragging from the **As BP Enemy** pin under the cast to **BP_Enemy** and, via the context-sensitive search, finding `Patrol Points`.

3. From the `Patrol Points` reference, you can *left-click* and drag to search for the `GetNextPoint` function that you created in *Exercise 13.08 – selecting a random point in an array*.

4. Now, you can connect the `NextPoint` vector output parameter of the `GetNextPoint` function to the `Set Blackboard Value as Vector` function and connect the execution pins from the cast to the `Set Blackboard Value as Vector` function. Now, each time the **BTTask_FindLocation** task is executed, a new random patrol point will be set.

5. Lastly, connect the `Set Blackboard Value as Vector` function to the `Finish Execute` function and manually set the `Success` parameter to `True` so that this task will always succeed if the cast is successful.

6. As a failsafe, create a duplicate of **Finish Execute** and connect it to the **Cast Failed** execution pin of the `Cast` function. Then, set the `Success` parameter to `False`. This will act as a failsafe so that if, for any reason, **Controlled Pawn** is not of the BP_Enemy class, the task will fail. This is a good debugging practice to ensure the functionality of the task for its intended AI class:

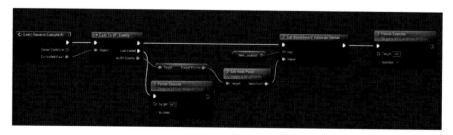

Figure 13.37 – It is always good practice to account for any casting failures in your logic

> **Note**
>
> You can find the preceding screenshot in full resolution for better viewing at the following link: `https://packt.live/3n58THA`.

With the **BTTask_FindLocation** task updated to use the random patrol point from the **BP_AIPoints** actor reference in the enemy, the enemy AI will now move between the patrol points at random:

Figure 13.38 – The enemy AI is now moving between the patrol point locations in the level

With this exercise complete, the enemy AI now uses the reference to the **BP_AIPoints** actor in the level to find and move to the patrol points in the level. Each instance of the enemy character in the level can have a reference to another unique instance of the **BP_AIPoints** actor or can share the same instance reference. It is up to you how you would like each enemy AI to move throughout the level.

Player projectile

For the last section of this chapter, you will focus on creating the base of the player projectile, which can be used to destroy enemies. The goal is to create the appropriate actor class, introduce the required collision and projectile movement components to the class, and set up the necessary parameters for the projectile's motion behavior.

For the sake of simplicity, the player projectile will not use gravity, will destroy enemies with one hit, and the projectile itself will be destroyed on hitting any surface; it will not bounce off walls, for example. The primary goal of the player projectile is to have a projectile that the player can spawn and use to destroy enemies throughout the level. In this chapter, you will set up the framework's basic functionality, while in *Chapter 14, Spawning the Player Projectile*, you will add sound and visual effects. Let's get started by creating the `PlayerProjectile` class.

Exercise 13.11 – creating the player projectile

So far, we have been working in the UE5 editor to create our enemy AI. For the player projectile class, we will be using C++ and Visual Studio. The player projectile will allow the player to destroy enemies that are placed in the level. This projectile will have a short lifespan, travel at a high speed, and collide with both enemies and the environment.

The goal of this exercise is to set up the base actor class for the player projectile and begin outlining the functions and components needed in the header file for the projectile.

Follow these steps to complete this exercise:

1. First, you will need to create a new C++ class by using the Actor class as the parent class for the player projectile. Next, name this new actor class PlayerProjectile and *left-click* on the **Create Class** option at the bottom right of the menu prompt.

    After creating the new class, Visual Studio will generate the required source and header files for the class and open these files for you. The Actor base class comes included with a handful of default functions that you will not need for the player projectile.

2. Find the following lines of code inside the PlayerProjectile.h file and remove them:

    ```
    protected:
        // Called when the game starts or when spawned
        virtual void BeginPlay() override;
    public:
        // Called every frame
        virtual void Tick(float DeltaTime) override;
    ```

    These lines of code represent the declarations of the Tick() and BeginPlay() functions that are included in every Actor-based class by default. The Tick() function is called on every frame and allows you to perform logic on every frame, which can get expensive, depending on what you are trying to do. The BeginPlay() function is called when this actor is initialized and play has started. This can be used to perform logic on the actor as soon as it enters the world. We are removing these functions because they are not required for the player projectile and will just clutter the code.

3. After removing these lines from the PlayerProjectile.h header file, you can remove the following lines from the PlayerProjectile.cpp source files as well:

    ```
    // Called when the game starts or when spawned
    void APlayerProjectile::BeginPlay()
    {
        Super::BeginPlay();
    }
    ```

```
// Called every frame
void APlayerProjectile::Tick(float DeltaTime)
{
   Super::Tick(DeltaTime);
}
```

These lines of code represent the function implementations of the two functions you removed in the previous step – that is, Tick() and BeginPlay(). Again, these are being removed because they serve no purpose for the player projectile and just add clutter to the code. Additionally, without the declarations inside the PlayerProjectile.h header file, you would receive a compilation error if you were to try to compile this code asis. The only remaining function will be the constructor for the projectile class, which you will use to initialize the components of the projectile in the next exercise. Now that you have removed the unnecessary code from the PlayerProjectile class, let's add the functions and components required for the projectile.

4. Inside the PlayerProjectile.h header file, add the following components:

```
public:
   //Sphere collision component
   UPROPERTY(VisibleDefaultsOnly, Category =
   Projectile)
   class USphereComponent* CollisionComp;

private:
   //Projectile movement component
   UPROPERTY(VisibleAnywhere, BlueprintReadOnly,
   Category = Movement, meta =
   (AllowPrivateAccess = "true"))
   class UProjectileMovementComponent*
   ProjectileMovement;

   //Static mesh component
   UPROPERTY(EditAnywhere, Category = Projectile)
   class UStaticMeshComponent* MeshComp;
```

You are adding three different components here. The first is the collision component, which you will use for the projectile to recognize collisions with enemies and environment assets. The next component is the projectile movement component, which you should be familiar with from the previous project. This will allow the projectile to behave like a projectile. The final component is `StaticMeshComponent`. You will use this to give the projectile a visual representation so that it can be seen in-game.

5. Next, add the following function signature code to the `PlayerProjectile.h` header file, under the `public` access modifier:

```
UFUNCTION()
void OnHit(UPrimitiveComponent* HitComp, AActor*
OtherActor,
    UPrimitiveComponent* OtherComp, FVector
    NormalImpulse, const FHitResult&
    Hit);
```

This final event declaration will allow the player projectile to respond to `OnHit` events from the `CollisionComp` component you created in the previous step.

6. To have this code compile, you will need to implement the function from the previous step in the `PlayerProjectile.cpp` source file. Add the following code:

```
void APlayerProjectile::OnHit(UPrimitiveComponent*
HitComp, AActor*
    OtherActor, UPrimitiveComponent* OtherComp, FVector
    NormalImpulse, const
    FHitResult& Hit)
{
}
```

The `OnHit` event provides you with a lot of information about the collision that takes place. The most important parameter that you will be working with in the next exercise is the `OtherActor` parameter. The `OtherActor` parameter will tell you the actor that this `OnHit` event is responding to. This will allow you to know if this other actor is an enemy. You will use this information to destroy the enemies when the projectile hits them.

7. Lastly, navigate back into the Unreal Engine editor and *left-click* the **Compile** option to compile the new code.

With this exercise complete, you now have the framework ready for the `PlayerProjectile` class. The class contains the required components for **Projectile Movement**, **Collision**, and **Static Mesh**, as well as the event signature for the `OnHit` collision so that the projectile can recognize collisions with other actors.

In the next exercise, you will continue to customize and enable parameters for `PlayerProjectile` so that it behaves the way you need it to for the `SuperSideScroller` project.

Exercise 13.12 – initializing the PlayerProjectile class's settings

Now that the framework of the `PlayerProjectile` class is in place, it's time to update the constructor of this class with the default settings needed for the projectile so that it moves and behaves as you want it to. To do this, you will need to initialize the **Projectile Movement**, **Collision**, and **Static Mesh** components.

Follow these steps to complete this exercise:

1. Open Visual Studio and navigate to the `PlayerProjectile.cpp` source file.

2. Before adding any code to the constructor, include the following files inside the `PlayerProjectile.cpp` source file:

    ```
    #include "GameFramework/ProjectileMovementComponent.h"
    #include "Components/SphereComponent.h"
    #include "Components/StaticMeshComponent.h"
    ```

    These header files will allow you to initialize and update the parameters of the projectile movement component, the sphere collision component, and `StaticMeshComponent`, respectively. Without these files, the `PlayerProjectile` class wouldn't know how to handle these components and how to access their functions and parameters.

3. By default, the `APlayerProjectile::APlayerProjectile()` constructor function includes the following line:

    ```
    PrimaryActorTick.bCanEverTick = true;
    ```

    This line of code can be removed entirely because it is not required in the player projectile.

4. In the `PlayerProjectile.cpp` source file, add the following lines to the `APlayerProjectile::APlayerProjectile()` constructor:

    ```
    CollisionComp = CreateDefaultSubobject
      <USphereComponent>(TEXT("SphereComp"));
    CollisionComp->InitSphereRadius(15.0f);
    CollisionComp->BodyInstance.
    SetCollisionProfileName("BlockAll");
    CollisionComp->OnComponentHit.AddDynamic(this,
    &APlayerProjectile::OnHit);
    ```

The first line initializes the sphere collision component and assigns it to the `CollisionComp` variable you created in the previous exercise. The sphere collision component has a parameter called `InitSphereRadius`. This will determine the size, or radius, of the collision actor by default; in this case, a value of `15.0f` works well. Next, `SetCollisionProfileName` sets the collision component to `BlockAll` so that the collision profile is set to `BlockAll`. This means this collision component will respond to OnHit when it collides with other objects. Lastly, the last line you added allows the `OnComponentHit` event to respond to the function you created in the previous exercise:

```
void APlayerProjectile::OnHit(UPrimitiveComponent*
HitComp, AActor*
  OtherActor, UPrimitiveComponent* OtherComp, FVector
  NormalImpulse, const
  FHitResult& Hit)
{
}
```

This means that when the collision component receives the `OnComponentHit` event from a collision event, it will respond with that function; however, this function is empty at the moment. You will add code to this function later in this chapter.

> **Note**
>
> You can learn more about how to create custom collision profiles at `https://docs.unrealengine.com/4.26/en-US/InteractiveExperiences/Physics/Collision/HowTo/AddCustomCollisionType/`.

5. The last thing you must do with `Collision Component` is set this component as the `Root Component` of the player projectile actor. Add the following line of code to the constructor, after the lines from *Step 4*:

```
// Set as root component
RootComponent = CollisionComp;
```

6. With the collision component set up and ready, let's move on to the `Projectile Movement` component. Add the following lines to the constructor:

```
// Use a ProjectileMovementComponent to govern this
projectile's movement
ProjectileMovement =
  CreateDefaultSubobject<
  UProjectileMovementComponent>(
  TEXT("ProjectileComp"))
```

```
;
ProjectileMovement->UpdatedComponent = CollisionComp;
ProjectileMovement->ProjectileGravityScale = 0.0f;
ProjectileMovement->InitialSpeed = 800.0f;
ProjectileMovement->MaxSpeed = 800.0f;
```

This first line initializes `ProjectileMovementComponent` and assigns it to the `ProjectileMovement` variable you created in the previous exercise. Next, we set `CollisionComp` as the updated component of the projectile movement component. The reason we're doing this is that `ProjectileMovementComponent` will use the `Root` of the actor as the component to move. Then, we set the gravity scale of the projectile to `0.0f` because the player projectile should not be affected by gravity; this behavior should allow the projectile to travel at the same speed, at the same height, and not be influenced by gravity. Lastly, we set both the `InitialSpeed` and `MaxSpeed` parameters to `500.0f`. This will allow the projectile to instantly start moving at this speed and remain at this speed for the duration of its lifetime. The player projectile will not support any kind of acceleration motion.

7. With the projectile movement component initialized and set up, it is time to do the same for `StaticMeshComponent`. Add the following code after the lines from the previous step:

```
MeshComp =
CreateDefaultSubobject<UStaticMeshComponent>(TEXT("Mesh-
Comp"));
MeshComp->AttachToComponent(RootComponent,
    FAttachmentTransformRules::KeepWorldTransform);
```

This first line initializes `StaticMeshComponent` and assigns it to the `MeshComp` variable you created in the previous exercise. Then, it attaches this `StaticMeshComponent` to `RootComponent` using a struct called `FAttachmentTransformRules` to ensure that `StaticMeshComponent` keeps its world transform during the attachment, which is `CollisionComp` from *Step 5* of this exercise.

Note

You can find more information about the `FAttachmentTransformRules` struct here: `https://docs.unrealengine.com/en-US/API/Runtime/Engine/Engine/FAttachmentTransformRules/index.html`.

8. Lastly, let's give `PlayerProjectile` an initial life span of 3 seconds so that the projectile will automatically be destroyed if it doesn't collide with anything after this time. Add the following code to the end of the constructor:

```
InitialLifeSpan = 3.0f;
```

9. Lastly, navigate back into the Unreal Engine editor and *left-click* the **Compile** option to compile the new code.

By completing this exercise, you have set up the groundwork for **Player Projectile** so that it can be created as a Blueprint actor inside the editor. All three required components have been initialized and contain the default parameters that you want for this projectile. All we need to do now is create the Blueprint from this class to see it in the level.

Activity 13.03 – creating the player projectile Blueprint

To conclude this chapter, you will create the Blueprint actor from the new `PlayerProjectile` class and customize this actor so that it uses a placeholder shape for **Static Mesh Component** for debugging purposes. This will allow you to view the projectile in the game world. Then, you will add a `UE_LOG()` function to the `APlayerProjectile::OnHit` function inside the `PlayerProjectile.cpp` source file so that you can ensure that this function is called when the projectile comes into contact with an object in the level.

Follow these steps:

1. Inside the **Content Drawer** interface, create a new folder called `Projectile` in the `/MainCharacter` directory.

2. In this directory, create a new Blueprint from the `PlayerProjectile` class, which you created in *Exercise 13.11 – creating the player projectile*. Name this Blueprint `BP_PlayerProjectile`.

3. Open **BP_PlayerProjectile** and navigate to its components. Select the `MeshComp` component to access its settings.

4. Add the `Shape_Sphere` mesh to the `Static Mesh` parameter of the `MeshComp` component.

5. Update the transform of `MeshComp` so that it fits the `Scale and Location of the CollisionComp` component. Use the following values:

```
Location: (X=0.000000,Y=0.000000,Z=-10.000000)
Scale:  (X=0.200000,Y=0.200000,Z=0.200000)
```

6. Compile and save the **BP_PlayerProjectile** Blueprint.

7. Navigate to the `PlayerProjectile.cpp` source file in Visual Studio and find the `APlayerProjectile::OnHit` function.

8. Inside the function, implement the UE_LOG call so that the logged line is of **LogTemp**, **Warning log level**, and displays the text HIT. UE_LOG , as covered back in *Chapter 11, Working with Blend Space 1D, Key Bindings, and State Machines.*

9. Compile your code changes and navigate to the level where you placed the **BP_PlayerProjectile** actor in the previous exercise. If you haven't added this actor to the level, do so now.

10. Before testing, make sure that you open **Output Log** under **Window**. From the **Window** dropdown, hover over the **Developers Tools** option and *left-click* to select **Output Log**.

11. Use PIE and watch out for the log warning inside **Output Log** when the projectile collides with something.

The following is the expected output:

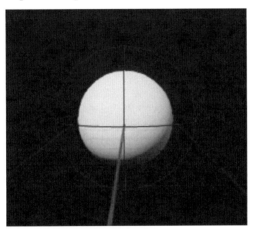

Figure 13.39 – The scale of MeshComp fits the size of CollisionComp better

The log warning should look as follows:

```
LogAudio: Display: Audio Device (ID: 2) registered with world 'ThirdPersonMap'.
LogLoad: Game class is 'BP_ThirdPersonGameMode_C'
LogWorld: Bringing World /Game/ThirdPerson/Maps/UEDPIE_0_ThirdPersonMap.ThirdPersonMap up for play (max t
LogWorld: Bringing up level for play took: 0.001596
LogOnline: OSS: Created online subsystem instance for: :Context_2
LogWorldPartition: New Streaming Source: PlayerController_0 -> Position: X=900.000 Y=1110.000 Z=92.013
LogWorldPartition: Warning: Invalid world bounds, grid partitioning will use a runtime grid with 1 cell.
LogTemp: Warning: HIT
LogBlueprintUserMessages: [BP_ThirdPersonCharacter_C_0] Hello
```

Figure 13.40 – When the projectile hits an object, HIT is shown in the Output Log area

With this final activity complete, **Player Projectile** is ready for the next chapter, where you will spawn this projectile when the player uses the Throw action. You will update the APlayerProjectile::OnHit function so that it destroys the enemy that it collides with and becomes an effective offensive tool for the player to use against the enemies.

> **Note**
>
> The solution for this activity can be found on GitHub here: `https://github.com/PacktPublishing/Elevating-Game-Experiences-with-Unreal-Engine-5-Second-Edition/tree/main/Activity%20solutions`.

Summary

In this chapter, you learned how to use the different aspects of the AI tools offered by UE5, including `Blackboards`, `Behavior Trees`, and AI Controllers. By using a combination of both custom-created tasks and default tasks provided by UE5, as well as a decorator, you were able to have the enemy AI navigate within the bounds of the Nav Mesh you added to your level.

On top of this, you created a new `Blueprint` actor that allows you to add patrol points with the use of a `Vector` array variable. Then, you added a new function to this actor that selects one of these points at random, converts its location from local space into world space, and then returns this new value for use by the enemy character.

With the ability to randomly select a patrol point, you updated the custom `BTTask_FindLocation` task to find and move to the selected patrol point, allowing the enemy to move from each patrol point at random. This brought the enemy AI character to a whole new level of interaction in terms of the player and the environment.

Lastly, you created the `PlayerProjectile` class, which the player will be able to use to destroy enemies within the environment. You took advantage of both `Projectile Movement Component` and `Sphere Component` to allow for both projectile movement and to recognize and respond to collisions within the environment.

With the `PlayerProjectile` class in a functional state, it is time to move on to the next chapter, where you will use `Anim Notifies` to spawn the projectile when the player uses the `Throw` action.

14
Spawning the Player Projectile

In the previous chapter, you made great progress with the enemy character's AI by creating a behavior tree that would allow the enemy to randomly select points from the `BP_AIPoints` actor you created. This gave the `SuperSideScroller` game more life as you can now have multiple enemies moving around your game world. Additionally, you learned about the different tools available in **Unreal Engine 5 (UE5)** that are used together to make AI of various degrees of complexity. These tools included the Navigation Mesh, behavior trees, and Blackboards.

Now that you have enemies running around your level, you need to allow the player to defeat these enemies with the player projectile you started to create at the end of the previous chapter. Our goal for this chapter is to use a custom `UAnimNotify` class that we will implement within our `Throw` Animation Montage to spawn the `Player Projectile`. Additionally, we will add polish elements to the projectile such as Particle Systems and Sound Cues.

In this chapter, we will cover the following topics:

- How to use the `UAnimNotify` class to spawn the player projectile during the `Throw` Animation Montage.

- Creating a new `Socket` for the main character skeleton from which the projectile will spawn.

- Learn how to use Particle Systems and Soundcues to add a layer of visual and audio polish to the game.

By the end of this chapter, you will be able to play Animation Montages in both Blueprints and C++ and know how to spawn objects into the game world using C++ and the `UWorld` class. These elements of the game will be given audio and visual components as an added layer of polish, and your `SuperSideScroller` player character will be able to throw projectiles that destroy enemies.

Technical requirements

For this chapter, you will need the following technical requirements:

- Unreal Engine 5 installed
- Visual Studio 2019 installed
- Unreal Engine 4.27 installed

The project for this chapter can be found in the `Chapter14` folder of the code bundle for this book, which can be downloaded here:

`https://github.com/PacktPublishing/Elevating-Game-Experiences-with-Unreal-Engine-5-Second-Edition`

Let's begin this chapter by learning about **Anim Notifies** and **Anim Notify States**. After that, you'll get your hands dirty by creating a `UAnimNotify` class so that you can spawn the player projectile during the `Throw` Animation Montage.

Anim Notifies and Anim Notify States

When it comes to creating polished and complex animations, there needs to be a way for animators and programmers to add custom events within the animation that will allow for additional effects, layers, and functionality to occur. The solution in UE5 is to use **Anim Notifies** and **Anim Notify States**.

The main difference between **Anim Notify** and **Anim Notify State** is that **Anim Notify State** possesses three distinct events that **Anim Notify** does not. These events are **Notify Begin**, **Notify End**, and **Notify Tick**, all of which can be used in Blueprints or C++. When it comes to these events, UE5 secures the following behaviors:

- **Notify State** will always start with **Notify Begin Event**
- **Notify State** will always finish with **Notify End Event**
- **Notify Tick Event** will always take place between the **Notify Begin** and **Notify End** events

Anim Notify, however, is a much more simplified version that uses just a single function, `Notify()`, to allow programmers to add functionality to the notify itself. It works with the mindset of *fire and forget*, meaning you don't need to worry about what happens at the start, end, or anywhere in-between the `Notify()` event. It is due to this simplicity of **Anim Notify**, and because we do not need the events included with **Anim Notify State**, that we will use **Anim Notify** to spawn the player projectile for the `SuperSideScroller` game.

Before moving on to the following exercise, where you will create a custom **Anim Notify** in C++, let's briefly discuss some examples of existing Anim Notifies that UE5 provides by default. A full list of default **Anim Notify** states can be seen in the following screenshot:

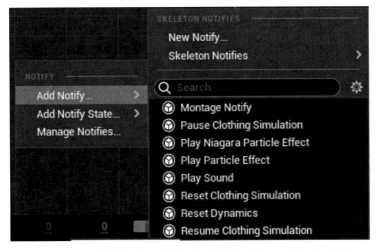

Figure 14.1 – The full list of default Anim Notifies provided in UE5

There are two **Anim Notifies** that you will be using later in this chapter: **Play Particle Effect** and **Play Sound**. Let's discuss these two in more detail so that you are familiar with them by the time you use them:

- **Play Particle Effect**: The **Play Particle Effect** notify, as its name suggests, allows you to spawn and play a Particle System at a certain frame of your animation. As shown in the following screenshot, you have options to change the **visual effects** (**VFX**) that are being used, such as updating the **Location Offset**, **Rotation Offset**, and **Scale** settings of the particle. You can even attach the particle to a specified **Socket Name** if you so choose:

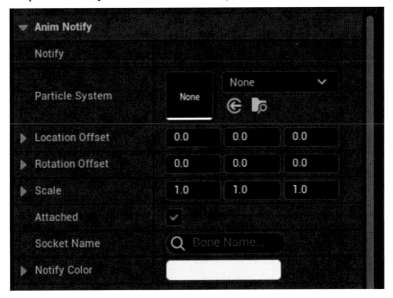

Figure 14.2 – The Details panel of the Play Particle Effect notify

> **Note**
>
> Visual effects, or VFX for short, are crucial elements for any game. VFX, in UE5, are created using a tool called **Niagara** inside the editor. Niagara has been around since Unreal Engine 4 version 4.20, as a free plugin to improve the quality and pipeline for how VFX are made. **Cascade**, the previous VFX tool, will become deprecated in a later version of UE5. You can learn more about Niagara here: `https://docs.unrealengine.com/en-US/Engine/Niagara/Overview/index.html`.

A very common example that's used in games is to use this type of notify to spawn dirt or other effects underneath the player's feet while they walk or run. Having the ability to specify at which frame of the animation these effects spawn is very powerful and allows you to create convincing effects for your character.

- **Play Sound**: The **Play Sound** notify allows you to play a **Soundcue** or **Soundwave** at a certain frame of your animation. As shown in the following screenshot, you have options for changing the sound being used, updating its **Volume Multiplier** and **Pitch Multiplier** values, and even having the sound follow the owner of the sound by attaching it to a specified **Attach Name**:

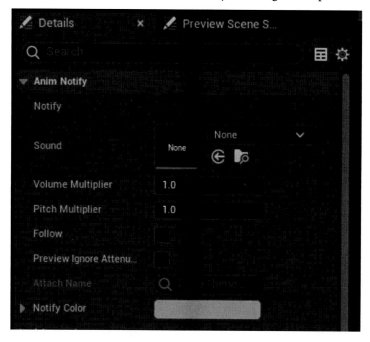

Figure 14.3 – The Details panel of the Play Sound notify

Much like the example given for the **Play Particle Effect** notify, the **Play Sound** notify can also be commonly used to play the sounds of footsteps while the character is moving. By having control of exactly where on the animation timeline you can play a sound, it is possible to create believable sound effects.

Although you will not be using an **Anim Notify State**, it is still important to at least know the options that are available to you by default, as shown in the following screenshot:

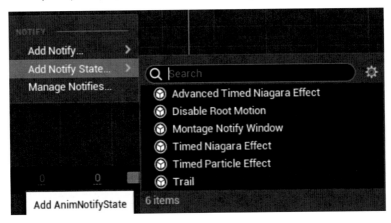

Figure 14.4 – The full list of default Anim Notify States provided to you in UE5

> **Note**
> The two Notify states that are not available in Animation Sequences are the **Montage Notify Window** and **Disable Root Motion** states, as shown in the preceding screenshot. For more information regarding notifies, please refer to the following documentation: `docs.unrealengine.com/en-US/Engine/Animation/Sequences/Notifies/index.html`.

Now that you are more familiar with **Anim Notify** and **Anim Notify State**, let's move on to the first exercise, where you will create a custom **Anim Notify** in C++ that you will use to spawn the player projectile.

Exercise 14.01 – creating a UAnimNotify class

The main offensive ability that the player character will have in the `SuperSideScroller` game is the projectile that the player can throw at enemies. In the previous chapter, you set up the framework and base functionality of the projectile, but right now, there is no way for the player to use it. To make spawning, or throwing, the projectile convincing to the eye, you need to create a custom **Anim Notify** that you will then add to the **Throw** Animation Montage. This **Anim Notify** will let the player know it's time to spawn the projectile.

Follow these steps to create the new `UAnimNotify` class:

1. Inside UE5, navigate to the **Tools** option and *left-click* on the **New C++ Class** option.

2. From the **Choose Parent Class** dialog window, search for `Anim Notify` and *left-click* the **AnimNotify** option. Then, *left-click* the **Next** option to name the new class.

3. Name this new class `Anim_ProjectileNotify`. Once it's been named, *left-click* the **Create Class** option so that UE5 recompiles and hot-reloads the new class in Visual Studio. Once Visual Studio opens, you will have both the header file, `Anim_ProjectileNotify.h`, and the source file, `Anim_ProjectileNotify.cpp`, available to you.

4. The `UAnimNotify` base class has one function that needs to be implemented inside your class:

    ```
    virtual void Notify(USkeletalMeshComponent*
    MeshComp, UAnimSequenceBase* Animation, const
    FAnimNotifyEventReference& EventReference);
    ```

    This function is called automatically when the notify is hit on the timeline it is being used in. By overriding this function, you will be able to add logic to the notify. This function also gives you access to both the `Skeletal Mesh` component of the owning notify and the Animation Sequence currently being played.

5. Next, let's add the override declaration of this function to the header file. In the `Anim_ProjectileNotify.h` header file, add the following code underneath `GENERATED_BODY()`:

    ```
    public:    virtual void Notify(USkeletalMeshComponent*
    MeshComp, UAnimSequenceBase* Animation, const
    FAnimNotifyEventReference& EventReference) override;
    ```

    Now that you've added the function to the header file, it is time to define the function inside the `Anim_ProjectileNotify` source file.

6. Inside the `Anim_ProjectileNotify.cpp` source file, define the function and add a `UE_LOG()` call that prints the text `"Throw Notify"`, as shown in the following code:

    ```
    void UAnim_
    ProjectileNotify::Notify(USkeletalMeshComponent*
    MeshComp, UAnimSequenceBase* Animation, const
    FAnimNotifyEventReference& EventReference)
    {
        Super::Notify(MeshComp, Animation, EventReference);
        UE_LOG(LogTemp, Warning, TEXT("Throw Notify"));
    }
    ```

    For now, you will just use this `UE_LOG()` debugging tool to know that this function is being called correctly when you add this notify to the **Throw** Animation Montage in the next exercise.

In this exercise, you created the groundwork necessary to implement your own `Anim Notify` class by adding the following function:

```
Notify(USkeletalMeshComponent* MeshComp, UAnimSequenceBase*
Animation, const FAnimNotifyEventReference& EventReference)
```

Inside this function, you are using `UE_LOG()` to print the custom text `"Throw Notify"` in the output log so that you know that this notify is working correctly.

Later in this chapter, you will update this function so that it calls logic that will spawn the player projectile, but first, let's add the new notify to the **Throw** Animation montage.

Exercise 14.02 – adding the new notify to the Throw Animation Montage

Now that you have your `Anim_ProjectileNotify` notify, it is time to add it to the **Throw** Animation Montage so that it can be of use to you.

In this exercise, you will add `Anim_ProjectileNotify` to the timeline of the **Throw** Animation Montage at the exact frame of the animation that you'd expect the projectile to spawn.

Follow these steps to achieve this:

1. Back inside UE5, navigate to the **Content Drawer** interface and go to the `/MainCharacter/ Animation/` directory. Inside this directory, *double-click* the `AM_Throw` asset to open the **Animation Montage** editor.

    At the very bottom of the **Animation Montage** editor, you will find the timeline for the animation. By default, you will observe that the *red-colored bar* will be moving along the timeline as the animation plays.

2. *Left-click* this red bar and manually move it to the 22nd frame, as close as you can, as shown in the following screenshot:

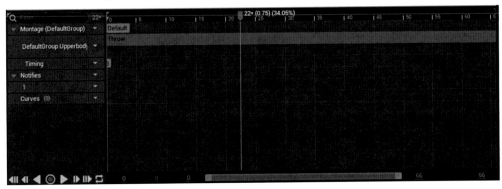

Figure 14.5 – The red-colored bar allows you to manually position notifies anywhere on the timeline

The 22nd frame of the **Throw** animation is the exact moment in the throw that you would expect a projectile to spawn and be thrown by the player. The following screenshot shows the frame of the **Throw** animation, as seen inside the editor within **Persona**:

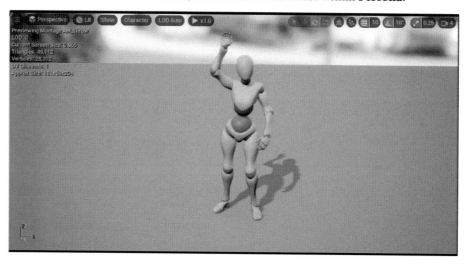

Figure 14.6 – The exact moment the player projectile should spawn

3.   Now that you know the position on the timeline that the notify should be played, you can *right-click* on the thin red line within the **Notifies** timeline.

A popup will appear where you can add a **Notify** or a **Notify State**. In some cases, the **Notifies** timeline may be collapsed and hard to find; simply left-click on the word **Notifies** to toggle between collapsed and expanded.

4.   Select **Add Notify** and, from the options provided, find and select **Anim Projectile Notify**.

5.   After adding **Anim Projectile Notify** to the **Notifies** timeline, you will see the following:

Figure 14.7 – Anim_ProjectileNotify successfully added to the Throw Animation Montage

6.   With the `Anim_ProjectileNotify` notify in place on the **Throw** Animation Montage timeline, save the montage.

7.   If the **Output Log** window is not visible, please re-enable the window by navigating to the **Window** option and hovering over it to find the option for **Output Log**. Then, *left-click* to enable it.

8.   Now, use `PIE` and, once in-game, use the *left mouse button* to start playing the **Throw** montage.

At the point in the animation where you added the notify, you will now see the `Throw Notify` debugging log text appear in the output log.

As you may recall from *Chapter 12, Animation Blending and Montages*, you added the `Play Montage` function to the player character Blueprint – that is, `BP_SuperSideScroller_MainCharacter`. For the sake of learning C++ in the context of UE5, you will be moving this logic from Blueprint to C++ in the upcoming exercises. This is so that we don't rely too heavily on Blueprint scripts for the base behavior of the player character.

With this exercise complete, you have successfully added your custom `Anim Notify` class, `Anim_ProjectileNotify`, to the **Throw** Animation Montage. This notify was added at the precise frame in which you expect a projectile to be thrown from the player's hand. Since you added the Blueprint logic to the player character in *Chapter 12, Animation Blending and Montages*, you can play this **Throw** Animation Montage when the `EnhancedInputAction` event, `ThrowProjectile`, is called when using the *left mouse button*. Before making the transition from playing the **Throw** Animation Montage in Blueprints to playing it in C++, let's discuss playing Animation Montages some more.

Playing Animation Montages

As you learned in *Chapter 12, Animation Blending and Montages*, these assets are useful for allowing animators to combine individual Animation Sequences into one complete montage. By splitting the montage into unique sections and adding notifies for particles and sound, animators and animation programmers can make complex sets of montages that handle all the different aspects of the animation.

But once the Animation Montage is ready, how do we play it on a character? You are already familiar with the first method, which is via Blueprints.

Playing Animation Montages in Blueprints

In Blueprints, the **Play Montage** function can be used, as shown in the following screenshot:

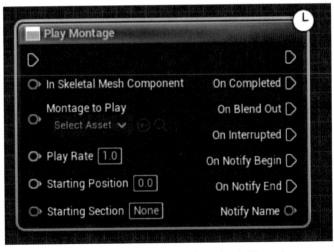

Figure 14.8 – The Play Montage function in Blueprints

You have already used the `Play Montage` function to play the `AM_Throw` Animation Montage. This function requires the **Skeletal Mesh** component that the montage must be played on, and it requires the Animation Montage to play.

The remaining parameters are optional, depending on how your montage will work. Let's have a quick look at these parameters:

- **Play Rate**: The **Play Rate** parameter allows you to increase or decrease the playback speed of the Animation Montage. For faster playback, you would increase this value; otherwise, you would decrease it.

- **Starting Position**: The **Starting Position** parameter allows you to set the starting position, in seconds, along the montage timeline from which the montage will start playing. For example, in an Animation Montage that has a 3-second timeline, you could choose to have the montage start at the `1.0f` position instead of at `0.0f`.

- **Starting Section**: The **Starting Section** parameter allows you to tell the Animation Montage to start at a specific section. Depending on how your montage is set up, you could have multiple sections created for different parts of the montage. For example, a shotgun weapon-reloading Animation Montage would include a section for the initial movement for reloading, a looped section for the actual bullet reload, and a final section for re-equipping the weapon so that it is ready to fire again.

When it comes to the outputs of the **Play Montage** function, you have a few different options:

- **On Completed**: The **On Completed** output is called when the Animation Montage has finished playing and has been fully blended out.

- **On Blend Out**: The **On Blend Out** output is called when the Animation Montage begins to blend out. This can occur during **Blend Out Trigger Time**, or if the montage ends prematurely.

- **On Interrupted**: The **On Interrupted** output is called when the montage begins to blend out due to it being interrupted by another montage that is trying to play on the same skeleton.

- **On Notify Begin** and **On Notify End**: Both the **On Notify Begin** and **On Notify End** outputs are called if you are using the **Montage Notify** option under the **Notifies** category in the Animation Montage. The name that's given to **Montage Notify** is returned via the **Notify Name** parameter.

Now that we have a better understanding of the Blueprint implementation of the **Play Montage** function, let's take a look at how to play animations in C++.

Playing Animation Montages in C++

On the C++ side, there is only one thing you need to know about, and that is the `UAnimInstance::Montage_Play()` function. This function requires the Animation Montage to play, the play rate in which to play back the montage, a value of the `EMontagePlayReturnType` type, a `float` value for determining the start position to play the montage, and a `Boolean` value for determining whether playing this montage should stop or interrupt all montages.

Although you will not be changing the default parameter of `EMontagePlayReturnType`, which is `EMontagePlayReturnType::MontageLength`, it is still important to know the two values that exist for this enumerator:

- `Montage Length`: The `Montage Length` value returns the length of the montage itself, in seconds.

- `Duration`: The `Duration` value returns the play duration of the montage, which is equal to the length of the montage, divided by the play rate.

> **Note**
>
> For more details regarding the UAnimMontage class, please refer to the following documentation:
> `https://docs.unrealengine.com/en-US/API/Runtime/Engine/Animation/UAnimMontage/index.html`.

You will learn more about the C++ implementation of playing an Animation Montage in the next exercise.

Exercise 14.03 – playing the Throw animation in C++

Now that you have a better understanding of how to play Animation Montages in UE5, both via Blueprints and C++, it is time to migrate the logic for playing the **Throw** Animation Montage from Blueprints to C++. The reason behind this change is that the Blueprint logic was put into place as a placeholder method so that you could preview the **Throw** montage. This book is a more heavily focused C++ guide to game development, and as such, it is important to learn how to implement this logic in code.

Let's begin by removing the logic from Blueprints, and then move on to recreating the logic in C++ inside the player character class.

Follow these steps to complete this exercise:

1. Navigate to the player character Blueprint, `BP_SuperSideScroller_MainCharacter`, which can be found in the `/MainCharacter/Blueprints/` directory. *Double-click* this asset to open it.

2. Inside this Blueprint, you will find the **EnhancedInputAction IA_Throw** event and the **Play Montage** function that you created to preview the **Throw** Animation Montage, as shown in the following screenshot. Delete this logic and then recompile and save the player character Blueprint:

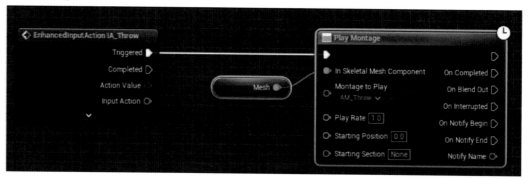

Figure 14.9 – You no longer need this placeholder logic inside the player character Blueprint

3. Now, use `PIE` and attempt to throw with the player character by using the *left mouse button*. You will observe that the player character no longer plays the **Throw** Animation Montage. Let's fix this by adding the required logic in C++.

4. Open the header file for the player character in Visual Studio – that is, `SuperSideScroller_Player.h`.

5. The first thing you need to do is create a new variable for the player character that will be used for the **Throw** animation. Add the following code under the `Private` access modifier:

    ```
    UPROPERTY(EditAnywhere)
    class UAnimMontage* ThrowMontage;
    ```

    Now that you have a variable that will represent the **Throw** Animation Montage, it is time to add the logic for playing the montage inside the `SuperSideScroller_Player.cpp` file.

6. Before you can make the call to `UAnimInstance::Montage_Play()`, you need to add the following `include` directory to the existing list at the top of the source file to have access to this function:

    ```
    #include "Animation/AnimInstance.h"
    ```

    As we know from *Chapter 9, Adding Audio-Visual Elements*, the player character already has a function called `ThrowProjectile` that is called whenever the *left mouse button* is pressed. As a reminder, this is where the binding occurs in C++:

    ```
    //Bind the pressed action Throw to your ThrowProjectile
    function
    ```

```
EnhancedPlayerInput->BindAction(IA_Throw,
ETriggerEvent::Triggered, this, &ASuperSideScroller_
Player::ThrowProjectile);
```

7. Update `ThrowProjectile` so that it plays `ThrowMontage`, which you set up earlier in this exercise. Add the following code to the `ThrowProjectile()` function. Then, we can discuss what is happening here:

```
void ASuperSideScroller_Player::ThrowProjectile()
{

  if (ThrowMontage)
  {
    const bool bIsMontagePlaying = GetMesh()
    ->GetAnimInstance()->
      Montage_IsPlaying(ThrowMontage);
    if (!bIsMontagePlaying)
    {
      GetMesh()->GetAnimInstance()
      ->Montage_Play(ThrowMontage,
        1.0f);
    }
  }   }
```

The first line is checking if `ThrowMontage` is valid; if we don't have a valid Animation Montage assigned, there is no point in continuing the logic. It can also be dangerous to use a `NULL` object in further function calls as it could result in a crash. Next, we are declaring a new Boolean variable, called `bIsMontagePlaying`, that determines whether `ThrowMontage` is already playing on the player character's skeletal mesh. This check is made because the **Throw** Animation Montage should not be played while it is already playing; this will cause the animation to break if the player repeatedly presses the *left mouse button*.

So long as the preceding conditions are met, it is safe to move on and play the Animation Montage.

8. Inside the `If` statement, you are telling the player's skeletal mesh to play `ThrowMontage` with a play rate of `1.0f`. This value is used so that the Animation Montage plays back at the speed it is intended to. Values larger than `1.0f` will make the montage play back faster, while values lower than `1.0f` will make the montage play back slower. The other parameters that you learned about, such as the start position or the `EMontagePlayReturnType` parameter, can be left at their defaults. Back inside the UE5 editor, perform a recompile of the code, as you have done in the past.

9. After the code recompiles successfully, navigate back to the player character Blueprint, BP_ SuperSideScroller_MainCharacter, which can be found in the /MainCharacter/ Blueprints/ directory. *Double-click* this asset to open it.

10. In the **Details** panel of the player character, you will now see the Throw Montage parameter that you added.

11. *Left-click* on the drop-down menu for the Throw Montage parameter to find the AM_Throw montage. *Left-click* again on the AM_Throw montage to select it for this parameter. Please refer to the following screenshot to see how the variable should be set up:

Figure 14.10 – The Throw montage has been assigned the AM_Throw montage

12. Recompile and save the player character Blueprint. Then, use PIE to spawn the player character and use the *left mouse button* to play Throw Montage. The following screenshot shows this in action:

Figure 14.11 – The player character is now able to perform the Throw animation again

By completing this exercise, you have learned how to add an `Animation Montage` parameter to the player character, as well as how to play the montage in C++. In addition to playing the **Throw** Animation Montage in C++, you added the ability to control how often the **Throw** animation can be played by adding a check for whether the montage is already playing. By doing this, you have prevented the player from spamming the `Throw` input and causing the animation to break or not play entirely.

> **Note**
>
> Try setting the play rate of `Animation Montage` from `1.0f` to `2.0f` and recompile the code. Observe how increasing the play rate of the animation affects how the animation looks and feels for the player.

Before moving on to spawning the player projectile, let's set up the `Socket` location in the player character's **Skeleton** so that the projectile can spawn from the *player's hand* during the **Throw** animation.

Exercise 14.04 – creating the projectile spawn socket

To spawn the player projectile, you need to determine the **Transform** properties in which the projectile will spawn while primarily focusing on **Location** and **Rotation**, rather than **Scale**.

In this exercise, you will create a new **Socket** on the player character's **Skeleton** that you can then reference in code to obtain the transform from which to spawn the projectile.

Let's get started:

1. Inside UE5, navigate to the **Content Drawer** interface and find the `/MainCharacter/ Mesh/` directory.

2. In this directory, find the **Skeleton** asset; that is, `MainCharacter_Skeleton.uasset`. *Double-click* to open this **Skeleton**.

   To determine the best position for where the projectile should spawn, we need to add the **Throw** Animation Montage as the preview animation for the skeleton.

3. In the **Preview Scene Settings** panel, under the **Animation** category, find the `Preview Controller` parameter and select the **Use Specific Animation** option.

4. Next, *left-click* on the drop-down menu to find and select the **AM_Throw** Animation Montage from the list of available animations.

Now, the player character's **Skeleton** will start previewing the **Throw** Animation Montage, as shown in the following screenshot:

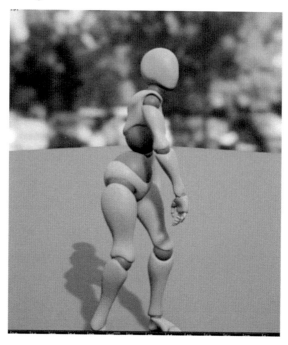

Figure 14.12 – The player character previewing the Throw Animation Montage

As you may recall from *Exercise 14.02 – adding the notify to the Throw montage*, you added `Anim_ProjectileNotify` at the 22nd frame of the **Throw** animation.

5.   Using the timeline at the bottom of the **Skeleton** editor, move the red bar to as close to the 22nd frame as you can. Please refer to the following screenshot:

Figure 14.13 – The same 22nd frame in which you added Anim_ProjectileNotify earlier

At the 22nd frame of the **Throw** animation, the player character should look as follows:

Figure 14.14 – The character's hand in position to release a projectile

As shown in the preceding screenshot, at the 22nd frame of the **Throw** Animation Montage, the character's hand is in position to release a projectile.

As you can see, the player character will be throwing the projectile from their *right hand*, so the new Socket should be attached to it. Let's take a look at the skeletal hierarchy of the player character, as shown in the following screenshot:

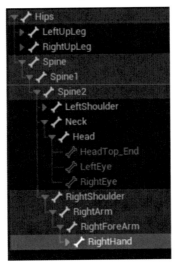

Figure 14.15 – The RightHand bone within the hierarchy of the player character's skeleton

6. From the skeletal hierarchy, find the **RightHand** bone. This can be found underneath the **RightShoulder** bone hierarchy structure.

7. *Right-click* on the **RightHand** bone and *left-click* the **Add Socket** option from the list of options that appears. Name this socket **ProjectileSocket**.

    Also, when adding a new `Socket`, the hierarchy of the entire **RightHand** will expand and the new socket will appear at the bottom.

8. With **ProjectileSocket** selected, use the **Transform** widget gizmo to position this `Socket` at the following location:

    ```
    Location = (X=30.145807,Y=36.805481,Z=-10.23186)
    ```

    The final result should look as follows:

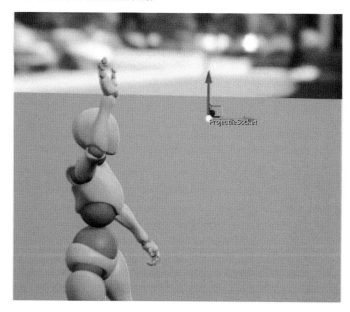

Figure 14.16 – The final position of ProjectileSocket at the 22nd
frame of the Throw animation in world space

If your gizmo looks a bit different, that is because the preceding screenshot shows the socket location in world space, not local space.

9. Now that **ProjectileSocket** is positioned where you want it, save the `MainCharacter_Skeleton` asset.

With this exercise complete, you now know the location that the player projectile will spawn from. Since you used the **Throw** Animation Montage in the preview and used the same 22nd frame of the animation, you know this position will be correct based on when `Anim_ProjectileNotify` will fire.

Now, let's spawn the player projectile in C++.

Exercise 14.05 – preparing the SpawnProjectile() Function

Now that you have **ProjectileSocket** in place and there is a location from which to spawn the player projectile, let's add the code necessary to spawn the player projectile.

By the end of this exercise, you will have the function ready to spawn the projectile and it will be ready to call from the `Anim_ProjectileNotify` class.

Follow these steps:

1. From Visual Studio, navigate to the `SuperSideScroller_Player.h` header file.

2. You need a class reference variable for the `PlayerProjectile` class. You can do this using the `TsubclassOf` variable template class type. Add the following code to the header file, under the `Private` access modifier:

    ```
    UPROPERTY(EditAnywhere)
    TSubclassOf<class APlayerProjectile> PlayerProjectile;
    ```

    Now that you have the variable ready, it is time to declare the function you will use to spawn the projectile.

3. Add the following function declaration under the declaration of the void `ThrowProjectile()` function and the `Public` access modifier:

    ```
    void SpawnProjectile();
    ```

4. Before preparing the definition of the `SpawnProjectile()` function, add the following `include` directories to the list of includes in the `SuperSideScroller_Player.cpp` source file:

    ```
    #include "PlayerProjectile.h"
    #include "Engine/World.h"
    #include "Components/SphereComponent.h"
    ```

    You need to include `PlayerProjectile.h` because it is required to reference the collision component of the projectile class. Next, you must use the `Engine/World.h` include to use the `SpawnActor()` function and access the `FActorSpawnParameters` struct. Lastly, you need to use the `Components/SphereComponent.h` include to update the collision component of the player projectile so that it will ignore the player.

5. Next, create the definition of the `SpawnProjectile()` function at the bottom of the `SuperSideScroller_Player.cpp` source file, as shown here:

```
void ASuperSideScroller_Player::SpawnProjectile()
{

}
```

The first thing this function needs to do is check whether the `PlayerProjectile` class variable is valid. If this object is not valid, there is no point in continuing to try and spawn it.

6. Update the `SpawnProjectile()` function so that it looks as follows:

```
void ASuperSideScroller_Player::SpawnProjectile()
{
    if(PlayerProjectile)
    {

    }
}
```

Now, if the `PlayerProjectile` object is valid, you'll want to obtain the `UWorld` object that the player currently exists in and ensure that this world is valid before continuing.

7. Update the `SpawnProjectile()` function to the following:

```
void ASuperSideScroller_Player::SpawnProjectile()
{
    if(PlayerProjectile)
    {
        UWorld* World = GetWorld();
        if (World)
        {

        }
    }
}
```

At this point, you have made safety checks to ensure that both `PlayerProjectile` and `UWorld` are valid, so now, it is safe to attempt to spawn the projectile. The first thing you must do is declare a new variable of the `FactorSpawnParameters` type and assign the player as the owner.

8. Add the following code within the most recent `if` statement so that the `SpawnProjectile()` function looks like this:

```
void ASuperSideScroller_Player::SpawnProjectile()
{
  if(PlayerProjectile)
    {
      UWorld* World = GetWorld();
      if (World)
        {
          FActorSpawnParameters SpawnParams;
          SpawnParams.Owner = this;
        }
    }
}
```

As you learned previously, the `SpawnActor()` function call from the `UWorld` object will require the `FActorSpawnParameters` struct as part of the spawned object's initialization. In the case of the player projectile, you can use the `this` keyword as a reference to the player character class for the owner of the projectile.

9. Next, you need to handle the `Location` and `Rotation` parameters of the `SpawnActor()` function. Add the following lines under the latest line – that is, `SpawnParams.Owner = this`:

```
const FVector SpawnLocation = this->GetMesh()-
  >GetSocketLocation(FName("ProjectileSocket"));
const FRotator Rotation = GetActorForwardVector().
Rotation();
```

In the first line, you declare a new `FVector` variable called `SpawnLocation`. This vector uses the `Socket` location of the `ProjectileSocket` socket that you created in the previous exercise. The `Skeletal Mesh` component returned from the `GetMesh()` function contains a function called `GetSocketLocation()` that will return the location of the socket with the `FName` property that is passed in – in this case, `ProjectileSocket`.

In the second line, you are declaring a new `FRotator` variable called `Rotation`. This value is set to the player's forward vector and converted into a `Rotator` container. This will ensure that the rotation – or in other words, the direction in which the player projectile will spawn – will be in front of the player, and it will move away from the player.

Now, all of the parameters required to spawn the projectile are ready.

10. Add the following line underneath the code from the previous step:

```
APlayerProjectile* Projectile = World-
   >SpawnActor<APlayerProjectile>(PlayerProjectile,
   SpawnLocation,
   Rotation, SpawnParams);
```

The `World->SpawnActor()` function will return an object of the class you are attempting to spawn in – in this case, `APlayerProjectile`. This is why you are adding `APlayerProjectile* Projectile` before the actual spawning occurs. Then, you are passing in the `SpawnLocation`, `Rotation`, and `SpawnParams` parameters to ensure that the projectile is spawning where and how you want.

11. Return to the editor to recompile the newly added code. After the code compiles successfully, this exercise is complete.

With this exercise complete, you now have a function that will spawn the player projectile class that is assigned inside the player character. By adding safety checks for the validity of both the projectile and the world, you can ensure that if an object is spawned, it is a valid object inside a valid world.

You set up the appropriate `location`, `rotation`, and `FActorSpawnParameters` parameters for the `UWorld SpawnActor()` function to ensure that the player projectile spawns at the right location, based on the socket location from the previous exercise, with the appropriate direction so that it moves away from the player, and with the player character as its owner.

Now, it is time to update the `Anim_ProjectileNotify` source file so that it spawns the projectile.

Exercise 14.06 – updating the Anim_ProjectileNotify class

The function that allows the player projectile to spawn is ready, but you aren't calling this function anywhere yet. Back in *Exercise 14.01 – creating a UAnim Notify class*, you created the `Anim_ProjectileNotify` class, while in *Exercise 14.02 – adding the notify to the Throw montage*, you added this notify to the **Throw** Animation Montage.

Now, it is time to update the `UanimNotify` class so that it calls the `SpawnProjectile()` function.

Follow these steps:

1. In Visual Studio, open the `Anim_ProjectileNotify.cpp` source file.

   In the source file, you have the following code:

```
#include "Anim_ProjectileNotify.h"

void UAnim_
ProjectileNotify::Notify(USkeletalMeshComponent*
```

```
MeshComp, UAnimSequenceBase* Animation, const
FAnimNotifyEventReference& EventReference)
{
    Super::Notify(MeshComp, Animation, EventReference);
    UE_LOG(LogTemp, Warning, TEXT("Throw Notify"));
}
```

2. Remove the UE_LOG() line from the Notify() function.

3. Next, add the following include lines underneath Anim_ProjectileNotify.h:

```
#include "Components/SkeletalMeshComponent.h"
#include "SuperSideScroller/SuperSideScroller_Player.h"
```

You need to include the SuperSideScroller_Player.h header file because it is required to call the SpawnProjectile() function you created in the previous exercise. We also included SkeletalMeshComponent.h because we will reference this component inside the Notify() function, so it's best to include it here too.

The Notify() function passes in a reference to the owning Skeletal Mesh, labeled MeshComp. You can use this skeletal mesh to get a reference to the player character by using the GetOwner() function and casting the returned actor to your SuperSideScroller_Player class. We'll do this next.

4. Inside the Notify() function, add the following line of code:

```
ASuperSideScroller_Player* Player =
    Cast<ASuperSideScroller_Player>(
    MeshComp->GetOwner());
```

5. Now that you have a reference to the player, you need to add a validity check for the Player variable before making a call to the SpawnProjectile() function. Add the following lines of code after the line from the previous step:

```
if (Player)
{
    Player->SpawnProjectile();
}
```

6. Now that the SpawnProjectile() function is being called from the Notify() function, return to the editor to recompile and hot-reload the code changes you have made.

Before you can use PIE to run around and throw the player projectile, you need to assign the Player Projectile variable from the previous exercise.

7. Inside the **Content Drawer** interface, navigate to the /MainCharacter/Blueprints

directory to find the `BP_SuperSideScroller_MainCharacter` Blueprint. *Double-click* to open the Blueprint.

8. In the **Details** panel, underneath the `Throw Montage` parameter, you will find the `Player Projectile` parameter. *Left-click* the drop-down option for this parameter and find `BP_ PlayerProjectile`. *Left-click* on this option to assign it to the `Player Projectile` variable.

9. Recompile and save the `BP_SuperSideScroller_MainCharacter` Blueprint.

10. Now, use `PIE` and use the *left mouse button*. The player character will play the **Throw** animation and the player projectile will spawn.

Notice that the projectile is spawned from the `ProjectileSocket` function you created and that it moves away from the player. The following screenshot shows this in action:

Figure 14.17 – The player can now throw the player projectile

With this exercise complete, the player can now throw the player projectile. The player projectile, in its current state, is ineffective against enemies and just flies through the air. It took a lot of moving parts between the **Throw** Animation Montage, the `Anim_ProjectileNotify` class, and the player character to get the player to throw the projectile.

In the upcoming section and exercises, you will update the player projectile so that it destroys enemies and play additional effects such as particles and sound.

Destroying actors

So far in this chapter, we have put a lot of focus on spawning, or creating, actors inside the game world; the player character uses the `UWorld` class to spawn the projectile. UE5 and its base `Actor` class come with a default function that you can use to destroy, or remove, an actor from the game world:

```
bool AActor::Destroy( bool bNetForce, bool bShouldModifyLevel )
```

You can find the full implementation of this function in Visual Studio by finding the `Actor.cpp` source file in the `/Source/Runtime/Engine/Actor.cpp` directory. This function exists in all the classes that extend from the `Actor` class, and in the case of UE5, it exists in all classes that can be spawned, or placed, inside the game world. To be more explicit, both the `EnemyBase` and `PlayerProjectile` classes are *children* of the `Actor` class, so they can be destroyed.

Looking further into the `AActor::Destroy()` function, you will find the following line:

```
World->DestroyActor( this, bNetForce, bShouldModifyLevel );
```

We won't be going into further detail about what exactly the `UWorld` class does to destroy an actor, but it is important to emphasize the fact that the `UWorld` class is responsible for both creating and destroying actors inside the world. Feel free to dig deeper into the source engine code to find more information about how the `UWorld` class handles destroying and spawning actors.

Now that you have more context regarding how UE5 handles destroying and removing actors from the game world, we'll implement this ourselves for the enemy character.

Exercise 14.07 – creating the DestroyEnemy() function

The main part of the gameplay for the `Super SideScroller` game is for the player to move around the level and use the projectile to destroy enemies. At this point in the project, you have handled the player movement and spawning the player projectile. However, the projectile does not destroy enemies yet.

To get this functionality in place, we'll start by adding some logic to the `EnemyBase` class so that it knows how to handle its destruction and remove it from the game once it collides with the player projectile.

Follow these steps to achieve this:

1. First, navigate to Visual Studio and open the `EnemyBase.h` header file.

2. In the header file, create the declaration of a new function called `DestroyEnemy()` under the `Public` access modifier, as shown here:

```
public:
    void DestroyEnemy();
```

Make sure this function definition is written underneath GENERATED_BODY(), within the class definition.

3. Save these changes to the header file and open the EnemyBase.cpp source file to add the implementation of this function.

4. Below the #include lines, add the following function definition:

```
void AEnemyBase::DestroyEnemy()
{
}
```

For now, this function will be very simple. All you need to do is call the inherited Destroy() function from the base Actor class.

5. Update the DestroyEnemy() function so that it looks like this:

```
void AEnemyBase::DestroyEnemy()
{
    Destroy();
}
```

6. With this function complete, save the source file and return to the editor so that you can recompile and hot-reload the code.

With this exercise complete, the enemy character now has a function that can easily handle the destruction of the actor whenever you choose. The DestroyEnemy() function is publicly accessible so that it can be called by other classes, which will come in handy later when you handle the destruction of the player projectile.

The reason you're creating a unique function to destroy the enemy actor is that you will use this function later in this chapter to add VFX and SFX to the enemy when they are destroyed by the player projectile.

Before polishing the elements of the enemy's destruction, let's implement a similar function inside the player projectile class so that it can also be destroyed.

Exercise 14.08 – destroying projectiles

Now that the enemy characters can handle being destroyed through the new DestroyEnemy() function you implemented in the previous exercise, it is time to do the same for the player projectile.

By the end of this exercise, the player projectile will have a unique function to handle it being destroyed and removed from the game world.

Let's get started:

1. In Visual Studio, open the header file for the player projectile – that is, `PlayerProjectile.h`.

2. Under the `Public` access modifier, add the following function declaration:

    ```
    void ExplodeProjectile();
    ```

3. Next, open the source file for the player projectile – that is, `PlayerProjectile.cpp`.

4. Underneath the void `APlayerProjectile::OnHit` function, add the definition of the `ExplodeProjectile()` function:

    ```
    void APlayerProjectile::ExplodeProjectile()
    {
    }
    ```

    For now, this function will work identically to the `DestroyEnemy()` function from the previous exercise.

5. Add the inherited `Destroy()` function to the new `ExplodeProjectile()` function, like so:

    ```
    void APlayerProjectile::ExplodeProjectile()
    {
        Destroy();
    }
    ```

6. With this function complete, save the source file and return to the editor so that you can recompile and hot-reload the code.

With this exercise complete, the player projectile now has a function that can easily handle the destruction of the actor whenever you choose. The reason you need to create a unique function to handle destroying the player projectile actor is the same reason you created the `DestroyEnemy()` function – you will use this function later in this chapter to add VFX and SFX to the player projectile when it collides with another actor.

Now that you have experience with implementing the `Destroy()` function inside both the player projectile and the enemy character, it is time to put these two elements together.

In the next activity, you will enable the player projectile to destroy the enemy character when they collide.

Activity 14.01 – Allow the projectile to destroy enemies

Now that both the player projectile and the enemy character can handle being destroyed, it is time to go the extra mile and allow the player projectile to destroy the enemy character when they collide.

Follow these steps to achieve this:

1. Add the `#include` statement for the `EnemyBase.h` header file toward the top of the `PlayerProjectile.cpp` source file.

2. Within the void `APlayerProjectile::OnHit()` function, create a new variable of the `AEnemyBase*` type and call this variable `Enemy`.

3. Cast the `OtherActor` parameter of the `APlayerProjectile::OnHit()` function to the `AEnemyBase*` class and set the `Enemy` variable to the result of this cast.

4. Use an `if()` statement to check the validity of the `Enemy` variable.

5. If the `Enemy` variable is valid, call the `DestroyEnemy()` function from this `Enemy`.

6. After the `if()` block, make a call to the `ExplodeProjectile()` function.

7. Save the changes to the source file and return to the UE5 editor.

8. Use `PIE` and then use the player projectile against an enemy to observe the results.

   The expected output is as follows:

Figure 14.18 – The player throwing the projectile

When the projectile hits the enemy, the enemy character is destroyed, as shown here:

Figure 14.19 – The projectile and enemy have been destroyed

With this activity complete, the player projectile and the enemy character can be destroyed when they collide with each other. Additionally, the player projectile will be destroyed whenever another actor triggers its `APlayerProjectile::OnHit()` function.

With that, a major element of the `Super SideScroller` game has been completed: the player projectile spawning and the enemies being destroyed when they collide with the projectile. You can observe that destroying these actors is very simple and not very interesting to the player.

This is why, in the upcoming exercises in this chapter, you will learn more about **visual effects** and **audio effects**, or **VFX** and **SFX**, respectively. You will also implement these elements for the enemy character and player projectile.

Now that both the enemy character and the player projectile can be destroyed, let's briefly discuss what VFX and SFX are, and how they will impact the project.

> **Note**
> The solution to this activity can be found on GitHub here: `https://github.com/PacktPublishing/Elevating-Game-Experiences-with-Unreal-Engine-5-Second-Edition/tree/main/Activity%20solutions`.

Understanding and implementing visual and audio effects

VFX such as Particle Systems and sound effects such as sound cues play an important role in video games. They add a level of polish on top of systems, game mechanics, and even basic actions that make these elements more interesting or more pleasing to perform.

Let's start by understanding VFX, followed by SFX.

VFX

VFX, in the context of UE5, are made up of what's called **particle systems**. Particle Systems are made up of emitters, and emitters consist of modules. In these modules, you can control the appearance and behavior of the emitter using materials, meshes, and mathematical modules. The result can be anything from a fire torch or snow falling to rain, dust, and so on.

> **Note**
> You can learn more here: `https://docs.unrealengine.com/en-US/Resources/Showcases/Effects/index.html`.

Audio effects (SFX)

SFX, in the context of UE5, are made up of a combination of sound waves and sound cues:

- Sound waves are `.wav` audio format files that can be imported into UE5.

- Sound cues combine sound wave audio files with other nodes such as **Oscillator**, **Modulator**, and **Concatenator** to create unique and complex sounds for your game.

> **Note**
> You can learn more here: `https://docs.unrealengine.com/en-US/Engine/Audio/SoundCues/NodeReference/index.html`.

In the context of UE5, VFX were created using a tool called **Cascade**, where artists could combine the use of **materials**, **static meshes**, and **math** to create interesting and convincing effects for the game world. This book will not dive into how this tool works, but you can find information about Cascade here: `https://docs.unrealengine.com/4.27/en-US/RenderingAndGraphics/ParticleSystems/`.

In more recent versions of the engine, starting in the 4.20 update, there is a plugin called **Niagara** that can be enabled to create VFX. Niagara, unlike Cascade, uses a system similar to Blueprints, where you can visually script the behaviors of the effect rather than use preset modules with predefined behavior. You can find more information about Niagara here: `https://docs.unrealengine.com/en-US/Engine/Niagara/Overview/index.html`. Furthermore, Cascade will be deprecated in new versions of UE5 and Niagara will be used. For the sake of this book, we will still use Cascade particle effects.

In *Chapter 9, Adding Audio-Visual Elements*, you learned more about audio and how audio is handled inside UE5. All you need to know right now is that UE5 uses the `.wav` file format to import audio into the engine. From there, you can use the `.wav` file directly, referred to as sound waves in the editor, or you can convert these assets into sound cues, which allow you to add audio effects on top of the sound wave.

Lastly, there is one important class to know about that you will be referencing in the upcoming exercises, and this class is called `UGameplayStatics`. This is a static class in UE5 that can be used from both C++ and Blueprints, and it offers a variety of useful gameplay-related functions. The two functions you will be working with in the upcoming exercise are as follows:

```
UGameplayStatics::SpawnEmitterAtLocation
UGameplayStatics:SpawnSoundAtLocation
```

These two functions work in very similar ways; they both require a `World` context object in which to spawn the effect, the Particle System or audio to spawn, and the location in which to spawn the effect. You will be using these functions to spawn the destroy effects for the enemy in the next exercise.

Exercise 14.09 – adding effects when the enemy is destroyed

In this exercise, you will add new content to the project that comes included with this chapter and exercise. This includes theVFX andSFX, and all of their required assets. Then, you will update the `EnemyBase` class so that it can use audio and Particle System parameters to add the layer of polish needed when the enemy is destroyed by the player projectile.

By the end of this exercise, you will have an enemy that is visually and audibly destroyed when it collides with the player projectile.

Let's get started:

1. To begin, we need to migrate specific assets from the **Action RPG** project, which can be found in the **Learn** tab of **Unreal Engine Launcher**.

2. From **Epic Games Launcher**, navigate to the **Samples** tab and, in the **UE Legacy Samples** category, you will find **Action RPG**:

Figure 14.20 – The Action RPG sample project

> **Note**
>
> You will be taking additional assets from the **Action RPG** project in later exercises of this chapter, so you should keep this project open to avoid redundantly opening the project. The assets for this exercise can be downloaded from https://github.com/PacktPublishing/ Elevating-Game-Experiences-with-Unreal-Engine-5-Second-Edition/ tree/main/Chapter14/Exercise14.09.

3. Left-click the **Action RPG** game project and then left-click the **Create Project** option.

4. From here, select engine version 4.27 and choose which directory to download the project to. Then, *left-click* the **Create** button to start installing the project.

5. Once the **Action RPG** project has finished downloading, navigate to the **Library** tab of **Epic Games Launcher** to find **ActionRPG** under the **My Projects** section.

6. *Double-click* the **ActionRPG** project to open it in the UE5 editor.

7. In the editor, find the **A_Guardian_Death_Cue** audio asset in the **Content Browser** interface. *Right-click* this asset and select **Asset Actions** and then **Migrate**.

8. After selecting **Migrate**, you will be presented with all the assets that are referenced in **A_ Guardian_Death_Cue**. This includes all audio classes and sound wave files. Choose **OK** from the **Asset Report** dialog window.

9. Next, you will need to navigate to the Content folder for your Super SideScroller project and *left-click* **Select Folder**.

10. Once the migration process is complete, you will see a notification in the editor stating that the migration was completed successfully.

11. Do the same migration steps for the `P_Goblin_Death` VFX asset. The two primary assets you will be adding to the project are as follows:

```
A_Guardian_Death_Cue
P_Goblin_Death
```

The `P_Goblin_Death` Particle System asset references additional assets such as materials and textures that are included in the `Effects` directory, while `A_Guardian_Death_Cue` references additional sound wave assets included in the `Assets` directory.

12. After migrating these folders into your `Content` directory, open the UE5 editor for your `SuperSideScroller` project to find the new folders included in your project's **Content Drawer**.

The particle you will be using for the enemy character's destruction is called `P_Goblin_Death` and can be found in the `/Effects/FX_Particle/` directory. The sound you will be using for the enemy character's destruction is called `A_Guardian_Death_Cue` and can be found in the `/Assets/Sounds/Creatures/Guardian/` directory. Now that the assets you need have been imported into the editor, let's move on to the code.

13. Open Visual Studio and navigate to the header file for the enemy base class – that is, `EnemyBase.h`.

14. Add the following `UPROPERTY()` variable. This will represent the Particle System for when the enemy is destroyed. Make sure this is declared under the `Public` access modifier:

```
UPROPERTY(EditAnywhere, BlueprintReadOnly)
class UParticleSystem* DeathEffect;
```

15. Add the following `UPROPERTY()` variable. This will represent the sound for when the enemy is destroyed. Make sure this is declared under the `Public` access modifier:

```
UPROPERTY(EditAnywhere, BlueprintReadOnly)
class USoundBase* DeathSound;
```

With these two properties defined, let's move on and add the logic required to spawn and use these effects for when the enemy is destroyed.

16. Inside the source file for the enemy base class, `EnemyBase.cpp`, add the following includes for the `UGameplayStatics` and `UWorld` classes:

```
#include "Kismet/GameplayStatics.h"
#include "Engine/World.h"
```

You will be using the `UGameplayStatics` and `UWorld` classes to spawn the sound and Particle System into the world when the enemy is destroyed.

17. Within the `AEnemyBase::DestroyEnemy()` function, you have one line of code:

```
Destroy();
```

18. Add the following line of code above the `Destroy()` function call:

```
UWorld* World = GetWorld();
```

It is necessary to define the `UWorld` object before attempting to spawn a Particle System or sound because a `World` context object is required.

19. Next, use an `if()` statement to check the validity of the `World` object you just defined:

```
if(World)
{
}
```

20. Within the `if()` block, add the following code to check the validity of the `DeathEffect` property, and then spawn this effect using the `SpawnEmitterAtLocation` function from `UGameplayStatics`:

```
if(DeathEffect)
{
    UGameplayStatics::SpawnEmitterAtLocation(World,
        DeathEffect, GetActorTransform());
}
```

It cannot be emphasized enough that you should ensure an object is valid before attempting to spawn or manipulate the object. By doing so, you can avoid engine crashes.

21. After the `if(DeathEffect)` block, perform the same validity check of the `DeathSound` property and then spawn the sound using the `UGameplayStatics::SpawnSoundAtLocation` function:

```
if(DeathSound)
{
    UGameplayStatics::SpawnSoundAtLocation(World,
        DeathSound, GetActorLocation());
}
```

Before calling the `Destroy()` function, you need to make checks regarding whether both the `DeathEffect` and `DeathSound` properties are valid, and if so, spawn those effects using the proper `UGameplayStatics` function. This ensures that regardless of whether either property is valid, the enemy character will still be destroyed.

22. Now that the `AEnemyBase::DestroyEnemy()` function has been updated to spawn these effects, return to the UE5 editor to compile and hot-reload these code changes.

23. Within the **Content Drawer** interface, navigate to the `/Enemy/Blueprints/` directory. *Double-click* the `BP_Enemy` asset to open it.

24. In the **Details** panel of the enemy Blueprint, you will find the `Death Effect` and `Death Sound` properties. *Left-click* on the drop-down list for the `Death Effect` property and find the `P_Goblin_Death` Particle System.

25. Next, underneath the `Death Effect` parameter, *left-click* on the drop-down list for the `Death Sound` property and find the **A_Guardian_Death_Cue** sound cue.

26. Now that these parameters have been updated and assigned the correct effect, compile and save the enemy Blueprint.

27. Using `PIE`, spawn the player character and throw a player projectile at an enemy. If an enemy is not present in your level, please add one. When the player projectile collides with the enemy, the VFX and SFX you added will play, as shown in the following screenshot:

Figure 14.21 – Now, the enemy explodes and gets destroyed in a blaze of glory

With this exercise complete, the enemy character now plays a Particle System and a sound cue when it is destroyed by the player projectile. This adds a nice layer of polish to the game, and it makes it more satisfying to destroy the enemies.

In the next exercise, you will add a new Particle System and audio components to the player projectile so that it looks and sounds more interesting while it flies through the air.

Exercise 14.10 – adding effects to the player projectile

In its current state, the player projectile functions the way it is intended to; it flies through the air, collides with objects in the game world, and is destroyed. However, visually, the player projectile is just a ball with a plain white texture.

In this exercise, you will add a layer of polish to the player projectile by adding both a Particle System and an audio component so that the projectile is more enjoyable to use.

Follow these steps to achieve this:

1. Much like the previous exercises, we will need to migrate assets from the **Action RPG** project to our **SuperSideScroller** project. Please refer to *Exercise 14.09 – adding effects when the enemy is destroyed*, on how to install and migrate assets from the **Action RPG** project.

   The two primary assets you will be adding to the project are as follows:

   ```
   P_Env_Fire_Grate_01
   A_Ambient_Fire01_Cue
   ```

   The P_Env_Fire_Grate_01 Particle System asset references additional assets, such as materials and textures, that are included in the Effects directory, while A_Ambient_Fire01_Cue references additional sound wave and sound attenuation assets included in the Assets directory.

   The particle you will be using for the player projectile is called P_Env_Fire_Grate_01 and can be found in the /Effects/FX_Particle/ directory. This is the same directory that's used by the P_Goblin_Death VFX from the previous exercise. The sound you will be using for the player projectile is called A_Ambient_Fire01_Cue and can be found in the /Assets/Sounds/Ambient/ directory.

2. *Right-click* on each of these assets in the **Content Browser** interface of the **Action RPG** project and select **Asset Actions** and then **Migrate**.

3. Make sure that you choose the directory of the **Content** folder for your **SuperSideScroller** project before confirming the migration.

   Now that the required assets have been migrated to our project, let's continue creating the player projectile class.

4. Open Visual Studio and navigate to the header file for the player projectile class – that is, PlayerProjectile.h.

5. Under the Private access modifier, underneath the declaration of the UStaticMeshComponent* MeshComp class component, add the following code to declare a new audio component for the player projectile:

   ```
   UPROPERTY(VisibleDefaultsOnly, Category = Sound)
   class UAudioComponent* ProjectileMovementSound;
   ```

6. Next, add the following code underneath the declaration of the audio component to declare a new Particle System component:

```
UPROPERTY(VisibleDefaultsOnly, Category = Projectile)
class UParticleSystemComponent* ProjectileEffect;
```

Instead of using properties that can be defined within the Blueprint, such as in the enemy character class, these effects will be components of the player projectile. This is because these effects should be attached to the collision component of the projectile so that they move with the projectile as it travels across the level when thrown.

7. With these two components declared in the header file, open the source file for the player projectile and add the following includes to the list of `include` lines at the top of the file:

```
#include "Components/AudioComponent.h"
#include "Engine/Classes/Particles/
ParticleSystemComponent.h"
```

You need a reference to both the audio component and the Particle System classes to create these subobjects using the `CreateDefaultSubobject` function, as well as to attach these components to **RootComponent**.

8. Add the following lines to create the default subobject of the `ProjectileMovementSound` component, and to attach this component to **RootComponent**:

```
ProjectileMovementSound =
CreateDefaultSubobject<UAudioComponent>
  (TEXT("ProjectileMovementSound"));
ProjectileMovementSound
->AttachToComponent(RootComponent,
FAttachmentTransformRules::KeepWorldTransform);
```

9. Next, add the following lines to create the default subobject for the `ProjectileEffect` component, and to attach this component to **RootComponent**:

```
ProjectileEffect = CreateDefaultSubobject<UParticle
SystemComponent>(TEXT("Projectile
  Effect"));
ProjectileEffect->AttachToComponent(RootComponent,
FAttachmentTransformRules::KeepWorldTransform);
```

10. Now that you have created, initialized, and attached these two components to **RootComponent**, return to the UE5 editor to recompile and hot-reload these code changes.

11. From the `Content Drawer` interface, navigate to the `/MainCharacter/Projectile/` directory. Find the `BP_PlayerProjectile` asset and *double-click* it to open the Blueprint.

   In the **Components** tab, you will find the two new components you added using the preceding code. Observe that these components are attached to the **CollisionComp** component, also known as **RootComponent**.

12. *Left-click* to select the **ProjectileEffect** component and, within the **Details** panel, assign the `P_Env_Fire_Grate_01` VFX asset to this parameter, as shown in the following screenshot:

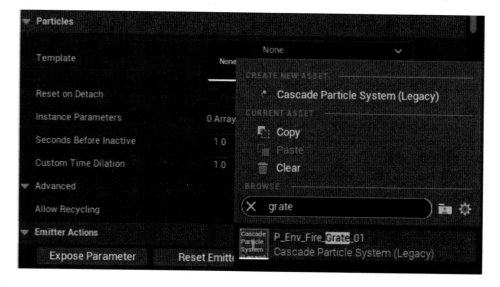

Figure 14.22 – Assigning the VFX to the particle system component

13. Before assigning the audio component, let's adjust the **Transform** property of the `ProjectileEffect` VFX asset. Update the **Rotation** and **Scale** values of the **Transform** property for the VFX so that they match what is shown in the following screenshot:

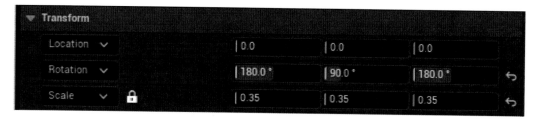

Figure 14.23 – The updated Transform of the Particle System
component so that it fits better with the projectile

14. Navigate to the `Viewport` tab within the Blueprint to view these changes to the **Transform** property. `ProjectileEffect` should look as follows:

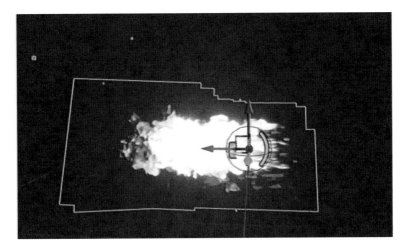

Figure 14.24 – Now, the fire VFX has been scaled and rotated appropriately

15. Now that the VFX has been set up, *left-click* the `ProjectileMovementSound` component and assign `A_Ambient_Fire01_Cue` to it.

16. Save and recompile the `BP_PlayerProjectile` Blueprint. Use `PIE` and observe that when you throw the projectile, it now shows the VFX asset and plays the assigned sound:

Figure 14.25 – The player projectile now has a VFX and an SFX as it flies through the air

With this exercise complete, the player projectile now has a VFX and an SFX that play together while it flies through the air. These elements bring the projectile to life and make the projectile much more interesting to use.

Since the VFX and SFX have been created as components of the projectile, they are also destroyed when the projectile is destroyed.

In the next exercise, you will add a particle notify and a sound notify to the **Throw** Animation Montage to provide more of an impact when the player throws the player projectile.

Exercise 14.11 – adding VFX and SFX notifies

So far, you have been implementing polish elements to the game via C++, which is a valid means of implementation. To give variety, and expand your knowledge of the UE5 toolset, this exercise will walk you through how to use notifies in Animation Montages to add Particle Systems and audio within the animation. Let's get started!

Much like the previous exercises, we will need to migrate assets from the `Action RPG` project to our **SuperSideScroller** project. Please refer to *Exercise 14.09 – adding effects when the enemy is destroyed*, to learn how to install and migrate assets from the **Action RPG** project.

Follow these steps:

1. Open the **ActionRPG** project and navigate to the **Content Browser** interface.

    The two primary assets you will be adding to the project are as follows:

    ```
    P_Skill_001
    A_Ability_FireballCast_Cue
    ```

    The `P_Skill_001` Particle System asset references additional assets such as *materials* and *textures* that are included in the `Effects` directory, while `A_Ability_FireballCast_Cue` references additional *sound wave* assets included in the `Assets` directory.

    The particle you will be using for the player when the projectile is thrown is called `P_Skill_001` and can be found in the `/Effects/FX_Particle/` directory. This is the same directory that was used by the `P_Goblin_Death` and `P_Env_Fire_Grate_01` VFX assets in the previous exercises. The sound you will be using for the enemy character destruction is called `A_Ambient_Fire01_Cue` and can be found in the `/Assets/Sounds/Ambient/` directory.

2. *Right-click* on each of these assets in the **Content Browser** interface of the **Action RPG** project and select **Asset Actions** and then **Migrate**.

3. Make sure that you choose the directory of the Content folder for your **SuperSideScroller** project before confirming the migration.

   Now that the assets you need have been migrated into your project, let's move on to adding the required notifies to the AM_Throw asset. Make sure that you return to your **SuperSideScroller** project before continuing with this exercise.

4. From the **Content Drawer** interface, navigate to the /MainCharacter/Animation/ directory. Find the AM_Throw asset and *double-click* it to open it.

5. Underneath the preview window in the center of the **Animation Montage** editor, find the **Notifies** section. This is the same section where you added Anim_ProjectileNotify earlier in this chapter.

6. To the left of the **Notifies** track, you will find a ▼ sign that allows you to use additional notify tracks. *Left-click* to add a new notify track, as shown in the following screenshot:

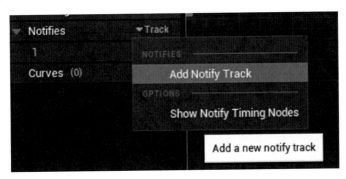

Figure 14.26 – Adding a new notify track

It is useful to add multiple tracks to the timeline to keep things organized when adding multiple notifies.

7. In the same frame as Anim_ProjectileNotify, *right-click* within the new track you created in the previous step. From the **Add Notify** list, *left-click* to select Play Particle Effect.

8.   Once created, *left-click* to select the new notify and access its **Details** panel. In **Details**, add the P_Skill_001 VFX asset to the Particle System parameter.

Once you've added this new VFX, you will notice that the VFX is placed almost toward the bottom, where the player character's feet are, but not exactly where you want it. This VFX should be placed directly on the floor, or at the base of the character. The following screenshot demonstrates this location:

Figure 14.27 – The location of the particle notify is not on the ground

To fix this, you need to add a new Socket to the player character's skeleton.

9.   Navigate to the /MainCharacter/Mesh/ directory. *Double-click* the MainCharacter_Skeleton asset to open it.

10. From the **Skeleton** bone hierarchy on the left-hand side, *right-click* on the **Hips** bone and *right-click* to select the **Add Socket** option. Name this new socket EffectSocket.

11. *Left-click* this socket from the hierarchy of bones to view its current location. By default, its location is set to the same position as the **Hips** bone. The following screenshot shows this location:

Figure 14.28 – The default location of this socket is in the center of the player's skeleton

Using the **Transform** gizmo widget, move the position of `EffectSocket` so that its position is set to the following:

`(X=0.000000,Y=100.000000,Z=0.000000)`

This position will be closer to the ground and the player character's feet. The final location can be seen in the following screenshot:

Figure 14.29 – Moving the socket's location to the base of the player skeleton

12. Now that you have a location for the particle notify, return to the AM_Throw Animation Montage.

13. Within the **Details** panel of the **Play Particle Effect** notify, there is the Socket Name parameter. Name it EffectSocket.

> **Note**
>
> If EffectSocket does not appear via the autocomplete, close and reopen the Animation Montage. Once it's reopened, the EffectSocket option should appear for you.

14. Lastly, the scale of the particle effect is a little too big, so adjust the scale of the projectile so that its value is as follows:

```
(X=0.500000,Y=0.500000,Z=0.500000)
```

Now, when the particle effect is played via this notify, its position and scale will be correct, as shown here:

Figure 14.30 – The particle now plays at the base of the player character's skeleton

15. To add the Play Sound notify, add a new track to the **Notifies** timeline section; you should have three in total.

16. On this new track, and at the same frame position as both the `Play Particle Effect` and `Anim_ProjectileNotify` notifies, *right-click* and select the **Play Sound** notify from the **Add Notify** selection. The following screenshot shows where this notify can be found:

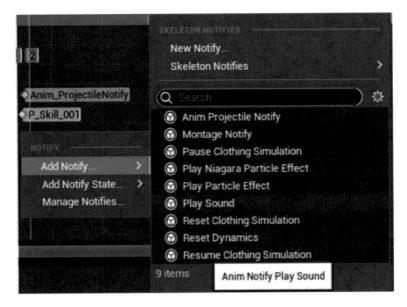

Figure 14.31 – The Play Sound notify that you learned about earlier in this chapter

17. Next, *left-click* to select the **Play Sound** notify and access its **Details** panel.

18. From the **Details** panel, find the **Sound** parameter and assign `A_Ability_FireballCast_Cue`.

    With the sound assigned, when the **Throw** animation is played back, you will see the VFX play and you will hear the sound. The **Notifies** tracks should look as follows:

Figure 14.32 – The final notify set up on the Throw Animation Montage timeline

19. Save the `AM_Throw` asset and use `PIE` to throw the player projectile.

20. Now, when you throw the projectile, you will see the particle notify play the `P_Skill_001` VFX and you will hear the `A_Ability_FireballCast_Cue` SFX. The result will look as follows:

Figure 14.33 – Now, when the player throws the projectile, powerful VFX and SFX are played

With this final exercise complete, the player now plays powerful VFX and SFX when the player projectile is thrown. This gives the throw animation more power and it feels like the player character is using a lot of energy to throw the projectile.

In the final activity, you will use the knowledge you've gained from the last few exercises to add VFX and SFX to the player projectile when it is destroyed.

Activity 14.02 – adding effects for when the projectile is destroyed

In this final activity, you will use the knowledge that you've gained from adding VFX and SFX elements to the player projectile and the enemy character to create an explosion effect for when the projectile collides with an object instead. The reason we're adding this additional explosion effect is to add a level of polish on top of destroying the projectile when it collides with environmental objects. It would look awkward and out of place if the player projectile were to hit an object and disappear without any audio or visual feedback from the player.

You will add both a Particle System and sound cue parameters to the player projectile and spawn these elements when the projectile collides with an object.

Follow these steps to achieve the expected output:

1. Inside the `PlayerProjectile.h` header file, add a new Particle System variable and a new sound base variable.

2. Name the Particle System variable `DestroyEffect` and name the sound base variable `DestroySound`.

3. In the `PlayerProjectile.cpp` source file, add the include for `UGameplayStatics` to the list of includes.

4. Update the `APlayerProjectile::ExplodeProjectile()` function so that it now spawns both the `DestroyEffect` and `DestroySound` objects. Return to the UE5 editor and recompile the new C++ code. Inside the `BP_PlayerProjectile` Blueprint, assign the `P_Explosion` VFX, which is already included in your project by default, to the `Destroy Effect` parameter of the projectile.

5. Assign the `Explosion_Cue` SFX, which is already included in your project by default, to the `Destroy Sound` parameter of the projectile.

6. Save and compile the player projectile Blueprint.

7. Use `PIE` to observe the new player projectile's destruction VFX and SFX.

   The expected output is as follows:

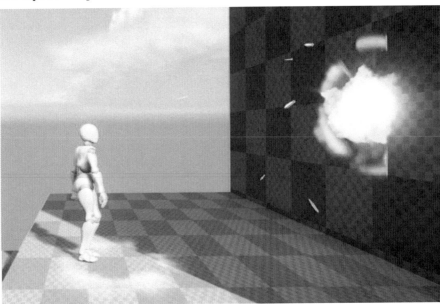

Figure 14.34 – Projectile VFX and SFX

With this activity complete, you now have experience with adding polished elements to the game. Not only have you added these elements through C++ code, but you've added elements through other tools from UE5. At this point, you have enough experience to add Particle Systems and audio to your game without having to worry about how to implement these features.

> **Note**
>
> The solution to this activity can be found on GitHub here: `https://github.com/ PacktPublishing/Elevating-Game-Experiences-with-Unreal-Engine- 5-Second-Edition/tree/main/Activity%20solutions`.

Summary

In this chapter, you learned about the importance of VFX and SFX in the world of game development. Using a combination of C++ code and notifies, you were able to bring gameplay functionality to the player projectile and the enemy character colliding, as well as a layer of polish to this functionality by adding VFX and SFX. On top of this, you learned about how objects are spawned and destroyed in UE5.

Moreover, you learned about how Animation Montages are played, both from Blueprints and through C++. By migrating the logic of playing the **Throw** Animation Montage from Blueprint to C++, you learned how both methods work and how to use both implementations for your game.

By adding a new Animation Notify using C++, you were able to add this notify to the **Throw** Animation Montage, which allows the player to spawn the player projectile you created in the previous chapter. By using the `UWorld->SpawnActor()` function and adding a new socket to the player skeleton, you were able to spawn the player projectile at the exact frame of the **Throw** animation, and at the exact position that you wanted to.

Lastly, you learned how to use the **Play Particle Effect** and **Play Sound** notifies within the **Throw** Animation Montage to add VFX and SFX to the throw of the player projectile. This chapter taught you about the different methods that exist inside UE5 when it comes to using VFX and SFX for your game.

Now that the player projectile can be thrown and destroy enemy characters, it is time to implement the final set of mechanics for the game. In the next chapter, you will create the collectibles that the player can collect, and you will also create a powerup for the player that will improve the player's movement mechanics for a short period.

15

Exploring Collectibles, Power-Ups, and Pickups

In the previous chapter, you created the player projectile and used `Anim Notifies` to spawn the player projectile during the `Throw` animation. The player projectile will serve as the player's main offensive gameplay mechanic to use against the enemies throughout the level. Due to the combination of default `Anim Notifies` provided by UE5 and your own custom `Anim_ProjectileNotify` class, the player projectile mechanic looks and feels great.

In this chapter, we will cover the following topics:

- How to create and integrate UI elements using the **Unreal Motion Graphics (UMG)** UI Designer system within UE5.

- Use the lessons learned from this project to create an interesting power-up that will increase the players' movement speed and jump height.

- How to use inheritance in C++ to derive multiple classes from one parent base class for both collectibles and power-ups. You will also be adding visual and audio elements to both the collectible and the power-up so that they are more polished.

- How to use `URotatingMovementComponent` to add rotation to actors in a very optimized and straightforward way.

By the end of this chapter, you will have the finished **SuperSideScroller** game project, complete with coin collectibles and a corresponding UI to track the number of coins collected, a new potion power-up that increases the player's movement speed and jump height, as well as a base class in which to derive potentially new power-ups and collectibles for the game.

Technical requirements

For this chapter, you will need the following technical requirements:

- Unreal Engine 5 installed

- Visual Studio 2019 installed
- Unreal Engine 4.27 installed

Let's begin this chapter by learning more about `URotatingMovementComponent`, which we will use for our collectibles.

The project for this chapter can be found in the Chapter15 folder of the code bundle for this book, which can be downloaded here: `https://github.com/PacktPublishing/Elevating-Game-Experiences-with-Unreal-Engine-5-Second-Edition`.

Understanding URotatingMovementComponent

`URotatingMovementComponent` is one of a few movement components that exists within UE5. You are already familiar with `CharacterMovementComponent` and `ProjectileMovementComponent` from the **SuperSideScroller** game project alone, and `RotatingMovementComponent` is just that – another movement component. As a refresher, movement components allow different types of movements to occur on actors, or characters, that they belong to.

> **Note**
>
> `CharacterMovementComponent`, which allows you to control the movement parameters of your character, such as their movement speed and jump height, was covered in *Chapter 10, Creating the SuperSideScroller Game*, when you created the **SuperSideScroller** player character. `ProjectileMovementComponent`, which allows you to add projectile-based movement functionality to actors, such as speed and gravity, was covered in *Chapter 14, Spawning the Player Projectile*, when you developed the player projectile.

`RotatingMovementComponent` is a very simple movement component compared to `CharacterMovementComponent` and that's because it only involves rotating the actor that `RotatingMovementComponent` is a part of; nothing more. `RotatingMovementComponent` continuously rotates a component based on the defined `Rotation Rate`, pivot translation, and the option to use rotation in local space or world space. Additionally, `RotatingMovementComponent` is much more efficient compared to other methods of rotating an actor, such as through `Event Tick` or `Timelines` within Blueprints.

> **Note**
>
> More information about movement components can be found here: `https://docs.unrealengine.com/en-US/Engine/Components/Movement/index.html#rotatingmovementcomponent`.

We will be using `RotatingMovementComponent` to allow the coin collectible and potion power-up to rotate in place along the Z-axis. This rotation will draw the player's attention to the collectible and give them a visual cue that the collectible is important.

Now that you have a better understanding of `RotatingMovementComponent`, let's move on and create the `PickableActor_Base` class, which is what the coin collectible and the potion power-up will derive from.

Exercise 15.01 – creating the PickableActor_Base class and adding URotatingMovementComponent

In this exercise, you will be creating the `PickableActor_Base` actor class, which will be used as the base class that both the collectible coin and potion power-up will derive from. You will also create a Blueprint class from this C++ base class to preview how `URotatingMovementComponent` works. Follow these steps to complete this exercise:

> **Note**
>
> You have performed many of the following steps numerous times throughout the **SuperSideScroller** game project, so there will be limited screenshots to help guide you. Only when introducing a new concept will there be an accompanying screenshot.

1. Inside the UE5 editor, click the **Tools** option at the top of the editor and then choose **New C++ Class**.

2. From the **Choose Parent Class** window, select the **Actor** option, and then click the **Next** button at the bottom of this window.

3. Name this class `PickableActor_Base` and leave the default `Path` directory as-is. Then, select the **Create Class** button at the bottom of this window.

4. After selecting the **Create Class** button, UE5 will recompile the project code and automatically open Visual Studio with both the header and source files for the `PickableActor_Base` class.

5. By default, `Actor` classes provide you with the `virtual void Tick(float DeltaTime) override;` function declaration inside the header file. For the `PickableActor_Base` class, we will not require the `Tick` function, so remove this function declaration from the `PickableActor_Base.h` header file.

6. Next, you will need to remove the function from the `PickableActor_Base.cpp` file; otherwise, you will receive a compile error. In this source file, find and remove the following code:

```
void PickableActor_Base::Tick(float DeltaTime)
{
    Super::Tick(DeltaTime);
}
```

> **Note**
>
> In many cases, the use of the `Tick()` function for movement updates can lead to performance issues as the `Tick()` function is called every single frame. Instead, try using `Gameplay Timer` functions to perform certain updates at specified intervals, rather than on each frame. You can learn more about `Gameplay Timers` here: `https://docs.unrealengine.com/4.27/en-US/ProgrammingAndScripting/ProgrammingWithCPP/UnrealArchitecture/Timers/`.

7. Now, it is time to add the components that the `PickableActor_Base` class requires. Let's start with `USphereComponent`, which you will use to detect overlap collision with the player. Add the following code underneath the `Protected` access modifier inside the `PickableActor_Base.h` header file:

    ```
    UPROPERTY(VisibleDefaultsOnly, Category = PickableItem)
    class USphereComponent* CollisionComp;
    ```

    The declaration of `USphereComponent` should be very familiar to you by now; we've done this in previous chapters, such as *Chapter 14, Spawning the Player Projectile*, when we created the `PlayerProjectile` class.

8. Next, add the following code underneath the declaration of `USphereComponent` to create a new `UStaticMeshComponent`. This will be used to visually represent either the coin collectible or the potion power-up:

    ```
    UPROPERTY(VisibleDefaultsOnly, Category = PickableItem)
    class UStaticMeshComponent* MeshComp;
    ```

9. Finally, add the following code underneath the declaration of `UStaticMeshComponent` to create a new `URotatingMovementComponent`. This will be used to give the collectible coin and potion power-up simple rotational movement:

    ```
    UPROPERTY(VisibleDefaultsOnly, Category = PickableItem)
    class URotatingMovementComponent* RotationComp;
    ```

10. Now that you have the components declared inside the `PickableActor_Base.h` header file, navigate to the `PickableActor_Base.cpp` source file so that you can add the required `#include` statements for these added components. Add the following lines after `#include "PickableActor_Base.h"`, at the top of the source file:

    ```
    #include "Components/SphereComponent.h"
    #include "Components/StaticMeshComponent.h"
    #include "GameFramework/RotatingMovementComponent.h"
    ```

11. Now that you have the necessary `#include` files for the components, you can add the necessary code to initialize these components within the `APickableActor_Base::APickableActor_Base()` constructor function:

```
APickableActor_Base::APickableActor_Base()
{

}
```

12. First, initialize the `USphereComponent` component variable, `CollisionComp`, by adding the following code to `APickableActor_Base::APickableActor_Base()`:

```
CollisionComp = CreateDefaultSubobject
    <USphereComponent>(TEXT("SphereComp"));
```

13. Next, initialize `USphereComponent` with a default sphere radius of `30.0f` by adding the following code underneath the code provided in the previous step:

```
CollisionComp->InitSphereRadius(30.0f);
```

14. Since the player character needs to overlap with this component, you will need to add the following code so that, by default, `USphereComponent` has the collision settings for `Overlap All Dynamic`:

```
CollisionComp->BodyInstance.
SetCollisionProfileName("OverlapAllDynamic");
```

15. Lastly, `CollisionComp USphereComponent` should be the root component of this actor. Add the following code to assign this:

```
RootComponent = CollisionComp;
```

16. Now that `CollisionComp USphereComponent` has been initialized, let's do the same for `MeshComp UStaticMeshComponent`. Add the following code. After, we'll discuss what the code is doing for us:

```
MeshComp = CreateDefaultSubobject<UStaticMeshComponent>(-
TEXT("MeshComp"));
MeshComp->AttachToComponent(RootComponent,
    FAttachmentTransformRules::KeepWorldTransform);
MeshComp->SetCollisionEnabled(ECollisionEnabled::NoColli-
sion);
```

The first line initializes `MeshComp UStaticMeshComponent` using the `CreateDefaultSubobject()` template function. Next, you are attaching `MeshComp` to the root component, which you made for `CollisionComp`, using the `AttachTo()` function. Lastly, `MeshComp UStaticMeshComponent` should not have any collision by default, so you are using the `SetCollisionEnabled()` function and passing in the `ECollisionEnable::NoCollision` enumerator value.

17. Lastly, we can initialize `URotatingMovementComponent RotationComp` by adding the following code:

```
RotationComp =
    CreateDefaultSubobject<URotatingMovementComponent>(
    TEXT("RotationComp"));
```

18. With all the components initialized, compile the C++ code and return to the UE5 editor. After compilation succeeds, you can start creating a Blueprint class for `PickableActor_Base`.

19. In the **Content Drawer** area, create a new folder called `PickableItems` by *right-clicking* on the `Content` folder and selecting the **New Folder** option.

20. In the `PickableItems` folder, *right-click* and select **Blueprint Class**. From the **Pick Parent Class** window, search for the `PickableActor_Base` class and *left-click* **Select** to create a new Blueprint.

21. Name this Blueprint `BP_PickableActor_Base` and *double-left-click* the Blueprint to open it.

22. In the **Components** tab, select **MeshComp UStaticMeshComponent** and assign the `Shape_Cone` static mesh to the `Static Mesh` parameter in the **Details** panel. Please refer to the following screenshot:

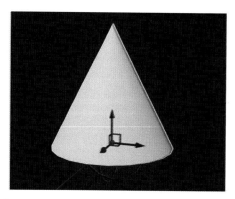

Figure 15.1 – The Shape_Cone mesh assigned to MeshComp StaticMeshComponent

23. Next, select **RotationComp URotatingMovementComponent** and find the **Rotation Rate** parameter in the **Rotating Component** category of the **Details** panel.

24. Set **Rotation Rate** to the following values:

```
(X=100.000000,Y=100.000000,Z=100.000000)
```

These values determine how fast the actor will rotate along each axis per second. This means that the cone-shaped actor will rotate along each axis at 100 degrees per second on each axis.

25. Compile the `PickableActor_Base` Blueprint and add this actor to your level.

26. Now, if you use `PIE` and look at the `PickableActor_Base` actor in the level, you will see that it is rotating. Please refer to the following screenshot:

Figure 15.2 – The BP_PickableActor_Base rotating in place

> **Note**
> You can find the assets and code for this exercise here: `https://github.com/ PacktPublishing/Game-Development-Projects-with-Unreal-Engine/ tree/master/Chapter15/Exercise15.01.`

With this exercise complete, you've created the base components required for the `PickableActor_ Base` class and learned how to implement and use `URotatingMovementComponent`. With the `PickableActor_Base` class ready, and with `URotatingMovementComponent` implemented on the Blueprint actor, we can complete the class by adding overlap detection functionality, destroying the collectible actor, and spawning audio effects when the actor is picked up by the player. In the following activity, you will add the remaining functionality required for the `PickableActor_Base` class.

Activity 15.01 – player overlap detection and spawning effects in PickableActor_Base

Now that the `PickableActor_Base` class has all the required components and has its constructor initializing the components, it is time to add the remaining aspects of its functionality. These will be inherited by the coin collectible and potion power-up later in this chapter. This additional functionality includes player overlap detection, destroying the collectible actor, and spawning an audio effect to give feedback to the player that it has been successfully picked up. Perform the following steps to add functionality that allows a `USoundBase` class object to be played when the collectible overlaps with the player:

1. Create a new function in the `PickableActor_Base` class that takes in a reference to the player as an input parameter. Call this function `PlayerPickedUp`.

2. Create a new UFUNCTION called `BeginOverlap()`. Make sure to include all the required input parameters for this function before moving on. Refer to *Chapter 6, Setting Up Collision Objects*, where you used this function inside the `VictoryBox` class.

3. Add a new UPROPERTY() for the `USoundBase` class and name it `PickupSound`.

4. In the `PickableActor_Base.cpp` source file, create the definitions for both the `BeginOverlap()` and `PlayerPickedUp()` functions.

5. Now, add the required `#include` files for the `SuperSideScroller_Player` class and the `GameplayStatics` class at the top of the source file.

6. In the `BeginOverlap()` function, create a reference to the player using the `OtherActor` input parameter of the function.

7. Next, if the player reference is valid, make a call to the `PlayerPickedUp()` function, passing in the player variable.

8. In the `PlayerPickedUp()` function, create a variable for the `UWorld*` object that's returned by the `GetWorld()` function.

9. Use the `UGameplayStatics` library to spawn `PickUpSound` at the location of the `PickableActor_Base` actor.

10. Then, call the `Destroy()` function so that the actor gets destroyed and removed from the world.

11. Finally, in the `APickableActor_Base::APickableActor_Base()` constructor, bind the `OnComponentBeginOverlap` event of `CollisionComp` to the `BeginOverlap()` function.

12. Download and install the `Unreal Match 3` project from the **Samples** tab of **Epic Games Launcher** under the **UE Legacy Samples** section. Migrate the `Match_Combo` soundwave asset from this project into your **SuperSideScroller** project using the knowledge you gained in *Chapter 14, Spawning the Player Projectile*.

13. Apply this sound to the `PickupSound` parameter of the `BP_PickableActor_Base` Blueprint.

14. Compile the Blueprint, and if one does not exist in your level, add the `BP_PickableActor_Base` actor to your level now.

15. In `PIE`, have your character overlap with the `BP_PickableActor_Base` actor.

Expected output:

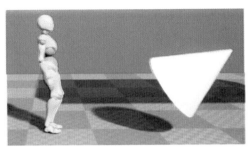

Figure 15.3 – The BP_PickableActor_Base object can be picked up by the player

---

Note

The solution for this activity can be found on `https://github.com/PacktPublishing/Elevating-Game-Experiences-with-Unreal-Engine-5-Second-Edition/tree/main/Activity%20solutions`.

With this activity complete, you have proven your knowledge regarding how to add the `OnBeginOverlap()` functionality to your actor classes and how to use this function to perform logic for your actor. In the case of `PickableActor_Base`, we added logic that will spawn a custom sound and destroy the actor.

Now that the `PickableActor_Base` class is set and ready, it is time to develop the collectible coin and power-up potion classes that will derive from it. The coin collectible class will inherit from the `PickableActor_Base` class you have just created. It will override key functionality, such as the `PlayerPickedUp()` function, so that we can implement unique logic for the collectible when it's picked up by the player. In addition to overriding functionality from the inherited parent `PickableActor_Base` class, the coin collectible class will have its own unique set of properties, such as its current coin value and unique pickup sound. We'll create the coin collectible class together in the next exercise.

Exercise 15.02 – creating the PickableActor_Collectable class

In this exercise, you will be creating the `PickableActor_Collectable` class, which will be derived from the `PickableActor_Base` class you created in *Exercise 15.01 – creating the PickableActor_Base class and adding URotatingMovement*, and finished in *Activity 15.01 – player overlap detection and spawning effects in PickableActor_Base*. This class will be used as the main collectible coin that the player can collect within the level. Follow these steps to complete this exercise:

1. Inside the UE5 editor, click the **Tools** option at the top of the editor and choose **New C++ Class**.

2. From the **Choose Parent Class** window, select the **PickableActor_Base** option, and then click the **Next** button at the bottom of this window.

3. Name this class `PickableActor_Collectable` and leave the default `Path` directory as-is. Then, select the **Create Class** button at the bottom of this window.

4. After selecting the **Create Class** button, UE5 will recompile the project code and will automatically open Visual Studio with both the header and source files for the `PickableActor_Collectable` class.

5. By default, the `PickableActor_Collectable.h` header file has no declared functions or variables within its class declaration. You will need to add the override for the `BeginPlay()` function underneath a new `Protected Access Modifier`. Add the following code:

```
protected:
    virtual void BeginPlay() override;
```

The reason we are overriding the `BeginPlay()` function is that `URotatingMovementComponent` requires the actor to initialize and use `BeginPlay()` to correctly rotate the actor. Therefore, we need to create the override declaration of this function and create a basic definition inside the source file. First, however, we need to override another important function from the `PickableActor_Base` parent class.

6. Override the `PlayerPickedUp()` function from the `PickableActor_Base` parent class by adding the following code under `Protected Access Modifier`:

```
virtual void PlayerPickedUp(class ASuperSideScroller_
Player* Player)override;
```

With this, we are saying that we are going to use, and override, the functionality of the `PlayerPickedUp()` function.

7. Lastly, create a new integer called `UPROPERTY()` that will hold the value that the coin collectible will have; in this case, it will have a value of `1`. Add the following code to do this:

```
public:
    UPROPERTY(EditAnywhere, Category = Collectable)
```

```
int32 CollectableValue = 1;
```

Here, we are creating the integer variable that will be accessible in Blueprints and has a default value of 1. If you so choose, with the EditAnywhere UPROPERTY() keyword, you can change how much a coin collectible is worth.

8. Now, we can move on to the PickableActor_Collectable.cpp source file and create the definition of the overridden PlayerPickedUp() function. Add the following code to the source file:

    ```
    void APickableActor_Collectable::PlayerPickedUp(class
      ASuperSideScroller_Player* Player)
    {
    }
    ```

9. For now, we need to make a call to the PlayerPickedUp() parent function by using the Super keyword. Add the following code to the PlayerPicked() function:

    ```
    Super::PlayerPickedUp(Player);
    ```

    The call to the parent function, which uses Super::PlayerPickedUp(Player), will ensure that the functionality you created in the PickableActor_Base class is called. As you may recall, the PlayerPickedUp() function in the parent class makes a call to spawn the PickupSound sound object and destroys the actor.

10. Next, create the definition of the BeginPlay() function inside the source file by adding the following code:

    ```
    void APickableActor_Collectable::BeginPlay()
    {
    }
    ```

11. Finally, in C++, once again make the call to the BeginPlay() parent function using the Super keyword. Add the following code to the BeginPlay() function inside the PickableActor_Collectable class:

    ```
    Super::BeginPlay();
    ```

12. Compile the C++ code and return to the editor.

Note

You can find the assets and code for this exercise at the following link: https://packt.live/35fRN3E.

Now that you've successfully compiled the `PickableActor_Collectable` class, you have created the framework needed for the coin collectible. In the following activity, you will create a Blueprint from this class and finalize the coin collectible actor.

Activity 15.02 – finalizing the PickableActor_Collectable actor

Now that the `PickableActor_Collectable` class has all of the necessary inherited functionality and unique properties it needs, it is time to create the Blueprint from this class and add a `Static Mesh`, update its `URotatingMovementComponent`, and apply a sound to the `PickUpSound` property. Perform the following steps to finalize the `PickableActor_Collectable` actor:

1. From **Epic Games Launcher**, find the **Content Examples** project in the **Samples** tab, underneath the **Engine Feature Samples** category.

2. Create and install a new project from the **Content Examples** project.

3. Migrate the `SM_Pickup_Coin` asset and all its referenced assets from the **Content Examples** project to your **SuperSideScroller** project.

4. Create a new folder within the `Content/PickableItems` directory in the **Content Drawer** window and name it `Collectable`.

5. In this new `Collectable` folder, create a new Blueprint from the `PickableActor_Collectable` class that you created in *Exercise 15.02 – creating the PickableActor_Collectable class*. Name this new Blueprint `BP_Collectable`.

6. In this Blueprint, set the `Static Mesh` parameter of the `MeshComp` component to the `SM_Pickup_Coin` mesh you imported earlier in this activity.

7. Next, add the `Match_Combo` sound asset to the `PickupSound` parameter of the collectible.

8. Lastly, update the `RotationComp` component so that the actor rotates along the *Z*-axis at 90 degrees per second.

9. Compile the Blueprint, place `BP_Collectable` in your level, and use `PIE`.

10. Overlap the player character with the `BP_Collectable` actor and observe the results.

    Expected output:

Figure 15.4 – The coin collectible rotates and can be overlapped by the player

> **Note**
> The solution for this activity can be found on `https://github.com/PacktPublishing/Elevating-Game-Experiences-with-Unreal-Engine-5-Second-Edition/tree/main/Activity%20solutions`.

With this activity complete, you have proven that you know how to migrate assets into your UE5 project and how to use and update `URotatingMovementComponent` to fit the needs of the coin collectible. Now that the coin collectible actor is complete, it is time to add functionality to the player so that the player can keep track of how many coins they have collected.

First, we will create the logic that will count the coins using `UE_LOG`. Later, we will implement the coin counter using the **Unreal Motion Graphics** (**UMG**) UI Designer system on the game's UI.

Logging variables using UE_LOG

In *Chapter 11, Working with Blend Space 1D, Key Bindings, and State Machines*, we used and learned about the `UE_LOG` function to log when the player should throw the projectile. Then, we used the `UE_LOG` function in *Chapter 13, Creating and Adding the Enemy Artificial Intelligence*, to log when the player projectile hit an object. `UE_LOG` is a robust logging tool we can use to output important information from our C++ functions into the **Output Log** window inside the editor when playing our game. So far, we have only logged `FStrings` to display general text in the **Output Log** window to know that our functions were being called. Now, it is time to learn how to log variables to debug how many coins the player has collected.

> **Note**
>
> There is another useful debug function available in C++ with UE5 known as `AddOnScreenDebugMessage`. You can learn more about this function here: `https://docs.unrealengine.com/en-US/API/Runtime/Engine/Engine/UEngine/AddOnScreenDebugMessage/1/index.html`.

When creating the `FString` syntax used by the `TEXT()` macro, we can add format specifiers to log different types of variables. We will only be discussing how to add the format specifier for integer variables.

> **Note**
>
> You can find more information on how to specify other variable types by reading the following documentation: `https://www.ue4community.wiki/Logging#Logging_an_FString`.

This is what `UE_LOG()` looks like when passing in `FString` "Example Text":

```
UE_LOG(LogTemp, Warning, TEXT("Example Text"));
```

Here, you have `Log Category`, `Log Verbose Level`, and the actual `FString`, "Example Text", to display in the log. To log an integer variable, you need to add `%d` to your `FString` within the `TEXT()` macro, followed by the integer variable name outside the `TEXT()` macro, separated by a comma. Here is an example:

```
UE_LOG(LogTemp, Warning, TEXT("My integer variable %d),
MyInteger);
```

The format specifier is identified by the `%` symbol, and each variable type has a designated letter that corresponds with it. In the case of integers, the letter `d` is used, representing a digit. You will be using this method of logging integer variables to log the number of coin collectibles the player has in the next exercise.

Exercise 15.03 – tracking the number of coins for the player

In this exercise, you will be creating the necessary properties and functions that will allow you to track how many coins the player collects throughout the level. You will use this tracking to show the player using UMG later in this chapter. Follow these steps to complete this exercise:

1. In Visual Studio, find and open the `SuperSideScroller_Player.h` header file.

2. Under `Private Access Modifier`, create a new `int` variable called NumberofCollectables, as shown here:

```
int32 NumberofCollectables;
```

This will be a private property that will keep track of the current number of coins the player has collected. You will be creating a public function that will return this integer value. We do this for safety reasons to ensure that no other classes can modify this value.

3. Next, under the existing `public` access modifier, create a new `UFUNCTION()` using the `BlueprintPure` keyword called `GetCurrentNumberOfCollectables()`. This function will return an `int`. The following code adds this as an inline function:

```
UFUNCTION(BlueprintPure)
int32 GetCurrentNumberofCollectables() { return
NumberofCollectables; };
```

Here, we are using `UFUNCTION()` and the `BlueprintPure` keyword to expose this function to Blueprints so that we can use it later in UMG.

4. Declare a new `void` function, under the `public` access modifier, called IncrementNumberofCollectables() that takes in a single integer parameter called Value:

```
void IncrementNumberofCollectables(int32  Value);
```

This is the main function you will use to keep track of how many coins the player has collected. We will also add some safety measures to ensure this value is never negative.

5. With the `IncrementNumberofCollectables()` function declared, let's create the definition of this function inside the `SuperSideScroller_Player.cpp` source file.

6. Write the following code to create the definition of the IncrementNumberofCollectables function:

```
void ASuperSideScroller_
Player::IncrementNumberofCollectables(int32 Value)
{

}
```

7. The main case to handle here is if the integer value that's passed into this function is less than or equal to 0. In this case, we do not want to bother incrementing the NumberofCollectables variable. Add the following code to the IncrementNumberofCollectables() function:

```
if(Value == 0)
{
```

```
    return;
  }
```

This `if()` statement says that if the `value` input parameter is less than or equal to 0, the function will end. With the `IncrementNumberofCollectables()` function returning `void`, it is perfectly okay to use the `return` keyword in this way.

We're adding this check of ensuring the `value` parameter that's passed into the `IncrementNumberofCollectables()` function is neither 0 nor negative because it is important to establish good coding practices; this guarantees that all possible outcomes are handled. In an actual development environment, there could be designers or other programmers who attempt to use the `IncrementNumberofCollectables()` function and try to pass in a negative value, or a value that equals 0. If the function does not take these possibilities into account, there is potential for bugs later on in development.

8. Now that we've handled the edge case where `value` is less than or equal to 0, let's continue with the function using an `else()` statement to increase `NumberofCollectables`. Add the following code under the `if()` statement from the previous step:

```
else
{
    NumberofCollectables += Value;
}
```

9. Next, let's log `NumberofCollectables` using `UE_LOG` and the knowledge we learned about logging variables. Add the following code after the `else()` statement to properly log `NumberofCollectables`:

```
UE_LOG(LogTemp, Warning, TEXT("Number of Coins: %d"),
NumberofCollectables);
```

With this `UE_LOG()`, we are making a more robust log to track the number of coins. This lays out the groundwork of how the UI will work. This is because we will be logging the same information to the player using UMG later in this chapter.

With `UE_LOG()` added, all we need to do is call the `IncrementNumberofCollectables()` function inside the `PickableActor_Collectable` class.

10. In the `PickableActor_Collectable.cpp` source file, add the following header:

```
#include "SuperSideScroller_Player.h"
```

11. Next, inside the `PlayerPickedUp()` function, add the following function call before the `Super::PlayerPickedUp(Player)` line:

```
Player->IncrementNumberofCollectables(CollectableValue);
```

12. Now that our `PickableActor_Collectable` class is calling our player's `IncrementNumberofCollectables` function, recompile the C++ code and return to the UE5 editor.

13. Within the UE5 editor, open the **Output Log** window by clicking **Window**, and then select **Output Log**.

14. Now, add multiple **BP_Collectable** actors to your level and use `PIE`.

15. When you overlap over each coin collectible, observe the **Output Log** window to find that each time you collect a coin, the **Output Log** window will show you how many coins you've collected.

> **Note**
> You can find the assets and code for this exercise here: `https://github.com/PacktPublishing/Game-Development-Projects-with-Unreal-Engine/tree/master/Chapter15/Exercise15.03`.

With this exercise completed, you have now completed half of the work needed to develop the UI element of tracking the number of coins collected by the player. The next half will involve using the functionality developed in this activity inside UMG to show this information to the player on-screen. To do this, we need to learn more about UMG inside UE5.

Introducing Unreal Motion Graphics UI

UMG UI Designer is UE5's main tool for creating UI menus, in-game HUD elements such as health bars, and other user interfaces you may want to present to the player.

In the **SuperSideScroller** game, we will only be using the **Text widget** to construct our **Coin Collection UI** in *Exercise 15.04 – creating the Coin Counter UI HUD element*. We'll learn more about the **Text widget** in the next section.

Understanding the Text widget

The **Text widget** is one of the simpler widgets that exists. This is because it only allows you to display text information to the user and customize the visuals of this text. Almost every single game uses text in one way or another to display information to its players. **Overwatch**, for example, uses a text-based UI to display crucial match data to its players. Without the use of text, it would be very difficult – maybe even impossible – to convey key pieces of statistical data to the player, such as total damage dealt, total time playing the game, and much more.

The **Text widget** appears in the **Palette** tab within UMG. When you add a **Text widget** to the **Canvas** panel, it will display the text `Text Block` by default. You can customize this text by adding your text to the `Text` parameter of the widget. Alternatively, you can use `Function Binding` to display more robust text that can reference internal or external variables. `Function Binding` should be used whenever you need to display information that can change; this could be text that represents a player's score, how much money the player has, or in our case, the number of coins the player has collected:

You will be using the `Function Binding` functionality of the **Text widget** to display the number of coins collected by the player using the `GetCurrentNumberofCollectables()` function you created in *Exercise 15.03 – tracking the number of coins for the player*.

Now that we have the **Text widget** in the **Canvas** panel, it is time to position this widget where we need it to be. For this, we will take advantage of anchors.

Anchors

Anchors are used to define where a widget's desired location should be on the **Canvas** panel. Once defined, this `Anchor` point will ensure that the widget will maintain this position with varying screen sizes through different platform devices such as phones, tablets, and computers. Without an anchor, a widget's position can become inconsistent between different screen resolutions, which is never desired.

> **Note**
> For more information about anchors, please refer to the following documentation: `https://docs.unrealengine.com/en-US/Engine/UMG/UserGuide/Anchors/index.html`.

For our **Coin Collection UI** and the **Text widget** you will use, the `Anchor` point will be at the top-left corner of the screen. You will also add a position offset from this `Anchor` point so that the text is more visible and readable to the player. Before moving on to creating our **Coin Collection UI**, let's learn about `Text Formatting`, which you will use to display the current number of collected coins to the player.

Text formatting

Much like the `UE_LOG()` macro available to us in C++, Blueprints offers a similar solution to display text and format it to allow custom variables to be added to it. The `Format Text` function takes in a single text input labeled `Format` and returns the `Result` text. This can be used to display information:

Figure 15.5 – The Format Text function

Instead of using the % symbol like `UE_LOG()` does, the `Format Text` function uses the { } symbols to denote arguments that can be passed into the string. In-between the { } symbols, you need to add an argument name; this can be anything you want, but it should be representative of what the argument is. Refer to the example shown in the following screenshot:

Figure 15.6 – An example integer in the Format Text function

The `Format Text` function only supports `Byte`, `Integer`, `Float`, `Text`, or `EText Gender` variable types, so if you are attempting to pass any other type of variable into the function as an argument, you must convert it into one of the supported types.

> **Note**
>
> The `Format Text` function is also used for **Text Localization**, where you can support multiple languages for your game. More information about how this can be done in both C++ and Blueprints can be found here: `https://docs.unrealengine.com/en-US/Gameplay/Localization/Formatting/index.html`.

You will be using the `Format Text` function in conjunction with the **Text widget** in UMG in the next exercise, where we will be creating the `Coin Counter UI` widget to display the number of coins that have been collected by the player. You will also be using `Anchor` points to position the **Text widget** at the top-left corner of the screen.

Exercise 15.04 – creating the Coin Counter UI HUD element

In this exercise, you will be creating the UMG UI asset, which will display and update the number of coins collected by the player. You will use the GetCurrentNumberofCollectables() inline function you created in *Exercise 15.02 – creating the PickableActor_Collectable class*, to display this value on the screen using a simple **Text widget**. Follow these steps to accomplish this:

1. Let's start by creating a new folder inside the **Content Drawer** area called UI. Do this by *right-clicking* on the Content folder at the top of the browser directory in the editor and selecting **New Folder**.

2. Inside the new /Content/UI directory, *right-click* and, instead of selecting **Blueprint Class**, hover over the **User Interface** option at the bottom of this list and *left-click* the **Widget Blueprint** option.

3. Name this new **Widget Blueprint** BP_UI_CoinCollection, and then *double-left-click* the asset to open the UMG editor.

4. By default, the **Widget** panel is empty, and you will find an empty hierarchy on the left-hand side, as shown in the following screenshot:

Figure 15.7 – The Widget panel's empty hierarchy

5. Above the **Hierarchy** tab is the **Palette** tab, which lists all the available widgets you can use inside your UI. We will only focus on the **Text widget**, which is listed under the **Common** category. Do not mistake this option with the **Rich Text Block** widget.

> **Note**
>
> For a more detailed reference regarding all the available widgets inside UMG, please read the following documentation from Epic Games: https://docs.unrealengine.com/en-US/Engine/UMG/UserGuide/WidgetTypeReference/index.html.

6. If one is not automatically created, add a **Canvas Panel** widget as the base of the **Hierarchy** area.

7. Add the **Text widget** to the **UI** panel by either *left-clicking* and dragging the **Text widget** from the **Palette** tab to the **Hierarchy** tab underneath the **Canvas** panel root, or by *left-clicking* and dragging the **Text widget** directly into the **Canvas** panel itself in the middle of the UMG editor.

   Before changing the text of this widget, we need to update its anchor, position, and font size so that it fits the needs we have for displaying the necessary information to the player.

8. With the **Text widget** selected, you will see many options under its **Details** panel to customize it. The first thing to do here is anchor the **Text widget** to the top-left corner of the **Canvas** panel. *Left-click* on the **Anchors** dropdown and select the top-left anchoring option, as shown in the following screenshot:

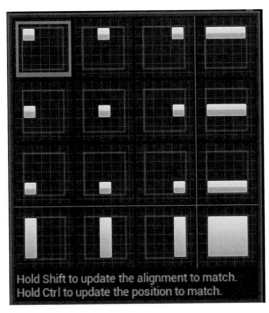

Figure 15.8 – By default, there are options to anchor a widget at different locations on the screen

Anchoring allows the widget to maintain its desired location within the **Canvas** panel, regardless of varying screen sizes.

Now that the **Text widget** is anchored to the top-left corner, we need to set its relative position to this anchor so that there is an offset for better positioning and readability of the text.

9. In the **Details** panel, underneath the **Anchors** option, are parameters for Position X and Position Y. Set both these parameters to 100.0f.

10. Next, enable the **Size To Content** parameter so that the **Text widget** will automatically resize itself depending on the size of the text it is displaying, as shown in the following screenshot:

Figure 15.9 – The Size To Content parameter will ensure that the Text widget won't be cut off

11. Lastly, we must update the size of the font that's used for the **Text widget**. Underneath the **Appearance** tab of the **Details** panel for the **Text widget**, you will find the **Size** parameter. Set its value to 48.

12. The final **Text widget** will look like this:

Figure 15.10 – The Text widget is now anchored to the top left of the Canvas panel

Now that we have the **Text widget** positioned and sized the way we need it to be, let's add a new binding to the text so that it will automatically update and match the value of the number of collectibles the player has.

13. With the **Text** widget selected, find the **Text** parameter in its **Details** panel, under the **Content** category. There, you will find the **Bind** option.

14. *Left-click* the **Bind** option and select **Create Binding**. When doing this, the new Function Binding will be created automatically and be given the name GetText_0. Please refer to the following screenshot:

Figure 15.11 – The new bound function of the text

15. Rename this function `Get Number of Collectables`.

16. Before continuing with this function, create a new object reference variable called `Player` that's of the `SuperSideScroller_Player` type. Make this variable **Public** and exposable on spawn by enabling both the **Instance Editable** and **Expose on Spawn** parameters of the variable, as shown in the following screenshot:

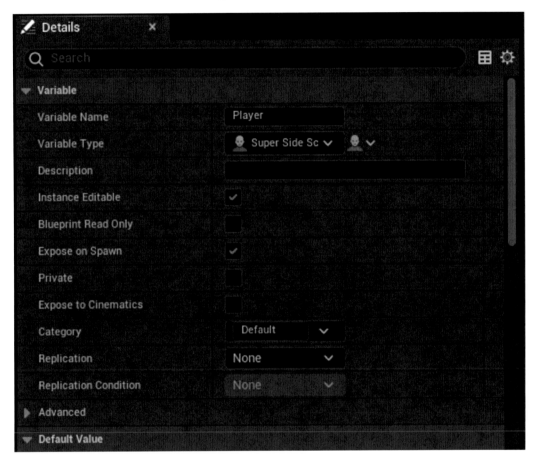

Figure 15.12 – The Player variable with the Instance Editable and Expose on Spawn parameters enabled

By making the `Player` variable **Public** and exposed on spawn, you will be able to assign this variable when creating the widget and adding it to the screen. We will do this in *Exercise 15.05 – adding the coin counter UI to the player screen*.

Now that we have a reference variable to `SuperSideScroller_Player`, let's continue with the `Get Number of Collectables` bind function.

17. Add a **Getter** of the `Player` variable to the `Get Number of Collectables` function.

18. From this variable, *left-click* and drag and from the context-sensitive drop-down menu, and find and select the `Get Current Number of Collectables` function. Please refer to the following screenshot:

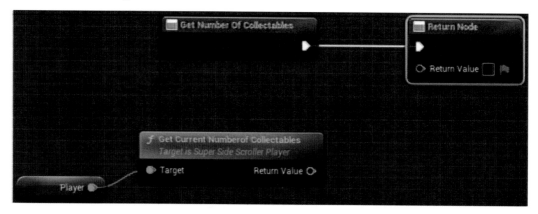

Figure 15.13 – The Get Current Number of Collectables function you created in Exercise 15.03

19. Next, *left-click* and drag out the `Return Value` text parameter of `Get Number of Collectables` to `Return Node`. From the context-sensitive drop-down menu, search for and select the **Format Text** option, as shown in the following screenshot:

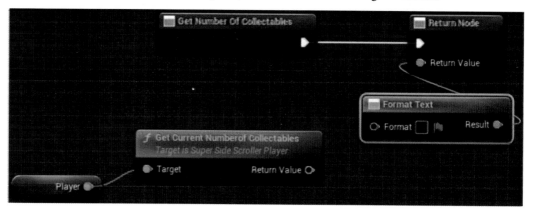

Figure 15.14 – Now, we can create customized and formatted text

20. Within the `Format Text` function, add the following text:

```
Coins: {coins}
```

Please refer to the following screenshot:

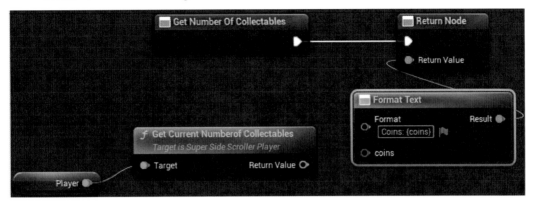

Figure 15.15 – Now, there is a new input argument for the formatted text

Remember that using the { } symbols denotes a text argument that allows you to pass variables into the text.

21. Finally, connect the `Return Value` int of the `GetCurrentNumberofCollectables()` function to the wildcard `coins` input pin of the `Format Text` function, as shown here:

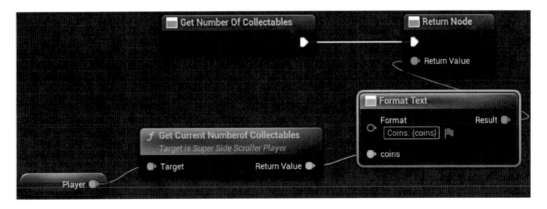

Figure 15.16 – The Text widget will update automatically based on
the Get Current Number of Collectables function

22. Compile and save the `BP_UI_CoinCollection` widget Blueprint.

With this exercise completed, you have created the `UI UMG` widget needed to display the current number of coins collected by the player. By using the `GetCurrentNumberofCollectables()` C++ function and the binding functionality of the **Text widget**, the UI will always update its value based on the number of coins collected. In the next exercise, we will add this UI to the player's screen, but first, we'll briefly learn about how to add and remove UMG from the player screen.

Adding and creating UMG user widgets

Now that we have created **Coin Collection UI** in UMG, it is time to learn how to add and remove the UI to and from the player screen, respectively. By adding **Coin Collection UI** to the player screen, the UI becomes visible to the player and can be updated as the player collects coins.

In Blueprints, there is a function called `Create Widget`, as shown in the following screenshot. Without a class assigned, it will be labeled `Construct None`, but do not let this confuse you:

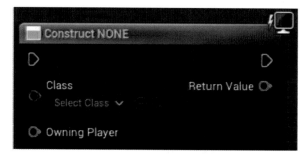

Figure 15.17 – The Create Widget function as-is by default, without a class applied

This function requires the class of the `User` widget to be created and requires a `Player Controller` that will be referenced as the owning player of this UI. This function then returns the spawned user widget as its `Return Value`, where you can then add it to the player's viewport using the `Add to Viewport` function. The `Create Widget` function only instantiates the widget object; it does not add this widget to the player's screen. It is the `Add to Viewport` function that makes this widget visible on the player's screen:

Figure 15.18 – The Add to Viewport function with ZOrder

The viewport is the game screen that overlays your view of the game world, and it uses what is called ZOrder to determine the overlay depth in cases where multiple UI elements need to overlap above or below one another. By default, the Add to Viewport function will add the User widget to the screen and make it fill the entire screen – that is, unless the Set Desired Size In Viewport function is called to set the size that it should fill manually:

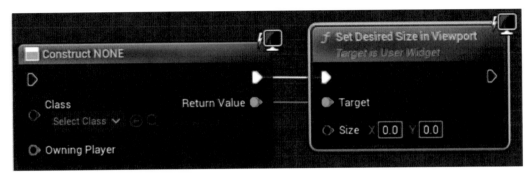

Figure 15.19 – The Size parameter determines the desired size of the passed in the User widget

In C++, you also have a function called CreateWidget():

```
template<typename WidgetT, typename OwnerT>
WidgetT * CreateWidget
(
    OwnerT * OwningObject,
    TSubclassOf < UUserWidget > UserWidgetClass,
    FName WidgetName
)
```

The CreateWidget() function is available through the UserWidget class, which can be found in /Engine/Source/Runtime/UMG/Public/Blueprint/UserWidget.h.

An example of this can be found in *Chapter 8, Creating User Interfaces with UMG*, where you used the CreateWidget() function to create BP_HUDWidget:

```
HUDWidget = CreateWidget<UHUDWidget>(this, BP_HUDWidget);
```

Refer back to *Chapter 8, Creating User Interfaces with UMG*, and *Exercise 8.06 – creating the health bar C++ logic*, for more information regarding the CreateWidget() function in C++.

This function works almost identically to its Blueprint counterpart because it takes in the Owning Object parameter, much like the Owning Player parameter of the Blueprint function, and it requires the User Widget class to be created. The C++ CreateWidget() function also takes in an FName parameter to represent the widget's name.

Now that we have learned about the methods to use to add a UI to the player screen, let's put this knowledge to the test. In the following exercise, you will be implementing the Create Widget and Add to Viewport Blueprint functions so that we can add the **coin collection UI** that we created in *Exercise 15.04 – creating the Coin Counter UI HUD element*, to the player screen.

Exercise 15.05 – Adding Coin Counter UI to the player screen

In this exercise, you will be creating a new Player Controller class so that you can use the player controller to add the BP_UI_CoinCollection widget Blueprint to the player's screen. From there, you will also create a new Game Mode class and apply this game mode to the **SuperSideScroller** project. Perform the following steps to complete this exercise:

1. In the UE5 editor, navigate to **Tools** and then **New C++ Class**.

2. From the **Choose Parent Class** dialog window, find and select the **Player Controller** option.

3. Name the new Player Controller class SuperSideScroller_Controller and then click the **Create Class** button. Visual Studio will automatically generate and open the source and header files for the SuperSideScroller_Controller class, but for now, we will stay inside the UE5 editor.

4. In the **Content Drawer** area, under the MainCharacter folder directory, create a new folder called PlayerController.

5. In the PlayerController folder, *right-click* and create a new Blueprint Class using the new SuperSideScroller_Controller class. Please refer to the following screenshot:

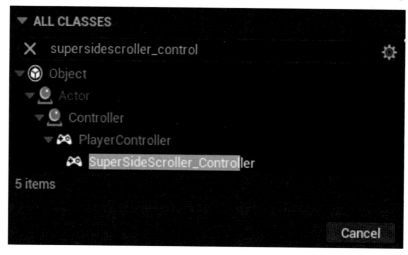

Figure 15.20 – Finding the new SuperSideScroller_Controller class to create a new Blueprint from

6. Name this new Blueprint `BP_SuperSideScroller_PC` and then *double-left-click* the asset to open it.

To add the `BP_UI_CoinCollection` widget to the screen, we need to use the `Add to Viewport` function and the `Create Widget` function. We want the UI to be added to the player's screen after the player character has been `Possessed` by the player controller.

7. *Right-click* inside the Blueprint graph and, from the context-sensitive menu, find the **Event On Possess** option and *left-click* to add it to the graph. Please refer to the following screenshot:

Figure 15.21 – Event On Possess

The **Event On Possess** event node returns **Possessed Pawn**. We will use this **Possessed Pawn** to pass into our BP_UI_CoinCollection UI Widget, but first, we need to **Cast To the SuperSideScroller_Player** class.

8. *Left-click* and drag the **Possessed Pawn** parameter of the `Event On Possess` node from the output. Then, search for and find the `Cast to SuperSideScroller_Player` node. Please refer to the following screenshot:

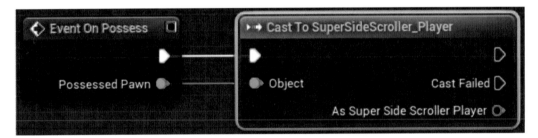

Figure 15.22 – We need to Cast To SuperSideScroller_Player

9. Now, *right-click* and search for the `Create Widget` function to add it to the Blueprint graph.

10. From the drop-down class parameter, find and assign the BP_UI_CoinCollection asset you created in *Exercise 15.04 – creating the Coin Counter UI HUD element*. Please refer to the following screenshot:

Figure 15.23 – The Create Widget function

After updating the Class parameter to the BP_UI_CoinCollection class, you will notice that the Create Widget function will update to show the Player variable you created, set to Exposed on Spawn.

11. *Right-click* in the Blueprint graph to search for and find the Self reference variable from the context-sensitive drop-down menu. Connect the Self object variable to the Owning Player parameter of the Create Widget function, as shown in the following screenshot:

Figure 15.24 – The Owning Player input parameter is of the Player Controller type

The Owning Player parameter refers to the Player Controller type that will show and own this UI object. Since we are adding this UI to the **SuperSideScroller_Controller** Blueprint, we can just use the **Self** reference variable to pass into the function.

12. Next, pass in the returned `SuperSideScroller_Player` variable from the `Cast` node to the `Player` input node of the `Create Widget` function. Then, connect the execution pins of the `Cast` node and the `Create Widget` function, as shown in the following screenshot:

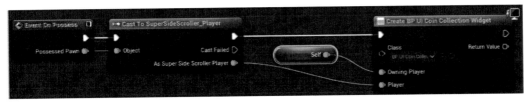

Figure 15.25 – Creating the BP_UI_CoinCollection widget

Note
You can find the preceding screenshot in full resolution for better viewing at the following link:
`https://github.com/PacktPublishing/Game-Development-Projects-with-Unreal-Engine/blob/master/Chapter15/Images/New_25.png`.

13. Upon pulling the `Create Widget` function from the `Return Value` parameter, search for and find the `Add to Viewport` function so that you can place it in the graph.

14. Connect the output `Return Value` parameter of the `Create Widget` function to the `Target` input parameter of the `Add to Viewport` function; do not change the `ZOrder` parameter.

15. Lastly, connect the execution pins of the `Create Widget` and `Add to Viewport` functions, as shown here:

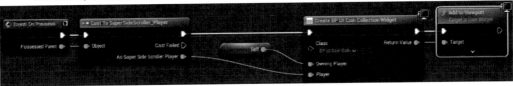

Figure 15.26 – After creating the BP_UI_CoinCollection widget, we can add it to the player viewport

Note
You can find the preceding screenshot in full resolution for better viewing at the following link:
`https://packt.live/2UwufBd`.

Now that the player controller adds the `BP_UI_CoinCollection` widget to the player's viewport, we need to create a `GameMode` Blueprint and apply both the `BP_SuperSideScroller_MainCharacter` and `BP_SuperSideScroller_PC` classes to this game mode.

16. In the **Content Drawer** area, create a new folder by *right-clicking* the Content folder and selecting **New Folder**. Name this folder GameMode.

17. Next, *right-click* and select **Blueprint Class** to begin creating the game mode Blueprint. From the **Pick Parent Class** dialog window, search for and find SuperSideScrollerGameMode under All Classes.

18. Name this new GameMode Blueprint BP_SuperSideScroller_GameMode. *Double-left-click* this asset to open it.

    The GameMode Blueprint contains a list of classes that you can customize with your unique classes. For now, we will only worry about Player Controller Class and Default Pawn Class.

19. Click the **Player Controller Class** dropdown to find and select the BP_SuperSideScroller_ PC Blueprint you created earlier in this exercise.

20. Then, click the **Default Pawn Class** dropdown to find and select the BP_SuperSideScroller_ MainCharacter Blueprint.

    Now that we have a custom GameMode that utilizes our custom Player Controller and Player Character classes, let's add this game mode to the **Project Settings** window so that the game mode is used by default when using PIE and when cooking builds of the project.

21. From the UE5 editor, navigate to the **Edit** option at the top of the screen. Click this option and from the drop-down menu, find and select the **Project Settings** option.

22. On the left-hand side of the **Project Settings** window, you will be provided with a list of categories divided into sections. Under the **Project** section, click the **Maps & Modes** category.

23. In the **Maps & Modes** section, you have a handful of parameters related to your project's default maps and game mode. At the top of this section, you have the **Default GameMode** option. Click this dropdown to find and select the **SuperSideScroller_GameMode** Blueprint you created earlier in this exercise.

> **Note**
>
> Changes made to the **Maps & Modes** section are automatically saved and written to the DefaultEngine.ini file, which can be found in your project's Config folder. Default GameMode can be overwritten per level by updating the **GameMode Override** parameter, which can be found in the **World Settings** window of your level.

24. Close the **Project Settings** window and return to your level. Use PIE and start collecting coins. Observe that the **BP_UI_CoinCollection** widget is shown and updated each time you collect a coin, as shown in the following screenshot:

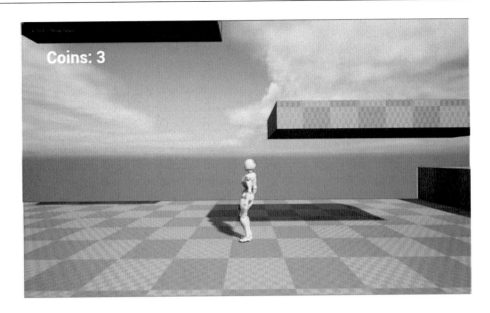

Figure 15.27 – Now, every coin you collect will appear on the player UI

> **Note**
> You can find the assets and code for this exercise here: `https://github.com/PacktPublishing/Game-Development-Projects-with-Unreal-Engine/tree/master/Chapter15/Exercise15.05`.

With this exercise complete, you have created the `UI UMG` widget needed to display the current number of coins collected by the player. By using the `GetCurrentNumberofCollectables()` C++ function and the binding functionality of the **Text widget**, the UI will always update its value based on the number of coins collected.

So far, we have focused on the collectible coin and allowing players to collect these coins and add the total coins collected to the player's UI. Now, we will focus on the potion power-up and granting movement speed and jump height increases to the player for a short period. To implement this functionality, we first need to study timers.

Using timers

Timers in UE5 allow you to perform actions after a delay or every *X* number of seconds. In the case of the **SuperSideScroller** potion power-up, a timer will be used to restore the player's movement and jump to their defaults after 8 seconds.

> **Note**
>
> In Blueprints, you can use a `Delay` node in addition to timer handles to achieve the same results. However, in C++, timers are the best means to achieve delays and reoccurring logic.

Timers are managed by `Timer Manager`, or `FTimerManager`, which exists in the `UWorld` object. There are two main functions that you will be using from the `FTimerManager` class, called `SetTimer()` and `ClearTimer()`:

```
void SetTimer
(
    FTimerHandle & InOutHandle,
    TFunction < void )> && Callback,
    float InRate,
    bool InbLoop,
    float InFirstDelay
)
void ClearTimer(FTimerHandle& InHandle)
```

You may have noticed that, in both functions, there is a required `FTimerHandle`. This handle is used to control the timer you have set. Using this handle, you can pause, resume, clear, and even extend the timer.

The `SetTimer()` function also has other parameters to help you customize this timer when initially setting it. The callback function will be called after the timer has been completed, and if the `InbLoop` parameter is `True`, it will continue to call the callback function indefinitely, until the timer has been stopped. The `InRate` parameter is the duration of the timer itself, while `InFirstDelay` is an initial delay that's applied to the timer before it begins its timer for `InRate`.

The header file for the `FTimerManager` class can be found here: `/Engine/Source/Runtime/Engine/Public/TimerManager.h`.

> **Note**
>
> You can learn more about timers and `FTimerHandle` by reading the documentation here: `https://docs.unrealengine.com/4.27/en-US/ProgrammingAndScripting/ProgrammingWithCPP/UnrealArchitecture/Timers/`.

In the following exercise, you will create your own `FTimerHandle` in the `SuperSideScroller_Player` class and use it to control how long the effects of the potion power-up last on the player.

Exercise 15.06 – adding the potion power-up behavior to the player

In this exercise, you will be creating the logic behind the potion power-up and how it will affect the player's character. You will take advantage of timers and timer handles to ensure that the power-up effects only last for a short duration. Follow these steps to accomplish this:

1. In Visual Studio, navigate to and open the `SuperSideScroller_Player.h` header file.

2. Under our `Private Access Modifier`, add a new variable of the `FTimerHandle` type and name it `PowerupHandle`:

   ```
   FTimerHandle PowerupHandle;
   ```

   This timer handle will be responsible for keeping track of how much time has elapsed since it was initiated. This will allow us to control how long the potion power-up's effects will last.

3. Next, add a Boolean variable under our `Private Access Modifier` called `bHasPowerupActive`:

   ```
   bool bHasPowerupActive;
   ```

   We will use this Boolean variable when updating the `Sprint()` and `StopSprinting()` functions to ensure we update the player's sprint movement speed appropriately based on whether the power-up is active.

4. Next, declare a new void function called `IncreaseMovementPowerup()` under our `Public Access Modifier`:

   ```
   void IncreaseMovementPowerup();
   ```

   This is the function that will be called from the potion power-up class to enable the effects of the power-up for the player.

5. Finally, you need to create a function that handles when the power-up effects end. Create a function called `EndPowerup()` under `Protected Access Modifier`:

   ```
   void EndPowerup();
   ```

   With all the necessary variables and functions declared, it's time to start defining these new functions and handling the power-up effects on the player.

6. Navigate to the `SuperSideScroller_Player.cpp` source file.

7. First, add the `#include "TimerManager.h"` header file to the top of the source file; we will need this class to use the timers.

8. Define the `IncreaseMovementPowerup()` function by adding the following code to the source file:

    ```
    void ASuperSideScroller_Player::IncreaseMovementPowerup()
    {
    }
    ```

9. When this function is called, the first thing we need to do is set the `bHasPowerupActive` variable to `true`. Add the following code to the `IncreaseMovementPowerup()` function:

    ```
    bHasPowerupActive = true;
    ```

10. Next, add the following code to increase both the `MaxWalkSpeed` and `JumpZVelocity` components of the player character's movement component:

    ```
    GetCharacterMovement()->MaxWalkSpeed = 500.0f;
    GetCharacterMovement()->JumpZVelocity = 1500.0f;
    ```

    Here, we are changing `MaxWalkSpeed` from the default value of `300.0f` to `500.0f`. As you may recall, the default sprinting speed is also `500.0f`. We will address this later in this activity to increase the sprinting speed when the power-up is active.

11. To take advantage of timers, we need to get a reference to the `UWorld` object. Add the following code:

    ```
    UWorld* World = GetWorld();
    if (World)
    {
    }
    ```

    As we've done many times before in this project, we're using the `GetWorld()` function to get a reference to the `UWorld` object and saving this reference in its variable.

12. Now that we have the reference to the `World` object and have performed a validity check, it is safe to use `TimerManager` to set the power-up timer. Add the following code within the `if()` statement shown in the previous step:

    ```
    World->GetTimerManager().SetTimer(PowerupHandle, this,
        &ASuperSideScroller_Player::EndPowerup, 8.0f, false);
    ```

Here, you are using the TimerManager class to set a timer. The SetTimer() function takes in the FTimerHandle component to use; in this case, the PowerupHandle variable you created. Next, we need to pass in a reference to the player class by using the this keyword. Then, we need to provide the callback function to call after the timer has ended, which in this case is the &ASuperSideScroller_Player::EndPowerup function. 8.0f represents the duration of the timer; feel free to adjust this as you see fit, but for now, 8 seconds is fine. Lastly, there is the final boolean parameter of the SetTimer() function that determines whether this timer should loop; in this case, it should not.

13. Create the function definition for the EndPowerup() function:

```
void ASuperSideScroller_Player::EndPowerup()
{
}
```

14. The first thing to do when the EndPowerup() function is called is set the bHasPowerupActive variable to false. Add the following code within the EndPowerup() function:

```
bHasPowerupActive = false;
```

15. Next, change the MaxWalkSpeed and JumpZVelocity parameters of the character movement component back to their default values. Add the following code:

```
GetCharacterMovement()->MaxWalkSpeed = 300.0f;
GetCharacterMovement()->JumpZVelocity = 1000.0f;
```

Here, we are changing both the MaxWalkSpeed and JumpZVelocity parameters of the character movement component to their default values.

16. Again, to take advantage of the timers and to clear the timer to handle PowerupHandle, we need to get a reference to the UWorld object. Add the following code:

```
UWorld* World = GetWorld();
if (World)
{
}
```

17. Finally, we can add the code to clear the timer handle's PowerupHandle:

```
World->GetTimerManager().ClearTimer(PowerupHandle);
```

By using the ClearTimer() function and passing in PowerupHandle, we are ensuring that this timer is no longer valid and will no longer affect the player.

Now that we have created the functions that handle the power-up effects and the timer associated with the effects, we need to update both the `Sprint()` and `StopSprinting()` functions so that they also take into account the speed of the player when the power-up is active.

18. Update the `Sprint()` function to the following:

```
void ASuperSideScroller_Player::Sprint()
{
  if (!bIsSprinting)
  {
    bIsSprinting = true;
    if (bHasPowerupActive)
    {
      GetCharacterMovement()->MaxWalkSpeed = 900.0f;
    }
    else
    {
      GetCharacterMovement()->MaxWalkSpeed = 500.0f;
    }
  }
}
```

Here, we are updating the `Sprint()` function to take into account whether `bHasPowerupActive` is true. If this variable is `true`, then we increase `MaxWalkSpeed` while sprinting from `500.0f` to `900.0f`, as shown here:

```
if (bHasPowerupActive)
{
  GetCharacterMovement()->MaxWalkSpeed = 900.0f;
}
```

If `bHasPowerupActive` is false, then we increase `MaxWalkSpeed` to `500.0f`, as we did by default.

19. Update the `StopSprinting()` function to the following:

```
void ASuperSideScroller_Player::StopSprinting()
{
  if (bIsSprinting)
  {
    bIsSprinting = false;
```

```
    if (bHasPowerupActive)
    {
        GetCharacterMovement()->MaxWalkSpeed = 500.0f;
    }
    else
    {
        GetCharacterMovement()->MaxWalkSpeed = 300.0f;
    }
}
}
```

Here, we are updating the `StopSprinting()` function to take into account whether `bHasPowerupActive` is true. If this variable is true, then we set the `MaxWalkSpeed` value to `500.0f` instead of `300.0f`, as shown here:

```
if (bHasPowerupActive)
{
    GetCharacterMovement()->MaxWalkSpeed = 500.0f;
}
```

If `bHasPowerupActive` is false, then we set `MaxWalkSpeed` to `300.0f`, as we did by default.

20. Finally, all we need to do is recompile the C++ code.

> **Note**
>
> You can find the assets and code for this exercise here: `https://github.com/PacktPublishing/Game-Development-Projects-with-Unreal-Engine/tree/master/Chapter15/Exercise15.06`.

With this exercise complete, you have created the potion power-up effects within the player character. The power-up increases both the default movement speed of the player and increases their jump height. Moreover, the effects of the power-up increase the sprinting speed. By using timer handles, you were able to control how long the power-up effect would last.

Now, it is time to create the potion power-up actor so that we can have a representation of this power-up in the game.

Activity 15.03 – creating the potion power-up actor

Now that the `SuperSideScroller_Player` class handles the effects of the potion power-up, it's time to create the potion power-up class and Blueprint. This activity aims to create the potion power-up class, inherit from the `PickableActor_Base` class, implement the overlapping functionality to grant the movement effects that you implemented in *Exercise 15.06 – adding the potion power-up behavior to the player*, and create the Blueprint actor for the potion power-up. Follow these steps to create the potion power-up class and create the potion Blueprint actor:

1. Create a new C++ class that inherits from the `PickableActor_Base` class and name this new class `PickableActor_Powerup`.

2. Add the override function declarations for both the `BeginPlay()` and `PlayerPickedUp()` functions.

3. Create the function definition for the `BeginPlay()` function. Within the `BeginPlay()` function, add the call to the parent class function of `BeginPlay()`.

4. Create the function definition for the `PlayerPickedUp()` function. Within the `PlayerPickedUp()` function, add the call to the `PlayerPickedUp()` parent class function.

5. Next, add the necessary `#include` file for the `SuperSideScroller_Player` class so that we can reference the player class and its functions.

6. In the `PlayerPickedUp()` function, use the `Player` input parameter of the function itself to make the function call to `IncreaseMovementPowerup()`.

7. From **Epic Games Launcher**, find the **Action RPG** project from the **Samples** tab, under the **UE Legacy Samples** category. Use this to create and install a new project.

8. Migrate the `A_Character_Heal_Mana_Cue` and `SM_PotionBottle` assets, as well as all of their referenced assets, from the **Action RPG** project to your **SuperSideScroller** project.

9. Create a new folder in the **Content Drawer** area within the `PickableItems` directory called `Powerup`. Create a new Blueprint within this directory based on the `PickableActor_Powerup` class and name this asset `BP_Powerup`.

10. In `BP_Powerup`, update the `MeshComp` component so that it uses the `SM_PotionBottle` static mesh.

11. Next, add `A_Character_Heal_Mana_Cue`, which you imported as the `Pickup Sound` parameter.

12. Finally, update the `RotationComp` component so that the actor will rotate 60 degrees per second around the `Pitch` axis (`Y` axis) and rotate 180 degrees per second around the `Yaw` axis (`X` axis).

13. Add `BP_Powerup` to your level and use `PIE` to observe the results when overlapping with the power-up.

Expected output:

Figure 15.28 – The potion power-up

> **Note**
>
> The solution for this activity can be found on https://github.com/PacktPublishing/
> Elevating-Game-Experiences-with-Unreal-Engine-5-Second-Edition/
> tree/main/Activity%20solutions.

With this activity complete, you were able to put your knowledge to the test in terms of creating a new C++ class that inherits from the `PickableActor_Base` class and overrides the `PlayerPickedUp()` function to add custom logic. By adding the call to the `IncreaseMovementPowerup()` function from the player class, you were able to add the movement power-up effects to the player when overlapping with the actor. Then, by using a custom mesh, material, and audio assets, you were able to bring the Blueprint actor to life from the `PickableActor_Powerup` class.

Now that we have created the coin collectible and the potion power-up, we need to implement a new gameplay feature into the project: the `Brick` class. In games such as *Super Mario*, bricks contain hidden coins and power-ups for the players to find. These bricks also serve as a means of reaching elevated platforms and areas within the level. In our **SuperSideScroller** project, the `Brick` class will serve the purpose of containing hidden coin collectibles for the player, and as a means of allowing the player to reach areas of the level by using the bricks as paths to access hard-to-reach locations. So, in the next section, we will create the `Brick` class, which needs to be broken to find the hidden coins.

Exercise 15.07 – creating the Brick class

Now that we have created the coin collectible and the potion power-up, it is time to create the `Brick` class, which will contain hidden coins for the player to collect. The brick is the final gameplay element of the **SuperSideScroller** project. In this exercise, you will be creating the `Brick` class, which will be used as part of the platforming mechanic of the **SuperSideScroller** game project, but also as a means to hold collectibles for players to find. Follow these steps to create this `Brick` class and its Blueprint:

1. In the UE5 editor, navigate to **Tools** and then **New C++ Class**.

2. From the **Choose Parent Class** dialog window, find and select the `Actor` class.

3. Name this class `SuperSideScroller_Brick` and click **Create Class**. Visual Studio and Unreal Engine will recompile the code and open this class for you.

    By default, the `SuperSideScroller_Brick` class comes with the `Tick()` function, but we will not need this function for the `Brick` class. Remove the function declaration for `Tick()` from the `SuperSideScroller_Brick.h` header file and remove the function definition from the `SuperSideScroller_Brick.cpp` source file before continuing.

4. Under `Private Access Modifier` for the `SuperSideScroller_Brick.h` file, add the following code to declare a new `UStaticMeshComponent* UPROPERTY()` function to represent the brick in our game world:

    ```
    UPROPERTY(VisibleDefaultsOnly, Category = Brick)
    class UStaticMeshComponent* BrickMesh;
    ```

5. Next, we need to create a `UBoxComponent UPROPERTY()` that will handle the collision with the player character. Add the following code to add this component under our `Private Access Modifier`:

    ```
    UPROPERTY(VisibleDefaultsOnly, Category = Brick)
    class UBoxComponent* BrickCollision;
    ```

6. Create the `UFUNCTION()` declaration for the `OnHit()` function under our `Private Access Modifier`. This will be used to determine when `UBoxComponent` is hit by the player:

    ```
    UFUNCTION()
    void OnHit(UPrimitiveComponent* HitComp, AActor*
    OtherActor,
      UPrimitiveComponent* OtherComp, FVector
      NormalImpulse,
      const FHitResult& Hit);
    ```

> **Note**
>
> Recall that you used the `OnHit()` function when developing the `PlayerProjectile` class in *Chapter 13, Creating and Adding the Enemy Artificial Intelligence*, for this project. Please review that chapter for more information about the `OnHit()` function.

7. Next, create a new Boolean called UPROPERTY() under our `Private Access Modifier` using the `EditAnywhere` keyword called `bHasCollectable`:

```
UPROPERTY(EditAnywhere)
bool bHasCollectable;
```

This Boolean will determine whether the brick contains a coin collectible for the player.

8. Now, we need a variable that holds how many coin collectibles are available within this brick for the player. We will do this by creating an integer variable called `Collectable Value`. Make this a UPROPERTY(), under `Private Access Modifier`, with the `EditAnywhere` keyword, and give it a default value of 1, as shown here:

```
UPROPERTY(EditAnywhere)
int32 CollectableValue = 1;
```

The brick will need to contain a unique sound and particle system so that it has a nice layer of polish for when the brick is destroyed by the player. We'll add these properties next.

9. Create a new `Public Access Modifier` in the `SuperSideScroller_Brick.h` header file.

10. Next, create a new UPROPERTY() using the `EditAnywhere` and `BlueprintReadOnly` keywords for a variable of the `USoundBase` class. Name this variable `HitSound`, as shown here:

```
UPROPERTY(EditAnywhere, BlueprintReadOnly, Category =
Brick)
class USoundBase* HitSound;
```

11. Then, create a new UPROPERTY() using the `EditAnywhere` and `BlueprintReadOnly` keywords for a variable of the `UParticleSystem` class. Make sure to put this under `Public Access Modifier` and name this variable `Explosion`, as shown here:

```
UPROPERTY(EditAnywhere, BlueprintReadOnly, Category =
Brick)
class UParticleSystem* Explosion;
```

Now that we have all the necessary properties for the `Brick` class, let's move on to the `SuperSideScroller_Brick.cpp` source file, where we will initialize the components.

12. Let's start by adding the following `#include` directories for `StaticMeshComponent` and `BoxComponent`. Add the following code to the `#include` list of the source file:

```
#include "Components/StaticMeshComponent.h"
#include "Components/BoxComponent.h"
```

13. First, initialize the `BrickMesh` component by adding the following code to the `ASuperSideScroller_Brick::ASuperSideScroller_Brick()` constructor function:

```
BrickMesh = CreateDefaultSubobject<UStaticMeshCompo-
nent>(TEXT("BrickMesh"));
```

14. Next, the `BrickMesh` component should have a collision so that the player can walk on top of it for platforming gameplay purposes. To ensure this occurs by default, add the following code to set the collision to "`BlockAll`":

```
BrickMesh->SetCollisionProfileName("BlockAll");
```

15. Lastly, the `BrickMesh` component will serve as the root component of the `Brick` actor. Add the following code to do this:

```
RootComponent = BrickMesh;
```

16. Now, add the following code to the constructor function to initialize our `BrickCollision` `UBoxComponent`:

```
BrickCollision = CreateDefaultSubobject<UBoxComponent>
    (TEXT("BrickCollision"));
```

17. Just like the `BrickMesh` component, the `BrickCollision` component will also need to have its collision set to "`BlockAll`" to receive the `OnHit()` callback events we will be adding later in this exercise. Add the following code:

```
BrickCollision->SetCollisionProfileName("BlockAll");
```

18. Next, the `BrickCollision` component needs to be attached to the `BrickMesh` component. We can do this by adding the following code:

```
BrickCollision->AttachToComponent(RootComponent,
    FAttachmentTransformRules::KeepWorldTransform);
```

19. Before we can finish the initialization of the `BrickCollision` component, we need to add the function definition for the `OnHit()` function. Add the following definition to the source file:

```
void ASuperSideScroller_Brick::OnHit(UPrimitiveComponent*
HitComp, AActor*
  OtherActor, UPrimitiveComponent* OtherComp, FVector
  NormalImpulse, const
  FHitResult& Hit)
{
}
```

20. Now that we have defined the `OnHit()` function, we can assign the `OnComponentHit` callback to the `BrickCollision` component. Add the following code to the constructor function:

```
BrickCollision->OnComponentHit.AddDynamic(this,
  &ASuperSideScroller_Brick::OnHit);
```

21. Compile the C++ code for the `SuperSideScroller_Brick` class and return to the UE5 editor.

22. In the **Content Drawer** area, *right-click* on the `Content` folder and select the **New Folder** option. Name this folder `Brick`.

23. *Right-click* inside the `Brick` folder and select `Blueprint Class`. From the `All Classes` search bar in the **Pick Parent Class** dialog window, search for and select the `SuperSideScroller_Brick` class.

24. Name this new Blueprint `BP_Brick`, and then *double-left-click* the asset to open it.

25. Select the `BrickMesh` component from the **Components** tab and set its `Static Mesh` parameter to the `Shape_Cube` mesh.

26. With the `BrickMesh` component still selected, set the `Element 0` material parameter to `M_Brick_Clay_Beveled`. This material is provided by Epic Games by default when creating a new project. It can be found within the `StarterContent` directory, in the **Content Drawer** area.

The last thing we need to do with the `BrickMesh` component is adjust its scale so that it fits the needs of the player character, as well as the platforming mechanics of the **SuperSideScroller** game project.

27. With the `BrickMesh` component selected, make the following change to its `Scale` parameter:

```
(X=0.750000,Y=0.750000,Z=0.750000)
```

Now that the `BrickMesh` component is 75% of its normal size, the `Brick` actor will become more manageable for us as designers when we place the actor into the game world, as well as when we're developing interesting platforming sections within the level.

The final step here is to update the location of the `BrickCollision` component so that it only has some of its collision sticking out from the bottom of the `BrickMesh` component.

28. Select the `BrickCollision` component from the **Components** tab and update its `Location` parameter to the following values:

```
(X=0.000000,Y=0.000000,Z=30.000000)
```

The `BrickCollision` component should now be positioned as follows:

Figure 15.29 – Now, the BrickCollision component is just barely outside the BrickMesh component

We are making this adjustment to the position of the `BrickCollision` component so that the player can only hit `UBoxComponent` when jumping underneath the brick. By making it slightly outside of the `BrickMesh` component, we can control it better and ensure that this component cannot be hit by the player in any other way.

> **Note**
>
> You can find the assets and code for this exercise here: `https://github.com/PacktPublishing/Game-Development-Projects-with-Unreal-Engine/tree/master/Chapter15/Exercise15.07`.

With this exercise complete, you were able to create the base framework for the `SuperSideScroller_Brick` class and put together the Blueprint actor to represent the brick in the game world. By adding a cube mesh and brick material, you added a nice visual polish to the brick. In the following exercise, you will add the remaining C++ logic to the brick. This will allow the player to destroy the brick and obtain a collectible.

Exercise 15.08 – adding the Brick class's C++ logic

In the previous exercise, you created the base framework for the `SuperSideScroller_Brick` class by adding the necessary components and creating the `BP_Brick` Blueprint actor. In this exercise, you will add on top of the C++ code of *Exercise 15.07 – creating the Brick class*, to grant logic to the `Brick` class. This will allow the brick to give players coin collectibles. Perform the following steps to accomplish this:

1. To begin, we need to create a function that will add the collectible to the player. Add the following function declaration to the `SuperSideScroller_Brick.h` header file, under our `Private Access Modifier`:

   ```
   void AddCollectable(class ASuperSideScroller_Player*
   Player);
   ```

   We want to pass in a reference to the `SuperSideScroller_Player` class so that we can call the `IncrementNumberofCollectables()` function from that class.

2. Next, create a void function declaration called `PlayHitSound()` under our `Private Access Modifier`:

   ```
   void PlayHitSound();
   ```

   The `PlayHitSound()` function will be responsible for spawning the `HitSound` property you created in *Exercise 15.07 – creating the Brick class*.

3. Finally, create another void function declaration called `PlayHitExplosion()` under our `Private Access Modifier`:

   ```
   void PlayHitExplosion();
   ```

   The `PlayHitExplosion()` function will be responsible for spawning the `Explosion` property you created in *Exercise 15.07 – creating the Brick class*.

   With the remaining functions needed for the `SuperSideScroller_Brick` class declared in the header file, let's move on and define these functions inside the source file.

4. At the top of the `SuperSideScroller_Brick.cpp` source file, add the following `#include` statements to the list of `#include` directories that already exist for this class:

   ```
   #include "Engine/World.h"
   #include "Kismet/GameplayStatics.h"
   #include "SuperSideScroller_Player.h"
   ```

The includes for the `World` and `GameplayStatics` classes are necessary to spawn both the `HitSound` and the `Explosion` effects for the brick. Including the `SuperSideScroller_Player` class is required to make the call to the `IncrementNumberofCollectables()` class function.

5. Let's start with the function definition for the `AddCollectable()` function. Add the following code:

```
void ASuperSideScroller_Brick::AddCollectable(class
    ASuperSideScroller_Player* Player)
{
}
```

6. Now, make the call to the `IncrementNumberofCollectables()` function by using the `Player` function input parameter:

```
Player->IncrementNumberofCollectables(CollectableValue);
```

7. For the `PlayHitSound()` function, you will need to get a reference to the `UWorld*` object and verify whether the `HitSound` property is valid before making the function call to `SpawnSoundAtLocation` from the `UGameplayStatics` class. This is a process you have done many times, so this is the entire function code:

```
void ASuperSideScroller_Brick::PlayHitSound()
{
    UWorld* World = GetWorld();
    if (World && HitSound)
    {
        UGameplayStatics::SpawnSoundAtLocation(World,
        HitSound,
            GetActorLocation());
    }
}
```

8. Just like the `PlayHitSound()` function, the `PlayHitExplosion()` function will work in an almost similar way, and it's a process you have done many times in this project. Add the following code to create the function definition:

```
void ASuperSideScroller_Brick::PlayHitExplosion()
{
    UWorld* World = GetWorld();
    if (World && Explosion)
```

```
    {
        UGameplayStatics::SpawnEmitterAtLocation(World,
        Explosion,
          GetActorTransform());

    }
    }
```

With these functions defined, let's update the OnHit() function so that if the player does hit the BrickCollision component, we can spawn HitSound and Explosion, and also add a coin collectible to the player's collection.

9. First, in the OnHit() function, create a new variable called Player of the ASuperSideScroller_Player type that equals Cast of the OtherActor input parameter of the function, as shown here:

    ```
    ASuperSideScroller_Player* Player =
        Cast<ASuperSideScroller_Player>(OtherActor);
    ```

10. Next, we only want to continue with this function if Player is valid and bHasCollectable is True. Add the following if() statement:

    ```
    if (Player && bHasCollectable)
    {
    }
    ```

11. If the conditions in the if() statement are met, that is when we need to make the calls to the AddCollectable(), PlayHitSound(), and PlayHitExplosion() functions. Make sure to also pass the Player variable inside the AddCollectable() function:

    ```
    AddCollectable(Player);
    PlayHitSound();
    PlayHitExplosion();
    ```

12. Finally, add the function call to destroy the brick inside the if() statement:

    ```
    Destroy();
    ```

13. With the OnHit() function defined as we need, recompile the C++ code but do not return to the UE5 editor just yet.

14. For the VFX and SFX of the brick's explosion, we will need to migrate assets from two separate projects available to us from **Epic Games Launcher**: the **Blueprints** project and the **Content Examples** project.

15. Using your knowledge from previous exercises, download and install these projects using Unreal Engine version 4.24. Both projects can be found in the **Samples** tab, in the **UE Legacy Samples** and **UE Feature Samples** categories, respectively.

16. Once installed, open the **Content Examples** project and find the P_Pixel_Explosion asset in the **Content Drawer** area.

17. *Right-click* this asset and select **Asset Actions**, then **Migrate**. Migrate this asset and all its referenced assets into your **SuperSideScroller** project.

18. Once this asset has been successfully migrated, close the **Content Examples** project and open the Blueprints project.

19. From the **Content Drawer** area of the Blueprints project, find the Blueprints_TextPop01 asset.

20. *Right-click* this asset, then select **Asset Actions**, and then **Migrate**. Migrate this asset and all its referenced assets into your **SuperSideScroller** project.

   With these assets migrated to your project, return to the Unreal Engine 5 editor of your **SuperSideScroller** project.

21. Navigate to the Brick folder in the **Content Drawer** window and *double-left-click* the BP_Brick asset to open it.

22. In the **Details** panel of the actor, find the **Super Side Scroller Brick** section and set the HitSound parameter to the Blueprints_TextPop01 soundwave you imported.

23. Next, add the P_Pixel_Explosion particle you imported into the Explosion parameter.

24. Recompile the BP_Brick Blueprint and add two of these actors to your level.

25. Set one of the bricks so that the bHasCollectable parameter is True; set the other to False. Please refer to the following screenshot:

Figure 15.30 – This Brick actor is set to have a collectible spawn

26. Using PIE, observe the differences in behavior between the two brick actors when you attempt to hit the bottom of the brick with the character's head when jumping, as shown in the following screenshot:

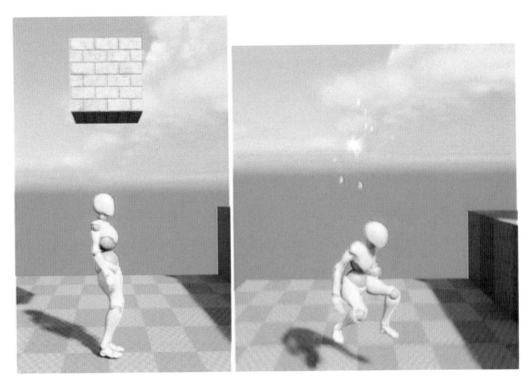

Figure 15.31 – Now, the player can hit the brick and it will be destroyed

When `bHasCollectable` is `True`, `SuperSideScroller_Brick` will play our `HitSound`, spawn the `Explosion` particle system, add a coin collectible to the player, and be destroyed.

> **Note**
>
> You can find the assets and code for this exercise here: `https://github.com/PacktPublishing/Game-Development-Projects-with-Unreal-Engine/tree/master/Chapter15/Exercise15.08`.

With this exercise complete, you have now finished developing the gameplay mechanics for the **SuperSideScroller** game project. Now, the `SuperSideScroller_Brick` class can be used for both the platforming gameplay and the coin-collecting mechanic that we want for the game.

Now that the brick can be destroyed and hidden coins can be collected, all the gameplay elements that we set out to create for the **SuperSideScroller** game project are complete.

Summary

In this chapter, you put your knowledge to the test to create the remaining gameplay mechanics for the **SuperSideScroller** game project. Using a combination of C++ and Blueprints, you developed the potion power-up and coins for the player to collect in the level. Also, by using your knowledge from *Chapter 14, Spawning the Player Projectile*, you added unique audio and visual assets to these collectible items to add a nice layer of polish to the game.

You learned and took advantage of the UMG UI system within UE5 to create a simple, yet effective, UI feedback system to display the number of coins that the player has collected. By using the binding feature of the **Text widget**, you were able to keep the UI updated with the number of coins the player has currently collected. Lastly, you created a `Brick` class using the knowledge you learned from the **SuperSideScroller** project to hide coins for the player so that they can collect and find them.

The **SuperSideScroller** project has been an extensive project that expanded upon many of the tools and practices available within UE5. In *Chapter 10, Creating the SuperSideScroller Game*, we imported custom skeleton and animation assets to use in developing the Animation Blueprint of the player character. In *Chapter 11, Working with Blend Space 1D, Key Bindings, and State Machines*, we used Blend Spaces to allow the player character to blend between idle, walking, and sprinting animations, while also using an `Animation State Machine` to handle the jumping and movement states of the player character. We then learned how to control the player's movement and jump height using the character movement component.

In *Chapter 12, Animation Blending and Montages*, we learned more about animation blending inside `Animation Blueprints` by using the `Layered Blend per Bone` function and `Saved Cached Poses`. By adding a new `AnimSlot` for the upper body animation of the player character's throw animation, we were able to have both the player movement animations and the throw animation blend together smoothly. In *Chapter 13, Creating and Adding the Enemy Artificial Intelligence*, we used the robust systems of behavior trees and Blackboards to develop AI behavior for the enemy. We created a `Task` that will allow the enemy AI to move in-between points from a custom Blueprint that we also developed to determine patrol points for the AI.

In *Chapter 14, Spawning the Player Projectile*, we learned how to create an `Anim Notify` and how to implement this notify in our `Animation Montage` for the player character's throw to spawn the player projectile. Then, we learned about how to create projectiles and how to use **Projectile Movement Component** to have the player projectile move in the game world.

Finally, in this chapter, we learned how to create UI using the UMG toolset for the coin collectible, as well as how to manipulate our **Character Movement Component** to create the potion power-up for the player. Lastly, you created a `Brick` class that can be used to hide coins for the player to find and collect.

In the next chapter, you will learn about the basics of multiplayer, server-client architectures, and the gameplay framework classes used for multiplayer inside UE5. You will use this knowledge to expand upon the multiplayer FPS project in UE5.

This summarization only really scratches the surface of what we learned and accomplished in the **SuperSideScroller** project. Before you move on, here are some challenges for you to test your knowledge and expand upon the project:

Additional Challenges

Test your knowledge from this section by adding the following functionality to the SuperSideScroller project.

1. Add a new power-up that lowers the gravity that's applied to the player character. Import a custom mesh and audio assets to give this power-up a unique look compared to the potion power-up you made.

2. When the player character collects 10 coins, grant the player a power-up.

3. Implement the functionality that allows the player to be destroyed when it's overlapping with the AI. Include being able to respawn the player when this happens.

4. Add another power-up that gives immunity to the player so that they cannot be destroyed when they're overlapping with an enemy. (In fact, when overlapping an enemy with this power-up, it could destroy the enemy.)

5. Using all the gameplay elements you've developed for the **SuperSideScroller** project, create a new level that takes advantage of these elements to make an interesting platforming arena to play in.

6. Add multiple enemies with interesting patrol points to challenge the player when they're navigating the area.

7. Place power-ups in hard-to-reach areas so that players need to improve their platforming skills to obtain them.

8. Create dangerous pitfalls for the player to navigate across and add functionality that will destroy the player if they fall off the map.

16

Getting Started with Multiplayer Basics

In the previous chapter, we completed the SuperSideScroller game and used 1D Blend Spaces, animation blueprints, and animation montages. In this chapter, we're going to build on that knowledge and learn how to add multiplayer functionality to a game using Unreal Engine.

Multiplayer games have grown quite a lot in the last decade. Games such as Fortnite, League of Legends, Rocket League, Overwatch, and Counter-Strike: Global Offensive have gained a lot of popularity in the gaming community and have had great success. Nowadays, almost all games need to have some kind of multiplayer experience to be more relevant and successful.

The reason for this is it adds a new layer of possibilities on top of the existing gameplay, such as being able to remotely play with friends in cooperative mode (also known as online co-op) or against people from all around the world, which greatly increases the longevity and value of a game.

In this chapter, we're going to cover the following main topics:

- Introduction to multiplayer basics
- Understanding the server
- Understanding the client
- Packaging the project
- Exploring connections and ownership
- Getting to know roles
- Understanding variable replication
- Exploring 2D Blend Spaces
- Transforming (modifying) bones

By the end of this chapter, you'll know basic multiplayer concepts such as the server-client architecture, connections, actor ownership, roles and variable replication so that you can create a multiplayer game of your own. You'll also be able to make a 2D Blend Space, which allows you to blend between animations laid out in a 2D grid. Finally, you'll learn how to use Transform (Modify) Bone nodes to control Skeletal Mesh bones at runtime.

Technical requirements

For this chapter, you will need the following technical requirements:

- Unreal Engine 5 installed
- Visual Studio 2019 installed

The project for this chapter can be found in the Chapter16 folder of the code bundle for this book, which can be downloaded here: https://github.com/PacktPublishing/Elevating-Game-Experiences-with-Unreal-Engine-5-Second-Edition.

In the next section, we will discuss the basics of multiplayer.

Introduction to multiplayer basics

You may have heard the term multiplayer a lot while gaming, but what does it mean for game developers? Multiplayer, in reality, is just a set of instructions sent through the network (internet or local area network) between the server and its connected clients to give players the illusion of a shared world.

For this to work, the server needs to be able to talk to clients, but also the other way around (client to server). This is because clients are typically the ones that affect the game world, so they need a way to be able to inform the server of their intentions while playing the game.

An example of this back and forth communication between the server and a client is when a player tries to fire a weapon during a game. Have a look at the following diagram, which shows a client-server interaction:

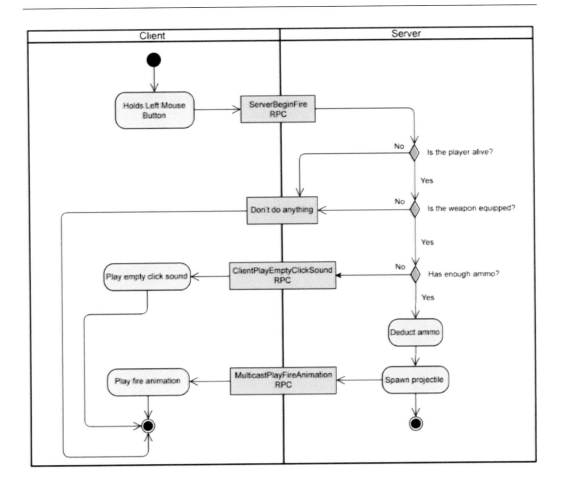

Figure 16.1 – Client-server interaction when firing a weapon

Let's understand the preceding diagram:

1. The player holds the left mouse button down and the client of that player tells the server that it wants to fire a weapon.

2. The server validates whether the player can fire the weapon by checking the following:

   - If the player is alive
   - If the player has the weapon equipped
   - If the player has enough ammo

3. If all of the conditions are valid, then the server will do the following:

- Run the logic to deduct ammo.

- Spawn the projectile actor on the server, which is automatically sent to all of the clients.

- Play the fire animation on that character instance in all of the clients to ensure synchronicity between all of them, which helps to sell the idea that it's the same world, even though it's not.

4. If any of the conditions fail, then the server tells the specific client what to do:

- The player is dead: Don't do anything.

- The player doesn't have the weapon equipped: Don't do anything.

- The player doesn't have enough ammo: Play an empty click sound.

Remember, if you want your game to support multiplayer, then it's highly recommended that you do that as soon as possible in your development cycle. If you try to run a single-player project with multiplayer enabled, you'll notice that some functionalities might just work, but probably most of them won't be working properly or as expected.

The reason for that is when you execute the game in single-player, the code runs locally and instantly, but when you add multiplayer into the equation, you are adding external factors such as an authoritative server that talks to clients on a network with latency, as you saw in *Figure 16.1*.

To get everything working properly, you need to break the existing code into the following components:

- Code that only runs on the server

- Code that only runs on the client

- Code that runs on both the server and the client

To add multiplayer support to games, UE5 comes with a very powerful and bandwidth-efficient network framework already built in that uses an authoritative server-client architecture.

Here is a diagram of how it works:

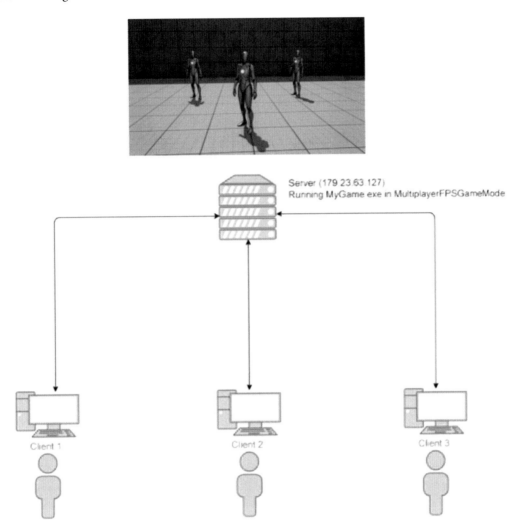

Figure 16.2 – Server-client architecture in UE5

Here, you can see how the server-client architecture works in UE5. Each player controls a client that communicates with the server using a two-way connection. The server runs a specific level with a game mode (that only exists in the server) and controls the flow of information so that the clients can see and interact with each other in the game world.

> **Note**
>
> Multiplayer can be a very advanced topic, so these next few chapters will serve as an introduction to help you understand the essentials, but it will not be an in-depth look. For that reason, some concepts might be omitted for the sake of simplicity.

At this point, you have an idea of how multiplayer basics work. Now, let's dive in and see how servers work and what their responsibilities are.

Understanding the server

The server is the most critical part of the architecture since it's responsible for handling most of the work and making important decisions.

Here is an overview of the main responsibilities of a server:

- **Creating and managing the shared world instance**: The server runs its instance of the game in a specific level and game mode (this will be covered in *Chapter 18, Using Gameplay Framework Classes in Multiplayer*), which will serve as the shared world between all of the connected clients. The level being used can be changed at any point in time and, if applicable, the server can bring along all of the connected clients with it automatically.

- **Handling client join and leave requests**: If a client wants to connect to a server, it needs to ask for permission. To do this, the client sends a join request to the server, through a direct IP connection (explained in the next section) or an online subsystem such as Steam. Once the join request reaches the server, it will perform some validations to determine whether the request is accepted or rejected.

  Some of the most common reasons why the server rejects a request are if the server is already at full capacity and can't take any more clients or if the client is using an out-of-date version of the game. If the server accepts the request, then a player controller with a connection is assigned to the client and the `PostLogin` function in the game mode is called. From that point on, the client will enter the game and is now part of the shared world, where the player will be able to see and interact with other clients. If a client disconnects at any point in time, then all of the other clients will be notified and the `Logout` function in the game mode will be called.

- **Spawning the actors that all of the clients need to know about**: If you want to spawn an actor that exists in all of the clients, then you need to do that on the server. The reason for this is that the server has the authority and is the only one that can tell each client to create an instance of that actor.

  This is the most common way of spawning actors in multiplayer since most actors need to exist in all of the clients. An example of this would be with a power-up, which is something that all clients can see and interact with.

- **Running critical gameplay logic**: To make sure that the game is fair to all of the clients, the critical gameplay logic needs to be executed on the server only. If the clients were responsible for handling the deduction of health, it would be very exploitable, because a player could use a tool to change the current value of health to 100% all the time in memory, so the player would never die in the game.

- **Handling variable replication**: If you have a replicated variable (covered in the *Understanding variable replication* section), then its value should only be changed on the server. This will ensure that all of the clients will have the value updated automatically. You can still change the value on the client, but it will always be replaced with the latest value from the server to prevent cheating and to make sure all of the clients are in sync.

- **Handling RPCs from the client**: The server needs to process the **remote procedure calls** (**RPCs**) (covered in *Chapter 17, Using Remote Procedure Calls*) that are sent from the clients.

Now that you know what a server does, we can talk about the two different ways of creating a server in UE5.

Dedicated server

The dedicated server only runs the server logic, so you won't see the typical window with the game running where you control a character as a normal player. This means that all the clients will connect to this server and its only job is to coordinate them and execute the critical gameplay logic. Additionally, if you run the dedicated server with the -log command prompt, you'll have a console window that logs relevant information about what is happening on the server, such as if a client has connected or disconnected, and so on. You, as a developer, can also log your information by using the UE_LOG macro.

Using dedicated servers is a very common way of creating servers for multiplayer games, and since it's more lightweight than a listen server (covered in the next section), you could just host it on a server stack and leave it running. Another advantage of dedicated servers is that it will make the game fairer for all players because the network conditions will be the same for everyone, and also because none of the clients has authority, so the possibility of a hack is reduced.

To start a dedicated server in UE5, you can use the following command arguments:

- Run the following command to start a dedicated server inside an editor through a shortcut or Command Prompt:

```
"<UE5 Install Folder>\Engine\Binaries\Win64\UnrealEditor.
exe"
"<UProject Location>" <Map Name> -server -game -log
```

Here's an example:

```
"C:\Program Files\Epic
Games\UE_5.0\Engine\Binaries\Win64\UnrealEditor.exe"
"D:\TestProject\TestProject.uproject" TestMap -server
-game -log
```

- Creating a packaged dedicated server requires a build of the project that's been built specifically to serve as a dedicated server.

> **Note**
>
> You can find out more about setting up a packaged dedicated server at https://docs.unrealengine.com/5.0/en-US/InteractiveExperiences/Networking/HowTo/DedicatedServers/.

The listen server

The listen server acts as a server and client at the same time, so you'll also have a window where you can play the game as a client with this server type. It also has the advantage of being the quickest way of getting a server running in a packaged build, but it's not as lightweight as a dedicated server, so the number of clients that can be connected at the same time will be limited.

To start a listen server, you can use the following command arguments:

- Run the following command to start a listen server inside an editor through a shortcut or Command Prompt:

```
"<UE5 Install Folder>\Engine\Binaries\Win64\UnrealEditor.exe"
"<UProject Location>" <Map Name>?Listen -game
```

Here's an example:

```
"C:\Program Files\Epic
Games\UE_5.0\Engine\Binaries\Win64\UnrealEditor.exe"
"D:\TestProject\TestProject.uproject" TestMap?Listen
-game
```

- Using a packaged development build through a shortcut or Command Prompt:

```
"<Project Name>.exe" <Map Name>?Listen -game
```

Here's an example:

```
"D:\Packaged\TestProject\TestProject.exe" TestMap?Listen
-game
```

Now that you know about the two different types of servers you have in Unreal Engine, we can now move on to its counterpart – the client and its responsibilities.

Understanding the client

The client is the simplest part of the architecture because most of the actors will have the authority on the server, so in those cases, the work will be done on the server and the client will just obey its orders.

Here is an overview of the main responsibilities of a client:

- **Enforcing variable replication from the server**: The server typically has authority over all of the actors that the client knows, so when the value of a replicated variable is changed on the server, the client needs to enforce that value as well.

- **Handling RPCs from the server**: The client needs to process the RPCs (covered in *Chapter 17, Using Remote Procedure Calls*) that are sent from the server.

- **Predicting movement when simulating**: When a client is simulating an actor (covered in the *Getting to know roles* section), it needs to locally predict where it's going to be based on the actor's velocity.

- **Spawning the actors that only a client needs to know about**: If you want to spawn an actor that only exists on a client, then you need to do it on that specific client.

  This is the least common way of spawning actors since there are fewer cases where you want an actor to only exist on a client. An example of this is the placement preview actor you see in multiplayer survival games, where the player controls a semi-transparent version of a wall that other players can't see until it's placed.

A client can join a server in a couple of different ways. Here is a list of the most common methods:

- By opening the UE5 console (by default, this can be done with the ` key) in a development build and typing the following:

  ```
  open <Server IP Address>
  ```

  Here's an example:

  ```
  open 194.56.23.4
  ```

- Using the `Execute Console Command` Blueprint node. An example is as follows:

Figure 16.3 – Joining a server with an example IP with the Execute Console Command node

- Using the `ConsoleCommand` function in `APlayerController`, as follows:

```
PlayerController->ConsoleCommand("open <Server IP
Address>");
```

Here's an example:

```
PlayerController->ConsoleCommand("open 194.56.23.4");
```

- Using the editor executable through a shortcut or Command Prompt:

```
"<UE5 Install Folder>\Engine\Binaries\Win64\UnrealEditor.
exe"
"<UProject Location>" <Server IP Address> -game
```

Here's an example:

```
"C:\Program Files\Epic Games\UE_5.0\Engine\Binaries\
Win64\UnrealEditor.exe" "D:\TestProject\TestProject.
uproject" 194.56.23.4 -game
```

- Using a packaged development build through a shortcut or Command Prompt:

```
"<Project Name>.exe" <Server IP Address>
```

Here's an example:

```
"D:\Packaged\TestProject\TestProject.exe" 194.56.23.4
```

In the following exercise, we will test the **Third Person** template that comes with UE5 in multiplayer.

Exercise 16.01 – Testing the Third Person template in multiplayer

In this exercise, we're going to create a **Third Person** template project and play it in multiplayer.

Follow these steps to complete this exercise:

1. Create a new **Third Person** template project using **Blueprints** called `TestMultiplayer` and save it to a location of your choosing.

   Once the project has been created, it should open the editor. Now, let's test the project in multiplayer to see how it behaves.

2. In the editor, to the right of the **Play** button, you have a button with three vertical dots. Click on it and you should see a list of options. Under the **Multiplayer Options** section, you can configure how many clients you want and specify the net mode, which has the following options:

   - **Play Standalone**: Runs the game in single player
   - **Play As Listen Server**: Runs the game with a listen server
   - **Play As Client**: Runs the game with a dedicated server

3. Make sure the **Net Mode** option is set to **Play As Listen Server**, change **Number of Players** to 3, and click on **New Editor Window (PIE)**.

   You should see three windows on top of each other representing the three clients:

Figure 16.4 – Launching three client windows with a listen server

As you can see, the server window is bigger than the client windows, so let's change its size. Press *Esc* on your keyboard to stop playing.

4. Once again, click on the button with the three vertical dots next to the **Play** button and pick the last option, **Advanced Settings**.

5. Search for the **Game Viewport Settings** section. Change **New Viewport Resolution** to 640x480 and close the **Editor Preferences** tab.

> **Note**
>
> This option will only change the size of the server window. If you want to change the size of the client window, you can modify the value of the **Multiplayer Viewport Size** option, which you can find by scrolling down a bit more in the same menu.

6. Play the game again; you should see the following:

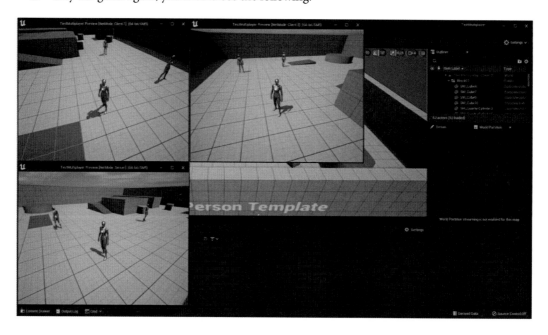

Figure 16.5 – Launching three client windows using a 640x480 resolution with a listen server

Once you start playing, you'll notice that the title bars of the windows say **Server**, **Client 1**, and **Client 2**. Since you can control a character in the **Server** window, that means we're running a listen server, where you have the server and a client running in the same window. When that happens, you should interpret the window title as **Server + Client 0** instead of just **Server** to avoid confusion.

By completing this exercise, you have a setup where you have a server and three clients running (**Client 0**, **Client 1**, and **Client 2**).

> **Note**
>
> When you have multiple windows running at the same time, you'll notice that you can only have input focus on one window at a time. To shift the focus to another window, just press *Shift + F1* to lose the current input focus, and then click on the new window you want to focus on.

If you play the game in one of the windows, you'll notice that you can move around and jump. When you do those actions the other clients will also be able to see that.

The reason why everything works is because the character movement component, which comes with the character class, replicates the location, rotation, and falling state (used to determine whether you are in the air or not) for you automatically. If you want to add a custom behavior such as an attack animation, you can't just tell the client to play an animation locally when a key is pressed, because that will not work on the other clients. That's why you need the server – to serve as an intermediary and tell all the clients to play the animation when one client presses the key.

In this exercise, we've learned how to test multiplayer in the editor. Now, let's learn how to do the same on a packaged build.

Packaging the project

Once you've finished the project, it's good practice to package it so that you have a pure standalone version that doesn't use the Unreal Engine editor. This will run faster and be more lightweight.

Follow these steps to create the packaged version of the file in *Exercise 16.01 – Testing the Third Person template in multiplayer*:

1. Go to **Platforms** (to the right of the **Play** button) | **Windows** | **Package Project**.

2. Pick a folder to place the packaged build and wait for it to finish.

3. Once it has finished, go to the selected folder and open the `Windows` folder inside it.

4. Right-click on **TestMultiplayer.exe** and pick **Create Shortcut**.

5. Rename the new shortcut **Run Server**.

6. Right-click on it and pick **Properties**.

7. On the target, append `ThirdPersonMap?Listen -server`, which will create a listen server using `ThirdPersonMap`. You should end up with this:

```
"<Packaged Path>\Windows\TestMultiplayer.exe"
    ThirdPersonMap?Listen -server
```

8. Click **OK** and run the shortcut.

9. You should get a Windows Firewall prompt; allow it.

10. Leave the server running, go back to the folder (using ALT+TAB or pressing the Windows Key and selecting another window from the taskbar), and create another shortcut from **TestMultiplayer.exe**.

11. Rename it `Run Client`.

12. Right-click on it and pick **Properties**.

13. On the target, append `127.0.0.1`, which is the IP of your local server. You should end up with `"<Packaged Path>\Windows\TestMultiplayer.exe" 127.0.0.1`.

14. Click **OK** and run the shortcut.

You are now connected to the listen server, which means you can see each other's characters. Every time you click on the **Run Client** shortcut, you'll add a new client to the server so that you can have a few clients running on the same machine.

Once you are done testing the packaged build, you can hit ALT+F4 to close each window.

Now that we know how to test our packaged project in multiplayer, let's take a look at connections and ownership, which allow us to have a two-way communication line between the server and the client.

Exploring connections and ownership

When using multiplayer in Unreal Engine, an important concept to understand is that of a connection. When a client joins a server, it will get a new Player Controller with a connection associated with it.

If an actor doesn't have a valid connection with the server, then it won't be able to do replication operations such as variable replication (covered in the *Understanding variable replication* section) or call RPCs (covered in *Chapter 17, Using Remote Procedure Calls*).

If the Player Controller is the only actor that holds a connection, then does that mean that it's the only place you can do replication operations? No, and that's where the `GetNetConnection` function, defined in `AActor`, comes into play.

When doing replication operations (such as variable replication or calling RPCs) on an actor, the network framework will get the actor's connection by calling the `GetNetConnection()` function on it. If the connection is valid, then the replication operation will be processed; if it's not, nothing will happen. The most common implementations of `GetNetConnection()` are from `APawn` and `AActor`.

Let's take a look at how the `APawn` class implements the `GetNetConnection()` function, which is typically used for characters:

```
class UNetConnection* APawn::GetNetConnection() const
{
  // If we have a controller, then use its net connection
  if ( Controller )
  {
    return Controller->GetNetConnection();
  }
  return Super::GetNetConnection();
}
```

The preceding implementation, which is part of the UE5 source code, will first check whether the pawn has a valid controller. If the controller is valid, then it will use its connection. If the controller is not valid, then it will use the parent implementation of the `GetNetConnection()` function, which is on `AActor`:

```
UNetConnection* AActor::GetNetConnection() const
{
  return Owner ? Owner->GetNetConnection() : nullptr;
}
```

The preceding implementation, which is also part of the UE5 source code, will check if the actor has a valid owner. If it does, it will use the owner's connection; if it doesn't, it will return an invalid connection. So, what is this `Owner` variable? Every actor has a variable called `Owner` (where you can set its value by calling the `SetOwner` function) that stores which actor owns it, so you can think of it as its parent actor.

> **Note**
> In a listen server, the connection for the character that's controlled by its client will always be invalid. This is because that client is already a part of the server and therefore doesn't need a connection.

Using the owner's connection in this implementation of `GetNetConnection()` will work like a hierarchy. If, while going up the hierarchy of owners, it finds an owner that is a Player Controller or is being controlled by one, then it will have a valid connection and will be able to process replication operations. Have a look at the following example:

Imagine that a weapon actor was placed in the world and it's just sitting there. In that situation, the weapon won't have an owner, so if the weapon tries to do any replication operations, such as variable replication or calling RPCs, nothing will happen.

However, if a client picks up the weapon and calls `SetOwner` on the server with the value of the character, then the weapon will now have a valid connection. The reason for this is because the weapon is an actor, so to get its connection, it will use the `AActor` implementation of `GetNetConnection()`, which returns the connection of its owner. Since the owner is the client's character, it will use the implementation of `GetNetConnection()` of `APawn`. The character has a valid Player Controller, so that is the connection returned by the function.

Here is a diagram to help you understand this logic:

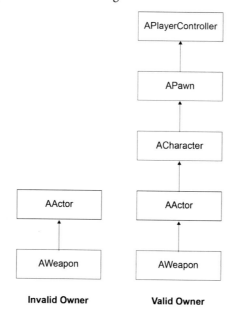

Figure 16.6 – Connections and ownership example of a weapon actor

If the weapon has an invalid owner, then this is what will happen:

- `AWeapon` doesn't override the `GetNetConnection` function, so it will call the first implementation found in the class hierarchy, which is `AActor::GetNetConnection`.

- The implementation of `AActor::GetNetConnection` calls `GetNetConnection` on its owner. Since there is no owner, the connection is invalid.

If the weapon has an valid owner, then this is what will happen:

- `AWeapon` doesn't override the `GetNetConnection` function, so it will call the first implementation found in the class hierarchy, which is `AActor::GetNetConnection`.

- The implementation of `AActor::GetNetConnection` calls `GetNetConnection` on its owner. Since the owner of the weapon is the character that picked it up, then it will call `GetNetConnection` on it.

- `ACharacter` doesn't override the `GetNetConnection` function, so it will call the first implementation found in the class hierarchy, which is `APawn::GetNetConnection`.

- The implementation of `APawn::GetNetConnection` uses the connection from the owning player controller. Since the owning player controller is valid, then it will use that connection for the weapon.

> **Note**
>
> For `SetOwner` to work as intended, it needs to be executed on the authority, which, in most cases, means the server. If you execute `SetOwner` on a game instance that is not the authority, it won't be able to execute replication operations.

In this section, we learned how connections and ownership allow the server and client to communicate in both directions. Next, we're going to learn about the concept of the roles of an actor, which tells us the version of the actor that is executing the code.

Getting to know roles

When an actor is spawned on the server, it will create a version on the server, as well as one on each client. Since there are different versions of the same actor on different instances of the game (`Server`, `Client 1`, `Client 2`, and so on), it is important to know which version of the actor is which. This will allow us to know what logic can be executed in each of these instances.

To help with this situation, every actor has the following two variables:

- **Local Role**: The role that the actor has on the current game instance. For example, if the actor was spawned on the server and the current game instance is also the server, then that version of the actor has authority, so you can run more critical gameplay logic on it. It's accessed by calling the `GetLocalRole()` function.

- **Remote Role**: The role that the actor has on remote game instances. For example, if the current game instance is the server, then it returns the role the actor has on clients and vice versa. It's accessed by calling the `GetRemoteRole()` function.

The return type of the `GetLocalRole()` and `GetRemoteRole()` functions is `ENetRole`, which is an enumeration that can have the following possible values:

- `ROLE_None`: The actor doesn't have a role because it's not being replicated.

- ROLE_SimulatedProxy: The current game instance doesn't have authority over the actor and it's not being controlled by a Player Controller. This means that its movement will be simulated/predicted by using the last value of the actor's velocity.

- ROLE_AutonomousProxy: The current game instance doesn't have authority over the actor, but it's being controlled by a Player Controller. This means that we can send more accurate movement information to the server, based on the player's inputs, instead of just using the last value of the actor's velocity.

- ROLE_Authority: The current game instance has complete authority over the actor. This means that if the actor is on the server, the changes that are made to its replicated variables will be treated as the value that every client needs to enforce through variable replication.

Let's have a look at the following example code snippet:

```
ENetRole MyLocalRole = GetLocalRole();
ENetRole MyRemoteRole = GetRemoteRole();
FString String;

if (MyLocalRole == ROLE_Authority)
{
  if (MyRemoteRole == ROLE_AutonomousProxy)
  {
    String = "This version of the actor is the authority
    and it's being controlled by a player on its client";
  }
  else if (MyRemoteRole == ROLE_SimulatedProxy)
  {
    String = "This version of the actor is the authority
    but it's not being controlled by a player on its
    client";
  }
}
else String = "This version of the actor isn't the authority";
GEngine->AddOnScreenDebugMessage(-1, 0.0f, FColor::Red,
String);
```

The preceding code snippet will store the values of the local role and remote role in MyLocalRole and MyRemoteRole, respectively. After that, it will print different messages on the screen, depending on whether that version of the actor is the authority or whether it's being controlled by a player on its client.

> **Note**
>
> It is important to understand that if an actor has a local role of `ROLE_Authority`, it doesn't mean that it's on the server; it means that it's on the game instance that originally spawned it and therefore has authority over it.
>
> If a client spawns an actor, even though the server and the other clients won't know about it, its local role will still be `ROLE_Authority`. Most of the actors in a multiplayer game will be spawned by the server; that's why it's easy to misunderstand that the authority is always referring to the server.

Here is a table to help you understand the roles that an actor will have in different scenarios:

	Server		Client	
	Local Role	Remote Role	Local Role	Remote Role
Actor spawned on the server	`ROLE_Authority`	`ROLE_SimulatedProxy`	`ROLE_SimulatedProxy`	`ROLE_Authority`
Actor spawned on the client	Won't exist	Won't exist	`ROLE_Authority`	`ROLE_SimulatedProxy`
Player-owned pawn spawned on the server	`ROLE_Authority`	`ROLE_AutonomousProxy`	`ROLE_AutonomousProxy`	`ROLE_Authority`
Player-owned pawn spawned on the client	Won't exist	Won't exist	`ROLE_Authority`	`ROLE_SimulatedProxy`

Figure 16.7 – Roles that an actor can have in different scenarios

In the preceding table, you can see the roles that an actor will have in different scenarios.

We'll analyze each scenario and explain why the actor has that role in the following sections.

Actor spawned on the server

The actor spawns on the server, so the server's version of that actor will have the local role of `ROLE_Authority` and the remote role of `ROLE_SimulatedProxy`. For the client's version of that actor, its local role will be `ROLE_SimulatedProxy` and the remote role will be `ROLE_Authority`.

Actor spawned on the client

The actor was spawned on the client, so the client's version of that actor will have the local role of `ROLE_Authority` and the remote role of `ROLE_SimulatedProxy`. Since the actor wasn't spawned on the server, then it will only exist on the client that spawned it.

Player-owned pawn spawned on the server

The pawn was spawned on the server, so the server's version of that pawn will have the local role of `ROLE_Authority` and the remote role of `ROLE_AutonomousProxy`. For the client's version of that pawn, its local role will be `ROLE_AutonomousProxy`, because it's being controlled by a Player Controller, and the remote role of `ROLE_Authority`.

Player-owned pawn spawned on the client

The pawn was spawned on the client, so the client's version of that pawn will have the local role of `ROLE_Authority` and the remote role of `ROLE_SimulatedProxy`. Since the pawn wasn't spawned on the server, then it will only exist on the client that spawned it.

Exercise 16.02 – Implementing ownership and roles

In this exercise, we're going to create a **C++** project that uses the **Third Person** template as a base and make it do the following:

- Create a new actor called **OwnershipTestActor** that has a static mesh component as the root component. On every tick, it'll do the following:

  - On the authority, it will check which character is closest to it within a certain radius (configured by the `EditAnywhere` variable called `OwnershipRadius`) and will set that character as its owner. When no character is within the radius, then the owner will be `nullptr`.

  - Display its local role, remote role, owner, and connection.

- Edit **OwnershipRolesCharacter** and override the **Tick** function so that it displays its local role, remote role, owner, and connection.

- Add a macro called **ROLE_TO_STRING** on **OwnershipRoles.h**, which converts `ENetRole` into an `FString` value that can be printed on the screen.

Follow these steps to complete this exercise:

1. Create a new **Third Person** template project using **C++** called **OwnershipRoles** and save it to a location of your liking.

2. Once the project has been created, it should open the editor as well as the Visual Studio solution.

3. Using the editor, create a new C++ class called **OwnershipTestActor** that derives from `Actor`.

4. Once it finishes compiling, Visual Studio should pop up with the newly created `.h` and `.cpp` files.

5. Close the editor and go back to Visual Studio.

6. In Visual Studio, open the `OwnershipRoles.h` file and add the following macro:

```
#define ROLE_TO_STRING(Value) FindObject<UEnum>(ANY_
PACKAGE, TEXT("ENetRole"), true)-
>GetNameStringByIndex(static_cast<int32>(Value))
```

This macro will be used to convert the `ENetRole` enumeration that we get from the `GetLocalRole()` function and `GetRemoteRole()` into an `FString`. The way it works is by finding the `ENetRole` enumeration type through Unreal Engine's reflection system. From there, it converts the `Value` parameter into an `FString` variable so that it can be printed on the screen.

7. Now, open the `OwnershipTestActor.h` file and declare the protected variables for the static mesh component and the ownership radius, as shown in the following code snippet:

```
UPROPERTY(VisibleAnywhere, BlueprintReadOnly, Category =
"Ownership Test Actor")
UStaticMeshComponent* Mesh;
UPROPERTY(EditAnywhere, BlueprintReadOnly, Category =
"Ownership Test Actor")
float OwnershipRadius = 400.0f;
```

In the preceding code snippet, we declared the static mesh component and the `OwnershipRadius` variable, which allows you to configure the radius of the ownership.

8. Next, delete the declaration of `BeginPlay` and move the constructor and the `Tick` function declarations to the protected area.

9. Now, open the `OwnershipTestActor.cpp` file and add the required header files, as shown in the following code snippet:

```
#include "OwnershipRoles.h"
#include "OwnershipRolesCharacter.h"
#include "Kismet/GameplayStatics.h"
```

In the preceding code snippet, we included `OwnershipRoles.h`, `OwnershipRolesCharacter.h`, and `GameplayStatics.h` because we'll be calling the `GetAllActorsOfClass` function.

10. In the constructor definition, create the static mesh component and set it as the root component:

```
Mesh =
CreateDefaultSubobject<UStaticMeshComponent>("Mesh");
RootComponent = Mesh;
```

11. Still in the constructor, set bReplicates to true to tell Unreal Engine that this actor replicates and should also exist in all of the clients:

```
bReplicates = true;
```

12. Delete the BeginPlay function definition.

13. In the Tick function, draw a debug sphere to help visualize the ownership radius, as shown in the following code snippet:

```
DrawDebugSphere(GetWorld(), GetActorLocation(),
OwnershipRadius, 32, FColor::Yellow);
```

14. Still in the Tick function, create the authority-specific logic that will get the closest AOwnershipRolesCharacter within the ownership radius. If it's different from the current one, set it as the owner:

```
if (HasAuthority())
{
    AActor* NextOwner = nullptr;
    float MinDistance = OwnershipRadius;
    TArray<AActor*> Actors;
    UGameplayStatics::GetAllActorsOfClass(this,
        AOwnershipRolesCharacter::StaticClass(), Actors);

    for (AActor* Actor : Actors)
    {
        const float Distance = GetDistanceTo(Actor);

        if (Distance <= MinDistance)
        {
            MinDistance = Distance;
            NextOwner = Actor;
        }
    }
    if (GetOwner() != NextOwner)
    {
        SetOwner(NextOwner);
    }
}
```

> **Note**
>
> The preceding code is for demonstration purposes only, because running `GetAllActorsOfClass` on the `Tick` function every frame will take a big toll on performance. Ideally, you should execute this code only once (on `BeginPlay`, for example) and store the values so that we can query them in `Tick`.

15. Still in the `Tick` function, convert the values for the local/remote roles (using the ROLE_TO_STRING macro we created earlier), the current owner, and the connection into strings:

```
const FString LocalRoleString = ROLE_TO_
STRING(GetLocalRole());

const FString RemoteRoleString = ROLE_TO_
STRING(GetRemoteRole());

const FString OwnerString = GetOwner() != nullptr ?
GetOwner()->GetName() : TEXT("No Owner");

const FString ConnectionString = GetNetConnection()
!= nullptr ? TEXT("Valid Connection") : TEXT("Invalid
Connection");
```

16. To finalize the `Tick` function, use `DrawDebugString` to print the strings we converted in the previous step on the screen:

```
const Fstring Values = Fstring::Printf(TEXT("LocalRole =
%s\nRemoteRole = %s\nOwner = %s\nConnection = %s"),
   *LocalRoleString, *RemoteRoleString, *OwnerString,
   *ConnectionString);

DrawDebugString(GetWorld(), GetActorLocation(), Values,
nullptr, Fcolor::White, 0.0f, true);
```

> **Note**
>
> Instead of constantly using `GetLocalRole() == ROLE_Authority` to check whether the actor has authority, you can use the `HasAuthority()` helper function, defined in `AActor`.

17. Next, open `OwnershipRolesCharacter.h` and declare the `Tick` function as protected:

```
virtual void Tick(float DeltaTime) override;
```

18. Now, open `OwnershipRolesCharacter.cpp` and include `OwnershipRoles.h`, as shown in the following code snippet:

```
#include "OwnershipRoles.h"
```

19. Implement the `Tick` function:

```
void AOwnershipRolesCharacter::Tick(float DeltaTime)
{
    Super::Tick(DeltaTime);
}
```

20. Inside of the Tick function, convert the values for the local/remote roles (using the ROLE_TO_STRING macro we created earlier), the current owner, and the connection into strings:

```
const FString LocalRoleString = ROLE_TO_
STRING(GetLocalRole());
const FString RemoteRoleString = ROLE_TO_
STRING(GetRemoteRole());
const FString OwnerString = GetOwner() != nullptr ?
GetOwner()->GetName() : TEXT("No Owner");
const FString ConnectionString = GetNetConnection() !=
nullptr ?
    TEXT("Valid Connection") : TEXT("Invalid
    Connection");
```

21. Use `DrawDebugString` to print the strings we converted in the previous step on the screen:

```
const FString Values = FString::Printf(TEXT("LocalRole =
    %s\nRemoteRole = %s\nOwner = %s\nConnection = %s"),
    *LocalRoleString, *RemoteRoleString, *OwnerString,
    *ConnectionString);
DrawDebugString(GetWorld(), GetActorLocation(), Values,
nullptr, FColor::White, 0.0f, true);
```

Finally, we can test the project.

22. Run the code and wait for the editor to fully load.

23. Create a new Blueprint called `OwnershipTestActor_BP` in the `Content` folder that derives from `OwnershipTestActor`. Set `Mesh` to use a cube mesh, and drop an instance of it in the world.

24. Go to `Multiplayer Options`, set **Net Mode** to **Play As Listen Server**, and set **Number of Players** to 2.

25. Set the window size to 800x600.

26. Play using **New Editor Window (PIE)**.

You should get the following output:

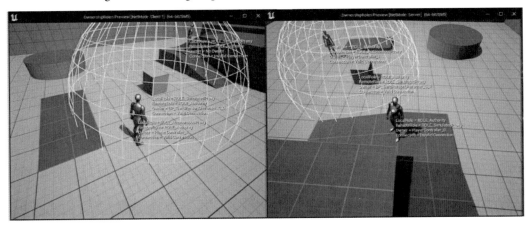

Figure 16.8 – Expected result on the Server and Client 1 windows

By completing this exercise, you'll have a better understanding of how connections and ownership work. These are important concepts to know as everything related to replication is dependent on them.

The next time you see that an actor is not doing replication operations, you'll know that you need to check whether it has a valid connection and an owner.

Now, let's analyze the values that are displayed in the server and client windows.

> **Note**
>
> The two figures for the server and client window will have three text blocks that say `Server Character`, `Client 1 Character`, and `Ownership Test Actor`, but that was added to the original screenshot to help you understand which character and actor are which.

Output for the Server window

Have a look at the following output screenshot of the **Server** window from the previous exercise:

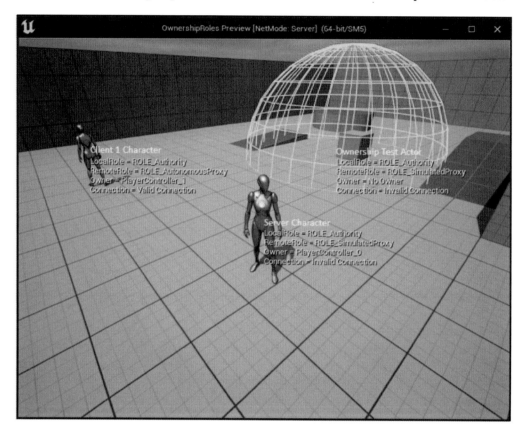

Figure 16.9 – The Server window

In the preceding screenshot, you can see **Server Character**, **Client 1 Character**, and the **Ownership Test** cube actor.

First, let's analyze the values for **Server Character**.

Server Character

This is the character that the listen server is controlling. The values associated with this character are as follows:

- `LocalRole = ROLE_Authority`: This character was spawned on the server, which is the current game instance.

- `RemoteRole = ROLE_SimulatedProxy`: Because this character was spawned on the server, the other clients should only simulate it.

- `Owner = PlayerController_0`: This character is being controlled by the client of the listen server, which uses the first `PlayerController` instance called `PlayerController_0`.

- `Connection = Invalid Connection`: Because we're the client of the listen server, there is no need for a connection.

Next, we are going to look at **Client 1 Character** in the same window.

Client 1 Character

This is the character that **Client 1** is controlling. The values associated with this character are as follows:

- `LocalRole = ROLE_Authority`: This character was spawned on the server, which is the current game instance.

- `RemoteRole = ROLE_AutonomousProxy`: Because this character was spawned on the server, but it's being controlled by another client.

- `Owner = PlayerController_1`: This character is being controlled by another client, which uses the second `PlayerController` instance called `PlayerController_1`.

- `Connection = Valid Connection`: Because this character is being controlled by another client, so a connection to the server is required.

Next, we are going to look at the **OwnershipTest** actor in the same window.

The OwnershipTest actor

This is the cube actor that will set its owner to the closest character within a certain ownership radius. The values associated with this actor are as follows:

- `LocalRole = ROLE_Authority`: This actor was placed in the level and spawned on the server, which is the current game instance.

- `RemoteRole = ROLE_SimulatedProxy`: This actor was spawned in the server, but it's not being controlled by any client.

- `Owner` and `Connection`: They will have their values based on the closest character. If there isn't a character inside the ownership radius, then they will have the values of `No Owner` and `Invalid Connection`, respectively.

Now, let's analyze the values that are displayed in the `Client 1` window.

Output for the Client 1 window

Have a look at the following output screenshot of the `Client 1` window from the previous exercise:

Figure 16.10 – The Client 1 window

The values for the `Client 1` window will be the same as those for the `Server` window, except the values of `LocalRole` and `RemoteRole` will be reversed because they are always relative to the game instance that you are in.

Another exception is that the server character has no owner and the other connected clients won't have a valid connection. The reason for that is that clients don't store player controllers and connections of other clients, only the server does, but this will be covered in more depth in *Chapter 18, Using Gameplay Framework Classes in Multiplayer*.

In this section, we've covered how roles are used to know which version of the actor the code is executing, which we can leverage to run specific code. In the next section, we will look at variable replication, which is one of the techniques that's used by the server to keep the clients synchronized.

Understanding variable replication

One of the ways the server can keep the clients synchronized is by using variable replication. The way it works is that every specific number of times per second (defined per actor in the `AActor::NetUpdateFrequency` variable, which is also exposed to blueprints) the variable replication system in the server will check whether there are any replicated variables (explained in the next section) in the client that need to be updated with the latest value.

If the variable meets all of the replication conditions, then the server will send an update to the client and enforce the new value.

For example, if you have a replicated `Health` variable and the client on its end uses a hacking tool to set the value of the variable from `10` to `100`, then the replication system will enforce the real value from the server and change it back to `10`, which nullifies the hack.

Variables are only sent to the client to be updated in the following situations:

- The variable is set to replicate.
- The value was changed on the server.
- The value on the client is different on the server.
- The actor has replication enabled.
- The actor is relevant and meets all of the replication conditions.

One important thing to take into consideration is that the logic that determines whether a variable should be replicated or not is only executed `Actor::NetUpdateFrequency` times a second. In other words, the server doesn't send an update request to a client immediately after you change the value of a variable on the server.

An example of this would be if you had an integer replicated variable called `Test` that has a default value of 5. If you call a function on the server that sets `Test` to 3 and in the next line changes it to 8, then only the latter change would send an update request to the clients. The reason for this is these two changes were made in-between the `NetUpdateFrequency` interval, so when the variable replication system executes, the current value is 8, and because that is different from the value stored on the clients (which is still 5), it will update them. If instead of setting it to 8, you set it back to 5, then no changes would be sent to the clients because the values haven't changed.

In the following sections, we are going to cover how to replicate variables by using the `Replicated` and `ReplicatedUsing` specifiers, as well as the `DOREPLIFETIME` and `DOREPLIFETIME_CONDITION` macros.

Replicated variables

In Unreal Engine, almost any variable type that can use the UPROPERTY macro can be set to replicate, and you can use two specifiers to do that. We will look at them in the following sections.

Replicated

If you just want to say that a variable is replicated, then you can use the `Replicated` specifier.

Have a look at the following example:

```
UPROPERTY(Replicated)
float Health = 100.0f;
```

In the preceding code snippet, we declared a float variable called `Health`, as we normally do. The difference is that we added UPROPERTY(Replicated) to let Unreal Engine know that the `Health` variable will be replicated.

ReplicatedUsing

If you want to say that a variable is replicated and should call a function every time it's updated, then you can use the `ReplicatedUsing=<Function Name>` specifier. Have a look at the following example:

```
UPROPERTY(ReplicatedUsing=OnRep_Health)
float Health = 100.0f;


UFUNCTION()
void OnRep_Health()
{
    UpdateHUD();
}
```

In the preceding code snippet, we declared a float variable called `Health`. The difference is that we added UPROPERTY(ReplicatedUsing=OnRep_Health) to let Unreal Engine know that this variable will be replicated and should call the `OnRep_Health` function every time it's updated, which, in this specific case, calls a function to update the HUD.

Typically, the naming scheme for the callback function is `OnRep_<Variable Name>`.

> **Note**
>
> The function that's used in the `ReplicatedUsing` specifier needs to be marked as `UFUNCTION()`.

GetLifetimeReplicatedProps

Besides marking the variable as replicated, you'll also need to implement the `GetLifetimeReplicatedProps` function in the actor's cpp file. One thing to take into consideration is that this function is automatically declared internally once you have at least one replicated variable, so you shouldn't declare it in the actor's header file. The purpose of this function is for you to tell how each replicated variable should replicate. You can do this by using the `DOREPLIFETIME` macro and its variants on every variable that you want to replicate.

DOREPLIFETIME

This macro specifies that the replicated variable in a class (entered as arguments) will replicate to all the clients, without an extra condition.

Here's its syntax:

```
DOREPLIFETIME(<Class Name>, <Replicated Variable Name>);
```

Have a look at the following example:

```
void
AVariableReplicationActor::GetLifetimeReplicatedProps(TArray<
  FLifetimeProperty >& OutLifetimeProps) const
{
  Super::GetLifetimeReplicatedProps(OutLifetimeProps);
  DOREPLIFETIME(AVariableReplicationActor, Health);
}
```

In the preceding code snippet, we used the `DOREPLIFETIME` macro to tell the replication system that the `Health` variable in the `AVariableReplicationActor` class will replicate without an extra condition.

DOREPLIFETIME_CONDITION

This macro specifies that the replicated variable in a class (entered as arguments) will replicate only to the clients that meet the condition (entered as an argument).

Here's the syntax:

```
DOREPLIFETIME_CONDITION(<Class Name>, <Replicated Variable
Name>, <Condition>);
```

The condition parameter can be one of the following values:

- COND_InitialOnly: The variable will only replicate once, with the initial replication.

- COND_OwnerOnly: The variable will only replicate to the owner of the actor.

- COND_SkipOwner: The variable won't replicate to the owner of the actor.

- COND_SimulatedOnly: The variable will only replicate to actors that are simulating.

- COND_AutonomousOnly: The variable will only replicate to autonomous actors.

- COND_SimulatedOrPhysics: The variable will only replicate to actors that are simulating or to actors with bRepPhysics set to true.

- COND_InitialOrOwner: The variable will only replicate once, with the initial replication or to the owner of the actor.

- COND_Custom: The variable will only replicate if its SetCustomIsActiveOverride Boolean condition (used in the AActor::PreReplication function) is true.

Have a look at the following example:

```
void
AVariableReplicationActor::GetLifetimeReplicatedProps(TArray<
    FLifetimeProperty >& OutLifetimeProps) const
{
    Super::GetLifetimeReplicatedProps(OutLifetimeProps);
    DOREPLIFETIME_CONDITION(AVariableReplicationActor,
    Health, COND_OwnerOnly);
}
```

In the preceding code snippet, we used the DOREPLIFETIME_CONDITION macro to tell the replication system that the Health variable in the AVariableReplicationActor class will replicate only for the owner of this actor.

> **Note**
>
> There are more DOREPLIFETIME macros available, but they won't be covered in this book. To see all of the variants, please check the `UnrealNetwork.h` file from the UE5 source code at `https://github.com/EpicGames/UnrealEngine/blob/release/Engine/Source/Runtime/Engine/Public/Net/UnrealNetwork.h`.

Now that you have an idea of how variable replication works, let's complete an exercise that uses the `Replicated` and `ReplicatedUsing` specifiers, as well as the DOREPLIFETIME and DOREPLIFETIME_CONDITION macros.

Exercise 16.03 – Replicating variables using Replicated, ReplicatedUsing, DOREPLIFETIME, and DOREPLIFETIME_CONDITION

In this exercise, we're going to create a C++ project that uses the **Third Person** template as a base and add two variables to the character that replicate in the following way:

- Variable A is a float that will use the `Replicated` specifier and the DOREPLIFETIME macro.

- Variable B is an integer that will use the `ReplicatedUsing` specifier and the DOREPLIFETIME_CONDITION macro.

- The Tick function of the character should increment A and B by 1 every frame, if it has authority, and call `DrawDebugString` to display theirs values on the location of the character.

Follow these steps to complete this exercise:

1. Create a new **Third Person** template project using C++ called `VariableReplication` and save it to a location of your choosing.

2. Once the project has been created, it should open the editor as well as the Visual Studio solution.

3. Close the editor and go back to Visual Studio.

4. Open the `VariableReplicationCharacter.h` file and declare the protected A and B variables as UPROPERTY using their respective replication specifiers:

    ```
    UPROPERTY(Replicated)
    float A = 100.0f;
    UPROPERTY(ReplicatedUsing = OnRepNotify_B)
    int32 B;
    ```

5. Declare the `Tick` function as protected:

    ```
    virtual void Tick(float DeltaTime) override;
    ```

6. Since we've declared the B variable as `ReplicatedUsing = OnRepNotify_B`, we also need to declare the protected `OnRepNotify_B` callback function as `UFUNCTION`:

```
UFUNCTION()
void OnRepNotify_B();
```

7. Now, open the `VariableReplicationCharacter.cpp` file and include the `UnrealNetwork.h` header file, which contains the definition of the `DOREPLIFETIME` macros that we're going to use:

```
#include "Net/UnrealNetwork.h"
```

8. Implement the `GetLifetimeReplicatedProps` function:

```
void
AVariableReplicationCharacter::GetLifetimeReplicatedProps
(TArray<FLifetimeProperty >& OutLifetimeProps) const
{
    Super::GetLifetimeReplicatedProps(OutLifetimeProps);
}
```

9. Let the replication system know that the A variable won't have any extra replication conditions:

```
DOREPLIFETIME(AVariableReplicationCharacter, A);
```

10. Let the replication system know that the B variable will only replicate to the owner of this actor:

```
DOREPLIFETIME_CONDITION(AVariableReplicationCharacter, B,
COD_OwnerOnly);
```

11. Implement the `Tick` function:

```
void AVariableReplicationCharacter::Tick(float DeltaTime)
{
    Super::Tick(DeltaTime);
}
```

12. Next, run the authority-specific logic that adds 1 to A and B:

```
if (HasAuthority())
{
    A++;
    B++;
}
```

Since this character will be spawned on the server, only the server will execute this logic.

13. Display the values of A and B on the location of the character:

```
const FString Values = FString::Printf(TEXT("A = %.2f
B = %d"), A, B);
DrawDebugString(GetWorld(), GetActorLocation(), Values,
nullptr, FColor::White, 0.0f, true);
```

14. Implement the RepNotify function for the B variable, which displays a message on the screen saying that the B variable was changed to a new value:

```
void AVariableReplicationCharacter::OnRepNotify_B()
{
    const FString String = FString::Printf(TEXT("B was
    changed by the server and is now %d!"), B);
    GEngine->AddOnScreenDebugMessage(-1, 0.0f,
    FColor::Red,String);
}
```

Finally, you can test the project.

15. Run the code and wait for the editor to fully load.

16. Go to Multiplayer Options, set **Net Mode** to **Play As Listen Server**, and set **Number of Players** to 2.

17. Set the window size to 800x600.

18. Play using New Editor Window (PIE).

By completing this exercise, you will be able to play on each client and you'll notice that the characters are displaying their respective values for A and B.

Now, let's analyze the values that are displayed in the Server and Client 1 windows.

> **Note**
>
> The two figures for the server and client window will have two text blocks that say Server Character and Client 1 Character, but that was added to the original screenshot to help you understand which character is which.

Output for the Server window

In the **Server** window, you have the values for **Server Character**, which is the character controlled by the server, while in the background, you have the values for **Client 1 Character**:

Figure 16.11 – The Server window

The outputs that can be observed are as follows:

- **Server Character**: A = 651.00 B = 551
- **Client 1 Character**: A = 592.00 B = 492

At this specific point in time, **Server Character** has a value of 651 for A and 551 for B. The reason why A and B have different values is that A starts at 100 and B starts at 0, which is the correct value after 551 ticks of A++ and B++.

Client 1 Character doesn't have the same values as **Server Character** because **Client 1** was created slightly after the server, so in this case, the count was off by 59 ticks of A++ and B++.

Next, we will look at the **Client 1** window.

Output for the Client 1 window

In the **Client 1** window, you have the values for **Client 1 Character**, which is the character controlled by **Client 1**, while in the background, you have the values for **Server Character**:

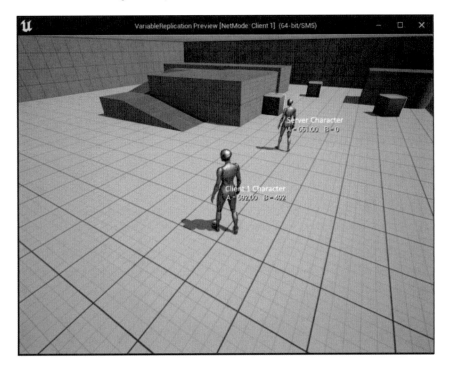

Figure 16.12 – The Client 1 window

The outputs that can be observed are as follows:

- **Server Character**: A = 651.00 B = 0
- **Client 1 Character**: A = 592.00 B = 492

Client 1 Character has the correct values from the server, so the variable replication is working as intended. If you look at **Server Character**, A is 651, which is correct, but B is 0. The reason for this is that A is using DOREPLIFETIME, which doesn't add any additional replication conditions, so it will replicate the variable and keep the client up to date every time the variable is changed on the server.

The B variable, on the other hand, uses DOREPLIFETIME_CONDITION with COND_OwnerOnly, and since **Client 1** is not the client that owns **Server Character** (the client of the listen server does), then the value is not replicated and remains unchanged from the default value of 0.

If you go back to the code and change the replication condition of B to use COND_SimulatedOnly instead of COND_OwnerOnly, you'll notice that the results will be reversed in the **Client 1** window. The value of B will be replicated for **Server Character**, but it won't replicate for its own character.

> **Note**
>
> The reason why the RepNotify message is showing in the **Server** window instead of the **Client** window is that, when playing in the editor, both windows share the same process, so printing text on the screen won't be accurate. To get the correct behavior, you'll need to run the packaged version of the game.

Exploring 2D Blend Spaces

In *Chapter 2, Working with Unreal Engine*, we created a 1D Blend Space to blend between the movement states (idle, walk, and run) of a character based on the value of the Speed axis. For that specific example, it worked pretty well because you only needed one axis, but if we wanted the character to also be able to strafe, then we couldn't do that.

To contemplate that case, Unreal Engine allows you to create 2D Blend Spaces. The concept is almost the same; the only difference is that you have an extra axis for animations, so you can blend between them not only horizontally, but also vertically.

Let's apply our knowledge of 1D Blend Spaces to the next exercise, where we will create a 2D Blend Space for the movement of a character that can also strafe.

Exercise 16.04 – Creating a movement 2D Blend Space

In this exercise, we're going to create a Blend Space that uses two axes instead of one. The vertical axis will be Speed, which will be between 0 and 200. The horizontal axis will be Direction, which represents the relative angle (-180 to 180) between the velocity and the rotation/forward vector of the pawn.

The following diagram will help you calculate the direction in this exercise:

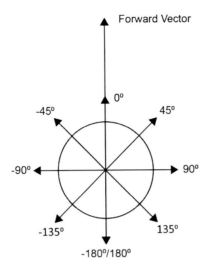

Figure 16.13 – Direction values based on the angle between the forward vector and the velocity

The preceding diagram shows how the direction will be calculated. The forward vector represents the direction that the character is currently facing, while the numbers represent the angle that the forward vector would make with the velocity vector if it was pointing in that direction. If the character was looking in a certain direction and you pressed a key to move the character to the right, then the velocity vector would be perpendicular to the forward vector. This would mean that the angle would be 90°, so that would be our direction.

If we set up our 2D Blend Space with that logic in mind, we can use the correct animation based on the character's movement angle.

Follow these steps to complete this exercise:

1. Create a new **Third Person** template project using **Blueprints** called Blendspace2D and save it to a location of your choosing.

2. Once the project has been created, it should open the editor.

3. Next, you will be importing the movement animations. In the editor, go to the **Content\Characters\Mannequins\Animations** folder.

4. Click on the **Import** button.

5. Go to the **Chapter16\Exercise16.04\Assets** folder, select all of the .fbx files, and hit the **Open** button.

6. In the import dialog, make sure you pick the SK_Mannequin skeleton and hit the **Import All** button.

7. Save all of the new files in the Assets folder.

    If you open any of the new animations, you will notice that the mesh is quite stretched on the Z-axis. So, let's fix that by adjusting the skeleton retargeting settings.

8. Go to **Content/Characters/Mannequins/Meshes/SK_Mannequin**. On the left, you should see the list of bones.

9. Click on the cog icon to the right of the search box on the top and enable **Show Retargeting Options**.

10. *Right-click* on the root bone and pick **Recursively Set Translation Retargeting Skeleton**.

11. Finally, pick **Animation** from the drop-down for the **root** and **pelvis** bones.

12. Save and close **SK_Mannequin**.

13. Once that's done, open the **Content Browser** area, click on the **Add** button, and pick **Animation | Blend Space**.

14. Next, select the **SK_Mannequin** skeleton.

15. Rename the Blend Space **BS_Movement** and open it.

16. Set the horizontal **Direction** axis to (-180 to 180) and the vertical **Speed** axis to (0 to 200), and make sure that you turn on Snap to Grid on both. You should end up with the following settings:

Figure 16.14 – 2D Blend Space – Axis Settings

17. Drag the **Idle_Rifle_Ironsights** animation where **Speed** is 0 and **Direction** is -180, 0, and 180.

18. Drag the **Walk_Fwd_Rifle_Ironsights** animation where **Speed** is 200 and **Direction** is 0.

19. Drag the **Walk_Lt_Rifle_Ironsights** animation where **Speed** is 200 and **Direction** is -90.

20. Drag the **Walk_Rt_Rifle_Ironsights** animation where **Speed** is 200 and **Direction** is 90.

21. Drag the **Walk_Bwd_Rifle_Ironsights** animation where **Speed** is 200 and **Direction** is -180 and 180.

    You should end up with a Blend Space that can be previewed by holding *Ctrl* and moving the mouse.

22. Now, on the **Asset Details** panel, set the **Weight Speed** variable to 5 to make the interpolation faster.

23. Save and close the Blend Space.

24. Now, let's update the animation Blueprint so that it uses the new Blend Space.

25. Go to **Content\Characters\Mannequins\Animations** and open **ABP_Manny**.

26. Next, go to the event graph and create a new float variable called `Direction`.

27. Add a new pin to the sequence and set the value of **Direction** with the result of the **Calculate Direction** function, which calculates the angle (-180 to 180) between the character's **velocity** and **rotation**:

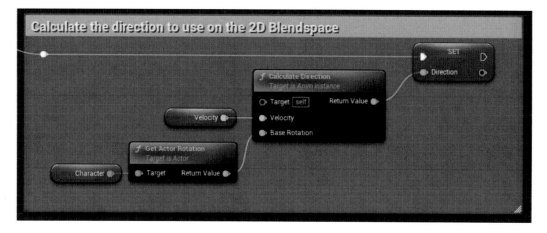

Figure 16.15 – Calculating the direction to use on the 2D Blend Space

28. In **AnimGraph**, find the **Control Rig** node and set **Alpha** to 0.0 to disable the automatic feet adjustment.

29. Go to the **Walk / Run** state inside the **Locomotion** state machine where the old 1D Blend Space is being used, as shown in the following screenshot:

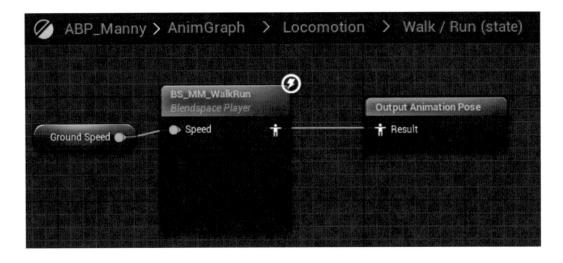

Figure 16.16 – The Walk / Run state in the AnimGraph

30. Replace that Blend Space with **BS_Movement** and use the **Direction** variable, like so:

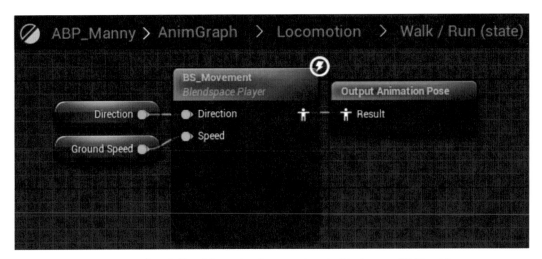

Figure 16.17 – The 1D Blend Space has been replaced with the new 2D Blend Space

31. Go to the Idle state inside the **Locomotion** state machine and change the animation to use **Idle_Rifle_Ironsights** instead.

32. Save and close the animation Blueprint. Now, you need to update the character.

33. Go to the **Content\ThirdPerson\Blueprints** folder and open **BP_ThirdPersonCharacter**.

34. On the **Details** panel for the character, set **Use Controller Rotation Yaw** to **true**, which will make the character's Yaw rotation always face the control rotation's Yaw.

35. Go to the character movement component and set **Max Walk Speed** to 200.

36. Set **Orient Rotation to Movement** to false, which will prevent the character from rotating toward the direction of the movement.

37. Select the Mesh component and on the **Details** panel, pick the **ABP_Manny** animation blueprint and the **SKM_Manny_Simple** skeletal mesh.

38. Save and close the character Blueprint.

If you play the game now with two clients and move the character, it will walk forward and backward, but it will also strafe, as shown in the following screenshot:

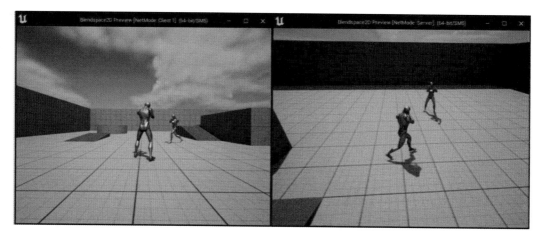

Figure 16.18 – Expected output on the Server and Client 1 windows

By completing this exercise, you have improved your understanding of how to create 2D Blend Spaces, how they work, and the advantages they provide compared to just using a regular 1D Blend Space.

In the next section, we will learn how to transform a character's bone so that we can rotate the torso of the player up and down based on the camera's pitch.

Transforming (modifying) bones

There is a very useful node that you can use in **AnimGraph** called the **Transform (Modify) Bone** node, which allows you to translate, rotate, and scale a bone of a skeleton at runtime.

You can add it to **AnimGraph** by *right-clicking* on an empty space, typing transform modify, and picking the node from the list. If you click on the **Transform (Modify) Bone** node, you'll have quite a few options on the **Details** panel.

Here's an explanation of what the most relevant options do:

- **Bone to Modify**: This option will tell the node what bone is going to be transformed.

  Slightly below that option, you have three sections representing each transform operation (**Translation**, **Rotation**, and **Scale**). In each section, you can do the following:

  - **Translation**, **Rotation**, **Scale**: This option will tell the node how much of that specific transform operation you want to apply. The final result will depend on the mode you have selected (covered in the next section).

  There are four ways you can set this value:

- Setting a constant value such as ($X=0.0, Y=0.0, Z=0.0$).

- Binding it to a function or a variable, by clicking on the drop-down on the right-hand side and picking one of the functions or variables available from the list.

- Using a dynamic value that can be set from a function, even if it's not exposed as a pin.

- Using a variable so that it can be changed at runtime. To enable this, you need to perform the following steps (this example is for **Rotation**, but the same concepts apply for **Translation** and **Scale**):

  I.   Click the dropdown to the right of the constant value and make sure that you select **Expose As Pin**. Once you do that, the text boxes for the constant value will disappear:

Figure 16.19 – Selecting Expose As Pin

  II. The **Transform (Modify) Bone** node will add an input so that you can plug in your variable:

Figure 16.20 – Variable used as an input on the Transform (Modify) Bone node

III.   Setting the mode

This will tell the node what to do with the value. You can pick from one of these three options:

- **Ignore**: Don't do anything with the supplied value.

- **Add to Existing**: Grab the current value of the bone and add the supplied value to it.

- **Replace Existing**: Replace the current value of the bone with the supplied value.

IV.   Setting the space

This will define the space where the node should apply the transform. You can pick from one of these four options:

- **World Space**: The transform will happen in the world space.

- **Component Space**: The transform will happen in the skeletal mesh component space.

- **Parent Bone Space**: The transform will happen in the parent bone's space of the selected bone.

- **Bone Space**: The transform will happen in the space of the selected bone.

V.   Alpha

This option allows you to control the amount of transform that you want to apply. As an example, if you have the `Alpha` value as a float, then you'll have the following behavior with different values:

- If `Alpha` is `0.0`, then no transform will be applied.

- If `Alpha` is `0.5`, then it will only apply half of the transform.

- If `Alpha` is `1.0`, then it will apply the entire transform.

In the next exercise, we will use the **Transform (Modify) Bone** node to enable the character from *Exercise 16.04 – creating a movement 2D Blend Space*, to look up and down based on the camera's rotation.

Exercise 16.05 – Creating a character that looks up and down

In this exercise, we're going to use the project from *Exercise 16.04 – Creating a movement 2D Blend Space*, and enable the character to look up and down based on the camera's rotation. To achieve this, we're going to use the **Transform (Modify) Bone** node to rotate the **spine_03** bone in the component space based on the pitch of the camera.

Follow these steps to complete this exercise:

1. First, you need to open the project from *Exercise 16.04 – Creating a movement 2D Blend Space*.

2. Go to **Content\Characters\Mannequins\Animations** and open **ABP_Manny**.

3. Go to **Event Graph** and create a float variable called **Pitch**.

4. Add a new pin to the sequence and set the value of **Pitch** with the subtraction (or delta) between the character's **rotation** and **base aim rotation**, as shown here:

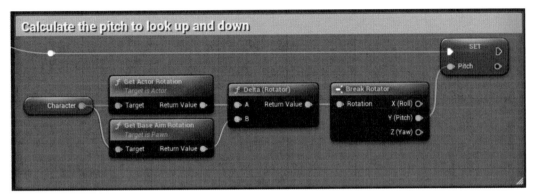

Figure 16.21 – Calculating the Pitch

This will allow you to get the value of **Pitch** from the rotator, which is the only part of the delta rotation that we are interested in.

> **Note**
>
> The **Break Rotator** node allows you to separate a **Rotator** variable into three float variables that represent **Pitch**, **Yaw**, and **Roll**. This is useful when you want to access the value of each component or if you only want to work with one or two components, and not with the whole rotation.

As an alternative to using the **Break Rotator** node, you can right-click on **Return Value** and pick **Split Struct Pin**. Take into consideration that the **Split Struct Pin** option will only appear if **Return Value** is not connected to anything. Once you do the split, it will create three separate wires for **Roll, Pitch**, and **Yaw,** just like a break but without the extra node.

You should end up with the following:

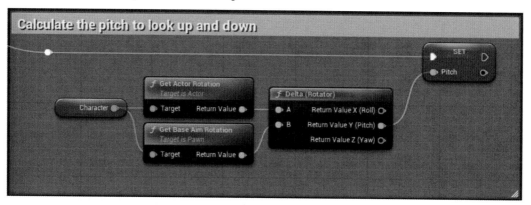

Figure 16.22 – Calculating the Pitch to look up using the Split Struct Pin option

This logic uses the rotation of the pawn and subtracts it from the camera's rotation to get the difference in **Pitch**, as shown in the following diagram:

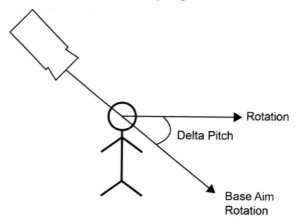

Figure 16.23 – How to calculate the delta Pitch

> **Note**
>
> You can double-click on a wire to create a reroute node, which allows you to bend the wire so that it doesn't overlap with other nodes, which makes the code easier to read.

5.   Next, go to **AnimGraph** and add a **Transform (Modify)** Bone node with the following settings:

Figure 16.24 – Settings for the Transform (Modify) Bone node

In the preceding screenshot, we've set **Bone to Modify** to **spine_03** because that is the bone that we want to rotate. We've also set **Rotation Mode** to **Add to Existing** because we want to keep the original rotation from the animation and add an offset to it. We can set the rest of the options to **Ignore** and remove **Expose As Pin** from the dropdown.

6. Connect the **Transform (Modify) Bone** node to **Control Rig** and the **Output Pose**, as shown in the following screenshot:

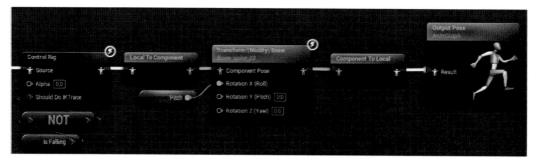

Figure 16.25 – The Transform (Modify) Bone node connected to Output Pose

In the preceding screenshot, you can see the **AnimGraph**, which will allow the character to look up and down by rotating the **spine_03** bone based on the camera's pitch. To connect the **Control Rig** node to the **Transform (Modify) Bone** node, we need to convert from local to component space. After the **Transform (Modify) Bone** node is executed we need to convert back to local space to be able to connect to the **Output Pose** node.

> **Note**
>
> We connect the **Pitch** variable to **Roll** because that bone in the skeleton is internally rotated that way. You can use **Split Struct Pin** on input parameters as well, so you don't have to add a **Make Rotator** node.

If you test the project with two clients and move the mouse up and down on one of the characters, you'll notice that it will pitch up and down, as shown in the following screenshot:

Figure 16.26 – Characters looking up and down, based on the camera rotation

By completing this final exercise, you should understand how to modify bones at runtime using the **Transform (Modify) Bone** node in an animation blueprint. This node can be used in various scenarios, so it may prove useful for you.

In the next activity, you're going to put everything you've learned to the test by creating the character we're going to use for our multiplayer FPS project.

Activity 16.01 – Creating the character for the multiplayer FPS project

In this activity, you'll create the character for the multiplayer FPS project that we're going to build in the next few chapters. The character will have a few different mechanics, but for this activity, you just need to create a character that walks, jumps, looks up/down, and has two replicated stats: health and armor.

Follow these steps to complete this activity:

1. Create a **Blank** project using **C++** called `MultiplayerFPS` without the starter content.

2. Import the skeletal mesh and the animations from the `Activity16.01\Assets` folder and place them in the **Content\Player\Mesh** and **Content\Player\Animations** folders, respectively.

3. Import the following sounds from the `Activity16.01\Assets` folder into `Content\Player\Sounds`:

   - `Jump.wav`: Play this sound on the `Jump_From_Stand_Ironsights` animation with a `Play Sound` anim notify.

   - `Footstep.wav`: Play this sound every time a foot is on the floor in every walk animation by using the `Play Sound` anim notify.

   - `Spawn.wav`: Use this on the `SpawnSound` variable in the character.

4. Set up the skeletal mesh by retargeting its bones and creating a socket called `Camera` that is a child of the head bone and has a `Relative Location` of (X=7.88, Y=4.73, Z=-10.00).

5. Create a 2D Blend Space in **Content\Player\Animations** called **BS_Movement** that uses the imported movement animations and a **Weight Speed** of 5.

6. Create the input actions using the knowledge you acquired in *Chapter 4, Getting Started with Player Input*:

   - **IA_Move (Axis 2D)**: W, S, A, D

   - **IA_Look (Axis 2D)**: Mouse X, Mouse Y

   - **IA_Jump (Digital)**: Spacebar

7. Add the new input actions to a new input mapping context called **IMC_Player**.

8. Create a C++ class called **FPSCharacter** that does the following:

   - Derives from the **Character** class.

   - Has a camera component attached to the skeletal mesh on the **Camera** socket and has **Pawn Control Rotation** set to **true**.

   - Has variables for **Health** and **Armor** that only replicate to the owner.

   - Has variables for **Max Health** and **Max Armor**.

   - Has a variable for `Armor Absorption`, which is the percentage of how much damage the armor absorbs.

   - Has a constructor that initializes the camera, disables ticking, and sets **Max Walk Speed** to 800 and **Jump Z Velocity** to 600.

   - On **BeginPlay**, plays the spawning sound and initializes **Health** with **Max Health** if it has authority.

   - Adds the input mapping context and binds the input actions.

   - Has functions to add/remove/set health. It also should have a function that returns where the character is dead or not.

   - Has functions to add/set/absorb armor. The armor absorption reduces the armor based on the `Armor Absorption` variable and changes the damage value based on the following formula:

   ```
   Damage = (Damage * (1 - ArmorAbsorption)) -
   FMath::Min(RemainingArmor, 0);
   ```

9. Create an animation Blueprint in `Content\Player\Animations` called `ABP_Player` that has a `State Machine` with the following states:

   - `Idle/Run`: Uses `BS_Movement` with the `Speed` and `Direction` variables.

   - `Jump`: Plays the jump animation and transitions from the `Idle/Run` states when the `Is Jumping` variable is `true`.

   - It also uses `Transform (Modify) Bone` to make the character look up and down based on the camera's pitch.

10. Create a UMG widget in `Content\UI` called `WBP_HUD` that displays the `Health` and `Armor` properties of the character in the `Health: 100` and `Armor: 100` formats using the knowledge you acquired in *Chapter 15, Exploring Collectibles, Power-Ups, and Pickups.*

11. Create a Blueprint in `Content\Player` called `BP_Player` that derives from `FPSCharacter`:

   - Set up the mesh component so that it has the following values:

     - **Skeletal Mesh**: `Content\Player\Mesh\SK_Mannequin`

     - **Animation Blueprint**: `Content\Player\Animations\ABP_Player`

     - **Location**: `(X=0.0, Y=0.0, Z=-88.0)`

     - **Rotation**: `(X=0.0, Y=0.0, Z=-90.0)`

     - **Move Input Action**: `Content\Player\Inputs\IA_Move`

     - **Look Input Action**: `Content\Player\Inputs\IA_Look`

     - **Jump Input Action**: `Content\Player\Inputs\IA_Jump`

     - On the `Begin Play` event, it needs to create a widget instance of `WBP_HUD` and add it to the viewport.

12. Create a Blueprint in **Content\Blueprints** called `BP_GameMode` that derives from **MultiplayerFPSGameModeBase**, which will use `BP_Player` as the **DefaultPawn** class.

13. Create a test map in **Content\Maps** called **DM-Test** and set it as the default map in **Project Settings**.

Expected output:

The result should be a project where each client will have a first-person character that can move, jump, and look around. These actions will also be replicated so that each client will be able to see what the other client's character is doing.

Each client will also have a HUD that displays the health and the armor values:

Figure 16.27 – Expected output

> **Note**
>
> The solution for this activity can be found on GitHub here: `https://github.com/PacktPublishing/Elevating-Game-Experiences-with-Unreal-Engine-5-Second-Edition/tree/main/Activity%20solutions`.

By completing this activity, you should have a good idea of how the server-client architecture, variable replication, roles, 2D Blend Spaces, and the **Transform (Modify) Bone** node work.

Summary

In this chapter, we learned about some critical multiplayer concepts, such as how the server-client architecture works, the responsibilities of the server and the client, how the listen server is quicker to set up than a dedicated server but not as lightweight, ownership and connections, roles, and variable replication.

We also learned about some useful techniques for animation, such as how to use 2D Blend Spaces, which allow you to have a two-axis grid to blend between animations, and the `Transform (Modify) Bone` node, which can modify the bones of a skeletal mesh at runtime. To finish off this chapter, we created a first-person multiplayer project where you have characters that can walk, look, and jump around. This will be the foundation of the multiplayer first-person shooter project that we will be working on for the next few chapters.

In the next chapter, we'll learn how to use RPCs, which allows clients and servers to execute functions on each other. We'll also cover how to use enumerations in the editor and how to use array index wrapping to iterate an array in both directions and loop around when you go beyond its limits.

17

Using Remote Procedure Calls

In the previous chapter, we covered some critical multiplayer concepts, including the server-client architecture, connections and ownership, roles, and variable replication. We also learned how to make 2D Blend Spaces and use the `Transform (Modify) Bone` node to modify bones at runtime. We used that knowledge to create a basic first-person shooter character that walks, jumps, and looks around.

In this chapter, we're going to cover **remote procedure calls** (**RPCs**), which is another important multiplayer concept that allows the server to execute functions on the clients and vice versa. So far, we've learned about variable replication as a form of communication between the server and the clients. However, to have proper communication, this isn't enough. This is because the server may need to execute specific logic on the clients that doesn't involve updating the value of a variable. The client also needs a way to tell its intentions to the server so that the server can validate the action and let the other clients know about it. This will ensure that the multiplayer world is synchronized between all of the connected clients. We'll also cover how to use enumerations and expose them to the editor, as well as array index wrapping, which allows you to iterate an array in both directions and loop around when you go beyond its limits.

In this chapter, we're going to cover the following main topics:

- Understanding remote procedure calls

- Exposing enumerations to the editor

- Using array index wrapping

By the end of this chapter, you'll understand how RPCs work to make the server and the clients execute logic on one another. You'll also be able to expose enumerations to the editor and use array index wrapping to cycle through arrays in both directions.

Technical requirements

For this chapter, you will need the following technical requirements:

- Unreal Engine 5 installed
- Visual Studio 2019 installed

The project for this chapter can be found in the `Chapter17` folder of the code bundle for this book, which can be downloaded here: `https://github.com/PacktPublishing/Elevating-Game-Experiences-with-Unreal-Engine-5-Second-Edition`.

In the next section, we will look at RPCs.

Understanding remote procedure calls

We covered variable replication in *Chapter 16, Getting Started with Multiplayer Basics*, and, while a very useful feature, it is a bit limited in terms of allowing custom code to be executed in remote game instances (client-to-server or server-to-client) for two main reasons:

- The first reason is that variable replication is strictly a form of server-to-client communication, so there isn't a way for a client to use variable replication to tell the server to execute some custom logic by changing the value of a variable.
- The second reason is that variable replication, as the name suggests, is driven by the values of variables, so even if variable replication allowed client-to-server communication, it would require you to change the value of a variable on the client to trigger a `RepNotify` function on the server to run the custom logic, which is not very practical.

To solve this problem, Unreal Engine supports RPCs, which work just like normal functions that can be defined and called. However, instead of executing them locally, they will be executed on a remote game instance, without being tied to a variable. To be able to use RPCs, make sure you are defining them in an actor that has a valid connection and replication turned on.

There are three types of RPCs, and each one serves a different purpose:

- Server RPC
- Multicast RPC
- Client RPC

Let's look at these three types in detail and explain when to use them.

Server RPC

You use a Server RPC every time you want the server to run a function on the actor that has defined the RPC. There are two main reasons why you would want to do this:

- The first reason is security. When making multiplayer games, especially competitive ones, you always have to assume that the client will try to cheat. The way to make sure there is no cheating is by forcing the client to go through the server to execute the functions that are critical to gameplay.

- The second reason is synchronicity. Since the critical gameplay logic is only executed on the server, the important variables are only going to be changed there, which will automatically trigger the variable replication logic to update the clients whenever they are changed.

An example of this would be when a client's character tries to fire a weapon. Since there's always the possibility that the client may try to cheat, you can't just execute the fire weapon logic locally. The correct way of doing this is by having the client call a Server RPC that tells the server to validate the `Fire` action by making sure the character has enough ammo, has the weapon equipped, and so on. If everything checks out, then it will deduct the ammo variable, and finally, it will execute a Multicast RPC (covered shortly) that will tell all of the clients to play the fire animation on that character.

Declaration

To declare a Server RPC, you can use the `Server` specifier on the `UFUNCTION` macro. Have a look at the following example:

```
UFUNCTION(Server, Reliable, WithValidation)
void ServerRPCFunction(int32 IntegerParameter, float
FloatParameter, AActor* ActorParameter);
```

In the preceding code snippet, the `Server` specifier is used on the `UFUNCTION` macro to state that the function is a Server RPC. You can have parameters on a Server RPC just like a normal function, but with some caveats that will be explained later in this topic, as well as the purpose of the `Reliable` and `WithValidation` specifiers.

Execution

To execute a Server RPC, you call it from a client on the actor instance that defined it. Take a look at the following example:

```
void ARPCTest::CallMyOwnServerRPC(int32 IntegerParameter)
{
    ServerMyOwnRPC(IntegerParameter);
}
```

The preceding code snippet implements the `CallMyOwnServerRPC` function, which calls the `ServerMyOwnRPC` RPC function, defined in its own `ARPCTest` class, with an integer parameter. This will execute the implementation of the `ServerMyOwnRPC` function on the server version of that actor's instance. We can also call a Server RPC from another actor's instance, like so:

```
void ARPCTest::CallServerRPCOfAnotherActor(AAnotherActor*
OtherActor)
{
   if(OtherActor != nullptr)
   {
      OtherActor->ServerAnotherActorRPC();
   }
}
```

The preceding code snippet implements the `CallServerRPCOfAnotherActor` function, which calls the `ServerAnotherActorRPC` RPC function, defined in `AAnotherActor`, on the `OtherActor` instance, so long as it's valid. This will execute the implementation of the `ServerAnotherActorRPC` function on the server version of the `OtherActor` instance.

Multicast RPC

You use a Multicast RPC when you want the server to instruct all of the clients to run a function on the actor that has defined the RPC.

An example of this is when a client's character tries to fire a weapon. After the client calls the Server RPC to ask permission to fire the weapon and the server has validated the request (the ammo has been deducted and the line trace/projectile was processed), we need to do a Multicast RPC so that all of the instances of that specific character play the fire animation.

Declaration

To declare a Multicast RPC, you need to use the `NetMulticast` specifier on the `UFUNCTION` macro. Have a look at the following example:

```
UFUNCTION(NetMulticast, Unreliable)
void MulticastRPCFunction(int32 IntegerParameter, float
FloatParameter, AActor* ActorParameter);
```

In the preceding code snippet, the `NetMulticast` specifier is used on the `UFUNCTION` macro to say that the function is a Multicast RPC. You can have parameters on a Multicast RPC just like a normal function, but with the same caveats as the Server RPC. The `Unreliable` specifier will be explained later in this topic.

Execution

To execute a Multicast RPC, you must call it from the server on the actor instance that defined it. Take a look at the following example:

```
void ARPCTest::CallMyOwnMulticastRPC(int32 IntegerParameter)
{
    MulticastMyOwnRPC(IntegerParameter);
}
```

The preceding code snippet implements the `CallMyOwnMulticastRPC` function, which calls the `MulticastMyOwnRPC` RPC function, defined in its own `ARPCTest` class, with an integer parameter. This will execute the implementation of the `MulticastMyOwnRPC` function on all of the clients' versions of that actor's instance. We can also call a Multicast RPC from another actor's instance, like so:

```
void ARPCTest::CallMulticastRPCOfAnotherActor(AAnotherActor*
OtherActor)
{
    if(OtherActor != nullptr)
    {
        OtherActor->MulticastAnotherActorRPC();
    }
}
```

The preceding code snippet implements the `CallMulticastRPCOfAnotherActor` function, which calls the `MulticastAnotherActorRPC` RPC function, defined in `AAnotherActor`, on the `OtherActor` instance, so long as it's valid. This will execute the implementation of the `MulticastAnotherActorRPC` function on all of the clients' versions of the `OtherActor` instance.

Client RPC

You use a Client RPC when you want the server to instruct only the owning client to run a function on the actor that has defined the RPC. To set the owning client, you need to call `SetOwner` on the server and set it with the client's player controller.

An example of this would be when a character is hit by a projectile and plays a pain sound that only that client will hear. By calling a Client RPC from the server, the sound will only be played on the owning client and not on the other clients.

Declaration

To declare a Client RPC, you need to use the `Client` specifier on the UFUNCTION macro. Have a look at the following example:

```
UFUNCTION(Client, Unreliable)
void ClientRPCFunction(int32 IntegerParameter, float
FloatParameter, Aactor* ActorParameter);
```

In the preceding code snippet, the `Client` specifier is being used on the UFUNCTION macro to say that the function is a Client RPC. You can have parameters on a Client RPC just like a normal function, but with the same caveats as the Server RPC and the Multicast RPC. The `Unreliable` specifier will be explained later in this topic.

Execution

To execute a Client RPC, you must call it from the server on the actor instance that defined it. Take a look at the following example:

```
void ARPCTest::CallMyOwnClientRPC(int32 IntegerParameter)
{
    ClientMyOwnRPC(IntegerParameter);
}
```

The preceding code snippet implements the `CallMyOwnClientRPC` function, which calls the `ClientMyOwnRPC` RPC function, defined in its own `ARPCTest` class, with an integer parameter. This will execute the implementation of the `ClientMyOwnRPC` function on the owning client's version of that actor's instance. We can also call a Client RPC from another actor's instance, like so:

```
void ARPCTest::CallClientRPCOfAnotherActor(AAnotherActor*
OtherActor)
{
    if(OtherActor != nullptr)
    {
        OtherActor->ClientAnotherActorRPC();
    }
}
```

The preceding code snippet implements the `CallClientRPCOfAnotherActor` function, which calls the `ClientAnotherActorRPC` RPC function, defined in `AAnotherActor`, on the `OtherActor` instance, so long as it's valid. This will execute the implementation of the `ClientAnotherActorRPC` function on the owning client's version of the `OtherActor` instance.

Important considerations when using RPCs

RPCs are very useful, but there are a couple of things that you need to take into consideration when using them.

Implementation

The implementation of an RPC differs slightly from that of a typical function. Instead of implementing the function as you normally do, you should only implement the `_Implementation` version of it, even though you didn't declare it in the header file. Have a look at the following examples.

Server RPC:

```
void ARPCTest::ServerRPCTest_Implementation(int32
IntegerParameter, float FloatParameter, AActor* ActorParameter)
{
}
```

In the preceding code snippet, we implemented the `_Implementation` version of the `ServerRPCTest` function, which uses three parameters.

Multicast RPC:

```
void ARPCTest::MulticastRPCTest_Implementation(int32
IntegerParameter, float FloatParameter, AActor* ActorParameter)
{
}
```

In the preceding code snippet, we implemented the `_Implementation` version of the `MulticastRPCTest` function, which uses three parameters.

Client RPC:

```
void ARPCTest::ClientRPCTest_Implementation(int32
IntegerParameter, float FloatParameter, AActor* ActorParameter)
{
}
```

In the preceding code snippet, we implemented the `_Implementation` version of the `ClientRPCTest` function, which uses three parameters.

As you can see from the previous examples, independent of the type of the RPC you are implementing, you should only implement the `_Implementation` version of the function and not the normal one, as demonstrated in the following code snippet:

```
void ARPCTest::ServerRPCFunction(int32 IntegerParameter, float
FloatParameter, AActor* ActorParameter)
{
}
```

In the preceding code, we're defining the normal implementation of `ServerRPCFunction`. If you implement the RPC like this, you'll get an error saying that it was already implemented. The reason for this is that when you declare the RPC function in the header file, Unreal Engine will automatically create the normal implementation internally, which once called, will execute the logic to send the RPC request through the network and when it reaches the remote computer it will call the `_Implementation` version there. Since you cannot have two implementations of the same function, it will throw a compilation error. To fix this, just make sure that you only implement the `_Implementation` version of the RPC.

Next, we will look at name prefixes.

Name prefixes

In Unreal Engine, it's good practice to prefix RPCs with their corresponding types. Have a look at the following examples:

- A **Server RPC** called `RPCFunction` should be named `ServerRPCFunction`
- A **Multicast RPC** called `RPCFunction` should be named `MulticastRPCFunction`
- A **Client RPC** called `RPCFunction` should be named `ClientRPCFunction`

Return value

Since the execution of RPCs is typically executed on different machines asynchronously, you can't have a return value, so it always needs to be void.

Overriding

You can override the implementation of an RPC to expand or bypass the parent's functionality by declaring and implementing the `_Implementation` function in the child class without the `UFUNCTION` macro. Let's look at an example.

The following is the declaration of the parent class:

```
UFUNCTION(Server, Reliable)
void ServerRPCTest(int32 IntegerParameter);
```

In the preceding code snippet, we have the declaration of the `ServerRPCTest` function in the parent class, which uses one integer parameter.

If we want to override the function on the child class, we would need to use the following declaration:

```
virtual void ServerRPCTest_Implementation(int32
IntegerParameter) override;
```

In the preceding code snippet, we have overridden the declaration of the `ServerRPCTest_Implementation` function in the child class header file. The implementation of the function is just like any other override, with the possibility of calling `Super::ServerRPCTest_Implementation` if you still want to execute the parent functionality.

Valid connection

For an actor to be able to execute its RPCs, they need to have a valid connection. If you try to call an RPC on an actor that doesn't have a valid connection, then nothing will happen on the remote instance. You must make sure that the actor is either a player controller, is being possessed by one (if applicable), or that its owning actor has a valid connection.

Supported parameter types

When using RPCs, you can add parameters just like any other function. At the time of writing, most common types are supported (such as `bool`, `int32`, `float`, `FText`, `FString`, `FName`, `TArray`, and so on), but not all of them, such as `TSet` and `TMap`. Among the types that are supported, the ones that you have to pay more attention to are the pointers to any `UObject` class or subclass, especially actors.

If you create an RPC with an actor parameter, then that actor also needs to exist on the remote game instance; otherwise, it will have a value of `nullptr`. Another important thing to take into account is that the instance name of each version of the actor can be different. This means that if you call an RPC with an actor parameter, then the instance name of the actor when calling the RPC might be different than the one when executing the RPC on the remote instance. Here is an example to help you understand this:

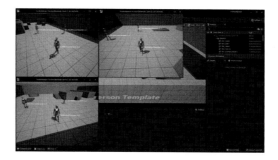

Figure 17.1 – Displaying the name of the character instances in three clients

In the preceding example, you can see three clients running (one of them is a listen server) and each window is displaying the name of all of the character instances. If you look at the **Client 1** window, its controlled character instance is called BP_ThirdPersonCharacter_C_0, but on the **Server** window, that equivalent character is called BP_ThirdPersonCharacter_C_1. This means that if **Client 1** calls a Server RPC and passes its BP_ThirdPersonCharacter_C_0 as an argument, then when the RPC is executed on the server, the parameter will be BP_ThirdPersonCharacter_C_1, which is the instance name of the equivalent character in that game instance.

Executing RPCs on the target machine

You can call RPCs directly on their target machine and they will still execute. In other words, you can call a Server RPC on the server and it will execute, as well as a Multicast/Client RPC on the client, but in the latter case, it will only execute the logic on the client that called the RPC. Either way, in these cases, you can call the _Implementation version directly instead, to execute the logic faster.

The reason for this is that the _Implementation version just holds the logic to execute and doesn't have the overhead of creating and sending the RPC request through the network that the regular call has.

Have a look at the following example of an actor that has authority on the server:

```
void ARPCTest::CallServerRPC(int32 IntegerParameter)
{
  if(HasAuthority())
  {
    ServerRPCFunction_Implementation(IntegerParameter);
  }
  else ServerRPCFunction(IntegerParameter);
}
```

In the preceding example, you have the `CallServerRPC` function, which calls `ServerRPCFunction` in two different ways. If the actor is already on the server, then it calls `ServerRPCFunction_Implementation`, which will skip the overhead, as mentioned previously.

If the actor is not on the server, then it executes the regular call by using `ServerRPCFunction`, which adds the required overhead for creating and sending the RPC request through the network.

Validation

When you define an RPC, you have the option of using an additional function to check whether there are any invalid inputs before the RPC is called. This is used to avoid processing the RPC if the inputs are invalid due to cheating or for some other reason.

To use validation, you need to add the `WithValidation` specifier to the `UFUNCTION` macro. When you use that specifier, you will be forced to implement the `_Validate` version of the function, which will return a Boolean stating whether the RPC can be executed.

Have a look at the following example:

```
UFUNCTION(Server, Reliable, WithValidation)
void ServerSetHealth(float NewHealth);
```

In the preceding code snippet, we've declared a validated Server RPC called `ServerSetHealth`, which takes a float parameter for the new value of `Health`. Take a look at its implementation:

```
bool ARPCTest::ServerSetHealth_Validate(float NewHealth)
{
    return NewHealth >= 0.0f && NewHealth <= MaxHealth;
}
void ARPCTest::ServerSetHealth_Implementation(float NewHealth)
{
    Health = NewHealth;
}
```

In the preceding code snippet, we implemented the `_Validate` function, which will check whether the new health is within 0 and the maximum value of the health. If a client tries to hack and call `ServerSetHealth` with `200` and `MaxHealth` is `100`, then the RPC won't be called, which prevents the client from changing the health with values outside a certain range. If the `_Validate` function returns `true`, the `_Implementation` function is called as usual, which sets `Health` with the value of `NewHealth`.

Reliability

When you declare an RPC, you are required to either use the `Reliable` or `Unreliable` specifier in the `UFUNCTION` macro. Here's a quick overview of what they do:

- `Reliable`: This is used when you want to make sure the RPC is executed, by repeating the request until the remote machine confirms its reception. This should only be used for RPCs that are very important, such as executing critical gameplay logic. Here is an example of how to use it:

    ```
    UFUNCTION(Server, Reliable)
    void ServerReliableRPCFunction(int32 IntegerParameter);
    ```

- `Unreliable`: This is used when you don't care whether the RPC is executed due to bad network conditions, such as playing a sound or spawning a particle effect. This should only be used for RPCs that aren't very important or are called very frequently to update values since it wouldn't matter if a couple didn't get through. Here is an example of how to use it:

    ```
    UFUNCTION(Server, Unreliable)
    void ServerUnreliableRPCFunction(int32 IntegerParameter);
    ```

> **Note**
>
> For more information on RPCs, please visit `https://docs.unrealengine.com/en-US/Gameplay/Networking/Actors/RPCs/index.html`.

In the following exercise, you will learn how to implement the different types of RPCs.

Exercise 17.01 – Using remote procedure calls

In this exercise, we're going to create a **C++** project that uses the **Third Person** template and we're going to expand it in the following way:

- Add a new `Ammo` integer variable that defaults to 5 and replicates to all of the clients.

- Add a fire animation that plays a fire sound and also create a **Fire Anim Montage** that is played when the server tells the client that the request to fire was valid.

- Add a **No Ammo Sound** that will play when the server tells the client that they didn't have sufficient ammo.

- Every time the player presses the left mouse button, the client will perform a reliable and validated Server RPC that will check whether the character has sufficient ammo. If it does, it will subtract 1 from the Ammo variable and call an unreliable Multicast RPC that plays the fire animation in every client. If it doesn't have ammo, then it will execute an unreliable Client RPC that will play No Ammo Sound that will only be heard by the owning client.

- Schedule a timer that will prevent the client from spamming the fire button for 1.5 s after playing the fire animation.

Follow these steps to complete this exercise:

1. Create a new **Third Person** template project using **C++** called RPC and save it to a location of your liking.

2. Once the project has been created, it should open the editor as well as the Visual Studio solution.

3. Close the editor and go back to Visual Studio.

4. Open RPCCharacter.h and declare the protected FireTimer variable, which will be used to prevent the client from spamming the Fire action:

```
FTimerHandle FireTimer;
```

5. Declare the protected replicated Ammo variable, which starts with 5 shots:

```
UPROPERTY(Replicated)
int32 Ammo = 5;
```

6. Next, declare the protected animation montage variable that will be played when the character fires:

```
UPROPERTY(EditDefaultsOnly, Category = "RPC Character")
UAnimMontage* FireAnimMontage;
```

7. Declare the protected sound variable that will be played when the character has no ammo:

```
UPROPERTY(EditDefaultsOnly, Category = "RPC Character")
USoundBase* NoAmmoSound;
```

8. Override the Tick function:

```
virtual void Tick(float DeltaSeconds) override;
```

9. Declare the reliable and validated Server RPC for firing:

```
UFUNCTION(Server, Reliable, WithValidation, Category =
"RPC Character")
void ServerFire();
```

10. Declare the unreliable Multicast RPC that will play the fire animation on all of the clients:

```
UFUNCTION(NetMulticast, Unreliable, Category = "RPC
Character")
void MulticastFire();
```

11. Declare the unreliable Client RPC that will play a sound only in the owning client:

```
UFUNCTION(Client, Unreliable, Category = "RPC Character")
void ClientPlaySound2D(USoundBase* Sound);
```

12. Now, open the RPCCharacter.cpp file and include GameplayStatics.h for the PlaySound2D function and the UnrealNetwork.h so we can use the DOREPLIFETIME_CONDITION macro:

```
#include "Kismet/GameplayStatics.h""
#include "Net/UnrealNetwork.h"
```

13. At the end of the constructor, enable the Tick function:

```
PrimaryActorTick.bCanEverTick = true;
```

14. Implement the GetLifetimeReplicatedProps function so that the Ammo variable will replicate to all of the clients:

```
void ARPCCharacter::GetLifetimeReplicatedProps(TArray<
    FLifetimeProperty >& OutLifetimeProps) const
{
    Super::GetLifetimeReplicatedProps(OutLifetimeProps);

    DOREPLIFETIME(ARPCCharacter, Ammo);
}
```

15. Next, implement the Tick function, which displays the value of the Ammo variable:

```
void ARPCCharacter::Tick(float DeltaSeconds)
{
    Super::Tick(DeltaSeconds);
    const FString AmmoString =
    FString::Printf(TEXT("Ammo = %d"), Ammo);
    DrawDebugString(GetWorld(), GetActorLocation(),
    AmmoString, nullptr, FColor::White, 0.0f, true);
}
```

16. At the end of the `SetupPlayerInputController` function, bind the `Fire` action to the `ServerFire` function:

```
PlayerInputComponent->BindAction("Fire", IE_Pressed,
this, &ARPCCharacter::ServerFire);
```

17. Implement the fire Server RPC validation function:

```
bool ARPCCharacter::ServerFire_Validate()
{
    return true;
}
```

18. Implement the fire Server RPC implementation function:

```
void ARPCCharacter::ServerFire_Implementation()
{

}
```

19. Now, add the logic to abort the function if the fire timer is still active since we fired the last shot:

```
if (GetWorldTimerManager().IsTimerActive(FireTimer))
{
    return;
}
```

20. Check whether the character has ammo. If it doesn't, then play NoAmmoSound only in the client that controls the character and abort the function:

```
if (Ammo == 0)
{
    ClientPlaySound2D(NoAmmoSound);
    return;
}
```

21. Deduct the ammo and schedule the `FireTimer` variable to prevent this function from being spammed while playing the fire animation:

```
Ammo--;
GetWorldTimerManager().SetTimer(FireTimer, 1.5f, false);
```

22. Call the fire Multicast RPC to make all the clients play the fire animation:

```
MulticastFire();
```

23. Implement the fire Multicast RPC, which will play the fire animation montage:

```
void ARPCCharacter::MulticastFire_Implementation()
{
    if (FireAnimMontage != nullptr)
    {
        PlayAnimMontage(FireAnimMontage);
    }
}
```

24. Implement the Client RPC that plays a 2D sound:

```
void ARPCCharacter::ClientPlaySound2D_
Implementation(USoundBase* Sound)
{
    UGameplayStatics::PlaySound2D(GetWorld(), Sound);
}
```

Finally, you can launch the project in the editor.

25. Compile the code and wait for the editor to fully load.

26. Go to **Project Settings**, go to **Engine**, then **Input**, and add the **Fire** action binding:

Figure 17.2 – Adding the new Fire action binding

27. Close **Project Settings**.

28. In the **Content Browser** area, go to the Content folder, create a new folder called Audio, and open it.

29. Click the **Import** button go to the Exercise17.01\Assets folder, and import NoAmmo.wav and Fire.wav.

30. Save both files.

31. Go to the `Content\Characters\Mannequins\Animations` folder.

32. Click the **Import** button, go to the `Exercise17.01\Assets` folder, and import the `ThirdPersonFire.fbx` file. Make sure it's using the `SK_Mannequin` skeleton and click **Import**.

33. Open the new animation and put a `Play Sound` anim notify at `0.3` seconds using the `Fire` sound.

34. On the **Details** panel, find the **Enable Root Motion** option and set it to **true**. This will prevent the character from moving when playing the animation.

35. Save and close `ThirdPersonFire`.

36. *Right-click* on `ThirdPersonFire` and pick **Create | Create AnimMontage**.

37. The `Animations` folder should look like this:

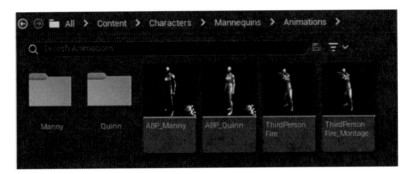

Figure 17.3 – The Animations folder for the Mannequin

38. Open `ABP_Manny` and go to `AnimGraph`.

39. Find the `Control Rig` node and set `Alpha` to `0.0` to disable the automatic feet adjustment. You should get the following output:

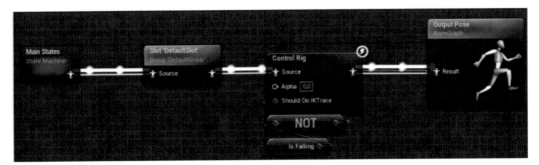

Figure 17.4 – Disabling the feet adjustment

40. Save and close `ABP_Manny`.

41. Open `SK_Mannequin` in the `Content\Characters\Mannequins\Meshes` folder and retarget (as shown in *Exercise 16.04*) the `root` and `pelvis` bones so that they use `Animation`. The remaining bones should use `Skeleton`.

42. Save and close `SK_Mannequin`.

43. Go to `Content\ThirdPerson\Blueprints` and open the `BP_ThirdPersonCharacter` blueprint.

44. In `Class Defaults`, set `No Ammo Sound` to use `NoAmmo`, and set `Fire Anim Montage` to use `ThirdPersonFire_Montage`.

45. Save and close `BP_ThirdPersonCharacter`.

46. Go to **Multiplayer Options** and set **Net Mode** to **Play As Listen Server** and **Number of Players** to 2.

47. Set the window size to `800x600` and play using **New Editor Window (PIE)**.

    You should get the following output:

Figure 17.5 – The result of this exercise

By completing this exercise, you can play on each client. Every time you press the left mouse button, the character of the client will play the **Fire Anim montage**, which all clients will be able to see, and its ammo will reduce by 1. If you try to fire when the ammo is 0, that client will hear `No Ammo Sound` and won't do the fire animation, because the server didn't call the Multicast RPC. If you try to spam the fire button, you'll notice that it will only trigger a new fire once the animation has finished.

In this section, you learned how to use all of the different types of RPCs and their caveats. In the next section, we will look at enumerations and how to expose them to the editor.

Exposing enumerations to the editor

An enumeration is a user-defined data type that holds a list of integer constants, where each item has a human-friendly name assigned by you, which makes the code easier to read. As an example, if we wanted to represent the different states that a character can be in, we could use an integer variable where 0 means it's idle, 1 means it's walking, and so on. The problem with this approach is that when you see code such as `if(State == 0)`, it's hard to remember what 0 means unless you are using some type of documentation or comments to help you. To fix this problem, you should use enumerations, where you can write code such as `if(State == EState::Idle)`, which is much more explicit and easier to understand.

In C++, you have two types of enums – the older raw enums and the new enum classes, which were introduced in C++11. If you want to use the new enum classes in the editor, your first instinct might be to do it in the typical way, which is by declaring a variable or a function that uses the enumeration with UPROPERTY or UFUNCTION, respectively.

The problem is, if you try to do that, you'll get a compilation error. Take a look at the following example:

```
enum class ETestEnum : uint8
{
    EnumValue1,
    EnumValue2,
    EnumValue3
};
```

In the preceding code snippet, we've declared an enum class called ETestEnum that has three possible values – EnumValue1, EnumValue2, and EnumValue3.

After that, try either of the following examples inside a class:

```
UPROPERTY(EditDefaultsOnly, BlueprintReadOnly, Category = "Test")
ETestEnum TestEnum;

UFUNCTION(BlueprintCallable, Category = "Test")
void SetTestEnum(ETestEnum NewTestEnum) { TestEnum = NewTestEnum; }
```

In the preceding code snippet, we declared a UPROPERTY variable and a UFUNCTION function that uses the ETestEnum enumeration. If you try to compile, you'll get the following compilation error:

```
error : Unrecognized type 'ETestEnum' - type must be a UCLASS, USTRUCT or UENUM
```

> **Note**
>
> In Unreal Engine, it's good practice to prefix the name of an enumeration with the letter E. For example, you could have `EWeaponType` and `EAmmoType`.

This error happens because when you try to expose a class, struct, or enumeration to the editor with the `UPROPERTY` or `UFUNCTION` macro, you need to add it to the Unreal Engine Reflection System by using the `UCLASS`, `USTRUCT`, and `UENUM` macros, respectively.

> **Note**
>
> You can learn more about the Unreal Engine Reflection System at `https://www.unrealengine.com/en-US/blog/unreal-property-system-reflection`.

With that knowledge in mind, it is simple to fix the previous error. Just do the following:

```
UENUM()
enum class ETestEnum : uint8
{
    EnumValue1,
    EnumValue2,
    EnumValue3
};
```

In the next section, we will look at the `TEnumAsByte` type.

TEnumAsByte

If you want to expose a variable to the engine that uses a raw enum, then you need to use the `TEnumAsByte` type. If you declare a `UPROPERTY` variable using a raw enum (not enum classes), you'll get a compilation error.

Have a look at the following example:

```
UENUM()
enum ETestRawEnum
{
    EnumValue1,
    EnumValue2,
    EnumValue3
};
```

Let's say you declare a UPROPERTY variable using ETestRawEnum, like so:

```
UPROPERTY(EditDefaultsOnly, BlueprintReadOnly, Category =
"Test")
ETestRawEnum TestRawEnum;
```

You'll get the following compilation error:

error : You cannot use the raw enum name as a type for member variables, instead use TEnumAsByte or a C++11 enum class with an explicit underlying type.

To fix this error, you need to surround the enum type of the variable, which in this case is ETestRawEnum, with TEnumAsByte<>, like so:

```
UPROPERTY(EditDefaultsOnly, BlueprintReadOnly, Category =
"Test")
TEnumAsByte<ETestRawEnum> TestRawEnum;
```

In the next section, we will look at the UMETA macro.

UMETA

When you use the UENUM macro to add an enumeration to the Unreal Engine Reflection System, you can use the UMETA macro on each value of the enum. The UMETA macro, just like with other macros, such as UPROPERTY or UFUNCTION, can use specifiers that will inform Unreal Engine of how to handle that value. Let's look at the most commonly used UMETA specifiers.

DisplayName

This specifier allows you to define a new name that is easier to read for the enum value when it's displayed in the editor.

Take a look at the following example:

```
UENUM()
enum class ETestEnum : uint8
{
   EnumValue1 UMETA(DisplayName = "My First Option"),
   EnumValue2 UMETA(DisplayName = "My Second Option"),
   EnumValue3 UMETA(DisplayName = "My Third Option")
};
```

Let's declare the following variable:

```
UPROPERTY(EditDefaultsOnly, BlueprintReadOnly, Category =
"Test")
ETestEnum TestEnum;
```

When you open the editor and look at the `TestEnum` variable, you will see a dropdown where `EnumValue1`, `EnumValue2`, and `EnumValue3` have been replaced with `My First Option`, `My Second Option`, and `My Third Option`, respectively.

Hidden

This specifier allows you to hide a specific enum value from the dropdown. This is typically used when there is an enum value that you only want to be able to use in C++ and not in the editor.

Take a look at the following example:

```
UENUM()
enum class ETestEnum : uint8
{
   EnumValue1 UMETA(DisplayName = "My First Option"),
   EnumValue2 UMETA(Hidden),
   EnumValue3 UMETA(DisplayName = "My Third Option")
};
```

Let's declare the following variable:

```
UPROPERTY(EditDefaultsOnly, BlueprintReadOnly, Category =
"Test")
ETestEnum TestEnum;
```

When you open the editor and look at the `TestEnum` variable, you will see a dropdown. You should notice that `My Second Option` doesn't appear in the dropdown and therefore can't be selected.

> **Note**
> For more information on all of the UMETA specifiers, visit `https://docs.unrealengine.com/en-US/Programming/UnrealArchitecture/Reference/Metadata/#enummetadataspecifiers`.

In the next section, we will look at the `BlueprintType` specifier for the UENUM macro.

BlueprintType

This UENUM specifier will expose the enumeration to blueprints. This means that there will be an entry for that enumeration in the dropdown that is used when making new variables or inputs/outputs for a function, as shown in the following example:

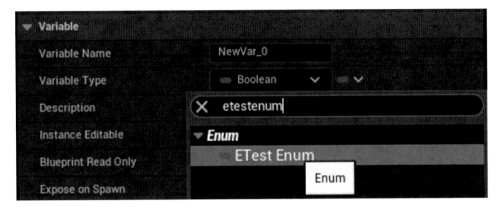

Figure 17.6 – Setting a variable to use the ETestEnum variable type

It will also create additional functions that you can call on the enumeration in the editor, as shown in the following example:

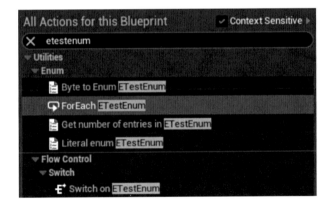

Figure 17.7 – List of additional functions available when using BlueprintType

MAX

When using enumerations, it's common to want to know how many values it has. In Unreal Engine, the standard way of doing this is by adding MAX as the last value, which will be automatically hidden in the editor.

Take a look at the following example:

```
UENUM()
enum class ETestEnum : uint8
{
   EnumValue1,
   EnumValue2,
   EnumValue3,
   MAX
};
```

If you want to know how many values ETestEnum has in C++, you just need to do the following:

```
const int32 MaxCount = static_cast<int32>(ETestEnum::MAX);
```

This works because enumerations in C++ are internally stored as numbers, where the first value is 0, the second is 1, and so on. This means that so long as MAX is the last value, it will always have the total number of values in the enumeration. An important thing to take into consideration is that for MAX to give you the correct value, you cannot change the internal numbering order of the enumeration, like so:

```
UENUM()
enum class ETestEnum : uint8
{
   EnumValue1 = 4,
   EnumValue2 = 78,
   EnumValue3 = 100,
   MAX
};
```

In this case, MAX will be 101 because it will use the number immediately next to the previous value, which is EnumValue3 = 100.

Using MAX is only meant to be used in C++ and not in the editor because the MAX value is hidden in blueprints, as mentioned previously. To get the number of entries of an enumeration in blueprints, you should use the BlueprintType specifier in the UENUM macro to expose some useful functions on the context menu. After that, you just need to type the name of your enumeration in the context menu. If you select the **Get number of entries in ETestEnum** option, you will have a function that returns the number of entries of that enumeration.

In the next exercise, you will be using C++ enumerations in the editor.

Exercise 17.02 – Using C++ enumerations in the editor

In this exercise, we're going to create a new **C++** project that uses the **Third Person** template. We're going to add the following:

- An enumeration called EWeaponType that contains **three** weapons – a pistol, a shotgun, and a rocket launcher.

- An enumeration called EAmmoType that contains **3** ammo types – bullets, shells, and rockets.

- A variable called Weapon that uses EWeaponType to tell the type of the current weapon.

- An integer array variable called Ammo that holds the amount of ammo for each type, which is initialized with a value of 10.

- When the player presses the 1, 2, or 3 key, the Weapon variable will be set to Pistol, Shotgun, or Rocket Launcher, respectively.

- When the player presses the left mouse button, the ammo for the current weapon will be consumed.

- With every Tick function call, the character will display the current weapon type and the equivalent ammo type and amount.

Follow these steps to complete this exercise:

1. Create a new **Third Person** template project using **C++** called Enumerations and save it to a location of your liking.

   Once the project has been created, it should open the editor as well as the Visual Studio solution.

2. Close the editor and go back to Visual Studio.

3. Open the Enumerations.h file.

4. Create a macro called ENUM_TO_INT32 that will convert an enumeration into an int32 data type:

   ```
   #define ENUM_TO_INT32(Value) static_cast<int32>(Value)
   ```

5. Create a macro called ENUM_TO_FSTRING that will get the display name for a value of an enum data type and convert it into an FString datatype:

   ```
   #define ENUM_TO_FSTRING(Enum, Value)
   FindObject<UEnum>(ANY_PACKAGE, TEXT(Enum), true)-
   >GetDisplayNameTextByIndex(ENUM_TO_INT32(Value)).
   ToString()
   ```

6. Declare the EWeaponType and EammoType enumerations:

```
UENUM(BlueprintType)
enum class EWeaponType : uint8
{
    Pistol UMETA(Display Name = "Glock 19"),
    Shotgun UMETA(Display Name = "Winchester M1897"),
    RocketLauncher UMETA(Display Name = "RPG"),
    MAX
};


UENUM(BlueprintType)
enum class EAmmoType : uint8
{
    Bullets UMETA(DisplayName = "9mm Bullets"),
    Shells UMETA(Display Name = "12 Gauge Shotgun
    Shells"),
    Rockets UMETA(Display Name = "RPG Rockets"),
    MAX
};
```

7. Open the EnumerationsCharacter.h file and add the Enumerations.h header before EnumerationsCharacter.generated.h:

```
#include "Enumerations.h"
```

8. Declare the protected Weapon variable that holds the weapon type of the selected weapon:

```
UPROPERTY(BlueprintReadOnly, Category = "Enumerations
Character")
EWeaponType Weapon;
```

9. Declare the protected Ammo array that holds the amount of ammo for each type:

```
UPROPERTY(EditDefaultsOnly, BlueprintReadOnly, Category =
"Enumerations Character")
TArray<int32> Ammo;
```

10. Declare the protected overrides for the `Begin Play` and `Tick` functions:

```
virtual void BeginPlay() override;
virtual void Tick(float DeltaSeconds) override;
```

11. Declare the protected input functions:

```
void Pistol();
void Shotgun();
void RocketLauncher();
void Fire();
```

12. Open the `EnumerationsCharacter.cpp` file and bind the new action bindings at the end of the `SetupPlayerInputController` function, as shown in the following code snippet:

```
PlayerInputComponent->BindAction("Pistol", IE_Pressed,
this, &AEnumerationsCharacter::Pistol);
PlayerInputComponent->BindAction("Shotgun", IE_Pressed,
this, &AEnumerationsCharacter::Shotgun);
PlayerInputComponent->BindAction("Rocket Launcher", IE_
Pressed, this, &AEnumerationsCharacter::RocketLauncher);
PlayerInputComponent->BindAction("Fire", IE_Pressed,
this, &AEnumerationsCharacter::Fire);
```

13. Next, implement the override for `BeginPlay` that executes the parent logic, but also initializes the size of the `Ammo` array with the number of entries in the `EAmmoType` enumeration. Each position in the array will also be initialized with a value of `10`:

```
void AEnumerationsCharacter::BeginPlay()
{
  Super::BeginPlay();
  constexpr int32 AmmoTypeCount =
  ENUM_TO_INT32(EAmmoType::MAX);
  Ammo.Init(10, AmmoTypeCount);
}
```

14. Implement the override for `Tick`:

```
void AEnumerationsCharacter::Tick(float DeltaSeconds)
{
  Super::Tick(DeltaSeconds);
}
```

15. Convert the `Weapon` variable into `int32` and the `Weapon` variable into an `FString`:

```
const int32 WeaponIndex = ENUM_TO_INT32(Weapon);
const FString WeaponString = ENUM_TO_
FSTRING("EWeaponType", Weapon);
```

16. Convert the ammo type into an `FString` and get the ammo count for the current weapon:

```
const FString AmmoTypeString = ENUM_TO_
FSTRING("EAmmoType", Weapon);
const int32 AmmoCount = Ammo[WeaponIndex];
```

We are using `Weapon` to get the ammo type string because the entries in `EAmmoType` match the type of ammo of the equivalent `EWeaponType`. In other words, `Pistol = 0` uses `Bullets = 0`, `Shotgun = 1` uses `Shells = 1`, and `RocketLauncher = 2` uses `Rockets = 2`, so it's a 1-to-1 mapping that we can use in our favor.

17. Display the name of the current weapon in the character's location and its corresponding ammo type and ammo count, as shown in the following code snippet:

```
const FString String = FString::Printf(TEXT("Weapon =
%s\nAmmo Type = %s\nAmmo Count = %d"), *WeaponString,
*AmmoTypeString, AmmoCount);
DrawDebugString(GetWorld(), GetActorLocation(), String,
nullptr, FColor::White, 0.0f, true);
```

18. Implement the equip input functions that set the `Weapon` variable with the corresponding value:

```
void AEnumerationsCharacter::Pistol()
{
    Weapon = EWeaponType::Pistol;
}
void AEnumerationsCharacter::Shotgun()
{
    Weapon = EWeaponType::Shotgun;
}
void AEnumerationsCharacter::RocketLauncher()
{
    Weapon = EWeaponType::RocketLauncher;
}
```

19. Implement the fire input function that will use the weapon index to get the corresponding ammo type count and subtract 1, so long as the resulting value is greater than or equal to 0:

```
void AEnumerationsCharacter::Fire()
{
    const int32 WeaponIndex = ENUM_TO_INT32(Weapon);
    const int32 NewRawAmmoCount = Ammo[WeaponIndex] - 1;
    const int32 NewAmmoCount =
    FMath::Max(NewRawAmmoCount, 0);
    Ammo[WeaponIndex] = NewAmmoCount;
}
```

20. Compile the code and run the editor.

21. Go to **Project Settings**, go to **Engine**, then **Input**, and add the new action bindings:

Figure 17.8 – Adding the Pistol, Shotgun, Rocket Launcher, and Fire bindings

22. Close **Project Settings**.

23. Make sure the **Net Mode** option is set to **Play Standalone** and that **Number of Players** is set to 1. Click on **New Editor Window (PIE)**; you should get the following result:

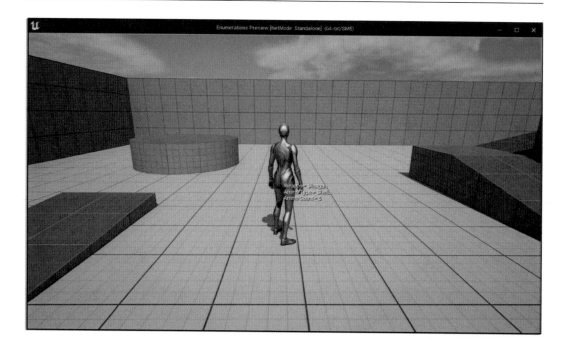

Figure 17.9 – The result of this exercise

By completing this exercise, you can use the **1**, **2**, and **3** keys to select the current weapon. You'll notice that every tick will display the type of the current weapon and its corresponding ammo type and ammo count. If you press the left mouse button, this will deduct the ammo count for the current weapon, but it will never go below 0.

In this section, you learned how to expose enumerations to the editor so that you can use them in blueprints. In the next section, we will look at array index wrapping, which allows you to iterate an array beyond its limits and wrap it back around from the other side.

Using array index wrapping

Sometimes, when you use arrays to store information, you may want to iterate it in both directions and be able to wrap the index so that it doesn't go beyond the index limit and crash the game. An example of this is the previous/next weapon logic in shooter games, where you have an array of weapons and you want to be able to cycle through them in a particular direction, and when you reach the first or the last index, you want to loop back around to the last and first index, respectively. The typical way of doing this would be as follows:

```
AWeapon * APlayer::GetPreviousWeapon()
{
```

```
  if(WeaponIndex - 1 < 0)
  {
     WeaponIndex = Weapons.Num() - 1;
  }
  else
  {
     WeaponIndex--;
  }

  return Weapons[WeaponIndex];
}
AWeapon * APlayer::GetNextWeapon()
{
  if(WeaponIndex + 1 > Weapons.Num() - 1)
  {
     WeaponIndex = 0;
  }
  else
  {
     WeaponIndex++;
  }

  return Weapons[WeaponIndex];
}
```

In the preceding code, we set the `WeaponIndex` variable (declared as a member of the class) to loop back if the new weapon index is outside the limits of the weapons array, which can happen in two cases. The first case is when the player has the last weapon of the inventory equipped and we want the next weapon. In this case, it should go back to the first weapon.

The second case is when the player has the first weapon of the inventory equipped and we want the previous weapon. In this case, it should go to the last weapon.

While the example code works, it's still quite a lot of code to solve such a trivial problem. To improve this code, there is a mathematical operation that will help you handle these two cases automatically in just one function. It's called the modulo (represented in C++ by the % operator), which gives you the remainder of a division between two numbers.

So, how do we use the modulo to wrap the index of an array? Let's rewrite the previous example using the modulo operator:

```
AWeapon * APlayer::GetNewWeapon(int32 Direction)
{
    const int32 WeaponCount = Weapons.Num();
    const int32 NewRawIndex = WeaponIndex + Direction;
    const in32 NewWrappedIndex = NewIndex % WeaponCount;

    WeaponIndex = (NewClampedIndex + WeaponCount) %
    WeaponCount;

    return Weapons[WeaponIndex];
}
```

This is the new version, and you can tell right away that it's a bit harder to understand, but it's more functional and compact. If you don't use the variables to store the intermediate values of each operation, you can probably make the entire function in one or two lines of code.

Let's break down the preceding code snippet:

- `const int WeaponCount = Weapons.Num()`: We need to know the size of the array to determine the index where it should go back to `0`. In other words, if `WeaponCount = 4`, then the array has the 0, 1, 2, and 3 indexes, which tells us that index 4 is the cutoff index where it should go back to 0.

- `const int32 NewRawIndex = WeaponIndex + Direction`: This is the new raw index that doesn't care about the limits of the array. The `Direction` variable is used to indicate the offset we want to add to the current index of the array. This is either `-1` if we want the previous index or `1` if we want the next index.

- `const int32 NewWrappedIndex = NewRawIndex % WeaponCount`: This will make sure that `NewWrappedIndex` is within the 0 to `WeaponCount - 1` interval and wrap around if needed, due to the modulo properties. So, if `NewRawIndex` is 4, then `NewWrappedIndex` will become 0, because there is no remainder from the division of 4 / 4.

If `Direction` is always `1`, meaning we only want the next index, then the value of `NewWrappedIndex` is enough for what we need. If we also want to use `Direction` with `-1`, then we'll have a problem, because the modulo operation won't wrap the index correctly for negative indexes. So, if `WeaponIndex` is `0` and `Direction` is `-1`, then `NewWrappedIndex` will be `-1`, which is not correct. To fix this limitation, we need to do some additional calculations:

- `WeaponIndex = (NewWrappedIndex + WeaponCount) % WeaponCount`: This will add `WeaponCount` to `NewWrappedIndex` to make it positive and apply the modulo again to get the correct wrapped index, which fixes the problem.

- `return Weapons[WeaponIndex]`: This returns the weapon in the calculated `WeaponIndex` index position.

Let's take a look at a practical example to help you visualize how all this works.

Weapons:

- `[0] Knife`

- `[1] Pistol`

- `[2] Shotgun`

- `[3] Rocket Launcher`

`WeaponCount = Weapons.Num()`, so it has a value of 4.

Let's assume that `WeaponIndex = 3` and `Direction = 1`.

Here, we would have the following:

- `NewRawIndex = WeaponIndex + Direction`, so `3 + 1 = 4`

- `NewWrappedIndex = NewRawIndex % WeaponCount`, so `4 % 4 = 0`

- `WeaponIndex = (NewWrappedIndex + WeaponCount) % WeaponCount`, so `(0 + 4) % 4 = 0`

In this example, the starting value for `WeaponIndex` is 3, which is `Rocket Launcher`, and we want the next weapon because `Direction` is set to 1. Performing the calculations, `WeaponIndex` will now be 0, which is `Knife`. This is the desired behavior because we have four weapons, so we circled back to the first index. In this case, since `NewRawIndex` is positive, we could've just used `NewWrappedIndex` without doing the extra calculations.

Let's debug it again using different values.

Let's assume that `WeaponIndex = 0` and `Direction = -1`:

- `NewRawIndex = WeaponIndex + Direction`, so `0 + -1 = -1`

- `NewWrappedIndex = NewIndex % WeaponCount`, so `-1 % 4 = -1`

- `WeaponIndex = (NewWrappedIndex + WeaponCount) % WeaponCount`, so `(-1 + 4) % 4 = 3`

In this example, the starting value for `WeaponIndex` is `0`, which is `Knife`, and we want the previous weapon because `Direction` is set to `-1`. Doing the calculations, `WeaponIndex` will now be 3, which is `Rocket Launcher`. This is the desired behavior because we have four weapons, so we circled back to the last index. In this case, since `NewRawIndex` is negative, we can't just use `NewWrappedIndex`; we need to do the extra calculation to get the correct value.

In the next exercise, you're going to use the knowledge you've acquired to cycle between an enumeration of weapons in both directions.

Exercise 17.03 – Using array index wrapping to cycle between an enumeration

In this exercise, we're going to use the project from *Exercise 17.02 – Using C++ enumerations in the editor*, and add two new action mappings for cycling the weapons. `Mouse Wheel Up` will go to the previous weapon type, while `Mouse Wheel Down` will go to the next weapon type.

Follow these steps to complete this exercise:

1. First, open the Visual Studio project from *Exercise 17.02 – Using C++ enumerations in the editor*.

    Next, you will be updating `Enumerations.h` and adding a macro that will handle the array index wrapping in a very convenient way.

2. Open `Enumerations.h` and add the `GET_WRAPPED_ARRAY_INDEX` macro. This will apply the modulo formula that we covered previously:

    ```
    #define GET_WRAPPED_ARRAY_INDEX(Index, Count) (Index %
    Count + Count) % Count
    ```

3. Open `EnumerationsCharacter.h` and declare the new input functions for the weapon cycling:

    ```
    void PreviousWeapon();
    void NextWeapon();
    ```

4. Declare the `CycleWeapons` function, as shown in the following code snippet:

    ```
    void CycleWeapons(int32 Direction);
    ```

5. Open `EnumerationsCharacter.cpp` and bind the new action bindings in the `SetupPlayerInputController` function:

```
PlayerInputComponent->BindAction("Previous Weapon", IE_
Pressed, this, &AEnumerationsCharacter::PreviousWeapon);

PlayerInputComponent->BindAction("Next Weapon", IE_
Pressed, this, &AEnumerationsCharacter::NextWeapon);
```

6. Now, implement the new input functions, as shown in the following code snippet:

```
void AEnumerationsCharacter::PreviousWeapon()
{
  CycleWeapons(-1);
}
void AEnumerationsCharacter::NextWeapon()
{
  CycleWeapons(1);
}
```

In the preceding code snippet, we defined the functions that handle the action mappings for `Previous Weapon` and `Next Weapon`. Each function uses the `CycleWeapons` function, with a direction of -1 for the previous weapon and 1 for the next weapon.

7. Implement the `CycleWeapons` function, which does the array index wrapping using the `Direction` parameter based on the current weapon index:

```
void AEnumerationsCharacter::CycleWeapons(int32
Direction)
{
  const int32 WeaponIndex = ENUM_TO_INT32(Weapon);
  const int32 AmmoCount = Ammo.Num();
  const int32 NextRawWeaponIndex = WeaponIndex +
  Direction;
  const int32 NextWeaponIndex =
  GET_WRAPPED_ARRAY_INDEX(NextRawWeaponIndex ,
  AmmoCount);

  Weapon = static_cast<EWeaponType>(NextWeaponIndex);
}
```

8. Compile the code and run the editor.

9. Go to **Project Settings**, go to **Engine**, then **Input**, and add the new action bindings:

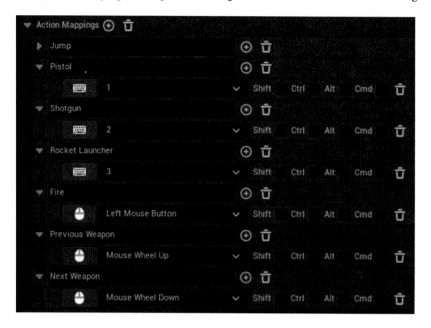

Figure 17.10 – Adding the Previous Weapon and Next Weapon bindings

10. Close **Project Settings**.

11. Make sure that the **Net Mode** option is set to **Play Standalone** and that **Number of Players** is set to 1. Click on **New Editor Window (PIE)**; you should get the following result:

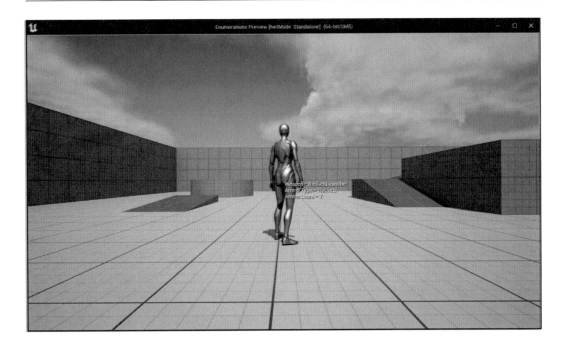

Figure 17.11 – The result of this exercise

By completing this exercise, you can use the mouse wheel to cycle between the weapons. If you select the rocket launcher and use the mouse wheel down to go to the next weapon, it will go back to the pistol. If you use the mouse wheel down to go to the previous weapon with the pistol selected, it will go back to the rocket launcher.

In the next activity, you will be adding the concept of weapons and ammo to the multiplayer FPS project we started in *Chapter 16, Getting Started with Multiplayer Basics.*

Activity 17.01 – Adding weapons and ammo to the multiplayer FPS game

In this activity, you'll add the concept of weapons and ammo to the multiplayer FPS project that we started in the previous chapter. You will need to use the different types of RPCs covered in this chapter to complete this activity.

Follow these steps to complete this activity:

1. Open the `MultiplayerFPS` project from *Activity 16.01 – Creating a character for the multiplayer FPS project.*

2. Create an `AnimMontage` slot called `Upper Body`.

3. Import the animations (`Pistol_Fire.fbx`, `MachineGun_Fire.fbx`, and `Railgun_Fire.fbx`) from the `Activity17.01\Assets` folder into `Content\Player\Animations`.

4. Create an `AnimMontage` for `Pistol_Fire`, `MachineGun_Fire`, and `Railgun_Fire`, and make sure they have the following configurations:

    -   **Pistol_Fire_Montage**: A `Blend In` time of `0.01` and a `Blend Out` time of `0.1`. Make sure it uses the `Upper Body` slot.

    -   **MachineGun_Fire_Montage**: A `Blend In` time of `0.01` and a `Blend Out` time of `0.1`. Make sure it uses the `Upper Body` slot.

    -   **Railgun_Fire_Montage**: Make sure it uses the `Upper Body` slot.

5. Import `SK_Weapon.fbx` (with Material Import Method set to Create New Materials), `NoAmmo.wav`, `WeaponChange.wav`, and `Hit.wav` from the `Activity17.01\Assets` folder into `Content\Weapons`.

6. Import `Pistol_Fire_Sound.wav` from `Activity17.01\Assets` into `Content\Weapons\Pistol` and use it on `Play Sound` in the `Pistol_Fire` animation.

7. Create a simple green-colored material instance from `M_FPGun` called `MI_Pistol` and place it on `Content\Weapons\Pistol`.

8. Import `MachineGun_Fire_Sound.wav` from `Activity17.01\Assets` into `Content\Weapons\MachineGun` and use it on `Play Sound` in the `MachineGun_Fire` animation.

9. Create a simple red-colored material instance from `M_FPGun` called `MI_MachineGun` and place it on `Content\Weapons\MachineGun`.

10. Import `Railgun_Fire_Sound.wav` from `Activity17.01\Assets` into `Content\Weapons\Railgun` and use it on `Play Sound` in the `Railgun_Fire` animation.

11. Create a simple white-colored material instance from `M_FPGun` called `MI_Railgun` and place it on `Content\Weapons\Railgun`.

12. Edit the `SK_Mannequin_Skeleton` and create a socket called `GripPoint` from `hand_r` with `Relative Location` set to `(X=-10.403845,Y=6.0,Z=-3.124871)` and `Relative Rotation` set to `(X=0.0,Y=0.0,Z=90.0)`.

13. Add the following input actions to `Content\Player\Inputs`, using the knowledge you acquired in *Chapter 4, Getting Started with Player Input*:

    -   **IA_Fire (Digital)**: *Left Mouse Button*

    -   **IA_Pistol (Digital)**: *1*

    -   **IA_MachineGun (Digital)**: *2*

    -   **IA_Railgun (Digital)**: *3*

- **IA_PreviousWeapon (Digital)**: *Mouse Wheel Up*

- **IA_NextWeapon (Digital)**: *Mouse Wheel Down*

14. Add the new input actions to `IMC_Player`.

15. In `MultiplayerFPS.h`, create the `ENUM_TO_INT32(Enum)` macro, which casts an enumeration to `int32`, and the `GET_WRAPPED_ARRAY_INDEX(Index, Count)` macro, which uses array indexing wrapping to make sure the index is within the limits of the array.

16. Create a header file called `EnumTypes.h` that holds the following enumerations:

    EWeaponType: `Pistol, MachineGun, Railgun, MAX`

    EWeaponFireMode: `Single, Automatic`

    EAmmoType: `PistolBullets, MachineGunBullets, Slugs, MAX`

17. Create a C++ class called `Weapon` that derives from the `Actor` class and has a skeletal mesh component called `Mesh` as the root component.

    In terms of variables, it stores the name, the weapon type, the ammo type, the fire mode, how far the hitscan goes, how much damage the hitscan does when it hits, the fire rate, the animation montage to use when firing, and the sound to play when it has no ammo. In terms of functionality, it needs to be able to start the fire (and also stop the fire, because of the automatic fire mode), which checks whether the player can fire. If it can, then it plays the fire animation in all of the clients and shoots a line trace in the camera position and direction with the supplied length to damage the actor it hits. If it doesn't have ammo, it will play a sound only on the owning client.

18. Edit `FPSCharacter` so that it supports the new input actions for `Fire, Pistol, Machine Gun, Railgun, Previous Weapon`, and `Next Weapon`. In terms of variables, it needs to store the amount of ammo for each type, the currently equipped weapon, all of the weapons classes and spawned instances, the sound to play when it hits another player, and the sound when it changes weapons. In terms of functions, it needs to be able to equip/cycle/add weapons, manage ammo (add, remove, and get), handle when the character is damaged, play an anim montage on all of the clients, and play a sound on the owning client.

19. Create `BP_Pistol` from `AWeapon`, place it on `Content\Weapons\Pistol`, and configure it with the following values:

    - **Skeletal Mesh**: `Content\Weapons\SK_Weapon`

    - **Material**: `Content\Weapons\Pistol\MI_Pistol`

    - **Name**: `Pistol Mk I`

    - **Weapon Type**: `Pistol`

    - **Ammo Type**: `Pistol Bullets`

- **Fire Mode**: `Automatic`
- **Hit Scan Range**: `9999.9`, **Hit Scan Damage**: `5.0`, **Fire Rate**: `0.5`
- **Fire Anim Montage**: `Content\Player\Animations\Pistol_Fire_Montage`
- **NoAmmoSound**: `Content\Weapons\NoAmmo`

20. Create `BP_MachineGun` from `AWeapon`, place it on `Content\Weapons\MachineGun`, and configure it with the following values:

- **Skeletal Mesh**: `Content\Weapons\SK_Weapon`
- **Material**: `Content\Weapons\MachineGun\MI_MachineGun`
- **Name**: `Machine Gun Mk I`
- **Weapon Type**: `Machine Gun`
- **Ammo Type**: `Machine Gun Bullets`
- **Fire Mode**: `Automatic`
- **Hit Scan Range**: `9999.9`, **Hit Scan Damage**: `5.0`, **Fire Rate**: `0.1`
- **Fire Anim Montage**: `Content\Player\Animations\MachineGun_Fire_Montage`
- **NoAmmoSound**: `Content\Weapons\NoAmmo`

21. Create `BP_Railgun` from `AWeapon`, place it on `Content\Weapons\Railgun`, and configure it with the following values:

- **Skeletal Mesh**: `Content\Weapons\SK_Weapon`
- **Material**: `Content\Weapons\Railgun\MI_Railgun`
- **Name**: `Railgun Mk I`
- **Weapon Type**: `Railgun`
- **AmmoType**: `Slugs`
- **Fire Mode**: `Single`
- **Hit Scan Range**: `9999.9`, **Hit Scan Damage**: `100.0`, **Fire Rate**: `1.5`
- **Fire Anim Montage**: `Content\Player\Animations\Railgun_Fire_Montage`
- **No Ammo Sound**: `Content\Weapons\NoAmmo`

22. Configure `BP_Player` with the following values:

- **Weapon Classes (Index 0**: `BP_Pistol`, **Index 1**: `BP_MachineGun`, **Index 2**: `BP_Railgun`)
- **Hit Sound**: `Content\Weapons\Hit`

- **Weapon Change Sound**: `Content\Weapons\WeaponChange`
- **Fire Input Action**: `Content\Player\Inputs\IA_Fire`
- **Pistol Input Action**: `Content\Player\Inputs\IA_Pistol`
- **Machine Gun Input Action**: `Content\Player\Inputs\IA_MachineGun`
- **Railgun Input Action**: `Content\Player\Inputs\IA_Railgun`
- **Previous Weapon Input Action**: `Content\Player\Inputs\IA_Previous`
- **Next Weapon Input Action**: `Content\Player\Inputs\IA_NextWeapon`

23. Make the mesh component block the visibility channel so that it can be hit by the hitscans of the weapons.

24. Edit `ABP_Player` so that it uses a *Layered blend Per bone* node, with `Mesh Space Rotation Blend` enabled, on the `spine_01` bone so that the upper body animations use the `Upper Body` slot.

25. Edit `WBP_HUD` so that it displays a white dot crosshair in the middle of the screen, the current weapon, and the ammo count under the `Health` and `Armor` indicators.

Expected output:

The result should be a project where each client will have weapons with ammo and will be able to use them to fire at and damage other players. You will also be able to select weapons by using the *1*, *2*, and *3* keys and by using the mouse wheel up and down to select the previous and next weapon, respectively:

Figure 17.12 – The expected result of this activity

> **Note**
> The solution to this activity can be found on GitHub here: `https://github.com/ PacktPublishing/Elevating-Game-Experiences-with-Unreal-Engine- 5-Second-Edition/tree/main/Activity%20solutions`.

By completing this activity, you should have a good idea of how RPCs, enumerations, and array index wrapping work.

Summary

In this chapter, you learned how to use RPCs to allow the server and the clients to execute logic on one another. You also learned how enumerations work in Unreal Engine by using the UENUM macro and how to use array index wrapping, which helps you iterate an array in both directions and loops around when you go beyond its index limits.

By completing this chapter's activity, you learned how to develop a basic playable game where players can shoot each other and switch between their weapons.

In the next chapter, we'll learn where the instances of the most common gameplay framework classes exist in multiplayer, as well as learn about the `Player State` and `Game State` classes. We'll also cover some new concepts in the game mode that are used in multiplayer matches, as well as some useful general-purpose, built-in functionality.

18

Using Gameplay Framework Classes in Multiplayer

In the previous chapter, we covered **remote procedure calls** (**RPCs**), which allow the server and the clients to execute remote functions on each other. We also covered enumerations and array index wrapping, which allow you to iterate an array in both directions and loop around when you go beyond its limits.

In this chapter, we're going to look at the most common gameplay framework classes and see where their instances exist in a multiplayer environment. This is important to understand so that you know which instances can be accessed in a specific game instance. An example of this is that only the server should be able to access the game mode instance because you don't want clients to be able to modify the rules of the game.

We'll also cover the game state and player state classes, which, as their names imply, store information about the state of the game and each player, respectively. Finally, toward the end of this chapter, we'll cover some new concepts in the game mode, as well as some useful built-in functionality.

In this chapter, we're going to cover the following main topics:

- Accessing Gameplay Framework instances in multiplayer
- Using Game Mode, Player State, and Game State

By the end of this chapter, you'll understand where the instances of the most important Gameplay Framework classes exist in multiplayer, as well as how the game state and player state store information that can be accessed by any client. You'll also know how to make the most out of the Game Mode class and other useful built-in functionality.

Technical requirements

This chapter has the following technical requirements:

- Unreal Engine 5 installed
- Visual Studio 2019 installed

The project for this chapter can be found in the `Chapter18` folder of the code bundle for this book, which can be downloaded here: `https://github.com/PacktPublishing/Elevating-Game-Experiences-with-Unreal-Engine-5-Second-Edition`.

In the next section, we will learn how to access the gameplay framework instances in multiplayer.

Accessing Gameplay Framework Instances in Multiplayer

Unreal Engine comes with a set of built-in classes (the Gameplay Framework) that provide the common functionality that most games require, such as a way to define the game rules (game mode), a way to control a character (the player controller and pawn/character class), and so on. When an instance of a gameplay framework class is created in a multiplayer environment, we need to know if it exists on the server, the clients, or the owning client. With that in mind, an instance of the gameplay framework class will always fall into one of the following categories:

- **Server Only**: The instance will only exist on the server.
- **Server and Clients**: The instance will exist on the server and the clients.
- **Server and Owning Client**: The instance will exist on the server and the owning client.
- **Owning Client Only**: The instance will only exist on the owning client.

Take a look at the following diagram, which shows each category and where the most common classes in the gameplay framework fall into:

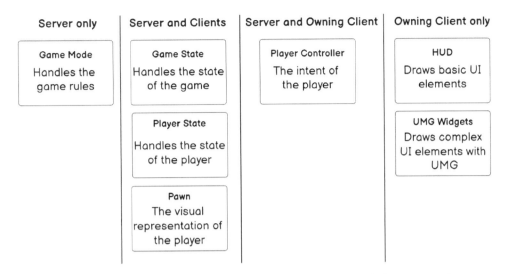

Figure 18.1 – The most common gameplay framework classes divided into categories

Let's look at each class in the preceding diagram in more detail:

- **Game Mode (Server Only)**: The Game Mode class defines the rules of the game and its instance can only be accessed by the server. If a client tries to access it, the instance will always be invalid, to prevent clients from changing the game rules.

- **Game State (Server and Clients)**: The Game State class stores the state of the game and its instance can be accessed both by the server and the clients. The game state will be covered in greater depth in the next topic.

- **Player State (Server and Clients)**: The Player State class stores the state of a player and its instance can be accessed both by the server and the clients. The player state will be covered in greater depth in the next topic.

- **Pawn (Server and Clients)**: The Pawn class is the visual representation of a player and its instance can be accessed by the server and the clients.

- **PlayerController (Server and Owning Client)**: The Player Controller class represents the intent of a player, which is relayed to the currently possessed pawn, and its instance can only be accessed on the server and the owning client. For security reasons, clients can't access other clients' player controllers, so they should use the server to communicate. If a client calls the UGameplayStatics::GetPlayerController function with an index other than 0 (which would return its player controller), the returned instance will always be invalid. This means that the server is the only place that has access to all of the player controllers. You can find out whether a player controller instance is in its owning client by calling the AController::IsLocalController function.

- **HUD (Owning Client Only):** The HUD class is used as an immediate mode to draw basic shapes and text on the screen. Since it's used for the UI, its instance is only available on the owning client, because the server and the other clients don't need to know about it.

- **UMG Widgets (Owning Client Only):** The UMG widget classes are used to display complex UI on the screen. Since it's used for the UI, its instance is only available on the owning client, because the server and the other clients don't need to know about it.

To help you understand these concepts, we will use *Dota 2* as an example:

- The game mode defines that there are different phases of the game (pre-game for hero picking, the actual game, and the post-game phase with the winner) and that the end goal is to destroy the other team's ancient. Since the game mode is a class that is critical to gameplay, clients can't be allowed to access it.

- The game state stores the elapsed time, whether it's day or night, the score of each team, and so on, so the server and the clients need to be able to access it.

- The player state stores the name, the hero selected, and the kill/death/assist ratio of a player, so the server and the clients need to be able to access it.

- The pawn would be the hero, the courier, the illusions, and so on, controlled by the player, so the server and the clients need to be able to access it.

- The player controller is what relays the input information to the controlled pawn, so only the server and the owning client need to be able to access it.

- The UI classes (HUD and User Widget) display all of the information on the owning client, so it only needs to be accessed there.

In the next exercise, you will display the instance values of the most common gameplay framework classes.

Exercise 18.01 – Displaying the Gameplay Framework instance values

In this exercise, we're going to create a new C++ project that uses the **Third Person** template, and we're going to add the following:

- On the owning client, the player controller creates and adds a simple UMG widget to the viewport that displays the name of the menu instance.

- On the Tick function, the character displays the value of its instance (as a pawn), as well as whether it has a valid instance for the game mode, game state, player state, player controller, and HUD.

Follow these steps to complete this exercise:

1. Create a new **Third Person** template project using **C++** called GFInstances (as in Gameplay Framework Instances) and save it to a location of your liking. Once the project has been created, it should open the editor as well as the Visual Studio solution.

2. In the editor, create a new C++ class called GFInstancePlayerController that derives from PlayerController. Wait for the compilation to end, close the editor, and go back to Visual Studio.

3. Open the GFInstancesCharacter.h file and declare the protected override for the Tick function:

```
virtual void Tick(float DeltaSeconds) override;
```

4. Open the GFInstancesCharacter.cpp file and implement the Tick function:

```
void AGFInstancesCharacter::Tick(float DeltaSeconds)
{
    Super::Tick(DeltaSeconds);
}
```

5. Get the instances for the game mode, game state, player controller, and HUD:

```
const AGameModeBase* GameMode = GetWorld()-
>GetAuthGameMode();
const AGameStateBase* GameState = GetWorld()-
>GetGameState();
const APlayerController* PlayerController =
    Cast<APlayerController>(GetController());
const AHUD* HUD = PlayerController != nullptr ?
PlayerController->GetHUD() : nullptr;
```

In the preceding code snippet, we stored the instances for the game mode, game state, player controller, and HUD in separate variables so that we can check whether they are valid.

6. Create a string for each gameplay framework class:

```
const FString GameModeString = GameMode != nullptr ?
    TEXT("Valid") : TEXT("Invalid");
const FString GameStateString = GameState != nullptr ?
    TEXT("Valid") : TEXT("Invalid");
const FString PlayerStateString = GetPlayerState() !=
nullptr ? TEXT("Valid") : TEXT("Invalid");
const FString PawnString = GetName();
```

```
const FString PlayerControllerString = PlayerController
!= nullptr ? TEXT("Valid") : TEXT("Invalid");
const FString HUDString = HUD != nullptr ? TEXT("Valid"):
  TEXT("Invalid");
```

Here, we have created strings to store the name of the pawn and checked whether the other gameplay framework instances are valid.

7. Display each string on the screen:

```
const FString String = FString::Printf(TEXT("Game Mode =
%s\nGame
  State = %s\nPlayerState = %s\nPawn = %s\nPlayer
Controller =
  %s\nHUD = %s"), *GameModeString, *GameStateString,
  *PlayerStateString, *PawnString,
  *PlayerControllerString,
  *HUDString);
DrawDebugString(GetWorld(), GetActorLocation(), String,
nullptr, FColor::White, 0.0f, true);
```

In the preceding code snippet, we have printed the strings that indicate the name of the pawn and whether the other gameplay framework instances are valid.

8. Before we can move on to the AGFInstancesPlayerController class, we need to tell Unreal Engine that we want to use the UMG functionality so that we can use the UUserWidget class. To do this, we need to open GFInstances.Build.cs and add UMG to the PublicDependencyModuleNames string array, like so:

```
PublicDependencyModuleNames.AddRange(new string[]
{ "Core", "CoreUObject", "Engine", "InputCore",
"HeadMountedDisplay", "UMG" });
```

If you try to compile and get errors from adding the new module, then clean and recompile your project. If that doesn't work, try restarting your IDE.

9. Open GFInstancesPlayerController.h and add the protected variables to create the UMG widget:

```
UPROPERTY(EditDefaultsOnly, BlueprintReadOnly, Category =
"GF Instance Player Controller")
TSubclassOf<UUserWidget> MenuClass;

UPROPERTY()
UUserWidget* Menu;
```

10. Declare the protected override for the `BeginPlay` function:

    ```
    virtual void BeginPlay() override;
    ```

11. Open `GFInstancesPlayerController.cpp` and include `UserWidget.h`:

    ```
    #include "Blueprint/UserWidget.h"
    ```

12. Implement the `BeginPlay` function:

    ```
    void AGFInstancePlayerController::BeginPlay()
    {
      Super::BeginPlay();
    }
    ```

13. Create the widget and add it to the viewport if it's a local controller and the `MenuClass` variable is valid:

    ```
    if (IsLocalController() && MenuClass != nullptr)
    {
      Menu = CreateWidget<UUserWidget>(this, MenuClass);
      if (Menu != nullptr)
      {
        Menu->AddToViewport(0);
      }
    }
    ```

14. Compile and run the code.

15. In the **Content Browser** area, go to the `Content` folder, create a new folder called `UI`, and open it.

16. Create a new widget blueprint called `WBP_Menu` and open it.

17. Add a `Canvas Panel` to the **Hierarchy** panel.

18. Add a **Text Block** called `Name` to the **canvas panel** and set it to be a variable.

19. Change the text block **Name** so that its **Size To Content** is `true`.

20. Go to the **Graph** section and, in **Event Graph**, implement `Event Construct` in the following manner:

Figure 18.2 – The Event Construct that displays the name of the WBP_Menu instance

21. Save and close `WBP_Menu`.

22. Go to the `Content` folder and create a blueprint called `BP_PlayerController` that derives from `GFInstancesPlayerController`.

23. Open `BP_PlayerController` and set `Menu Class` to use `WBP_Menu`.

24. Save and close `BP_PlayerController`.

25. Create a blueprint called `BP_GameMode` that derives from `GFInstancesGameMode`.

26. Open `BP_GameMode` and set `Player Controller Class` to use `BP_PlayerController`.

27. Save and close `BP_GameMode`.

28. Go to **World Settings**, set **GameMode Override** to **None**, and save the map.

29. Go to **Project Settings** and pick **Maps & Modes** from the left panel, which can be found in the **Project** category.

30. Set the `Default` Game Mode to use `BP_GameMode`.

31. Close **Project Settings**.

    Finally, you can test the project.

32. Go to **Multiplayer Options**, set **Net Mode** to **Play As Listen Server**, and set the **Number of Players** to 2.

33. Set the window sizes to 800x600 and play using **New Editor Window (PIE)**.

You should get the following output:

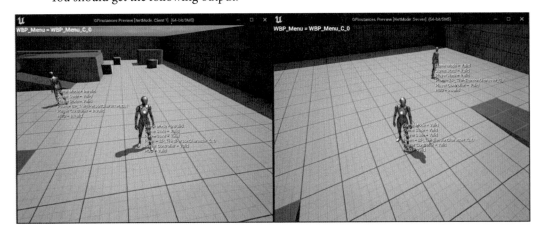

Figure 18.3 – Expected result on the Server and Client 1 windows

Now that you've completed this exercise, you'll notice that each character displays its name, as well as if the instances for the game mode, game state, player state, player controller, and HUD are valid. It also displays the instance name of the WBP_Menu UMG widget in the top-left corner of the screen.

Now, let's analyze the values that are displayed in the Server and Client 1 windows.

> **Note**
>
> The two figures for the Server and Client 1 window will have two text blocks that say Server Character and Client 1 Character. These were added to the original screenshot to help you understand which character is which.

Output for the Server window

Have a look at the following output of the `Server` window from the previous exercise:

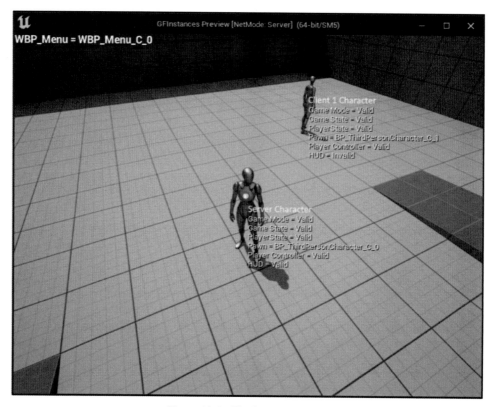

Figure 18.4 – The Server window

In the preceding screenshot, you have the values for `Server Character` and `Client 1 Character`. The `WBP_Menu` UMG widget is displayed in the top-left corner and is only created for the player controller of `Server Character` since it's the only player controller in this window that controls a character.

First, let's analyze the values for `Server Character`.

Server Character

This is the character that the listen server is controlling. The values that are displayed on this character are as follows:

- **Game Mode = Valid** because the game mode instance only exists in the server, which is the case here

- **Game State = Valid** because the game state instance exists on the clients and the server, which is the case here

- **Player State = Valid** because the player state instance exists on the clients and the server, which is the case here

- **Pawn = BP_ThirdPersonCharacter_C_0** because pawn instances exist on the clients and the server, which is the case here

- **Player Controller = Valid** because player controller instances exist on the owning client and the server, which is the case here

- **HUD = Valid** because HUD instances only exist on the owning client, which is the case here

Next, we are going to look at `Client 1 Character` in the same window.

Client 1 Character

This is the character that `Client 1` is controlling. The values that are displayed on this character are as follows:

- **Game Mode = Valid** because the game mode instance only exists in the server, which is the case here

- **Game State = Valid** because the game state instance exists on the clients and the server, which is the case here

- **Player State = Valid** because the player state instance exists on the clients and the server, which is the case here

- **Pawn = BP_ThirdPersonCharacter_C_1** because pawn instances exist on the clients and the server, which is the case here

- **Player Controller = Valid** because player controller instances exist on the owning client and the server, which is the case here

- **HUD = Invalid** because HUD instances only exist on the owning client, which is not the case here

Output for the Client 1 window

Have a look at the following output of the `Client 1` window from the previous exercise:

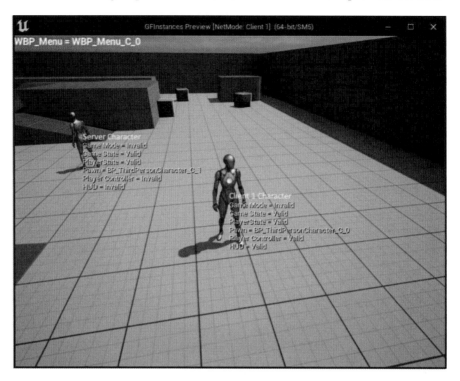

Figure 18.5 – The Client 1 window

In the preceding screenshot, you have the values for `Client 1 Character` and `Server Character`. The `WBP_Menu` UMG widget is displayed in the top-left corner and is only created for the player controller of `Client 1 Character` since it's the only player controller in this window that controls a character.

First, let's analyze the values for `Client 1 Character`.

Client 1 Character

This is the character that `Client 1` is controlling. The values that are displayed on this character are as follows:

- **Game Mode = Invalid** because the game mode instance only exists in the server, which is not the case here

- **Game State** = **Valid** because the game state instance exists on the server and the clients, which is the case here

- **Player State** = **Valid** because the player state instance exists on the server and the clients, which is the case here

- **Pawn** = **BP_ThirdPersonCharacter_C_0** because pawn instances exist on the server and the clients, which is the case here

- **Player Controller** = **Valid** because player controller instances exist on the server and the owning client, which is the case here

- **HUD** = **Valid** because HUD instances only exist on the owning client, which is the case here

Next, we are going to look at `Server Character` in the same window.

Server Character

This is the character that the listen server controls. The values that are displayed on this character are as follows:

- **Game Mode** = **Invalid** because the game mode instance only exists in the server, which is not the case here

- **Game State** = **Valid** because the game state instance exists on the server and the clients, which is the case here

- **Player State** = **Valid** because the player state instance exists on the server and the clients, which is the case here

- **Pawn** = **BP_ThirdPersonCharacter_C_1** because pawn instances exist on the server and the clients, which is the case here

- **Player Controller** = **Invalid** because player controller instances exist on the server and the owning client, which is not the case here

- **HUD** = **Invalid** because HUD instances only exist on the owning client, which is not the case here

By completing this exercise, you should have a better understanding of where each instance of the gameplay framework class exists and where it doesn't. In the next section, we're going to cover the player state and game state classes, as well as some additional concepts regarding the game mode and useful built-in functionalities.

Using Game Mode, Player State, and Game State

So far, we've covered most of the important classes in the gameplay framework, including the game mode, player controller, and the pawn. In this section, we're going to cover the player state, game state, and some additional concepts regarding the game mode, as well as some useful built-in functionalities.

Game mode

We've already talked about the game mode and how it works, but there are a few concepts that are useful to know about. Let's take a look.

Constructor

To set the default class values, you can use a constructor like so:

```
ATestGameMode::ATestGameMode()
{
  DefaultPawnClass = AMyCharacter::StaticClass();
  PlayerControllerClass =
  AMyPlayerController::StaticClass();
  PlayerStateClass = AMyPlayerState::StaticClass();
  GameStateClass = AMyGameState::StaticClass();
}
```

The preceding code lets you specify which classes to use when spawning pawns, player controllers, player states, and game states when we are using this game mode.

Getting the game mode instance

If you want to access the game mode instance, you need to get it from the `GetWorld` function by using the following code:

```
AGameModeBase* GameMode = GetWorld()->GetAuthGameMode();
```

The preceding code allows you to access the current game mode instance, but you have to make sure that you are calling it on the server since this will be invalid on the clients due to security reasons.

Match states

So far, we've only been using the `AGameModeBase` class, which is the most basic game mode class in the framework. Although it's more than enough for certain types of games, there will be cases where you will require a bit more functionality. An example of this would be if we wanted to do a lobby system, where the match only starts if all the players have marked that they are ready. This example wouldn't be possible to do with just the built-in function of the `AGameModeBase` class. For these cases, it's better to use the `AGameMode` class instead, which is a child class of `AGameModeBase` that adds support for match states. The way match states work is by using a state machine that can only be in one of the following states at a given time:

- `EnteringMap`: This is the starting state when the world is still loading and the actors aren't ticking yet. It will transition to the `WaitingToStart` state once the world finishes loading.

- `WaitingToStart`: This state is set when the world has finished loading and the actors are ticking, although the pawns for the players won't be spawned because the game hasn't started yet. When the state machine enters this state, it will call the `HandleMatchIsWaitingToStart` function. The state machine will transition to the `InProgress` state if the `ReadyToStartMatch` function returns `true` or if the `StartMatch` function is called somewhere in the code.

- `InProgress`: This state is where the actual game takes place. When the state machine enters this state, it will spawn the pawns for the players, call `BeginPlay` on all of the actors in the world, and call the `HandleMatchHasStarted` function. The state machine will transition to the `WaitingPostMatch` state if the `ReadyToEndMatch` function returns `true` or if the `EndMatch` function is called somewhere in the code.

- `WaitingPostMatch`: This state is set when the match ends. When the state machine enters this state, it will call the `HandleMatchHasEnded` function. In this state, actors still tick, but new players cannot join. It will transition to the `LeavingMap` state when it starts unloading the world.

- `LeavingMap`: This state is set while it's unloading the world. When the state machine enters this state, it will call the `HandleLeavingMap` function. The state machine will transition to the `EnteringMap` state when it starts loading the new level.

- `Aborted`: This is a failed state that can only be set by calling the `AbortMatch` function, which is used to flag that something went wrong that prevented the match from happening.

To help you understand these concepts better, we can use *Dota 2* again as an example:

- `EnteringMap`: The state machine will be in this state when the map is loading.

- `WaitingToStart`: The state machine will be in this state once the map is loaded and the players are picking their heroes. The `ReadyToStartMatch` function will check whether all the players have selected their heroes; if they have, then the match can start.

- `InProgress`: The state machine will be in this state when the game is underway. The players control their heroes to farm and fight other players. The `ReadyToEndMatch` function will constantly check the health of each ancient to see whether one of them was destroyed; if it was, then the match ends.

- `WaitingPostMatch`: The state machine will be in this state when the game has ended and you can see the destroyed ancient, as well as a message that displays the name of the winning team.

- `LeavingMap`: The state machine will be in this state when it's unloading the map.

- `Aborted`: The state machine will be in this state if one of the players failed to connect in the initial stage, therefore aborting the whole match.

Respawning the player

When the player dies and you want to respawn it, you typically have two options. The first option is to reuse the same pawn instance, manually reset its state back to the defaults, and teleport it to the respawn location. The second option is to destroy the current pawn instance and spawn a new one, which will already have its state reset. If you prefer the latter option, then the `AGameModeBase::RestartPlayer` function handles the logic of spawning a new pawn instance for a certain player controller for you and places it on a player start.

One important thing to take into consideration is that the function only spawns a new pawn instance if the player controller doesn't already possess a pawn, so make sure to destroy the controlled pawn before calling `RestartPlayer`.

Take a look at the following example:

```
void ATestGameMode::OnDeath(APlayerController*
VictimController)
{
  if(VictimController == nullptr)
  {
    return;
  }


  APawn* Pawn = VictimController->GetPawn();

  if(Pawn != nullptr)
  {
    Pawn->Destroy();
  }
```

```
    RestartPlayer(VictimController);
}
```

In the preceding code, we have the `OnDeath` function, which takes the player controller of the player that died, destroys its controlled pawn, and calls the `RestartPlayer` function to spawn a new instance. By default, the new pawn instance will spawn in the player start actor that was used when the player spawned for the first time. Alternatively, you can tell the game mode that you want to spawn on a random player start. To accomplish that, all you need to do is override the `AGameModeBase::ShouldSpawnAtStartSpot` function and force it to `return false`, like so:

```
bool ATestGameMode::ShouldSpawnAtStartSpot(AController* Player)
{
    return false;
}
```

The preceding code will make the game mode use a random player start instead of always using the first one that was used.

> **Note**
>
> For more information about the game mode, please visit `https://docs.unrealengine.com/en-US/Gameplay/Framework/GameMode/#gamemodes` and `https://docs.unrealengine.com/en-US/API/Runtime/Engine/GameFramework/AGameMode/index.html`.

Player state

The player state class stores the information that other clients need to know about a specific player (such as their current score, kills/deaths/assists, and so on) since they can't access its player controller. The most widely used built-in functions are `GetPlayerName()`, `GetScore` and `GetPingInMilliseconds()`, which give you the name, score, and ping of the player, respectively.

A good example of how to use the player state is a scoreboard entry on a multiplayer shooter such as *Call Of Duty*, because every client needs to know the name, kills/deaths/assists, and ping for that player. The player state instance can be accessed in various ways, so let's take a look at the most common ones:

AController::PlayerState

This variable contains the player state associated with the controller and can only be accessed by the server and the owning client. The following example shows how to use the variable:

```
APlayerState* PlayerState = Controller->PlayerState;
```

AController::GetPlayerState()

This function returns the player state associated with the controller and can only be accessed by the server and the owning client. This function also has a template version so that you can cast it to your own custom player state class. The following example shows how to use the default and template versions of this function:

```
// Default version
APlayerState* PlayerState = Controller->GetPlayerState();


// Template version
ATestPlayerState* MyPlayerState = Controller->GetPlayerState<AT
estPlayerState>();
```

APawn::GetPlayerState()

This function returns the player state associated with the controller that is possessing the pawn and can be accessed by the server and the clients. This function also has a template version so that you can cast it to your own custom player state class. The following example shows how to use the default and template versions of this function:

```
// Default version
APlayerState* PlayerState = Pawn->GetPlayerState();


// Template version
ATestPlayerState* MyPlayerState = Pawn-
   >GetPlayerState<ATestPlayerState>();
```

AGameState::PlayerArray

This variable in the game state (covered in the next section) stores the player state instances for each player and can be accessed on the server and the clients. The following example shows how to use this variable:

```
TArray<APlayerState*> PlayerStates = GameState->PlayerArray;
```

To help you understand these concepts better, we will use *Dota 2* again as an example. The player state would have at least the following variables:

- **Name**: The name of the player
- **Hero**: The selected hero
- **Health**: The health of the hero
- **Mana**: The mana of the hero
- **Stats**: The hero stats
- **Level**: The level the hero is currently in
- **Kill/Death/Assist**: The kill/death/assist ratio for the player

> **Note**
>
> For more information about the player state, please visit `https://docs.unrealengine.com/en-US/API/Runtime/Engine/GameFramework/APlayerState/index.html`.

Game State

The game state class stores the information that other clients need to know about the game (such as the match's elapsed time and the score required to win the game) since they can't access the game mode. The most widely used variable is `PlayerArray`, which is an array that provides the player state of every connected client. A good example of how to use the game state is a scoreboard on a multiplayer shooter such as *Call Of Duty* because every client needs to know how many kills are required to win, as well as the names, kills/deaths/assists, and pings for every connected player.

The game state instance can be accessed in various ways. Let's take a look.

UWorld::GetGameState()

This function returns the game state associated with the world and can be accessed on the server and the clients. This function also has a template version so that you can cast it to your own custom game state class. The following example shows how to use the default and template versions of this function:

```
// Default version
AGameStateBase* GameState = GetWorld()->GetGameState();


// Template version
AMyGameState* MyGameState = GetWorld()-
>GetGameState<AMyGameState>();
```

AGameModeBase::GameState

This variable contains the game state associated with the game mode and can only be accessed on the server. The following example shows how to use the variable:

```
AGameStateBase* GameState = GameMode->GameState;
```

AGameModeBase::GetGameState()

This function returns the game state associated with the game mode and can only be accessed on the server. This function also has a template version so that you can cast it to your own custom game state class. The following example shows how to use the default and template versions of this function:

```
// Default version
AGameStateBase* GameState = GameMode->GetGameState<AGameStateB
ase>();

// Template version
AMyGameState* MyGameState = GameMode-
>GetGameState<AMyGameState>();
```

To help you understand these concepts better, we will use *Dota 2* again as an example. The game state will have the following variables:

- **Elapsed Time**: How long the match has been going on for
- **Radiant Kills**: How many Dire heroes the Radiant team has killed
- **Dire Kills**: How many Radiant heroes the Dire team has killed
- **Day/Night Timer**: Used to determine whether it is day or night

> **Note**
>
> For more information about the game state, please visit `https://docs.unrealengine.com/en-US/API/Runtime/Engine/GameFramework/AGameState/index.html`.

Useful built-in functionality

UE5 comes with a lot of functionality built in. Let's look at some examples that are useful to know about when developing a game.

void AActor::EndPlay(const EEndPlayReason::Type EndPlayReason)

This function is called when the actor has stopped playing, which is the opposite of the `BeginPlay` function. This function has a parameter called `EndPlayReason`, which tells you why the actor stopped playing (if it was destroyed, if you stopped `PIE`, and so on). Take a look at the following example, which prints to the screen that the actor has stopped playing:

```
void ATestActor::EndPlay(const EEndPlayReason::Type
EndPlayReason)
{
   Super::EndPlay(EndPlayReason);
   const FString String = FString::Printf(TEXT("The actor %s
   has just stopped playing"), *GetName());
   GEngine->AddOnScreenDebugMessage(-1, 2.0f, FColor::Red,
   String);
}
```

void ACharacter::Landed(const FHitResult& Hit)

This function is called when a player lands on a surface after being in the air. Take a look at the following example, which plays a sound when a player lands on a surface:

```
void ATestCharacter::Landed(const FHitResult& Hit)
{
   Super::Landed(Hit);
   UGameplayStatics::PlaySound2D(GetWorld(), LandSound);
}
```

bool UWorld::ServerTravel(const FString& FURL, bool bAbsolute, bool bShouldSkipGameNotify)

This function will make the server load a new map and bring all of the connected clients along with it. This is different from using other methods that load maps, such as the `UGameplayStatics::OpenLevel` function, because it won't bring the clients along; it will just load the map on the server and disconnect the clients.

Take a look at the following example, which gets the current map name and uses server travel to reload it and bring along the connected clients:

```
void ATestGameModeBase::RestartMap()
{
    const FString URL = GetWorld()->GetName();
    GetWorld()->ServerTravel(URL, false, false);
}
```

void TArray::Sort(const PREDICATE_CLASS& Predicate)

The TArray data structure comes with the Sort function, which allows you to sort the values of an array by using a lambda function that returns whether the A value should be ordered first, followed by the B value. Take a look at the following example, which sorts an integer array from the smallest value to the highest:

```
void ATestActor::SortValues()
{
    TArray<int32> SortTest;

    SortTest.Add(43);
    SortTest.Add(1);
    SortTest.Add(23);
    SortTest.Add(8);

    SortTest.Sort([](const int32& A, const int32& B) { return
    A < B; });
}
```

The preceding code will sort the SortTest array's values of [43, 1, 23, 8] from smallest to highest – that is, [1, 8, 23, 43].

void AActor::FellOutOfWorld(const UDamageType& DmgType)

In Unreal Engine, there is a concept called **Kill Z**, which is a plane on a certain value in Z (set in the **World Settings** panel). If an actor goes below that Z value, it will call the `FellOutOfWorld` function, which, by default, destroys the actor. Take a look at the following example, which prints to the screen that the actor fell out of the world:

```
void AFPSCharacter::FellOutOfWorld(const UDamageType& DmgType)
{
  Super::FellOutOfWorld(DmgType);

  const FString String = FString::Printf(TEXT("The actor %s
  has fell out of the world"), *GetName());

  GEngine->AddOnScreenDebugMessage(-1, 2.0f, FColor::Red,
  String);
}
```

URotatingMovementComponent

This component rotates the owning actor along time with a certain rate on each axis, defined in the `RotationRate` variable. To use it, you need to include the following header:

```
#include "GameFramework/RotatingMovementComponent.h"
```

You must also declare the component variable:

```
UPROPERTY(VisibleAnywhere, BlueprintReadOnly, Category = "Test
Actor")
URotatingMovementComponent* RotatingMovement;
```

Finally, you must initialize it in the actor constructor, like so:

```
RotatingMovement = CreateDefaultSubobject
   <URotatingMovementComponent>("Rotating Movement");
RotatingMovement->RotationRate = FRotator(0.0, 90.0f, 0);
```

In the preceding code, `RotationRate` is set to rotate 90 degrees per second on the Yaw axis.

Exercise 18.02 – Making a simple multiplayer pickup game

In this exercise, we're going to create a new C++ project that uses the **Third Person** template. The following will happen:

- On the owning client, the player controller will create and add to the viewport a UMG widget that, for each player, displays the score, sorted from highest to lowest, and how many pickups it has collected.

- Create a simple pickup actor class that gives 10 points to the player that picked it up. The pickup will also rotate 90 degrees per second on the Yaw axis.

- Set the Kill Z to -500 and make the player respawn and lose 10 points every time they fall from the world.

- The game will end when there are no more pickups available. Once the game ends, all characters will be destroyed and after 5 seconds, the server will do a server travel call to reload the same map and bring along the connected clients.

Follow these steps to complete the C++ part of this exercise:

1. Create a new **Third Person** template project using **C++** called Pickups and save it to a location of your liking.

2. Once the project has been created, it should open the editor, as well as the Visual Studio solution.

   Now, let's create the new C++ classes we're going to use.

3. Create a Pickup class that derives from Actor.

4. Create a PickupsGameState class that derives from GameState.

5. Create a PickupsPlayerState class that derives from PlayerState.

6. Create a PickupsPlayerController class that derives from PlayerController.

7. Close the editor and open Visual Studio.

Next, we're going to work on the PickupsGameState class:

1. Open PickupsGameState.h and declare the protected replicated integer variable, PickupsRemaining, which tells all clients how many pickups remain in the level:

   ```
   UPROPERTY(Replicated, BlueprintReadOnly)
   int32 PickupsRemaining;
   ```

2. Declare the protected override for the BeginPlay function:

   ```
   virtual void BeginPlay() override;
   ```

3. Declare the protected `GetPlayerStatesOrderedByScore` function:

```
UFUNCTION(BlueprintCallable)
TArray<APlayerState*> GetPlayerStatesOrderedByScore()
const;
```

4. Implement the public `RemovePickup` function, which removes one pickup from the `PickupsRemaining` variable:

```
void RemovePickup() { PickupsRemaining--; }
```

5. Implement the public `HasPickups` function, which returns whether any pickups remain:

```
bool HasPickups() const { return PickupsRemaining > 0; }
```

6. Open `PickupsGameState.cpp` and include `Pickup.h`, `GameplayStatics.h`, `UnrealNetwork.h`, and `PlayerState.h`:

```
#include "Pickup.h"
#include "Kismet/GameplayStatics.h"
#include "Net/UnrealNetwork.h"
#include "GameFramework/PlayerState.h"
```

7. Implement the `GetLifetimeReplicatedProps` function and make the `PickupRemaining` variable replicate to all clients:

```
void APickupsGameState::GetLifetimeReplicatedProps(TArray<
  FLifetimeProperty >& OutLifetimeProps) const
{
  Super::GetLifetimeReplicatedProps(OutLifetimeProps);
  DOREPLIFETIME(APickupsGameState, PickupsRemaining);
}
```

8. Implement the `BeginPlay` override function and set the value of `PickupsRemaining` by getting all the pickups in the world:

```
void APickupsGameState::BeginPlay()
{
  Super::BeginPlay();
  TArray<AActor*> Pickups;
  UGameplayStatics::GetAllActorsOfClass(this,
    APickup::StaticClass(), Pickups);
```

```
        PickupsRemaining = Pickups.Num();
    }
```

9. Implement the `GetPlayerStatesOrderedByScore` function, which duplicates the `PlayerArray` variable and sorts it so that the players with the highest scores show up first:

```
TArray<APlayerState*>
APickupsGameState::GetPlayerStatesOrderedByScore() const
{
    TArray<APlayerState*> PlayerStates(PlayerArray);
    PlayerStates.Sort([](const APlayerState& A, const
    APlayerState&
      B) { return A.GetScore() > B.GetScore(); });
    return PlayerStates;
}
```

Next, let's work on the `PickupsPlayerState` class. Follow these steps:

1. Open `PickupsPlayerState.h` and declare the protected replicated integer variable, `Pickups`, which indicates how many pickups a player has collected:

```
UPROPERTY(Replicated, BlueprintReadOnly)
int32 Pickups;
```

2. Implement the public `AddPickup` function, which adds one pickup to the `Pickups` variable:

```
void AddPickup() { Pickups++; }
```

3. Open `PickupsPlayerState.cpp` and include `UnrealNetwork.h`:

```
#include "Net/UnrealNetwork.h"
```

4. Implement the `GetLifetimeReplicatedProps` function and make the `Pickups` variable replicate to all clients:

```
void
APickupsPlayerState::GetLifetimeReplicatedProps(TArray<
    FLifetimeProperty >& OutLifetimeProps) const
{
    Super::GetLifetimeReplicatedProps(OutLifetimeProps);
    DOREPLIFETIME(APickupsPlayerState, Pickups);
}
```

Next, let's work on the `PickupsPlayerController` class.

5. Open `PickupsPlayerController.h` and declare the protected `ScoreboardMenuClass` variable, which will set the UMG widget class we want to use for our scoreboard:

```
UPROPERTY(EditDefaultsOnly, BlueprintReadOnly, Category =
"Pickup Player Controller")
TSubclassOf<class UUserWidget> ScoreboardMenuClass;
```

6. Declare the protected `ScoreboardMenu` variable, which stores the scoreboard UMG widget instance we will create on the `BeginPlay` function:

```
UPROPERTY()
class UUserWidget* ScoreboardMenu;
```

7. Declare the protected override for the `BeginPlay` function:

```
virtual void BeginPlay() override;
```

8. Open `PickupsPlayerController.cpp` and include `UserWidget.h`:

```
#include "Blueprint/UserWidget.h"
```

9. Implement the `BeginPlay` override function, which, for the owning client, creates and adds the scoreboard UMG widget to the viewport:

```
void ApickupsPlayerController::BeginPlay()
{
  Super::BeginPlay();
  if (IsLocalController() && ScoreboardMenuClass !=
  nullptr)
  {
    ScoreboardMenu = CreateWidget<UUserWidget>(this,
    ScoreboardMenuClass);
    if (ScoreboardMenu != nullptr)
    {
      ScoreboardMenu->AddToViewport(0);
    }
  }
}
```

Now, let's edit the `PickupsGameMode` class:

1. Open `PickupsGameMode.h` and replace the `#include` statement for `GameModeBase.h` with `GameMode.h`:

    ```
    #include "GameFramework/GameMode.h"
    ```

2. Make the class derive from `AGameMode` instead of `AGameModeBase`:

    ```
    class APickupsGameMode : public AGameMode
    ```

3. Declare the protected game state variable, `MyGameState`, which holds the instance of the `APickupsGameState` class:

    ```
    UPROPERTY()
    class APickupsGameState* MyGameState;
    ```

4. Move the constructor to the protected area and delete the public area.

5. Declare the protected override for the `BeginPlay` function:

    ```
    virtual void BeginPlay() override;
    ```

6. Declare the protected override for the `ShouldSpawnAtStartSpot` function:

    ```
    virtual bool ShouldSpawnAtStartSpot(AController* Player)
        override;
    ```

7. Declare the protected overrides for the match state functions of the game mode:

    ```
    virtual void HandleMatchHasStarted() override;
    virtual void HandleMatchHasEnded() override;
    virtual bool ReadyToStartMatch_Implementation() override;
    virtual bool ReadyToEndMatch_Implementation() override;
    ```

8. Declare the protected `RestartMap` function:

    ```
    void RestartMap() const;
    ```

9. Open `PickupsGameMode.cpp` and include `GameplayStatics.h` and `PickupGameState.h`:

    ```
    #include "Kismet/GameplayStatics.h"
    #include "PickupsGameState.h"
    ```

10. Implement the `BeginPlay` override function, which stores the `APickupGameState` instance:

```
void APickupsGameMode::BeginPlay()
{
  Super::BeginPlay();
  MyGameState = GetGameState<APickupsGameState>();
}
```

11. Implement the `ShouldSpawnAtStartSpot` override function, which indicates that we want the players to respawn on a random player start and not always on the same one:

```
bool APickupsGameMode::ShouldSpawnAtStartSpot
  (AController* Player)
{
  return false;
}
```

12. Implement the `HandleMatchHasStarted` override function, which prints to the screen, informing players that the game has started:

```
void APickupsGameMode::HandleMatchHasStarted()
{
  Super::HandleMatchHasStarted();
  GEngine->AddOnScreenDebugMessage(-1, 2.0f,
  FColor::Green, "The game has started!");
}
```

13. Implement the `HandleMatchHasEnded` override function, which prints to the screen, informing players that the game has ended, destroys all characters, and schedules a timer to restart the map:

```
void APickupsGameMode::HandleMatchHasEnded()
{
  Super::HandleMatchHasEnded();
  GEngine->AddOnScreenDebugMessage(-1, 2.0f,
  FColor::Red, "The game has ended!");
  TArray<AActor*> Characters;
    UGameplayStatics::GetAllActorsOfClass(this,
    APickupsCharacter::StaticClass(), Characters);
  for (AActor* Character : Characters)
```

```
        {
            Character->Destroy();
        }
        FTimerHandle TimerHandle;
        GetWorldTimerManager().SetTimer(TimerHandle, this,
            &APickupsGameMode::RestartMap, 5.0f);
    }
```

14. Implement the `ReadyToStartMatch_Implementation` override function, which indicates that the match can start straight away:

```
bool APickupsGameMode::ReadyToStartMatch_Implementation()
{
    return true;
}
```

15. Implement the `ReadyToEndMatch_Implementation` override function, which indicates that the match ends when the game state has no more pickups remaining:

```
bool APickupsGameMode::ReadyToEndMatch_Implementation()
{
    return MyGameState != nullptr && !MyGameState
    ->HasPickups();
}
```

16. Implement the `RestartMap` function, which performs a server travel to the same level and brings all clients along:

```
void APickupsGameMode::RestartMap() const
{
    GetWorld()->ServerTravel(GetWorld()->GetName(),
    false, false);
}
```

Now, let's edit the `PickupsCharacter` class. Follow these steps:

1. Open `PickupsCharacter.h` and declare the protected sound variables for falling and landing:

    ```
    UPROPERTY(EditDefaultsOnly, BlueprintReadOnly, Category =
      "Pickups Character")
    USoundBase* FallSound;
    UPROPERTY(EditDefaultsOnly, BlueprintReadOnly, Category =
      "Pickups Character")
    USoundBase* LandSound;
    ```

2. Declare the protected override functions:

    ```
    virtual void EndPlay(const EEndPlayReason::Type
    EndPlayReason) override;
    virtual void Landed(const FHitResult& Hit) override;
    virtual void FellOutOfWorld(const UDamageType& DmgType)
    override;
    ```

3. Declare the public functions that add scores and pickups to the player state:

    ```
    void AddScore(const float Score) const;
    void AddPickup() const;
    ```

4. Declare the public client RPC that plays a sound on the owning client:

    ```
    UFUNCTION(Client, Unreliable)
    void ClientPlaySound2D(USoundBase* Sound);
    ```

5. Open `PickupsCharacter.cpp` and include `PickupsPlayerState.h`, `GameMode.h`, `PlayerState.h`, and `GameplayStatics.h`:

    ```
    #include "PickupsPlayerState.h"
    #include "GameFramework/GameMode.h"
    #include "GameFramework/PlayerState.h"
    #include "Kismet/GameplayStatics.h"
    ```

6. Implement the `EndPlay` override function, which plays the fall sound if the character was destroyed:

```
void APickupsCharacter::EndPlay(const
EEndPlayReason::Type EndPlayReason)
{
  Super::EndPlay(EndPlayReason);
  if (EndPlayReason == EEndPlayReason::Destroyed)
  {
    UGameplayStatics::PlaySound2D(GetWorld(),
    FallSound);
  }
}
```

7. Implement the `Landed` override function, which plays the landed sound:

```
void APickupsCharacter::Landed(const FHitResult& Hit)
{
  Super::Landed(Hit);
  UGameplayStatics::PlaySound2D(GetWorld(), LandSound);
}
```

8. Implement the `FellOutOfWorld` override function, which stores the controller, removes 10 points from the score, destroys the character, and tells the game mode to restart the player using the previous controller:

```
void APickupsCharacter::FellOutOfWorld(const UDamageType&
  DmgType)
{
  AController* TempController = Controller;
  AddScore(-10);
  Destroy();
  AGameMode* GameMode = GetWorld()
  ->GetAuthGameMode<AGameMode>();
  if (GameMode != nullptr)
  {
    GameMode->RestartPlayer(TempController);
  }
}
```

9. Implement the `AddScore` function, which adds a certain amount to the `score` in the player state:

```
void APickupsCharacter::AddScore(const float Score) const
{
  APlayerState* MyPlayerState = GetPlayerState();
  if (MyPlayerState != nullptr)
  {
    const float CurrentScore = MyPlayerState->GetScore();
    MyPlayerState->SetScore(CurrentScore + Score);
  }
}
```

10. Implement the `AddPickup` function, which adds a pickup to the `Pickup` variable in our custom player state:

```
void APickupsCharacter::AddPickup() const
{
  APickupsPlayerState* MyPlayerState =
    GetPlayerState<APickupsPlayerState>();
  if (MyPlayerState != nullptr)
  {
    MyPlayerState->AddPickup();
  }
}
```

11. Implement the `ClientPlaySound2D_Implementation` function, which plays a sound on the owning client:

```
void APickupsCharacter::ClientPlaySound2D_
Implementation(USoundBase* Sound)
{
  UGameplayStatics::PlaySound2D(GetWorld(), Sound);
}
```

Now, let's work on the `Pickup` class. Follow these steps:

1. Open `Pickup.h` and clear all existing functions and delete the public areas.

2. Declare the protected `Static Mesh` component called `Mesh`:

```
UPROPERTY(VisibleAnywhere, BlueprintReadOnly, Category =
    "Pickup")
UStaticMeshComponent* Mesh;
```

3. Declare the protected rotating movement component called `RotatingMovement`:

```
UPROPERTY(VisibleAnywhere, BlueprintReadOnly, Category =
    "Pickup")
class URotatingMovementComponent* RotatingMovement;
```

4. Declare the protected `PickupSound` variable:

```
UPROPERTY(EditDefaultsOnly, BlueprintReadOnly, Category =
    "Pickup")
USoundBase* PickupSound;
```

5. Declare the protected constructor and `BeginPlay` override:

```
APickup();
virtual void BeginPlay() override;
```

6. Declare the protected `OnBeginOverlap` function:

```
UFUNCTION()
void OnBeginOverlap(UPrimitiveComponent* OverlappedComp,
AActor*
    OtherActor, UPrimitiveComponent* OtherComp, int32
    OtherBodyIndex, bool bFromSweep, const FHitResult&
    Hit);
```

7. Open `Pickup.cpp` and include `PickupsCharacter.h`, `PickupsGameState.h`, and `RotatingMovementComponent.h` after `Pickup.h`:

```
#include "PickupsCharacter.h"
#include "PickupsGameState.h"
#include "GameFramework/RotatingMovementComponent.h"
```

8. In the constructor, initialize the `Mesh` component so that it overlaps everything and make it the root component:

```
Mesh =
CreateDefaultSubobject<UStaticMeshComponent>("Mesh");
Mesh->SetCollisionProfileName("OverlapAll");
RootComponent = Mesh;
```

9. Still in the constructor, initialize the rotating movement component so that it rotates 90 degrees per second on the `Yaw` axis:

```
RotatingMovement = CreateDefaultSubobject
  <URotatingMovementComponent>("Rotating Movement");
RotatingMovement->RotationRate = FRotator(0.0, 90.0f, 0);
```

10. To finalize the constructor, enable replication and disable the `Tick` function:

```
bReplicates = true;
PrimaryActorTick.bCanEverTick = false;
```

11. At the end of the `BeginPlay` function, bind the begin overlap event of `Mesh` to the `OnBeginOverlap` function:

```
Mesh->OnComponentBeginOverlap.AddDynamic(this,
&APickup::OnBeginOverlap);
```

12. Delete the definition for the `Tick` function.

13. Implement the `OnBeginOverlap` function, which checks whether the character is valid and has authority, removes the pickup from the game state, plays the pickup sound on the owning client, and adds `10` points and the pickup to the character. Once all of that is done, the pickup will destroy itself:

```
void APickup::OnBeginOverlap(UPrimitiveComponent*
OverlappedComp,
  AActor* OtherActor, UPrimitiveComponent* OtherComp,
  int32
  OtherBodyIndex, bool bFromSweep, const FHitResult&
  Hit)
{
  APickupsCharacter* Character =
    Cast<APickupsCharacter>(OtherActor);
  if (Character == nullptr || !HasAuthority())
```

```
    {
      return;
    }
    APickupsGameState* GameState =
      Cast<APickupsGameState>(GetWorld()
    ->GetGameState());
    if (GameState != nullptr)
    {
      GameState->RemovePickup();
    }
    Character->ClientPlaySound2D(PickupSound);
    Character->AddScore(10);
    Character->AddPickup();
    Destroy();
}
```

14. Open `Pickups.Build.cs` and add the `UMG` module to `PublicDependencyModuleNames`, like so:

```
PublicDependencyModuleNames.AddRange(new string[] {
"Core",
    "CoreUObject", "Engine", "InputCore",
    "HeadMountedDisplay",
    "UMG" });
```

If you try to compile and get errors from adding the new module, then clean and recompile your project. If that doesn't work, try restarting your IDE.

15. Compile and run the code until the editor loads.

Once it's loaded, we're going to import some assets and create some blueprints that derive from the C++ classes we've just created.

First, let's import the sound files:

1. In the **Content Browser**, create and go to the `Content\Sounds` folder.

2. Import `Pickup.wav`, `Footstep.wav`, `Jump.wav`, `Land.wav`, and `Fall.wav` from the `Exercise18.02\Assets` folder.

3. Save the new files.

    Next, we will add the `Play Sound` anim notifies to some of the character's animations.

4. Open the `MM_Jump` animation, located in `Content\Characters\Mannequins\Animations\Manny`, and add a `Play Sound` anim notify at frame 0 using the `Jump` sound.

5. Save and close `MM_Jump`.

6. Open the `MF_Run_Fwd` animation, located in `Content\Characters\Mannequins\Animations\Quinn`, and add `Play Sound` anim notifies using the `Footstep` sound at `0.24`, `0.56`, `0.82`, `1.12`, `1.38`, and `1.70` seconds.

7. Save and close `MF_Run_Fwd`.

8. Open the `MF_Walk_Fwd` animation, located in `Content\Characters\Mannequins\Animations\Quinn`, and add two `Play Sound` anim notifies using the `Footstep` sound at `0.33`, `0.72`, `1.23`, and `1.7` seconds.

9. Save and close `MF_Walk_Fwd`.

Now, let's set the sounds to use on the character blueprint:

1. Open the `BP_ThirdPersonCharacter` blueprint, located in `Content\ThirdPerson\Blueprints`, and set `Fall Sound` and `Land Sound` so that they use the `Fall` and `Land` sounds, respectively.

2. Save and close `BP_ThirdPersonCharacter`.

    Now, let's create the blueprint for the pickup.

3. Create and open the `Content\Blueprints` folder.

4. Create a new blueprint called `BP_Pickup` that derives from the `Pickup` class and open it.

5. Configure the `Static Mesh` component in the following way:

    - **Scale**: `(X=0.5, Y=0.5, Z=0.5)`

    - **Static Mesh**: `Engine\BasicShapes\Cube`

    - **Material**: `Engine\EngineMaterials\CubeMaterial`

> **Note**
>
> To display the Engine content, you need to click on the dropdown for the static mesh, click on the cog icon next to the filter box, and make sure that the **Show Engine Content** flag is set to `true`.

6. Set the `Pickup Sound` variable to use the `Pickup` sound.

7. Save and close `BP_Pickup`.

Now, let's create the scoreboard UMG widgets. Follow these steps:

1. Create and go to the `Content\UI` folder.

2. Create a new widget blueprint called `WBP_Scoreboard_Header`:

    • Add a **Canvas Panel** to the **Hierarchy** panel.

    • Add a text block called **Name** to the canvas panel with **Is Variable** set to `true`, **Size To Content** set to `true`, **Text** set to `Player Name`, and **Color and Opacity** set to use the color `green`.

    • Add a text block called **Score** to the canvas panel with **Is Variable** set to `true`, **Position X** = `500`, **Alignment** = `1.0, 0.0`, **Size To Content** set to `true`, **Text** set to `Score`, and **Color and Opacity** set to use the color `green`.

    • Add a text block called **Pickups** to the canvas panel with **Is Variable** set to `true`, **Position X** = `650`, **Alignment** = `1.0, 0.0`, **Size To Content** set to `true`, **Text** set to `Pickups`, and **Color and Opacity** set to use the color `green`.

3. Save and close `WBP_Scoreboard_Header`.

4. Go back to **Content\UI**, duplicate `WBP_Scoreboard_Header`, rename it to `WBP_Scoreboard_Entry`, and open it.

5. Change the color of all of the text blocks to `white` instead of `green`.

6. Go to the **Graph** section and create the `Player State` variable with the following configuration:

Figure 18.6 – Creating the Player State variable

7. Go back to the **Designer** section and create a text block called `Name` with **Text** set to `Player Name` and bind it to the `GetPlayerName` function from the dropdown, like so:

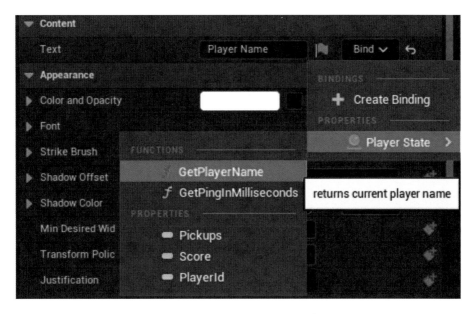

Figure 18.7 – Binding the player name function

8. Create a text block called Score with **Text** set to Score and bind it to the Score variable from the dropdown, like so:

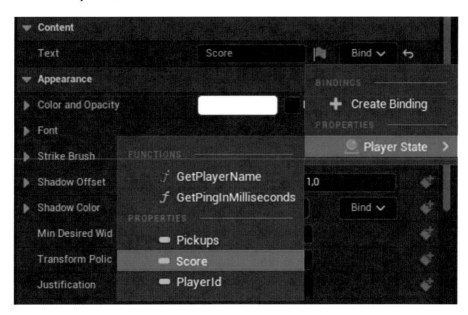

Figure 18.8 – Binding the player score function

9. Create a text block called `Pickups` with **Text** set to `Pickups` and bind it to the `Pickups` variable from the dropdown, like so:

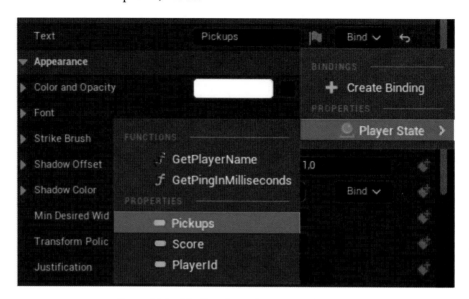

Figure 18.9 – Binding the pickups count function

10. Create a pure function called `Get Typeface` that does the following:

Figure 18.10 – Determining whether the entry should be displayed in Bold or Regular

In the preceding code, we used a `Select` node, which can be created by dragging a wire from the return value and releasing it on an empty space, and then typed `Select` on the filter. From there, we picked the `Select` node from the list. Here, we are using the `Select` node to pick the name of the typeface we're going to use, so it should return `Regular` if the player state's pawn is not the same as the pawn that owns the widget and `Bold` if it is. We do this to highlight the player's state entry in bold so that the player knows what their entry is.

11. Implement `Event Construct` in the following way:

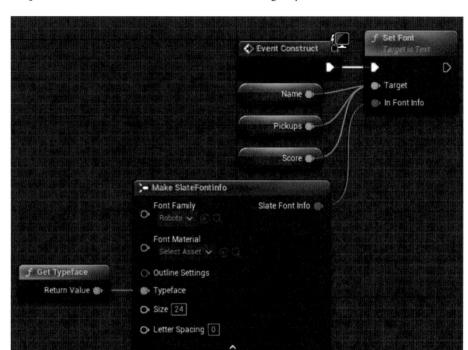

Figure 18.11 – The Event Graph that sets the text for the name, score, and pickups count

In the preceding code, we set the font for `Name`, `Score`, and `Pickups` to use the `Bold` typeface to highlight which scoreboard entry is relative to the player of the current client. For the remainder of the players, use the `Regular` typeface. If you can't find the **Roboto** font, then pick **Show Engine Content** from the dropdown options.

12. Save and close `WBP_Scoreboard_Entry`.

13. Open `WBP_Scoreboard` and add a **Canvas Panel** to the **Hierarchy** panel.

14. Go to the **Graph** section and create a new variable called `Game State` of the `Pickups Game State` type.

15. Go back to the **Designer** section and add a vertical box called `Scoreboard` to the canvas panel with **Size To Content** set to `true`.

16. Add a text block to `Scoreboard` called `PickupsRemaining` with `Text` set to `100 Pickup(s) Remaining`.

17. Add a vertical box to **Scoreboard** called `PlayerStates` with `Is Variable` set to `true` and a top padding of `50`. You should have the following:

Figure 18.12 – The WBP_Scoreboard widget hierarchy

18. Bind the `Text` value for the `PickupsRemaining` text block with the following function:

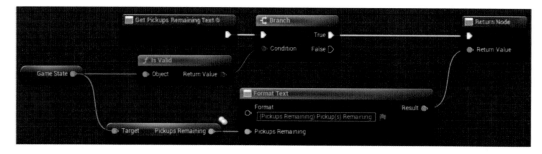

Figure 18.13 – Displaying the number of pickups remaining in the world

19. Go to **Event Graph** and create a new event called `Add Scoreboard Header` that adds an instance of `WBP_Scoreboard_Header` to `Player States`, as shown in the following screenshot:

Figure 18.14 – The Add Scoreboard Header event

20. Create a new event called `Add Scoreboard Entries`. This goes through all of the player states ordered by score and adds an instance of `WBP_Scoreboard_Entry` to `Player States`, as demonstrated in the following screenshot:

Figure 18.15 – The Add Scoreboard Entries event

21. Create a new event called **Update Scoreboard**. This event clears the widgets in **Player States** and calls **Add Scoreboard Header** and **Add Scoreboard Entries**, as shown in the following screenshot:

Figure 18.16 – The Update Scoreboard event

22. Implement **Event Construct** in the following way:

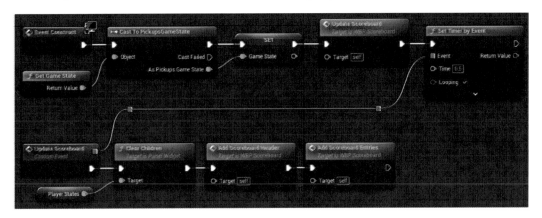

Figure 18.17 – Event Construct

In the preceding code, we get the game state instance, update the scoreboard, and schedule a timer to automatically call the **Update Scoreboard** event every **0.5** seconds.

23. Save and close **WBP_Scoreboard**.

Now, let's create the blueprint for the player controller. Follow these steps:

1. Go to `Content\Blueprints` and create a new blueprint called `BP_PlayerController` that derives from the `PickupsPlayerController` class.

2. Open the new blueprint and set `Scoreboard Menu` to use `WBP_Scoreboard`.

3. Save and close `BP_PlayerController`.

   Next, let's create the blueprint for the game mode.

4. Create a new blueprint called `BP_GameMode` that derives from the `PickupsGameMode` class, open it, and change the following variables:

   • **Game State Class**: `PickupsGameState`

   • **Player Controller Class**: `BP_PlayerController`

   • **Player State Class**: `PickupsPlayerState`

5. Save and close `BP_GameMode`.

6. Next, let's configure **Project Settings** so that it uses the new game mode.

7. Go to **Project Settings** and pick **Maps & Modes** from the left panel, which is in the **Project** category.

8. Set **Default GameMode** to use `BP_GameMode`.

9. Close **Project Settings**.

Now, let's modify the main level. Follow these steps:

1. Make sure you have `ThirdPersonMap` opened, located in `Content\ThirdPerson\Maps`.

2. Add some cube actors to act as platforms. Make sure they have gaps between them to force the player to jump on them and possibly fall from the level.

3. Add a couple of player start actors spread throughout the map.

4. Add at least 50 instances of `BP_Pickup` and spread them across the entire map.

5. Here is an example of a possible way of configuring the map:

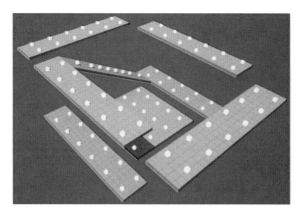

Figure 18.18 – An example of a map configuration

6. Go to **World Settings**, set **GameMode Override** to **None,** and save everything.

7. Go to **Multiplayer Options**, set **Net Mode** to **Play As Listen Server**, and set **Number of Players** to 2.

8. Set the window sizes to 800x600 and play using **New Editor Window (PIE).**

    You should get the following output:

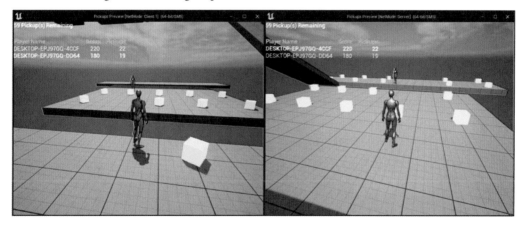

Figure 18.19 – The listen Server and Client 1 picking up cubes in the world

By completing this exercise, you can play on each client. You'll notice that the characters can collect pickups and gain **10** points just by overlapping with them. If a character falls from the level, they will respawn on a random player start and lose **10** points.

Once all the pickups have been collected, the game will end, and after **5** seconds, it will perform a server travel to reload the same level and bring all the clients with it. You will also see that the UI displays how many pickups are remaining in the level, as well as the scoreboard with information about the name, score, and pickups for each player.

In the next activity, you're going to add a scoreboard, kill limit, the concept of death/respawning, and the ability for the characters to pick up weapons, ammo, armor, and health in our multiplayer FPS game.

Activity 18.01 – Adding death, respawning, a scoreboard, kill limit, and pickups to the multiplayer FPS game

In this activity, you'll add the concept of death/respawning and the ability for a character to collect pickups to our multiplayer FPS game. We'll also add a scoreboard and a kill limit to the game so that it has an end goal.

Follow these steps to complete this activity:

1. Open the `MultiplayerFPS` project from *Activity 17.01 – Adding weapons and ammo to the multiplayer FPS game*. Compile the code and run the editor.

2. Create a C++ class called `FPSGameState`, which derives from the `GameState` class, and has a kill limit variable and a function that returns the player states ordered by kills.

3. Create a C++ class called `FPSPlayerState`, which derives from the `PlayerState` class, and stores the number of kills and deaths of a player.

4. Create a C++ class called `PlayerMenu`, which derives from the `UserWidget` class, and has some `BlueprintImplementableEvent` functions to toggle the scoreboard visibility, set the scoreboard visibility, and notify when a player was killed.

5. Create a C++ class called `FPSPlayerController`, which derives from `APlayerController`, that creates the `PlayerMenu` UMG widget instance on the owning client.

6. Create a C++ class called `Pickup`, which derives from the `Actor` class, and has a static mesh that rotates 90 degrees per second on the `Yaw` axis and can be picked up by the player on overlap. Once picked up, it plays a pickup sound and disables collision and visibility. After a certain amount of time, it will make it visible and able to collide again.

7. Create a C++ class called `AmmoPickup`, which derives from the `Pickup` class, and adds a certain amount of an ammo type to the player.

8. Create a C++ class called `ArmorPickup`, which derives from the `Pickup` class, and adds a certain amount of armor to the player.

9. Create a C++ class called `HealthPickup`, which derives from the `Pickup` class, and adds a certain amount of health to the player.

10. Create a C++ class called `WeaponPickup`, which derives from the `Pickup` class, and adds a certain weapon type to the player. If the player already has the weapon, it will add a certain amount of ammo.

11. Edit the `FPSCharacter` class so that it does the following:

    • After the character is damaged, it checks whether it's dead. If it's dead, it registers the kill for the killer character and the death of the player and respawn it. If the character is not dead, then it plays the pain sound on the owning client.

    • When the character dies and executes the `EndPlay` function, it should destroy all of its weapon instances.

    • If the character falls from the world, it will register the death of the player and respawn it.

    • If the player presses the *Tab* key, it will toggle the visibility of the scoreboard menu.

12. Edit the `MultiplayerFPSGameModeBase` class so that it does the following:

    • Uses the `GameMode` class instead of `GameModeBase`

    • Stores the number of kills necessary to win the game.

    • Uses our custom player controller, player state, and game state classes.

    • Makes it implement the match state functions so that the match starts immediately and ends if there is a player that has the required number of kills.

    • When the match ends, it will perform a server travel to the same level after 5 seconds.

    • Handles when a player dies by adding the kill (when killed by another player) and the death to the respective player state, as well as respawn the player on a random player start.

13. Import `AmmoPickup.wav` from `Activity18.01\Assets` into `Content\Pickups\Ammo`.

14. Create `BP_PistolBullets_Pickup` from `AmmoPickup`, place it in `Content\Pickups\Ammo`, and configure it with the following values:

    • **Scale**: `(X=0.5, Y=0.5, Z=0.5)`

    • **Static Mesh**: `Engine\BasicShapes\Cube`

    • **Material**: `Content\Weapon\Pistol\MI_Pistol`

    • **Ammo Type**: `Pistol Bullets`

    • **Ammo Amount**: `25`

    • **Pickup Sound**: `Content\Pickup\Ammo\AmmoPickup`

15. Create `BP_MachineGunBullets_Pickup` from `AmmoPickup`, place it in `Content\Pickups\Ammo`, and configure it with the following values:

  - **Scale**: `(X=0.5, Y=0.5, Z=0.5)`
  - **Static Mesh**: `Engine\BasicShapes\Cube`
  - **Material**: `Content\Weapon\MachineGun\MI_MachineGun`
  - **Ammo Type**: `Machine Gun Bullets`
  - **Ammo Amount**: `50`
  - **Pickup Sound**: `Content\Pickup\Ammo\AmmoPickup`

16. Create `BP_Slugs_Pickup` from `AmmoPickup`, place it in `Content\Pickups\Ammo`, and configure it with the following values:

  - **Scale**: `(X=0.5, Y=0.5, Z=0.5)`
  - **Static Mesh**: `Engine\BasicShapes\Cube`
  - **Material**: `Content\Weapon\Railgun\MI_Railgun`
  - **Ammo Type**: `Slugs`
  - **Ammo Amount**: `5`
  - **Pickup Sound**: `Content\Pickup\Ammo\AmmoPickup`

17. Import `ArmorPickup.wav` from `Activity18.01\Assets` into `Content\Pickups\Armor`.

18. Create the `M_Armor` material in `Content\Pickups\Armor`, which has `Base Color` set to blue and `Metallic` set to `1`.

19. Create `BP_Armor_Pickup` from `ArmorPickup`, place it in `Content\Pickups\Armor`, and configure it with the following values:

  - **Scale**: `(X=1.0, Y=1.5, Z=1.0)`
  - **Static Mesh**: `Engine\BasicShapes\Cube`
  - **Material**: `Content\Pickup\Armor\M_Armor`
  - **Armor Amount**: `50`
  - **Pickup Sound**: `Content\Pickup\Armor\ArmorPickup`

20. Import `HealthPickup.wav` from `Activity18.01\Assets` into `Content\Pickups\Health`.

21. Create the M_Health material in Content\Pickups\Health, which has Base Color set to green and Metallic/Roughness set to 0.5.

22. Create BP_Health_Pickup from HealthPickup, place it in Content\Pickups\Health, and configure it with the following values:

- **Static Mesh**: Engine\BasicShapes\Sphere

- **Material**: Content\Pickup\Health\M_Health

- **Health Amount**: 50

- **Pickup Sound**: Content\Pickup\Health\HealthPickup

23. Import WeaponPickup.wav from Activity18.01\Assets into Content\Pickups\Weapon.

24. Create BP_Pistol_Pickup from WeaponPickup, place it in Content\Pickups\Weapon, and configure it with the following values:

- **Static Mesh**: Content\Pickup\Weapon\SM_Weapon

- **Material**: Content\Weapon\Pistol\MI_Pistol

- **Weapon Type**: Pistol

- **Ammo Amount**: 25

- **Pickup Sound**: Content\Pickup\Weapon\WeaponPickup

25. Create BP_MachineGun_Pickup from WeaponPickup, place it in Content\Pickups\Weapon, and configure it with the following values:

- **Static Mesh**: Content\Pickup\Weapon\SM_Weapon

- **Material**: Content\Weapon\MachineGun\MI_MachineGun

- **Weapon Type**: Machine Gun

- **Ammo Amount**: 50

- **Pickup Sound**: Content\Pickup\Weapon\WeaponPickup

26. Create BP_Railgun_Pickup from WeaponPickup, place it in Content\Pickups\Weapon, and configure it with the following values:

- **Static Mesh**: Content\Pickup\Weapon\SM_Weapon

- **Material**: Content\Weapon\Railgun\MI_Railgun

- **Weapon Type**: Railgun

- **Ammo Amount**: 5
- **Pickup Sound**: Content\Pickup\Weapon\WeaponPickup

27. Import Land.wav and Pain.wav from Activity18.01\Assets into Content\Player\Sounds.

28. Edit BP_Player so that it uses the Pain and Land sounds, as well as deletes all of the nodes that create and add the WBP_HUD instance to the viewport in the Begin Play event.

29. Create a UMG widget called WBP_Scoreboard_Entry in Content\UI that displays the name, kills, deaths, and ping of FPSPlayerState.

30. Create a UMG widget called WBP_Scoreboard_Header that displays the headers for the name, kills, deaths, and ping.

31. Create a UMG widget called WBP_Scoreboard that displays the kill limit from the game state, a vertical box that has WBP_Scoreboard_Header as the first entry, and then add a WBP_Scoreboard_Entry for each FPSPlayerState in the game state instance. The vertical box will update every 0.5 seconds, through a timer, by clearing its children and adding them again.

32. Edit WBP_HUD so that it adds a new text block called Killed that starts with Visibility set to Hidden. When the player kills someone, it will make the text block visible, display the name of the killed player, and hide after 1 second.

33. Create a new blueprint called WBP_PlayerMenu from PlayerMenu and place it in Content\UI. Use a widget switcher with an instance of WBP_HUD to index 0 and an instance of WBP_Scoreboard to index 1. In the event graph, make sure that you override the Toggle Scoreboard, Set Scoreboard Visibility, and Notify Kill events that were set as BlueprintImplementableEvent in C++. The Toggle Scoreboard event toggles the widget switcher's active index between 0 and 1, the Set Scoreboard Visibility event sets the widget switcher's active index to 0 or 1, and the Notify Kill event tells the WBP_HUD instance to set the text and hide it after 1 second.

34. Create BP_PlayerController from FPSPlayerController, place it in the Content folder, and set the PlayerMenuClass variable to use WBP_PlayerMenu.

35. Edit BP_GameMode and set Player Controller Class to use BP_PlayerController.

36. Create the input action IA_Scoreboard to toggle the scoreboard with the *Tab* key and update IMC_Player.

37. Edit the DM-Test level so that you have at least three new player starts placed in different locations. Then, place an instance of every different pickup.

38. In **World Settings**, set **Kill Z** to -500.

Expected output:

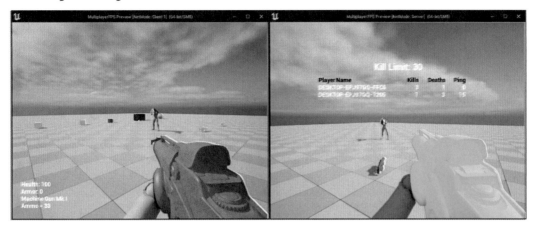

Figure 18.20 – The expected output of the activity

The result should be a project where each client's character can use and switch between three different weapons. If a character kills another, it should register the kill and the death, as well as respawn the character that died at a random player start. You should have a scoreboard that displays the name, kill count, death count, and ping for each player. A character can fall from the level, which should only count as a death, and respawn at a random player start. The character should also be able to pick up the different pickups in the level to get ammo, armor, health, and weapons. The game should end when the kill limit has been reached by showing the scoreboard and server travel to the same level after 5 seconds.

> **Note**
> The solution to this activity can be found on GitHub here: `https://github.com/PacktPublishing/Elevating-Game-Experiences-with-Unreal-Engine-5-Second-Edition/tree/main/Activity%20solutions`.

Summary

In this chapter, you learned that the instances of the gameplay framework classes exist in some specific game instances, but not in others. You also learned about the purpose of the game state and player state classes, as well as new concepts for the game mode and some useful built-in functionalities.

At the end of this chapter, you made a basic but functional multiplayer shooter that can be used as a foundation to build upon. You added new weapons, ammo types, fire modes, pickups, and so on to make it more feature-complete and fun.

Having completed this book, you should now have a better understanding of how to use UE5 to make games come to life. We've covered a lot of topics in this book, ranging from the simple to more advanced. You started by learning how to create projects using the different templates and how to use Blueprints to create actors and components. Then, you learned how to create a fully functioning **Third Person** template from scratch by importing the required assets and setting up the Animation Blueprint, Blend Space, game mode, and character, as well as defining and handling the inputs.

Then, you moved on to your first project – a simple stealth game that uses game physics and collisions, projectile movement components, actor components, interfaces, blueprint function libraries, UMG, sounds, and particle effects. Following this, you learned how to create a simple side-scrolling game by using AI, Anim Montages, and Destructible Meshes. Finally, you learned how to create a first-person multiplayer shooter by using the Server-Client architecture, variable replication, and RPCs, as well as how the Player State, Game State, and Game Mode classes work.

By working on various projects that use different parts of Unreal Engine, you now have a strong understanding of how UE5 works. Although this is the end of this book, this is just the beginning of your journey into the world of game development using UE5.

Index

C

L

layered blend per bone

about 396

animation, blending with Upper
   Body Anim Slot 397-401

Throw animation, previewing 401-403

level 64

level blockout

about 289

building 290, 291, 293

Level Blueprint 64

level design

exploring 289

levels 11

Line Traces

about 139

functionalities 140

Trace Channels feature 140

visualizing 146

listen server 576, 577

LookAtActor function

creating 147, 148

LookAtActor logic

moving, to Actor component 226-228

loose coupling

about 210

best practices 210

M

Main Character Animation Blueprint

about 344

Blend Space, adding to 345-350

graphs 344

using 344

mannequin animation

creating 74-86

mannequin skeleton weights

manipulating 308-318

Material Instances

about 408

applying 409

Blend Weights, updating 413-415

enemy Material Instance, applying 411-413

enemy Material Instance, creating 410-413

example 409

materials

about 38, 408

manipulating, in UE5 39-43

menus, game UI 232

meshes

about 166

procedural meshes 166

skeletal meshes 166

static meshes 166

Mixamo

reference link 321

MixamoAnimPack assets

reference link 95

movement 2D Blend Space

creating 606-612

Movement state machine

completing 382-384

Move tool 12, 13

Multicast RPC

about 626

declaration 626

example 626

execution 627

Multi Line Traces 156-158

multiplayer

basics 570-573

connections and ownership,
   exploring 582-584

W

`Packt.com`

Subscribe to our online digital library for full access to over 7,000 books and videos, as well as industry leading tools to help you plan your personal development and advance your career. For more information, please visit our website.

Why subscribe?

- Spend less time learning and more time coding with practical eBooks and Videos from over 4,000 industry professionals

- Improve your learning with Skill Plans built especially for you

- Get a free eBook or video every month

- Fully searchable for easy access to vital information

- Copy and paste, print, and bookmark content

Did you know that Packt offers eBook versions of every book published, with PDF and ePub files available? You can upgrade to the eBook version at `packt.com` and as a print book customer, you are entitled to a discount on the eBook copy. Get in touch with us at `customercare@packtpub.com` for more details.

At `www.packt.com`, you can also read a collection of free technical articles, sign up for a range of free newsletters, and receive exclusive discounts and offers on Packt books and eBooks.

Other Books You May Enjoy

If you enjoyed this book, you may be interested in these other books by Packt:

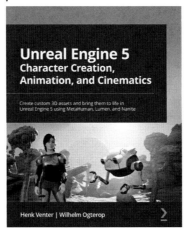

Unreal Engine 5 Character Creation, Animation, and Cinematics

Henk Venter , Wilhelm Ogterop

ISBN: 978-1-80181-244-3

- Create, customize, and use a MetaHuman in a cinematic scene in UE5
- Model and texture custom 3D assets for your movie using Blender and Quixel Mixer
- Use Nanite with Quixel Megascans assets to build 3D movie sets
- Rig and animate characters and 3D assets inside UE5 using Control Rig tools
- Light your 3D movie set using Lumen lighting in UE5

Blueprints Visual Scripting for Unreal Engine 5 - Third Edition

Marcos Romero , Brenden Sewell

ISBN: 978-1-80181-158-3

- Understand programming concepts in Blueprints
- Create prototypes and iterate new game mechanics rapidly
- Build user interface elements and interactive menus
- Use advanced Blueprint nodes to manage the complexity of a game
- Explore all the features of the Blueprint editor, such as the Components tab, Viewport, and Event Graph

Packt is searching for authors like you

If you're interested in becoming an author for Packt, please visit `authors.packtpub.com` and apply today. We have worked with thousands of developers and tech professionals, just like you, to help them share their insight with the global tech community. You can make a general application, apply for a specific hot topic that we are recruiting an author for, or submit your own idea.

Hi!

Gonçalo Marques, Devin Sherry, David Pereira, and Hammad Fozi, authors of *Elevating Game Experiences with Unreal Engine 5*, really hope you enjoyed reading this book and found it useful for increasing your productivity and efficiency in Unreal Engine 5.

It would really help us (and other potential readers!) if you could leave a review on Amazon sharing your thoughts on this book.

Go to the link below or scan the QR code to leave your review:

`https://packt.link/r/1803239867`

Your review will help us to understand what's worked well in this book, and what could be improved upon for future editions, so it really is appreciated.

Best wishes,

Gonçalo Marques

Devin Sherry

David Pereira

Hammad Fozi

Made in the USA
Las Vegas, NV
06 February 2023

67013000R00454